Convergence of Broadband, Broadcast, and Cellular Network Technologies

Ramona Trestian
Middlesex University, UK

Gabriel-Miro Muntean
Dublin City University, Ireland

A volume in the Advances in Wireless Technologies and Telecommunication (AWTT) Book Series

Information Science
REFERENCE
An Imprint of IGI Global

Managing Director:	Lindsay Johnston
Production Editor:	Jennifer Yoder
Development Editor:	Austin DeMarco
Acquisitions Editor:	Kayla Wolfe
Typesetter:	Christina Henning
Cover Design:	Jason Mull

Published in the United States of America by
Information Science Reference (an imprint of IGI Global)
701 E. Chocolate Avenue
Hershey PA 17033
Tel: 717-533-8845
Fax: 717-533-8661
E-mail: cust@igi-global.com
Web site: http://www.igi-global.com

Library of Congress Cataloging-in-Publication Data

Convergence of broadband, broadcast, and cellular network technologies / Ramona Trestian and Gabriel-Miro Muntean, editors.
    pages cm
  Includes bibliographical references and index.
    ISBN 978-1-4666-5978-0 (hardcover) -- ISBN 978-1-4666-5979-7 (ebook) -- ISBN 978-1-4666-5981-0 (print & perpetual access) 1. Wireless communication systems. 2. Telecommunication systems. I. Trestian, Ramona, 1983- II. Muntean, Gabriel-Miro, 1972-
  TK5103.2.C657 2014
  384.5--dc23
                              2014006041

This book is published in the IGI Global book series Advances in Wireless Technologies and Telecommunication (AWTT) (ISSN: 2327-3305; eISSN: 2327-3313)

British Cataloguing in Publication Data
A Cataloguing in Publication record for this book is available from the British Library.

For electronic access to this publication, please contact: eresources@igi-global.com.

Advances in Wireless Technologies and Telecommunication (AWTT) Book Series

Xiaoge Xu
The University of Nottingham Ningbo China

ISSN: 2327-3305
EISSN: 2327-3313

MISSION

The wireless computing industry is constantly evolving, redesigning the ways in which individuals share information. Wireless technology and telecommunication remain one of the most important technologies in business organizations. The utilization of these technologies has enhanced business efficiency by enabling dynamic resources in all aspects of society.

The **Advances in Wireless Technologies and Telecommunication Book Series** aims to provide researchers and academic communities with quality research on the concepts and developments in the wireless technology fields. Developers, engineers, students, research strategists, and IT managers will find this series useful to gain insight into next generation wireless technologies and telecommunication.

COVERAGE

- Cellular Networks
- Digital Communication
- Global Telecommunications
- Grid Communications
- Mobile Technology
- Mobile Web Services
- Network Management
- Virtual Network Operations
- Wireless Broadband
- Wireless Sensor Networks

IGI Global is currently accepting manuscripts for publication within this series. To submit a proposal for a volume in this series, please contact our Acquisition Editors at Acquisitions@igi-global.com or visit: http://www.igi-global.com/publish/.

Titles in this Series

For a list of additional titles in this series, please visit: www.igi-global.com

Convergence of Broadband, Broadcast, and Cellular Network Technologies
Ramona Trestian (Middlesex University, UK) and Gabriel-Miro Muntean (Dublin City University, Ireland)
Information Science Reference • copyright 2014 • 323pp • H/C (ISBN: 9781466659780) • US $235.00 (our price)

Handbook of Research on Progressive Trends in Wireless Communications and Networking
M.A. Matin (Institut Teknologi Brunei, Brunei Darussalam)
Information Science Reference • copyright 2014 • 592pp • H/C (ISBN: 9781466651708) • US $380.00 (our price)

Broadband Wireless Access Networks for 4G Theory, Application, and Experimentation
Raul Aquino Santos (University of Colima, Mexico) Victor Rangel Licea (National Autonomous University of Mexico, Mexico) and Arthur Edwards-Block (University of Colima, Mexico)
Information Science Reference • copyright 2014 • 452pp • H/C (ISBN: 9781466648883) • US $235.00 (our price)

Multidisciplinary Perspectives on Telecommunications, Wireless Systems, and Mobile Computing
Wen-Chen Hu (University of North Dakota, USA)
Information Science Reference • copyright 2014 • 305pp • H/C (ISBN: 9781466647152) • US $175.00 (our price)

Mobile Networks and Cloud Computing Convergence for Progressive Services and Applications
Joel J.P.C. Rodrigues (Instituto de Telecomunicações, University of Beira Interior, Portugal) Kai Lin (Dalian University of Technology, China) and Jaime Lloret (Polytechnic University of Valencia, Spain)
Information Science Reference • copyright 2014 • 408pp • H/C (ISBN: 9781466647817) • US $180.00 (our price)

Research and Design Innovations for Mobile User Experience
Kerem Rızvanoğlu (Galatasaray University, Turkey) and Görkem Çetin (Turkcell, Turkey)
Information Science Reference • copyright 2014 • 377pp • H/C (ISBN: 9781466644465) • US $190.00 (our price)

Cognitive Radio Technology Applications for Wireless and Mobile Ad Hoc Networks
Natarajan Meghanathan (Jackson State University, USA) and Yenumula B. Reddy (Grambling State University, USA)
Information Science Reference • copyright 2013 • 370pp • H/C (ISBN: 9781466642218) • US $190.00 (our price)

Evolution of Cognitive Networks and Self-Adaptive Communication Systems
Thomas D. Lagkas (University of Western Macedonia, Greece) Panagiotis Sarigiannidis (University of Western Macedonia, Greece) Malamati Louta (University of Western Macedonia, Greece) and Periklis Chatzimisios (Alexander TEI of Thessaloniki, Greece)
Information Science Reference • copyright 2013 • 438pp • H/C (ISBN: 9781466641891) • US $195.00 (our price)

www.igi-global.com

701 E. Chocolate Ave., Hershey, PA 17033
Order online at www.igi-global.com or call 717-533-8845 x100
To place a standing order for titles released in this series, contact: cust@igi-global.com
Mon-Fri 8:00 am - 5:00 pm (est) or fax 24 hours a day 717-533-8661

Editorial Advisory Board

Table of Contents

Section 1
Convergent Evolution

Chapter 1
Andreea Molnar, Arizona State University, USA
Cristina Hava Muntean, National College of Ireland, Ireland

Chapter 2
Irina Tal, Dublin City University, Ireland
Gabriel-Miro Muntean, Dublin City University, Ireland

Chapter 3
Chetna Singhal, Indian Institute of Technology Delhi, India
Swades De, Indian Institute of Technology Delhi, India

Chapter 4
Giuseppe Araniti, University Mediterranea of Reggio Calabria, Italy
Massimo Condoluci, University Mediterranea of Reggio Calabria, Italy
Antonella Molinaro, University Mediterranea of Reggio Calabria, Italy

Chapter 12

Detailed Table of Contents

Section 1
Convergent Evolution

Chapter 1

> *Andreea Molnar, Arizona State University, USA*
> *Cristina Hava Muntean, National College of Ireland, Ireland*

The high usage of multimedia content in daily activities has put strains on the network operators as the transmitted content can lead to network congestion. In an effort to control and reduce the traffic, network operators have capped their billing plans. A capped billing plan may require the user to pay extra money when exceeding the quota, and this can result in undesirably high bills for the mobile users. A solution that has been shown to reduce the size of transmitted data and also addresses user needs in terms of billing cost was presented in Molnar and Muntean (2013a). This solution involves personalising the multimedia content based on the user attitude towards risk. It makes use of a model that assesses the user attitude towards risk by considering the user age, gender, and risk attitude self-assessment. The research presented in this chapter adds to the state of the art by presenting an improvement to the user risk attitude model (Molnar & Muntean, 2012) that takes into account the user context (e.g. whether the user uses the roaming service or not, the current data consumption) as well as the user input. The improved model may be used to provide a more accurate trade-off: quality vs. price (Molnar & Muntean, 2013a) and this leads to an increase in user satisfaction and better service quality.

Chapter 2

> *Irina Tal, Dublin City University, Ireland*
> *Gabriel-Miro Muntean, Dublin City University, Ireland*

This chapter highlights the importance of Vehicular Ad-Hoc Networks (VANETs) in the context of smarter cities and roads, a topic that currently attracts significant academic, industrial, and governmental planning, research, and development efforts. In order for VANETs to become reality, a very promising avenue is to bring together multiple wireless technologies in the architectural design. Clustering can be employed in designing such a VANET architecture that successfully uses different technologies. Moreover, as clustering addresses some of VANETs' major challenges, such as scalability and stability, it seems clustering will have an important role in the desired vehicular connectivity in the cities and roads of the future. This chapter presents a comprehensive survey of clustering schemes in the VANET research area, covering aspects that have never been addressed before in a structured manner. The survey presented in this chapter provides a general classification of the clustering algorithms, presents some of the most advanced and latest algorithms in VANETs, and in addition, constitutes the only work in the literature to the best of authors' knowledge that also reviews the performance assessment of clustering algorithms.

    Chetna Singhal, Indian Institute of Technology Delhi, India
    Swades De, Indian Institute of Technology Delhi, India

The advent of heterogeneous Broadband Wireless Access Networks (BWANs) has been to support the ever increasing cellular networks' data requirements by increasing capacity, spectrum efficiency, and network coverage. The focus of this chapter is to discuss the implementation details (i.e. architecture and network components), issues associated with heterogeneous BWANs (i.e. handovers, network selection, and base station placement), and also the various resource allocation schemes (i.e. shared resource allocation in split handover and inter-RAT self-organizing networks) that can improve the performance of the system by maximizing the capacity of users.

    Giuseppe Araniti, University Mediterranea of Reggio Calabria, Italy
    Massimo Condoluci, University Mediterranea of Reggio Calabria, Italy
    Antonella Molinaro, University Mediterranea of Reggio Calabria, Italy

In recent years, mobile operators are observing a growing demand of multicast services over radio cellular networks. In this scenario, multicasting is the technology exploited to serve a group of users which simultaneously request the same data content. Since multicast applications are expected to be massively exchanged over Fourth Generation (4G) systems, the Third Generation Partnership Project (3GPP) defined the Multimedia Broadcast Multicast Service (MBMS) standard. MBMS allows supporting multicast services over Long Term Evolution (LTE), the 4G wireless technology able to provide high quality services in mobile environments. Nevertheless, several issues related to the management of MBMS services are still open. The aim of this chapter is to analyze the challenges in supporting multicast services over LTE with particular attention to resource management, considered the key aspect for an effective provisioning of MBMS services over cellular networks.

    José André Moura, ISCTE-IUL, Portugal
    Rui Neto Marinheiro, ISCTE-IUL, Portugal
    João Carlos Silva, ISCTE-IUL, Portugal

Cooperative strategies have the great potential of improving network performance and spectrum utilization in future networking environments. This new paradigm in terms of network management, however, requires a novel design and analysis framework targeting a highly flexible networking solution with a distributed architecture. Game Theory is very suitable for this task, since it is a comprehensive mathematical tool for modeling the highly complex interactions among distributed and intelligent decision makers. In this way, the more convenient management policies for the diverse players (e.g. content providers, cloud providers, home providers, brokers, network providers or users) should be found to optimize the performance of the overall network infrastructure. The authors discuss in this chapter several Game Theory models/concepts that are highly relevant for enabling collaboration among the diverse players, using different ways to incentivize it, namely through pricing or reputation. In addition, the authors highlight several related open problems, such as the lack of proper models for dynamic and incomplete information games in this area.

Chapter 6
Chungang Yang, Xidian University, China
Jiandong Li, Xidian University, China

In Long Term Evolution (LTE) 4G systems, coexistence of multiple in-band smallcells defines what is called heterogeneous cellular networks. There is no doubt that the development of heterogeneous networks and the popularization of intelligent terminals facilitate subscribers with great convenience, better Quality of Experience (QoE) guarantee, and much higher traffic rate. However, interference management will be indispensable in heterogeneous networks. Meanwhile, with emerging various energy-hungry services of subscribers, energy-aware design attracts a wide attention. Motivated by interference mitigation and energy-saving challenges of the heterogeneous networks and the promising cognitive radio techniques, more advanced energy-saving and interference control techniques based on cognitive radio should be developed for better QoE. In this chapter, the authors first review cognitive radios, multiple types of smallcells, and introduce the benefits of cognitive radio-enabled heterogeneous networks. Then, focusing on the scheme design of cognitive interference management and energy management, finally, simulation results are provided to show the improved performance of these proposed cognitive schemes.

Section 2
QoS Provisioning Solutions

Chapter 7
Lejla Rovcanin, Dublin City University, Ireland
Gabriel-Miro Muntean, Dublin City University, Ireland

Multimedia streaming has major commercial potential as the global community of online video viewers is expanding rapidly following the proliferation of low-cost multimedia-enabled mobile devices. These devices enable increasing amounts of video-based content to be acquired, stored, and distributed across existing best effort networks that also carry other traffic types. Although a number of protocols are used for video transfer, a significant portion of the Internet streaming media is currently delivered over Hypertext Transfer Protocol (HTTP). Network congestion is one of the most important issues that affects networking traffic in general and video content delivery. Among the various solutions proposed, adaptive delivery of content according to available network bandwidth was very successful. In this context, the most recent standardisation efforts have focused on the introduction of the Dynamic Adaptive Streaming over HTTP (DASH) (ISO, 2012) standard. DASH offers support for client-based bitrate video streaming adaptation, but as it does not introduce any particular adaptation mechanism, it relies on third party solutions to complement it. This chapter provides an overview of the DASH standard and presents a short survey of currently proposed mechanisms for video adaptation related to DASH. It also introduces the DASH-aware Performance-Oriented Adaptation Agent (dPOAA), which improves user Quality of Experience (QoE) levels by dynamically selecting best performing sources for the delivery of video content. dPOAA, in its functionality, considers the characteristics of the network links connecting clients with video providers. dPOAA can be utilised as a DASH player plugin or in conjunction with the DASH-based performance-oriented Adaptive Video Distribution solution (DAV) (Rovcanin & Muntean, 2013), which considers the local network characteristics, quantity of requested content available locally, and device and user profiles.

Chapter 8

Kevin Collins, Dublin City University, Ireland
Gabriel-Miro Muntean, Dublin City University, Ireland

Traffic congestion is a major issue in the modern society, and unfortunately, it continues to worsen as the number of cars on the road grows behind the ability of existing road infrastructures to cope. Additionally, vehicle fuel consumption and gas emissions are increasing, and concentrated efforts to propose solutions to reduce these and consequently the pollution are needed. In this context, this chapter presents TraffCon, an innovative vehicle route management solution, which makes use of a novel best route selection algorithm for vehicular traffic routing and of vehicular wireless communications to reduce not only journey times but also fuel consumption and as a direct consequence vehicle gas emissions. The chapter shows how TraffCon can be supported by an IEEE 802.11p sparse roadside-vehicle network with very good results in comparison with classic approaches.

Chapter 9

Dan Pescaru, Politehnica University of Timisoara, Romania
Daniel-Ioan Curiac, Politehnica University of Timisoara, Romania

This chapter presents the main challenges in developing complex systems built around the core concept of Video-Based Wireless Sensor Networks. It summarizes some innovative solutions proposed in scientific literature on this field. Besides discussion on various issues related to such systems, the authors focus on two crucial aspects: video data processing and data exchange. A special attention is paid to localization algorithms in case of random deployment of nodes having no specific localization hardware installed. Solutions for data exchange are presented by highlighting the data compression and communication efficiency in terms of energy saving. In the end, some open research topics related with Video-Based Wireless Sensor Networks are identified and explained.

Chapter 10

João Paulo Ribeiro Pereira, Polytechnic Institute of Bragança, Portugal

Like in a real competitive market situation, Next Generation Networks (NGN) competitors need to adapt their strategy to face/react the strategies from other players. To better understand the effects of interaction between different players, the authors build a Game Theory model in which the profit of each operator will be dependent not only on their actions but also on the actions of the other operators in the market. This chapter analyzes the impact of the price (retail and wholesale) variations on several output results: players' profit, consumer surplus, welfare, costs, and service adoption. The authors assume that two competing FTTH networks (incumbent operator and new entrant) are deployed in two different areas. They also propose in this chapter an adoption model use in a way that reflects the competition between players and that the variation of the services prices of one player has an influence on the market share of all players. Finally, the model uses the Nash equilibrium to find the best strategies.

Chapter 11
Haymen Shams, University College London, UK

There is a continuous demand for increasing wireless access broadband services to the end users, especially with widespread high quality mobile devices. The Internet mobile applications and multimedia services are constantly hungry for broadband wireless bandwidth. In order to overcome this bandwidth limitation, a frequency band (57-64 GHz) has recently been assigned for short range indoor wireless broadband signals due to the large available bandwidth. However, the transmission at this band is limited to a few meters due to the high atmospheric absorption loss. Radio over Fiber (RoF) technology was considered an efficient solution to extend the distribution range and wireless capacity services. This chapter presents an introduction to RoF technology and its basic required optical components for indoor short range wireless millimeter waves (mm-waves). The limiting factors of RoF and its impairments are also described. Moreover, optical mm-wave generation solutions are explained and followed by the recent optical 60GHz activities and upcoming research areas such as THz and optical wireless.

Chapter 12
Rastislav Róka, FEI STU Bratislava, Slovakia

With the emerging applications and needs of ever increasing bandwidth, it is anticipated that the Next-Generation Passive Optical Network (NG-PON) with much higher bandwidth is a natural path forward to satisfy these demands and for network operators to develop valuable access networks. NG-PON systems present optical access infrastructures to support various applications of many service providers. Therefore, some general requirements for NG-PON networks are characterized and specified. Hybrid Passive Optical Networks (HPON) present a necessary phase of the future transition between PON classes with TDM or WDM multiplexing techniques utilized on the optical transmission medium – the optical fiber. Therefore, some specific requirements for HPON networks are characterized and presented. For developing hybrid passive optical networks, there exist various architectures and directions. They are also specified with emphasis on their basic characteristics and distinctions. Finally, the HPON network configurator as the interactive software tool is introduced in this chapter. Its main aim is helping users, professional workers, network operators and system analysts to design, configure, analyze, and compare various variations of possible hybrid passive optical networks. Some of the executed analysis is presented in detail.

Foreword

The evolution of networking is continuing apace with advances flourishing in both the optical and wireless domains. The demands that users are placing on these networks has increased rapidly with the explosion of both Web-based applications and smart phones. People expect to have connections available at all times, in all places, and with the same quality. This translates to many difficult technical goals. In the optical domain, both radio over fiber and next generation passive optical networks are still to be conquered. In the wireless areas, there is an abundance of different technologies, some for the home and office, some for travel in cars, and some for both. The full range of applications available today, including video and voice communications and Internet usage, must be delivered to the end device now, and the networks have to be ready for those that will no doubt arrive in the next decade.

It is clear that there will be many networks that will provide services, and one of the major goals is to find methods not merely to have these coexist but to have them work efficiently and to optimize their performance and the user experience. The changes of the wireless environments (LTE) and the explosion of vehicular network research (VANETS) have meant there is a massive increase in the number of researchers working in these fields. The editors Gabriel-Miro Muntean and Ramona Trestian have made a significant contribution to the overall area by focusing attention for their book on the convergence evolution and Quality of Service (QoS) provisioning in these current and future networks. These two key aspects have been carefully chosen, and an exciting and an excellent selection of up-to-date chapters addressing these aspects are presented in this book.

The international set of experts chosen from around the world provide insights from clustering algorithms in VANETS to game theory for either collaboration or competition from next generation optical networks to resource allocation in wireless LTE and from interference mitigation in radio to video quality improvements. There is much to enjoy in this book for either a student or researcher, and they will get valuable insights into current research approaches. This would give those in industry a snapshot of the many methods by which problems they are no doubt aware of are being addressed in research. I am sure that *Convergence of Broadband, Broadcast, and Cellular Network Technologies* will serve as an important link between academics and industrialists, and it will be an important reference for this field for many years to come.

John Murphy
University College Dublin, Ireland
February 2014

John Murphy *is an Associate Professor in Computer Science and Informatics at University College Dublin. He got a first class honours degree in electronic engineering (B.E.) in 1988 from the National University of Ireland (UCD), an M.Sc. in electrical engineering from the California Institute of Technology in 1990, and a Ph.D. in electronic engineering from Dublin City University in March 1996. He is an IBM Faculty Fellow, a Senior Member of the IEEE, a Fellow and Chartered Engineer with Engineers Ireland, and a Fellow of the Irish Computer Society. For many years, he held an academic part-time position at the Jet Propulsion Laboratory in Pasadena and acted as a consultant to the US Department of Justice. Prof. Murphy is an associate editor for IEEE Communications Letters Journal, a member of the Editorial Board for the IET Communications (formerly IEE Proc Communications), and an associate editor for Telecommunications Systems Journal. He was the guest editor (along with Prof. Perros) for a special issue of IET Communications on Optical Burst and Packet Switching in 2009. He has published over 100 peer-reviewed journal articles or international conference full papers in performance engineering of networks and distributed systems and has been awarded over 20 competitive research grants (over 5 million euro). He has supervised 13 Ph.D. students to completion.*

Preface

In the ever-evolving telecommunication industry, smart mobile computing devices have become increasingly affordable and powerful, leading to a significant growth in the number of advanced mobile users and their bandwidth demands. People can now connect to the Internet from anywhere at any time, while on the move (e.g. on foot, in the car, on the bus, stuck in traffic, etc.) or stationary (e.g. at home/office/airport/coffee bars, etc.). The connection to the Internet is possible and can be done via wireline or wireless solutions. Depending on the user location, wireless connectivity is enabled by different Radio Access Technologies (RATs) such as: Global System for Mobile Communications (GSM), Enhanced Data Rates for GSM Evolution (EDGE), Universal Mobile Telecommunications System (UMTS), High Speed Packet Access (HSPA), Long-Term Evolution (LTE), Worldwide Interoperability for Microwave Access (WiMAX), Wireless Local Area Networks (WLAN), Wireless Personal Area Network (WPAN), etc. Use of all these RATs is rapidly spreading, covering various geographical locations in an overlapping manner. Moreover, RATs differ in capacity, coverage area, monetary cost, connection speed, and can be deployed by one or more network operators.

The "Always Best Connected" vision is built around the scenario of a mobile user seamlessly roaming within a multi-operator, multi-technology, multi-terminal, multi-application, multi-user environment supported by the next generation of wireless networks. In this heterogeneous environment, users equipped with multi-mode wireless mobile devices will be able to get online anytime and anywhere. The heterogeneous environment will enable them to use the e-mail system to keep in touch or close deals, take part in video conferencing, perform video streaming, use Voice over IP (VoIP), mobile TV, entertainment services, download music or videos with the preferred band, watch a movie of interest, transfer files to and from business contacts or friends, to do online shopping, and use many other applications. Among these, using social networking applications based on Web sites such as Twitter, Facebook, Linkedin, MySpace, etc. is also a possibility. These have become a part of one's daily life and are often used for business (e.g., to post a profile or look for a job), to connect to people (e.g., share videos, music, photos), or share social media (e.g., news, personal experience, reviews). All these applications can be accessed by any network-connected user from a variety of devices. Nowadays, with the advances in technology, mobile computing devices such as smartphones, PDAs, small netbooks, tablets, and other integrated mobile devices have become more and more affordable, easy to use, and powerful, mobile users expect rich services at higher quality levels.

This increase in the number of mobile users and their applications demands led to an exponential increase in the mobile broadband usage, which puts an unprecedented level of pressure on the capacity of wireless networks. No single network technology will be equipped to deal with this explosion of mobile broadband data, making the coexistence of the most advanced broadband, broadcast, and cellular technologies a key solution.

THE CHALLENGES

Looking at the rapidly evolving Information Communications Technology (ICT) industry, it can be noticed that a stealth but very powerful service-oriented revolution takes place step-by-step.

First, smart mobile computing devices have become increasingly powerful and affordable, determining a significant growth in their number, their user number, and their processing, communication, and display capabilities. Due to these advances in technologies (e.g., improved CPU, graphics, display, etc.) and the mass-market adoption of the new multi-mode high-end devices—smartphones, iPhones, netbooks, and laptops—the mobile operators are confronting massive traffic growth.

Second, a wide range of diverse services are being launched including those offered by video sharing sites such as YouTube, social Websites, mobile TV, banking, gaming, and other entertainment services. Moreover, Cisco noted that the global IP traffic has increased eight fold in the past 5 years and will further increase fourfold by 2016, so it estimates that more than 110 Exabytes of data per month will be transferred, out of which 61% will be exchanged wireless and 55% will be rich media-based (Cisco, 2011). Some of these services (e.g. HD TV, 3D TV) put important pressure on both content processing and delivery.

Third, a wide range of technologies enable Internet connectivity and access to various services from anywhere at any time, while on the move or stationary. They include broadcast (e.g. DVB-T2, DVB-H, etc.), broadband (e.g. IEEE 802.11g, IEEE 802.11n, etc.), and cellular (e.g. LTE, UMTS, etc.) technologies. Multiple coexisting radio access technologies will be fundamental for the next generation of wireless network in order to handle the volume and diversity of user traffic demands.

Fourth, there is a definite trend towards using cloud computing for next generation business processing and communication needs, offering both robustness and flexibility. By making use of cloud computing, a mass-market adoption of the mobile devices has been observed that became as powerful as the PCs are today with the advantage of enabling the ubiquitous availability of mobile broadband. This requires data exchange and processing both in the foreground and background. Moreover, there is an important increase in inter-communicating non-PC-like objects, including machines, appliances, sensors, and vehicles.

Last but not least, there are important efforts put in energy consumption optimization and in finding sustainable solutions in diverse areas, including ICT and networking in particular. The increased competition in the networked-based services and the current worldwide economic situation determines increased efforts for reducing the costs by making use of optimization and/or finding innovative more efficient research and development directions.

For many years, ICT has focused on providing solutions for supporting a wide range of service types and then on increasing user quality of experience only. However, in recent years, a rising concern on finding sustainable and energy-efficient solutions appeared. This was driven by both the evolved societal interests and the user conscience and was backed by EU and worldwide policies related to the reduction of the gas emissions. Additionally, the latest economic situation has determined all the important market players to work at reducing costs in order to make their businesses more efficient. However, these cost- and energy-efficiency targets contrast severely with both the user demand expectations of high quality levels and service providers' need to introduce new various interactive rich media services. All these new rich media data services are known for being bandwidth hungry applications and highly power intensive.

The very recent digital dividend (i.e. there are no analog TV broadcasts as of 2012), and the new high spectrum efficient solutions (i.e. DVB-T2) in broadcast world, the proliferation of broadband wireless networks and gigabit wired communication support in broadband networking, and the increase in cellular technology penetration in the developing countries and the introduction of the latest technology (i.e. LTE) in cellular technology space enable the use of additional spectrum, support more efficient communications, and reach more users. However, in this multi-service, multi-technology, multi-provider, multi-device, multi-user environment there is a need for the development of a coherent framework and a set of new solutions to support cost and energy consumption optimization while offering a high quality of experience levels for the users when they avail from diverse services.

SEARCHING FOR A SOLUTION

According to Cisco (2012a), the global IP traffic has increased eight fold in the past 5 years and will further increase fourfold by 2016. It is estimated that more than 110 Exabytes of data per month will be transferred, out of which 61% will be exchanged wireless (Cisco, 2011) and 55% will be rich media-based (Cisco, 2012b). It is estimated that networked delivered digital media, especially over a heterogeneous environment to mobile customers will become one of main economic driving forces in the coming years. However, this will only be possible by having the necessary infrastructure to accommodate the increasing number of mobile users and supporting their expected high Quality of Experience (QoE) levels. There are many Internet Service Providers that provide excellent wired connectivity to residential and business users alike. For local network access and service support, wireless technologies such as Wireless Local Area Network (WLAN) and Wireless Personal Area Network (WPAN) can be employed. Additionally, full wireless connectivity is supported via different radio access technologies, offered by different operators. These operators can provide connectivity by making use of different technologies such as: GSM, EDGE, UMTS, HSPA, LTE, WiMAX, etc. One operator can cover different regions with different technologies. However, no single network technology and no single network provider will be capable of dealing with this explosion of mobile broadband traffic and the diverse services demands, making the optimized innovative use of the co-existing broadband, broadcast, and cellular network technologies a key solution. In order to deal with this explosion of mobile broadband data, network operators have started deploying different radio access technologies in overlapping areas. This solution enables them to accommodate more mobile users and to keep up with traffic demands. In this context, the new challenge that the network operators are facing is to ensure seamless rich media service delivery experience at high quality levels to the end-user in a heterogeneous environment.

This multi-user, multi-technology, multi-application, multi-provider environment requires the development of new technologies and standards that seek to ensure the quality of experience for the global end-users. While wireless technologies had a spectacular evolution over the past years, the present trend is to adopt a global network of shared standards, which comes to meet user applications' requirements. For example, the new Long-Term Evolution Advanced (LTE Advanced) technology represents the next-generation all-IP Mobile Broadband network solution with data rates of 1Gbps for stationary users, and up to 100Mbps for mobile users. LTE was designed to ensure enhanced data throughput speeds, to increase the capacity, and to improve the user quality of experience. It is built on the concept of self-organizing and self-optimizing network, which intends to break the network into smaller pieces and to make use of the femtocells. The femtocells are small cellular base stations designed for indoor solutions. The use of the femtocells is also becoming successful, as they are an efficient solution for improving the capacity and the coverage area for a mobile operator, especially indoors. Moreover, LTE includes a mobile broadband component suitable for Video on Demand services and a mobile broadcast component (enhanced

Multimedia Broadcast and Multicast System [eMBMS]) for broadcast services. In this context, network operators will be able to offer mobile and interactive TV. Another broadcast technology solution for 3G mobile broadband is represented by the Integrated Mobile Broadcast (IMB), which is designed to work with Time Division Duplex (TDD) spectrum. An optimal solution would be to build out a mobile TV network by making use of the coexistence of the broadcast, broadband, and cellular technologies, which could be led by a Mobile Virtual Network Operator (MVNO). This solution could bridge the digital divide and can bring economic, social, and technological benefits by enabling innovations in mobile broadcast devices and applications. Moreover, by converging the different delivery mechanisms and making use of the additional Digital Dividend spectrum, it can make mobile broadband more affordable for the masses, especially to the far reaching regions; it can bring education to the remote regions; it can contribute to enabling innovations in healthcare (e.g. remote monitoring and diagnostics), smart grid solutions, social networking sites, economy, etc.

Another solution adopted by the network operators to help them deal with this explosion of mobile broadband data is the use of WLAN offload. WLAN networks have had an important impact in the area of mobile communications and their use has grown significantly in recent years (e.g., extended coverage, low-latency, power-efficient connection, reduced loads, etc.). The Wireless-Fidelity (Wi-Fi) offload solution is already adopted by many service providers (e.g., Deutsche Telekom and iPass launched WiFi Mobilize). This solution enables the transfer of some of the mobile broadband traffic from the core cellular network to the WiFi network at peak times. In this way, users can avail of a wider service offering. However, the overall user experience is still far from optimal as providing high quality mobile video services with QoS (Quality of Service) provisioning over resource-constrained wireless networks remains a challenge. Moreover, user mobility, as well as the heterogeneity of mobile devices (e.g., different operating systems, display size, CPU capabilities, battery limitations, etc.),and the wide range of the video-centric applications (e.g., VoD [Video On Demand], video games, live video streaming, video conferences, surveillance, etc.) opens up the demand for user-centric solutions that adapt the application to the underlying network conditions and device characteristics. In the current environment, mobile users want to be connected to the best value network that best satisfies their preferences for their current application(s) requirements. On the other hand, the network operators want to maximize their revenue by efficiently using their networks to satisfy and retain the most customers possible. Challenges for the operators include network optimization, especially for video traffic, if it is to represent two-thirds of the overall wireless traffic. Uninterrupted, continuous, and smooth video streaming, minimal delay, jitter, and packet loss must be provided in order to avoid degradation in the application quality and user experience. The main challenge for the users is to select the best available Radio Access Network (RAN). For example, there is a need for an efficient solution for selecting the best value network for the user, considering the user preferences, application requirements, and network conditions. The network selection decision is a complex one, with the challenge of trading-off different decision criteria (e.g. service class type, users' preferences, mobile device being used, battery level, network load, time of day, price, etc.). This is further complicated by the combination of static and dynamic information involved, the accuracy of the information available, and the effort in collecting all of this information with a battery, memory, and processor-limited device. This selection decision needs to be made once for connection initiation and subsequently as part of all handover decisions.

Another challenge is the multimedia service delivery with QoS provisioning over wireless networks. This is due to the constraints of wireless links and the user mobility. In this context, it is essential to provide QoS mechanisms to cater for the rich media throughput, delay, and jitter constraints, especially within the wireless environment where connections are prone to interference, high data loss rates, and/ or disconnection. The aim of these mechanisms is to maintain an acceptable user-perceived quality and make efficient use of the wireless network resources.

The energy consumption is another key component that consumers care highly about. Handsets are used as mobile work and entertainment centres (e.g. for communications, listening to music/radio, taking photos, GPS services, playing games, and for rich media playback/streaming). It is known that real-time applications, and in particular those which are based on multimedia, have strict QoS requirements, but they are also the most power-hungry. In this context, one of the impediments of progress is the battery lifetime of the mobile device. With advances in technology, the mobile user has a wide choice of high capability mobile devices, from laptop computers and netbooks to PDAs, tablets, and smart phones. However, the batteries have not evolved as much as processors and memory, and their capability is very much limited. This deficiency in battery power and the need for reduced energy consumption provides motivation for the development of more energy efficient solutions while enabling always best connectivity and always best experience to mobile users.

This continuing growth of video content creates challenges for the network service providers in ensuring seamless multimedia experience at high end-user perceived quality levels, given the device characteristics and network resources. Technologies improvements alone would not be able to keep up with this explosion of mobile broadband traffic. Thus, even though LTE-Advanced is seen as a dominant player in offering support for mobile broadband and broadcast technologies, making use of the Digital Dividend spectrum allocation for mobile networks could bring game-changing benefits to all parties involved. Bringing together broadband, broadcast, and cellular technologies for global consumers could contribute to the economical, social, and technological benefits.

ORGANIZATION OF THE BOOK

The book will cover important aspects of the emerging technologies in this multi-technology, multi-application, multi-terminal, multi-user environment with the main focus on the convergence problems and quality of service provisioning. It presents various convergence approaches and adaptive techniques identifying the main research issues and challenges and presents a survey of the proposed solutions in the literature.

The manuscript is structured in two main sections. The first section on "Convergent Evolution" describes the current wireless multi-access environment, which leads towards the next generation of wireless networks. It includes important chapters written by researchers from prestigious laboratories from USA, Ireland, India, Portugal, and China that present the current state of the art in the heterogeneous wireless communication environment, including economical aspects, mobility challenges, resource allocation and management, ensuring always best experience, multimedia content distribution, energy management and interference mitigation, etc. The "Convergence Evolution" section consists of six chapters. A brief description of each of the chapters in this section is given below.

Chapter 1 identifies the economical aspects of the heterogeneous network environment. The increase usage of the multimedia content by the mobile users on a daily basis puts high pressure on the network operators in terms of network resources, which might lead to network congestion. In order to provide a better control and reduce the network traffic, the network operators have capped their billing plans, which might require the mobile user to pay extra money when exceeding the quota. However, this might result in undesirably high bills for the mobile user, which could lead to their dissatisfaction and increased churn rate. The chapter introduces a model that involves personalising the multimedia content based on the user attitude towards risk. It makes use of a model that assesses the user attitude towards risk by considering the user age, gender, and risk attitude self-assessment. The research presented in this chapter adds to the state of the art by taking into account the user context (e.g. whether the user uses the roaming service or not, the current data consumption) as well as the user input. The improved model may be used to provide a more accurate trade-off: quality vs. price resulting in an increase of user satisfaction and a better service quality.

Chapter 2 highlights the importance of Vehicular Ad-Hoc Networks (VANETs) in the context of smarter cities and roads. Currently, VANET attracts significant academic, industrial and governmental planning, research, and development efforts. A very promising avenue in VANET is to bring together multiple wireless technologies in the architectural design. One of the solutions that can be employed in designing such a VANET architecture that successfully uses different technologies is clustering. Clustering will have an important role in the desired vehicular connectivity in the future cities and roads, as it addresses some of VANETs' major challenges such as scalability and stability. This chapter presents a comprehensive survey of clustering schemes in the VANET research area, covering aspects that have never been addressed before in a structured manner. Moreover, the survey provides a general classification of the clustering algorithms, presents some of the most advanced and latest algorithms in VANETs, and in addition, reviews the performance assessment of clustering algorithms.

Chapter 3 discusses the implementation details (i.e. architecture and network components), issues associated with heterogeneous Broadband Wireless Access Networks (BWANs) (i.e. handovers, network selection, and base-station placement), and the various resource allocation schemes (i.e. shared resource allocation in split handover and inter-RAT self-organizing networks) that can improve the performance of the system by maximizing the capacity and accommodating more users. The chapter looks at the existing solutions that have been proposed in the literature in order to support the ever-increasing cellular networks' data requirements by increasing capacity, spectrum efficiency, and network coverage.

Chapter 4 analyzes the possible challenges that might exist when supporting multicast services over Long-Term Evolution (LTE), with particular attention to resource management, considered as the key aspect for an effective provisioning of Multimedia Broadcast Multicast Service (MBMS) services over cellular networks. Recently, the mobile operators observed a growing demand of multicast services over their radio cellular networks. Since multicast applications are expected to be massively exchanged over Fourth Generation (4G) systems, the Third Generation Partnership Project (3GPP) defined the MBMS standard that offers support for multicast services over LTE, the 4G wireless technology able to provide high quality services in mobile environments. Nevertheless, several issues related to the management of MBMS services are still open and are discussed in this chapter.

Chapter 5 looks into the use of Game Theory for collaboration in future next generation networks. It has been shown that cooperative strategies have the great potential of improving network performance and spectrum utilization in future networking environments. This represents a new paradigm in terms of network management. However, this requires a novel design and analysis framework targeting a highly flexible networking solution with a distributed architecture. Game Theory is a comprehensive mathematical tool suitable for modeling highly complex interactions among distributed and intelligent decision makers. In this way, the more convenient management policies for the diverse players (e.g. content providers, cloud providers, home providers, brokers, network providers, or users) should be found to optimize the performance of the overall network infrastructure. This chapter discusses several Game Theory models that are highly relevant for enabling collaboration among the diverse players, using different ways to incentivize it, namely through pricing or reputation. Additionally, several related open problems, such as the lack of proper models for dynamic and incomplete information games in this area, are highlighted.

Chapter 6 introduces the benefits of cognitive radio-enabled heterogeneous networks and introduces a scheme design of cognitive interference mitigation and energy management in heterogeneous networks. The wide deployment of heterogeneous networks and the increased popularization of intelligent terminals facilitate subscribers with great convenience, better Quality of Experience (QoE) guarantee, and much higher traffic rates. However, interference management will be indispensable in this heterogeneous network environment. Moreover, with the emerging energy-hungry riche media services for subscribers, energy-aware solutions become popular. To this end, motivated by interference mitigation and energy-saving challenges of the heterogeneous networks and the promising cognitive radio techniques, more advanced energy saving and interference control techniques based on cognitive radio should be developed for ensuring a better QoE to the mobile users. This chapter presents a review of the cognitive radios, multiple types of smallcells, and introduces the benefits of cognitive radio-enabled heterogeneous networks.

The second section titled "QoS Provisioning Solutions" presents various solutions proposed by world-known researchers in different areas of wireless communications. It includes important chapters written by researchers from prestigious laboratories from Ireland, Romania, Portugal, UK, and Slovakia, presenting results in the area of enhanced video delivery, vehicular networks, wireless sensor networking, wireless broadband communications and fibre networking, game theory model for next generation networks, etc. The "QoS Provisioning Solutions" section consists of six chapters with a brief description given below:

Chapter 7 presents Dynamic Adaptive Streaming over HTTP (DASH), a solution for improving video delivery quality over heterogeneous network environments. Following the proliferation of low-cost rich media-enabled mobile devices, the global community of online video viewers is expanding rapidly, especially with multimedia streaming seen as a major commercial potential. All these high-end devices enable increasing amounts of video-based content to be acquired, stored, and distributed across existing best effort networks that also carry other traffic types. In this context, network congestion is one of the most important issues that affects networking traffic in general and video content delivery. Among the various solutions proposed in the literature, adaptive delivery of content according to available network bandwidth was very successful. This chapter provides an overview of the DASH standard and presents a survey of currently proposed mechanisms for video adaptation related to DASH. It also introduces the DASH-Aware Performance Oriented Adaptation Agent (dPOAA), which improves user Quality of Experience (QoE) levels by dynamically selecting best performing sources for the delivery of video content.

Chapter 8 introduces TraffCon, an innovative vehicle route-management solution based on IEEE 802.11p sparse roadside-vehicle networking. The chapter looks at the traffic congestion representing a major issue in the modern society that continues to worsen as the number of cars on the road increases behind the ability of the existing infrastructure to cope with this growth. Additionally, research efforts are needed to address the problem of reducing vehicle fuel consumption and gas emissions and consequently reducing pollution. To this end, this chapter shows how TraffCon makes use of a novel best route selection algorithm for vehicular traffic routing and of vehicular wireless communications to reduce not only the journey time but also the fuel consumption and vehicle gas emissions.

Chapter 9 presents the main challenges that can be arise when developing complex systems using the core concept of Video-Based Wireless Sensor Networks. The chapter summarizes innovative solutions proposed in the literature on this area with the main focus on two crucial aspects: video data processing and data exchange. The chapter looks into localization algorithms in case of random deployment of wireless sensor nodes having no specific localization hardware installed. Solutions for data exchange are presented by highlighting the data compression and communication efficiency in terms of energy saving. Moreover, several open research topics related to Video-Based Wireless Sensor Networks are identified and discussed.

Chapter 10 builds a Game Theory model in order to analyse the competition in next generation networks. Similar to a real competitive market situation, the next generation networks are seen as the competitors that need to adapt their strategy to react to the other players' strategies. The profit of each network operator will be dependent not only on their actions but also on the actions of the other operators in the market. This chapter analyzes the impact of the price (retail and wholesale) variations on several output results: players' profit, consumer surplus, welfare, costs, and service adoption. An adoption model is proposed that reflects the competition between players and that the variation of the service prices of one player has an influence on the market share of all players.

Chapter 11 proposes an Optical Fiber distribution solution for indoor short-range wireless broadband communications. This chapter presents an introduction to Radio over Fiber (RoF) technology, which is considered to be an efficient solution to extend the distribution range and wireless capacity services to the end-user for the short range indoor wireless broadband signal. The basic requirements in terms of optical components for indoor short-range wireless millimeter waves, the limiting factor, and the impairments are identified and described. The optical millimeter-wave generation solutions are explained followed by the recent optical activities at the 60GHz band and upcoming research areas such as THz and optical wireless.

Chapter 12 explores the use of the Hybrid Passive Optical Networks (HPON) configurator in designing broadband Next Generation Passive Optical Networks (NG-PON). Looking at the emerging applications and the needs of ever increasing bandwidth demands, it is anticipated NG-PON will require higher bandwidth to satisfy all the end-user demands and for the network operators to develop valuable access networks. Therefore, this chapter identifies several general requirements for NG-PON networks, which are characterized and described. As the HPON presents a necessary phase of the future transition towards optical fiber, the specific requirements of the HPON networks are also presented. The various architectures of the HPON with their characteristics and distinctions are discusses, and the HPON network configurator is introduced with the main aim on helping users, professional workers, network operators, and system analysts to design, configure, analyze, and compare various variations of possible hybrid passive optical networks.

The prospective audience of this book is mainly undergraduate students, postgraduate students, and researchers who are interested in learning more about the latest developments in the area of mobile and wireless communications. It also targets industry professionals who are working or are interested in this area, providing them with a reference of the latest efforts, which take the research further by addressing some of the shortcomings of the existing solutions.

The editors wish you a pleasant reading.

Ramona Trestian
Middlesex University, UK

Gabriel-Miro Muntean
Dublin City University, Ireland

REFERENCES

Cisco. (2011). *Cisco visual networking index: Global mobile data traffic forecast update, 2010–2015*. Cisco.

Cisco. (2012a). *Cisco visual networking index: The zettabyte era*. Cisco.

Cisco. (2012b). *Cisco visual networking index: Forecast and methodology, 2011-2016*. Cisco.

Acknowledgment

The *Convergence of Broadband, Broadcast, and Cellular Network Technologies* book would not exist without the effort of many people whose names may not appear on the cover of the book. However, their hard work, cooperation, friendship, and understanding were very important to the preparation and production of the book.

The editors would like to sincerely thank the entire team at IGI Global for their support and help in the publication of this book. In particular, we wish to thank Austin M. DeMarco the Managing Editor – Book Development. His patience was amazing and appreciated, while his guidance was always timely, useful, and valued.

Prof. John Murphy deserves special attention, as he very generously provided his time and expertise to help in writing the foreword. As the success of this book depends on the high quality chapters submitted, the editors wish to express their deep appreciation to the authors of each chapter for their significant contribution. Without their insights and expertise, this book would not be possible.

As in general the work associated with the chapter review is underestimated and forgotten, we would like to thank the team of reviewers for their generous commitment of time and effort they have put into the reviewing process and for providing their expertise to ensure a high-quality review process. We also thank the Editorial Advisory Board members for their implication in this project.

Last but not least, we would like to thank our families for being the "center of gravity" and for their continuous support along the way. In particular, Gabriel-Miro would like to thank his dear parents, Dora and Ivo, for being an immense source of inspirations throughout his life. His special gratitude is for his wife, Cristina, for her immense love, patience, and support. His lovely kids: his smart son, Daniel-Sasha, and beautiful daughter, Alexandra, for making him such a proud dad and making his life worth living. Ramona would like to thank her wonderful and loving parents, Maria and Vasile, for providing her the opportunity to study and be where she is today. Their unconditional love and care is a source of inspiration in everything that she is doing. Her special gratitude goes to her dear brother, Ionut, and his lovely wife, Andreea. She also owes a special thank you to Kumar for his continued patience and support, which were essential to this project.

Ramona Trestian
Middlesex University, UK

Gabriel-Miro Muntean
Dublin City University, Ireland

Section 1
Convergent Evolution

Chapter 1
Economical Aspects of Heterogeneous Networks:
When Money, Quality, and Context Matter

Andreea Molnar
Arizona State University, USA

Cristina Hava Muntean
National College of Ireland, Ireland

ABSTRACT

The high usage of multimedia content in daily activities has put strains on the network operators as the transmitted content can lead to network congestion. In an effort to control and reduce the traffic, network operators have capped their billing plans. A capped billing plan may require the user to pay extra money when exceeding the quota, and this can result in undesirably high bills for the mobile users. A solution that has been shown to reduce the size of transmitted data and also addresses user needs in terms of billing cost was presented in Molnar and Muntean (2013a). This solution involves personalising the multimedia content based on the user attitude towards risk. It makes use of a model that assesses the user attitude towards risk by considering the user age, gender, and risk attitude self-assessment. The research presented in this chapter adds to the state of the art by presenting an improvement to the user risk attitude model (Molnar & Muntean, 2012) that takes into account the user context (e.g. whether the user uses the roaming service or not, the current data consumption) as well as the user input. The improved model may be used to provide a more accurate trade-off: quality vs. price (Molnar & Muntean, 2013a) and this leads to an increase in user satisfaction and better service quality.

INTRODUCTION

The increased popularity of user generated multimedia content (Traverso et al., 2012), enormous peer to peer traffic volume (Mondal et al., 2012), and an increase in mobile data traffic (Trestian et al., 2012b) as a result of high usage and accessibility of multimedia through mobile phones and mobile devices with video streaming capabilities, have made video to become "casual and conversational," a "primary form of communication" between many young people (Bell & Bull, 2010).

DOI: 10.4018/978-1-4666-5978-0.ch001

These have led mobile operators, and not only, to cap mobile data billing plans in an effort to increase their revenues and impede congestion (Sen et al., 2013; Oeldorf-Hirsch et al., 2012). Most capped billing plans currently have "very strict quotas" (Raj et al., 2013) that can lead to high bills as the user has to pay extra for exceeding the quota (Molnar & Muntean, 2013a, 2013b). This aspect creates problems for the users that are not willing/do not afford to pay the required price but still want to access multimedia content over the Internet.

A price reduction for the user, as well as reduced bandwidth consumption can be obtained as a trade-off in multimedia quality (Molnar & Muntean, 2013b; Oeldorf-Hirsch et al., 2012). However, not all users are affected in the same way by the content delivery cost. Some people prefer to pay as much as it is required for an excellent multimedia quality while others being sensitive to a price increase and they prefer to trade-off for quality (Molnar & Muntean, 2010). It has been shown that the difference in the attitude of people when choosing a certain video quality over the price to be paid can be explained by people's attitude towards risk (Molnar & Muntean, 2012). A method that classifies people either in willing to pay for high video quality (risk seekers) or not willing to pay (risk averse) based on their age, gender and their risk attitude self-assessment was proposed in (Molnar & Muntean, 2012). This classification may be used to personalise the content. This chapter adds to the state of the art in user modelling and adaptive multimedia areas by presenting a context-aware user risk attitude model that extends the model presented in Molnar & Muntean (2012) by considering different contextual factors. The following factors are considered: user's location and degree of billing plans usage. User location (i.e. in or out of the country where the billing plan was acquired) is given by the activation of the roaming service.

The rest of this chapter is organised as follows. The next section provides an overview on the fol-

lowing aspects: personalisation, focusing on the context based personalisation, research on user risk attitude and types of user models. The following section presents the context aware based extension proposed for the user risk attitude model presented in Molnar & Muntean (2012) and the considered contextual factors are presented and discussed. An exemplification of the extended model is also provided. The chapter continues with a discussion on the usefulness of the proposed model and ends with conclusions.

BACKGROUND AND MOTIVATION

This section briefly presents previous work done in the area of personalisation focusing on context based personalisation. It continues by introducing various research studies that assess and analyse user risk attitude. The section ends by presenting different types of user models and focusing on the open user type models.

Personalisation

User Profile Based Personalisation

User profile based personalisation builds a profile that stores information about the user such as: the user's knowledge, background, past interaction, preferred media type, etc. User based personalisation is used a lot in the area of e-learning, with the aim to improve learner experience and learning outcomes. Two projects in this area are JPELAS2 (Yin et al., 2010) and EducaMovil (Molnar & Frias-Martinez, 2011).

JPELAS2 stores information about the user such as: name, gender, number of years in school, friends and relatives. This information is introduced by the user when s/he first enters into the system. In addition, the system automatically detects the user comprehension. The aim of the JPELAS2 is to facilitate learning of Japanese and its politeness rules.

EducaMovil considers the required time for a user to answer a question, the number of correctly answered questions and the number of errors done in order to determine the educational content to be shown to the user.

When personalising multimedia content, several adaptation algorithms have considered adapting the multimedia content based on the user region of interest (Muntean at el., 2008; Nemoianu & Pesquet-Popescu, 2013, Ciubotaru, et al., 2009). This approach assumes that there are certain regions in a video clip that are of a higher interest to the user than the other regions where a more aggressive degradation of quality can be applied without affecting as much the user perceived user video quality as degrading equally the whole video clip.

Device Based Personalisation

The diversity of devices user may have when accessing a multimedia clip, and the device characteristics have always been considered a challenge when it comes to personalisation. Devices can have different screen size, screen colour depth (bits/pixel), screen mode (it refers to whether the screen has portrait or landscape mode and if it supports switching between them), capabilities (i.e. whether the device is capable of displaying multimedia, audio or images), memory and type of supported network connectivity (WiMax, 3G, 802.11, etc.). For example, Karadeniz (2011) designed a mobile application that takes into account the screen size of the user's mobile phone when delivering multimedia; Huang et al. (2012) proposed a system that adapts the content regardless of the used device by taking into account the device resolution and supported colours. Ding & Muntean (2013) and Moldovan & Muntean (2011) have proposed adaptive mechanisms that consider the device characteristics in order to deliver multimedia content in an energy efficient manner. Device's battery load was also considered in the

adaptation process of multimedia type content (Moldovan et al., 2011; Moldovan & Muntean, 2012). Concerning the content delivered to a mobile phone the browser optimization of the content is typically done automatically by the browser by compressing the text and images (Oeldorf-Hirsch, et al., 2012). However, the browser currently does not consider optimisations for video content although of the video has a considerable bigger size (Oeldorf-Hirsch, et al. 2012).

Context Based Personalisation

Mobile services are different from traditional ones that make use of desktop computers, by the fact that users could be anywhere and the information access may occur in any circumstance. The user context refers to the location of the user and the environment in which the user watches the content. Examples of context aware personalised systems are JAPELAS2 - Japanese Polite-Expressions Learning Assisting System (Yin et al., 2010) and AmI – Ambient Intelligence (Varela, 2013). JAPELAS2 aims at suggesting which Japanese polite expression may be used in a given context. The users have a PDA equipped with IR (infrared), RFID (Radio Frequency Identification) tag, GPS and wireless LAN. Information about the user location is obtained through the RFID tag attached to the doors when the user is located inside the building, or by using GPS when the user is located outside. IR is used for simplifying the communication targets; instead of entering the interlocutor name, the user just points to him. The users are required to introduce information about them when they use the system for the first time. Based on this information, the system suggests the appropriate "level of politeness". Four "levels of politeness" were considered: casual, basic, formal, more formal. The level of politeness the user has to use changes according to hyponymy (e.g. age, position, etc.), social distance (e.g. family, colleagues, etc.), and formality of the situation (e.g.

meeting). AmI application considers the variable environment conditions and available interaction resources in order to adapt the application interface to the user environment and available device in a proactive and transparent manner. The research presented in this chapter considers the location of the user (whether s/he is using the roaming service or not) and how much the user has consumed from the available bundle, in order to provide a better user risk attitude model.

Risk Attitude

One of the dispositions that drive economic decisions is the human attitude towards risk. Risk is considered "the pivotal element in consumer behaviour" (Taylor, 1974), a central element to economics and finances (Bucciol & Zarri, 2013). It is most often associated with uncertainty (e.g. missing information – making decisions about an unfamiliar brand, however "full information" contexts do not imply missing uncertainty).

It has been found that risk attitude has a great impact on many of the person's decisions such as those involving investment, educational attainment, ownership of a home and occupational choices (Dohmen et al., 2008). Understanding people's attitude towards risk is linked to predicting the consumer behaviour (Dohmen et al., 2011).

Purchase decisions are one of the arenas which involve perceived risk. Five kinds of risks that affect purchase decisions are presented in Solomon et al. (2010): monetary risk, functional risk, physical risk, social risk and psychological risk. Items which are perceived as having a high price are more susceptible to monetary risk. Functional risk refers to the performance of the product. The physical risk is greater when the accident is bigger. Social risk involves the pressure put by the peers when buying visible goods (e.g. when the choice is visible to other peers, there is a risk of embarrassment if the work decision is made). Psychological risk refers to how satisfied

the consumer will be when acquiring a certain product. Risk is perceived differently by different consumers. For example, a self-confident consumer will not be so much affected by peer choices; person's wealth can also influence how monetary risk is perceived. As price is an issue in the capped billing plans provided by the mobile network operators, monetary risk is of a greater importance for the research community. However, by adopting an open user model the user is able to modify its profile and have an impact if, for example a peer manifest has an influence on his/her choices.

Based on people's attitude towards risk, previous studies have shown that certain categories of people tend to be more risk averse than others. For example, women are less willing to take risks than men in general (Ding et al., 2010; Grossman, 2013; Hügelschäfer & Achtziger, 2013) and in different contexts (Dohmen & Falk, 2011; Karhunen & Ledyaeva, 2010; Hügelschäfer & Achtziger, 2013); and older people are less willing to take risks (Dohmen et al., 2011) .

Based on their attitude towards risk people can be classified into:

- **Risk Averse:** They prefer not to assume risks;
- **Risk Neutral:** Who are neutral to risk;
- **Risk Seekers:** They love risk.

However, these three categories are not always used as they are. The first and last one are the most used ones, risk neutral people being included in any of the previous two categories. Depends on the relevance of the three categories and if the system is able to determine the risk neutral category, not all three categories are used. Experimental studies involving lottery and hypothetical questions are typically able to determine a risk neutral person. Studies that ask people to assess on a scale their attitude towards risk in general or in a certain context, were not able to place on the scale a risk neutral person The three risk type categories were used to determine the user attitude towards risk across different domains such as health, financial matters, and career, in order to predict the economic behaviour or to explain different decisions taken by people (Hammitt & Haninger, 2010; Dohmen et al., 2011).

A controversy concerning whether the person's risk attitudes is constant or not across different contexts exists among neo-classical economics and psychology. Neo-classical economists believe that risk preference is the same across all contexts, and psychology challenges this idea. More recent studies show that a stable risk attitude exists but it may vary across the contexts (Dohmen et al., 2011; Lauriola et al., 2013), therefore, when taking into account people's attitude towards risk, the context should also be considered in order to obtain better results. The proposed context aware user risk model presented in this chapter aims to model better the user's risk attitude by enhancing an already existing model that does not take into account the contextual factors.

User Model

Typically, a user model is constructed to inform the system about the user. Based on the information contained in the user model, the system personalises the content delivered to the user. However, some systems (Xu & Bull, 2010, Muntean & Muntean, 2009) have adopted an 'open user model' that allows the users to see and even to modify the information saved in the model. Previous research has shown that users prefer models over which they have control (Ahn et al., 2007). An open user model is used in this research because we wanted the users to be able to see and modify their individual profiles regarding their economic behaviour, as it has been shown that the risk behaviour can vary across contexts (Dohmen et al., 2011; Guiso, et al., 2013).

CONTEXT AWARE OPEN USER RISK MODEL

The aim of this section is to present the extension brought to the the risk attitude model presented in (Molnar & Muntean, 2012). The proposed enhancement considers contextual factors (i.e. user data consumption and if the roaming service is activated or not). The proposed open risk attitude user model allows the users to directly adjust their risk attitude and any other user related information stored by the model.

Risk Attitude Model

A user model that assesses user risk attitude by taking into account the user age, gender and his answer to the general risk question has been proposed in (Molnar & Muntean, 2012). This model assumes that a user who is risk averse will be willing to switch to a lower multimedia quality if monetary cost benefits are obtained, whereas a user who is a risk seeker prefers to pay for maintaining the multimedia quality (Molnar & Muntean, 2011). For the purpose of this chapter, the user risk value computed as in Equation (1) and presented in more details in (Molnar & Muntean, 2012) is named a general user risk model, as it can be applied regardless of the user context.

$$
\begin{aligned}
RV_{General} = w_1 \\
* RV_{GeneralRiskQuestion} + w_2 * RV_{AgeGender}
\end{aligned}
\tag{1}
$$

where, w1 + w2 = 1.

$RV_{GeneralRiskQuestion}$ and $RV_{AgeGender}$ take values between 0 and 10 and therefore the computed $RV_{General}$ value will also be in the range of 0 to 10. If the $RV_{General}$ is a value between zero and less than or equal to 5, the user is classified as a risk averse. If the value is greater than 5 is considered as risk seeker.

The value of the first parameter, RV-
GeneralRiskQuestion, is computed based on the answer
given by the user to the general risk question
(Figure 1). The general risk question asks users
to assess their attitude towards risk on a 0 (risk
averse) to 10 (fully prepared to take risks) scale.
Users who pick a value between 0 and 5 (inclusive) are classified as risk averse, and the ones
that select a value higher than 5 are classified as
risk seekers (Dohmen et al. 2011).

The second parameter, $RV_{AgeGender}$ considers the
age and the gender of the person and it is computed
based on an analysis performed on the SOEP data
set (SOEP v.26). SOEP is a survey performed
by the German Institute. It is a longitudinal research study, the survey taking place each year
since 1984 and it is used for economic research.
In 2009, the SOEP survey was administered to
20,869 people, 52% were women, and 48% men
and they age varied from 17 up to 100 years old.
The survey required the participants to provide,
among others, information about their gender,
the year when they were born, and to answer the
general risk question. As users' attitude towards
risk differs with age and between the two genders
we have analysed the results of the SOEP study.

A general formula for the computation of a user
risk value based on person's age and gender was
proposed and presented in Equation (2).

$$RV_{AgeGender} = \sum_{i=0}^{10} RiskValue_i * ProbabilityRiskValue_i \tag{2}$$

For a given person, $RV_{AgeGender}$ is computed
as the sum of probabilities of having a certain
risk value i for a certain gender and certain age
($ProbabilityRiskValue_i$), multiplied by the risk
value i ($RiskValue_i$), where i can have a value
from 0 up to 10, as the risk values scale from the
general risk question.

For example, for a 24 years old female, the
percentage of subjects from the SOEP survey that
have assigned a particular risk value is presented
in Table 1. The first row represents the 0 to 10 risk
value range, and the second column the percentage
of 24 years old females that were assigned for each
risk value based on the SOEP survey analysis.
Similar tables were created based on the SOEP
data analysis for each age between 17 and 100.

When $RV_{AgeGender}$ value is computed, $RiskValue_i$
represents a particular risk value from the first

Figure 1. User's risk attitude assessment based on the general risk question

How do you see yourself:
Are you generally a person who is fully prepared to take risks or do you try to avoid taking risks?
Please tick a box on the scale, where the value 0 means: "risk averse"
and the value 10 means: "fully prepared to take risks".
You can use the values in between to make your estimate.

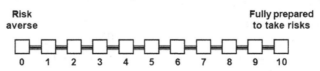

Table 1. Percentages of 24 years old females for each risk value (RV) on the 1-10 scale, based on SOEP data set

RV	0	1	2	3	4	5	6	7	8	9	10
%	2.10	3.50	10.49	11.19	9.09	23.08	13.29	16.78	8.39	0.70	1.40

row of the Table 1, and *ProbabilityRisk Value*$_i$ represents the percentage of people being assigned to *RiskValue*$_i$.

Therefore, for a 24 years old female, $RV_{AgeGender}$ is computed as presented in Equation (3).

$RV_{24Female} = 0 * 0.021 + 1 * 0.0035 + 2 * 0.1049 + 3 * 0.1109 + 4 * 0.0909 + 5 * 0.2308 + 6 * 0.1329 + 7 * 0.1678 + 8 * 0.0839 + 9 * 0.007 + 10 * 0.014$

$$RV_{24Female} = 4.94 \qquad (3)$$

The computed value is less than 5, therefore, all 24 years old female persons have $RV_{AgeGender}$ equal to 4.94 and they are classified as risk averse just based on their age and gender. $RV_{AgeGender}$ is combined with $RV_{GeneralRiskQuestion}$ and an individual risk attitude value is computed for a particular person.

The general user risk model described above has been validated and results have been presented in (Molnar & Muntean, 2012). A multimedia delivery mechanism that uses the general user risk model has been already proposed in (Molnar & Muntean, 2013a).

CONTEXT AWARE EXTENSION FOR THE USER RISK ATTITUDE MODEL

Although it is considered that a stable attitude towards risk exists, it has been shown that it can vary across different contexts (Dohmen et al., 2011; Lauriola et al., 2013). Among the factors that influence people decisions when it comes to paying for multimedia quality is whether the user still has data available in the bundle and the price to be paid when exceeding the quota (Molnar & Muntean, 2011). Therefore, this research considers two contextual factors: user billing plan usage, and whether or not the user is using the roaming service as major price differences can be noticed when the roaming service is used (Molnar, 2011).

Since a user has a different billing plan when using the mobile phone abroad (roaming) than in the home country, and as some users could have multiple billing plans even in the home country (i.e. an increasing number of people use multiple SIMs to access the best tariff (Molnar & Muntean, 2009; Page, Molina & Jones, 2013)), the risk attitude model presented in the next subsection computes a RV value for each of the billing plans the user has. The reason for this is that a different billing plan could influence the outcome and the user switching from one to another could lead to different attitudes. Therefore, if the user has just one billing plan in his home country, and another one when travelling to Country X, two RVs are computed, one for the home country and another one for the Country X. The user is however not restricted to two billing plans and can have different billing plans in the same country, see for example users who have access to multiple SIM phones, or they have multiple billing plans for the roaming service based on the country they travel to.

Open User Risk Attitude Model

The idea behind the user model in this case is to allow the user to see and update his profile, depending on the context s/he is in, as we acknowledge that the current model is not able to consider all factors that may affect people's attitude towards risk. The user may change directly the user risk attitude model information. When the user updates his profile, by changing the risk attitude value, with a new value named $RV_{UserUpdate}$, the new risk attitude value will be considered for the duration of the session, unless the user specifies otherwise.

Real Time Update of the User Risk Attitude Value

At a certain point, multiple factors can trigger a change of the user risk attitude such as user changes his risk value, billing plan data, and/or activation of the roaming service. As consequence the computed risk value RV is updated. Two cases can be distinguished. If one of the factors is a user action that triggers the computation of the $RV_{UserUpdate}$ this value overwrites all the changes the other factors can have on the user model. If the user does not update his risk attitude value $RV_{UserUpdate}$, an average of the computed RV values corresponding to each ctivated factor is computed as in Equation (4). This approach has the advantage that multiple factors can be introduced in the model. The research presented in this chapter considers only two factors, except for $RV_{UserUpdate}$. The following two user risk attitude values are computed for the two factors: RV_{Data} as in Equation (7), and $RV_{Roaming}$ as in Equation (8), where $RV_{Factor1} \ldots RV_{FactorM}$ are risk attitude values computed for each activated factor.

$$RV_{RealTime} = Avg(RV_{Factor1}, RV_{Factor2}, \cdots RV_{FactorM})$$

$$RV_{RealTime} = RV_{Factor1} \text{ when only one factor was activated} \tag{4}$$

The risk attitude value RV_i stored in the user profile is updated with a new value RV_{i+1} as in Equation (5) every time when $RV_{RealTime}$ is computed due to a re-computation of $RV_{UserUpdate}$, RV_{Data}, and/or $RV_{Roaming}$ values. The weight values, w'_1 and w'_2, are in this case 0.1 is 0.9. These values were taken in order to ensure a slow modification of the stored user risk attitude value over time, such that a certain change which might be triggered by an occasional change of context for the user, will not have a big effect on the user risk attitude value as a whole. A slow modification of the values is recommended when the initial value is a reasonable approximation (Rich, 1979). As previous research has shown (Molnar & Muntean, 2012) it is hold true for this case. The selected weight values were considered based on the TCP/IP model (RFC: 793, 1981). TC/IP model is used with the aim of ensuring that there are no sudden spikes in the traffic, and in this case is used to ensure that there are no sudden changes in the

user model. The computed value will be used for the next session.

$$RV_1 = RV_{General}$$

$$RV_{i+1} = w'_1 * RV_{RealTime} + w'_2 * \frac{RV_i + RV_{General}}{2} \tag{5}$$

where,

$$w'_1 + w'_2 = 1$$

RV_{Data} Computation

Bundle based billing plans (capped billing plans) are the most common billing plans currently used by mobile network operators (Molnar & Muntean, 2013a). A bundle billing plan requires the user to pay for a certain data quota in advance. When the data quota included in the bundle is exceeded, the user can be penalised in two ways: either to pay extra for the exceed quantity (most often at a higher price than the charge for the quantity of data contained in the bundle) or to throttle the user's bandwidth (Molnar, 2011). When the user has a bundle based billing plan (a capped billing plan) the personal consumption is monitored though the user risk attitude model. The aim is to maintain data consumption in the limits of the bundle quota. Therefore, when the user requests multimedia content, an estimation of the remaining data quantity from the bundle is computed as in Equation (6), where *DataQuota* represents the original data quota included in the bundle when the plan was bought; *TimeLimitInterval* the time interval for which the bundle is available, *CurrInterval* is the time period elapsed since the plan was activated. For example, if the bundle has an availability of 30 days, *CurrInterval* will be the number of the day when the multimedia was requested, counting as day one the day when the plan was activated. *DataCons* represents the quantity of data used so far from the bundle.

$$EstimatedRemainingData = \frac{DataQuota}{TimeLimitInterval} * CurrInterval - DataCons. \quad (6)$$

If the *EstimatedRemainingData* has a negative value, the estimated user risk attitude value RV_{Data} is computed as in Equation (7), where RV_i is the last user risk attitude value saved in the user profile.

$$RV_{Data} = RV_i - RV_i * 10\% \quad (7)$$

Once the RV_{Data} was computed due to a multimedia clip request, the $RV_{RealTime}$ value will also be updated considering the new value of the RV_{Data}. As result a new user risk attitude value is computed and saved in the profile. This value becomes the new risk value, until the user requests data again, or particular contextual factor is activated. If the *EstimatedRemainingData* has a positive value, the risk value remains unchanged.

The proposed computation of the RV_{Data} can also be applied for a data based billing plans that is used when the user uses the roaming service. A data based billing plan requires the user to pay for the amount of data consumed. In this case the user could specify how much data he wants to consume and this would act as a bundle cap.

RV_Roaming Computation

The use of the roaming service is another situation the user could find herself/himself. The cost of the roaming service is typically higher than the one for using the phone service in the home country. A change in price to be paid in a certain context has been shown to affect the user preference towards the multimedia content. Regardless of the person risk attitude most of the users became more careful with their spending (Molnar & Muntean, 2012) when using the mobile Internet through the roaming service. Different roaming zones exist depending on the mobile network operator, and the price the user has to pay for the accessing data varies depending on the roaming zone s/he is in (Molnar, 2011). Therefore, depending on the zone the user is travelling to, a user risk attitude value ($RV_{Roaming}$) corresponding to the activation of the roaming service is computed as presented in Equation (8). The RV_i represents the current user risk attitude value stored in the user profile, reduced by a percentage. The percentage of reduction (x) depends on the roaming zone the user is. For example a 10% reduction is used for Zone 1 - Europe and 20% reduction for Zone 2 - Middle East.

$$RV_{Roaming} = RV_i - RV_i * x\% \quad (8)$$

This roaming related risk value is considered for the duration of the session, unless other contextual factors are activated.

Exemplification of the User Risk Attitude Value Computation

A person living in Ireland has acquired a bundle plan with a 500MB data quota, valid for a 30 days period. The person has the current risk attitude value RV_i equal to 5.1 and the $RV_{General}$ value equal to 5. As the current risk attitude value is higher than 5 the person is classified as risk seeker. By the third day s/he has already consumed 100MB. The estimated remaining data in the budle is computed as in Equation (9) and it is equal to -50, which means that the person has exceeded its quota for the first 3 days by 50MB. If a person exceeds the daily quota multiply by the number of days the bundle is already activated, the model assumes that by the end of the bundle period the user will be exceeding the bundle quota.

$$\text{EstimatedRemainingData}$$
$$= \frac{500}{30} * 3 - 100 \tag{9}$$

$$\text{EstimatedRemainingData} = -50$$

As the estimated remaining data is negative the RV_{Data} value is computed and presented in Equation (10).

$$RV_{Data} = 5.1 - 5.1 * 10\% \tag{10}$$

$$RV_{Data} = 4.59$$

The person is currently located in China and uses through the roaming service the mobile phone in order to access data over the Internet As China is considered as part of Zone 3 – Fat East, a 30% reduction is used for the $RV_{Roaming}$ computation as in Equation (11) .

$$RV_{Roaming} = 5.1 - 5.1 * 30\% \tag{11}$$

$$RV_{Roaming} = 3.57$$

As the user has requesred some data over the Internet and uses the roaming service, the $RV_{RealTime}$ value is computed as the average of RV_{Data} and $RV_{Roaming}$ values ans presented in Equation (12).

Therefore, $RV_{RealTime}$ is computed as the average of the newly computed $RV_{Roaming}$ and RV_{Data} values as presented in Equation (12).

$$RV_{RealTime} = (4.59 + 3.57)/2 \tag{12}$$

$$RV_{RealTime} = 4.08$$

As result of the $RV_{RealTime}$ computation, the user risk attitude value stored in the user profile is updated with a new value computed as in Equation (13).

$$RV_{i+1} = 0.1 * 4.08 + 0.9 * \frac{5.1 + 5}{2} \tag{13}$$

$$RV_{i+1} = 4.963$$

The newly computed risk attitude value is lower than the previous value. The value is also lower than 5. Therefore, the model will consider from now on the person being a risk averse and the person may accept a degradation of the quality with the aim to reduce the cost related to accessing the multimedia content via the roaming service.

DISCUSSIONS

The work presented in this chapter discusses a context aware user risk attitude model. The research extends the model that computes the user risk attitude ($RV_{General}$) and was presented in Molnar & Muntean (2012), by considering contextual factors such as the user changes the risk attitude value, activation of the roaming service and or bundle data quota. The model may be further improved by increasing its granularity. Instead of stereotyping the people in two categories: risk averse and risk seekers other categories may be used to classify those persons that have a moderate opinion with regards to how much they are willing to trade-off. Another way of improving the model is to consider categories of multimedia clips for which the risk averse users are willing to pay for quality due to other extraneous benefits. For example, in the case of tele-monitoring glaucoma patients, it is a requirement of the doctor to have a very good (high definition) video image of the patient's eye in order to be able to consult the patient (Molnar & Weerakkody, 2013). In this case the patient is reducing the health related cost through other means such as avoiding the cost of travelling to the hospital, not queuing in the hospital anymore and/

or the necessity to ask somebody to accompany her/him to the hospital, as the patients suffering from glaucoma are typically older – therefore giving more independence to the patient. A cost reduction for the hospital is also obtained due to the usage of tele-monitoring. A better patient management and hence a more efficient use of the ophthalmologists time may be obtain (Molnar & Weerakkody, 2013).

As the network capacity is affected due to increase the proposed model could be used to incentivize a user to accept a lower multimedia quality that requires lower bandwidth thus allowing a critical application, such as ambulance service to make use of a higher bandwidth (Weerakkody et al., 2013). In the context of an emergency service the ability to obtain fast and good quality data (e.g. videos, images) about the patient could improve patient health or even save the patient life.

The context aware user risk attitude model may also be used by the Internet service providers as part of an adaptive mechanism with the aim to reduce the network congestion or by the service providers to reduce the traffic to the server/proxy. Most adaptive multimedia applications take into account technical aspects (Muntean & Murphy, 2002; Trestian et al., 2012a, Muntean et al., 2002) only recently the user risk attitude has been taken into account (Molnar & Muntean, 2013a).

Another direction is to use the model as an input for a handover mechanism. There are some studies that consider the cost of data delivery when performing a handover operation (Bakmaz, 2013) and risk attitude as a willingness to trade-off for handover related waiting time (Ormond et al., 2006). The risk averse users could prefer a network which has more bandwidth constraints as long as the price is reduced, whereas risk seekers would prefer a network that ensures high quality content delivery even if the delivery cost is high. If this affirmation is verified it could be used to further enhanced the handover mechanism.

CONCLUSION

This chapter presented a model that assesses the user risk attitude by considering contextual factors such as whether the use is using the roaming service, the quantity of data consumed from the bundle plan and user's own update of the risk attitude value. The proposed model can be used by adaptive mechanisms for multimedia content distribution which would incentivize users to accept a lower multimedia quality for allowing a better management of the network resources.

ACKNOWLEDGMENT

This work was supported by Irish Research Council for Science, Engineering, and Technology.

REFERENCES

Ahn, J. W., Brusilovsky, P., Grady, J., He, D., & Syn, S. Y. (2007). Open user profiles for adaptive news systems: Help or harm? In *Proceedings of ACM International Conference on World Wide Web*. Alberta, Canada: ACM.

Bakmaz, B. M. (2013). Network selection equilibrium in heterogeneous wireless environment. *Electronics and Electrical Engineering*, *19*(4), 91–96. doi:10.5755/j01.eee.19.4.4058

Bell, L., & Bull, G. (2010). Digital video and teaching. *Contemporary Issues in Technology & Teacher Education*, *10*(1), 1–6.

Bucciol, A., & Zarri, L. (2013). *Financial risk aversion and personal life history*. Retrieved September 16, 2013, from http://leonardo3.dse.univr.it/home/workingpapers/risk_events_BZ.pdf

Ciubotaru, B., Muntean, G. M., & Ghinea, G. (2009). Objective assessment of region of interest-aware adaptive multimedia streaming quality. *IEEE Transactions on Broadcasting*, *55*(2), 202–212. doi:10.1109/TBC.2009.2020448

Ding, R., & Muntean, G. M. (2013). Device characteristics-based differentiated energy-efficient adaptive solution for video delivery over heterogeneous wireless networks. In *Proceedings of IEEE Wireless Communications and Networking Conference*. Shanghai, China: IEEE.

Ding, X., Hartog, J., & Sun, Y. (2010). *Can we measure individual risk attitudes in a survey?* (IZA Discussion Paper No 4807). Retrieved August 22, 2011, from http://ftp.iza.org/dp4807.pdf

Dohmen, T., & Falk, A. (2011). Performance pay and multidimensional sorting - Productivity, preferences and gender. *The American Economic Review*, *101*(2), 556–590. doi:10.1257/aer.101.2.556

Dohmen, T., Falk, A., David, H., & Sunde, U. (2008). *The intergenerational transmission of risk and trust attitudes* (IZA Discussion Paper No 2380). Retrieved August 22, 2011, from http://www.swarthmore.edu/Documents/academics/economics/huffman/Intergenerational_ReStud_revision2_v6.pdf

Dohmen, T., Falk, A., Huffman, D., Sunde, U., Schupp, J., & Wagner, G. (2011). Individual risk attitudes: Measurement, determinants and behavioural consequences. *Journal of the European Economic Association*, *9*(3), 522–550. doi:10.1111/j.1542-4774.2011.01015.x

Grossman, P. J. (2013). Holding fast: The persistence and dominance of gender stereotypes. *Economic Inquiry*, *51*(1), 747–763. doi:10.1111/j.1465-7295.2012.00479.x

Guiso, L., Sapienza, P., & Zingales, L. (2013). *Time varying risk aversion*. The National Bureau of Economic Research. Retrieved September 16, 2013, from http://www.econ.yale.edu/~shiller/behfin/2013_04/Guiso_Sapienza_Zingales.pdf

Hammitt, J., & Haninger, K. (2010). Valuing fatal risks to children and adults: Effects of disease, latency, and risk aversion. *Journal of Risk and Uncertainty*, *40*(1), 57–83. doi:10.1007/s11166-009-9086-9

Huang, H. C., Wang, T. Y., & Hsieh, F. M. (2012). Constructing an adaptive mobile learning system for the support of personalized learning and device adaptation. *Procedia-Social and Behavioral Sciences*, *64*, 332–341. doi:10.1016/j.sbspro.2012.11.040

Hügelschäfer, S., & Achtziger, A. (2013). On confident men and rational women: It's all on your mind (set). *Journal of Economic Psychology*. ISSN 0167-4870

Karadeniz, S. (2011). Effects of gender and test anxiety on student achievement in mobile based assessment. *Procedia Social and Behavioral Sciences*, *15*, 3173–3178. doi:10.1016/j.sbspro.2011.04.267

Karhunen, P., & Ledyaeva, S. (2010). Determinants of entrepreneurial interest and risk tolerance among Russian university students: Empirical study. *Journal of Enterprising Culture*, *18*(3), 229–263. doi:10.1142/S0218495810000574

Lauriola, M., Panno, A., Levin, I. P., & Lejuez, C. W. (2013). Individual differences in risky decision making: A meta-analysis of sensation seeking and impulsivity with the balloon analogue risk task. *Journal of Behavioral Decision Making*. doi: doi:10.1002/bdm.1784

Moldovan, A. N., Molnar, A., & Muntean, C. H. (2011). EcoLearn: Battery power friendly e-learning environment for mobile device users. In *Learning-oriented technologies, devices and networks-Innovative case studies*. Saarbrücken, Germany: LAP LAMBERT Academic Publishing.

Moldovan, A. N., & Muntean, C. H. (2011). Towards personalized and adaptive multimedia in m-learning systems. In *Proceedings of 16th AACE World Conference on E-Learning in Corporate, Government, Healthcare, and Higher Education* (E-Learn). AACE.

Moldovan, A.-N. & Muntean, C. H. (2012). Subjective assessment of BitDetect – A mechanism for energy-aware adaptive multimedia. *IEEE Transactions on Broadcasting Journal, 58*(3), 480-492.

Molnar, A. (2011). *Cost efficient educational multimedia delivery.* (Doctoral thesis). National College of Ireland, Dublin, Ireland. Retrieved August 26, 2013, from http://trap.ncirl.ie/762/

Molnar, A., & Frias-Martinez, V. (2011). EducaMovil: Mobile educational games made easy. In *Proceedings of AACE EDMEDIA 2011 World Conference on Educational Multimedia, Hypermedia & Telecommunications*. Lisbon, Portugal: AACE.

Molnar, A., & Muntean, C. H. (2009). Performance aware and cost oriented adaptive e-learning framework. In *Proceedings of IADIS International Conference e-Learning*. Algarve, Portugal: IADIS.

Molnar, A., & Muntean, C. H. (2010). *Educational content delivery: An experimental study assessing student preference for multimedia content when monetary cost is involved.* Paper presented at the 10th International Conference on Intelligent Systems Design and Applications. Cairo, Egypt.

Molnar, A., & Muntean, C. H. (2011). Mobile learning: An economic approach. In *Intelligent and adaptive learning systems: Technology enhanced support for learners and teachers*. Hershey, PA: IGI Global. doi:10.4018/978-1-60960-842-2.ch020

Molnar, A., & Muntean, C. H. (2012). Consumer' risk attitude based personalisation for content delivery. In *Proceedings of Consumer Communications and Networking Conference*. Las Vegas, NV: Academic Press.

Molnar, A., & Muntean, C. H. (2013a). Cost oriented adaptive multimedia delivery. *IEEE Transactions on Broadcasting, 59*(3), 484–499. doi:10.1109/TBC.2013.2244786

Molnar, A., & Muntean, C. H. (2013b). Comedy: Viewer trade-off between multimedia quality and monetary benefits. In *Proceedings of IEEE International Symposium on Broadband Multimedia Systems and Broadcasting*. London, UK: IEEE.

Molnar, A., & Weerakkody, V. (2013). Defining key performance indicators for evaluating the use of high definition video-to-video services in eHealth. In *Proceedings of Artificial Intelligence Applications and Innovations, 2nd Workshop on Intelligent Video-to-Video Communications in Modern Smart Cities*. Paphos, Cyprus: Academic Press.

Mondal, A., Trestian, I., Qin, Z., & Kuzmanovic, A. (2012). P2P as a CDN: A new service model for file sharing. *Computer Networks, 56*(14), 3233–3246. doi:10.1016/j.comnet.2012.06.010

Muntean, C. H., McManis, J., & Murphy, J. (2002). The influence of web page images on the performance of the web servers. In *Proceedings of Int. Conference of Networking (ICN 2001)* (LNCS), (vol. 2093, pp. 821–828). Berlin: Springer.

Muntean, C. H., & Muntean, G. M. (2009). Open corpus architecture for personalized ubiquitous e-learning. *Personal and Ubiquitous Computing, 13*(3), 197–205. doi:10.1007/s00779-007-0189-5

Muntean, G. M., Ghinea, G., & Sheehan, T. N. (2008). Region of interest-based adaptive multimedia streaming scheme. *IEEE Transactions on Broadcasting, 54*(2), 296–303. doi:10.1109/TBC.2008.919012

Muntean, G. M., & Murphy, L. (2002). Adaptive pre-recorded multimedia streaming. In *Proceedings of IEEE Global Telecommunications Conference,* (Vol. 2, pp. 1728-1732). IEEE.

Nemoianu, I. D., & Pesquet-Popescu, B. (2013). Network coding for multimedia communications. In *Intelligent multimedia technologies for networking applications: Techniques and tools.* Academic Press.

Oeldorf-Hirsch, A., Donner, J., & Cutrell, E. (2012). How bad is good enough? Exploring mobile video quality trade-offs for bandwidth-constrained consumers. In *Proceedings of ACM 7th Nordic Conference on Human-Computer Interaction: Making Sense through Design.* Copenhagen, Denmark: ACM.

Ormond, O., Murphy, J., & Muntean, G. M. (2006). Utility-based intelligent network selection in beyond 3G systems. In *Proceedings of IEEE International Conference on Communications* (Vol. 4, pp. 1831-1836). IEEE.

Page, M., Molina, M., & Jones, G. (2013). The mobile economy. *GSMA.* Retrieved November 1, 2013, from http://www.atkearney.com/documents/10192/760890/The_Mobile_Economy_2013.pdf/

Raj, H., Saroiu, S., Wolman, A., & Padhye, J. (2013). Splitting the bill for mobile data with SIMlets. In *Proceedings of ACM Workshop on Mobile Computing Systems and Applications.* Santa Barbara, CA: ACM.

RFC 793. (1981). *Transmission control protocol.* Retrieved August 26, 2013, from http://www.ietf.org/rfc/rfc793.txt

Rich, E. (1979). User modelling via stereotypes. *Cognitive Science, 3*(4), 329–354. doi:10.1207/s15516709cog0304_3

Sen, S., Joe-Wong, C., Ha, S., Bawa, J., & Chiang, M. (2013). When the price is right: Enabling time-dependent pricing of broadband data. In *Proceedings of SIGCHI Conference on Human Factors in Computing Systems.* Paris, France: ACM.

Solomon, M. R., Bamossy, G., Askegaard, S., & Hogg, M. K. (2010). *Consumer behaviour: A European perspective.* New York: Prentice Hall.

Taylor, J. W. (1974). The role of risk in consumer behaviour. *Journal of Marketing, 38,* 54–60. doi:10.2307/1250198

Traverso, S., Huguenin, K., Trestian, I., Erramilli, V., Laoutaris, N., & Papagiannaki, K. (2012). Tailgate: Handling long-tail content with a little help from friends. In *Proceedings of ACM International Conference on World Wide Web.* Lyon, France: ACM.

Trestian, I., Ranjan, S., Kuzmanovic, A., & Nucci, A. (2012b). Taming the mobile data deluge with drop zones. *IEEE/ACM Transactions on Networking, 20*(4), 1010–1023. doi:10.1109/TNET.2011.2172952

Trestian, R., Moldovan, A. N., Muntean, C. H., Ormond, O., & Muntean, G. M. (2012a). Quality utility modelling for multimedia applications for android mobile devices. In *Proceedings of IEEE International Symposium on Broadband Multimedia Systems and Broadcasting*. Seoul, Republic of Korea: IEEE.

Varela, G. (2013). Autonomous adaptation of user interfaces to support mobility in ambient intelligence systems. In *Proceedings of ACM SIGCHI Symposium on Engineering Interactive Computing Systems* (pp. 179-182). ACM.

Weerakkody, V., Molnar, A., Irani, Z., & El-Haddadeh, R. (2013). A research proposition for using high definition video in emergency medical services. *Health Policy and Technology*, *2*(3), 131–138. doi:10.1016/j.hlpt.2013.04.001

Xu, J., & Bull, S. (2010). Encouraging advanced second language speakers to recognise their language difficulties: A personalised computer-based approach. *Computer Assisted Language Learning*, *23*(2), 111–127. doi:10.1080/09588221003666206

Yin, C., Ogata, H., Tabata, Y., & Yano, Y. (2010). JAPELAS2: Japanese polite expressions learning assisting system in ubiquitous environments. *International Journal of Mobile Learning and Organisation*, *4*(2), 214–234. doi:10.1504/IJMLO.2010.032637

KEY TERMS AND DEFINITIONS

Bundle Based Billing (Capped Billing Plan): A bundle based billing is characterised by the fact that the user has to pay for a specific amount of data (bundle) in advance. That may be used over a given period of time. If the amount of data used is exceeded during the given period, the user may have the following options: (i) pays a different price for the exceeding quantity; (ii) buys a new bundle at the same or different price; (iii) the bandwidth is throttled.

Multimedia Adaptation: Adapting the multimedia properties (e.g. bit rate, frame rate) such that they satisfy certain constraints.

Open User Model: A user model that shows the user the information stored about him. Some open user models would also allow the user to modify the information stored.

Personalised Systems: Systems that adapt their results based on user characteristics, context etc.

Risk Averse Person: A person who prefers stability to risk.

Risk Neutral Person: A person whose decision is not influenced by the uncertainty.

Risk Seeking Person: A person who prefers to assume risks.

Chapter 2
Towards Smarter Cities and Roads:
A Survey of Clustering Algorithms in VANETs

Irina Tal
Dublin City University, Ireland

Gabriel-Miro Muntean
Dublin City University, Ireland

ABSTRACT

This chapter highlights the importance of Vehicular Ad-Hoc Networks (VANETs) in the context of smarter cities and roads, a topic that currently attracts significant academic, industrial, and governmental planning, research, and development efforts. In order for VANETs to become reality, a very promising avenue is to bring together multiple wireless technologies in the architectural design. Clustering can be employed in designing such a VANET architecture that successfully uses different technologies. Moreover, as clustering addresses some of VANETs' major challenges, such as scalability and stability, it seems clustering will have an important role in the desired vehicular connectivity in the cities and roads of the future. This chapter presents a comprehensive survey of clustering schemes in the VANET research area, covering aspects that have never been addressed before in a structured manner. The survey presented in this chapter provides a general classification of the clustering algorithms, presents some of the most advanced and latest algorithms in VANETs, and in addition, constitutes the only work in the literature to the best of authors' knowledge that also reviews the performance assessment of clustering algorithms.

INTRODUCTION

Nowadays, smart cities represent a very important research direction for academia, industry and governments that are eager to embrace various technologies, which will make cities "smarter".

The main purpose of smart cities is to improve all the facilities provided in a city (e.g. buildings, infrastructure, transportation, energy distribution, etc.) in order to improve the citizens' quality of life, while creating a sustainable environment by reducing gas emissions and energy consump-

DOI: 10.4018/978-1-4666-5978-0.ch002

tion. IBM has launched in 2010 IBM Smarter Cities[1] challenge, aiming to support 100 cities in addressing some of their critical challenges, and Dublin Ireland is one of them. In the same year, the European Commission has launched the European Initiative on Smart Cities[2] that addresses four dimensions of the city: buildings, heating and cooling systems, electricity and transport. Related to the transport, the declared aim is to promote sustainable forms of transportation, to build intelligent public transportation systems based on real-time information, traffic management systems for congestion avoidance, safety applications (e.g. collision avoidance) and green applications (e.g. intelligent routing aiming to reduce fuel consumption, gas emissions or energy consumption).

In this context, Vehicular Ad-hoc Networks (VANETs) or simply vehicular networks represent a hot research topic both for academia and industry due to their high potential to create not only smarter cities, but also smarter roads. This potential relies in the *on the wheels connectivity* provided by VANETs that can also meet the *always connected* need of drivers and passengers. Statistics shows that vehicles occupy the third position, after homes and offices, in the top of the places where people spend their time on a daily basis (Araniti, Campolo, Condoluci, Iera, & Molinaro, 2013). VANETs are based on "smart" vehicles that are able to communicate to each other and to the infrastructure via vehicle-to-vehicle (V2V) and vehicle-to-infrastructure (V2I) communications, known under the generic term of V2X communications, but also via other wireless communications technologies (e.g. cellular, WLAN).

V2X communications are considered the main enabling technology of VANETs. They have exclusively dedicated spectrum that is of high importance particularly for safety applications. As this technology has a low penetration rate and also some limitations (i.e. short-lived and intermittent connectivity), in some architectures, other access technologies are employed as well, in order to support the diversity of VANET applications (i.e. safety, traffic management and infotainment applications). Best candidates among the other access technologies are cellular technologies due to their theoretically ubiquitous coverage. First considered was Universal Mobile Telecommunication System (UMTS), but its limited capacity and data rates impose significant challenges in the case of infotainment applications for example. Long Term Evolution (LTE) appears to be the most promising enabling technology for vehicular applications due to the high data rates provided, support for high mobility (up to 350km/h) and high market penetration – LTE was confirmed as the fastest developing mobile system technology ever[3]. However, cellular technologies do not provide built-in support for direct communication between vehicles. Therefore they are appropriate mainly for the communication between vehicle and infrastructure. In addition, according to the studies performed so far, it is more likely that not even LTE can support the huge amount of messages exchanged by vehicles during rush hours. Moreover, the latest statistics show a huge growth in mobile data (without considering the vehicular space) that appears to be impossible to be accommodated by the cellular technologies only. Consequently, VANETs cannot rely on a single type of access technologies, thus there is a need of bringing together multiple technologies, V2X communications, cellular technologies and WLAN, in order to enable support for a wide range of VANET applications.

In this context, clustering can play a very important role in the design of VANET architectures: on one hand clustering addresses some of the V2X communications limitations such as sparse deployment of the infrastructure, and intermittent connections and on the other hand it optimizes the communication via cellular access technology. In addition, clustering algorithms in VANET address some of the main VANET challenges: scalability and stability, and have been integrated in a various range of applications. This chapter presents a thorough survey of clustering algorithms in VANETs. To the best knowledge of the authors there is only a single review in the literature of clustering algorithms in VANETs (Vodopivec, Bester & Kos, 2012). This review is focused on summarizing some of the clustering algorithms in VANETs, but there is no classification provided and no overview on the performance assessment of these algorithms. There still remains a huge gap in the literature: there is no well structured analysis of the performance assessment of clustering algorithms in VANETs. In this chapter this gap is covered and a detailed survey of clustering algorithms is performed. The clustering algorithms are classified in general categories depending on the context they are applied to and depending on the structural criterion. Moreover, compared to the review presented by Vodopivec et al. (2012), the survey presented here covers new and significant stages in this research field.

The structure of the chapter is as follows. In the first sections, an overview of vehicular networks, their enabling technologies, applications and challenges is presented. The following sections are dedicated to clustering: general concepts of clustering, survey of clustering in VANETs – application, classification, performance assessment and representative algorithms. The chapter ends with future directions and conclusions.

BACKGROUND

Introduction to VANETs

Vehicular Ad-hoc Networks (VANETs) or simply vehicular networks are a novel class of mobile ad-hoc networks (MANETs), where the mobile nodes are represented by vehicles. Although they are a class of MANETs, they have specific characteristics that differentiate them, characteristics which will be discussed in a dedicated section. VANETs are mostly based on the com-munication between vehicle-to-vehicle (V2V), vehicle-to-infrastructure (V2I) or infrastructure-to-vehicle (I2V), generally referred to as V2X communications. This type of communications is supported by a novel type of wireless access called Wireless Access for Vehicular Environment (WAVE). Note that in this chapter V2X commu-nications refer exclusively to the communications supported by WAVE (e.g. if the communication between a vehicle and another vehicle is done via another type of access technology such as WiFi for instance, this communication will not be referred to as V2V communication). WAVE contains all the standards dedicated to vehicular environment (Uzcategui & Acosta-Marum, 2009): IEEE 802.11p and IEEE P1609.x standards. IEEE 802.11p, developed to provide wireless access in vehicles, is a new amendment of IEEE 802.11 standard body (IEEE 802.11p, 2010). This is a justified decision in the context of the wide adoption and subsequently the low cost of IEEE 802.11 technologies. Both, IEEE 802.11p and IEEE 1609.x standards, are based upon the alloca-tion of Dedicated Short Range Communications (DSRC) spectrum band. This initiative, started in USA in 1999, allocated dedicated spectrum of frequency to be used exclusively by V2X com-munications. In Europe, spectrum allocation was harder to achieve, as each country has different regulations, but agreement was eventually made on a spectrum similar to the USA. Seven channels of 10MHz in the 5.9GHz range are allocated for use in DSRC/IEEE 802.11p standard. Out of the 7 channels, 6 are service channels (SCH), while the one left is the control channel (CCH). CCH is reserved for system control and safety messages, an SCH channel is dedicated to safety messages as well, whereas the rest of SCHs are mainly used to exchange non-safety and larger data.

While IEEE 802.11p covers the Physical and MAC layers, IEEE P1609.x covers the entire VANET scope of services from application down to the MAC layer.

- **IEEE P1609.1:** (IEEE P1609.1, 2006) is the WAVE Resource Manager standard, defining the interfaces and services of WAVE applications and the format of data messages.
- **IEEE P1609.2:** (IEEE P1609.2, 2006) is the WAVE Security Services for Applications and Management Messages standard that defines the WAVE security: anonymity, authenticity and confidentiality and also the exchange of messages.
- **IEEE P1609.3:** (IEEE P1609.3, 2007) is the WAVE Networking Services that defines routing and transport services. It provides description and management to the protocol stack, network configuration management and also provides the transmission and reception of WAVE short messages.
- **IEEE P1609.4:** (IEEE P1609.4, 2006) is the WAVE Multi-channel Operations that provides the DSRC frequency band coordination and management.

In addition to V2X communications, other types of technologies are also used in supporting vehicular applications. Depending on how these VANET enabling technologies are employed in the vehicular applications, three types of VANET architectures (Figure 1) are defined: pure ad-hoc, pure WLAN/cellular and hybrid (K.C. Lee, U. Lee & Gerla, 2010; Moustafa, Senouci, Jerbi, 2009).

In the ad-hoc architecture, there is V2V communication only, without any infrastructure support. This scenario is feasible since the in-frastructure and wireless access points are not everywhere and their deployment is limited by the cost or geography. Information exchanged between vehicles can be of extreme value, especially in difficult conditions or special circumstances (e.g. an icy road section previously detected by another car or an accident blocking the road).

In WLAN/cellular architecture, cellular base stations and WLAN access points facilitate vehicles' connection to the Internet and provide support for vehicular communications-based applications. In this type of architecture the vehicles do not have support for directly communication with each other in a distributed manner with few exceptions. Such exception is the case when the vehicles are travelling in groups and they can communicate via WiFi. However, if the vehicles do not have similar mobility, the communication via WiFi is not possible as this standard does not support mobility. Cellular networks have a centralized architecture so they do not provide any native support for direct communication between vehicles. All the communication is done via infrastructure support. This can lead to vehicles that are not interested in the messages to receive those messages (e.g. vehicles travelling in a different direction). Among the cellular technologies, LTE looks the most promising in enabling vehicular applications and therefore studies have been performed in order to see how appropriate is LTE in this context. However, so far, it appears to be more likely that LTE alone is not capable of supporting vehicular applications, especially applications that require an intense exchange of

Figure 1. VANET architectures

information between vehicles or during rush hours (Araniti et al., 2013). Moreover, there are already many studies showing that the huge growth in data will be almost impossible to be supported by the cellular networks at all in the near future (Goldsmith, 2012). Therefore, even if cellular technology is used in VANET architecture is preferably to limit the communication via these technologies as much as possible. In this context, clustering can be successfully employed to limit the cellular network communications.

In the hybrid architecture all types of communications are present. Vehicles can talk to each other and exchange information (V2V communications), but also can communicate with fixed infrastructure that is deployed alongside the road also referred to as *road side unit* (RSU) (V2I) or with access points, or wireless towers (WLAN, cellular). This is the most complex architecture and provides support for more complex applications. Especially infotainment applications which require richer content are based on this type of architecture, but also complex traffic management systems. Similar to the previous architecture, clustering can be a viable solution for an optimal communication between vehicle to infrastructure, if this is done via cellular technologies. In the case of V2I communications, clustering can be the response to limited range of communications, sparse deployment of RSUs and intermittent communication.

In VANET architectures the communication capabilities of a vehicle are provided by an in-vehicle component referred to as the *on-board unit* (OBU) that can have multiple network interfaces (V2X, UMTS, LTE, etc.). Note that this component was envisioned to be integrated in the cars by the car manufactures, but in the latter VANET solutions OBU can stand for different devices with wireless capabilities such as the driver's smartphone. OBU also supports intra-vehicle communication needed to collect the data from the vehicle's sensors and devices, data that is then used in the applications enabled by VANET. Most

VANET applications assume that the position of the vehicle is known, so a GPS or other positioning system is considered to be integrated in OBU (or co-exist with OBU).

VANET Applications

A large plethora of applications have been envisioned and proposed for VANETs. These can be categorized in three big classes (Karagiannis et al., 2011): active road safety applications, traffic efficiency and management applications and infotainment applications.

Active Road Safety Applications: Aim to provide a safer driving environment by reducing the probability of accidents and preventing the loss of lives. Such applications are traffic signal violation warning, emergency electronic brake light, pre-crash sensing, lane change warning, cooperative forward collision warning, etc. (Toulminet, Boussuge & Laurgeau, 2008). These are mainly pro-active approaches that are trying to avoid accidents. Reactive safety approach based on VANETs can be developed in the context of emergency systems. "Green" routes for emergency vehicles can lead to saving many human lives. In a recent survey, Martinez, Toh, Cano, Calafate, & Manzoni, (2010) emphasized both the great potential of V2I/V2V communications in enhancing the emergency services and the need of designing systems based on this type of communications that ensure efficient emergency service delivery. The architecture and principles of a complete solution, a VANETs-based traffic management system ensuring "green" routes for emergency vehicles has been proposed by Djahel and his colleagues in (Djahel, Salehie, Tal, & Jamshidi, 2013).

Traffic Efficiency and Management Applications' Goal: Is to improve the overall efficiency of transportation by managing the navigation of the vehicles via cooperative co-ordination (e.g. cooperative adaptive cruise control (Ploeg, Serrarens, & Heijenk, 2011)). Also, they aim to improve not only the overall efficiency, but the efficiency per vehicle via speed management applications (e.g. avoiding stopping to the intersections (Rakha & Kamalanathsharma, 2011; Barth, Mandava, Boriboonsomsin & Xia, 2011)). This type of applications are situated somewhere at the border between safety and infotainment applications.

Infotainment Applications: Are applications that are not directly related to traffic safety or efficiency, but they are designed for the needs and comfort of the users. These applications can be split into two big classes: entertainment applications and driver assistance applications.

Entertainment applications include solutions for different service delivery such as multimedia delivery and live video streaming over VANETs (Yang, Li, & Lou, 2010; Razzaq & Mehaoua, 2010), file-sharing and gaming platforms over VANETs (Hartenstein et al., 2001; Tonguz & Boban 2010).

Driver assistance applications comprise countless VANETs-based solutions. This type of applications provide driver with useful information in driving process, but not only (e.g. applications that provide valuable information for driver, such as price of fuel or closest charging station, etc, are also included). Example of such applications are routing applications (Doolan & Muntean, 2013), free parking discovery applications (Lu, Lin, Zhu & Shen, 2009), tolling applications (Gomes, Vieira & Ferreira, 2013), applications that give driving/riding advices based on certain criteria (e.g. how to drive/ride in certain conditions in order to reduce gas emissions, fuel (Rakha el al., 2011) or energy consumption in the case of electric cars (Tielert, Rieger, Hartenstein, Luz & Hausberger, 2012) or electric bicycles (Tal & Muntean, 2013b; Tal, Tianhua & Muntean, 2013)), etc.

VANET Characteristics and Challenges

VANETs have specific characteristics that differentiate them from any other type of ad-hoc networks. Some of these characteristics are very attractive for the researchers, while the others are creating new technical challenges that need to be addressed. The following features are among the attractive ones:

Theoretical Unlimited Power: Is considered due to the fact that any vehicle-node is capable of generating power while moving. In the case of classic MANET mobile nodes, power is a very serious issue. However, this VANET characteristic is not applicable to the case of electric vehicles (EVs), where energy preservation is vital for increasing the travel range.

High Computational and Storage Capabilities: Unlike the handheld devices in classic MANETs, vehicles can afford significant computational, storage and communication capabilities. This capability is partially made possible by the previously mentioned characteristic.

Predictable Mobility: Is possible in VANETs due to the fact that vehicle movement is constrained by the roads, traffic regulations and driver behavior. So, given parameters such as the current position, current speed, route, average speed and/or learning about driver behavior, it is possible to predict the next position of the vehicle. On the contrary, the node mobility in classic MANETs is very hard to predict.

The challenging set of VANET features includes:

High Mobility: Vehicle-nodes have very high speed compared to the nodes from MANETs. In highway scenarios speeds of up to 300km/h may occur, while in city scenarios speeds of up to 70km/h.

Rapidly Changing Topology: The aforementioned high node mobility in VANETs leads to a frequent link disconnection between the vehicle-nodes and consequently to a rapidly changing network topology.

Diversity of Conditions: Mainly refers to the diversity of the network density that can be very sparse or on the contrary, very dense. In a city scenario, especially during rush hours, the network is extremely dense, while in a highway scenario the network can be very sparse.

Frequent disconnections in the Network: Mainly caused by the two previously mentioned characteristics. Road dead-ends is another factor that can produce frequent disconnections in VANETs.

Potentially Large Scale VANETs: Are networks with a potential high number of nodes. There is no limitation in terms of number of nodes, as it is in the case of other networks, so vehicle-nodes can potentially expand over the entire road network.

Diversity of Applications: As presented in the previous section, a large plethora of applications have been envisioned for VANETs in the areas of traffic safety, traffic management and efficiency, and infotainment ranging from multimedia applications to driver assistance services. The requirements of these applications are as diverse as their range is. Consequently, much VANET- dedicated technology needs to be designed so these networks can cope with all this diversity of applications.

In the presence of these characteristics, some of the main technical challenges of VANETs are imposed in the context of MAC protocols, security, routing and data dissemination protocols and service delivery architectures due to the frequent disconnections (Moustafa et. al, 2009). MAC protocols are considered to be a key issue in the design of VANETs (Karagiannis et al., 2011). Efficient MAC protocols need to be specifically designed for VANETs in order to cope with the high dynamic environment caused by the high mobility and rapidly changing topology. In addition, MAC protocols designed for VANETs need to fulfill the requirements of all the diversity of applications. As such, they need to be able to provide quality of experience (QoS) for non-safety applications (such as infotainment applications) and reliability for safety applications. Routing protocols in VANETs need to be able to cope with their rapidly changing topology, but also with the different types of networks densities and diversity of applications. Data dissemination in the conditions of potentially

large number of nodes must take into account the efficient usage of the available bandwidth. Data aggregation addresses this issue in the context of data collection, avoiding the dissemination of similar information in the network. In such a dynamic environment, security protocols become a challenge as an optimal trade-off should be found between safety and complexity.

Socio-economic challenges (i.e. the cost of the infrastructure needed for the deployment of VANET solutions and the market penetration of V2X communication technologies) were included as well among the main challenges of VANETs (Hartenstein & Laberteaux, 2008). Two solutions were proposed for the latter problem that either enforce a regulative order, or deploy user-oriented applications in order to advertise the added value of the technology. While it appears credible that in the future the governments will impose the adoption of the V2X communication technologies for new vehicles through regulation, there will be long periods of time during which the penetration rate of these technologies will be very low (e.g. in USA alone it is estimated it will take more than 10 years to acquire 100% penetration rate if a new technology starts to be deployed on vehicles now (Santi, 2012)). In this context, the deployment of applications that demonstrate the added-value of the V2X communications and bringing other types of technologies in the vehicular networks appears to be the best solution to fasten the market penetration of WAVE technology.

CLUSTERING AND VANETS

Introduction to Clustering

Clustering is a division technique that creates groups of similar objects (Wanner, 2009) mainly with the purpose of dealing with scalability. The similarity between objects is built upon one or more clustering metrics that are extremely varied and highly dependent on the context clustering is applied in. Clustering is widely used in data analysis, data mining, statistics, text mining, information retrieval, etc. Clustering has been widely adopted in MANETs (Figure 2), as it provides support for good system performance, good management and stability of the networks in the presence of mobility and large number of terminals (Yu & Chong, 2005). Thus, clustering helps solve some of the main issues in MANETs: scalability and stability (Wanner, 2009).

In MANETs, clustering involves dividing the nodes into virtual groups based on some rules that establish if a node is suitable to be within a cluster or not. These rules are defined based on clustering metrics that in MANETs can be node type, battery energy level, mobility pattern, etc.

In general, a clustering scheme considers that a node can be in one the following situations (Yu & Chong, 2005), based on the node membership and task associated to the node. If node situations are associated with states, one could consider the following as possible node states:

- **Unclustered:** Also known as non-clustered or independent, when it does not pertain to any cluster.
- **Cluster Member:** Or clustered when the node is within a cluster.
- **Cluster Head (Ch):** When the node has extra-responsibilities in a cluster. Usually, CH is the main controller of the cluster,

the main coordinator of the communication within the cluster (i.e. intra-cluster communication) and has a main role in the functionality that is supposed to be provided by the cluster.

- **Gateway Node:** Is the node that ensures the communication between the clusters, also called inter-cluster communications.

A general classification of MANET clustering schemes is based upon the following criterion: *CH-based clustering*, if there is a CH in the clusters created or *non-CH-based clustering*, if there is no CH in the cluster created. Note that in CH-based clustering, the performance of clustering is highly dependent on CH election as this node has the main responsibilities in its cluster. Therefore in this type of clustering algorithms the focus is mainly on CH selection algorithms. Another general classification of clustering is based upon the number of hops between node pairs in the cluster: *1-hop clustering* or *multi-hop clustering*.

Successfully applied in MANETs to address stability and scalability, clustering was adopted in VANETs, where these issues are even more augmented. At the beginning, MANET clustering algorithms were adopted and directly applied to VANETs without any modifications, but as this research direction evolved, new clustering algorithms dedicated to VANETs were designed to address their specific characteristics.

Figure 2. Illustration of node states in MANET clustering

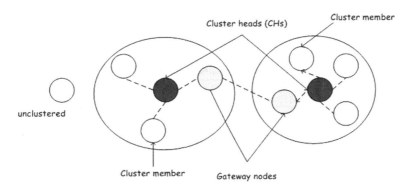

Clustering in VANETs

The clustering concepts presented in the context of MANETs are valid in VANETs context as well, especially given the fact that clustering in VANETs has evolved from MANETs. There are only some additional aspects that need to be mentioned and that derive from the adaptation of clustering to VANET-specific conditions.

Clustering metrics were adapted not only to address VANET challenges imposed by their specific characteristics such as high mobility, rapidly changing topology and diversity of conditions, but also to take advantage of some of these characteristics, such as predictability of their movement. Therefore, clustering in VANETs is based upon more metrics than in MANETs that need to describe the complexity of VANET environment. Among the most common metrics in VANET clustering are direction, vehicle's relative speed in comparison to other neighbouring vehicles, vehicle's relative position, but also traffic flow, the lane in urban scenarios (e.g. right lane, left lane, and ahead lane), predicted future speed and position, density of vehicles (sparse or dense), etc.

In the context of node states, as already described, additional node states have to be added in VANETs in order to address its more dynamic environment. These intermediate states include the *candidate node* and *CH backup* or *CH candidate states*. The candidate state was introduced by some approaches in order to obtain a better stability of the cluster. A node is not immediately given the cluster member state; it goes into the candidate state until it proves that it has certain stability in the cluster. The CH backup/CH candidate (quasi-CH in other approaches) state was introduced to make faster and smoother the process of changing the CH. Clustering in VANETs can be represented as a state machine, where the machine is the vehicle-node that can be in one of the following states: *unclustered, cluster member, CH* (in the case of CH-based clustering) and, optionally, in an intermediate state *candidate* and *CH backup/ candidate* as previously defined (Figure 3).

Once adopted in VANETs, clustering gained popularity mostly due to its efficiency in addressing network stability issues. Clustering algorithms were implemented in the design of a large variety of VANET solutions: MAC

Figure 3. State machine representing CH-based clustering in VANETs

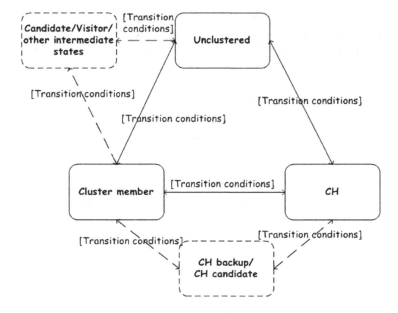

protocols, routing protocols, data aggregation, security protocols, inter-vehicle communication, and data and infotainment dissemination solutions and architectures. In addition, various generic clustering algorithms were defined for VANETs. The distribution of the clustering algorithms in VANETs is presented in Figure 4.

Independent of the type of VANET solution the clustering algorithm is designed for, one of the main purpose of clustering is to achieve network stability. Therefore, the clustering metrics are focusing mainly on this aspect and they relate to VANET's dynamic environment. Thus independently of the context in which clustering is applied (i.e. MAC protocols, routing protocols, etc), clustering metrics focus on the same issues

and they are similar to each other. They are only dependent on the ingeniously modeling of the VANET environment and they are different from solution to solution as researchers are experimenting in trying to find the best clustering metrics to express the dynamicity of the VANETs. Similarly, in clustering performance assessment, usually first the network stability achieved is measured and then, the overall assessment of the clustering solution is performed (the overall solution where clustering is integrated; e.g. MAC protocol, data aggregation, etc). All these considerations allows for a uniform analysis of clustering algorithms in VANETs, independent of the type of solution/application in which they are integrated.

Figure 4. Clustering algorithms in VANETs

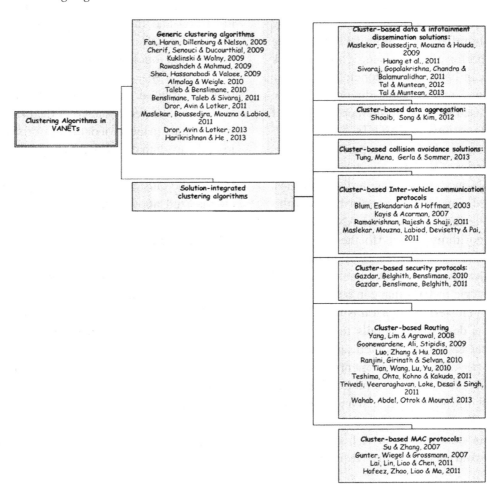

Although there is a considerable number of clustering solutions in VANETs, this research direction is still not mature. A closer analysis of the existent solutions in the literature reveals some major issues that relate to the performance assessment of clustering solutions in VANETs. So far, no analysis on this topic was provided in the literature and this is reflected by the fact that the existing clustering solutions use intuitively-defined performance assessment metrics or re-defined metrics similar with already existing ones mostly because researchers were not aware that such metrics have already been proposed in the literature. This resulted in metrics having various name versions. In particular this is the case for the metrics used to measure the stability of the clusters, which contributes to network stability. These metrics are a direct measure of the performance of clustering algorithms in the context of VANETs, where the performance of clustering algorithms is reflected in how well clustering algorithms perform in achieving good network stability. It can be therefore concluded that the aforementioned major issues directly relate to the metrics used to evaluate the performance of clustering algorithms in VANETs.

In the absence of a study on performance assessment metrics of VANETs clustering solutions and in the absence of the standardized metrics, we performed a survey of the performance evaluation of clustering solutions in VANETs and of clustering algorithms designed for these solutions. This survey resulted in the identification and comprehensive definition, including in mathematical terms, of generic metrics that can be used in the evaluation of clustering algorithms in VANETs. Next sections describe in details the results of the study that can be considered an invaluable guide for the performance assessment of VANETs cluster-based solutions in general and VANETs clustering algorithms in particular and could support the standardization effort of these general metrics. This standardization is highly needed in order to avoid metrics being "re-invented" or

intuitive assessment of the clustering solutions in VANETs to be performed. Moreover, evaluating the performance of clustering algorithms via these general metrics can greatly facilitate the comparison between clustering algorithms, independent from their type (i.e. generic algorithms or solution-specific).

Performance Assessment of Clustering in VANETs

The study conducted aimed to exhaustively analyze clustering solutions in VANETs. First, the focus was on the performance assessment of clustering solutions in general. Then the focus was moved on the evaluation of clustering algorithms designed for these solutions. As a result of the analysis performed, three major classes of performance assessment metrics for clustering solutions were identified and they are illustrated in Figure 5: network-specific metrics, application-specific metrics and topology-based metrics.

Network-Specific Metrics: Are well-known metrics applied in network communications, evaluating the performance of the clustered network mainly in terms of data transfer: throughput, loss, delay, data delivery ratio, overhead, etc.

Application-Specific Metrics: Depend on the type of the cluster-based solution employed. As emphasized above, clustering algorithms were implemented in the design of a large variety of VANET solutions: data aggregation solutions, MAC and routing protocols, security, etc. Therefore, this class includes a large variety of metrics as well. For instance, a data aggregation cluster-based solution is evaluated by measuring the size of data that needs to be disseminated, as the goal of a data aggregation scheme is to reduce the size of the data that needs to be disseminated. Note that these metrics and network-specific metrics are evaluating the performance of the overall solution based on clustering.

Topology-based metrics (hashed in Figure 5) evaluate the stability and robustness of the resulted clusters. Cluster stability translates into network stability, thus topology-based metrics are measuring the network stability. Network stability is emphasized as an important issue in VANETs due to their rapidly changing topology. Therefore, topology-related metrics are of great importance, fact acknowledged by researchers: the majority of proposed clustering solutions are using topology-based metrics in the performance assessment.

Independent of the type of VANET solution the clustering algorithm is designed for, the general aim of a clustering algorithm is to achieve network stability. In this context, the performance of clustering algorithms is not seen from a computational point of view (e.g. complexity of the algorithms). The focus is on how well clustering algorithms perform in achieving good network stability. Based on these considerations it can be said that in the context of VANETs, topology-based metrics are a measure of clustering algorithms performance.

TOPOLOGY-BASED METRICS FOR CLUSTERING ALGORITHMS ASSESSMENT IN VANETS

In the previous section, topology-based metrics were identified as the metrics suitable for the evaluation of clustering algorithms in VANETs.

Therefore, this section contains an in-depth analysis of the topology-based metrics. The comprehensive definition of the performance metrics subscribing to the general topology-based class from the solution-dependent topology-based class is one of the purposes of this work. The first class contains the metrics we called as being general metrics for the evaluation of clustering algorithms in VANETs.

Next the topology-based metrics identified during the analysis of VANET clustering algorithms are presented. Several aspects regarding the form of presentation need to be mentioned before getting to the presentation of the topology-based metrics. These aspects relate to several issues revealed during the study performed on the clustering solutions in VANETs.

An important issue is the inconsistency in naming the metrics. As already mentioned some of the metrics have been re-defined and consequently bare different names. In some cases of re-defining, general metrics are constrained by particular conditions/characteristics of the algorithm they are used to assess: general metrics are defined either using particular conditions/assumptions of the algorithm or using particular parameters of the current algorithm. This is not necessary wrong as it is perfectly applicable for that particular algorithm, but can lead to misconceptions and misusing in case of other clustering

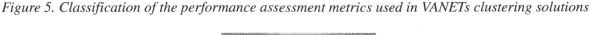

Figure 5. Classification of the performance assessment metrics used in VANETs clustering solutions

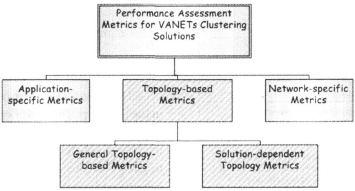

algorithms. In addition, there are a considerable number of metrics that are not provided with a mathematical definition at all, being described in words only. So far, a single work in the literature (Su & Zhang, 2007) has provided mathematical definitions for some general metrics used in the evaluation of clustering.

Due to the aforementioned aspects, when presenting the metrics in the next sections, all naming versions are provided. The most representative name was chosen based on either the popularity or the degree of match with the metric description. In addition, general mathematical definitions for each of the general metrics were provided. The mathematical formulas were proposed based on the textual definitions of the metrics and the in-depth analysis of the results. The general mathematical definitions provided to some of the general metrics in by Su & Zhang (2007) were taken in the same form as presented in their work. Together with these metrics were taken the notations used in their definitions (i.e. first 6 notations from Table 1).

Table 1. Notations used in topology-based metrics definition

Notation	Explanation
$|V(t)|$	Total number of vehicles at time t
$|C(t)|$	Numbers of clusters at time t
$|CH_i(t)|$	Number of cluster members in cluster i at time t
$\overrightarrow{SP}_i(t)$	Velocity vector of vehicle i at time t
$|\overrightarrow{SP}_i(t)|$	Speed of vehicle i at time t
S	Simulation time
$CHL_i(t)$	Time period between time t, when vehicle i becomes a CH, and the moment of time vehicle i changes to another state.
$CL_i(t)$	Time period between time t, when cluster i is formed and the moment of time cluster i is dismissed.
$CMT_j^i(t)$	Time period between time t, when vehicle j becomes a cluster-member of cluster i, and the moment of time vehicle j leaves cluster i.

General Topology-based Metrics or General Metrics for the Evaluation of Clustering Algorithms in VANETs

Average CH Lifetime ($\overline{CHL}$): (Average CH duration, CH time) is one of the most popular topology-based metrics. It is applicable to the CH-based clustering algorithms only. It was used for the evaluation of VANET clustering algorithms in a considerable number of works (see Table 2). The popularity of this metric is explainable: the importance of CHs lifetime is crucial as, usually, the CH is the main controller and content forwarder in the CH-based clustered networks. Smaller CH lifetime affects the overall performance of the clustering algorithm. Higher CH lifetime implies more stable cluster topologies are found, leading to a decrease in number of re-clusterings, and consequently avoiding the waste of system resources and excessive use of computation time.

The mathematical definition of ($\overline{CHL}$), as given by Su & Zhang (2007), is shown in Equation (1).

$$\overline{CHL} = \sum_{t=0}^{S} \frac{\sum_{i=1}^{|V(t)|} CHL_i(t)}{\sum_{i=1}^{|V(t)|} BC_i(t)} \qquad (1)$$

In Equation (1), $BC_i(t)$ represents a function that defines the transition of a node (vehicle i) to the CH state as described by Equation (2).

$$BC_i(t) = \begin{cases} 1, & \text{if vehicle } i \text{ changes to cluster head at time } t \\ 0, & \text{otherwise} \end{cases} \qquad (2)$$

$\overline{CHL}$ is one of the metrics that were re-defined in the literature. In the work proposed by Rawashdesh & Mahmud (2009), this metric is given a mathematical definition dependent on the particularity of the clustering algorithm shown in Equation (3).

$$\overline{CHL} = \frac{1}{L} \sum {}_{i=1}^{L} C_i^{life},\qquad(3)$$

where L is the number of clusters created throughout the session and C_i^{life} .has the same meaning as $CHL_i(t)$. This is not a general definition, as the clusters are dismissed when the CH is changed. There are clustering algorithms (Hafeez et al., 2011) where clusters have back-up CHs. Often,

when the vehicle CH changes its state, its role is taken by its back-up and the cluster is not dismissed. In this situation, Equation (3) cannot be used in all CH-based clustering algorithms evaluation.

Average Number of Clusters ($\overline{NoC}$): is a very popular metric used to assess the performance of a large number of clustering algorithms (see Table 2). $\overline{NoC}$ is a general metric that can be applied to assess the performance of all the cat-

Table 2. General metrics for the evaluation of clustering algorithms in VANETs – summary

Metric	Mathematical Definition	Popularity	Restriction
Average CH Lifetime ($\overline{CHL}$)	$\overline{CHL} = \sum {}_{t=0}^{S} \dfrac{\sum_{i=1}^{\|V(t)\|} CHL_i(t)}{\sum_{i=1}^{\|V(t)\|} BC_i(t)}$ where $BC_i(t) = \begin{cases} 1, & \text{if vehicle } i \text{ changes to} \\ & \text{cluster head at time } t \\ 0, & \text{otherwise} \end{cases}$	Blum et al., 2003 Gunteret al., 2007 Su & Zhang, 2007 Rawashdesh & Mahmed, 2009 Shea et al., 2009 Huang et al., 2011 Lai et al., 2011 Tal & Muntean, 2012 Harikrishnan & He, 2013 Tal & Muntean, 2013a Ucar et al., 2013	CH-based algorithms only
Average number of clusters ($\overline{NoC}$)	$\overline{NoC} = \dfrac{1}{S} \sum {}_{t=0}^{S} \|C(t)\|$	Wolny, 2008 Rawashdesh &Mahmed, 2009 Shea et al., 2009 Gazdar et al., 2010 Dror et al., 2011 Maslekar et al., 2011 Shoaib et al., 2012 Dror et. al, 2013 Tal & Muntean, 2013a Harikrishnan & He, 2013	-
Average cluster size ($\overline{CS}$)	$\overline{CS} = \dfrac{1}{S} \sum {}_{t=0}^{S} \sum_{i \in C(t)} \|CH_i(t)\|$	Fan et al., 2005 Su & Zhang, 2007 Kuklinski &Wolny, 2009 Hafeez et al., 2011 Teshima et al., 2011 Harikrishnan & He, 2013	-
Average CH change rate ($\overline{CHCR}$)	$\overline{CHCR} = \dfrac{1}{S} \sum {}_{t=0}^{S} \sum_{i=1}^{\|v(t)\|} CHD_i(t)$, where $CHD_i(t) = \begin{cases} 1, & \text{if vehicle } i \text{ changes from} \\ & \text{cluster head to another type} \\ & \text{of node at moment } t \\ 0, & \text{otherwise} \end{cases}$	Fan et al., 2005 Kuklinski &Wolny, 2009 Shea et al., 2009 Almalag & Weigle, 2010 Ucar et al., 2013	CH-based algorithms only

continued on following page

Table 2. Continued

Metric	Mathematical Definition	Popularity	Restriction
Average cluster member lifetime ($\overline{CML}$)	$\overline{CML} = \dfrac{1}{\left|C(t)\right|}\sum_{t=0}^{S}\sum_{i\in C(t)}\dfrac{\sum_{j\in CH_i(t)}CMT_j^i(t)CMD_j^i(t)}{\sum_{k=0}^{S}\sum_{j\in CH_i(t)}CMD_j^i(k)}$ where $CMD_i^j(t) = \begin{cases} 1, & \text{if vehicle } j,\text{ cluster member of} \\ & \text{cluster } i \text{ is dissmissed} \\ & \text{from the cluster } i \text{ at moment } t \\ 0, & \text{otherwise} \end{cases}$	Goonewardene et al., 2009 Shea et al., 2009 Huang et al., 2011 Ucar et al., 2013	-
Cluster changes per node ($\overline{CC}$)	$\overline{CC} = \sum_{t=0}^{S}\sum_{i\in C(t),\,j\in CH_i(t)}CMD_j^i(t)$ where CMD is defined as above	Wolny, 2008 Dror et al., 2011 Dror et al, 2013	-
Average cluster lifetime ($\overline{CL}$)	$\overline{CL} = \dfrac{\sum_{t=0}^{S}\sum_{i\in C(t)}CL_i(t)}{\sum_{t=0}^{S}\left|C(t)\right|}$	Cherif et al., 2009 Rawashdesh &Mahmed, 2009	-
Cluster reconfiguration rate ($\overline{CRR}$)	$\overline{CRR} = \sum_{t=0}^{S}\sum_{i=1}^{\left|C(t)\right|}CD_i(t)$ where $CD_i(t) = \begin{cases} 1, & \text{if cluster } i \text{ was dissmissed} \\ & \text{at moment } t \\ 0, & \text{otherwise} \end{cases}$	Wang et al., 2008 Huang et al., 2011	-
Average relative speed compared to the CH within a cluster ($\overline{RSWC}$)	$\overline{RSWC} = \dfrac{1}{\left|C(t)\right|S}\sum_{t=0}^{S}\sum_{i\in C(t)}\dfrac{\sum_{j\in CH_i(t)}\left|\overrightarrow{SP_i}(t)-\overrightarrow{SP_j}(t)\right|}{\left|CH_i(t)\right|}$	Su & Zhang, 2007 Hafeez et al., 2011	CH-based algorithms only
Average relative speed among CHs ($\overline{RSCH}$)	$\overline{RSCH} = \dfrac{1}{S}\sum_{t=0}^{S}\dfrac{\sum_{i,j\in C(t)^\wedge i\neq j}\left|\overrightarrow{SP_i}(t)-\overrightarrow{SP_j}(t)\right|}{\left|C(t)\right|^2}$	Su & Zhang, 2007	CH-based algorithms only

egories of clustering algorithms. $\overline{NoC}$ is a measure of network stability. When there are fewer clusters, better network stability is obtained. Equation (4) is proposed as a general mathematical definition of $\overline{NoC}$.

$$\overline{NoC} = \frac{1}{S}\sum_{t=0}^{S}\left|C(t)\right| \qquad (4)$$

It can be stated that the same metric is used by Maslekar et al. (2011), although instead of number of clusters, the number of CHs is measured. This is due to the fact that in this particular solution, a cluster is dismissed when its CH is dismissed. In consequence, the number of CHs is equal to the number of clusters created.

Average Cluster Size ($\overline{CS}$): Metric (average number of cluster members) measures the average size of the clusters throughout the session. This size of a cluster is considered to be determined by the number of vehicles in the cluster. $\overline{CS}$ is a metric applicable to all clustering algorithms and was highly used in the literature (see Table 2). Its general definition, as given by Su & Zhang (2007), is shown in Equation (5).

$$\overline{CS} = \frac{1}{S} \sum\nolimits_{t=0}^{S} \sum\nolimits_{i \in C(t)} \left| CH_i\left(t\right) \right| \qquad (5)$$

Average CH Change Rate ($\overline{CHCR}$): Is another popular metric (see Table 2) and it is seen as a measure of cluster stability. In more stable clusters, nodes in general and CHs in particular change their cluster membership or their state less often. It is a metric that can be used for the performance assessment of CH-based algorithms. Equation (6) is proposed as the general mathematical definition of $\overline{CHCR}$.

$$\overline{CHCR} = \frac{1}{S} \sum\nolimits_{t=0}^{S} \sum\nolimits_{i=1}^{|v(t)|} CHD_i\left(t\right) \qquad (6)$$

where CHD_i *(t)* is the CH dismissed function of vehicle *i*, that was defined in Equation (7) to express the transitions from CH to another type of node.

$$CHD_i\left(t\right) =
\begin{cases}
1, & \textit{if vehicle } i \\
& \textit{changes from cluster head} \\
& \textit{to another type of node at time } t \\
0, & \textit{otherwise}
\end{cases} \qquad (7)$$

Average Cluster Member Lifetime ($\overline{CML}$): (Average cluster member duration, cluster residence time) was used as a performance metric by Goonewardene et al. (2009); Shea et al. (2009)

and Huang et al. (2011). It is a general topology-based metric measuring the overall stability of clustering. $\overline{CML}$ is a similar metric to the average CH lifetime just that the lifetime is computed for all the nodes in the cluster members not only for the CH. Same as for $\overline{CML}$, longer average cluster member lifetime indicates a more stable clustering topology. A general mathematical definition of $\overline{CML}$ is provided in Equation (8).

$$\overline{CML} = \frac{1}{\left| C\left(t\right) \right|} \sum\nolimits_{t=0}^{S} \sum\nolimits_{i \in C(t)} \\ \frac{\sum\nolimits_{j \in CH_i(t)} CMT_j^i\left(t\right) CMD_j^i\left(t\right)}{\sum\nolimits_{k=0}^{S} \sum\nolimits_{i \in C(t)} CMD_j^i\left(k\right)} \qquad (8)$$

where CMD_j^i (t) is the cluster member dismissed function of vehicle *j* from cluster *i* being defined in Equation (9).

$$CMD_j^i\left(t\right) =
\begin{cases}
1, & \textit{if vehicle } j, \textit{cluster member of} \\
& \textit{cluster } i \textit{ is dissmissed} \\
& \textit{from the cluster } i \textit{ at time } t \\
0, & \textit{otherwise}
\end{cases} \qquad (9)$$

Cluster Changes per Node ($\overline{CC}$): (Average number of cluster switches per node) measures the number of transitions of a vehicle between clusters and is used in order to measure cluster stability. The less number of transitions indicates better cluster stability. In the work proposed by Dror et al. (2011), the metric is called improperly cluster stability and was measured through average number of cluster switches per node.

Based on the descriptions provided by Shea et al. (2009) and Wolny (2008) and on the evaluation of the results, Equation (10) is proposed as the general mathematical formula for $\overline{CC}$, applicable to all clustering algorithms.

$$\overline{CC} = \sum\nolimits_{t=0}^{S} \sum\nolimits_{i \in C(t), j \in CH_i(t)} CMD_j^i(t) \qquad (10)$$

where CMD_j^i (t) was defined in Equation (9).

Cluster stability is stated as a metric by Wolny (2008), Dror et al. (2011) and Wahab et al. (2013). In the latter work, it is described and measured in terms of the average number of cluster switches per node during the simulation. As stated before, this metric is actually $\overline{CC}$. Wolny (2008) states that the cluster stability metric depends on the change rate of the cluster and provide a formula that is not generic, but solution-dependent and uses some undefined terms. A solution-dependent description is provided by Wahab et al. (2013) for what they call network stability metric. However, we argue that no metric can be called *cluster stability* until it is not able to comprise all the metrics that were defined so far for its measurement. In addition, cluster stability is a property of the VANETs which is assessed by most of the topology-related metrics defined and not only a metric. In consequence, cluster stability is not proposed and considered as a general metric in this work.

Average Cluster Lifetime ($\overline{CL}$): (Rawashdesh & Mahmud, 2009) (Average cluster lifecycle (Cherif et al. 2009)) is another general metric that can be used for assessing the performance of any type of VANETs clustering algorithm. It is a measure of cluster stability: larger average cluster lifetime translates into more stable clusters, thus a more stable network. Rawashdesh & Mahmud (2009) consider the average cluster lifetime equal to the average CH lifetime, as the clusters are dismissed whenever their CH changes. The authors define $\overline{CL}$ through Equation (2) which was considered not to be an appropriate general formula for CH lifetime. It is obvious that Equation (2) cannot be also considered a general formula for the $\overline{CL}$ as the cluster duration is not always de-

pendent on the CH lifetime. This is valid in non-CH schemes and even in CH-based schemes. Equation (11) is proposed as a general mathematical definition for $\overline{CL}$.

$$\overline{CL} = \frac{\sum\nolimits_{t=0}^{S} \sum\nolimits_{i \in C(t)} CL_i(t)}{\sum\nolimits_{t=0}^{S} |C(t)|} \qquad (11)$$

Cluster Reconfiguration Rate ($\overline{CRR}$): (Wang et al. 2008) (Number of re-clusterings (Huang et al., 2011)) is a metric defined to measure cluster stability based on the fact that a good clustering algorithm should be stable and it should not change the cluster configuration too drastically when few nodes are moving and the topology changes rapidly. This metric does not have a mathematical definition in none of the solutions that use it. Moreover, these solutions are both CH-based algorithms and they state that the re-clustering/reconfiguration happens when CH changes. Described like this, the metric becomes identical to $\overline{CHCR}$. However, equation (12) proposed a general mathematical description for the $\overline{CRR}$ applicable to all clustering algorithms.

$$\overline{CRR} = \frac{1}{S} \sum\nolimits_{t=0}^{S} \sum\nolimits_{i=1}^{|C(t)|} CD_i(t)$$

where CD_i (t) is the cluster dismissed (*CD*) function for cluster *i* as defined in Equation (13).

$$CD_i(t) = \begin{cases} 1, & \textit{if cluster i was dissmissed} \\ & \textit{at moment t} \\ 0, & \textit{otherwise} \end{cases} \qquad (13)$$

Average Relative Speed Compared to the CH within a Cluster ($\overline{RSWC}$) (Su & Zhang, 2007) (average cluster stability factor (Hafeez et al.,

2011)) measures the topology stability of clusters. It is a general topology-based metric for all the CH-based algorithms. In all CH-based algorithms, a smaller average speed of the cluster member compared to that of the CH is translated into an increased stability of the cluster. However, $\overline{RSWC}$ is not a very common metric. It was defined and used as in equation (14) by Su & Zhang (2007). Hafeez et al. (2011) re-defined this metric as the *average cluster stability factor* and it is described depending on some particular parameters of the solution. However, deeper analysis reveals that average cluster stability factor is identical to $\overline{RSWC}$.

$$\overline{RSWC} =$$

$$\frac{1}{|C(t)|S} \sum_{t=0}^{S} \sum_{i \in C(t)} \cdot$$

$$\frac{\sum_{j \in CH_i(t)} \left| \overrightarrow{SP_i}(t) - \overrightarrow{SP_j}(t) \right|}{|CH_i(t)|}$$

Average Relative Speed Among CHs ($\overline{RSCH}$): (Su & Zhang, 2007) Is a general topology-based metric for CH-based algorithms. It measures the global topology of the network. Equation (15) represents the general mathematical definition of this metric as given by Su & Zhang (2007).

$$\overline{RSCH} =$$

$$\frac{1}{S} \sum_{t=0}^{S} \frac{\sum_{i,j \in C(t)^\wedge i \neq j} \left| \overrightarrow{SP_i}(t) - \overrightarrow{SP_j}(t) \right|}{|C(t)|^2} \quad (15)$$

$\overline{RSWC}$ and $\overline{RSCH}$ are more complex metrics for CH-based algorithms that are indicators of both CH and network stability, as this type of metrics are measuring better the cluster stability in general. This statement also sustained by Fan et al. (2005), that fist assessed the clustering al-

gorithms defined using $\overline{CS}$ and $\overline{CHCR}$ and then using relative measure ($\overline{CS}$ / $\overline{CHCR}$) arguing that this is a better measurement of cluster stability.

All the general metrics presented and defined (except the cluster stability which is not considered a metric) are summarized in Table 2. This section and the table-based summary provided represent an invaluable guide for the performance assessment of VANETs clustering algorithms in particular and of VANETs cluster-based solutions in general. Evaluating the performance of clustering algorithms via these general metrics can greatly facilitate the comparison between the clustering algorithms, independent from their type: generic algorithms or integrated in a specific solution (e.g. clustering algorithm implemented in a MAC protocol).

Solution-Dependent Topology-Based Metrics

Node re-clustering time (Goonewardene et al., 2009)/*Re-affiliation frequency* (Blum, 2003) are metrics very differently named, but both described as being the time between cluster associations for a given node. Solutions using this metric consider that this is a measure of the stability of a cluster membership and shorter node re-clustering time/re-affiliation frequency means an increased stability of a cluster membership. However, we consider that average cluster membership lifetime and average CH lifetime (in case of CH-based algorithms) are a better indicator of the stability of cluster membership and we base this statement on the following considerations. Particularly in VANET clustering, as emphasized before, the nodes can be in intermediate states. They have different states like candidate, visitor and they are not clustered until they demonstrate their future stability in the cluster, meaning a long lifetime as a cluster member. This translates into longer period of re-clustering/re-affiliation frequency, but this does not mean that the topology is less stable. These considerations represent also the motivation of including this metric in the class of solution-dependent topology-based clustering metrics. In this class, we also include the *average percentage of clustered nodes* metric (Kuklinski & Wolny, 2009). A bigger average percentage of clustered nodes it is usually translated into a better stability of the network topology. However, in the aforementioned particular clustering algorithms, this metric is not applicable because at some moments of time there can be a considerable number of nodes not-clustered (candidates or visitors).

CLUSTERING ALGORITHMS IN VANETS

Initial approaches of clustering in VANETs used clustering algorithms designed for MANETs. Lowest Id (Yu & Chong, 2005) is a state-of-the-art clustering algorithm in ad-hoc networks and was borrowed in VANETs from MANETs. Its principle is very simple. The nodes have assigned a unique fixed id which is broadcasted periodically in the network. The clusters are formed around the node with the lowest id among them, which is chosen as CH. Although its principle is very simple, it is a very efficient algorithm, more efficient than other clustering schemes, such as Highest-Degree (Yu & Chong, 2005), that take into consideration more factors (Fan et al., 2005). Highest-Degree is another state-of-the-art clustering algorithm in the area of ad-hoc networks. Its principle is similar to the Lowest Id algorithm, but the clusters are formed around the node with the highest number of neighbors. These two algorithms, as state-of-the-art algorithms in the area of ad-hoc networks, are very often used in the comparison-based assessment of the VANETs clustering algorithms and served as source of inspiration for many VANETs clustering approaches.

As emphasized before, although VANETs represent an instantiation of MANETs, they have unique features that need to be considered in order to design appropriate clustering algorithms for vehicular networks. On one hand some of the VANET's characteristics need to be overcome by the clustering schemes, such as their rapidly changing topology, high mobility and scalability, while on the other hand clustering schemes can make use of other characteristics such as predictable mobility due to the road topology, traffic regulations and driver's behavior. Researchers acknowledged these facts and VANET-dedicated clustering solutions have been proposed. After an overview of VANET clustering solutions in the literature, a very broad classification is provided here and several approaches are presented for each class for exemplification. The classification is made based on the cluster formation criterion: is the cluster formation dependent on some fixed structures such as road segments, grids, etc, or is it independent on any kind of structure and it is just following the traffic flow, vehicle's movement? In the first case, vehicles from the same structure (road segment, grid, etc) are grouped into a cluster. Thus static clusters are created bounded by this structure. Therefore, we called this type of VANET clustering algorithm under the generic name of *static clustering algorithms*. In the second case, cluster formation does not depend on any type of structures. Clusters are created by following the movement of the vehicles: vehicles with similar mobility patterns such as neighboring vehicles are grouped into clusters through exchange of clustering messages. In this type of approaches there is usually a beaconing message (a periodically broadcasted message in the network) sent either by the unclustered vehicle, either by a CH or a node with extra-responsibilities in the cluster. In the absence of predefined structures, this is necessary in order to announce the availability of joining the cluster or the availability of a cluster in zone so that a vehicle can join a cluster. The clusters created following this approach are mobile clusters, following the mobility of the vehicles and therefore we name this class of VANET clustering algorithms, *mobile clustering algorithms*.

Static Clustering Algorithms

Cherif et al. (2009) propose a CH-based clustering algorithm where the cluster formation is depended on fixed road segments. The communication area where vehicles can be reached by RSU via multi-hop communication is called extended communication area. This area is split into fixed length segments, vehicles located into the same segment forming a cluster. Beside CH and simple cluster member, nodes can have another status inside a cluster, called super-member. This is a node that has been a CH and is yielding the job to another node. Inside the cluster, a main area of interest is conceptually partitioned in the centre of the segment. This area is called central zone and has the radius equal to the transmission range. Central zone has an important role in the distributed election of the CH. Initially, each member in the cluster estimates the time period it is going to spend in the central zone. The main principle behind CH election algorithm is to choose as CH the vehicle with the highest probability to spend the longest duration in the central zone. The speed and the position of the vehicle are also taken into consideration. All these parameters are used in the computation of each vehicle's electing factor, based on which the CH is selected. After that, each vehicle periodically examines its status and, by using the laws of uniform motion from Physics (*distance = speed* x *time*) predicts its future position in the immediate next moment of time. If a CH determines that it will be leaving the central zone in this moment of time, it will resign as CH, and a new CH is elected following the same procedure.

The proposed algorithm takes into consideration the high mobility of VANET nodes and movement predictability. Algorithm's assessment is performed both via general topology-based metrics – $\overline{CL}$ – and network metrics – overhead, end to end delay and delivery ratio. These are evaluated in relation to network density, but it is

to be mentioned as a limitation the fact that the solution is not compared against any other clustering scheme.

Luo et al. (2010) propose a CH-based clustering algorithm where the cluster's formation is based on square grids. The geographical area is divided into a subset of square grids. All the vehicles pertaining to a grid form a cluster. The vehicle having the closest position to the centre of the grid is elected as CH. This clustering scheme is implemented in a cluster and position-based routing protocol dedicated to VANETs and claims to reduce the overhead and packet delivery delay. CHs are the main data forwarders, a packet is sent from CH to CH until it gets to the CH that governs in the cluster where the destination node is positioned. The performance assessment is not very thoroughly, the authors presenting just a small analysis where they make some observation about their algorithm in comparison with state-of-the-art routing algorithms. Moreover, the clustering scheme neither tries to address any of VANETs challenging characteristics nor does it take advantage of any of VANETs characteristics. Thus, the clustering scheme, only by itself is not VANETs dedicated, but the routing protocol is taking advantage of the vehicle's knowledge about their own positioning via the GPS integrated in their OBU.

Ramakrishnan et al. (2011) adopt a similar approach in their proposed CH-based clustering algorithm to the one previously discussed: cluster formation is based on road segments called clustering areas. However, these clustering areas are not assigned with a fixed length value. Their size varies depending on the average speed of the vehicles within them. If the average speed is small then the cluster size is smaller, otherwise bigger. However, it is not mathematically described what smaller or bigger means. If an RSU is inside a cluster, then this is elected as CH. Otherwise, CH election is based on a single metric that is the velocity. As the clusters are static, the vehicle with the lowest speed in the cluster is going to spend the more time inside the cluster. Thus this vehicle is elected as CH. However, although the CHCR is reduced, is not clear how the fact that the position of CH related to the other cluster members is not taken into consideration is affecting the communication between CH and cluster members.

Performance assessment is done via topology metrics only, which are quite different than the ones typically used. Instead of measuring directly the rate of changes in CH or clusters, the times of creation of clusters or the time of electing CH is measured. However, these are not good measurements of the stability in clusters; instead these assess the initial performance of clustering.

Mobile Clustering Algorithms

Su and Zhang (2007) proposed a CH-based clustering algorithm in the design of a dedicated VANET MAC protocol. The cluster formation is based on beaconing messages (an initial message periodically broadcast in the network either by a vehicle recently entered in the network, either by CHs) and other cluster messages among the same-direction neighbours. Thus in cluster formation the main criterion considered is the direction of the vehicles based on the assumption that vehicles flowing in the same direction have similar speeds and moving patterns that are regulated by the traffic rules. Another criterion considered in cluster formation is signal strength and its role is revealed in the next paragraph.

The possible states of a vehicle-node in this clustering algorithm are: CH, quasi-CH, cluster member and quasi-cluster member. Each vehicle is seen from the moment of entering on the road a potential CH, so it receives the quasi-CH state. If after a predefined period of time it does not receive any valid *invite-to-join* beaconing message from a CH, the vehicle elects himself as a CH, otherwise the vehicle joins the cluster and its state changes to cluster member. Note that valid *invite-to-join* message must have the signal

strength greater than a predefined threshold. Thus the size of the cluster is determined by the signal strength threshold.

This algorithm is among the first mobile VANETs clustering algorithms. Its principle is simple, the only clustering metrics considered are direction and signal strength and the CH election is very simple, no decision process based on multiple metrics is involved. However, it is the first that considered direction metric in clustering the vehicles. In addition, this is the first approach in the literature that thoroughly defined some of the most popular general topology metrics in VANETs: $\overline{CHL}$ and $\overline{CS}$. Also, they defined 2 relative topology metrics, previously discussed: $\overline{RSWC}$ and $\overline{RSCH}$. These metrics are used to illustrate the performances of the clustering algorithm, but no other clustering algorithm is used as reference. The focus of the authors is on testing the MAC protocol where the clustering solution has been integrated. Tests show that this MAC protocol outperforms the standard IEEE 802.11p.

Kuklinski and Wolny (2009) propose a mobile clustering algorithm where mobile clusters are formed by the neighbouring vehicles through beaconing and other messages exchange. Multiple clustering metrics are considered in creating stable clusters such as: connectivity level that is actually measuring the density, link quality estimated by SNR, relative nodes position and the prediction of this position in the future (based on speed and position) and nodes reputation built upon the history of node connections. The prediction of vehicle positions aims on one hand to avoid situations like clustering the vehicles that are moving in different directions with high speed. On the other hand, it allows for clustering the vehicles that are moving in different directions but with a low speed (e.g. vehicles in traffic jam). This approach leads to a greater stability of the clusters. Moreover, in order to avoid a high rate of re-clusterings, a node is given three possible states, excepting the CH state: member, candidate and visitor. Vehicles must prove they are potentially stable members of the clusters before they can join. First, a vehicle is in the visitor change, then after a time threshold is given the candidate state and only after applying the other clustering metric (connectivity, future position, etc), its state is changed into a member. Candidate and visitor nodes do not have the same rights as members do. They are not provided with the services that are provided in the cluster and they only have the right to exchange clustering messages. CH election algorithm is not described, although in each cluster a vehicle is assigned with this role. In addition, it is not clear what the CH responsibilities are.

The proposed solution is compared against the state-of-the-art algorithm, Highest Degree and proves better performances in terms of $\overline{CS}$ and $\overline{CHCR}$ topology metrics.

Almalag and Weigle (2010) introduced a CH-based clustering algorithm designed mainly for urban scenarios that uses traffic flow in cluster formation. The authors focus on the CH election algorithm as it is a well-known fact that stable CHs conduct to stable clusters. This algorithm is based on multiple clustering parameters: density, distance between vehicles, speed and the lane of travelling. This last parameter is a new parameter considered so far in the clustering schemes and the key novelty of the algorithm. The rationale behind considering this parameter is that CH should be selected from a lane that the majority of vehicles are travelling in. Each vehicle first determines its own lane. Then each lane, referred as traffic flow, is given a weight. It is not explained what is the rationale behind weights' assignment for each traffic flow. Then for each vehicle it is determined on one hand the number of vehicles it is connected to (density), the comparison of its speed compared to others within its range and the comparison of its distance from all other vehicles within its range and on the other hand all these parameters but within their own traffic flows. The first group of parameters are multiplied with the traffic flow

weights and then added to the second group in order to obtain the CH level of each vehicle. The vehicle with the highest CHL is selected as CH.

The proposed algorithm is compared against other three algorithms: the well known Lowest Id, Highest Degree and against what authors generic named the Utility Function algorithm for VANETs. The latter clustering approach was proposed by Fan et al. (2005) having as models Lowest Id and Highest Degree and it is probably the first clustering scheme proposed for VANETs. The focus in this scheme is fully on the CH election that is suggested to be chosen for VANETs as the vehicle having the speed closest to the average and the distance between vehicles closest to the average. Although the authors do not provide details about what closest to the average means, they state that simulation results show better performance of their approach compared to Lowest-Id and Highest Degree. In the performance assessment of the traffic flow based algorithm, the authors use their own understanding of what closest to the average means for both speed and distance parameters. This is the same understanding that they used for implementing their own algorithm with respect to speed and distance metrics. The traffic flow-based algorithm outperforms all three algorithms (i.e. Lowest Id, Highest Degree and Utility Function) in terms of the topology metric used, $\overline{CHCR}$.

Shea et al. (2009) proposed another mobility-based clustering algorithm for VANETs with focus on the stability of the resulted clustered network. The novelty of the algorithm consists in employing affinity propagation (Frey & Dueck, 2007), a clustering technique that is borrowed from data clustering field. Same pattern for clustering formation is followed as in the other structure-free discussed algorithms: exchange of clustering messages between vehicles in 1-hop neighbourhood. Direction is the first parameter considered in clustering formation: the vehicles form clusters with their 1-hop same-direction neighbours. The focus is again on the CH election algorithm where the affinity propagation technique applies. This technique is based upon a similarity function that is tailored for VANETs. Thus it is based on the Euclidean distance between the position of the node and the positions of its same-direction neighbours and the Euclidean distance between the next position of the node and the next positions of its same-direction neighbours. The efficiency of the algorithm is demonstrated against the previously discussed clustering algorithm proposed by Su & Zhang (2007) by applying the most popular topology-based metrics: $\overline{CHL}$, $\overline{CML}$, $\overline{NoC}$ and $\overline{CHCR}$.

Goonewardene et al. (2009) proposed a mobile clustering algorithm based on exchange of clustering messages between 1-hop neighbours designed with a robust adaptability to mobility – RMAC (i.e .robust mobility adaptive clustering). The algorithm is designed to support geographic routing, although no routing protocol is proposed. An unclusterd node first makes a list of its 1-hop neighbours that answer to its beaconing messages with a message containing their speed, location and direction of travelling. Based on these metrics, the list is then sorted so that the most appropriate neighbour of the unclustered node to be selected as its CH. The appropriateness is decided as follows. First the position parameter is considered. Based on this the Euclidean distance is computed between the node and its neighbours. If the distances are comparable, then the next parameters, speed and location are considered. Based on these two parameters the next locations of the node and its neighbours are computed. The first neighbour in the list, the most appropriate to become the CH, is the one closer in the current moment of time and in the next one. This is quite a new approach in the literature, as usually a CH is elected in the cluster based on some values (id, computed weight using different techniques) that applies globally. The clustering algorithm proposed here is node-oriented – node precedence algorithm –

as each node elects its own CH. If the first node in its 1-hop neighbours list is already a CH then the unclustered node becomes a member of its CH cluster. Otherwise, the vehicle selects this node as its CH and e new cluster is formed. Thus, beside cluster member and CH, a node can be in a dual state that is when it is a CH of a cluster and a member of another cluster. This leads to overlapping neighbouring clusters and no message overhead in case of a cluster member transition to a neighbouring cluster.

Another novel concept introduced by this algorithm is the zone of interest that enables each vehicle to keep an updated table of its neighbours that goes beyond their transmission range. Zone of interest' radius is established as two times their transmission range. Thus vehicles have prior knowledge about the network while they are travelling into the neighbourhood which it's translated into an optimized and smoother process of re-clustering.

The algorithm is compared against an algorithm proposed by Basagni (1999) that is shortly called DMAC (Distributed and Mobility Adaptive Clustering). DMAC is a generalised clustering algorithm designed for MANETs where the CH election is done globally and is not node-oriented. Each vehicle has a weight associated. The clustering process begins with each node examining the weights of all nodes within its own transmission range. The node with the highest weight becomes the CH. This algorithm can be tailored for VANETS where the weight of a vehicle is calculated using metrics such as distance/speed/acceleration. RMAC outperforms DMAC in terms of $\overline{CML}$, and in terms of another topology metric: node re-clustering time.

Hafeez et al. (2011) introduced a clustering algorithm in the context of a new MAC protocol. Vehicles are organized in clusters on the basis of the beaconing and clustering messages they exchange in their neighbourhood. The focus is again on the CH election as CH is assigned with the main organizing and communication roles inside its cluster. The vehicles can have 5 different states: lone (not clustered), member, temporal CH, backup CH and CH. Temporal CH and backup CH roles aim to provide on one hand a stable CH in the cluster, a temporal Ch must prove that it is the most stable selection, and on the other hand to ensure a smoother CH re-election, backup CH is ready to take over the CH role. CH election algorithm is based on a weighted stability factor that is built upon the exponential-weighted moving average of the previous stability factors. Stability factor is computed for each vehicle and it is based on the relative movement between the neighbouring vehicles reflected in the average speed difference between the vehicle speed and its neighbours' speed. The novelty of this clustering scheme consists in the technique implemented in order to provide a smoother CH re-election and consequently to improve the cluster stability. Basically, this technique states how backup CH is taking over the CH role. The implementation of this technique is based on a Fuzzy Logic system that aims to predict and learn driver's behaviour. Based on this the next position and speed of the vehicles are computed. If in this next moment of time if not all the member of its cluster are in its range anymore, but they are still in the range of the backup CH, then CH hands over its role to the backup CH.

The proposed clustering solution is assessed using a large variety of metrics from all the classes presented. Thus, the MAC protocol integrating the clustering solution is assessed as well. However as our interest relays in the clustering schemes we mention the topology-based metrics employed in assessment: , , . The proposed clustering algorithm is demonstrated to overcome the performances of another cluster algorithm designed for a VANETs MAC protocol that was previously discussed (Su & Zhang, 2007). Moreover, the MAC protocol based on the proposed clustering solution proves better performances than the protocol used as comparison.

Tal and Muntean (2013a) proposed a new CH-based scheme that has as main novelty the employment of Fuzzy Logic as decisional framework in selecting the CH. Fuzzy Logic is an excellent mathematical framework for dealing with imprecision and multiple parameters. This is what needs to be modelled in VANET clustering: imprecision – it is impossible to define precisely how each of the clustering metrics influences the stability of CH in particular and clusters in general – and multiple clustering metrics that are imposed by the dynamicity and complex vehicular networking environment. The clustering metrics considered are the average relative distance, average relative velocity, direction of travelling and the average relative compatibility. This later parameter was introduced as a novelty by Tal & Muntean (2012) and measures the compatibility in the users (vehicles' drivers/passengers) preferences in certain data/content. The aim is to increase the probability of users being provided with data/content of their interest inside the cluster. Thus both clustering schemes aim to provide a cluster-based architecture for disseminating data/content of users' interest inside the cluster. In addition, these two approaches emphasize on the capability of clustering of designing efficient and optimized VANET architectures where the communication with infrastructure is limited (only CH is communicating with RSU) and in the same time the communication range can be extended via multi-hop communication inside the cluster in case of a multi-hop clustering.

In an assessment that compares these both algorithms and in addition the Lowest Id it is shown that the Fuzzy Logic-based clustering algorithm performs better than others two. The performance metrics used were $\overline{CHL}$, $\overline{CS}$ and a solution–dependent relative topology metric.

Wahab et al. (2013) is a very recently proposed two-hop CH-based clustering scheme for VANETs that is also incorporating computational intelligence. This is one of the proposed clustering algorithm novelties: the employment of Ant Colony Optimization in selecting the nodes having a state called multi point relay. These nodes are selected by CH for inter-cluster communication. The other novelty of this approach consist in building 5 new clustering metrics models with the focus on QoS. The most complex one combines bandwidth, connectivity and mobility metrics specific to VANETs (i.e. relative speed and distance). The output of the model is a QoS factor that is computed for each vehicle. Each of these models can be employed in further QoS-oriented clustering algorithms for VANETs, the authors describing each model's recommended scenario. This QoS factor is used to elect the most suitable CH and the multi point relays, while the clustering formation is done only on the basis of 2-hop neighbouring.

The clustering algorithm is designed in the context of a new routing protocol dedicated for VANETs that derivates from a MANET routing protocol designed to improve QoS, QoS-OLSR that on its turns derives from the state-of-the-art routing protocol for MANETs, QLSR (Optimized Link State Routing). Thus the performance assessment aims to demonstrate on one hand the efficiency of the clustering algorithm in terms of network stability and on the other hand to prove the efficiency of this algorithm in the designed routing protocol. In the first case, the performance is tested using a solution-dependent topology metric defined by the authors that is generic entitled stability. The metric is highly dependent on the clustering parameters. The authors show the performances of the algorithm in terms of stability and network metrics (e.g. packet delivery ratio) in 5 different cases corresponding to the 5 different clustering metrics models. No comparison is done with other clustering schemes. The comparison-based assessment is done only when showing the performances of the overall solution. The cluster-based routing protocol outperforms QoS-OLSR and OLSR both.

Tung et al. (2013) proposed a clustering algorithm designed in the context of an intersec-tion collision avoidance service. This clustering algorithm is employed in the design of a novel VANET WLAN-cellular architecture. This architecture is based on a heterogeneous network: LTE and WiFi. The communication messages inside the cluster are done via WiFi and they are called beacons, while CHs only are using the LTE interface for communicating with the base stations. This algorithm bridges the two types of clustering algorithms as it uses both static and mobile approach. On one hand, the clustering is bounded by the so called service region, region that is placed in the nearby of the intersection, but on the other hand it follows the mobility of the vehicles taking into account their direction. The proposed clustering algorithm is very specific to the solution built within. However, it indicates an efficient modality of bringing LTE in the vehicular networking context, as at this moment it appears to be more likely that LTE cannot handle the multiple messages that can be generated in VANET, especially during rush hours and in the traffic collision related applications when a huge number of messages can be generated. This solution was preceded by (Sivaraj et al., 2011) that employed a clustering algorithm to design a LTE-WAVE network architecture dedicated to multimedia delivery. This latest work uses a similar principle as in (Taleb & Benslimane, 2010; Benslimane et al., 2011), where a generic VANET UMTS-WAVE architecture based on clustering is designed, but instead of 3G brings 4G in the VANET context. The principle of these three works differ from (Tung et al., 2013) by delegating the responsibility of communicating to infrastructure (via 3G or 4G) to another node, a gateway node, while CH is the main forwarder of messages inside the cluster. Multiple metrics are involved in both selection procedures: CH and gateway node as both states are of great importance. Independently of the type of node that has the responsibility of communicating with the infrastructure, CH or gateway, there is a single node in each cluster that is accessing the cellular network interface. This leads to an optimized architecture that it is also proven to be reliable even for applications that require a rich content such as multimedia applications.

In (Tung et al., 2013), the procedure of selecting the CH is based on a single metric: the proximity to the base station. The algorithm is evaluated in the context of the overall solution using solution-dependent metrics. Although WiFi standard is chosen for the inter-vehicle communications, the authors suggest that this can be replaced with V2V communication (IEEE 802.11p). Such architecture is used in the clustering solution proposed by Harikrishnan & He (2013): IEEE 802.11p – V2V communication – for intra-cluster communication and LTE for the communication between CH and base station. This algorithm is a general CH-based clustering algorithm for VANETs. The clustering metrics are not clearly stated, but the CH is selected following the same policy as above: minimum distance to the base station. The algorithm is evaluated in terms of both network-specific performance metrics and topology-based performance metrics, namely: $\overline{CHL}$, $\overline{CS}$ and $\overline{NoC}$.

FUTURE RESEARCH DIRECTIONS

In a roadmap of clustering algorithms in the VANET research area, its start is recorded in 2005 when the first studies have been performed by employing Lowest Id and Highest Degree in VANETs scenarios and by suggesting new approaches that relate to these (e.g. Fan et al. (2005)). Actually, most of the VANET mobile clustering algorithms are using the basic principles that fundament Lowest Id and Highest Degree algorithms. Back in 2005 some of the main clustering challenges in VANETs have been outlined as well: rapidly changing topology of VANETs, scalability, multiple services to be provided with different requirements (real-time traffic, non-real time traffic) (Reumerman, Roggero & Ruffini,

2005). Based on the latter outlined challenge, the authors of the study suggest as a new direction for VANET clustering algorithms, when compared to MANETs clustering techniques, the application or service-oriented clustering. As such, a vehicle can be included in multiple overlaid clusters depending on the interest of driver/passengers (i.e. user).

Since then, the clustering algorithms evolved, many approaches have been proposed to tackle especially the rapidly changing topology of VANETs. More and more mobility parameters have been considered in clustering: direction, lanes, speed, position, predicted speed and position and combined with other parameters such bandwidth, connectivity (or density of the vehicles) and signal strength. These parameters are mainly considered in selecting the nodes with extra-responsibilities in the cluster, especially CH. CH election algorithms are of high importance and some of the researchers are actually focusing on this aspect of clustering only. Usually CH has the main responsibilities in the cluster and therefore a stable CH is required. In addition, the stability of CH is highly influencing the stability of the cluster itself, as most of the times when CH is re-elected a cluster reconfiguration is required, too. Therefore, researchers employed all kind of techniques to combine the clustering parameters and to decide which is the most suitable CH. The predominant techniques are utility functions and weight-based techniques, but recently more innovatory techniques such as Affinity Propagation have been employed (Shea et al., 2009).

One of the newest trends in VANET clustering algorithms is the employment of computational intelligence such as Fuzzy Logic (Hafeez et al., 2011) and Ant Colony Optimization (Wahab et al., 2013) in some secondary roles in clustering such as predicting the future positions of the vehicles. Fuzzy Logic decisional systems, known as very powerful decisional systems, have just started to be employed as main players in CH election algorithms (Tal & Muntean, 2013a). Fuzzy Logic is the perfect mathematical framework for dealing with imprecise information such as the one used in clustering (it is impossible to precisely define how each of the clustering parameters influence the stability of CH) and with multiple parameters.

Another trend in VANET clustering is the employment of clustering algorithms in designing reliable and efficient VANET architectures that bring together multiple access technologies. The need to converge multiple types of technologies in VANET context in order to enable the diversity of vehicular applications is underlined more and more in the literature and is also enforced by the low penetration rate of the WAVE technology. Thus, design techniques of VANET architectures that bring together multiple access technologies are of high interest. First, VANET cluster-based 3G-WAVE architectures were envisioned and very recently, VANET cluster-based architectures using 4G together with other technologies (WLAN or WAVE) were proposed. Due to its superior suitability for VANET environment compared to 3G technologies, the interest in bringing LTE in vehicular networks is far higher and considerable research efforts are done in this direction (Araniti, 2013). Although, LTE has high data rates and supports high mobility, it does not support direct communication between vehicles and from the studies performed so far it appears that it also cannot support the high number of messages exchanged by vehicles in certain scenarios (e.g. rush hours, applications that request an exchange of many messages such as collision avoidance applications). In addition, statistics

have shown that the huge growth in mobile data will be almost impossible to be accommodated in cellular networks (Goldsmith, 2012). Therefore, if brought in the context of VANETs, either 3G or 4G (LTE) technologies, these technologies need to be used in an optimum manner and they are mostly suitable for the communication between vehicles to infrastructure.

The cluster-based solutions presented in this chapter demonstrated that clustering is suitable for designing multiple access technologies-based VANET architectures with the previous recommendations. Two instances of this type of architecture can be outlined: one in which the communication with the infrastructure is done via CHs and the other one in which the communication with the infrastructure is done via gateways (Figure 6).

As a conclusion to the aforementioned aspects, the future directions in this research area of clustering in VANETs can be summarized as follows:

- More mathematical frameworks incorporating computational intelligence should be experimented in trying to find the most appropriate method of combining the clustering parameters in order to obtain stable CHs and stable networks.
- Although this chapter does some significant steps forward in the context of performance assessment of clustering algorithms in VANETs, this remains still an open challenge. The analysis of the VANET cluster-

Figure 6. Cluster and multiple access technologies-based VANETs architectures

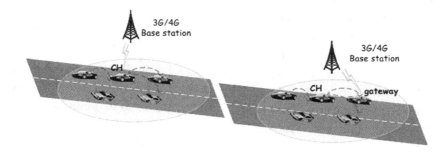

ing algorithms conducted in this work, leads to the idea that there is a need of standardizing clustering performance metrics, especially the general topology metrics. In addition, there is a huge need of traffic and mobility models for performing the testing of VANETs clustering algorithms.

- Although from the beginning of this research direction, application-oriented clustering was suggested for satisfying user requirements and interests, to our best knowledge so far this suggestion has not yet been explored. So far, the main clustering approaches were focused on a clustering that controls the topology and scalability of the VANETs. However, in this stage, clustering algorithms should also focus on user preferences, especially when clustering is integrated in information dissemination solutions or service-delivery solutions. To date user preferences have been considered in (Tal & Muntean, 2012; Tal & Muntean, 2013a), but among the neighbours only. Neighbouring can be the first criterion, but clustering solutions that are driven by preferences, application types, etc. are still expected to be proposed. These solutions are suitable for urban busy scenarios.

- A direction to be followed is the one that relates to clustering capabilities of conducting to a reliable and optimized design of VANET architecture based on multiple access technologies that is able to support the diversity of VANET applications. A comparison between the two outlined instances of VANET cluster and multiple access technologies-based architectures (Figure 6) in diverse scenarios and application types would be of high interest. This research direction could lead in the future to a generalized VANET cluster and multiple access technologies-based architecture or to guidelines in designing this type of architectures that are application-oriented, adapted to the type of application aiming to support.

CONCLUSION

This chapter has emphasized the high importance of VANETs in the context of smarter cities and roads. Initially, VANET was mainly associated with V2X communications/WAVE but this work has underlined and motivated the need for the convergence of multiple wireless technologies for support of a reliable VANET architecture that is able to provide a variety of services and to cope with the multiple challenges of VANETs. Clustering can be employed in designing such a VANET architecture that successfully uses different wireless communications technologies in an optimal manner. Moreover, clustering addresses some of VANETs major challenges such as scalability and stability.

This work presents a comprehensive survey of clustering schemes in the VANET research area covering aspects that have never been addressed before in a structured manner. To the best knowledge of the authors, this works complements the single review of clustering algorithms in VANETs which mainly summarizes some of the clustering algorithms in VANETs. The survey presented in this chapter provides a general classification of the clustering algorithms, presents some of the most advanced and latest algorithms in VANETs, and in addition, this is the only work that also reviewed the performance assessment of clustering algorithms. The latter is probably one of the biggest gaps of clustering in VANETs: there is so far, no analysis of the performance assessment metrics, and these metrics were not summarized nor standardized. In this chapter, we discussed the performance assessment metrics used in clustering in VANETs, provided a classification, identified and defined general performance metrics to be used in the evaluation of clustering algorithms in VANETs.

REFERENCES

Almalag, M. S., & Weigle, M. C. (2010). Using traffic flow for cluster formation in vehicular ad-hoc networks. In Proceedings of Local Computer Networks (LCN), (pp. 631-636). IEEE.

Araniti, G., Campolo, C., Condoluci, M., Iera, A., & Molinaro, A. (2013). LTE for vehicular networking: A survey. *IEEE Communications Magazine, 51*(5), 148–157. doi:10.1109/MCOM.2013.6515060

Barth, M., Mandava, S., Boriboonsomsin, K., & Xia, H. (2011). Dynamic ECO-driving for arterial corridors. In Proceedings of Integrated and Sustainable Transportation System (FISTS), (pp. 182-188). IEEE.

Basagni, S. (1999). Distributed clustering for ad hoc networks. In Proceedings of Parallel Architectures, Algorithms, and Networks, (pp. 310-315). IEEE.

Benslimane, A., Taleb, T., & Sivaraj, R. (2011). Dynamic clustering-based adaptive mobile gateway management in integrated VANET—3G heterogeneous wireless networks. *IEEE Journal on Selected Areas in Communications, 29*(3), 559–570. doi:10.1109/JSAC.2011.110306

Blum, J., Eskandarian, A., & Hoffman, L. (2003). Mobility management in IVC networks. In *Proceedings of Intelligent Vehicles Symposium,* (pp. 150-155). IEEE.

Cherif, M. O., Senouci, S. M., & Ducourthial, B. (2009). A new framework of self-organization of vehicular networks. In *Proceedings of Information Infrastructure Symposium,* (pp. 1-6). IEEE.

Djahel, S., Salehie, M., Tal, I., & Jamshidi, P. (2013). Adaptive traffic management for secure and efficient emergency services in smart cities. In *Pervasive computing and communications* (pp. 340–343). Academic Press. doi:10.1109/PerComW.2013.6529511

Doolan, R., & Muntean, G. M. (2013). VANET-enabled eco-friendly road characteristics-aware routing for vehicular traffic. In *Proceedings of IEEE Vehicular Technology Conference* (pp. 1-5). IEEE.

Dror, E., Avin, C., & Lotker, Z. (2011). Fast randomized algorithm for hierarchical clustering in vehicular ad-hoc networks. In *Proceedings of Ad Hoc Networking Workshop (Med-Hoc-Net),* (pp. 1-8). IEEE.

Dror, E., Avin, C., & Lotker, Z. (2013). Fast randomized algorithm for 2-hops clustering in vehicular ad-hoc networks. *Ad Hoc Networks, 11*(7), 2002–2015. doi:10.1016/j.adhoc.2012.02.006

Fan, P., Haran, J. G., Dillenburg, J., & Nelson, P. C. (2005). Cluster-based framework in vehicular ad-hoc networks. In *Proceedings of Ad-Hoc, Mobile, and Wireless Networks* (pp. 32–42). Berlin: Springer. doi:10.1007/11561354_5

Frey, B. J., & Dueck, D. (2007). Clustering by passing messages between data points. *Science, 315*(5814), 972–976. doi:10.1126/science.1136800 PMID:17218491

Gazdar, T., Belghith, A., & Benslimane, A. (2010). A cluster based secure architecture for vehicular ad hoc networks. In Proceedings of Computer Systems and Applications (AICCSA), (pp. 1-8). IEEE.

Gazdar, T., Benslimane, A., & Belghith, A. (2011). Secure clustering scheme based keys management in VANETs. In *Proceedings of Vehicular Technology Conference (VTC Spring),* (pp. 1-5). IEEE.

Girinath, D. R., & Selvan, S. (2010). A novel cluster based routing algorithm for hybrid mobility model in VANET. *International Journal of Computers and Applications, 1*(15), 35–42. doi:10.5120/326-495

Goldsmith, A. (2012). Beyond 4G: What lies ahead for cellular system design. In *Proceedings of Wireless Communications and Networking Conference* (WCNC). IEEE.

Gomes, P., Vieira, F., & Ferreira, M. (2013). Sustainable highways with shadow tolls based on VANET advertising. In *Proceeding of the Tenth ACM International Workshop on Vehicular Inter-Networking, Systems, and Applications* (pp. 71-76). ACM.

Goonewardene, R. T., Ali, F. H., & Stipidis, E. L. I. A. S. (2009). Robust mobility adaptive clustering scheme with support for geographic routing for vehicular ad hoc networks. *Intelligent Transport Systems*, *3*(2), 148–158. doi:10.1049/iet-its:20070052

Gunter, Y., Wiegel, B., & Großmann, H. P. (2007). Medium access concept for VANETs based on clustering. In *Proceedings of Vehicular Technology Conference,* (pp. 2189-2193). IEEE.

Hafeez, K. A., Zhao, L., Liao, Z., & Ma, B. N. W. (2011). Clustering and OFDMA-based MAC protocol (COMAC) for vehicular ad hoc networks. *EURASIP Journal on Wireless Communications and Networking*, (1): 1–16.

Harikrishnan, Y., & He, J. (2013). Clustering algorithm based on minimal path loss ratio for vehicular communication. In Proceedings of Computing, Networking and Communications (ICNC), (pp. 745-749). IEEE.

Hartenstein, H., Bochow, B., Ebner, A., Lott, M., Radimirsch, M., & Vollmer, D. (2001). Position-aware ad hoc wireless networks for inter-vehicle communications: The Fleetnet project. In *Proceedings of the 2nd ACM International Symposium on Mobile Ad Hoc Networking & Computing* (pp. 259-262). ACM.

Huang, C. J., Lin, C. F., Li, C. Y., Lee, C. Y., Chen, H. M., Shen, H. Y., & Chen, I. F. (2011). Service-oriented routing and clustering strategies for vehicle infotainment dissemination. *International Journal of Innovative Computing, Information, & Control*, *7*(3), 1467–1480.

Karagiannis, G., Altintas, O., Ekici, E., Heijenk, G., Jarupan, B., Lin, K., & Weil, T. (2011). Vehicular networking: A survey and tutorial on requirements, architectures, challenges, standards and solutions. *IEEE Communications Surveys & Tutorials*, *13*(4), 584–616. doi:10.1109/SURV.2011.061411.00019

Kayis, O., & Acarman, T. (2007). Clustering formation for inter-vehicle communication. In *Proceedings of Intelligent Transportation Systems Conference,* (pp. 636-641). IEEE.

Kuklinski, S., & Wolny, G. (2009). Density based clustering algorithm for VANETs. In Proceedings of Testbeds and Research Infrastructures for the Development of Networks & Communities and Workshops, (pp. 1-6). IEEE.

Lee, K. C., Lee, U., & Gerla, M. (2009). Survey of routing protocols in vehicular ad hoc networks. In *Advances in vehicular ad-hoc networks: Developments and challenges*. Hershey, PA: IGI Global.

Lu, R., Lin, X., Zhu, H., & Shen, X. (2009). SPARK: A new VANET-based smart parking scheme for large parking lots. [IEEE.]. *Proceedings of INFOCOM*, *2009*, 1413–1421.

Luo, Y., Zhang, W., & Hu, Y. (2010). A new cluster based routing protocol for VANET. [NSWCTC]. *Proceedings of Networks Security Wireless Communications and Trusted Computing*, *1*, 176–180.

Martinez, F. J., Toh, C. K., Cano, J. C., Calafate, C. T., & Manzoni, P. (2010). Emergency services in future intelligent transportation systems based on vehicular communication networks. *IEEE Intelligent Transportation Systems Magazine, 2*(2), 6–20. doi:10.1109/MITS.2010.938166

Maslekar, N., Boussedjra, M., Mouzna, J., & Houda, L. (2009). Direction based clustering algorithm for data dissemination in vehicular networks. In *Proceedings of Vehicular Networking Conference (VNC),* (pp. 1-6). IEEE.

Maslekar, N., Boussedjra, M., Mouzna, J., & Labiod, H. (2011). A stable clustering algorithm for efficiency applications in VANETs. In *Proceedings of Wireless Communications and Mobile Computing Conference (IWCMC),* (pp. 1188-1193). IEEE.

Maslekar, N., Mouzna, J., Labiod, H., Devisetty, M., & Pai, M. (2011). Modified C-DRIVE: Clustering based on direction in vehicular environment. In *Proceedings of Intelligent Vehicles Symposium (IV),* (pp. 845-850). IEEE.

Moustafa, H., Senouci, S. M., & Jerbi, M. (2009). Introduction to vehicular networks. In H. Moustafa, & Y. Zhang (Eds.), *Vehicular networks: Techniques, standards and applications.* Boca Raton, FL: CRC Press. doi:10.1201/9781420085723

Ploeg, J., Serrarens, A. F., & Heijenk, G. J. (2011). Connect & drive: Design and evaluation of cooperative adaptive cruise control for congestion reduction. *Journal of Modern Transportation, 19*(3), 207–213. doi:10.1007/BF03325760

Rakha, H., & Kamalanathsharma, R. K. (2011). Eco-driving at signalized intersections using V2I communication. In Proceedings of Intelligent Transportation Systems (ITSC), (pp. 341-346). IEEE.

Ramakrishnan, B., Rajesh, R. S., & Shaji, R. S. (2011). CBVANET: A cluster based vehicular adhoc network model for simple highway communication. *J. Advanced Networking and Applications, 2*(4), 755–761.

Razzaq, A., & Mehaoua, A. (2010). Video transport over VANETs: Multi-stream coding with multi-path and network coding. In Proceedings of Local Computer Networks (LCN), (pp. 32-39). IEEE.

Reumerman, H. J., Roggero, M., & Ruffini, M. (2005). The application-based clustering concept and requirements for intervehicle networks. *IEEE Communications Magazine, 43*(4), 108–113. doi:10.1109/MCOM.2005.1421913

Santi, P. (2012). *Mobility models for next generation wireless networks.* Sussex, UK: Wiley. doi:10.1002/9781118344774

Shea, C., Hassanabadi, B., & Valaee, S. (2009). Mobility-based clustering in VANETs using affinity propagation. In *Proceedings of Global Telecommunications Conference,* (pp. 1-6). IEEE.

Shoaib, M., Song, W. C., & Kim, K. H. (2012). Cluster based data aggregation in vehicular ad-hoc network. In *Proceedings of Communication Technologies for Vehicles* (pp. 91–102). Berlin: Springer. doi:10.1007/978-3-642-29667-3_8

Sivaraj, R., Gopalakrishna, A. K., Chandra, M. G., & Balamuralidhar, P. (2011). QoS-enabled group communication in integrated VANET-LTE heterogeneous wireless networks. In Proceedings of Wireless and Mobile Computing, Networking and Communications (WiMob), (pp. 17-24). IEEE.

Su, H., & Zhang, X. (2007). Clustering-based multichannel MAC protocols for QoS provisionings over vehicular. *IEEE Transactions on Vehicular Technology, 56*(6), 3309–3323. doi:10.1109/TVT.2007.907233

Tal, I., & Muntean, G. M. (2012). User-oriented cluster-based solution for multimedia content delivery over VANETs. In Proceedings of Broadband Multimedia Systems and Broadcasting (BMSB), (pp. 1-5). IEEE.

Tal, I., & Muntean, G. M. (2013a). User-oriented fuzzy logic-based clustering scheme for vehicular ad-hoc networks. In *Proceedings of Vehicular Technology Conference* (pp. 1-5). IEEE.

Tal, I., & Muntean, G.-M. (2013b). V2X communication-based power saving strategy for electric bicycles. In *Proceedings of Global Telecommunications Conference Workshops,* (pp. 1-6). Academic Press.

Tal, I., Tianhua, Z., & Muntean, G.-M. (2013). On the potential of V2X communications in helping electric bicycles save energy. In *Proceedings of Vehicular Networking Conference,* (pp. 1-4). Academic Press.

Taleb, T., & Benslimane, A. (2010). Design guidelines for a network architecture integrating VANET with 3G & beyond networks. In *Proceedings of Global Telecommunications Conference (GLOBECOM 2010),* (pp. 1-5). IEEE.

Teshima, S., Ohta, T., Kohno, E., & Kakuda, Y. (2011). A data transfer scheme using autonomous clustering in VANETs environment. In Proceedings of Autonomous Decentralized Systems (ISADS), (pp. 477-482). IEEE.

Tian, D., Wang, Y., Lu, G., & Yu, G. (2010). A VANETs routing algorithm based on Euclidean distance clustering. [ICFCC]. *Proceedings of Future Computer and Communication, 1,* V1–V183.

Tielert, T., Rieger, D., Hartenstein, H., Luz, R., & Hausberger, S. (2012). Can V2X communication help electric vehicles save energy? In *Proceedings of ITS Telecommunications (ITST),* (pp. 232-237). IEEE.

Tonguz, O. K., & Boban, M. (2010). Multiplayer games over vehicular ad hoc networks: A new application. *Ad Hoc Networks, 8*(5), 531–543. doi:10.1016/j.adhoc.2009.12.009

Toulminet, G., Boussuge, J., & Laurgeau, C. (2008). Comparative synthesis of the 3 main European projects dealing with Cooperative Systems (CVIS, SAFESPOT and COOPERS) and description of COOPERS demonstration site 4. In Proceedings of Intelligent Transportation Systems, (pp. 809-814). IEEE.

Trivedi, H., Veeraraghavan, P., Loke, S., Desai, A., & Singh, J. (2011). SmartVANET: The case for a cross-layer vehicular network architecture. In Proceedings of Advanced Information Networking and Applications (WAINA), (pp. 362-368). IEEE.

Tung, L.-C., Mena, J., Gerla, M., & Sommer, C. (2013). A cluster based architecture for intersection collision avoidance using heterogeneous networks. In *Proceedings of Annual Mediterranean Ad Hoc Networking Workshop* (Med-Hoc-Net 2013). IFIP/IEEE.

Ucar, S., Ergen, S. C., & Ozkasap, O. (2013). VMaSC: Vehicular multi-hop algorithm for stable clustering in vehicular ad hoc networks. In *Proceedings of Wireless Communications and Networking Conference* (WCNC), (pp. 2381-2386). IEEE.

Uzcategui, R. A., & Acosta-Marum, G. (2009). Wave: A tutorial. *IEEE Communications Magazine, 47*(5), 126–133. doi:10.1109/MCOM.2009.4939288

Vodopivec, S., Bester, J., & Kos, A. (2012). A survey on clustering algorithms for vehicular ad-hoc networks. In Proceedings of Telecommunications and Signal Processing (TSP), (pp. 52-56). IEEE.

Wahab, O. A., Otrok, H., & Mourad, A. (2013). VANET QoS-OLSR: QoS-based clustering protocol for vehicular ad hoc networks. *Computer Communications*. doi:10.1016/j.comcom.2013.07.003 PMID:23805013

Wang, Z., Liu, L., Zhou, M., & Ansari, N. (2008). A position-based clustering technique for ad hoc intervehicle communication. *IEEE Transactions on Systems, Man and Cybernetics. Part C, Applications and Reviews*, 38(2), 201–208. doi:10.1109/TSMCC.2007.913917

Wanner, L. (2004). *Introduction to clustering techniques*. International Union of Local Authorities.

Wolny, G. (2008). Modified DMAC clustering algorithm for VANETS. In *Proceedings of Systems and Networks Communications* (pp. 268–273). IEEE.

Yang, Q., Lim, A., & Agrawal, P. (2008). Connectivity aware routing in vehicular networks. In *Proceedings of Wireless Communications and Networking Conference,* (pp. 2218-2223). IEEE.

Yang, Z., Li, M., & Lou, W. (2010). Codeplay: Live multimedia streaming in VANETS using symbol-level network coding. In Proceedings of Network Protocols (ICNP), (pp. 223-232). IEEE.

Yu, J. Y., & Chong, P. H. J. (2005). A survey of clustering schemes for mobile ad hoc networks. *IEEE Communications Surveys and Tutorials*, 7(1-4), 32–48. doi:10.1109/COMST.2005.1423333

Zaydoun, Z. Y., & Mahmud, S. M. (2009). Toward strongly connected clustering structure in vehicular ad hoc networks. In *Proceedings of Conference on Vehicular Technology,* (pp. 1-5). IEEE.

ADDITIONAL READING

Al-Sultan, S., Al-Doori, M. M., Al-Bayatti, A. H., & Zedan, H. (in press). A comprehensive survey on vehicular Ad Hoc network. *Journal of Network and Computer Applications*.

Amadeo, M., Campolo, C., & Molinaro, A. (2012). Enhancing IEEE 802.11p/WAVE to provide infotainment applications in VANETs. *Ad Hoc Networks*, 10(2), 253–269. doi:10.1016/j.adhoc.2010.09.013

Campolo, C., Iera, A., Molinaro, A., Paratore, S. Y., & Ruggeri, G. (2012, November). SMaRTCaR: An integrated smartphone-based platform to support traffic management applications. In *Vehicular Traffic Management for Smart Cities (VTM), 2012 First International Workshop on* (pp. 1-6). IEEE.

Chen, T. M. (2010). Smart grids, smart cities need better networks [Editor's Note]. *Network, IEEE*, 24(2), 2–3. doi:10.1109/MNET.2010.5430136

Eltoweissy, M., Olariu, S., & Younis, M. (2010). Towards autonomous vehicular clouds. In *Ad Hoc Networks* (pp. 1–16). Springer Berlin Heidelberg. doi:10.1007/978-3-642-17994-5_1

Fan, P., Haran, J., Dillenburg, J., & Nelson, P. C. (2006, January). Traffic model for clustering algorithms in vehicular ad-hoc networks. In *Proc. of CCNC* (pp. 168-172).

Gerla, M. (2012). Vehicular Cloud Computing. In *Ad Hoc Networking Workshop (Med-Hoc-Net), 2012 The 11th Annual Mediterranean* (pp. 152-155). IEEE.

Gerla, M. (2013). Safe driving in Crowded Spectrum: Cognitive radios for VANETs. Keynote presentation at *Network Protocols (ICNP), IEEE International Conference on, Workshop on Vehicular Communications and Applications.*

Gerla, M., & Kleinrock, L. (2011). Vehicular networks and the future of the mobile Internet. *Computer Networks, 55*(2), 457–469. doi:10.1016/j.comnet.2010.10.015

Gerla, M., & Tsai, J. T. C. (1995). Multicluster, mobile, multimedia radio network. *Wireless Networks, 1*(3), 255–265. doi:10.1007/BF01200845

Hartenstein, H., & Laberteaux, K. P. (2008). A tutorial survey on vehicular ad hoc networks. *Communications Magazine, IEEE, 46*(6), 164–171. doi:10.1109/MCOM.2008.4539481

Hossain, E., Chow, G., Leung, V., McLeod, R. D., Mišić, J., Wong, V. W., & Yang, O. (2010). Vehicular telematics over heterogeneous wireless networks: A survey. *Computer Communications, 33*(7), 775–793. doi:10.1016/j.comcom.2009.12.010

Ide, C., Dusza, B., Putzke, M., & Wietfeld, C. (2012, June). Channel sensitive transmission scheme for V2I-based Floating Car Data collection via LTE. In *Communications (ICC), 2012 IEEE International Conference on* (pp. 7151-7156). IEEE.

Ide, C., Niehoefer, B., Knaup, T., Weber, D., Wietfeld, C., Habel, L., & Schreckenberg, M. (2012, September). Efficient Floating Car Data Transmission via LTE for Travel Time Estimation of Vehicles. In *Vehicular Technology Conference (VTC Fall), 2012 IEEE* (pp. 1-5). IEEE.

Kihl, M., Bur, K., Mahanta, P., & Coelingh, E. (2012, July). 3GPP. LTE downlink scheduling strategies in vehicle-to-infrastructure communications for traffic safety applications. In *Computers and Communications (ISCC), 2012 IEEE Symposium on* (pp. 448-453). IEEE.

Lottermann, C., Botsov, M., Fertl, P., & Mullner, R. (2012, November). Performance evaluation of automotive off-board applications in LTE deployments. In *Vehicular Networking Conference (VNC), 2012 IEEE* (pp. 211-218). IEEE.

Mangel, T., Kosch, T., & Hartenstein, H. (2010, December). A comparison of UMTS and LTE for vehicular safety communication at intersections. In *Vehicular Networking Conference (VNC), 2010 IEEE* (pp. 293-300). IEEE.

Morgan, Y. L. (2010). Notes on DSRC & WAVE standards suite: Its architecture, design, and characteristics. *Communications Surveys & Tutorials, IEEE, 12*(4), 504–518. doi:10.1109/SURV.2010.033010.00024

Net!Works European Technology Platform (2011). Expert Working Group on Smart Cities and Requirements [white paper]. Retrieved from: http://www.networks-etp.eu/fileadmin/user_upload/Publications/Position_White_Papers/White_Paper_Smart_Cities_Applications.pdf

Phan, M. A., Rembarz, R., & Sories, S. (2011). A Capacity Analysis for the Transmission of Event and Cooperative Awareness Messages in LTE Networks. In *18th ITS World Congress.*

Rémy, G., Senouci, S., Jan, F., & Gourhant, Y. (2011, December). LTE4V2X: LTE for a Centralized VANET Organization. In *Global Telecommunications Conference (GLOBECOM 2011), 2011 IEEE* (pp. 1-6). IEEE.

Remy, G., Senouci, S. M., Jan, F., & Gourhant, Y. (2012, June). LTE4V2X—Collection, dissemination and multi-hop forwarding. In *Communications (ICC), 2012 IEEE International Conference on* (pp. 120-125). IEEE.

Toor, Y., Muhlethaler, P., & Laouiti, A. (2008). Vehicle ad hoc networks: Applications and related technical issues. *Communications Surveys & Tutorials, IEEE, 10*(3), 74–88. doi:10.1109/COMST.2008.4625806

Vegni, A. M., Biagi, M., & Cusani, R. (2013). Smart Vehicles, Technologies and Main Applications in Vehicular Ad hoc. *Networks*. doi: doi:10.5772/55492

Vinel, A. (2012). 3GPP. LTE Versus IEEE802.11p/WAVE: Which Technology is Able to Support Cooperative Vehicular Safety Applications. *Communications Letters, IEEE, 1*(2), 125–128. doi:10.1109/WCL.2012.022012.120073

Whaiduzzaman, M., Sookhak, M., Gani, A., & Buyya, R. (in press). A survey on vehicular cloud computing. *Journal of Network and Computer Applications*.

Wu, X., Subramanian, S., Guha, R., White, R., Li, J., & Lu, K. et al. (2013). Vehicular communications using DSRC: challenges, enhancements, and evolution. *Selected Areas in Communications. IEEE Journal on, 31*(9), 399–408.

KEY TERMS AND DEFINITIONS

3G/4G: 3rd/4th Generation of mobile cellular communications.

Clustering: Technique of grouping similar objects used mainly to deal with scalability, but its aim depends on the context it is applied in.

Performance Assessment: Evaluation – in the context of this chapter, the evaluation of clustering algorithms in VANETs.

Smart Cites: Cities of the future that provide increased comfort to their citizens while creating a sustainable environment.

V2X Communications: The main enabling technology of VANETs.

VANET: Vehicular ad-hoc networks.

WAVE: WIRELESS Access Vehicular Environment – V2X communications standardization.

WLAN: Wireless Local Area Network.

ENDNOTES

[1]   http://smartercitieschallenge.org/
[2]   http://setis.ec.europa.eu/implementation/technology-roadmap/european-initiative-on-smart-cities
[3]   http://www.gsacom.com/news/statistics

Chapter 3
Resource Allocation in Heterogeneous Broadband Wireless Access Networks

Chetna Singhal
Indian Institute of Technology Delhi, India

Swades De
Indian Institute of Technology Delhi, India

ABSTRACT

The advent of heterogeneous Broadband Wireless Access Networks (BWANs) has been to support the ever increasing cellular networks' data requirements by increasing capacity, spectrum efficiency, and network coverage. The focus of this chapter is to discuss the implementation details (i.e. architecture and network components), issues associated with heterogeneous BWANs (i.e. handovers, network selection, and base station placement), and also the various resource allocation schemes (i.e. shared resource allocation in split handover and inter-RAT self-organizing networks) that can improve the performance of the system by maximizing the capacity of users.

INTRODUCTION

Emergence of BWAN as a popular alternative to the wire-line access infrastructure is primarily associated with steady increase in data rate support and has inherent advantages, such as: easy scalability; ease of use in the end system; and low deployment and maintenance cost. According to Dahlman et al. (2008), the 4th generation (4G) BWAN, like LTE-A (long term evolution-advanced) and WiMAX-Mobile (world-wide interoperability for microwave access-mobile),

have a maximum data rate of approximately 1 Gbps in downlink and 300Mbps in uplink as per the IMT-Advanced (international mobile telecommunications-advanced) specification. According to the data published by Ericson (2012) and Cisco (2012), the mobile broadband data traffic has been increasing exponentially every year and the increase was nearly 885 petabytes per month by the end of 2012. Traffic forecast update by Cisco (2012) also projects a 13-fold increase in global mobile data traffic and a 7-fold increase in network connection speeds by 2017. Latouche

DOI: 10.4018/978-1-4666-5978-0.ch003

et al. (2013) has suggested value-added services (based on end-user information and user identification) and industry "coopetation" (simultaneous cooperation and competition between service providers) as feasible solutions for the predicted mobile data explosion. Mobile data offloading (such as Wi-Fi offloading discussed by Cisco (2012)) is a cost-effective solution for delivering cellular network data that eases network congestion, provides seamless connectivity, and offers higher bandwidth to end-users.

The future heterogeneous network would efficiently and effectively integrate the prevailing heterogeneities as discussed by Chan et al. (2011), such as: communication modalities, channel types, technology generations, protocol types, and QoS requirements. To address dynamic, distributed, and unpredictable nature of these networks, they need to have self-organisation properties that range from self-configuration during startup, to self-adaptation to dynamic changes in operating environment, to self-healing in presence of failures and losses, as has been discussed by Razzaque et al. (2010). Among the standardization groups in this domain, are next generation mobile networks (NGMN) alliance that aims to bring affordable mobile broadband services to the LTE and LTE-A end users and Small Cell Forum/Femto Forum that works towards adoption of small cell technologies to improve coverage, capacity, and services delivered by mobile networks.

The prominent need to enhance network capacity, throughput and users' quality of service (QoS) has led to the advent of heterogeneous next generation networks, comprising of different RAN (radio access networks) connected to a single core network. Implementing these networks, while ensuring high data rates in the wireless environment, poses certain resource allocation challenges such as: positioning the base station (BS) transceiver, handovers and network selection etc. In this chapter, we discuss: the architecture of heterogeneous BWAN; the issues associated with their implementation such as handover, network selection and BS placement; shared resource al-

location solution to maximize the users capacity; and the idea of self-organizing network (SON) based inter-RAT (radio access technology) MRO (mobility robustness optimization). [1]

ARCHITECTURE

Heterogeneous network (het-net) architecture is a prominent low-cost approach where an operator can exploit the different BWANs to provide additional areal capacity gain, indoor coverage improvement, and improved quality of service (QoS) in the network, as per Yeh et al. (2011).

Deployment Scenarios

Multitier Architecture Network Components

A heterogeneous BWAN architecture consisting of hierarchical multitier multiple radio access technologies (RAT) deployments is shown in Figure 1. This multitier deployment improves capacity and coverage by enabling dense reuse of the spectrum and enhancing link quality. The role of tiers and the larger and smaller footprint devices is examined as follows:

1. **Macrocells/Microcells:** Macrocells are deployed in rural or suburban areas with a coverage distance of more than 500m. The advantage of having large macrocells is that it provides support for high mobility users with reduced frequency of handovers. Both the macrocell and microcells provide essential coverage in het-nets.
2. **Picocells:** Pico BS (PBS) are deployed as hotspots to serve capacity hungry locations (example: airports, stadiums) where the serving area is smaller than micro-cells. PBSs are low cost, low power, simplified MBSs (macro/micro BS) that are accessible to all cellular users. MBSs and PBSs are planned and controlled by operators and horizontal

Figure 1. Heterogeneous network (het-net) architecture

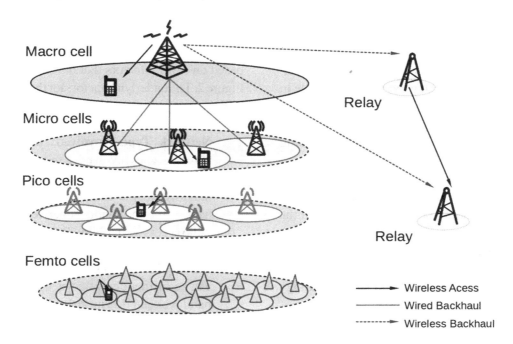

optimization is beneficial across tiers. MBSs and PBSs are connected to the network through operator-owned backhaul.

3. **Femtocells:** Femto access point (FAP) covers a very small area (10-50m, in a house). These utilize residential backhaul links (digital subscriber line (DSL) or cable). FAPs are privately owned and deployed according to users' needs. FAPs are configured in closed subscriber groups (CSG), where FAP is accessible to only restricted users. CSG FAPs causes excessive interference to the network when the same spectrum is shared with other tiers. CSG FAP interference and network scalability to support large number of FAPs are important research challenges.

4. **Relays:** Relay stations serve similar sizes of footprints as PBSs. They provide coverage extension and throughput enhancement by forwarding an enhanced version of the received signal from BSs to mobile stations. Relays use wireless backhaul, so no landline resource is required; however, this reduces

the amount of spectrum available for access. Operators may choose to implement infrastructural relays over PBSs at coverage holes where wired backhaul is unavailable or difficult to implement.

5. **Client Relay:** Client relay is the client cooperation (CC) tier that lies between clients comprising of very short range links. Utilizing good links between clients and BS, it improves the successful transmission probability for and virtual link quality for users in poor locations (i.e., cell edge users), thereby reducing the amount of channel resources, battery power consumption, and interference caused to other cells. CC improves average network throughput.

It is efficient to deploy small cells in significant data generation sites (shopping mall, stadium, university campus, public transportation hub, etc.) and where subscribers spend considerable amount of time (home, office, etc.).

HANDOVER

Handover is the process of transferring an active call or data session of a mobile user from one cell in a cellular network to another or from one channel in a cell to another. It plays a very vital role in mobile wireless networks, to ensure a seamless service to a mobile user. Because of high data rates in broadband wireless access networks, providing a seamless handover is a challenging issue.

Before performing handover, an appropriate BS candidate must be chosen and then the handover procedure should be continued based on the current technology and the specific application constraints of the MS (mobile station/subscriber). The exact procedures vary depending on the used technology, and usually within the technology several alternatives are available as well.

Classification and Associated Factors

The various handover schemes in het-nets are based on several factors that have been shown in Figure 2. The underlying factors for these handover schemes are enlisted as follows:

1. **Network Types Involved:** Based on the network types involved, handovers are classified as vertical handover and horizontal handover (depicted in Figure 2). Horizontal handover is the handover between two same radio access technology (RAT) networks and vertical handover is the handover between two different RATs. Vertical handovers can be further classified as upward vertical handover and downward vertical handover.

Figure 2. Handover classification

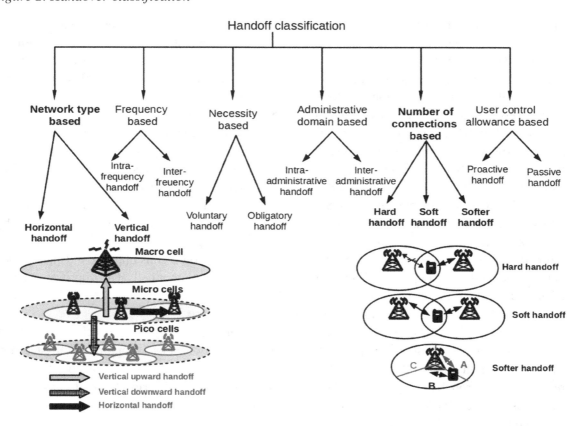

In upward vertical handover the user device connects to a cell with larger coverage area and lower bandwidth than its source cell. In downward vertical handover the user device connects to a cell with lower coverage area and higher bandwidth. Downward handover is less critical as the device can stay connected to upper layer. In vertical handover, the decision of when to carry out handover itself is a complex problem since in vertical handover we cannot consider only the signal strength like we do in horizontal handover due to different physical techniques that are used by different overlay networks. In vertical handovers, the two key issues to be considered are network conditions for vertical handover and connection maintenance which have been discussed by Guo et al. (2004). Both the vertical and horizontal handover process constitute of three phases – handover decision, radio link transfer, and channel assignment, as discussed by Nasser (2006). These handover process phases are elaborately discussed later in the chapter.

2. **Frequencies Engaged:** Based on the frequencies engaged, handovers are classified as intra-frequency handover and inter-frequency handover. Intra-frequency handover is the handover between same frequency access points. Example: handovers in CDMA. Inter-frequency handover is the handover between different frequency access points. Example: handovers in GSM.

3. **Number of Connections Involved:** Based on the number of connections involved, handovers are classified as hard handover, soft handover, and softer handover. These are depicted in Figure 2. In a hard handover, the new connection will only be established after disconnecting from source base station. In hard handover the user device maintains only single connection at a time. In a soft handover, the user device maintains con-

nection with atleast two base stations in an overlapping handover region. These types of handovers are possible when handover is between cells operating with same frequency. Softer handover is soft handover between sectors of a given cell. Different variants of hard handover and soft handover are semi-soft handover and fractional handover in OFDM based systems that have been discussed by Lee et al. (2011) and Chang et al. (2011), fast base station switching (FBSS) and macro-diversity handover (MDHO) specified in IEEE Standard for Local and Metropolitan Area Networks-Part 16. (2005). Soft and softer handovers improve forward link capacity and signal to interference ratio for mobile users near the cell and sector boundaries, as per Lee et al. (1998).

4. **Administrative Domains Involved:** Based on the administrative domains involved, handovers are classified as intra-administrative handover and inter-administrative handover. In intra-administrative handover the user device moves from one network to another which belongs to same operator. In Inter administrative handover the user device moves from one network to another which is operated by different operators.

5. **Necessity of Handover:** Based on the necessity of handover, handovers are classified as obligatory handover and voluntary handover. Obligatory handover is necessary to avoid connection termination. Voluntary handover is optional and mostly used in scenarios in order to improve QOS.

6. **User Control Allowance:** Based on the user control allowance, handovers are classified as proactive handover and passive handover. In proactive handovers, user can give preferences which will affect the handover decision. In passive handover, the handover decision is not controlled by the user.

As compared to soft/softer handover schemes, a further increase in capacity is achieved by using a split handover procedure as discussed by Singhal et al. (2012), which results in a capacity gain by employing a 2-dimensional shared resource allocation for cell edge users in orthogonal frequency division multiple access (OFDMA) networks. Here, the MSs at the cell-edge can maintain parallel connections with more than one BS when it is in their coverage area. A MS, before handover to a new BS, seeks to utilize additional resources from the other BSs if the BS through which its current session is registered is not able to satisfy its requirements. The BSs participate in split handover operation while guaranteeing that they are able to maintain QoS of the existing connections associated with them.

Handover Process Operations

The handover process constitutes of three phases (handover decision, radio link transfer, and channel assignment) and the following discussion is in context of hard and soft handover.

1. **Handover Decision:** In horizontal handover, the decision is mainly reflected by the QoS which in turn depends mainly on signal strength since the source and target base station are using the same physical techniques. So a horizontal handover is executed if the signal strength from the source BS is less than the threshold value and signal strength from neighboring BS is more than the threshold. Unlike in horizontal handover there are many network parameters that will affect the handover decision in vertical handover since it is between the BSs with different access technologies. These parameters are - quality of service, cost of service, power requirement, velocity, and proactive handover etc. Here the network selection which we will discuss subsequently comes into picture. Based on the above parameters, if a better

network is available when the current one is not able to service then vertical handover will be executed. The handover parameters are briefly stated as follows:

a. **Quality of Service (QOS):** Handing over to a better network with better QoS parameters such as - transmission rates, error rates, delay and connectivity etc.

b. **Cost of Service:** It is one of the important parameter as some users are not willing to pay more than a certain limit and may want to connect to the cheapest network available with minimum requirements. Different access technologies have different costs, hence it is critical in vertical handover decision making.

c. **Velocity:** It is also an important parameter because if the user is moving with higher velocity then it is better to connect him to a cell with larger radius (macro cell) rather than connecting him to a cell with smaller radius (micro or pico cell) which in turn increases the handovers.

d. **Power Requirements:** The mobile devices have the limited battery power and when the battery level decreases it is better to handover to a network which consumes less battery power.

e. **Proactive Handover:** By proactive handover, it means that the ultimate decision is with the user to satisfy their special requirement. If a user wants to handover to a network regardless of network conditions the vertical handover decision is executed.

2. **Radio Link Transfer:** There are two approaches for radio link transfer they are forward handover and backward handover. In forward handover the radio link transfer is initiated by the target BS unlike the backward handover in which the source BS initiates the radio link transfer. Both have their

advantages and disadvantages, for instance the advantage of backward handover is that in this the initial signaling information is transmitted through the existing connection and thus does not need establishment of a new channel. However, the disadvantage of backward handover as per Shen & Zeng (2007) is that if the link quality of source BS is too poor, then the signaling information might be lost leading to unsuccessful handover. Backward handover is used in most cellular networks.

3. The final handover stage is the channel assignment stage, in which allocation of resources to the mobile node is done by the target BS. In this stage a call admission control (CAC) algorithm will take decision of accepting or rejecting the new mobile node based on the available amount of resources and the effect of existing connection on QoS that may have been caused due to a new connection.

NETWORK SELECTION

Network selection in het-nets is a challenge as the user device has to select from radio access networks (RANs) with different latency, coverage area, cost etc (Figure 3). These RANs may belong to different service providers who are competing with each other to maximize their own revenue or cooperating with each other for mutual benefit. The network selection may be needed mainly at two stages, while requesting for a new connection and in the handover process. Proper modeling of network selection by user device is important, since a bad network selection algorithm results in unnecessary handovers which in turn decreases the QoS of the users.

The network selection in het-nets is modeled mainly by using two different approaches that are: user oriented approach and network oriented approach. In network oriented approach, a central node runs the decision algorithm to assign the access networks to the users and users bind by the

Figure 3. User oriented network selection process

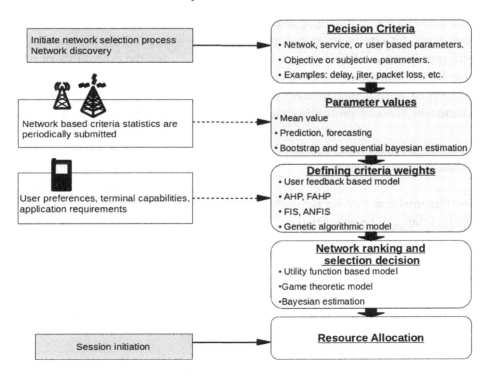

decision. The above approach mainly enhances the network capacity. It is very complex to implement and it creates extensive overhead in networks. On the contrary, in user oriented approach given by Charilas & Panagopoulous (2010), the users' mobile device executes the algorithms for network selection and implements them. This approach is more dynamic and it has less communication overhead and low complexity of implementation.

Steps Involved in Network Selection

Network selection for heterogeneous networks mainly involves the following five steps:

1. **Selection of Decision Criteria:** The user device is responsible for determining the set of decision criteria to be used. The decision criteria are classified into the following three categories:
   a. **Network Based Parameters:** Utilization, reliability, coverage, anonymity, security, seamless number of active users, etc.
   b. **Service Based Parameters:** Delay, jitter, packet loss, throughput average in kbps, bit error rate, signal-to-interference ratio in dB, etc.
   c. **User Based Parameters:** Sojourn time, forced termination probability for handover, blocking probability, etc.

The above mentioned parameters can also be classified into two groups, as follows:

1. **Objective Parameters:** Can be measured accurately and thus can be quantified.
2. **Subjective Parameters:** Can only be estimated usually in the form of fuzzy numbers (i.e., a number that refers to a set of possible values between 0 and 1), as given by Zhang (2004).

Parameters like jitter, packet loss are to be given low priority because they cannot be measured before establishing the connection to the network whereas parameters such as bandwidth, signal-to-interference ratio, and coverage area should be given comparatively higher priority since information about these can be known before connecting to the network.

1. **Collection of Values for Selected Criteria:** After listing of the available RANs, value of parameters for each RAN is collected, and monitoring of the network conditions is also done. The following four ways are used for collecting the parameter values:
   a. Collecting mean values from previous sessions. This is suitable when the network is not prone to abrupt changes.
   b. Collecting most recent values that reflect current status of the network.
   c. Predicting and forecasting the values of the parameters. The forecasting can be done by two techniques such as: direct estimation of parameters like load on the hot spot by using past values in weighted moving average or simple moving average methods; and predicting the probability of parameter (like SNR, blocking probability, termination probability) using markov chains for modeling, as discussed by Shen & Zeng (2007).
   d. Bootstrap and sequential Bayesian estimation of dynamic QoS parameters discussed by Ong & Khan (2008) and Zoubir & Boashash (1998). The bootstrap estimation generates probability distribution of parameters using samples collected from parameter values.
2. Defining criteria weights in the final outcome based on their importance and also user or application context based requirements.

This can be performed by the following six models:

a. **User Feedback Based Evaluation of Weights:** i.e. obtained through questionnaire and provided to the device. Since this model depends on overall users' perception of the service, it cannot guarantee accurate results for objective criteria. However, in scenarios where user always wants to select the cheapest network, this model is helpful.

b. **Analytical Hierarchy Process (AHP):** Given by Pervaiz & Bigham (2009) is widely used in multi criteria models by dividing the decision problem into multi-level hierarchical model and determining weights by paired comparisons between parameters. When AHP is followed by game theory modeling for ranking, it results in achieving optimum network utility and customer's satisfaction in competing wireless networks.

c. **Fuzzy Analytical Hierarchy Process (FAHP):** Is an extension of AHP that solves hierarchical fuzzy problems, since AHP cannot handle imprecise data represented in fuzzy numbers. The outputs of pair-wise comparison in FAHP are fuzzy numbers. Shen (2010) uses FAHP for access selection among various RATs and for optimizing system performance by considering multiple criterions of QoE to cater to user-preferences and experiences. Sgora (2010) combines two Multi Attribute Decision Making (MADM) methods, the AHP method to determine weights of the criteria and the fuzzy Total Order Preference by Similarity to the Ideal Solution (TOPSIS) method to obtain the final access network ranking.

d. **Fuzzy Inference System (FIS):** Input is converted to linguistic variables by fuzzier; system is controlled using if-then rules (based on questionnaires, network measurement, and previous system knowledge) by the inference engine. The main disadvantage of this system is that it is not scalable, since the weights of all parameters are determined by all the combination of large number of rules in the inference engine.

e. **Adaptive Network Based Fis (Anfis):** Is developed to add scalability and adaptability for FIS. The advantage of this system is that the user need not develop all the rules, instead a training data set is the input to ANFIS and the rules are automatically adapted. However, in FIS and ANFIS the number of rules increases exponentially with increase in the number of RANs. Jang (2002) presented FIS based architecture and learning procedure for adaptive networks.

f. **General Algorithms (GA):** Can also be implemented to determine the weights. Unlike FIS and AFIS, genetic algorithms can be used when large numbers of RANs are involved. They can also be used to implement fuzzy logic for network selection, as have been discussed by Alkhawlani (2008).

3. Ranking the networks and network selection decision: The network selection decision is initiated by a new call connection or by handover of existing connection. The best network is selected by ranking of the available networks based on evaluation of the parameters collected in the previous step. The various procedures for ranking of networks are given as follows:

a. **Utility Function:** This is an easy way to rank the available networks by maximizing the utility function value. Network with highest utility function value is selected. The networks are ranked in the decreasing order of utility function value. For example, according to Ormond et al. (2006), a possible utility function used for ranking can be consumer surplus (Datavolume -ServiceCost). A disadvantage of this method is that every user tries to maximize its own utility function irrespective of others.

b. **Game Theory Model:** It is the best tool to model the competitive environment where different players interact to maximize their utility functions, as has been discussed by Trestian et al. (2012). There are six different approaches of using game theory to model network selection:

    i. **Users vs. Users Cooperative Approach:** Where users mutually cooperate with each other for mutual benefit.

    ii. **Users vs. Users Non-Cooperative Approach:** Where users compete with each other to maximize their own utility function.

    iii. **Users vs. networks cooperative approach:** Where users and networks mutually cooperate with each other for mutual benefit.

    iv. **Users vs. Networks Non-Cooperative Approach:** Where users and networks compete with each other for their own benefits.

    v. **Networks vs. Networks Cooperative Approach:** Where networks mutually cooperate with each other for mutual benefit.

    vi. **Networks vs. Networks Non-Cooperative Approach:** Where networks mutually compete with each other for their own revenue maximization.

Non-cooperative game model is mostly used as compared to cooperative (i.e. cooperative behavior between BSs) game model. In the above scenario, users try to maximize their utility function and networks try to maximize their revenue and capacity. The various game theory models like trading market game, auction game, repeated game, bargaining game and strategic game (prisoners dilemma) etc. can be used in different approaches. Watanabe et al. (2008) have used Evolutionary game for network selection and parameters considered for payoff function are loss rate, mean burst size and delay jitter; Zhu et al. (2010) have used Bayesian game and parameters considered for payoff function are bandwidth and price; Khan et al. (2010) and Khan et al. (2009) used Auction game for network selection and parameters considered are bandwidth, Delivery and response time, application requirements; Charilas (2009) used Prisoners dilemma game for network selection and parameters considered are delay, jitter, throughput, packet loss and cost; Niyato & Hossain (2008) have used Trading market game for network selection and parameters considered are bandwidth and network load. Bargaining game and repeated game are cooperative games while others are non-cooperative games.

    a. **Bayesian Estimation:** It is the fundamental statistical approach for decision making in the presence of uncertain values. It is based on Bayes theorem. It maximizes the probability average values ($\leq$ corresponding thresholds) estimated and thus selects the network with highest probability.

4. **Resource Allocation at the New Base Station:** For network selection initiated by handover, after the network is selected, protocol is transferred from source BS to target BS and resource is allocated at target BS.

BASE STATION PLACEMENT

BS placement is also a very important challenge in heterogeneous networks because poor placement leads to wastage of resources or inefficient utilization which in turn decreases the capacity and revenue etc. Choosing the optimal places for BSs in heterogeneous networks is a complex problem because of its multi-layer structure (usage of macro, micro, pico and femto cells) and different radio access technologies with different coverage areas should coexist to enhance the effective coverage and increase spectrum efficiency. The parameters to be considered to find an optimal position for BSs for different radio access technologies are coverage area, capacity, available bandwidth, cell structure (antenna height), maintenance cost, and deployment cost etc.

There are several algorithms proposed in the literature and some of these are discussed here. Guruprasad (2011) proposed a Generalized Vornoi partition scheme. Vornoi partition also known as Dirchlet tessellation is mainly used in homogeneous scenario. So generalization of standard Vornoi partition is used in order to corporate the heterogeneity of BSs. Wen (2009) formulated the BS placement problem as an integer-nonlinear programming problem. In this the algorithms used to choose BS position are based on simulated annealing approaches and Lagrangian relaxation. The methods used by Wen (2009) mainly focused on decreasing the deployment cost of the heterogeneous network while satisfying users' QoS requirements.

Relay Based Heterogeneous Network

The relay based het-net improves the effective coverage area, and QoS, etc,and have been discussed in Peng et al. (2011). In relay based het-net, the relay nodes (relay stations) are introduced which will receive the signal from the BS, enhances it and retransmit it so that the cell edge users' QoS is improved. An iterative algorithm that has been discussed by Isalm et al. (2012), determines the optimum positions for the BSs and relay stations. Islam et al. (2012) showed that by using relays, the total transmitted power is significantly reduced and is thus preferred over increasing the number of BSs instead.

SHARED RESOURCE ALLOCATION IN HET-NETS

A significant improvement in capacity and QoS of the het-nets can be achieved by using shared resource allocation scheme (split handover) and network selection, wherein the resources of multiple RATs are pooled together so as to enhance the user experience in a mobile network environment. Here, we discuss the architecture, capacity enhancement analysis, and protocol functionalities in split handover with network selection facilitating differentiated QoS provisioning that accounts for MS speed, channel quality and load of different RAN involved in resource sharing.

System Model

With the advent of LTE and use of 2G and 3G being prevalent, the inter-RAT handover between LTE to 3G and from 3G to 2G, would gain significance due to limited LTE and 3G coverage since LTE is deployed more in areas having high traffic overlaying with the legacy 2G and 3G mobile systems. We consider BWA (broadband wireless access) system with LTE, 3G, and 2G mobile systems deployed. In order to incorporate the flexibility in the scheme Figure 4 depicts a new transport layer, two-level queueing system model, for minimized impact of user movement on the connection for active users. Queueing is applied at the data link control (DLC) layer and the transport control (TCP) layer, to distribute the traffic to the BSs which are participating in data transmission of the users in the shared region. This scheduling principle applies to both downlink and

Figure 4. System architecture and downlink queuing model, with different queue structure for the shared and non-shared users

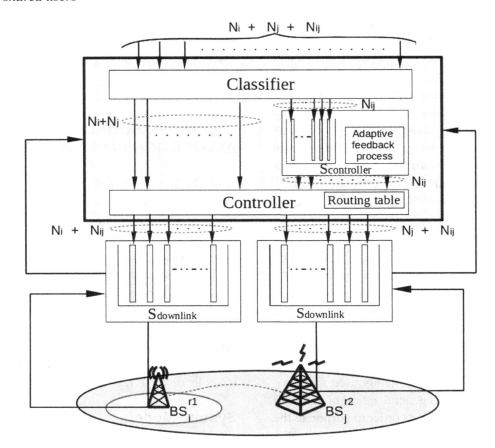

uplink (control message exchange related modifications) traffic. In Figure 4, the node architecture and its interaction with other network entities is presented. This resource sharing between two BSs can be extended to three or more BSs.

Two BSs, BS_i^{r1} and BS_j^{r2} are shown in the figure belonging to different RAT *r1* and *r2* with an overlapping coverage. There are N_i users which are served only by BS_i^{r1}, N_j users served only by BS_j^{r2}, and N_{ij} users served by both BS_i^{r1} and BS_j^{r2} in shared mode. $BS r1 i$ maintains queues for N_i + N_{ij} users and serves them using its $S_{downlink}$ scheduler. Likewise, BS_j^{r2} maintains queues for $N_j + N_{ij}$ users and serves them using $S_{downlink}$. It is assumed that one user has only one class of service at a time. If a single user maintains multiple parallel connections with different QoS requirements, then the scheduling can be easily handled by additional queues, called priority queues, at a BS. A controller directs the flows from the classifier according to the routing table maintained at the controller. Controller and classifier are the two logical entities which can be physically co-located. Based on the feedback from the BSs, the classifier is used to distinguish the incoming/outgoing flows if they are of a shared user - served by two BSs, or a non-shared user - served by only one BS. The controller also maintains the queues for all users which can be served by both BSs. Flow scheduling at the controller is according to the rule provided by $S_{controller}$. The parameters considered for splitting of traffic are fed back to the controller using feedback links.

Some of the advantages of the given architecture are: (i) centralized routing information maintenance for the subscribers to create multiple parallel connections when necessary; (ii) avoidance of packet duplication, by distributing packets for a cell-edge user across the BSs, thereby minimizing resource wastage; (iii) rule based splitting of traffic by using scheduler $S_{controller}$; (iv) possibility of resource allocation based on traffic classification.

The controller in split handover is connected to the BSs via high-speed wireline or wireless links. Beyond signal transmission-reception over the radio links, the BSs have a very little role to play. Functionality-wise, a controller will perform some extended tasks beyond a conventional BSC (base station controller) or a RNC (radio network controller). The specific activities of a controller in split handover are: (i) construction of universal DL-map and broadcasting to all BSs, and (ii) scheduling and traffic load balancing by accounting the CINR (carrier-to-interference- and-noise ratio) at the MS from the connected BS and the neighboring BSs, available resources of the neighboring BSs, and QoS requirements of subscribers. The participating BSs are assumed synchronized through the controller.

The split-handover of the MS occurs between the primary BS (PBS) (the BS with which a MS exchanges the management messages as well as data and the secondary BS (SBS) (a BS with which the MS exchanges only data).

The WiMAX multi-tier architecture's BS specification for each tier is given in Table 1. For an inter-tier handover the PBS and SBS belong to different tiers. This concept is equally applicable to multi-tier architecture of other 3G and 4G wireless technologies.

Multi-Tier and Intra-RAT Split Handover Scheme for WiMAX

WiMAX standard based shared resource split-handover system functionalities for multi-tier architecture has been explained in the following discussion and an extension of this scheme is applicable to other RATs. Following the WiMAX standard notations for channel usage, the downlink interval usage code (DIUC) used by a MS with the PBS is denoted as DIUC1, and the DIUC used by a MS with the SBS is denoted as DIUC2. As indicated in the proposed system architecture (Section VI-A), traffic splitting is done at the transport layer. The controller stores the BS IDs and their associated loads. With respect to a particular MS, it stores the MS ID, its MAC address, PBS ID, DIUC1, priority calculated based on the service flow QoS parameters, and SBS ID and DIUC2 - in case the MS is in contact with two BSs. The timing diagram of a MS session and a split handover process is shown in Figure 5, in which only downlink data traffic is considered. The initialization procedure is similar as in a standard service flow set up. The MAC information and DIUC1 of the MS is passed to the controller at the network entry phase. During data and management message exchange with the PBS, the MS sends scanning

Table 1. WiMAX multi-tier architecture base stations

Tier	Range	No. of Users per Sector	Typical RF Output Power	No. of Sectors
Macro	up to 5 km	>200	10W	3
Micro	up to 3km	<200	4W	3
Outdoor pico	1km	up to 100	1W	1
Indoor pico	100m	up to 50	500mW	1
Femto	20-30m	<10	100mW	1

Figure 5. Timing diagram of a MS session and split handoff process, where only the downlink traffic is considered

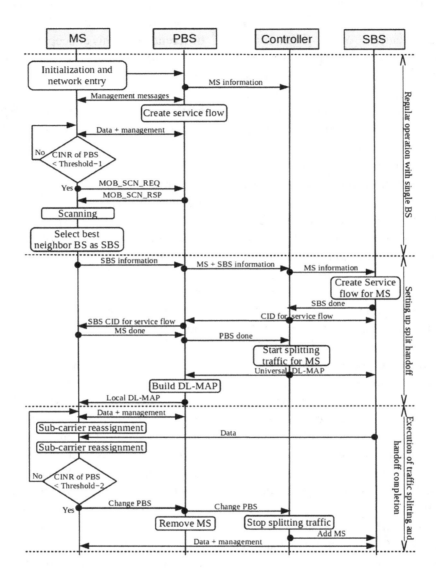

request (MOB_SCN_REQ) to the PBS when the CINR from the PBS falls below Threshold-1 (which corresponds to a higher-than-the-lowest modulation and coding rate).

If the response (MOB_SCN_RSP) from the PBS is positive, the MS starts scanning for a SBS and synchronizes with one, initiating the split handover set up phase. Otherwise it continues its connection with the PBS only. During scanning,

the MS sends (via the PBS) the SBS information (BS ID, DIUC2, traffic load) to the controller. Subsequently, a new CID for data connection with the SBS is created by the controller, which is forwarded to the MS. With the ongoing CID for the PBS and the new CID for the SBS, the user-level split handover procedure starts. The timing information of the bursts (slots) for connecting to the PBS and SBS is notified to the MS by the controller via a universal DL-map. To address user QoS and cell load imbalance, the controller accounts for the QoS priority, buffer status at the MS, and the BS traffic load at the time of burst scheduling. The burst timings for the PBS and SBS are separated within a frame such that the sub-carrier frequency reassignment latency of the MS is sufficiently accommodated. Note that, with frequency reuse factor = 1, it may be possible that the MS is connected to the BSs at different time slots over the same assignment of sub-carriers, in which case no reassignment is necessary. On the other hand, in case the adjacent BSs operate at different carrier frequencies, i.e., with frequency reuse factor < 1, split handover involves sub-carrier reassignment latency. Finally, when the CINR from the PBS falls below Threshold-2 (corresponding to the lowest allowable data rate), a PBS change request is sent to the controller. At that point the SBS assumes the responsibility of PBS for the MS. This process marks the *end of split handover*.

Analytical Model for Shared Resource Allocation in Het-Nets

In the following discussion an analytical framework for shared resource allocation is shown to result in capacity gain.

1. Maximizing Capacity by Scheduling Shared Users

Theoretically, QoS is defined by the maximum tolerable delay D_{max} for a user (traffic type) beyond which the delay violation probability exceeds a predefined threshold ε i.e.:

$$\sup_{t} \Pr\{D(t) \geq D_{\max}\} \leq \varepsilon$$

Also for a dynamic Also for a dynamic queuing system, where the arrival and service processes are stationary and ergodic, the probability that the delay at time t, $D(t)$ exceeds the threshold D_{max} can be accurately given as:

$$\sup_{t} \Pr\{D(t) \geq D_{\max}\} \approx \gamma(\Omega) e^{\theta(\Omega) D_{\max}},$$

where $\theta(\Omega)$ is a function of constant source rate Ω, D_{max} is a sufficiently large quantity, and $\gamma(\Omega)$ is the probability that the delay of a particular packet is non-zero, i.e.:

$$\gamma(\Omega) = \Pr\{D(t) > 0\}$$

at a randomly chosen time instant t. Here, $\theta(\Omega)>0$ is a parameter describing the exponential decay rate of probability of QoS violation. $\theta(\Omega)$ is referred as the QoS exponent. A large value of $\theta(\Omega)$ corresponds to stringent QoS requirement and a smaller value corresponds to a loose QoS requirement.

The effective capacity for a given QoS exponent $\theta(\Omega)$ specifies the maximum constant arrival rate that can be supported by the system at the link layer. Applying the effective capacity concept to wireless channels with arbitrary physical-layer characteristics, for a discrete-time stationary and ergodic service process with rate $\mu(n)$ and channel service rate:

$$R(m) = \sum_{n=0}^{m} \mu(n),$$

the effective capacity is given as:

$$E_c(\theta) \overset{def}{=} - \lim_{m \to \infty} \frac{1}{\theta_m} \ln E\{e^{-\theta R(m)}\},$$

where m is the block length. For uncorrelated block fading channels, where the service process $\mu(n)$, $n=1,2,\cdots$ is also uncorrelated, the expression is reduced to:

$$E_c(\theta) = \frac{1}{\theta} \ln E\{e^{-\theta\mu(n)}\},$$

where the product T_fB is the total time-frequency resources available in one frame $S = T_fB$.

A saturation condition arises when the total resource demand is more than the available resources at the BS such that:

$$\sum_{u=1}^{N_i} S^u = S_i,$$

where S_i is the total resource available per frame in BS_i and $(0 \le S_u \le S_i)$ is the resource allocated to the user u from BS_i, in order to maintain its QoS demand. It is assumed that the total resource available, at each BS in a cluster with FFR plan, is equal, i.e.:

$$S_i = S \forall i \in N_c.$$

The effective capacity of user u scheduled from BS_i, is:

$$E_{C,i}^u(\theta^u) = -\frac{1}{\theta^u S} \ln E\{e^{\theta^u \mu_i^u}\},$$

where θ^u is the QoS exponent of user u and $\mu_i^u = r_i^u S^u$ is the rate provided to user u from BS_i, with modulation index r_i^u. The *joint effective capacity* when the user u is scheduled from two BSs i.e. BS_i and Bs_j is:

$$E_{C,joint}^u(\theta^u) = -\frac{1}{\theta^u S} \ln[E\{e^{\theta^u \mu_{i(1)}^u}\}E\{e^{\theta^u \mu_{j(2)}^u}\}],$$

such that:

$$S^u = S_{i(1)}^u + S_{j(2)}^u,$$

$$S^u > S_{i(1)}^u,$$

$$S^u > S_{j(2)}^u > 0,$$

$$\gamma_i > \gamma_{th}$$

and

$$\gamma_j > \gamma_{th}$$

i.e. joint resources from BS_i and BS_j are the same as before and the CINR of these BSs is above acceptable threshold. Considering $\Pr\{\gamma_i^u \le \gamma_{th}\}$ and $\Pr\{\gamma_j^u \le \gamma_{th}\}$. Assuming the same modulation index (i.e. r) for the user u from the two BSs then:

$$E_{C,joint}^u(\theta^u) = -\frac{1}{\theta^u S} \ln[\{e^{-\theta^u r S_{i(1)}^u}(1-p_i) + p_i\} \cdot \{e^{-\theta^u r S_{j(1)}^u}(1-p_j) + p_j\}]$$

By substituting $S_{i(1)}^u$ with $S^u - S_{j(2)}^u$ in the expression for $E_{C,joint}^u(\theta^u)$ and differentiating with respect to $S_{j(2)}^u$ and equating it to zero, we have:

$$S_{j(2)}^u = \frac{S^u}{2} + \frac{S^u}{2\theta^u r} \ln\left[\frac{(1-p_j)/p_j}{(1-p_i)/p_i}\right],$$

$$S_{i(1)}^u = \frac{S^u}{2} + \frac{S^u}{2\theta^u r} \ln\left[\frac{(1-p_i)/p_i}{(1-p_j)/p_j}\right]$$

that maximize the joint effective capacity. Hence for a MS in the coverage regions of two or more BSs and when the resource allocation is done from these BSs as per the iterated scheme increases the total effective capacity.

2. Class Based Shared Resource Allocation for Mobile Users

Class based resource allocation policy which is also influenced by the dynamic availability of bandwidth, cell load conditions, and shared BS resource usage. The usual standard service differentiation suggests division of user traffic into service classes. For differentiated shared resource usage, the following three classes categorize the user traffic of user: P_0 (voice packets), P_1 (video traffic), and P_2 (data traffic). P_0 is most delay sensitive and needs a guaranteed bandwidth; P_1 requires a minimum bandwidth and has more delay flexibility. P_2 traffic does not have delay or bandwidth guarantee constraints. Since P_0 traffic is most delay sensitive, initially the resources are allocated to this traffic class, then the resources are allocated to P_1 traffic and the remaining resources of each BS are allocated to P_2 traffic.

For resource allocation to mobile users in a class P_c, $c \in \{0, 1, 2\}$, the user with the maximum scheduling function $\psi^n = \max\{\frac{\rho^u}{\tau^u}\}$, is successively selected. To maximize throughput the current bit rate of user u, ρ^u, ensures the user with best channel conditions is selected while the user throughput, τ^u, ensures none of users' experience starves. Fairness is ensured with the selection of the user with high ρ^u and /or low τ^u. The resource allocation for mobile users is influenced by statistical characteristics of the traffic arrival and channel behavior and backlog history usage. The resource required over a time frame interval T_f for the incoming traffic using a linear predictor is given as:

$$\tilde{S}_{P_C}^{u(v)}(n+1) = \sum_{l=0}^{L_{P_C}-1} \xi_{P_C,l}^{u(v)}(n-l),$$

where the prediction order L_{P_C} is a function of the traffic type P_C, $\xi_{P_C,l}^{u}$ is the parameter that in-

dicates the impact of actual resource requirements $\tilde{S}_{P_C}^{u(v)}(n-l)$ due to new arrivals in frame *(n-l)*. $\xi_{P_C,l}^{u}$ is updated by least mean square (LMS) algorithm as:

$$\xi_{P_C,l}^{u}(n+1) = \xi_{P_C,l}^{u}(n) + \eta_{P_C}^{u}(n)\frac{\varepsilon_{P_C}^{u}(n)}{S_{P_C}^{u(v)}(n)},$$

where the prediction error

$$\varepsilon_{P_C}^{u}(n) = S_{P_C}^{u(v)}(n) - \tilde{S}_{P_C}^{u(v)}(n),$$

and

$$\eta_{P_C}^{u}(n) = \frac{L_{P_C}}{\sum_{l=0}^{L_{P_C}-1}[S_{P_C}^{u(v)}(n-1)]^2}.$$

The requested resource for frame $(n+1)$ and P_c traffic type is given as:

$$S_{P_C}^{u(r)}(n+1) = S_{P_C}^{u(q)}(n) - \tilde{S}_{P_C}^{u(v)}(n),$$

where $S_{P_C}^{u(q)}(n)$ is the resource required from nth frame due to user u's queued traffic and service type. For any given traffic type P_C, it is important to choose an important optimum number of taps that maximizes the quality of prediction using historical prediction. A higher value of L_{P_C} increases the prediction accuracy as it sharply predicts the burstiness of the traffic, but also causes increased lag in predicted traffic and detrimental to prediction quality. A small value of L_{P_C} tracks the traffic fast but is unable to track burstiness.

Shared Resource Allocation for Split Handover in Comparison to MDHO and FBSS

Prior to discussing the advantage that shared resource allocation has in comparison to the other soft handover scheme variants like MDHO and FBSS (shown in Figure 6), it is necessary to briefly discuss about these soft handover techniques.

Macro Diversity Handover (MDHO): MS maintains a diversity set that constitutes a group of BSs that operate on same frequency channel and are synchronized on time and frame level. The BSs having a considerable CINR are selected for the diversity set by the MS by the exchange of MAC context between BS and MS. All the BSs in the diversity set have the information of the MS and the MAC context and are said to be active BSs. The BS, with which the MS is registered or is handed over to, is the active BS. All the other BSs that are not a part of the diversity set and do not have any traffic exchange with MS but the MS is still able to perform signal strength measurement with these BSs, are said to be the neighbor BSs. The diversity set is updated when

the CINR of the serving BS falls below a pre-defined threshold or when CINR of a BS is above another predefined threshold. In MDHO, during downlink communication MS receives data from all the active BSs in the diversity set and the MS combines the multiple signals by the virtue of diversity combining to obtain an improved data signal. During uplink communication the MS's data signal is received by different active BSs and the BS with the strongest signal finally makes the transmission after performing selection diversity.

Fast Base Station Switching (FBSS): During handover the MS receives signal from all the BSs of diversity set and then from these BSs, MS selects one BS for exchanging uplink or downlink data. This BS is known as the anchor BS. MS registers and shares MAC context information with this anchor BS only. Anchor BS can be updated at a MS based on CINR levels

In the case of class based shared resource allocation, intelligent scheduling of MS by multiple BSs to increase users' capacity and QoS. In case of schemes like MDHO the diversity combining underutilizes the resources in the shared cell region, resulting in a poorer data rate for the users

Figure 6. Soft handover scheme: MDHO and FBSS

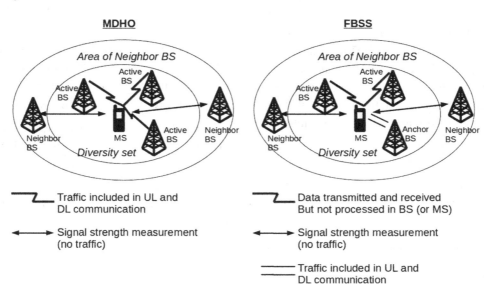

in this region as compared to the split-handover scheme. Since the class based traffic is scheduled by two different BSs (several BSs as the case may be), it results in increase in the effective throughput and data rate provided to the mobile user. These metrics are significantly higher than the hard handover or the other soft handover scheme variants (MDHO and FBSS). This is also reflected in the Figure 7, wherein the data rate of MS in shared cell region is highest by the split handover scheme, intermediate for MDHO soft handover scheme, and least for hard handover scheme.

SON Based Inter-RAT MRO

The increasing demand for high speed communication services has led to the deployment of the new radio access technologies (RATs) (LTE overlaying legacy 3G and 2G mobile systems). Inter-RAT handover is necessary to fully utilize the capabilities of the various RATs to provide best QoS and meet users' demands. While discussing the heterogeneous networks, an important concept is that of SON (self-organizing network) and its important use case of MRO (mobility robustness optimization). SON is a technology that simplifies and speeds up the planning, management, configuration, healing and optimization of NGMN (Next Generation Mobile Networks) that comprises of several RATs deployed. An inter-RAT MRO algorithm given by Awada et al. (2013) automates the adjustment of handover threshold of each cell. Various measurement quantities such as SS (signal strength) and SQ (signal quality) form the basis for measurement event.

Inter-RAT Handover Procedure

At any given time the UE is served by an LTE, 3G or 2G cell. A UE u being served by a cell c experiences a radio link failure (RLF) when its SINR ($\gamma_{u,c}(t)$) falls below a threshold (Q_{out}) for a certain interval of time $T_{Q_{out}}$ i.e. $\gamma_{u,c}(t) < Q_{out}$ for $t_0 - T_{Q_{out}} < t < t_0$. The serving BS in LTE,

Figure 7. Two cell scenario, comparison of data rate for the hard, soft (MDHO), and split handover schemes

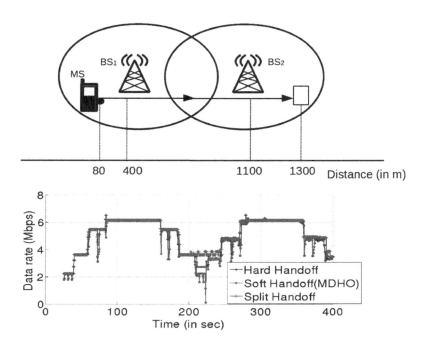

3G or 2G network configures the UE to perform signal strength measurement for intra or inter-RAT neighboring cells and the serving cell and sending a report to the serving BS periodically or by means of event trigger mechanism (report sent on fulfillment entering condition of measurement event). The handover is triggered by serving BS after receiving the measurement report. For LTE to 3G handover the serving LTE BS configures UE with measurement *event B2*. For a handover from 3G cell to LTE or 2G, the measurement event is *event 3A*. The measurements of the signal strength by UE in LTE cell is of received signal received power (RSRP), in 3G it is of received signal code power (RSCP). RSRP is the linear average of power contributions of the resource elements carrying cell-specific reference signals within the measurement frequency bandwidth considered, and RSCP is the received power measured on primary common pilot channel (CPICH). These measurements are inclusive of path loss, antenna gain, log-normal shadowing and fast fading. The phases before handover comprise of handover triggering condition, measurement by mobile UE of neighboring cells, and selection of the best candidate cell that fulfills the handover criteria condition.

The entering condition for the event 3A or B2 is fulfilled when serving cell's signal (i.e. $S_{u,c}(t)$) falls below threshold S_{thr} in dBm and the target cell's signal $T_{u,C_0}(t)$ greater than threshold (i.e., T_{thr}) in dBm. The entering condition needs to be fulfilled for time duration T_T for the measurement report to be sent by the UE i.e.:

$$S_{u,c}(t) < S_{thr} \cap T_{u,C_0}(t) > T_{thr}$$

for

$$-T_T < t < t_0.$$

After receiving the measurement report from the UE u, the serving cell c sends a handover request to the target handover cell c_0 in order to prepare handover of UE. An additional delay termed as handover preparation time (i.e. T_{HP}) during which c waits for acknowledgement from c_0. Handover occurs after T_{HP} seconds after the measurement event trigger and the UE's SINR $\gamma_{u,c}(t)$ being greater than the threshold Q_{fail}. Thus, the execution of handover is based on the following conditions' fulfillment, i.e.:

$$S_{u,c}(t) < S_{thr} \cap T_{u,C_0}(t) > T_{thr}$$

for

$$t_{HO} - T_{HP} - T_T < t < t_{HO} - T_{HP},$$

and

$$\gamma_{u,C}(t_{HO}) > Q_{fail}.$$

The key performance indicators (KPI) for inter-RAT mobility are to capture the radio link failure (RLF) events and the costly inter-RAT handover like ping-pongs (PPs). There are three RLF mobility events: Too late inter-RAT handover (TLH), too early inter-RAT handover (TEH), and inter-RAT handover to wrong cell (HWC). There are two kinds of costly inter-RAT HOs: Inter-RAT PPs, and unnecessary HOs (UHs) from LTE to 3G. It is essential to minimize UHs to enable users to benefit from the newly deployed, higher priority LTE network. These KPIs are briefly described as follows:

- **TLH:** The UE is dropped before handover is executed or has been initiated from one RAT to another and subsequently the UE reconnects to a RAT that is different from the previous serving cell. This occurs when the entering condition of the measurement event is not fulfilled or the RLF occurs before the inter-RAT handover is executed inspite of the fulfillment of the entering condition of the measurement event. There are four cases (illustrated in Figure 8) in which TLH for inter-RAT handover scenario occurs.

Case A: $S_{u,c}(t) < S_{thr} \cap T_{u,C_0}(t) < T_{thr}$, misconfiguration of T_{thr} is the root cause for TLH.

Case B: $S_{u,c}(t) > S_{thr} \cap T_{u,C_0}(t) > T_{thr}$, misconfiguration of S_{thr} is the root cause for TLH.

Case C: $S_{u,c}(t) > S_{thr} \cap T_{u,C_0}(t) < T_{thr}$, misconfiguration of the threshold corresponding to the smallest values of Δ_S and Δ_T, is the root cause for TLH. (iv) Case D: Entering condition of measurement event is fulfilled but RLF occurs before inter-RAT HO, and the misconfiguration of one of the two thresholds that is reached later is the root cause for TLH.

- **TEH:** An RLF happens shortly after the UE is successfully handed over to a cell of a different RAT, and the UE reconnects to a previous RAT cell. Also when the UE fails to connect to c_0 using random access channel (RACH), the inter-RAT handover fails and is considered as a TEH. Misconfiguration of T_{thr} is the root cause of TEH. T_{thr} needs to be increased to ensure that signal of target cell of a different RAT i.e., c_0 is strong enough.

- **HWC:** Shortly after the UE is successfully handed over to a cell c_0 of a different RAT, an RLF happens and UE connects to a cell c_0 of the same RAt as c_0. Similar to TEH, misconfiguration of T_{thr} is the root cause for HWC. T_{thr} should be increased to guarantee that other RAT's cell signal is strong enough.

Figure 8. Four cases of inter-RAT TLH

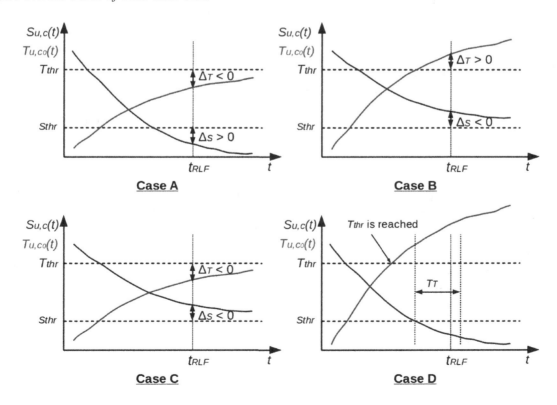

- **PP:** When the UE is handed over to a cell of a different RAT and then handed over back to the same cell or a different cell of the previous RAT within a time interval of T_{PP}. By delaying the first inter-RAT handover by either increasing T_{thr} or decreasing S_{thr}, it is possible to resolve inter-RAT HO.

- **UH:** The UE is handover from a cell of high priority RAT to a cell of low priority RAT, even though the signal quality of the previous RAT is good enough. This can be evaluated in terms of reference signal received quality (RSRQ) of the previous LTE cell is higher than Q_{RSRQ} threshold for $T_{Q_{RSRQ}}$ time interval. To resolve UHs it is essential to decrease S_{thr} thereby increasing the LTE cell coverage.

The SON with inter-RAT MRO needs that the two thresholds (i.e. S_{thr} and T_{thr}) should be adjusted properly for the above mentioned KPIs, and for this purpose a feedback controller can be used to determine magnitude change in the handover threshold.

Although the above discussion is more focused on LTE to 3G cell inter-RAT HO, however this same analytical framework is equally applicable to 3G to 2G cell inter-RAT handover and had been discussed by Mohammed et al. (2007).

CONCLUSION AND FUTURE RESEARCH DIRECTIONS

According to ITUs vision of optimally connected anytime, anywhere, mobile users are free to roam between different RATs that are provided by different service providers, has resulted in advent of heterogeneous networks. Next generation networks are based on these heterogeneous networks with heterogeneity in terms of communication modalities, channel types, technology generations, protocol types, and QoS requirements. This chapter has discussed several issues faced in heterogeneous networks in network selection, inter/intra-RAT handovers, BS placement, and resource allocation. These issues can be very complex mainly because of heterogeneity in radio access networks. Selection of suitable scheme depends on many parameters which have been discussed. In different scenarios different parameters should be weighted with high priority, for which the various existing schemes in the literature have also been enlisted in this chapter.

Although, several aspects of next-generation heterogeneous networks have been studied by researchers in the recent times and are discussed in this chapter. However, still there are some other issues in heterogeneous wireless access networks that still needs to be focused upon, like pricing schemes, and several approaches where network operators or service providers will compete with each other to maximize their revenue and users will compete with each other to maximize their QoS, which will have effects in decision taken in network selection and handover. In addition to this, it is essential to also consider simultaneous cooperation and competition by the service providers in an optimized manner to integrate resources and provide users with improved service experience, and also consider user-preferences while configuring the network system in an automated manner. Even though any optimization is often based on tradeoffs and also since each of the solutions discussed previously look into a subset of the factors concerning heterogeneous network. Hence, a collated, well-balanced, and comprehensive solution is the need-of-hour, which would integrate the network heterogeneities to the advantage of users as well as the service providers, while utilizing the available resources in the best possible manner.

REFERENCES

Alkhawlani, M., & Ayesh, A. (2008). Access network selection based on fuzzy logic and genetic algorithm. *Advances in Artificial Intelligence*, (1): 1–12. doi:10.1155/2008/793058

Awada, A., Wegmann, B., Viering, I., & Klein, A. (2013). A SON-based algorithm for the optimization of inter-RAT handover parameters. *IEEE Transactions on Vehicular Technology*, *62*(5), 1906–1923. doi:10.1109/TVT.2013.2251923

Chan, V., Chapin, J., Elson, P., Fisher, D., Frost, V., Jones, K., & Miller, G. (2011). *Workshop on future heterogeneous networks*. Mountain View.

Chang, J., Li, Y., Feng, S., Wang, H., Sun, C., & Zhang, P. (2009). A fractional soft handover scheme for 3GPP LTE-advanced system. In *Proceedings of IEEE International Conference on Communications Workshops* (pp. 1-5). IEEE.

Charilas, D., & Panagopoulous, A. (2010). Multi-access radio network enviroments. *IEEE Vehicular Technology Magazine*, *5*(4), 40–49. doi:10.1109/MVT.2010.939107

Charilas, D. E., Panagopoulos, A. D., Vlacheas, P., Markaki, O. I., & Constantinou, P. (2009). *Mobile lightweight wireless systems congestion avoidance control through non-cooperative games between customers and service providers*. Berlin: Springer.

Cisco. (2012). *Architecture for mobile data offload over wi-fi access networks* (Cisco White Paper). Cisco.

Cisco. (2012). *Cisco visual networking index, 2012-2017*. Cisco.

Dahlman, E., Parkvall, S., & Skold, J. (2008). *3G evolution: HSPA and LTE for mobile broadband*. Burlington, MA: Academic Press.

Ericson. (2012). *Traffic and market report*. Ericson.

Guo, C., Guo, Z., Zhang, Q., & Wenwu, Z. (2004). A seamless and proactive end-to-end mobility solution for roaming across heterogeneous wireless networks. *IEEE Journal on Selected Areas in Communications*, *22*(5), 834–848. doi:10.1109/JSAC.2004.826921

Guruprasad, K. R. (2011). Generalized Vornoi partition: A new tool for optimal placement of base stations. In *Proceedings of IEEE International Conference on Advanced Networks and Telecommunication Systems* (pp. 1-3). IEEE.

IEEE Standard for Local and Metropolitan Area Networks-Part 16. (2005) Air interface for fixed broadband wireless access systems (Incorporated into IEEE Standard 802.16e-2005 and IEEE Standard 802.16-2004/Cor 1-2005 E). *IEEE Standard P802.16/Cor1/D5*. IEEE.

Islam, M. H., Dziong, Z., Sohraby, K., Daneshmand, M. F., & Jana, R. (2012). Capacity-optimal relay and base station placement in wireless networks. In *Proceedings of International Conference on Information Networking* (pp. 358-363). Academic Press.

Jang, J.-S. R. (2002). ANFIS: Adaptive-network-based fuzzy inference system. *IEEE Transactions on Systems, Man, and Cybernetics*, *23*(3), 665–685. doi:10.1109/21.256541

Khan, M. A., Sivrikaya, F., Albayrak, S., & Mengaly, K. Q. (2009). Auction based interface selection in heterogeneous wireless networks. In *Proceedings of Second IFIP Wireless Days* (pp. 1-6). IFIP.

Khan, M. A., Toseef, U., Marx, S., & Goerg, C. (2010). Auction based interface selection with media independent handover services and flow management. In *Proceedings of European Wireless Conference* (pp. 429-436). Academic Press.

Khan, M. A., Toseef, U., Marx, S., & Goerg, C. (2010). Game-theory based user centric network selection with media independent handover services and flow management. In *Proceedings of Eighth Annual Communication Networks and Services Research Conference* (pp. 248-255). Academic Press.

Latouche, M., Rauschen, C., Oszabó, O., Creusat, J.-B., & Belmans, W. (2013). *Mobile data explosion how mobile service providers can monetize the growth in mobile data through value-added services* (Cisco White Paper). Cisco Internet Business Solutions Group (IBSG).

Lee, C. C., & Steele, R. (1998). Effect of soft and softer handoffs on CDMA system capacity. *IEEE Transactions on Vehicular Technology, 47*(3), 830–841. doi:10.1109/25.704838

Lee, H., Son, H., & Lee, S. (2009). Semisoft handover gain analysis over OFDM-based broadband systems. *IEEE Transactions on Vehicular Technology, 58*(3), 1443–1453. doi:10.1109/TVT.2008.927041

Mohammed, A., Kamal, H., & AbdelWahab, S. (2007). 2G/3G inter-RAT handover performance analysis. In *Proceedings of the Second European Conference on Antennas and Propagation* (pp. 1-8). Academic Press.

Nasser, N., Hasswa, A., & Hassanein, H. (2006). Handoffs in fourth generation heterogeneous networks. *IEEE Communications Magazine*, 96–103. doi:10.1109/MCOM.2006.1710420

Niyato, D., & Hossain, E. (2008). A noncooperative game-theoretic framework for radio resource management in 4G heterogeneous wireless access networks. *IEEE Transactions on Mobile Computing, 7*(3), 332–345. doi:10.1109/TMC.2007.70727

Ong, E. H., & Khan, J. (2008). Dynamic access network selection with QoS parameters estimation: A step closer to ABC. In *Proceedings of IEEE Vehicular Technology Conference* (pp. 2671-2676). IEEE.

Ormond, O., Murphy, J., & Muntean, G. M. (2006). Utility-based intelligent network selection in beyond 3G systems. In *Proceedings of IEEE International Conference on Communications* (pp. 1831-1836). IEEE.

Peng, M., Liu, Y., Wei, D., Wang, W., & Chen, H.-H. (2011). Hierarchical cooperative relay based heterogeneous networks. *IEEE Wireless Communications Magazine, 18*(3), 48–56. doi:10.1109/MWC.2011.5876500

Pervaiz, H., & Bigham, J. (2009). Game theoretical formulation of network selection in competing wireless networks: An analytic hierarchy process model. In *Proceedings of Third International Conference on Next Generation Mobile Applications, Services and Technologies* (pp. 292–297). Academic Press.

Razzaque, M. A., Dobson, S., & Nixon, P. (2010). *Enhancement of self-organisation in wireless networking through a cross-layer approach*. Berlin: Springer. doi:10.1007/978-3-642-11723-7_10

Sgora, A., Chatzimisios, P., & Vergados, D. D. (2010). *Mobile lightweight wireless systems: Access network selection in a heterogeneous environment using the AHP and fuzzy TOPSIS methods*. Berlin: Springer.

Shen, D. M. (2010) The QoE-oriented heterogeneous network selection based on fuzzy AHP methodology. In *Proceedings of the Fourth International Conference on Mobile Ubiquitous Computing, Systems, Services and Technologies* (pp. 275-280). Academic Press.

Shen, W., & Zeng, Q.-A. (2007). Cost-function-based network selection strategy in integrated wireless and mobile networks. In *Proceedings of 21st International Conference on Advanced Information Networking and Applications Workshops* (vol. 2, pp. 314-319). Academic Press.

Singhal, C., Kumar, S., De, S., Panwar, N., Tonde, R., & De, P. (2012). Class-based shared resource allocation for cell-edge users in OFDMA networks. *IEEE Transactions on Mobile Computing, 99*(PrePrints), 1.

Trestian, R., Ormond, O., & Muntean, G.-M. (2012). Game theory-based network selection: Solutions and challenges. *IEEE Communications Surveys & Tutorials, 14*(4), 1212–1231. doi:10.1109/SURV.2012.010912.00081

Watanabe, E. H., Nenasche, D. S., de Souza, S., & Leao, R. M. M. (2008). Modeling resource sharing dynamics of VoIP users over a WLAN using a game-theoretic approach. In *Proceedings of IEEE International Conference on Computer Communications*. IEEE.

Wen, Y. F. (2009). Heterogeneous base station placement for wireless networks. In *Proceedings of IEEE Mobile WiMAX Symposium* (pp. 87-92). IEEE.

Yeh, S., Talwar, S., Wu, G., Himayat, N., & Johnsson, K. (2011). Capacity and coverage enhancement in heterogeneous networks. *IEEE Wireless Communications, 18*(3), 32–38. doi:10.1109/MWC.2011.5876498

Zhang, W. (2004). Handover decision using fuzzy MADM in heterogeneous networks. In *Proceedings of IEEE Wireless Communications and Networking Conference* (vol. 2, pp. 653-658). IEEE.

Zhu, K., Niyato, D., & Wang, P. (2010). Network selection in heterogeneous wireless networks: Evolution with incomplete information. In *Proceedings of IEEE Wireless Communications and Networking Conference* (pp. 1-6). IEEE.

Zoubir, A., & Boashash, B. (1998). The bootstrap and its application in signal processing. *IEEE Signal Processing Magazine, 15*(1), 56–76. doi:10.1109/79.647043

KEY TERMS AND DEFINITIONS

Broadband Wireless Access (BWA) Networks: BWA technologies provide broadband data access over wireless LAN (Local Area Network), 3G, MAN (Metropolitan Area Network).

Differentiated QoS: It is an end-to-end, application-level, QoS-management technique that classifies application-traffic into multiple classes with different QoS parameters.

Effective Capacity: Effective capacity of a system is the maximum constant arrival rate that can be supported by the system at the link layer.

Mobility Robustness Optimization (MRO): It is an algorithmic optimization framework that automates the adjustment of handover threshold of each cell based on measurement quantities such as SS (signal strength) and SQ (signal quality).

Multi-Tier Handover: It is an intra-RAT handover technique where handover occurs between hierarchical tiers (macrocell, picocell, and femtocalls) of an infrastructural RAT deployment.

Network Selection: Network selection is a process in which the user devices (while requesting for a new connection or during the handover process) select from the radio access networks (RANs) that belong to competing service providers having different latency, coverage area, and cost.

Radio Access Technology (RAT): RAT is the underlying physical connection method for a radio based mobile communication network such as Bluetooth, Wi-Fi, 3G, 4G, and LTE.

Self-Organizing Network (SON): SON is a technology that simplifies and speeds up the planning, management, configuration, healing and optimization of NGMN (Next Generation Mobile Networks) that comprises of several RATs deployed.

Shared Resource Allocation: Resource allocation technique wherein resources of multiple RATs are pooled together to improve capacity and QoS in a mobile network environment.

Split Handover: Shared resource allocation technique for cell edge users in orthogonal frequency division multiple access (OFDMA) networks, where MSs maintain parallel connections with more than one BS.

ENDNOTES

[1] This work has been partly supported by the Department of Science and Technology (DST) under the grant no. SR/S3/EECE/0122/2010.

Chapter 4
Resource Management of Multicast Services Over LTE

Giuseppe Araniti
University Mediterranea of Reggio Calabria, Italy

Massimo Condoluci
University Mediterranea of Reggio Calabria, Italy

Antonella Molinaro
University Mediterranea of Reggio Calabria, Italy

ABSTRACT

In recent years, mobile operators are observing a growing demand of multicast services over radio cellular networks. In this scenario, multicasting is the technology exploited to serve a group of users which simultaneously request the same data content. Since multicast applications are expected to be massively exchanged over Fourth Generation (4G) systems, the Third Generation Partnership Project (3GPP) defined the Multimedia Broadcast Multicast Service (MBMS) standard. MBMS allows supporting multicast services over Long Term Evolution (LTE), the 4G wireless technology able to provide high quality services in mobile environments. Nevertheless, several issues related to the management of MBMS services are still open. The aim of this chapter is to analyze the challenges in supporting multicast services over LTE with particular attention to resource management, considered the key aspect for an effective provisioning of MBMS services over cellular networks.

INTRODUCTION

The increase in the content availability and the growing number of available devices with enhanced media capabilities (i.e., smartphones and tablets) enabled a tremendous growth in the demand of advanced services over mobile radio systems. Among those, *multicast* services are expected to be massively transmitted over Fourth Generation (4G) wireless systems and allow groups of users to simultaneously access services with high Quality of Service (QoS) (such as Mobile TV, news forecast, video calls, video conferencing, Internet video streaming). Since multicasting is considered as one of the main value-added services for 4G systems, standardization bodies

DOI: 10.4018/978-1-4666-5978-0.ch004

and network providers are currently working to suitably support multicast services over Long Term Evolution (LTE), the most promising wireless technology that will lead the growth of mobile broadband services in the next years (Third Generation Partnership Project, 2012). With this aim, the Third Generation Partnership Project (3GPP) standardized the Multimedia Broadcast Multicast Service (MBMS). This standard, which defines all networks enhancements necessary to support the transmission of multicast services over LTE, introduces the *Point-to-Multipoint (PtM)* transmission mode and covers different functionalities related to the management of multicast services (e.g., service announcement, joining and leaving procedures, session setup and re-configuration). An example of PtM transmission mode is shown in Figure 1, where the main differences between PtM and the traditional unicast transmission mode, i.e., Point-to-Point (PtP), are highlighted. In particular, PtM simultaneously serves all users interested to a given multicast service through a shared channel, with the aim to improve the system capacity and "theoretically" serve an unlimited number of users per group (Lecompte & Gabin, 2012).

Although MBMS improves the capabilities of LTE in supporting multicast services, the main challenge in multicast environments is related to the Radio Resource Management (RRM), which includes all functionalities necessary to manage the radio resources available in the cellular system (Richard, Dadlani & Kim, 2013). In particular, the RRM is in charge of performing *link adaptation* procedures, i.e., the selection of the transmission parameters, such as the Modulation and Coding Scheme (MCS), for multicast content delivery according to the channel conditions experienced by the User Equipments (UEs). Indeed, in a multicast scenario, link adaptation must be accomplished on a per-group basis, i.e., by taking into account the channel state information of all terminals interested to a given multicast service. This may limit the session quality performance achieved by multicast members, due to the presence of cell-edge users which experience poor channel conditions and consequently cannot support high data rates. Moreover, the delivery of typical multicast applications (e.g., mobile TV) requires a large amount of radio resources and this further challenges the spectrum efficiency and the coexistence with other services (e.g., unicast flows) in the cell.

In this Chapter we will focus on the challenges related to the RRM of multicast services over LTE. We firstly will present an overview on the most typical multicast applications, with the related requirements in terms of QoS, and we will discuss about the MBMS standard, by introducing the

Figure 1. A comparison of multicast service delivery through Point-to-Point (PtP) and Point-to-Multipoint (PtM) transmission modes

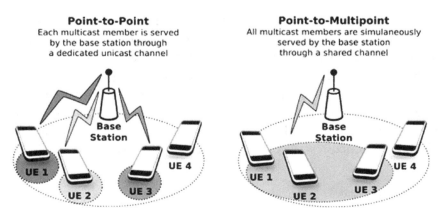

network architecture and the system features of LTE/MBMS. Then, we will address the structure of LTE packet scheduler, by underling the aspects related to the RRM. Finally, we will focus on the issues related to RRM in multicast environments over LTE, and we will present an overview of the different approaches defined in literature for multicast service delivery.

MULTICAST SERVICES

A multicast service is defined as a service which is simultaneously transmitted towards a set of managed UEs, namely *multicast members*. Each multicast service transmitted in a given cell of a mobile radio system is associated to only one *multicast group*. The terminals can receive only those services related to the multicast group they belong to. A multicast service is announced by the base station through several advertising messages and, through this procedure, interested cellular users may join the multicast group. Once the multicast group is formed, the base station will send data content only towards those nodes that joined the multicast group. The multicast service delivery can be considered similar to a traditional broadcast transmission. Indeed, while at the physical layer the transmission of both broadcast and multicast services is the same, the difference between these two modes lies in the set of involved users: broadcast services are available to *all* users of a given mobile network (i.e., there is no need for subscriptions), whereas multicast services are restricted only to those UEs belonging to a multicast group.

In the following of this Section we will discuss the multicast applications commonly exchanged over mobile radio systems.

Multicast Applications

Multicast services can cover several types of applications, each one characterized by different QoS

requirements. One of the main multicast services expected to be massively exchanged over LTE is *audio and/or video streaming,* which can range over a wide set of applications such as standard video (e.g., Mobile TV) or audio streaming (e.g., Web radio), news (e.g., weather forecasts) or advertisement message distribution, video or audio conference calls, and so on. The management of multicast audio/video streaming sessions poses several challenges since these services are characterized by strict QoS constraints. In particular, the most relevant QoS issues are related to the provisioning of a minimum data rate, a maximum packet transfer delay and tolerated jitter.

Another important multicast application is the *file downloading*. Multicast file downloading can be suitable for software update transmission (e.g., codec or plug-in), for image and text distribution and for multimedia content delivery (e.g., video or audio files) for off-line use. The management of these multicast services does not pose strict constraints in terms of delay and guaranteed bit rate are, but it is characterized by strict requirements in terms of packet loss ratio.

Recently, the transmission of *geographic information updates* is growing in importance in the mobile market scenario. Typical examples of such services are traffic reports, local news, weather forecast, stock prices and location-based advertisement. In these cases, data must be delivered only to those users located in a given area. The management of these services is quiet similar to the typical management of multicast file downloading, but additional issues must be considered in order to perform multicast group formation according to users' position. Moreover, additional procedures are required to dynamically update the members belonging to a given group by taking into account the users' direction and mobility speed.

The applications considered above can be divided into two categories. The *single-rate* applications require all multicast users to be served with the same session quality. Examples of single-rate services are file downloading and geographic information updates. On the contrary, for the *multi-rate* applications the original information is split into different levels of "quality," and the better the channel condition of a given multicast user the higher the quality experienced by such a user. Multi-rate services cover a large set of multicast applications, e.g., audio/video streaming, and they will be explored in the following of this Section.

Multi-Rate Services

Multi-rate applications foresee to split the original data stream into different sub-streams, where each sub-stream represents a "portion" of the overall information to be transmitted to multicast group members. The idea at the basis of multi-layer techniques is that the perceived session quality improves as users receive a higher number of sub-streams. As a consequence, a minimal service, namely *base sub-stream* (or base layer), is received by *all* multicast users, while terminals with higher channel gain (which potentially support less robust MCS and can accordingly attain higher data rates) can also receive additional *enhancement sub-streams*, and consequently experience improved session quality.

Currently, two categories of multi-layer schemes are largely used: Multiple Description Coding (MDC) and Scalable Video Coding (SVC). In MDC, multimedia data is split into multiple descriptors, where each descriptor represents a given sub-stream of the original information. According to MDC, the higher the number of successfully received descriptors the higher the session quality experienced by a given user. It is worth noticing that the quality improvement is not related to the priority of each descriptor. Indeed, in MDC, all descriptors have equal priority and any combinations of the received descriptors can be decoded independently. Because of its sub-stream independence feature MDC has received high attention from researchers, though MDC suffers of several limitations in case of real-time audio/video streaming applications. Concerning this

latter type of multicast services, SVC represents a more attractive solution, which is based on the idea to dynamically adapt the quality of the streaming to the various needs or preferences of multicast users (as well as to varying capabilities of involved UEs or to different network conditions and loads) by removing one or more parts of the original audio/video data. Being similar to MDC, the term "scalable" refers to the fact that, also in the case one or more sub-streams of the original content are not successfully received by a UE, the received sub-stream (or sub-streams) represents a valid information for some target decoders. SVC applications enable three different types of scalability: temporal, spatial, and quality. Spatial and temporal scalabilities refer to the cases where the reception of only a subset of original sub-streams involves the reception of a video stream with a reduced picture size (i.e., spatial resolution) or frame rate (i.e., temporal resolution), respectively. With quality scalability, the sub-stream provides the same spatio-temporal resolution as the reception of the overall available sub-streams, but with a lower fidelity (where fidelity is often informally referred to as signal-to-noise ratio, i.e., SNR). The main difference between MDC and SVC is related to the order in the reception of the sub-streams. In SVC, a given sub-stream n can be considered as successfully received (i.e., it represents a valid information for the decoder) only if the sub-stream $n-1$ has been previously received by the user. This involves that, in SVC applications, all available sub-streams are hierarchically ordered.

MULTICASTING OVER LTE

The 3GPP, motivated by the increasing demand for high-quality services over mobile broadband networks, carried out several activities under the LTE and System Architecture Evolution (SAE) projects, finalized to respectively define the radio access and the core network for the next generation of mobile radio systems. The LTE system is one of the most promising wireless technologies able to support the growing demand of high-quality multicast services. LTE offers several benefits in terms of *(i)* high data rates in both downlink and uplink directions, *(ii)* low latency, *(iii)* low cost per bit, *(iv)* high spectrum efficiency even for cell-edge users, *(v)* high system capacity.

LTE is very appealing to network providers as a means to deliver high quality services with strict QoS constraints. With the aim to efficiently support multicast services, the 3GPP defined the MBMS standard, which will be the main topic addressed in this Section.

Multimedia Broadcast Multicast Service

The LTE/MBMS architecture, depicted in Figure 2, is based on a *flat all-IP* network infrastructure where both control and data information is transmitted through IP-based connections. This characteristic introduces great flexibility in the management of network devices and allows mobile operators to reduce installation and configuration costs.

The LTE/MBMS network is composed of:

- **eNodeB:** The eNodeB (i.e., the LTE base station) is the entry point for UE to the

LTE network. It is responsible for RRM procedures. In particular, it handles the configuration of transmission parameters (i.e., link adaptation) in single-cell MBMS mode (i.e., a MBMS service transmitted by only one eNodeB). The eNodeB is also in charge of collecting the channel state information of LTE subscribers and performs handover procedures.

- **MultiCell/Multicast Coordination Entity (MCE):** It is a logical entity (it can also be deployed within the eNodeB) involved in session control signaling towards multiple eNodeBs (the MCE does not perform signaling towards the MBMS receivers). One eNodeB is managed by one MCE while one MCE could manage multiple eNodeBs. The MCE covers different functionalities. Among those, the admission control and the allocation of the radio resources used by all the eNodeBs involved in a multi-cell MBMS transmission are the most important. This is typically the case of broadcast services simultaneously delivered by several base stations through single-frequency transmissions. In particular, in a multi-cell scenario, the MCE selects the transmission parameters (i.e., MCSs) to be simultaneously exploited by involved eNodeBs.

Figure 2. The network architecture of LTE/MBMS

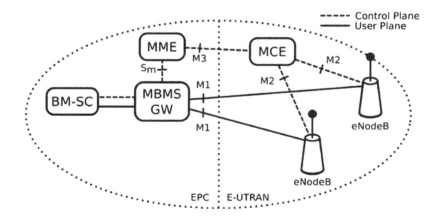

The MCE performs the selection between multi- and single-cell transmission modes in the setup (or network reconfiguration) phase of the MBMS Service. The MCE also performs MBMS session suspension/resumption based on the counting results for the corresponding MBMS service. The MCE is connected to the served eNodeB via the *M2* interface, used for MBMS session management and radio configuration signaling. The Stream Control Transmission Protocol (SCTP) is used over the *M2* interface to carry the control traffic.

- **Mobility Management Entity (MME):** It performs authentication and security procedures for subscriber's identification when a UE establishes a connection to the LTE network. The MME is also in charge for mobility management by storing the serving eNodeB for each terminal in *active*-mode while it stores the Tracking Area (which indicates a set of base stations relevant to a specific area) for UEs in *idle*-mode. Finally, the MME allocates the multicast IP address (in addition to the IP address relevant to the multicast source) to the eNodeB(s) that joined the MBMS session. The *M3* interface connects the MME and the MCE for conveying MBMS session management signaling. The SCTP is used over the *M3* interface to carry the control traffic.

- **MBMS-Gateway (MBMS-GW):** It is a logical entity (i.e., it may be a stand-alone device or it may be co-located with other network nodes) which accomplishes data content forwarding to the eNodeB(s) involved in the MBMS session. The MBMS-GW is in charge of maintaining the IP multicast groups. In particular, it allocates the multicast IP address to a multicast group. The eNodeB joins the IP multicast group to receive the data relevant to the MBMS

user plane when the session starts, while it leaves the IP multicast group when the session stops. The *M1* interface connects the MBMS-GW and the eNodeB(s) in the user plane. The data delivery over the *M1* interface is performed by exploiting IP multicast transmissions (there is no uplink data over *M1* radio network layer). The MBMS synchronization protocol (SYNC) is used over the *M1* interface to allow content synchronization for MBMS service data transmission.

- **Broadcast Multicast-Service Center (BM-SC):** It is a functional entity which represents the entry point for content provider transmissions. It authorizes and initiates MBMS Bearer Services by performing several procedures relevant to service provisioning. Indeed, The BM-SC should be used for scheduling and delivery procedures relevant to a MBMS transmission. In addition, the BM-SC is able to accomplish service announcement and membership functions and performs functions such as security operations and content synchronization. Finally, the BM-SC is in charge for header compression in multi-cell MBMS services.

Multicast Session Procedures

The provisioning of a multicast service involves different procedures necessary for service announcement, multicast group formation and service delivery. In details, the phases to be accomplished for a MBMS multicast session set up are:

- **Subscription:** It is an agreement between the UE and the service provider for the reception of the MBMS service(s). The BM-SC stores the subscription information. At the end of this phase, the subscriber's terminal is updated with MBMS-specific information (MBMS service keys and user keys) useful to decipher the received data traffic.

- **Service Announcement:** It allows the MBMS members to collect service activation information (e.g., multicast IP address, service start time) about the available MBMS services. Service provider may consider different discovery mechanisms: *(i)* Point-to-Point or Cell Broadcast SMS; *(ii)* MBMS Broadcast mode to announce both multicast and broadcast services; *(iii)* MBMS Multicast mode for MBMS Multicast services advertising; *(iv)* URL (HTTP, FTP); *(v)* PUSH mechanisms (WAP, SMS-PP, MMS).
- **Joining:** The subscriber joins the multicast group. In this phase, the UE becomes a multicast group member and it initiates the relevant MBMS bearer services in order to receive the multicast data content.
- **Session Start:** The BM-SC performs the transmission of MBMS data content. A Session Start message is sent for each MBMS bearer service involved in the MBMS session. The Session Start message does not depend on the activation of the service by the user (i.e., the service activation can be performed by the user before or after the transmission of the Session Start message).
- **MBMS Notification:** In this phase multicast members are informed about forthcoming MBMS multicast data transfer.
- **Data Transfer.** In this phase the MBMS traffic is delivered to the multicast group members.
- **Session Stop:** The BM-SC stops data transmission and the MBMS bearers are accordingly released.
- **Leaving:** In this phase a subscriber leaves a multicast group.

Subscription, joining and leaving phases are performed on a *per-user* basis. On the contrary, other phases involve the whole set of users interested in the MBMS multicast session and are accordingly performed on a *per-group* basis.

MBMS Channels

The MBMS standard defines two logical channels to be exploited for multicast content delivery: the *Multicast Traffic Channel (MTCH)* and the *Multicast Control Channel (MCCH)*. The MTCH is a PtM downlink channel for data transmission. Multiple MBMS services can therefore be transmitted using a single MTCH. The MTCH exploits the Radio Link Control (RLC) unacknowledged mode. According to this mode, no retransmissions at the RLC layer of LTE protocol stack are used, i.e., multicast terminals do not send any acknowledgement message to the eNodeB.

The MCCH is a PtM downlink channel for signaling traffic transmission. One MCCH carries information regarding one or several MTCHs, including the sub-frame allocation and the MCS relevant to each MTCH. The MCCH exploits the RLC unacknowledged mode.

In single-cell mode, these channels are mapped on the Downlink Shared Channel (DL-SCH). The design of the MCCH is a key challenge in order to efficiently manage the MBMS signaling traffic. The number of MCCHs varies according to the data transmission mode and, for single-cell MBMS deployments, one MCCH is activated for each MBMS service transmitted by the eNodeB.

RESOURCE MANAGEMENT OF MULTICAST SERVICES

The eNodeB is in charge of performing RRM procedures in LTE systems. The RRM covers different functionalities at different layers of the LTE protocol stack. In particular, by considering layer 1, the RRM manages channel state information by allowing multicast members to transmit channel state feedback to the eNodeB. At layer 2, the RRM performs dynamic scheduling and link adaptation procedures. Finally, at layer 3, the RRM accomplish QoS management, admission control and semi-persistent scheduling.

In this Section, we will focus on the RRM procedures relevant to the multicast services management. After an overview on the LTE packet scheduler, we will analyze the issues related to link adaptation in multicast environments.

LTE Packet Scheduler

The LTE air interface exploits Orthogonal Frequency Division Multiple Access (OFDMA) for transmissions on the downlink direction. Multiple orthogonal sub-carriers spaced 15 kHz apart are used to carry data. A sub-channel of 180 kHz is named Resource Block (RB) and corresponds to 12 consecutive and equally spaced sub-carries. The RB is the smallest frequency resource which can be assigned to a terminal in the frequency domain. The number of RBs depends on the system bandwidth configuration and varies from 6 (i.e., 1.4 MHz) and 100 (i.e., 20 MHz). In the time domain, every Transmission Time Interval (TTI), which lasts 1 ms, radio resources are allocated on a RB-pair basis.

The set of available RBs is managed by the LTE Packet scheduler, implemented at the Medium Access Control (MAC) layer of the eNodeB to efficiently handle resource allocation to mobile users in the time/frequency domain. The main functionalities of the packet scheduler are depicted in Figure 3 and can be summarized in three steps, performed according to the QoS parameters and the channel quality experienced by each UE.

During the first step, namely the *schedulability check*, the scheduler collects information relevant to the set of services to be considered for scheduling opportunities in the current scheduling frame. In this step, the eNodeB collects information regarding: *(i)* the number of subscribers requiring LTE services; *(ii)* QoS parameters (e.g., minimum requested data rate, jitter, delay, packet loss ratio) which must be guaranteed to each service; *(iii)* the amount of traffic generated and queued into the buffers.

The second step is performed by the *Time Domain Packet Scheduler (TDPS)*. It selects the multicast services which must be served in the current scheduling frame to guarantee their QoS constraints. This step is performed according to the QoS profile associated to the multicast service. In particular, the QoS profile of each data flow (i.e., bearer) is described by the following downlink parameters: *(i)* Allocation retention priority (ARP); *(ii)* Guaranteed bit rate (GBR) and *(iii)* QoS class identifier (QCI). The GBR parameter is only specified for GBR bearers, i.e., for those services which need a minimum requested data rate, whereas for non-GBR bearers an aggregate maximum bit rate is indicated. The ARP parameter, represented by an integer which

Figure 3. The structure of LTE packet scheduler

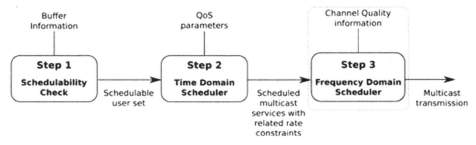

varies in the range 1-16, indicates the priority of a given service. Finally, the QCI is a pointer to a set of QoS attributes (QCI levels defined in LTE are listed in Table 1). The QCI includes several parameters such as the flow priority level and the delay budget relevant to the layer 2 of LTE protocol stack.

Finally, on the basis of the channel quality experienced by UEs, the *Frequency Domain Packet Scheduler (FDPS)* executes the link adaptation procedures by selecting, for each multicast service scheduled in the previous step, the most appropriate: *(i)* modulation technique (from QPSK to 64-QAM), *(ii)* coding scheme, *(iii)* number of RBs. In details, according to the Signal to Interference and Noise Ratio (SINR) and the target Block Error Rate (BLER), each UE estimates and forwards the Channel Quality Indicator (CQI) feedback to the eNodeB. The CQI is an integer value varying from 1 to 15 which indicates the maximum supported MCS by a given UE. The CQI values defined by LTE are listed in Table 2. The CQI report cycle can last one or several TTIs and it is selected by the eNodeB depending on the channel variations due to the user mobility. It is worth remarking that a given MCS is related to each CQI, while the number of RBs can vary between a minimum and maximum value (i.e., 1 and 50 RBs for system bandwidth equal to 10 MHz) that depends on the implemented FDPS algorithm.

Conservative Approach

An important topic regarding the multicast services management over mobile radio systems is related to the *link adaptation* procedures. Such procedures are accomplished by the base station in order to dynamically update the transmission parameters, such as the MCSs, according to the time variations in the radio channel of served users. With this aim, group members periodically report their channel state information, i.e., CQI, to the serving base station. Consequently, the portion of system resources assigned to a multicast group may vary as well as the appropriate MCS (or MCSs) for the assigned resources. In addition, due to errors in channel state estimation, user mobility and traffic fluctuations, link adaptation errors may occur resulting in either unnecessarily high robustness of the transmission or block errors due to the exploitation of less robust MCSs.

The PtP and PtM transmissions modes are defined to convey data content to the set of users in a multicast group. According to the PtP mode, the same content is conveyed to each multicast member on a UE-dedicated channel through standard unicast transmissions. Such a channel can be used to transfer both control information related to multicast service and UE-dedicated information between the base station and a given terminal. Each member is scheduled individually,

Table 1. QCI characteristics for the bearer QoS profile

QCI	Priority	L2 Packet Delay Budget	Example Services
1 (GBR)	2	100 ms	Conversational voice
2 (GBR)	4	150 ms	Conversational video
3 (GBR)	5	300 ms	Buffered streaming
4 (GBR)	3	50 ms	Real-time gaming
5 (non-GBR)	1	100 ms	IMS signaling
6 (non-GBR)	7	100 ms	Live streaming
7 (non-GBR)	6	300 ms	Buffered streaming, TCP, email, P2P file sharing, etc.
8 (non-GBR)	8	300 ms	
9 (non-GBR)	9	300 ms	

Table 2. CQI values defined by LTE

CQI Index	Modulation	Coding Rate x 1024	Efficiency [bps/Hz]
0	Out of range		
1	QPSK	78	0.1523
2	QPSK	120	0.2344
3	QPSK	193	0.3770
4	QPSK	308	0.6016
5	QPSK	449	0.8770
6	QPSK	602	1.1758
7	16-QAM	378	1.4766
8	16-QAM	490	1.9141
9	16-QAM	616	2.4063
10	64-QAM	466	2.7305
11	64-QAM	567	3.3223
12	64-QAM	666	3.9023
13	64-QAM	772	4.5234
14	64-QAM	873	5.1152
15	64-QAM	948	5.5547

and this implies that link adaptation is performed on a *per-user basis*. As a consequence, PtP mode is link efficient, but the number of required radio resources increases linearly with the number of members in a multicast group. This limits the effectiveness of PtP transmissions in scenarios with large multicast groups; indeed, the exploitation of PtP in such scenarios causes a network capacity reduction with consequent quality degradation for multicast and other services transmitted in the cell.

In PtM mode, the same content is conveyed to all multicast members on a shared channel. By exploiting the broadcast nature of a radio transmission, all users are simultaneously served through only one transmission. As a consequence, group members are scheduled all together. Compared to PtP, PtM is a broadcast delivery approach because the amount of required radio resources has no direct relation to the number of multicast members. Therefore, the spectral efficiency increases and this is more evident in scenarios where the number of multicast terminals is high.

Concerning the link adaptation procedures, PtM exploits uplink dedicated feedback channels, as in the case of PTP mode, in order to maximize the reuse of existing protocols and functionalities of mobile radio systems. In contrast to user individual MCS selection, the PtM mode requires to process multiple channel state information reports before choosing an appropriate MCS for a single downlink transmission. As a consequence, the advantage of this scheme compared to PtP increases as the number of users in the multicast group becomes large, though, the uplink traffic caused by the transmission of channel state feedbacks would rise accordingly (however, the issue related to the uplink load may be reduced by omitting redundant information). In addition, due to the fact that link adaptation procedures are performed on *per-group basis* since radio transmission is simultaneously delivered to multiple users, the performance of PtM mode is mainly influenced by the presence of user(s) which experience poor channel conditions.

The basic scheduling strategy adopted in LTE systems is a single-rate scheme known as *conservative* approach. This is based on the idea that all members in a given multicast group are served with the same QoS. According to this idea, a system based on PtM transmissions is only as strong as its weakest link (Alexious, Bouras, Kokkinos & Tsichritzis, 2010). So, the conservative scheme adaptively sets the group transmission parameters (i.e., MCS) to suit the user with the worst (minimum) channel quality, usually located at the edge-cell. Although the conservative scheme overcomes the performance of traditional PtP communications, this policy is highly spectrum inefficient, since users within the group which experience good channel gains (commonly located close to the eNodeB) are severely hindered from utilizing link adaptation modes that fully exploit their good channel state. In addition, as the group size increases, the data capacity of the multicast group becomes limited, because more users share resources assigned to the group, consequently, capacity benefits of the multicast system drastically decreases as the number of users increases.

Opportunistic Multicasting

Opportunistic multicasting is proposed in literature to overcome the limitations in terms of multicast session quality and spectral efficiency of the conservative approach and to efficiently exploit the multiuser diversity while guaranteeing adequate multicast gain (Low, Pun, Hong & Kuo, 2009). As depicted in Figure 4, the opportunistic multicasting is based on the fact that each user experiences independent fading over different time slots; hence, in any given time slot, a portion of users (the best ones) can be selected for service delivery. As a consequence, the aim of the opportunistic strategy is to efficiently select the most suitable MCS for multicast delivery in any given time slot and to select the portion of multicast members to serve accordingly.

Several research works proposed different strategies for the selection of the most suitable portions of users to serve in any given time slot. Such strategies can be summarized in the following approaches:

- **Pre-Defined Fixed MCS:** The idea at the basis of this approach is to set the MCS for multicast content delivery and to exploit such a MCS during the entire multicast session delivery. Accordingly, a multicast member will receive the multicast content only if the experienced channel conditions allow the terminal to successfully support the MCS adopted by the eNodeB. The selection of the MCS for content delivery follows different strategies. For instance,

Figure 4. Opportunistic multicast scheme

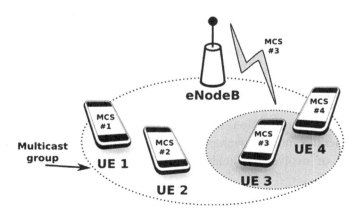

the MCS can be selected to achieve a pre-defined spectral efficiency target value (where the spectral efficiency is defined as the ratio between the mean throughput experienced by multicast users and the channel bandwidth exploited for multicast session delivery). Another strategy is to select the most reliable MCS to maximize either the spectral efficiency or the achievable system throughput. The fixed MCS approach involves severe restrictions on achievable session coverage (i.e., the portion of users served by the eNodeB compared to the whole set of terminals joined to multicast group) and system throughput, especially when users experience different channel conditions. In addition, this approach does not allow to effectively consider intra-group and inter-group user throughput fairness in resource allocation.

- **Average Group Throughput:** Another strategy to improve the system capacity and to simultaneously exploit the multiuser channel dynamics is enabling the eNodeB to transmit towards a given multicast group based on the long-term moving average throughput of the group. Different averaging strategies can be exploited to perform this task. For instance, a suitable approach is to order the multicast users according to the instantaneous achievable throughput and to select the median user, i.e. multicast content will be transmitted by the eNodeB with the MCS supported by half (50%) of all group members. Despite its good performance as compared to PtP and pure PtM, the optimality of fixing the selection ratio at 50% has not been clearly addressed. Another strategy is to select the most appropriate data transmission rate based on the exponential moving average of throughput values of involved terminals.

Similarly to the fixed MCS approach, the average group throughput suffers in terms of poor intra- and inter-group fairness.

The approaches mentioned above can be extended to allow the eNodeB to dynamically change the portion of users to serve in any time slot. According to this approach, known as *Opportunistic Multicast Scheduling (OMS)*, the eNodeB changes on a per-slot basis the MCS for multicast transmission according to the users' channel conditions. OMS can support both single- and multi-rate applications. Since the portion of users served by the scheduler dynamically changes within the frame, OMS-based strategies must couple with rateless coding schemes. A rateless code allows users to recover the full original content of a message once a minimum set of encoded symbols is received, regardless of the specific received sequence of encoded symbols. The strategy at the basis of rateless codes is in sharp contrast with conventional schemes where the eNodeB must keep track of the data that each user has received throughout the content delivery process, and this is obviously a huge burden for networks with a large number of multicast users and several multicast services transmitted in the cell. Example of rateless codes are *fountain* and *erasure* codes. Such codes are rateless in the sense that the number of encoded packets that can be generated from the multicast source is potentially unlimited, and the number of generated encoded packets can be determined on the fly. Rateless codes are record-breaking sparse-graph codes for channels with erasures, such as the radio channel of cellular networks, where files are transmitted in multiple small packets, each of which is either received without error or not received if an error on the radio channel occurred. Standard file transfer protocols simply split a file up into K packet-sized pieces, then the eNodeB transmits each packet until it is successfully received. This approach asks for a back channel for the transmitter to find out which packets need retransmitting. In contrast, rateless codes make packets that are functions of the whole original file. The transmitter sprays packets at the receiver without any knowledge of which packets are received. Once the receiver has received any N packets (where N is just slightly greater than the original file size K) the whole file can be recovered. The computational costs of the best rateless codes are astonishingly small, scaling linearly with the file size. Nevertheless, the adoption of rateless codes involves further issues in terms of computational burden, buffer size, and decoding delay. In addition, a very challenging issue related to OMS is that it cannot guarantee adequate fairness among multicast members on a short term. Above mentioned issues are exacerbated when considering real-time video streams characterized by strict QoS constraints in terms of delivery delay and jitter.

Multicast Subgrouping

Multicast subgrouping is considered as a hybrid scheme to reduce the bottleneck effects of conservative schemes influenced by the presence of users with poor channel qualities located at the cell-edge. As shown in Figure 5, subgrouping foresees to split the multicast members into different subgroups, each one including users with similar channel conditions, and to adopt a different MCS for each served subgroup (Araniti, Scordamaglia, Condoluci, Molinaro & Iera, 2012). The goals of subgrouping are to serve the whole multicast group within every time slot while guaranteeing improvements in terms of session quality, user satisfaction and spectrum utilization. Subgrouping efficiently supports both single- and multi-. rate multicast services.

The subgroup formation can be accomplished with different strategies. A basic approach is to split the multicast group into two subgroups and to define a single multicast transmission rate for such subgroups. For instance, the cell is divided into two QoS regions. The eNodeB transmits two data streams with different transmission parameters, i.e., MCS, and power level, according to the QoS definitions. Each stream corresponds to a different QoS region. Users with high channel gain can receive both streams (i.e., they will achieve the highest quality session) while the users with poor channel qualities will receive only one stream (i.e., basic video quality).

Another strategy for multicast subgrouping is to design the subgroup formation according to an optimization problem. In this way, the most suitable subgroup configuration (i.e., number of subgroups with the related MCS, portion of

Figure 5. Multicast subgrouping

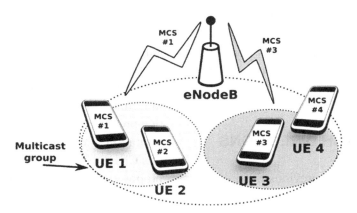

users, assigned resources, and data rate for each enabled subgroup) is dynamically selected by the eNodeB based on the an optimization problem which takes into account the users' CQI values and the QoS constraints of multicast session. The optimization problem can be formulated in order to achieve different goals, for example to maximize the system throughput or the spectral efficiency. Another strategy is to recast the subgroup creation phase with the aim to minimize the amount of RBs needed for multicast content delivery. Finally, another suitable approach is to enable the best subgroups in order to achieve proportional fairness allocation with the aim to attain both intra- and inter-group fairness.

The subgrouping approach can be extended through the exploitation of short-range links to improve the multicast service performance according to the users' channel qualities, while simultaneously improve the system capacity and reducing the consumption of system resources (Condoluci, Militano, Araniti, Molinaro & Iera, 2013). In this scenario, short-range communication can be supported over LTE Device-to Device (D2D) or Wi-Fi links. In this case, a subset of the MBMS UEs will act as *relay* nodes by receiving the data content from the eNodeB and then forwarding it to the connected multicast member(s). In particular, cellular mode D2D connections can be supported on Frequency Division Duplex (FDD) and Time Division Duplex (TDD) modes, although the FDD mode poses additional issues in terms of terminal design, cost and complexity. The logic followed by eNodeB to select the relays is to activate the short-range links for serving the nodes with worse channel conditions and so maximize the throughput performance.

FUTURE RESEARCH DIRECTIONS

From the discussion in the previous Sections, it clearly emerges that the design of an effective RRM policy for the management of multicast

services over LTE is still an open issue. Among the addressed solutions, multicast subgrouping is the most promising scheme since it allows to improve the multicast session quality by efficiently exploiting multi-user diversity while guaranteeing full coverage. For this reason, future researches are required to definitively demonstrate the effectiveness of multicast subgrouping in several cell deployment scenarios and load conditions. Furthermore, since RRM procedures must be accomplished with strict time constraints (link adaptation is performed every 1ms-long TTI), a further challenge is related to the design of low-complexity subgrouping schemes which can perform subgroup formation without requiring high computational cost at the eNodeB.

Another important scenario to consider is related to the management of multiple multicast services transmitted in a cell. Indeed, since multicast services are considered as the value-added of 4G wireless systems, it is expected that several multicast sessions are simultaneously served by a given eNodeB. This scenario poses several challenges since the delivery of several multicast applications could meaningfully reduce the capacity of LTE systems. Finally, further investigations are still required to assess the impact of multicast subgrouping on the management of typical unicast services transmitted in a LTE cell.

CONCLUSION

This Chapter focused on the issues and the challenges related to the RRM of multicast services over LTE systems. Multicasting is expected to be massively used over LTE, and effective solutions in terms of resource allocation and link adaptation procedures are still required to overcome the limitation of conventional multicast schemes. In this Chapter we analyzed the different strategies proposed in literature for multicast environments. Among those, multicast subgrouping appears as the most promising solution able to efficiently support practical implementation of multicast services over LTE systems.

Further research is still required to address the effectiveness of multicast subgrouping in scenarios with multiple multicast services and to analyze the impact of multicast content delivery on the traditional unicast services transmitted in LTE.

REFERENCES

Alexious, A., Bouras, C., Kokkinos, V., & Tsichritzis, G. (2010). *Communication cost analysis of MBSFN in LTE*. Paper presented at the Institute of Electrical and Electronics Engineers 21st International Symposium on Personal Indoor and Mobile Radio Communications. Istanbul, Turkey.

Araniti, G., Scordamaglia, V., Condoluci, M., Molinaro, A., & Iera, A. (2012). *Efficient frequency domain packet scheduler for point-to-multipoint transmissions in LTE networks*. Paper presented at the IEEE International Conference on Communications. Ottawa, Canada.

Condoluci, M., Militano, L., Araniti, G., Molinaro, A., & Iera, A. (2013). *Multicasting in LTE-A networks enhanced by device-to-device communications*. Paper presented at the IEEE Global Telecommunications Conference. Atlanta, GA.

Lecompte, D., & Gabin, F. (2012). Evolved multimedia broadcast/multicast service (eMBMS) in LTE-advanced: Overview and Rel-11 enhancements. *IEEE Communications Magazine, 50*(11), 68–74. doi:10.1109/MCOM.2012.6353684

Low, T. P., Pun, M. O., Hong, Y. W. P., & Kuo, C. C. J. (2009). Optimized opportunistic multicast scheduling (OMS) over wireless cellular networks. *IEEE Transactions on Wireless Communications, 9*(2), 791–801. doi:10.1109/TWC.2010.02.090387

Richard, A., Dadlani, A., & Kim, A. (2013). Multicast scheduling and resource allocation algorithms for OFDMA-based systems: A survey. *IEEE Communications Surveys and Tutorials, 15*(1), 240–254. doi:10.1109/SURV.2012.013012.00074

Third Generation Partnership Project. (2012). *TS 36.300, evolved universal terrestrial radio access (E-UTRA) and evolved universal terrestrial radio access network (E-UTRAN) (Release 11)*. Academic Press.

ADDITIONAL READING

Akyildiz, I. F., Gutierrez-Estevez, D. M., & Chavarria Reyes, E. (2010). The evolution to 4G cellular systems: LTE-Advanced. *Physical Communication, 3*(4), 217–244. doi:10.1016/j.phycom.2010.08.001

Alexious, A., Bouras, C., Kokkinos, V., Papazois, A., & Tsichritzis, G. (2010, October). *Efficient MCS selection for MBSFN transmissions over LTE networks*. Paper presented at the IFIP Wireless Days (WD), Venice, Italy.

Araniti, G., Condoluci, M., Militano, L., & Iera, A. (2013). Adaptive resource allocation to multicast services in LTE systems. *IEEE Transactions on Broadcasting, 59*(4), 658–664. doi:10.1109/TBC.2013.2271387

Bakanoglu, K., Mingquan, W., Hang, L., & Saurabh, M. (2010, April). *Adaptive resource allocation in multicast OFDMA systems*. Paper presented at the IEEE Wireless Communications and Networking Conference, Sydney, Australia.

Belleschi, M., Gabor, F., & Abrardo, A. (2011, December). *Performance analysis of a distributed resource allocation scheme for D2D communications*. Paper presented at the IEEE Global Telecommunications Conference, Houston, Texas, USA.

Condoluci, M., Araniti, G., Molinaro, A., & Iera, A. (2013, September). *Exploiting Frequency-Selectivity in Real-Time Multicast Services over LTE Networks*. Paper presented at the IEEE 24rd International Symposium on Personal, Indoor and Mobile Radio Communications. London, UK.

Condoluci, M., Araniti, G., Molinaro, A., Iera, A., & Cosmas, J. (2013, June). *On the Impact of Frequency Selectivity on Multicast Subgroup Formation in 4G Networks*. Paper presented at the IEEE International Symposium on Broadband Multimedia Systems and Broadcasting, London, UK.

Deb, S., Jaiswal, S., & Nagaraj, K. (2008, April). *Real-Time Video Multicast in WiMAX Networks*. Paper presented at the IEEE 27th Conference on Computer Communications, Phoenix, AZ.

Gopala, P. K., & Gamal, H. E. (2004, November). *Opportunistic multicasting*. Paper presented at the Thirty-Eighth Asilomar Conference on Signals, Systems and Computers, Pacific Groove, California.

Huang, C. W., Huang, S. M., Wu, P. H., Lin, S. J., & Hwang, J. N. (2012). OLM: Opportunistic Layered Multicasting for Scalable IPTV over Mobile WiMAX. *IEEE Transactions on Mobile Computing*, *11*(3), 453–463. doi:10.1109/TMC.2011.34

Kuo, W. H., Liu, T., & Liao, W. (2007, June). *Utility-based resource allocation for layer-encoded IPTV multicast in IEEE 802.16 (WiMAX) wireless networks*. Paper presented at the IEEE International Conference on Communications, Glasgow, Scotland.

Li, P., Zhang, H., Zhao, B., & Rangarajan, S. (2009, October). *Scalable video multicast in multi-carrier wireless data system*, Paper presented at the IEEE 17th International Conference on Network Protocols, Princeton, New Jersey, USA.

Ma, Y., Letaief, K., Wang, Z., Murch, R., & Wu, Z. (2010, December). *Multiple description coding-based optimal resource allocation for OFDMA multicast service*. Paper presented at the IEEE Global Telecommunications Conference, Miami, Florida, USA.

Militano, L., Condoluci, M., Araniti, G., & Iera, A. (2013, June). *Multicast service delivery solutions in LTE-Advanced systems*. Paper presented at the IEEE International Conference on Communications, Budapest, Hungary.

Ngo, D. T., Tellambura, C., & Nguyen, H. H. (2009, January). *Efficient resource allocation for OFDMA multicast systems with fairness consideration*. Paper presented at the IEEE Radio and Wireless Symposium, San Diego, CA, USA.

Pyattaev, A., Johnsson, K., Andreev, S., & Koucheryavy, Y. (2013, June). *Proximity based data offloading via network assisted device-to-device communications*. Paper presented at the IEEE Vehicular Technology Conference, Dresden, Germany.

Rhee, W., & Cioffi, J. (2000, May). *Increase in capacity of multiuser OFDM systems using dynamic subchannel allocation*. Paper presented at the IEEE 51st Vehicular Technology Conference, Tokyo, Japan.

Schwarz, H., Marpe, D., & Wiegand, T. (2007). Overview of the Scalable Video Coding Extension of the H.264/AVC Standard. *IEEE Transactions on Circuits and Systems for Video Technology*, *17*(9), 1103–1120. doi:10.1109/TCSVT.2007.905532

Sharangi, S., Krishnamurti, R., & Hefeeda, M. (2011). Energy-Efficient Multicasting of Scalable Video Streams Over WiMAX Networks. *IEEE Transactions on Multimedia*, *13*(1), 102–115. doi:10.1109/TMM.2010.2076799

Suh, C., & Mo, J. (2006, April). *Resource Allocation for Multicast Services in Multicarrier Wireless Communications*. Paper presented at the IEEE 25th International Conference on Computer Communications, Barcelona, Spain.

Third Generation Partnership Project (2006, October). *TR 25.814, Physical layer aspect for evolved Universal Terrestrial Radio Access (UTRA)*, Release 7.

Third Generation Partnership Project (2012, March). *TS 23.246, Multimedia Broadcast/Multicast Service (MBMS), Architecture and functional description*, Release 11.

Third Generation Partnership Project (2012, September). *TS 36.213, Evolved Universal Terrestrial Radio Access (E-UTRA), Physical layer procedures*, Release 11.

Third Generation Partnership Project (2012, December). *TS 36.201, LTE physical layer, General description*, Release 11.

Third Generation Partnership Project (2012, September). *TS 36.440, General aspects and principles for interfaces supporting Multimedia Broadcast Multicast Service (MBMS) within E-UTRAN*, Release 11.

Zhang, L., He, Z., Niu, K., Zhang, B., & Skov, P. (2009, September). *Optimization of coverage and throughput in single-cell E-MBMS*. Paper presented at the IEEE 70th Vehicular Technology Conference Fall, Anchorage, AK.

KEY TERMS AND DEFINITIONS

CQI: Channel State Information transmitted by a UE to the base station.

FDPS: The unit responsible of link adaptation procedures over LTE.

Link Adaptation: Selection of the most suitable transmission parameters according to users' CQI.

LTE: Radio mobile system able to support high data rate even for users located at the cell-edge.

MBMS: Standard allowing to efficiently support multicast services over LTE.

Multicast: A service which is simultaneously transmitted towards multiple users.

RRM: Set of functionalities relevant to the management of radio resources over cellular networks.

UE: Mobile terminal connected to the LTE system.

Chapter 5
Game Theory for Collaboration in Future Networks

José André Moura
ISCTE-IUL, Portugal

Rui Neto Marinheiro
ISCTE-IUL, Portugal

João Carlos Silva
ISCTE-IUL, Portugal

ABSTRACT

Cooperative strategies have the great potential of improving network performance and spectrum utilization in future networking environments. This new paradigm in terms of network management, however, requires a novel design and analysis framework targeting a highly flexible networking solution with a distributed architecture. Game Theory is very suitable for this task, since it is a comprehensive mathematical tool for modeling the highly complex interactions among distributed and intelligent decision makers. In this way, the more convenient management policies for the diverse players (e.g. content providers, cloud providers, home providers, brokers, network providers or users) should be found to optimize the performance of the overall network infrastructure. The authors discuss in this chapter several Game Theory models/concepts that are highly relevant for enabling collaboration among the diverse players, using different ways to incentivize it, namely through pricing or reputation. In addition, the authors highlight several related open problems, such as the lack of proper models for dynamic and incomplete information games in this area.

1. INTRODUCTION

Game Theory (GT) techniques have recently emerged in many engineering applications, notably in communications and networking. With the emergence of cooperation as a new communication paradigm, alongside the need for self-organizing, decentralized, and autonomic networks, it has become imperative to seek suitable GT tools to analyze and study the behavior and interactions of nodes in Future Networks (FNs). The final goal is to find low-complexity distributed algorithms

DOI: 10.4018/978-1-4666-5978-0.ch005

that can efficiently manage the highly-complex future network environment formed by heterogeneous technologies, enhancing collaboration among players and punish selfish or misbehaving nodes. In addition, the new management solutions should reduce the unwanted effects of stale information (e.g. oscillation around a specific network status) by choosing the proper values, namely, for both sampling rate of network status and delay associated to the dissemination of status information amongst the network nodes. This chapter fills a hole in existing communications literature, by providing a comprehensive review about GT models/concepts that are highly relevant for enabling collaboration in FNs environments.

In FNs, incentive mechanisms should be applied to the network infrastructure as distributed and intelligent management algorithms, forcing players to cooperate instead of pursuing their own interest. This novel player's behavior aims to efficiently use the available network resources and to satisfy the heterogeneous requirements of data flows. Broadly speaking, the current literature highlights two different ways to encourage cooperation (collaboration) among the players: one with a short-term control effect and the other with a long-term control effect. The first approach makes use of virtual payments (credit-based games) to relieve costs for relaying traffic, and the second approach is related to community (or group) enforcement to establish long-term relationships among the nodes (reputation-based games). Cooperation is sustained in reputation-base games because defection against a specific node causes personal retaliation or sanction by others. In the limit, nodes that do not cooperate will not be able to use the network themselves. Effective corrective actions against cheating nodes are also required with either permanent or temporary measures. In addition, there is also a relatively new and a very interesting set of games designated by evolutionary coalitional games that can enable more intelligent, self-adjustable, and

robust algorithms for the management of FNs. Furthermore, the social networks like Facebook or Flickr currently have a large popularity, and following very recent work (Apicella, 2012) (Bond, 2012), these networks could rapidly disseminate the positive impact of collaborative actions among the users of FNs. This fast dissemination will be anchored by the convergence of distinct wireless access technologies, and the deployment in large scale of vehicular networks as well as wireless sensor networks. Finally, it should be also interesting to investigate the deployment of hybrid solutions combining credit-based and reputation-based methods to enhance collaboration amongst players.

The current chapter reviews the literature to find and discuss the more promising GT proposals that can incentivize the collaboration among the diverse players to use more intelligently and efficiently the available resources of FNs. This chapter is organized as follows. Section 2 introduces and discusses important GT aspects for FNs. Section 3 gives the background and highlights collaborative strategies in FNs. It also presents our vision about FNs. Then, section 4 describes how GT can enable and enhance collaboration in FNs. In particular, section 5 offers a broad GT literature survey in wireless networking. Section 6 discusses some relevant research work on how GT can be used to address the more significant operational or functional aspects we expect to be present in FN environments. Several guidelines to apply game theory on future networks using different application examples are given in this section. Finally, Section 7 concludes and discusses relevant GT open problems to support collaboration in FNs.

2. DISCUSSING GAME THEORY

The current section introduces and discusses relevant aspects of GT, which can be very useful to model the emergent network environments of FNs.

Roots and Scope

The earliest predecessors of GT are economic analysis of imperfectly competitive markets of the French economist Augustin Cournot in 1838 (Dutta, 1999). The next great advance is due to John Nash who, in 1950, introduced the Nash equilibrium (NE) which is the most widely used concept in modern GT. This was built on the earlier work of Cournot about oligopolistic markets. The NE consists on a game status where no rational actor playing that game has enough incentives to deviate from. In fact, as any player would decide to use a different strategy from the one used to immediately reach the Nash Equilibrium then that player would be punished in the sense that its reward is reduced. Nash´s initial work created a new branch in GT grouping all the non-cooperative games. Further historical evolution in GT is available in (Dutta, 1999).

GT is the study of multi-person decision problems (which differentiates it from the classical decision theory) in applications drawn from industrial organization, labor economics, macroeconomics, financial economics, and international economics (Gibbons, 1992). Alongside with previous applications in Economics and Finance, GT could be applied also to other completely different real world scenarios, like Art auctions, voting at the United Nations, animal conflicts, sustainable use of natural resources, random drug testing at sports, bankruptcy law, takeover of one company by other, trench warfare in World War I, and a group project preparing a case study for a GT class (Dutta, 1999).

Classical GT essentially requires that all of the specified players of a specific game make rational choices among a pre-defined set of static strategies. As a consequence, it is fundamental in GT that each player must consider the strategic analysis that the players' opponents are making in determining that his (her) own static strategic choice is appropriate to receive the best payoff (reward) as possible (Vincent, 2011). Otherwise,

if a player's reward is not influenced by other players, then GT cannot be used. In this last case, constrained optimization should be used in the place of GT. Following, some classical examples are discussed to illustrate how GT can be applied to create a mathematical model (e.g. matrix form) that mimics real-life scenarios with conflict situations among the players, trying to solve those conflict situations.

Matrix Games

Matrix games are those in which the payoff to a player can be determined from a matrix of payoffs. The payoffs are assigned to each element of the matrix assuming that interactions among players are pairwise (Vincent, 2011). One player chooses a row of the matrix and the other chooses a column of the matrix. The intersection between the row and the column points out a unique element of the matrix. As an example, if player A's strategy is to choose the third row and player B's strategy is to choose the first column, the resultant payoff to player A is the value in the third row and first column of the matrix. A consequence of this is that the number of strategies available to the players is finite and discrete.

The matrix games can be asymmetric or symmetric. On one hand, a game is asymmetric if players have different set of strategies and/or if players are distinctively rewarded from choosing a given strategy against an opponent with a particular strategy. A classic example of an asymmetric game is the battle of sexes that is modelled by two distinct payoff matrixes. On the other hand, a game is symmetric if players have the same set of strategies and experience the same reward of using a given strategy against an opponent with a particular strategy. A classic example of a symmetric game is the prisoner's dilemma, which can be modelled with a single matrix. Following, we discuss with further detail the prisoner's dilemma because is the classical GT approach to solve the dilemma of an individual choice between cooperate or defect (not cooperate) with others, which is the main focus of the current chapter.

The prisoner's dilemma can be formulated in terms of a single payoff matrix with two players, each one with two possible strategies, as shown in Table 1. Suppose that two individuals are being held in a prison in isolated cells. In this game, regardless of what the other prisoner decides, each prisoner gets a higher pay-off by betraying the other ("defecting"). The reasoning involves an argument by dilemma: B will either cooperate or defect. If B cooperates, A should defect, since going free is better than serving 1 year. If B defects, A should also defect, since serving 2 years is better than serving 3. So either way, A should defect. Parallel reasoning shows that B should also defect. As both players choose to defect, they will be serving 2 years. Yet both players choosing to cooperate obtain a higher payoff (serving only 1 year) than both players defecting! In this way, GT results in both players being worse off than if each chose to lessen the sentence of his accomplice at the cost of spending more time in jail himself. Later on, in the current chapter, this game will be used to show the cooperation among network operators is very useful to all of them.

Evolutionary Game Theory

In opposition to the classical GT, a recent branch of GT - Evolutionary GT (EGT), states that the players aren´t completely rational, the players have limited information about available choices and consequences, and the strategies are not static (the strategies evolve). The players have a preferred strategy that continuously compare with other alternative strategies, checking if they need to change their current strategy to get a better reward (fitness). The decision to change the preferred strategy can be also influenced by other neighboring players belonging to the same population (by observation and strategy optimization based on what has been learned). In this way, the strategy with the highest selection score inside a group of individuals forming a community will become the predominant strategy for that generation of individuals, and it will be transferred to the next generation of individuals (evolutionary aspect). Following, we discuss EGT that could be seen as an interesting alternative paradigm to model realistically more complex and very dynamic wireless networking scenarios that potentially will occur in FNs. In Table 2, we briefly compare traditional GT with EGT.

EGT has been developed as a mathematical framework to study the interaction among rational biological agents in a population. In evolutionary games, the agent revolves the chosen strategy based on its payoff. In this way, both static and

Table 1. Payoff matrix of prisoner's dilemma

		Prisoner B	
		Cooperate (Silent)	Defect (Betray)
Prisoner A	Cooperate (Silent)	1, 1	3, free
	Defect (Betray)	free, 3	2, 2

Table 2. Comparison between traditional GT and EGT

Game Characteristic	Traditional GT	EGT
Pure strategies	Yes	No
Strategy adaption over time	No	Yes
Hyper rational behavior	Yes	No
Equilibria is always possible	No (in some particular scenarios due to restrictions on the strategy options)	Yes (i.e. at least it discovers an asymptotic equilibrium due to unrestricted strategy options space)
Model dynamic and high complex game	No	Yes

dynamic behavior of the game can be analyzed (Han, 2012). In this way, on one hand, evolutionary stable strategies (ESS) are used to study a static evolutionary game. On the other hand, replicator dynamics is used to study a dynamic evolutionary game.

EGT usually considers a set of players that interact within a game and then die, giving birth to a new player generation that fully inherits its ancestor's knowledge. The new player strategy is evaluated against the one of its ancestors and its current environmental context. Also, through mutation, a slightly distinct strategy may be selected by a set of players belonging to a specific generation, probably offering better payoffs. Next, each player competes with the other players within the evolutionary game using a strategy that increases its payoff. In this way, strategies with high payoffs will survive inside the system as more players will tend to choose them, while weak strategies will eventually disappear. Following, we present a tutorial in how EGT can be applied to wireless networks (Zhang, 2011).

Formally, we should consider within an evolutionary game an infinite population of individuals that react to changes of their environmental surroundings using a finite set of n pure strategies S $= \{s_1, s_2, ..., s_n\}$. There is also a population profile, i.e. x $= \{x_1, x_2, ..., x_n\}$, which denotes the popularity of each strategy $s_i \in S$ among the individuals. This means that x_i is the probability that a strategy s_i is played by the individuals. By this reason, x is also designated by the set of mixed strategies.

Consider an individual in a population with profile x. Its expected payoff when choosing to play strategy s_i is given by f (s_i, x). In a two-player game, if an individual chooses strategy s_i and its opponent responds with strategy s_j, the payoff of the former player is given by f (s_i, s_j). In a more generic way, the expected payoff of strategy s_i is evaluated by (1), whereas the average payoff is given by (2).

The replicator dynamics is a differential equation that describes the dynamics of an evolutionary game without mutation (Zhang, 2011) (Taylor,

1978). According to this differential equation, the rate of growth of a specific strategy is proportional to the difference between the expected payoff of that strategy and the overall average payoff of the population, as stated in (3). Using this equation, if a strategy has a much better payoff than the average, the number of individuals from the population that tend to choose it increases. On the contrary, a strategy with a lower payoff than the average is preferred less and eventually is eliminated from the system set of strategies.

Considering now the mutation issue, suppose that a small group of mutants $m \in [0,1]$ with a profile $x' \neq x$ invades the previous population. The profile of the newly formed population is given by (4). Hence, the average payoff of non-mutants will be given by (5) and the average payoff of mutants will be given by (6). In this context, a strategy x is called evolutionary stable strategy (ESS) if for any $x' \neq x$, $m_{mut} \in [0,1]$ exists such that for all $m \in [0, m_{mut}]$, then Equation (7) holds true. In this way, when an ESS is reached, the population is immune from being invaded by other groups with different population profiles. By other words, in this context the population is not affected by mutation issues.

$$f_i = \sum_{j=1}^{n} x_j \cdot f\left(s_i, s_j\right) \tag{1}$$

$$f_x = \sum_{i=1}^{n} x_i \cdot f_i \tag{2}$$

$$\dot{x} = x_i \cdot \left(f_i - f_x\right) \tag{3}$$

$$x_{final} = m.x' + \left(1 - m\right).x \tag{4}$$

$$f_{x_{final}}^{non-mutant} = f\left(x, x_{final}\right)$$
$$= \sum_{j=1}^{n} x_j \cdot f\left(j, x_{final}\right) \tag{5}$$

$$f_{x_{final}}^{mutant} = f\left(x', x_{final}\right)$$
$$= \sum_{j=1}^{n} x_j' \cdot f\left(j, x_{final}\right) \tag{6}$$

$$f_{x_{final}}^{non-mutant} > f_{x_{final}}^{mutant} \qquad (7)$$

EGT may be successfully applied to model a variety of network problems. The authors of (Zhang, 2011) review the literature concerning the applications of EGT to distinct network types such as wireless sensor networks, delay tolerant networks, peer-to-peer networks and wireless networks in general, including heterogeneous 4G networks and cloud environments. In addition, (Han, 2012) discusses selected applications of EGT in wireless communications and networking, including congestion control, contention-based (i.e. Aloha) protocol adaptation, power control in CDMA, routing, cooperative sensing in cognitive radio, TCP throughput adaptation, and service-provider network selection. By service-provider network selection, (Han, 2012) suggests EGT to study different scenarios:

- User churning behavior that impacts the revenue of service providers;
- User choice among candidate service providers of the access network that maximizes the perceived QoS for a particular service type.

In (Nazir, 2010), an evolutionary game based on replicator dynamics is formulated to model the dynamic competition in network selection among users. Each user can choose a particular service class from a certain service provider (i.e. available access network). They present two algorithms, namely, population evolution and reinforcement-learning for network selection. Although the network-selection algorithm based on population evolution can reach the evolutionary equilibrium faster, it requires a centralized controller to gather, process, and broadcast information about the users within the corresponding service area. In contrast, with reinforcement learning, a user can gradually learn (by interacting with the service provider) and adapt the decision on network selection (through a trial-and-error learning method)

to reach evolutionary equilibrium without any interaction with other users.

Some work (Nazir, 2010) (Bennis, 2011) investigated and compared the convergence behavior of Q-learning with EGT to enable a satisfactory performance of cellular networks with femtocells. The authors of (Nazir, 2010) introduce two mechanisms for interference mitigation supported by EGT and machine learning. In the first mechanism, stand-alone femtocells choose their strategies, observe the behavior of other players, and make the best decision based on their instantaneous payoff, as well as the average payoff of all other femtocells. They also formulate the interactions among selfish femtocells using evolutionary games and demonstrate how the system converges to equilibrium. By contrast, using the second mechanism (i.e. reinforcement learning), the information exchange among femtocells is no longer possible and hence each femtocell adapts its strategy and gradually learns by interacting with its environment (i.e., neighboring interferers). The femtocells can self-organize by relying only on local information, while mitigating interference inside the macrocell. In this way, the macrocell user can meet its Quality of Service requirements. They reach the final conclusion that the biologically-inspired evolutionary approach converges more rapidly to the desired equilibrium as compared to the reinforcement learning and random approach. Nevertheless, this faster convergence requires more context information at the femtocells. The authors of (Bennis, 2011) reached equivalent results as (Nazir, 2010).

Further references that address EGT applications to the networking area are available for wireless (Khan, 2012a) and wireline (Altman, 2009) networks.

Mechanism Design

There is a subfield of GT designated by Mechanism Design (MD) that allows a game designer to define initially the desired outcome and then specify the game rules to achieve that outcome (Han, 2012, 221-252). This is the opposite of game analysis, in which the game rules are predefined and then the outcome is investigated, as shown in Figure 1. That is why MD is also designated as reverse GT.

A very important result in MD is the Revelation Principle that states for any Bayesian Nash Equilibrium is associated a Bayesian game with the same equilibrium outcome but in which players truthfully report their choices (it could be a preference list), which simplifies the game analysis, eliminating the need to consider either strategic behavior or lying. So, no matter what the mechanism, a designer can confine attention to equilibrium in which players only report truthfully. To accomplish this, the model needs to consider incentives for players to truthfully cooperate among them, optimizing the game outcome.

3. BACKGROUND AND TRENDS IN FUTURE NETWORKS

According to the Cisco Global Forecast (Cisco, 2013), during 2012, more than 50 percent of the total mobile traffic was video, average smartphone usage grew 81 percent and, globally 33 percent of the total mobile data traffic was offloaded onto the fixed network through Wifi or femtocells. This traffic offloading occurs due to the lack of capacity in the mobile network infrastructure,

originally dimensioned to support only voice and messages. The traffic offloading is one possible solution to mitigate congestion, avoiding the loss on the perceived quality by users' applications.

However, the first approach to the problem has been to perform an inter-technology handover between available technologies, with all the traffic routed through the most convenient access technology. A survey about mobility is available in (Fernandes, 2012). In our opinion, a better usage of available resources on the network-edge with a more fine-grained traffic management based on flows (e.g., Web traffic, VoIP) should alleviate the negative impact of network congestion, which has been reported very often essentially in the mobile broadband access. Multi-interface handheld terminals will soon have the battery autonomy and the capability to perform network access using simultaneous multi-radio access technologies (RAT). In addition, of particular interest is the support of simultaneous data/multimedia flows through different access systems (LTE-A, WLAN, Wimax). Recent works (Yap, 2013; Silva, 2013) propose that mobile multimode terminal should use all the available connectivity options simultaneously. The mobile terminal should choose dynamically the most suitable network to each flow, obtaining faster connections by stitching flows over multiple networks, decrease the usage cost by choosing the most cost-effective network that meets application requisites, and reduce the energy consumption by selecting the technologies with the lowest energy-usage per byte.

This concept for FNs contributes to the perspective of integrating complementary access technologies with overlapping coverage to provide the expected ubiquitous coverage and to achieve the Always Best Connected (ABC) concept (Louta, 2011). This concept allows a flow to use at any time the most suitable access network/Network Attachment Point (NAP). This management of flows should be done in a distributed way with low complexity and reliable algorithms/protocols in networks formed by heterogeneous access

Figure 1. Game Theory (GT) vs. Mechanism Design (MD)

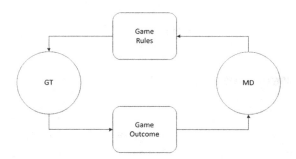

technologies, where the most part of involved nodes should cooperate. Network brokers such as in (Moura, 2012) follow on this idea. Brokerage systems, possibly implementing GT algorithms, can manage the network architecture, in which distributed nodes discover relevant context information to enhance the usage of local available connectivity resources (Mateus, 2010). In this way, mobile operators can develop policies for IP flow mobility, and control which traffic is routed over different access technologies.

Another aspect to consider is that the Internet was initially designed to support communications between remote hosts. Since its early days the Internet has evolved drastically, with a huge evolution in broadband access penetration and dissemination of mobile terminals with unforeseen capacities. This evolution has altered the Internet into a medium to connect people in multiple ways with content made available in completely new and complex modes through the entire network infrastructure. In fact, current users are more interested in searching for information over Google, watch videos on YouTube, and share files via Dropbox than to worry about connectivity to a particular host.

This content demand has catalyzed an exponential growth of Internet traffic volume and content distribution is increasingly becoming more centric in the Internet, and this is challenging and changing how the Internet is being organized.

Content delivery network (CDN) operators, content providers as well as ISPs are important players to consider in more content centric FNs. But todays these players interact with a mix of technologies that are difficult to manage in a comprehensive and global ways.

Research efforts have been made to move the Internet away from its current reliance on purely point-to-point primitives and, to this end, have proposed detailed designs that make the Internet more data-oriented or content-centric. As such Information-centric networking has emerged as a new approach in the research community (Gritter, 2000; Ahlgren, 2012) to integrate content delivery as a native network feature and make networks natively content-aware.

Due to this, FNs most probably will sustain the next generation of the Internet infrastructure, interconnecting people and content through mobile cloud networks (as said before, the Internet is evolving from a node discovery to enable the discovery of specialized objects). These cloud networks will operate on an always best connected scenario, where a person is allowed to choose the best available access technology (from small cells to standard base stations), access network and terminal device at any point in time. Generally, the idea is to enhance FNs to automatically interpret, process, and move content (information) independently of users' location.

Of course that this scheme to operate in a satisfactory way, a great number of very demanding requirements has to be fulfilled, not only technical ones (e.g. autonomic self-x requisites with cognitive radios like self-learning) but also in terms of business relationships among operators and service providers, as well as, the handling of the service subscription.

The course of finding a solution that can satisfy all the involved entities in the high complex network environment of FNs, like content providers, cloud providers, home providers, brokers, network providers or users, can be found by means of GT. In this way, as the players define their strategies then the GT can find ways to build-up win-win situations for all of them. Cooperation between technologies and/or providers, alongside Machine to Machine (M2M) communications or Internet of Things deployment will require complex and dynamic management algorithms to maximize network efficiency, pricing, Quality of Service (QoS), Quality of Experience (QoE) and ultimately, profit.

Considering all previous facets, we foresee that FNs will have to form a network infrastructure with a collective intelligence, as shown in Figure 2. This intelligence is very pertinent in FNs to address emergent traffic requisites, the management complexity of the heterogeneous wireless access

Figure 2. Collective Intelligence in FNs to manage emergent traffic and functional requisites

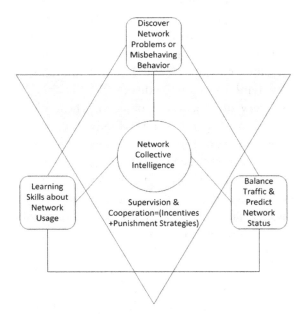

technologies, and the challenges faced by a more content and data centric network.

To enhance the network intelligence, the future network infrastructure needs to be supervised in order to enable learning processes on management algorithms when these control some network problems (e.g. congestion situation, node misbehaving behavior). In this way, the network intelligence will be enhanced, enabling the network infrastructure to manage the high complex future heterogeneous access infrastructure in a much more efficient way. As an example, the load could be balanced among the diverse wireless access technologies, reacting to a detected congestion situation in order to mitigate its negative effects. Alternatively, the load could be also balanced in a flash crowd scenario where a network problem is predicted and some policies are applied to the network to avoid the occurrence of that problem, e.g. offloading flows from the technology that soon could become disrupted to other available technologies with low levels of traffic load. In addition, congestion situations could be controlled

by limiting the transmission rate of some users and freeing network resources to others. The one billion dollar question that remains to be answered is to find out the more efficient levels of aggressiveness of the algorithm that dynamically increases/decreases the rate transmission in a high complex networking scenario with diverse wireless access technologies and flow requirements.

To enable the network collective intelligence, we argue that it is important to obtain cooperation among the nodes. In this way, the network nodes need to be incentivized to cooperate, and the nodes that do not cooperate should be detected in a truthful way and be gradually penalized (e.g. their access rate is diminished). Eventually, uncooperative nodes that afterwards would change to a cooperative behavior, they could have their reputation values being restored to values that allow them to use again the network resources without any restriction on their access rate.

In practical terms, the FNs should require distributed management algorithms to support the network self-configuring feature. GT seems a very important area to model, analyze and decide how these distributed algorithms need to be deployed.

4. GAME THEORY CONTRIBUTIONS FOR ENHANCING NETWORK COOPERATION

FNs will be demanding for the deployment of novel management solutions aiming more efficiently and fairly usage of the available network resources. In order to accomplish the overall network goals, the nodes should collaborate or cooperate essentially in a multi-hop network topology, the typical scenario of future heterogeneous and high-complexity networks. For example, a terminal node should process both related and non-related traffic, whereas non-related classifies traffic not originated (not destined) from (to) that node. This new collaborative functionality will become possible at the physical layer in future multi-hop wireless networks because the network edge infrastructure will be vastly deployed by radio technologies, which allow the easy share of data messages among local terminals due to their broadcast transmission characteristic.

A very significant number of researchers have proposed GT models to encourage players (terminals and networks) to cooperate and enhance the overall network performance instead for acting selfishly to optimize their own performance. In this way, some additional incentives are required in FNs to enable collaboration among the nodes, defeating eventual misbehaving nodes like selfish or malicious ones. A selfish node may refuse to forward a non-related message in order to save its battery. In this way, this node needs a correct incentive to forward traffic, e.g. the network could increase the throughput of flows originated (destined) from (to) that node as a reward to previous collaboration in forwarding non-related traffic. Alternatively, a malicious node may try to disrupt the network functionality; in this case, the network could isolate that node from the network for a certain period as a punishment to that wrong procedure.

Broadly discussing, the right incentives to the nodes collaborate among them can be divided in two large groups: monetary-based and reputation-based. On one hand, the monetary-based solutions typically aim to achieve short/medium-term

relationships among nodes. On the other hand, the reputation-based solutions typically aim to establish long-term relationships among nodes. This section will be highlighting some relevant work from these two groups (Charilas, 2011), which is summarized in Figure 3.

The first group of contributions makes use of virtual payments for channel use and to incentive the collaboration among nodes in a multi-hop wireless network topology, as shown in Figure 4. Here, there are typically three types of nodes: the senders, the forwarders (intermediates) and the destination nodes. Some proposed credit-based systems suggest that distinct node types should be charged to cover the costs for packet forwarding. In fact, some proposals suggest that only the senders should be charged with a tariff initially specified (Zhong, 2003) (Buttyán, 2000) (Buttyán, 2003) (Ileri, 2005) (Shastry, 2006) (Chen, 2005) (Alpcan, 2002) (Saraydar, 2002) (Vassaki, 2009). Alternatively, the destination nodes are charged (Buttyán, 2000) (Liu, 2006) or destination and senders are both charged (Buttyán, 2001) (Zhang, 2004). In addition, an incentive mechanism called bandwidth exchange was proposed in (Zhang, 2008), where a node can delegate a portion of its bandwidth to another node in exchange for relay cooperation. Finally, a different approach of credit-based schemes appear in (Chen, 2004) (Demir, 2007), where auction-based incentive models are

Figure 3. Summary of game theory work supporting cooperation incentives

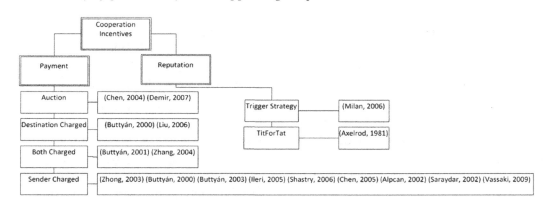

Figure 4. Credit-based incentive mechanism

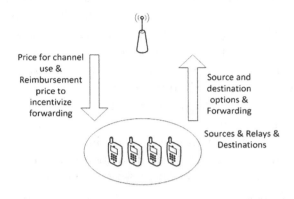

Price for channel use & Reimbursement price to incentivize forwarding

Source and destination options & Forwarding

Sources & Relays & Destinations

proposed. The basic idea of these schemes is that each intermediate node operates as a market; the users of the network put bids for their packets, the packets are accordingly scheduled to transmission and then charged after their transmission. The goals to achieve with auction models could be node truthful bidding and social network welfare maximization (Chen, 2004) or balancing residual battery energy and the current currency (credit) levels of the nodes in the network (Demir, 2007).

The main advantage of credit-based approaches is that they succeed in large scale networks to enforce a distributed cooperation mechanism among selfish nodes. Moreover, credits are useful when an action and its reward are not simultaneous. This is valid for multi-hop wireless networks: the action is packet forwarding and the reward is being possible later on to send their own packets. These approaches could be useful to discover the more convenient routing policies, solving very challenging dilemmas in multi-hop networks. For example, these approaches could help to choose the cheapest route between a source and a destination node either by minimizing the total number of hops (to minimize the end-to-end flow delay) or by choosing the less-congested hops (to increase the end-to-end flow data rate). The drawbacks of credit-based proposals are additional overhead and complexity to charge users fairly and avoid cheating, turning these proposals hard to deploy (Charilas, 2011).

In FNs, customers can be billed using a congestion-sensitive tariff, where prices are set in real time according to current load and taking full advantage of demand elasticity to maximize efficiency and fairness (Saraydar, 2002). The demand elasticity utilizes historical information about expected peak load periods. According to (Felegyhazi, 2006), an investigation area where pricing has practical relevance is service provisioning among operators (e.g., renting transmission capacity).

The second group of contributions makes use of reputation-based proposals (Trestian, 2011) to incentivize the collaboration among nodes in a multi-hop wireless network topology. The reputation metric is defined as the amount of trust inspired by a particular member (node) on the network community. Figure 5 illustrates the diverse typical phases of a reputation system to incentivize a correct behavior in the network nodes.

During the initial phase, the reputation information of each node is collected to a central node connected to the wired network. After receiving the new reputation information, the central node updates a reputation matrix, which stores the reputation information from all the nodes (second phase). Then, in the next phase, management decisions are selected, which, during the fourth and last phase, are applied to the network infrastructure. In this way, as an example, members that have good reputation, because they helpfully contribute to the community welfare, are able to use the network resources; while nodes with a bad reputation, because they usually refuse to cooperate, are excluded from that community.

The most accepted game-theoretic approach for reputation analysis is the repeated game (Aberer, 2004) because in this context it does not make sense that a game for reputation is based uniquely in its current (instantaneous) value; in fact, the reputation should be also evaluated through a historical term, normally with a higher weight than the one associated with the instantaneous value of reputation. In this way, it is possible to avoid

Figure 5. Reputation-based incentive mechanism

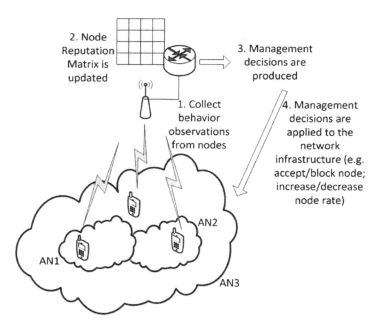

false misbehavior detections due to temporary link communications failures. In addition, the uncertainty about the information that is available to other players and their decisions is normally modeled with Bayesian Game or Game with Incomplete Information (Harsanyi, 1967). Finally, to correctly model the robustness to changes on the behavior of the participants, auction games are normally preferred (Nurmi, 2006).

There are at least two different strategies on how the reputation could incentivize cooperation among nodes (or players). One of the ways is to develop a strategy such that the cooperation of a node is measured and if the fraction of packets it has dropped is above a threshold, it is considered selfish and is disconnected for a given amount of time. This strategy is known as a Trigger Strategy (Milan, 2006). An alternative way is designated by Tit For Tat (TFT) (Axelrod, 1981). A player using this strategy will cooperate initially and then act regarding the opponent´s previous action: if the opponent previously was cooperative then the former player will be cooperative as well; otherwise, the former player will not cooperate.

To illustrate the advantages of the TFT strategy being used by game players, a Finite Repeated Prisoner's Dilemma Game was simulated via Matlab (5000 iterations). The game is between two players. Each player tries to score the most number of points against each opponent player during each game. In this case, the player Operator1 can choose in each game's iteration between 'cooperate' or 'defect', like player Operator2. In each game's iteration, points are then awarded to both players based on the combination of their choices, following what is shown in Table 3.

The maximum number of points a player can win during a game's iteration is five. This maximum score only occurs if that player defects and

Table 3. Points awarded to each player based on individual player's choices

		Operator2	
		Cooperate	Defect
Operator1	Cooperate	3, 3	0, 5
	Defect	5, 0	1, 1

the opponent cooperates. Nevertheless, the former player scores one point instead five points if both players defect. As one can easily conclude, the main difficulty imposed to each player of the current game is to choose the option that maximizes his reward because he ignores the opponent's choice, as both players, during a game's iteration, perform their choices simultaneously. The previous difficulty in a player choosing the right option to maximize the reward points won by that player is perfectly evident from the simulation results presented in Figure 6. In fact, the random strategy used by each player to make a choice gives the worst performance. In opposition, TFT strategy shows a better performance.

In spite of the good performance of TFT, it could reveal some drawbacks in a wireless scenario. As an example, TFT does not distinguish uncooperative behavior from a transmission failure due to a collision. In this way, TFT could penalize a collaborative player that had the bad luck of suffering a collision during a data transmission tentative. Consequently, a few TFT variants have been proposed (Milan, 2006) (Jaramillo, 2007) to correct that problem.

For a multi-hop wireless network, there is an interesting tradeoff between the amount of available information to evaluate a node´s behavior (reputation) and the protocol overhead/complexity used to disseminate the necessary information through the network. Some proposals are more concerned with all the nodes having access to the full information about node behavior (Buchegger, 2002) (Mundinger, 2005) (He, 2004) to enhance the accuracy on how the reputation is evaluated. These proposals could have problems related with fake information disseminated among the nodes that create wrong reputation values. To avoid these problems, the protocol used to disseminate the reputation values through the network must be enriched with additional authentication and trust functional features. Alternatively, to keep the protocol overhead low, each node should only disseminate the reputation values he directly measured to its neighbors (it only uses first-hand reputation changes) (Bansal, 2003).

Recent work proposed dynamic reputation-based incentives for cooperative relays present in a network topology formed by heterogeneous networks (Hwang, 2008) (Skraparlis, 2009). The

Figure 6. Outcomes of a finite repeated prisoner's dilemma game using two distinct strategies

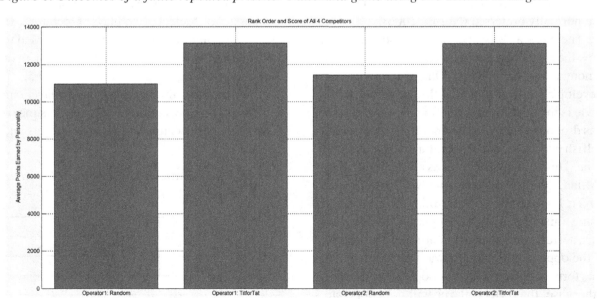

incentive for cooperation among nodes can be given either by additional throughput (Hwang, 2008) or by additional time-slots for transmission (Skraparlis, 2009).

Regarding strategies for penalizing misbehaving users, the research community has proposed several ways to perform it: isolate misbehaving users from the network (Buchegger, 2002), reduce misbehaving users' bandwidth (Hwang, 2008) or reduce the transmission slots of misbehaving users (Skraparlis, 2009).

The main advantage of reputation-based proposals is that they rely on observations from multiple sources, turning it relatively resistant to the diffusion of false information from a small number of lying nodes. Some potential problems are the usage of additional bandwidth and battery energy to intensively monitor the behavior of each network node. In addition, some nodes could collude to cheat the reputation of other nodes by the dissemination of false information through the network about the latter nodes to the former nodes increase their benefits (Charilas, 2011).

The development of more suitable and fair schemes to incentivize cooperation in FNs is a challenging research direction. According to the authors of (Han, 2012) hybrid schemes that combine both reputation and credit aspects are of particular interest to be further investigated. Lastly, by defining mechanisms of incentives for cooperation and disincentives against cheating or selfish behavior, and applying repeatedly both of these mechanisms, the cooperation among the players apparently becomes stronger in a distributed way without the need to sign a contract among the players (Trestian, 2011).

5. GAME THEORY FOR WIRELESS NETWORKING

In this section, we revise the literature in terms of how GT can be successfully applied to wireless communications and networking areas. (Mackenzie, 2006) describes ways in which GT

can be applied to real applications in wireless communications and networking, such as: pricing, flow control, power control, medium access and interference avoidance. They also pointed out some appealing future applications of GT: cognitive networks and learning, mobility support and cooperation in wireless networks. (Zhang, 2011) explores applications of different economic approaches, including bargaining, auctions, cooperation incentives and dynamic coalition games for cooperation. (Han, 2012) discusses game-theoretic models in a wide range of wireless and communication applications such as cellular and broadband wireless access networks, wireless local area networks, multi-hop networks, cooperative networks, cognitive-radio networks, and Internet networks. In addition, some relevant Internet problems such as, congestion control, pricing, revenue sharing among Internet service providers, and incentive mechanisms to enable cooperation into peer-to-peer applications, are also discussed.

(Huang, 2010) presents several GT models/ concepts that are highly relevant for spectrum sharing, including iterative water-filling, potential game, supermodular game, bargaining, auction, and correlated equilibrium. (Huang, In Press) outlines a taxonomy to systematically understand and tackle the issue of economic viability of cooperation in dynamic spectrum management. The framework divides the problem space according to four orthogonal dimensions, including complete/incomplete network information, loose/ tight decision couplings, user/operator interactions, and static/dynamic decision processes. The vast majority of the key methodologies for each dimension involve GT. (Saad, 2011) reviews coalitional GT for cooperative cellular wireless networks. (Marina, 2011) revises GT work about malicious behavior.

From the literature a significant number of surveys have been found about GT application in wireless communications and networking, as summarized in Figure 7. These surveys cover the following areas: wireless networks (Charilas, 2010) (Akkarajitsakul, 2011) (Ghazvini, 2013)

Figure 7. Summary of Game Theory surveys

(Niyato, 2007) (Trestian, 2011) (Larsson, 2009) (Khan, 2012a), wireless Ad Hoc networks (Srivastava, 2005), wireless sensor networks (WSNs) (Machado, 2008) (Shen, 2011) (Shi, 2012), MIMO systems (Scutari, 2008), cognitive radio networks (Wang, 2010) (Wang, 2011), 4G networks (Khan, 2012b), smart grids (Fadlullah, 2011) (Saad, 2012), and telecommunications (Altman, 2006).

Covering the area of wireless networks where GT is applied, we can explicit the following surveys: a significant number of GT proposals are discussed in a network-layered perspective (Charilas, 2010); multiple access games are analyzed in (Akkarajitsakul, 2011); games of random access with Carrier Sense Multiple Access (CSMA) are covered in (Ghazvini, 2013); games about resource management and admission control are addressed by (Niyato, 2007); games for network selection and resource allocation are available in (Trestian, 2011); games of spectrum allocation, power control, interference are covered in (Larsson, 2009); and finally, evolutionary coalitional games for wireless networking and communications are available in (Khan, 2012a).

Since the application of GT to enhance cooperation in FNs, formed by heterogeneous wireless access networks, is the main focus of the present chapter, we particularize now some surveys related to Wireless Sensor Networks (WSNs), cognitive radio networks and 4G networks. (Machado, 2008) reviewed the literature about the usage of game-theoretic approaches to address problems related to security and energy efficiency in WSNs. (Shen, 2011) main concern was to revise GT approaches towards the enhancement of WSN security. Finally, (Shi, 2012) offered a more comprehensive survey than previous referred ones about GT applied to WSNs.

The games for cognitive radio networks are classified by (Wang, 2010) into four categories: non-cooperative spectrum sharing, spectrum trading and mechanism design, cooperative spectrum sharing, and stochastic spectrum sharing games. For each category, they explained the fundamental concepts and properties, and provided a detailed discussion about the methodologies on how to apply these games in spectrum sharing protocol design. They also discussed some research challenges and future research directions related to game theoretic modeling in cognitive radio networks.

Cognitive attackers may exist in a cognitive radio network, who can adapt their attacking strategy to the time-varying spectrum opportunities and secondary users' strategy. To alleviate the damage caused by cognitive attackers, a dynamic security mechanism is investigated in (Wang, 2011) by a stochastic game modeling. The state of the anti-jamming game includes the spectrum availability, channel quality, and the status of jammed channels observed at the current time slot. The action of the secondary users reflects how many channels they should reserve for transmitting control and data messages and how to switch between the different channels. Since the secondary users and attackers have opposite goals, the antijamming game can be classified as a zero-sum game.

The authors of (Khan, 2012b) study game dynamics and learning schemes for heterogeneous 4G networks. They propose a novel learning scheme called cost-to-learn that incorporates the cost to switch, the switching delay, and the cost of changing to a new action. Considering a dynamic and uncertain environment, where the users and operators have only a numerical value of their own payoffs as information, and strategy reinforcement learning (CODIPAS-RL) is used, they show the users are able to learn their own optimal payoff and their optimal strategy simultaneously. Using evolutionary game dynamics, they prove the convergence and stability properties in specific classes of dynamic robust games. They also provide various numerical and simulation results in the context of network selection in wireless local area networks (WLAN) and Long Term Evolution (LTE). In addition, a very recent work (Silva, In Press) clearly shows the main advantages of cooperation among wireless access technologies. The following sections justify why the collaboration aspect should be very important in FNs and how GT can help to study the best ways to deploy this new functionality in a distributed way.

6. GUIDELINES TO APPLY GAME THEORY ON FUTURE NETWORKS

The current section discusses some relevant research work in how GT can be used to address the more significant operational or functional expected aspects of Future Network (FN) environments. The most-part of the discussed scenarios belongs to the network edge of Internet. More specifically, these scenarios are concerned in how the heterogeneous wireless access infrastructure can be efficiently used by multimode terminals, as well as, to guarantee a reliable access to the Internet through wireless backhaul links. In this way, several possible functional/operational enhancements are envisioned to use efficiently the heterogeneous wireless access infrastructure in the following topics: network planning, multi-technology wireless networks, network management, Internet of Things (multi-hop reliable networks) and reliable wireless backhaul. All of these should be hot research areas in FNs and are summarized in Table 4 together with references for relevant work that should be initially studied in order to find innovative ways to plan, control, manage and operate FNs.

Table 4. Relevant FN topics/areas where GT can be successfully applied

Topic/Area	Scenario/Game Type	Reference
Network Planning	Stackelberg game to control power transmission in a network formed by macrocells and femtocells	(Guruacharya, 2010
Multi-Technology Wireless Networks	Bayesian game to study vertical-handovers in which the users have distinct bandwidth requirements	(Kun, 2010)
Network Management	Evolutionary game to study rate selection for VoIP service; non-zero sum game for studying user admission control to avoid congestion	(Watanabe, 2008) (Kuo, 2004)
Internet of Things (Multi-Hop Reliable Networks)	Hop price-based routing game; auction theory to support truthfulness and security;	(Liu, 2006) (Anderegg, 2003 & Eidenbez, 2008)
Reliable Wireless Backhaul	Evolutionary game to study traffic routing through multi-hop wireless backhaul links	(Anastasopoulos, 2008)

Network Planning

Imperfect network coverage, especially in indoor locations is an important problem in existing cellular networks. To overcome this problem, the concept of Femtocell Access Points (FAPs) has recently been proposed as a means to overlay, on existing mobile networks, low-power and low-cost Base Stations (BSs). FAPs are connected by an IP backhaul through a local broadband connection such as DSL, cable or fiber.

Notably, various benefits of using FAP technology have been already identified:

- Enhances indoor coverage
- Provides high data rates
- Improves Quality-of-Service (QoS) to subscribers
- Ensures longer battery life for handheld terminals
- Offloads traffic from the mobile operator's backhaul to the wired residential broadband connection, reducing the backhaul cost of the mobile operator.

When FAPs are deployed on top of an existing cellular system, and since FAPs operate on the same frequency bands as macrocell BSs, a new problem arises. This problem is related with the interference among channels that can impair the overall network performance. In such a network scenario, it is of interest to study the problem of transmit-power control in the downlink, minimizing the interference problem and ensuring an acceptable network performance.

In this section, we adopt the approach of (Guruacharya, 2010), also thoroughly discussed in (Han, 2012), for studying the transmit-power control in the downlink from a game-theory perspective. First, we model the scenario as a Stackelberg game. Then, we discuss the properties of the considered game and its solution. Finally, we present a low-complexity algorithm to reach the desired outcome (Han, 2012).

Stackelberg Game to Control Transmission Power

In order to tackle the power-control problem using GT, a framework of a Stackelberg game has been used (Han, 2012). In the studied femtocell deployment model, it is considered that the macrocell BSs are the leaders and the FAPs are the followers in a Stackelberg game, as summarized in Table 5. In this multi-leader multi-follower Stackelberg game, there exists a competitive game among the leaders and a competitive game among the followers. The Stackelberg game keeps a distinct hierarchy among leaders and followers such that the leaders can anticipate, and take this into consideration, the behavior of the followers (the reciprocal is not true), before making their own decisions to maximize their data rate.

It was considered a Stackelberg game with complete and perfect information. As already mentioned, the leaders are the set of macrocell BS transceivers M, the followers are the set of FAPs N. Therefore, the total set of players in this game is $M \cup N$. The strategy space of the leaders is given by $P^{up} = \Pi_{i \in M} P_i$, and any point in P^{up} is called a leader strategy. Let P_i denote the set of all feasible power vectors of transmitter i. The leaders compete with each other in a non-cooperative way to maximize their individual data rate,

Table 5. Summary of relevant characteristics of Femtocell deployment game (Guruacharya, 2010)

Scenario	Game Type	Player	Player's Strategy	Payoff
Femtocell deployment	Stackelberg with complete and perfect information to control power	Base-stations (leaders)/ femtocell access points (followers)	Choose the maximum transmission power constrained by power constraints	Maximize Shannon data rate that each player can achieve

while always anticipating the strategic responses of the followers. This game among the leaders is referred as the upper subgame, and its equilibrium is referred as the upper subgame equilibrium. After the leaders apply their strategies, the followers make their moves in response to the leaders' strategies.

The strategy space of the followers is $P^{low} = \Pi_{i \in M} P_i$, and any point in P^{low} is called a follower strategy. The followers also compete with each other in a non-cooperative way to maximize their own data rate, and this competition among the followers is referred as the lower subgame. It is expected this game could offer an equilibrium state designated by the lower subgame equilibrium.

For any user $i \in \{M \bigcup N\}$, it is defined the best-response function as shown in (8).

$$p_i = argmax_{p_i} C_i\left(p_i, p_{-i}\right) = b_i\left(p_{-i}, \overline{p}_i, \overline{m}_i\right) \tag{8}$$

where the notation $-i$ refers to all of the users in the set $\{M\ U\ N\}$ except user i; $\overline{p}_i$ is the total power constraint; $\overline{m}_i$ is the individual power constraint, where $\overline{m}_i$ is chosen so as to maximize user i's capacity function subject to the power constraints. C_i is the maximal data rate that user i can achieve from the channel.

Lower Subgame Equilibrium

It is defined the lower subgame equilibrium as any fixed point $p^{low*} = (p_1^*, \dots p_N^*) \in P^{low}$ such that expression in (9) is satisfied.

$$p_i^* = b_i(p_{-i}^*, p^{up}, \overline{p}_i, \overline{m}_i) \tag{9}$$

where $p^{up} \in P^{up}$ is a fixed but arbitrary leader strategy for all the $i \in N$. Note that this definition is the same as a Nash Equilibrium (NE) of the lower subgame.

Following (Han, 2012), since every user participating in the lower subgame will maximize in a myopic way their individual data rate, the best response $b_i(.)$ of each user in the subgame can be given by the following water-filling game function (Lai, 2008), as shown in (10).

$$p_i = F\left(p_{-i}, \overline{p}_i, \overline{m}_i\right) = w_i\left(A_i\right)v_i + r_i\left(A_i, S_i\right) \tag{10}$$

where $W_i(A_i)$ is an $L_i \times L_i$ symmetric matrix which contents is explained in more detail in (Han, 2012); $r_i(A_i, S_i)$ is an L_i-dimensional column vector detailed in (Han, 2012).

The main goal of a water-filling game is to identify a set of resource allocation strategies distributed among rational and selfish users (i.e. not interested in the overall system performance), who are interested in maximizing the utilities they obtain from the network (Lai, 2008).

By letting $b^{low} \equiv (b_i(.))^N_{i=1}$, it is possible to express the lower subgame equilibrium as any fixed point of the system-power space $p* \in P$ such that $p* = b^{low}(p*)$.

Note that the function $b^{low}(.)$ does not impact the upper subgame strategy.

Upper Subgame Equilibrium

It is defined the upper subgame equilibrium as any fixed point $p^{up*} = (p_1^*, \dots, p_M^*) \in P^{up}$ such that the expression in (11) is satisfied.

$$p_i^* = b_i\left(p_{-i}^*, p^{low*}, \overline{p}_i, \overline{m}_i\right) \tag{11}$$

where $p^{low*} \in P^{low}$ is an equilibrium follower strategy conditioned on the upper subgame strategy, for all $i \in M$.

Equivalently, let $b^{up} \equiv (b_i(.))^M_{i=1}$; then the upper subgame equilibrium as the fixed point $p^{up*} \in P^{up}$ such that (12) is a valid expression.

$$p^{up*} = b^{up}\left(p^{up*}, b^{low}\left(p^{low*}, p^{up*}\right)\right) \qquad (12)$$

For convenience, the notation can be further simplified by writing the upper subgame equilibrium in terms of a system-power vector, i.e. as any fixed point $p* \in P$ such that (13) is true.

$$p^* = b^{up}\left(b^{low}\left(p^*\right)\right) \qquad (13)$$

Note that although the function $b^{up}(.)$ acts only on the upper subgame strategy, the lower subgame equilibrium strategy (the reaction of the followers) associated with each upper subgame strategy needs to be computed as well, since the leaders compute their strategies given their knowledge of what the followers might play.

Multi-Leader Multi-Follower Stackelberg Equilibrium

A suitable solution for the formulated hierarchical game between the base stations and the FAPs is the Stackelberg equilibrium. In such a multi-leader multi-follower game, the Stackelberg equilibrium is defined as any fixed-point $(p^{up*}, p^{low*}) = p* \in P$ that satisfies both conditions as shown in (14).

$$\begin{cases} p^* = b^{low}\left(p^*\right) \\ p^* = b^{up}\left(b^{low}\left(p^*\right)\right) \end{cases} \qquad (14)$$

Algorithm for Reaching the Stackelberg Equilibrium

Finding, iteratively, the fixed point of the lower subgame using the water-filling algorithm usually yields an unstable system for a random channel gain matrix (Han, 2012). Therefore, it can be used a technique designated by Mann iterative methods, which allows a weaker stability criterion but it ensures that a stable system status point can

be reached. To achieve this further discussion is available in (Han, 2012).

Multi-Technology Wireless Networks

The FN environment will be a heterogeneous network infrastructure composed by distinct wireless access technologies and several users/terminals aiming to monitor and select the best technology/Access Point (AP)/ Base Station (BS) to connect to, depending on their Quality-of-Service (QoS) requirements. One possible QoS requirement is the best throughput as possible each user can have through each AP/BS taking in consideration the overload imposed by the other attached users. Each user (the player of this network selection/vertical handover game) after its monitoring phase about all the available AP/BS connection possibilities should choose the one that ensures the maximum throughput value among all the options. Most of the existing work on vertical handover assumes that users have complete information on one another (Han, 2012). In FNs, the users will lack the ability to predict the behaviors of others based on past actions. In this case, it is more convenient to utilize a game with incomplete information, i.e. a Bayesian game, like the one adopted by (Zhu, 2010). Since the payoff (i.e. utility) for a mobile user is composed by private information (see Table 6), each user has to make a network selection given only the distribution of the preferences of other users (Han, 2012). In this game, it is very interesting to investigate the impact of different system parameters on the game performance itself using a practical setting, like the one composed by three different access technologies (Wifi, Wimax and cellular). The studied system parameters have been the convergence property of the aggregate best-response dynamics for the considered network selection game, the game adaptation for different handover costs (delay or packet loss), the impact of connection price on the equilibrium distribution and the impact of learning (i.e. user strategy adjustment) rate on game dynamics. The obtained results are discussed in (Han, 2012).

Table 6. Summary of relevant characteristics of network selection with incomplete information game (Zhu, 2010)

Scenario	Game Type	Player	Player's Strategy	Payoff
Network selection with incomplete information	Bayesian game	Users in a service area with K available access networks	Represents the probability of choosing an access network K and the minimum user bandwidth requirement (only the user knows about this, which turns this game an incomplete one)	User utility combines user achieved throughput above a minimum threshold (user private information) vs. price paid for the connection

Network Management

The support of voice service in FNs will be a challenging task due the heterogeneity of both the network infrastructure and user requirements. A very interesting starting point to this problem is available in (Watanabe, 2008). It is proposed an analytical model based on Evolutionary Game Theory (EGT) (see Table 7) to analyze the consequences of a situation in which all users are allowed to freely choose the transmission rate. They perform that by selecting the codec and Forward Error Correction (FEC) mode to maximize the voice quality (payoff), which can be experienced by them. They show that in a scenario where the users know only their own perceived voice quality, the system converges to a total transmission rate close to that of the effective cell's capacity. They concluded that each individual user's MOS, which is estimated by a Random Neural Network (RNN), can also be satisfied. Further, cell's congestion is avoided by local user adaptation (dynamically changing its codec/FEC to maximize its perceived quality) without any intervention from a centralized controller.

Internet of Things (Multi-Hop Reliable Networks)

FN environments will have a large-scale deployment of wireless networks, which consist of small, low-cost nodes with simple processing and networking capabilities. This emergent environment is commonly designated inside the research community as the Internet of Things. In order to reach the desired destination such as the data sink node, transmissions depending on multiple hops are necessary (Han, 2012). As a consequence of this, the routing optimization is a pertinent problem that involves many aspects but the one more relevant for the current work is the nodes not willing to fully cooperate in the routing process through multiple wireless hops, forwarding traffic from other nodes, because relaying external traffic consumes their limited battery power. Hence, it is crucial to design a distributed –control mechanism encouraging cooperation among the nodes in the routing process (see Table 8). The literature describes two typical approaches to enforce cooperation. First, in a price-based approach, each hop has a price and the game outcome is controlled between the

Table 7. Summary of relevant characteristics of an evolutionary game to study rate selection for VoIP service (Watanabe, 2008)

Scenario	Game Type	Player	Player's Strategy	Payoff
Study rate selection to guarantee the QoS offered to VoIP users	Evolutionary game	VoIP users in a service area	Each user selects the transmission rate through the codec and FEC mode	Voice quality experienced by the user and measured via a Mean Opinion Score (MOS) technique

Table 8. Summary of characteristics of Games to incentivize cooperation among multi-hop nodes

Scenario	Game Type	Player	Player's Strategy	Payoff
Incentivize cooperation among nodes (Liu, 2006)	Hop price-based reliable routing game	All the nodes except the destination one	A node to participate in this game should at least choose one next hop node in the path from the source to the destination; otherwise it is out of this game	The source's utility is the expected income (destination payment minus the payments to all of the intermediate nodes, times the probability that the packet will be delivered over the route) minus the link set-up cost for the first hop of the route; The utility for each intermediate routing node equals the expected payment that it obtains from the source node, times the ongoing route reliability minus the transmission cost per packet to its next-hop neighbor. If any node does not participate in the routing, it gains (and loses) nothing.
Incentivize cooperation among nodes (Eidenbez, 2008)	Vickrey-Clarke-Groves (VCG) auction to prevent players from lying and to route messages along the most energy-efficient paths (as defined by the topology control protocol)	All the network nodes	A strategy is a combination of strategies from the following base space: 1. a node can declare any value for its type; 2. a node can drop control messages that it should forward; 3. a node can modify messages before forwarding, and 4. a node can create bogus messages.	Maximizing the node's utility. The sender's node utility is the difference between the amount of money it is willing to pay for the connection and the amount it effectively pays for that; the intermediate's node utility is the difference about the amount of money received from the sender and the total cost incurred by relaying the sender's packet.

source-destination pair and the intermediate hops. Second, an auction-based approach is suggested to ensure that users reveal their information truthfully to others for network cooperation, because this strategy will bring them the best benefits.

Reliable Wireless Backhaul

In FN environments wireless multi-hop backhaul links are expected to be very popular deployments. In this case, the channel quality between relay stations can fluctuate because of fading. Therefore, the users (players) at the source node

have to be able to observe, learn, and change the routing strategy to achieve the most reliable path from source node to the Internet gateway, as summarized in Table 9.

7. CONCLUSION

Cooperation: Current Status and Open Issues

Cooperation is a revolutionary wireless communication paradigm that can achieve much higher

Table 9. Summary of relevant characteristics of game to study traffic routing through multi-hop wireless backhaul links (Anastasopoulos, 2008)

Scenario	Game Type	Player	Player's Strategy	Payoff
Multi-hop Wireless Backhaul Links	Evolutionary game	Users	Users periodically and randomly sampling different wireless backhaul links to select a convenient path between a source node and an Internet gateway	Find a backhaul link that ensures the smallest number of packet errors due to rain attenuation

network performance and spectrum utilization in future networking environments. Many technical challenges, however, still remain to be solved to make this vision a reality. In particular, the distributed and dynamic nature of the sharing of information about node cooperation requires a new design and analysis framework. GT provides a very solid solution for this challenging task. In this book chapter, we describe several GT models that have been successfully used to solve various problems associated with node cooperation and related issues.

The most part of discussed models relies on the concept of Nash Equilibrium (NE) in games with complete information and static strategies. Although mathematically convenient, this may not be the most suitable GT model in practice. For example, the complete information assumption is difficult to be satisfied in practice, due to the dynamic and uncertain environment associated to FNs formed by heterogeneous wireless access technologies and a huge variety of flow

types. A model of incomplete games will be more suitable. Moreover, NE assumes rational players and static strategies but the players in FNs aren´t completely rational; the players have limited information about available choices and consequences of others; the game strategies are not static (in fact, the strategies are highly dynamic). A recent branch of GT - Evolutionary GT (EGT) seems a very promising alternative to the traditional GT in order to be applied in FNs. Some preliminary work has been reported along these directions (Khan, 2012a) (Nazir, 2010) (Bennis, 2011) (Altman, 2009) and definitely much more is required. As a pertinent example, evolutionary network models can provide useful guidelines for upgrading protocols/algorithms to achieve stable infrastructure functionality around preferred status/configuration in FNs. Finally, in Table 10, some relevant contributions found in the literature, which can be the foundations for new work in the FN area, are listed together with some associated open issues.

Table 10. Open issues in applying GT to future wireless networking scenarios

Scenario	Reference	Open Issue
Network Planning	(Guruacharya, 2010	Due to the notorious computational burden of estimating the Stackelberg equilibrium, a low complexity algorithm based on Lagrangian dual theory was chosen. However the numerical results show that the adopted algorithm is suboptimal.
Multi-Technology Wireless Networks	(Zhu, 2010)	Future work can study based on the Equilibrium distribution, how the service providers can adjust the system capacity and price accordingly to maximize the profits
Network Management	(Watanabe, 2008)	The experiments were performed with small populations. Future work can devise more scalable experiments.
Internet of Things (Multi-Hop Reliable Networks)	(Liu, 2006)	Add the destination as a player; consider scenarios where the destination can choose from several source nodes for a given piece of information. This will allow for an auction to be held among the source nodes to optimize destination's payoff
Internet of Things (Multi-Hop Reliable Networks)	(Eidenbez, 2008)	Enhance previous protocol to be robust against malicious nodes and collusion
Reliable Wireless Backhaul	(Anastasopoulos, 2008)	Extend previous work in the direction of IEEE 802.11s (wireless mesh networking)

REFERENCES

Aberer, K., & Despotovic, Z. (2004). *On reputation in game theory application on online settings* (Working Paper). Unpublished.

Ahlgren, B., Dannewitz, C., Imbrenda, C., Kutscher, D., & Ohlman, B. (2012). A survey of information-centric networking. *IEEE Communications Magazine, 50*(7), 26–36. doi:10.1109/MCOM.2012.6231276

Akkarajitsakul, K., Hossain, E., Niyato, D., & Dong, I. K. (2011). Game theoretic approaches for multiple access in wireless networks: A survey. *IEEE Communications Surveys & Tutorials, 13*(3), 372–395. doi:10.1109/SURV.2011.122310.000119

Alpcan, T., Basar, T., Srikant, R., & Altman, E. (2002). CDMA uplink power control as a noncooperative game. *Wireless Networks, 8*(6), 659–670. doi:10.1023/A:1020375225649

Altman, E., Boulogne, T., El-Azouzi, R., Jimenez, T., & Wynter, L. (2006). A survey on networking games in telecommunications. *Computers & Operations Research, 33*(2), 286–311. doi:10.1016/j.cor.2004.06.005

Altman, E., El-Azouzi, R., Hayel, Y., & Tembine, H. (2009). The evolution of transport protocols: An evolutionary game perspective. *Computer Networks, 53*(10), 1751–1759. doi:10.1016/j.comnet.2008.12.023

Anastasopoulos, M. P., Arapoglou, P. D., Kannan, R., & Cottis, P. G. (2008). Adaptive routing strategies in IEEE 802.16 multi-hop wireless backhaul networks based on evolutionary game theory. *IEEE Journal on Selected Areas in Communications, 26*(7), 1218–1225. doi:10.1109/JSAC.2008.080918

Anderegg, L., & Eidenbenz, S. (2003). Ad hoc-VCG: A truthful and cost-efficient routing protocol for mobile ad hoc networks with selfish agents. In *Proceedings of the ACM International Conference on Mobile Computing and Networking*, (pp. 245-259). ACM.

Axelrod, R. (1981). The emergence of cooperation among egoists. *The American Political Science Review, 75*(2), 306–318. doi:10.2307/1961366

Bansal, S., & Baker, M. (2003). *Observation-based cooperation enforcement in ad hoc networks (Stanford Technical Report)*. Palo Alto, CA: Stanford University.

Bennis, M., Guruacharya, S., & Niyato, D. (2011). Distributed learning strategies for interference mitigation in femtocell networks. In *Proceedings of IEEE Global Telecommunications Conference* (GLOBECOM). IEEE.

Buchegger, S., & Boudec, J.-Y. L. (2002). Performance analysis of the CONFIDANT protocol. In *Proceedings of the 3rd ACM International Symposium on Mobile Ad Hoc Networking & Computing* (MobiHoc '02), (pp. 226-236). ACM.

Buttyán, L., & Hubaux, J.-P. (2000). Enforcing service availability in mobile ad-hoc WANs. In *Proceedings of the 1st ACM International Symposium on Mobile Ad Hoc Networking & Computing* (MobiHoc '00), (pp. 87-96). ACM.

Buttyán, L., & Hubaux, J.-P. (2001). *Nuglets: A virtual currency to stimulate cooperation in self organized ad hoc networks* (Technical Report DSC/2001/001). Lausanne, Switzerland: Swiss Federal Institute of Technology.

Buttyán, L., & Hubaux, J.-P. (2003). Stimulating cooperation in self-organizing mobile ad hoc networks. *Mobile Networks and Applications, 8*(5), 579–592. doi:10.1023/A:1025146013151

Charilas, D., Athanasios, E., & Panagopoulos, D. (2010). A survey on game theory applications in wireless networks. *Computer Networks, 54*(18), 3421–3430. doi:10.1016/j.comnet.2010.06.020

Charilas, D., Vassaki, S., Panagopoulos, A., & Constantinou, P. (2011). Cooperation incentives in 4G networks. In *Game theory for wireless communications and networking*. Boca Raton, FL: CRC Press. doi:10.1201/b10975-17

Chen, K., & Nahrstedt, K. (2004). iPass: An incentive compatible auction scheme to enable packet forwarding service in MANET. In *Proceedings of the 24th International Conference on Distributed Computing Systems*, (pp. 534-542). Academic Press.

Chen, K., Yang, Z., Wagener, C., & Nahrstedt, K. (2005). Market models and pricing mechanisms in a multihop wireless hotspot network. In *Proceedings of the Second Annual International Conference on Mobile and Ubiquitous Systems: Networking and Services* (MOBIQUITOUS '05), (pp. 73-84). Academic Press.

Cisco Data Traffic Forecast Update, 2012–2017. (n.d.). Retrieved from http://www.cisco.com/en/US/solutions/collateral/ns341/ns525/ns537/ns705/ns827/white_paper_c11-520862.pdf

Demir, C., & Comaniciu, C. (2007). An auction based AODV protocol for mobile ad hoc networks with selfish nodes. In *Proceedings of IEEE International Conference on Communications* (ICC '07), (pp. 3351-3356). IEEE.

Dutta, P. (1999). *Strategies and games, theory and practice*. Cambridge, MA: MIT Press.

Eidenbenz, S., Resta, G., & Santi, P. (2008). The commit protocol for truthful and cost-efficient routing in ad hoc networks with selfish nodes. *IEEE Transactions on Mobile Computing, 7*(1), 19–33. doi:10.1109/TMC.2007.1069

Fadlullah, Z. M., Nozaki, Y., Takeuchi, A., & Kato, N. (2011). A survey of game theoretic approaches in smart grid. In *Proceedings of International Conference on Wireless Communications and Signal Processing* (WCSP), (pp. 1-4). WCSP.

Felegyhazi, M., & Hubaux, J. (2006). *Game theory in wireless networks: A tutorial (EPFL Technical Report, 2006-002)*. EPFL.

Fernandes, S., & Karmouch, A. (2012). Vertical mobility management architectures in wireless networks: A comprehensive survey and future directions. *IEEE Communications Surveys & Tutorials, 14*(1), 45–63. doi:10.1109/SURV.2011.082010.00099

Ghazvini, M., Movahedinia, N., Jamshidi, K., & Moghim, N. (2013). Game theory applications in CSMA methods. *IEEE Communications Surveys & Tutorials, 15*(3), 1062–1087. doi:10.1109/SURV.2012.111412.00167

Gibbons, R. (1992). *A primer in game theory*. Upper Saddle River, NJ: Pearson Education Limited.

Gritter, M., & Cheriton, D. R. (2000). *TRIAD: A new next-generation internet architecture*. Retrieved from http://www-dsg.stanford.edu/triad/

Guruacharya, S., Niyato, D., Hossain, E., & Kim, D. I. (2010). Hierarchical competition in femtocell-based cellular networks. In *Proceedings of IEEE Global Telecommunications Conference* (GLOBECOM), (pp. 1-5). IEEE.

Han, Z., Niyato, D., Saad, W., Basar, T., & Hjorungnes, A. (Eds.). (2012). *Game theory in wireless communications and networks: Theory, models, and applications*. Cambridge, UK: Cambridge University Press.

Harsanyi, J. (1967). Games with incomplete information played by Bayesian players, part I, the basic model. *Management Science, 14*(3), 159–182. doi:10.1287/mnsc.14.3.159

He, Q., Wu, D., & Pradeep, K. (2004). SORI: A secure and objective reputation-based incentive scheme for ad-hoc networks. In *Proceedings of IEEE Wireless Communications and Networking Conference* (WCNC'04), (vol. 2, pp. 825-830). IEEE.

Huang, J. (in press). Economic viability of dynamic spectrum management. In *Mechanisms and games for dynamic spectrum allocation*. Cambridge, UK: Cambridge University Press. doi:10.1017/CBO9781139524421.018

Huang, J. H., & Han, Z. (2010). Game theory for spectrum sharing. In *Cognitive radio networks: Architectures, protocols, and standards*. Auerbach Publications, CRC Press. doi:10.1201/EBK1420077759-c10

Hwang, J., Shin, A., & Yoon, H. (2008). Dynamic reputation-based incentive mechanism considering heterogeneous networks. In *Proceedings of the 3rd ACM Workshop on Performance Monitoring and Measurement of Heterogeneous Wireless and Wired Networks* (PM2HW2N '08), (pp. 137-144). ACM.

Ileri, O., Siun-Chuon, M., & Mandayam, N. B. (2005). Pricing for enabling forwarding in self-configuring ad hoc networks. *IEEE Journal on Selected Areas in Communications*, *23*(1), 151–162. doi:10.1109/JSAC.2004.837356

Jaramillo, J. J., & Srikant, R. (2007). Darwin: Distributed and adaptive reputation mechanism for wireless ad-hoc networks. In *Proceedings of the 13th Annual ACM International Conference on Mobile Computing and Networking* (MobiCom '07), (pp. 87-98). ACM.

Khan, M., Tembine, H., & Vasilakos, A. (2012a). Evolutionary coalitional games: design and challenges in wireless networks. *IEEE Wireless Communications*, *19*(2), 50–56. doi:10.1109/MWC.2012.6189413

Khan, M., Tembine, H., & Vasilakos, A. (2012b). Game dynamics and cost of learning in heterogeneous 4G networks. *IEEE Journal on Selected Areas in Communications*, *30*(1), 198–213. doi:10.1109/JSAC.2012.120118

Kuo, Y., Wu, E., & Chen, G. (2004). Non-cooperative admission control for differentiated services in IEEE 802.11 WLANs. In *Proceedings of the IEEE Global Telecommunications Conference* (GLOBECOM 2004), (vol. 5, pp. 2981-2986). IEEE.

Lai, L., & el Gamal, H. (2008). The water-filling game in fading multiple-access channels. *IEEE Transactions on Information Theory*, *54*(5), 2110–2122. doi:10.1109/TIT.2008.920340

Larsson, E. G., Jorswieck, E. A., Lindblom, J., & Mochaourab, R. (2009). Game theory and the flat-fading Gaussian interference channel: Analyzing resource conflicts in wireless networks. *IEEE Signal Processing Magazine*, *26*(5), 18–27. doi:10.1109/MSP.2009.933370

Liu, H., & Krishnamachari, B. (2006). A price-based reliable routing game in wireless networks. In *Proceedings of the ACM Workshop on Game Theory for Communications and Networks* (GameNets '06). ACM.

Louta, M., Zournatzis, P., Kraounakis, S., Sarigiannidis, P., & Demetropoulos, I. (2011). Towards realization of the ABC vision: A comparative survey of access network selection. In *Proceedings of IEEE Symposium on Computers and Communications* (ISCC), (pp. 472-477). IEEE.

Machado, R., & Tekinay, S. (2008). A survey of game-theoretic approaches in wireless sensor networks. *Computer Networks*, *52*, 3047–3061. doi:10.1016/j.gaceta.2008.07.003

Mackenzie, A., & DaSilva, L. (2006). *Game theory for wireless engineers*. Morgan & Claypool Publishers.

Marina, N., Saad, W., Han, Z., & Hjorungnes, A. (2011). Modeling malicious behavior in cooperative cellular wireless networks. In *Cooperative cellular wireless networks*. Cambridge, UK: Cambridge University Press. doi:10.1017/CBO9780511667008.015

Mateus, A., & Marinheiro, R. N. (2010). A media independent information service integration architecture for media independent handover. In *Proceedings of Ninth International Conference on Networks* (ICN), (pp. 173-178). ICN.

Milan, F., Jaramillo, J. J., & Srikant, R. (2006). Achieving cooperation in multihop wireless networks of selfish nodes. In *Proceedings from the 2006 ACM Workshop on Game Theory for Communications and Networks* (GameNets '06). ACM.

Moura, J., Silva, J., & Marinheiro, R. N. (2012). A brokerage system for enhancing wireless access. In *Proceedings of International Conference on Communications and Signal Processing* (MIC-CSP), (vol. 1, pp. 45-50). Academic Press.

Mundinger, J., & Boudec, J.-Y. L. (2005). Analysis of a robust reputation system for self-organized networks. *European Transactions on Communications*, *16*(5), 375–384.

Nazir, M., Bennis, M., Ghaboosi, K., MacKenzie, A. B., & Latva-Aho, M. (2010). Learning based mechanisms for interference mitigation in self-organized femtocell networks. In *Proceedings of Conference Record of the Forty Fourth Asilomar Conference on Signals, Systems and Computers*, (pp. 1886-1890). Academic Press.

Niyato, D., & Hossain, E. (2007). Radio resource management games in wireless networks: An approach to bandwidth allocation and admission control for polling service in IEEE 802.16 (Radio Resource Management and Protocol Engineering for IEEE 802.16). *IEEE Wireless Communications*, *14*(1), 27–35. doi:10.1109/MWC.2007.314548

Nurmi, P. (2006). *Bayesian game theory in practice: A framework for online reputation systems* (Technical Report C-2005-10). Academic Press.

Saad, W., Han, Z., & Hjorungnes, A. (2011). Coalitional games for cooperative wireless cellular networks. In *Cooperative cellular wireless networks*. Cambridge, UK: Cambridge University Press. doi:10.1017/CBO9780511667008.014

Saad, W., Han, Z., Poor, H. V., & Başar, T. (2012). *Game theoretic methods for the smart grid*. Eprint arXiv:1202.0452.

Saraydar, C. U., Mandayam, N. B., & Goodman, D. (2002). Efficient power control via pricing in wireless data networks. *IEEE Transactions on Communications*, *50*(2), 291–303. doi:10.1109/26.983324

Scutari, G., Palomar, D., & Barbarossa, S. (2008). Competitive design of multiuser MIMO systems based on game theory: A unified view. *IEEE Journal on Selected Areas in Communications*, *26*(7), 1089–1103. doi:10.1109/JSAC.2008.080907

Shastry, N., & Adve, R. S. (2006). Stimulating cooperative diversity in wireless ad hoc networks through pricing. In *Proceedings of IEEE International Conference on Communications* (ICC '06.), (vol. 8, pp. 3747-3752). IEEE.

Shen, S., Yue, G., & Cao, Q. (2011). A survey of game theory in wireless sensor networks security. *Journal Networks*, *6*(3), 521–532. doi:10.4304/jnw.6.3.521-532

Shi, H.-Y., Wang, W.-L., Kwok, N.-M., & Chen, S.-Y. (2012). Game theory for wireless sensor networks: A survey. *Sensors (Basel, Switzerland)*, *12*, 9055–9097. doi:10.3390/s120709055 PMID:23012533

Silva, J., Marinheiro, R., Moura, J., & Almeida, J. (2013). Differentiated classes of service and flow management using an hybrid broker. *ACEEE International Journal on Communication*, *4*(2), 13–22.

Silva, J. C., Moura, J. A., Marinheiro, R. N., & Almeida, J. (2013). Optimizing 4G networks with flow management using an hybrid broker. In *Proceedings of International Conference on Advances in Information Technology and Mobile Communication* (AIM). Academic Press.

Skraparlis, D., Sakarellos, V. K., Panagopoulos, A. D., & Kanellopoulos, J. D. (2009). *Outage performance analysis of cooperative diversity with MRC and SC in correlated lognormal channels* (p. 707839). Article, ID: EURASIP Journal on Wireless Communications and Networking.

Srivastava, V., Neel, J., MacKenzie, A. B., Menon, R., Dasilva, L. A., & Hicks, J. E. et al. (2005). Using game theory to analyze wireless ad hoc networks. *IEEE Communications Surveys & Tutorials*, *7*(4), 46–56. doi:10.1109/COMST.2005.1593279

Taylor, P., & Jonker, L. (1978). Evolutionary stable strategies and game dynamics. *Mathematical Biosciences*, *40*, 145–156. doi:10.1016/0025-5564(78)90077-9

Trestian, R., Ormond, O., & Muntean, G.-M. (2011). Reputation-based network selection mechanism using game theory. *Physical Communication*, *4*(3), 156–171. doi:10.1016/j.phycom.2011.06.004

Vassaki, S., Panagopulos, A., & Constantinou, P. (2009). *A game-theoretic approach of power control schemes in DVB-RCS networks*. Paper presented at the 15th Ka and Broadband Communications, Navigation and Earth Observation Conference. Cagliari, Italy.

Wang, B., Wu, Y., & Liu, K. (2010). Game theory for cognitive radio networks: An overview. *Computer Networks*, *54*(14), 2537–2561. doi:10.1016/j.comnet.2010.04.004

Wang, B., Wu, Y., Liu, K. J. R., & Clancy, T. C. (2011). An anti-jamming stochastic game for cognitive radio networks. *IEEE Journal on Selected Areas in Communications*, *29*(4), 877–889. doi:10.1109/JSAC.2011.110418

Watanabe, E. H., & Menasché, D. S. de Souza e Silva, E., & Leao, R. M. M. (2008). Modeling resource sharing dynamics of VoIP users over a WLAN using a game-theoretic approach. In *Proceedings of IEEE Conference on Computer Communications* (INFOCOM 2008), (pp. 915-923). IEEE.

Yap, K.-K. (2013). *Using all networks around us*. (PhD Thesis). Stanford University, Palo Alto, CA.

Zhang, D., Ileri, O., & Mandayam, N. (2008). Bandwidth exchange as an incentive for relaying. In *Proceedings of 42nd Annual Conference on Information Sciences and Systems*, (pp. 749-754). Academic Press.

Zhang, Y., & Guizani, M. (Eds.). (2011). *Game theory for wireless communications and networking*. Boca Raton, FL: CRC Press.

Zhang, Y., Lou, W., & Fang, Y. (2004). SIP: A secure incentive protocol against selfishness in mobile ad hoc networks. In *Proceedings of IEEE Conference Wireless Communications and Networking* (WCNC), (vol. 3, pp. 1679-1684). IEEE.

Zhong, S., Chen, J., & Yang, Y. R. (2003). Sprite: A simple, cheat-proof, credit-based system for mobile ad hoc networks. []. INFOCOM.]. *Proceedings of INFOCOM*, *3*, 1987–1997.

Zhu, K., Niyato, D., & Wang, P. (2010). Network selection in heterogeneous wireless networks: Evolution with incomplete information. In *Proceedings of IEEE Wireless Communications and Networking Conference* (WCNC 2010), (pp. 1-6). IEEE.

ADDITIONAL READING

Ackermann, H., Briest, P., Fanghänel, A., & Vöcking, B. (2008). Who Should Pay for Forwarding Packets? *Internet Mathematics*, *5*(4), 459–475. doi:10.1080/15427951.2008.10129168

Akyildiz, I., Lee, W.-Y., Vuran, M., & Mohanty, S. (2006). NeXt generation/dynamic spectrum access/cognitive radio wireless networks: A survey. *Computer Networks*, *50*(13), 2127–2159. doi:10.1016/j.comnet.2006.05.001

Al-Manthari, B., Nasser, N., & Hassanein, H. (2011). Congestion Pricing in Wireless Cellular Networks. *IEEE Communications Surveys & Tutorials*, *13*(3), 358–371. doi:10.1109/SURV.2011.090710.00042

Alayesh, M., & Ghani, N. (2012). Performance of a primary-secondary user power control under rayleigh fast flat fading channel with pricing. 19th International Conference on Telecommunications (ICT), 1(5), 23-25.

Anggraeni, P., & Wardana, S. (2007). Cooperation in Wireless Grids-An Energy Efficient MAC Protocol for Cooperative Network with Game Theory Model. Master Thesis, Aalborg University.

Apicella, C., Marlowe, F., Fowler, J., & Christakis, N. (2012). Social networks and cooperation in hunter-gatherers. *Nature*, *481*, 497–501. doi:10.1038/nature10736 PMID:22281599

Bond, R., Fariss, C., Jones, J., Kramer, A., Marlow, C., Settle, J., & Fowler, J. (2012). A 61-million-person experiment in social influence and political mobilization. *Nature*, *489*(7415), 295–298. doi:10.1038/nature11421 PMID:22972300

Buddhikot, M. (2007). Understanding Dynamic Spectrum Access: Models, Taxonomy and Challenges. In Proceedings of IEEE DySPAN, 649-663.

Buddhikot, M., & Ryan, K. (2005). Spectrum management in coordinated dynamic spectrum access based cellular networks. In Proceedings of IEEE DySPAN, 299-307.

Buttyan, L., & Hubaux, J.-P. (2007). *Security and cooperation in wireless networks*. Cambridge University Press. doi:10.1017/CBO9780511815102

Courcoubetis, C., & Weber, R. (2003). Pricing communication networks: economics, technology and modeling. Wiley-Interscience series in systems and optimization, ISBN 0-470-85130-9.

DaSilva, L. (2000). Pricing for QoS-enabled networks: A survey. *IEEE Communications Surveys & Tutorials*, *3*(2), 2–8. doi:10.1109/COMST.2000.5340797

Etkin, R., Parekh, A., & Tse, D. (2007). Spectrum Sharing for Unlicensed Bands. IEEE Journal on Selected Areas in Communications, Special Issue on Adaptive. *Spectrum Agile and Cognitive Wireless Networks*, *25*(3), 517–528.

Felegyhazi, M., & Cagalj, M., & Bidokhti, S., & Hubaux, J.-P. (2007). Non-cooperative multi-radio channel allocation in wireless networks. In Proceedings of INFOCOM, 1442-1450.

Halpern, J. (2008). *Computer Science and Game Theory: A Brief Survey. In the New Palgrave Disctionary of Economics* (S. Durlauf, & L. Blurne, Eds.). Palgrave MacMillan. doi:10.1057/9780230226203.0287

Heikkinen, T. (2002). On congestion pricing in a wireless network. *Wireless Networks*, *8*(4), 347–354. doi:10.1023/A:1015578321066

Heikkinen, T. (2004). Distributed scheduling and dynamic pricing in a communication network. *Wireless Networks*, *10*(3), 233–244. doi:10.1023/B:WINE.0000023858.20849.ab

Heikkinen, T. (2006). A potential game approach to distributed power control and scheduling. *Computer Networks*, *50*(13), 2295–2311. doi:10.1016/j.comnet.2005.09.010

Huang, J., Berry, R., & Honig, M. (2006a). Distributed interference compensation for wireless networks. *IEEE Journal on Selected Areas in Communications*, *24*(5), 1074–1084. doi:10.1109/JSAC.2006.872889

Huang, J., Berry, R., & Honig, M. (2006b). Auction-based spectrum sharing. *Mobile Networks and Applications*, *11*(3), 405–418. doi:10.1007/s11036-006-5192-y

Ileri, O., Samardzija, D., & Mandayam, N. (2005). Demand responsive pricing and competitive spectrum allocation via spectrum server. In Proceedings of IEEE DySPAN, 194-202.

Inaltekin, H., Wexler, T., & Wicker, S. (2007). A Duopoly Pricing Game for Wireless IP Services. IEEE SECON, 600-609.

Jia, J., & Zhang, Q. (2008). Competitions and dynamics of duopoly wireless service providers in dynamic spectrum market. In Proceedings of the 9th ACM International Symposium on Mobile Ad Hoc Networking and Computing (MobiHoc), 313-322.

Koutsopoulou, M., Kaloxylos, A., Alonistioti, A., Merakos, L., & Kawamura, K. (2004). Charging, accounting and billing management schemes in mobile telecommunication networks and the Internet. *IEEE Communications Surveys & Tutorials*, *6*(1), 50–58. doi:10.1109/COMST.2004.5342234

Lee, J.-W., Tang, A., Huang, J., Chiang, M., & Calderbank, A. (2007). Reverse-Engineering MAC: a non-cooperative game model. *IEEE Journal on Selected Areas in Communications*, *25*(6), 1135–1147. doi:10.1109/JSAC.2007.070808

MacKenzie, A., & Wicker, S. (2003). Stability of multipacket slotted aloha with selfish users and perfect information. In Proceedings of INFOCOM, 1583-1590.

Maharjan, S., Zhang, Y., & Gjessing, S. (2011). Economic Approaches for Cognitive Radio Networks: A Survey. *Wireless Personal Communications*, *57*(1), 33–51. doi:10.1007/s11277-010-0005-9

Maille, P., & Tuffin, B. (2006). Pricing the Internet With Multibid Auctions. *IEEE/ACM Transactions on Networking*, *14*(5), 992–1004. doi:10.1109/TNET.2006.882861

Maskery, M., Krishnamurthy, V., & Zhao, Q. (2009). Decentralized dynamic spectrum access for cognitive radios: cooperative design of a non-cooperative game. *IEEE Transactions on Communications*, *57*(2), 459–469. doi:10.1109/TCOMM.2009.02.070158

Meshkati, F., Poor, H., & Schwartz, S. (2007). Energy-Efficient Resource Allocation in Wireless Networks. *IEEE Signal Processing Magazine*, *24*(3), 58–68. doi:10.1109/MSP.2007.361602

Nguyen, D. N., & Krunz, M. (2012). Price-Based Joint Beamforming and Spectrum Management in Multi-Antenna Cognitive Radio Networks. *IEEE Journal on Selected Areas in Communications*, *30*(11), 2295–2305. doi:10.1109/JSAC.2012.121221

Nie, N., & Comaniciu, C. (2006). Adaptive channel allocation spectrum etiquette for cognitive radio networks. *Mobile Networks and Applications*, *11*(6), 779–797. doi:10.1007/s11036-006-0049-y

Niyato, D., & Hossain, E. (2009b). Dynamics of Network Selection in Heterogeneous Wireless Networks: An Evolutionary Game Approach. *IEEE Transactions on Vehicular Technology*, *58*(4), 2008–2017. doi:10.1109/TVT.2008.2004588

Niyato, D., Hossain, E., & Han, Z. (2009a). Dynamic spectrum access in IEEE 802.22- based cognitive wireless networks: a game theoretic model for competitive spectrum bidding and pricing. *IEEE Wireless Communications, 16*(2), 16–23. doi:10.1109/MWC.2009.4907555

Rasti, M., Sharafat, A., & Seyfe, B. (2009). Pareto-Efficient and Goal-Driven Power Control in Wireless Networks: A Game-Theoretic Approach With a Novel Pricing Scheme. *IEEE/ACM Transactions on Networking, 17*(2), 556–569. doi:10.1109/TNET.2009.2014655

Ren, W., Zhao, Q., & Swami, A. (2008). Power control in spectrum overlay networks: how to cross a multi-lane highway? IEEE International Conference Acoustics, Speech, Signal Processing (ICASSP), 2773-2776.

Sengupta, S., Anand, S., Chatterjee, M., & Chandramouli, R. (2009). Dynamic pricing for service provisioning and network selection in heterogeneous networks. *Physical Communication, 2*(1-2), 138–150. doi:10.1016/j.phycom.2009.02.009

Shroff, N., Xiao, M., & Chong, E. (2001). Utility based power control in cellular radio systems. In Proceedings of INFOCOM, 1, 412-421.

Thomas, R. (2007). Cognitive Networks. PhD thesis, Virginia Polytechnic Institute and State University.

Vincent, T., & Brown, J. (2011). *Evolutionary Game Theory, Natural Selection, and Darwinian Dynamics*. Cambridge University Press.

Wang, D., Comaniciu, C., & Tureli, U. (2006). A fair and efficient pricing strategy for slotted Aloha in MPR models. IEEE VTC, 1-5.

Youngmi, J., & Kesidis, G. (2002). Equilibria of a noncooperative game for heterogeneous users of an aloha network. *IEEE Communications Letters, 6*(7), 282–284. doi:10.1109/LCOMM.2002.801326

Zhang, J., & Zhang, Q. (2009). Stackelberg game for utility-based cooperative cognitive radio networks. In Proceedings of ACM MobiHoc, 23-32.

Zhao, L., Zhang, J., & Zhang, H. (2008). Using Incompletely Cooperative Game Theory in Wireless Mesh Networks. *IEEE Network, 22*(1), 39–44. doi:10.1109/MNET.2008.4435901

Zhao, Q., & Sadler, B. (2007). A survey of dynamic spectrum access. *IEEE Signal Processing Magazine, 24*(3), 79–89. doi:10.1109/MSP.2007.361604

Chapter 6
Interference Mitigation and Energy Management in Heterogeneous Networks:
A Cognitive Radio Perspective

Chungang Yang
Xidian University, China

Jiandong Li
Xidian University, China

ABSTRACT

In Long Term Evolution (LTE) 4G systems, coexistence of multiple in-band smallcells defines what is called heterogeneous cellular networks. There is no doubt that the development of heterogeneous networks and the popularization of intelligent terminals facilitate subscribers with great convenience, better Quality of Experience (QoE) guarantee, and much higher traffic rate. However, interference management will be indispensable in heterogeneous networks. Meanwhile, with emerging various energy-hungry services of subscribers, energy-aware design attracts a wide attention. Motivated by interference mitigation and energy-saving challenges of the heterogeneous networks and the promising cognitive radio techniques, more advanced energy-saving and interference control techniques based on cognitive radio should be developed for better QoE. In this chapter, the authors first review cognitive radios, multiple types of smallcells, and introduce the benefits of cognitive radio-enabled heterogeneous networks. Then, focusing on the scheme design of cognitive interference management and energy management, finally, simulation results are provided to show the improved performance of these proposed cognitive schemes.

INTRODUCTION AND MOTIVATION

Next generation (xG) wireless networks will contain a number of radio access networks (RANs). Different RANs employ different radio access technologies (RATs). Meanwhile, subscribers who are equipped with smart terminals are pursuing much better user experience with multi-mode, reconfigurable and cognitive equipments. In long term evolution (LTE) 4G systems, coexistence of multiple in-band smallcells defines what is called heterogeneous cellular networks. Since

DOI: 10.4018/978-1-4666-5978-0.ch006

its first introduction, the LTE standard has significantly evolved toward LTE-Advanced one, where numerous spectral efficiency and peak data rate improvements have been introduced. Meanwhile, various transmission techniques are introduced to approach the limites of these point-to-point capacity rate requirements. Among those advanced techniques, it is worth mentioning the improved multiple input multiple-output (MIMO) techniques (e.g., the 3D and massive MIMO), carrier aggregation (CA), and enhanced intercell interference coordination (R1-101369, 2010; R1-104968, 2010; R1-104661, 2010). However, as the spectral efficiency of a point-to-point link in cellular networks approaches its theoretical limits, with the fore-casted explosion of data traffic, there is a need for an increase in the node density to further improve network capacity due to its proved powerful network enhanced capacity space. However, in already dense deployments in today's networks, cell splitting gains can be severely limited by high inter-cell interference. Moreover, high capital expenditure cost associated with high power macro nodes further limits viability of such an approach. Therefore, the promisingly discussed scheme is the need for an alternative strategy, where low power nodes are overlaid within a macro network, creating what is referred to as a heterogeneous network (R4-110284,2011).

The rational behind the heterogeneous network is that macrocell-only networks may not be able to carry the predicted future broadband traffic. Therefore, the next big leap in cellular system performance improvement is estimated to come from the introduction of additional smallcells to complement traditional macrocell installations. This raises the questions on how smallcells are most spectrally efficiently introduced, and how to integrate them with the macro-tier to maximize the performance benefits while keeping capital expenditures (CAPEX) and operational expenditure (OPEX) at tolerable levels. For this purpose, two state-of-the-art LTE-Advanced heterogeneous

network integration schemes should be examined: co-tier and cross-tier interference management between macrocells and smallcells, or among themself, and energy-aware resource management strategy design between tiers, especially in the scenario of massive deployment of smallcells. In both use cases, we will highlight the benefits of cognitive radio-motivated schemes to push the system performance to its maximum, and in fact, extensive cognitive radio-based schemes have been poured attentions in the cellular systems, for example, cognitive LTE and cognitive femtocell networks (Lopez-Perez, Guvenc, & Roche, 2011).

Spectrum and energy are both scarce resources for wireless networks, specifically, the spectrum resource is the real source of the interference. Effective and efficient interference management and dynamic energy management with respect to the variations of the traffic and channel state, are both critical and important to further enhance the capacity and improve the quality of user experience. In this chapter, we concentrate on the cognitive radio based interference management and energy management, since they have shown a strong capabilities on the resource management and energy harvesting, and in the future they will play a greater role. We first summarize the current research and the necessary conditions of interference management and control, especially, the inter-cell interference coordination and energy management strategies using cognitive radios (Attar, Krishnamurthy & Gharehshiran, 2011; Li & Sousa, 2010; Viering, Dottling, & Lobinger, 2011; Saatsakis, Tsagkaris & Von-Hugo 2008; Wang, Yu & Huang, 2013; Yang, Li, 2012), finally we verify cognitive energy management for the heterogeneous networks to enhance the network energy efficiency and cognitive interference shift (capacity offload) for two-tiered heterogeneous networks, respectively. Meanwhile, the future research directions and typical issues on cognitive ideas for heterogeneous networks are summarized, which conclude the chapter.

COGNITIVE RADIO ENABLED HETEROGENEOUS NETWORKS

Cognitive Radio

As known, most of the already allocated spectrum are significantly underutilized or even unused worldwide temporally or geographically. Recently, many researchers and organizations are seeking alternatives to unlocking the spectrum resource. Cognitive radio technology has been proposed to effectively resolve the dilemma between the increasing spectrum requirements and scarce spectrum resources. With cognitive radio technology, secondary users (SUs) sense the spectrum environment from time to time, and then choose idle channels for opportunistic transmissions. Once the primary user (PU) returns to the channel, the SU should switch to a different channel to avoid interference to the PU or simply the SUs terminate the current transmission if there is no idle channel available. In summary, such a cognitive implementation of SU's opportunistic use of the licensed spectrum resource should be supported by the following functions including 1) spectrum sensing and analysis of the current spectrum and the activity of the PUs; 2) dynamic spectrum management and handoff; 3) flexible spectrum allocation and sharing. Such a typical duty cycle of cognitive radio, as illustrated in Figure 1, includes detecting spectrum white space, selecting the best frequency bands, coordinating

Figure 1. A typical duty cycle of cognitive radio

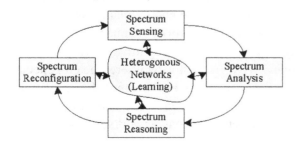

spectrum access with other users, and vacating the frequency when a primary user appears.

Cognitive radio technology can provide abundant new spectrum opportunities by opportunistically exploiting underutilized spectrum. There have been numerous research efforts and outcomes on cognitive radio technology since its inception. Cognitive radio has emerged as a promising technology to maximize the utilization of the limited radio spectrum while accommodating the increasing amount of services and applications in wireless networks. Key cognitive radio technology evolutions and innovations make LTE working in the expanded white space spectrum more feasible, which can be well found in the current research and the necessary conditions of interference management and control, especially, the interference and energy management strategies using cognitive radios (Attar, Krishnamurthy & Gharehshiran, 2011; Li & Sousa, 2010; Viering, Dottling & Lobinger, 2011; Saatsakis, Tsagkaris & Von-Hugo 2008; Wang, Yu & Huang, 2013; Yang, Li, 2012). Specifically, cognitive radio has been recommended as a key technology to solve the spectrum scarcity problem in the next generation wireless networks. For example, IEEE standards series (e.g., IEEE 802.11af, 802.16h, 802.19) constitute the cognitive radio technique standardization over TVWS. IEEE 802.11af is an amendment to the IEEE 802.11 baseline standard and intends to operate in the TV white spaces. IEEE 802.16h is designed to enable coexistence among license-exempt systems based on IEEE 802.16 and to facilitate the coexistence of such systems with primary users. IEEE 802.19 is focused on developing coexistence scenarios and possible coexistence metrics to enable the family of IEEE 802 wireless standards to most effectively use TV white space. On the other hand, many efforts are being made to introduce cognitive radio features into 3GPP LTE-A systems (Xiao, HU, Qian & Gong, 2013).

Heterogeneous Networks with Multiple Types of Smallcells

A heterogeneous network is a network consisting of infrastructure points with various wireless access technologies, each of them having different capabilities, constraints, and operating functionalities. Specifically, in LTE-Advanced, multi-tier network roll-outs, involving remote radio heads (RRHs), picocells, femtocells, as well as relay stations underlaying the existing macrocell layout are envisaged. These low-power overlaid base stations can be either operator deployed or user deployed, and may coexist in the same geographical area, potentially sharing the same spectrum. Deploying such smallcells aims at offloading the macrocells, improving indoor coverage and cell-edge user performance, and boosting spectral efficiency per area unit via spatial reuse. They can be deployed with relatively low network overhead, and have high potentials for reducing the energy consumption of future wireless networks. Also, this new palette of low-power smallcells requires little or no upfront planning and lease costs, therefore drastically reducing the operational and capital expenditures of networks. According to Table 1, the details of the different elements of heterogeneous networks are provided as follows (Lopez-Perez, Guvenc & Roche, 2011):

1. Macrocellular networks consist of conventional operator-installed BSs, providing open public access and a wide area coverage typically on the order of few kilometers. In LTE, they are also called enhanced NodeBs (eNBs). Usually destined to provide guaranteed minimum data rate under maximum tolerable delay and outage constraints, macrocells typically emit up to 46 dBm, serving thousands of customers and using a dedicated backhaul.

2. Picocells are low-power operator-installed cell towers with the same backhaul and access features as macrocells. They are usually deployed in a centralized way, serving a few tens of users within a radio range of 300 m or less, and have a typical transmit power range from 23 to 30 dBm. Picocells are mainly utilized for capacity and outdoor or indoor coverage infill in environments with insufficient macro penetration.

3. Femtocells, also known as home eNBs, are low-cost low-power user deployed access points, offloading data traffic using consumers' broadband connection, cable, or fiber, and serving a dozen active users in homes or enterprises. Typically, the femtocell range is less than 50 m and its transmit power less than 23 dBm. They operate in open or restricted access.

4. Relays are usually operator-deployed access points that route data from the macro BS to end users and vice versa. They are positioned so as to increase signal strength and to improve reception in poor coverage areas and dead spots in the existing networks. They

Table 1. Multiple types of smallcells

Types of Smallcells	Transmit Power (dBm)	Coverage (m)	Backhaul	Deployment
Macrocell	46	km	S1	Operator
Picocell	23-30	<300	X2	Operator
Femtocell	<23	<50	IP	User
Relay	30	300	Wireless	Operator
RRH	46	km	Fiber	Operator

can operate in transparent or non-transparent modes, with little to no incremental backhaul expense and with similar transmit power as picocells.

5. RRHs are compact-size high-power and low-weight units, which are mounted outside the conventional macro BS and connected to it generally through a fiber optic cable, thus creating a distributed BS. The central macro BS is in charge of control and baseband signal processing. Moving some radio circuitry into the remote antenna, RRHs eliminate power losses in the antenna cable and reduce power consumption. They also enhance flexibility to network deployments for operators that face site acquisition challenges and/or physical limitations.

Heterogeneous networks entail a significant paradigm shift transitioning from "traditional" centralized macrocell/microcell approaches to more autonomous, uncoordinated, and intelligent rollouts. However, this paradigm shift, which can be seen as an excellent opportunity for enhancements, also introduces challenges. For instance, although the advantage of deploying femtocells is supported by recent studies suggesting that 50 percent of all voice calls and more than 70 percent of data traffic originate indoors, cross-tier interference and traffic load variability may become a barrier to a successful deployment of this type of network. Hence, heterogeneous networks bring into play significant technical issues and raise substantial challenges that are presented as follows. In heterogeneous networks, the deployment of smallcell eNodeBs, overlaid on existing macrocell controlled by the macrocell eNodeB is widely accepted as a key solution for offloading traffic, optimizing coverage, and boosting the capacity of future cellular wireless systems. However, both the smallcell and macrocell may suffer significant performance degradation due to inter-and intra-tier interference. In addition, no matter from the financial or the environmental

considerations or better quality of user experience (QoE), reducing the amount of energy consumption has become an important way to increase the profits of both operators and users in mobile communications industry. In addition, in order not to repeat the same mistake of the one-sided pursuit of spectral efficiency, the next generation of communications should meanwhile care about the EE. Energy efficient design/networking means the monetary profit for the operators and much better QoE for prolonging the battery life of user terminals by deploying new network architectures with low signaling overhead.

Cognitive Enabled Heterogeneous Networks

We describe the cognitive radio-enabled heterogeneous networks in Figure 2. Figure 2 depicts a two-tier macro-small network, where the K smallcell eNodeBs (SeNBs) overlay on the only existing macrocell eNodeB (MeNB). Both SeNB and MeNB are backhauled to the core network using the wired connections, e.g., the fiber or cable. Also, we assume that the MeNB always can obtain the information of the multiple SeNBs, for instance, the interference information, through X2 interface or other transmission media. The M macrocell user equipments (MUEs) are associated to the sole MeNB. Here, we divide the multiple MUEs into two types of "Local_MUE," e.g., MUE_1 and "Wide_MUE," e.g., MUE_2 according to their locations with respect to their associated MeNB. Each SeNB $k \in K$ serves N_k smallcell user equipments (SUEs), for instance, SUE_1 is associated to SeNB_1\$ for service forming the communication pair of SeNB_1→FUE_1. At the same time, there is macrocellular downlink of MeNB→MUE_1. We illustrate the cognitive benefits to the interference management and energy saving using Figure 2.

As illustrated in case 1 in Figure 2, both the SeNB and MeNB may suffer significant performance degradation due to inter/intra-tier interfer-

Figure 2. Cognitive radio-motivated heterogeneous networks

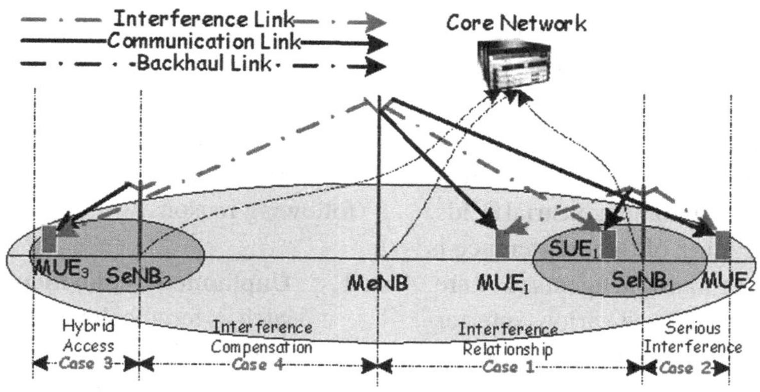

ence. This situation will be even worse in case 2 in Figure 2, where the "Wide_MUE," e.g., MUE_2 receives a less useful power on the communication link from its associated MeNB, but a large harmful power on the interference link from its nearest SeNB_1. Therefore, the SINR achieved by MUE_2 will be very low due to the serious interference. However, if the SeNB permits these "Wide_MUEs" to access in, that is, MeNB can capacity offload these users to their corresponding most serious interferer, then the SINR performance will be improved. As illustrated in case 3 in Figure 2, where we use a hybrid access femtocell as an example, the SeNB_2 helps to offload the MUE_3. Then MUE_3 will receive a large useful power on the new communication link from its nearest SeNB_1, but a less useful power on the interference link from its originally associated MeNB, since it is far away from the MeNB. By now, we can see that the serious interference problems can be well solved. Furthermore, the MeNB will moderately coordinate its downlink power according to its currently associated MUEs without affecting the coverage and mobility, which will provide a further interference compensation to the multiple SeNBs resulting a win-win situation shown in case 4 in Figure 2. More important, the energy consumption of the MeNB is largely saved, since the downlink

power of the MeNB is much larger than that of femtocell. In summary, cognition and intercell cooperation scheme design will help to improve the performance of both spectral efficiency and energy efficiency through the collaboration behaviors between SeNBs and MeNB.

INTERFERENCE CONCEPT AND MANAGEMENT

As mentioned above, heterogeneous networks have been regarded as one of the promising techniques to enhance capacity by exploring and exploiting both frequency and and spatial diversities. In heterogeneous networks, the deployment of smallcell eNodeBs overlaid on existing macrocell controlled by the macrocell eNodeB is widely accepted as a key solution for offloading traffic, optimizing coverage, and boosting the capacity of future cellular wireless systems. Smallcell in LTE networks is a general term used to refer to femtocells and picocells with he coverage radius around 10-300 m. However, both the smallcell eNodeBs and macrocell eNodeB may suffer significant performance degradation due to inter and intra-tier interference.

Basics of Interference and Inference Management

There are so many interference management schemes and techniques including interference cancellation/mitigation/avoidance/alignment, which have been extensively studied, examined and standardized in the academic and industrial fields. However, the real meaning of the interference is the resource conflict of multiple agents to share. Therefore, we can divided these various interference management schemes into the resource/user scheduling on the dimension of time, frequency, space or code, certainly the combination of several of them. Suppose the smallcell, using the femtocell access point as an example, operates on the same spectrum band as the macrocell base station, shown in Figure 3. Three types of interference exist with different impact to the entire network capacity: interference from femtocells to macrocell, interference from macrocell to femtocells, and interference between femtocells.

Furthermore, considering that femto-macrocell networks comprise two tiers (the macrocell and femtocell tiers), interference in these heterogeneous networks on the downlink can be typically classified as follows:

1. **Cross-Tier Interference:** Interference is caused by an entity in one tier to an entity, which belongs to another tier (e.g., interference caused by a femtocell to a macrocell user).

2. **Co-Tier Interference:** Interference is caused by an entity to another entity that belongs to the same tier (e.g., interference caused by a femtocell to the user of another femtocell).

The interference problem in heterogeneous networks is especially challenging due to the following reasons:

1. **Unplanned Deployment:** Low-power nodes such as femtocells are typically deployed in an ad hoc manner by users. They can even be moved or switched on/off at any time. Hence, traditional network planning and optimization becomes inefficient because operators do not control neither the number nor the location of these cells. This motivates the need for new decentralized interference avoidance schemes that operate independently in each cell, utilizing only local information, whereas achieving an efficient solution for the entire network.

2. **Closed Subscriber Group (CSG) Access:** The fact that some cells may operate in CSG mode, in which cell access is restricted and nonsubscribers are thus not always connected to the nearest BS, originates significant cross-tier interference components.

3. **Power Difference Between Nodes:** Picocells and relays usually operate in open access mode, meaning that all users of a given operator can access them. Open access helps minimize DL interference as

Figure 3. Two-tiered heterogeneous networks of smallcell and macrocell

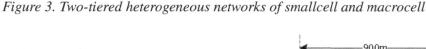
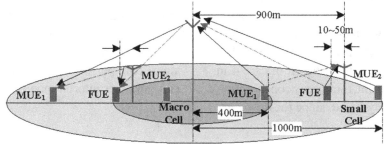

end users always connect to the strongest cell, thus avoiding the CSG interference issue. However, in heterogeneous networks, being attached to the cell that provides the strongest DL received signal strength (RSS) may not be the best strategy since users tend to connect to macrocells, not to the cells at the shortest path loss distance. This is due to the large difference in transmission power between macrocells and low-power nodes.

4. **Range Expanded Users:** To address the problems arising due to the power difference between the nodes in heterogeneous networks, new cell selection methods that allow user association with cells that provide a weaker downlink pilot signal quality are necessary.

Current Studies from Different Dimensions

In essence, interference is generated when a predetermined signal fails to occupy its licensed resource of some specific dimension (i.g., time, frequency, space and power), causing the corresponding legal signal of this licensed resource does not work normally. Therefore, an enhanced inter-cell interference coordination (eICIC) is investigated in (Ghosh, Mangalvedhe & Ratasuk et al., 2012; Supratim, Pantelis, Jerzy & James, 2013) from the dimension of time, a downlink dynamic frequency-reuse-based interference avoidance scheme with inter-cell coordination (Rahman & Yanikomeroglu, 2010) and a cooperative game-theoretic collaborative sub-channel allocation scheme (Gharehshiran, Attar & Krishnamurthy, 2013) are proposed from the frequency use dimension, an interference alignment for cooperative femtocell networks is studied using coalitional game-theoretic approach in (Rahman & Yanikomeroglu, 2010), which employs the spatial viewpoint. The ICIC methods specified in Releases 8 and 9 of 3GPP do not specifically

consider heterogeneous network settings and may not be effective for dominant heterogeneous network interference scenarios (Figure 3). In order to address such dominant interference scenarios, eICIC techniques have recently been developed for Release 10, which can be grouped under three major categories:

1. **Time-Domain Techniques:** In time-domain eICIC methods, transmissions of the victim users are scheduled in time-domain resources where the interference from other nodes is mitigated. They can be classified into two categories as follows.

2. **Frequency-Domain Techniques:** In frequency-domain eICIC solutions, control channels and physical signals (i.e., synchronization and reference signals) of different cells are scheduled in reduced bandwidths in order to have totally orthogonal transmission of these signals at different cells. While frequency-domain orthogonalization may be achieved in a static manner, it may also be implemented dynamically through victim UE detection.

3. **Power Control Techniques:** One last approach that has been heavily discussed in 3GPP for handling dominant interference scenarios is to apply different power control techniques at femtocells. While reducing the radiated power at a femtocell also reduces the total throughput of femtocell users, it may significantly improve the performance of victim MUEs. Finally from 3GPP Release 7 standards, also known as HSPA+, the the power self-calibration is proposed as a key interference management method Contrary to other dimensions of interference mitigation, power control is more flexible and efficient, especially, it is largely determined the energy consumption. Interference-aware power coordination helps to avoid severe interference and thus enhance their SINR-

related spectral efficiency performance. Therefore, to fully explore the benefits of the heterogeneous networks, the well defined power control-related interference managements have widely appeared in the literatures.

Considering interference among different cooperating base stations, (Yavuz, Meshkati & Nanda, et al, 2009) formulates a non-cooperative game to refine the conventional power water-filling algorithm for interference coordination and improving the individual throughput. A distributed utility-based SINR adaptation of Foschini-Miljanic algorithm at femtocells is proposed in order to alleviate cross-tier interference at the macrocell from co-channel femtocells in (Fu, Wu, Ho & Ling, 2012). The data rate is enhanced by finding the optimum transmit power for each co-channel user using game theory-based scheme (Chandrasekhar, Andrews & Muharemovic, et al., 2009). Assuming that the central MeNB considered as a leader sells transmission power quota to femtocells, several Stackelberg games are formulated and constraints to avoid unnecessary high transmission power are designed in (Al-Zahrani & Yu, 2011; Li, Zhu, Wu & Sandrasegaran, 2013; Kang, Zhang & Motani, 2012), where (Al-Zahrani & Yu 2011) is with pricing function design, (Zhu, Wu & Sandrasegaran, 2013) protects the leader MeNB by pricing the interference from femtocell users, and (Kang, Zhang & Motani, 2012) addresses the problem of allocating downlink transmit power over OFDMA cellular networks. The objective of each femtocell is to maximize its individual capacity under power constraints.

Actually, we can see from above listed works that game-theoretical formulations have found a wide use in interference/resource management in heterogeneous networks, since it can well describe the rational behaviors and the interference relationship among MeNBs or SeNBs, and between them . However, most of the current

works are formulated as non-cooperative game, or Stackelberg game (Al-Zahrani & Yu, 2011; Li, Zhu Wu & Sandrasegaran, 2013; Kang, Zhang & Motani, 2012) due to their selfish and rational behaviors and intrinsic hierarchy of leaders and followers, which coincides with the MeNB and SeNB in the multi-tier heterogeneous networks. Essentially, Stackelberg game is also non-cooperative game, which always leads to an inefficient equilibrium, further sometimes results in the tragedy of commons, specially, in the scenario of densely deployed SeNBs, which has been widely proved. Furthermore, it cannot well characterize resource conflict and interference coordination relationships. Meanwhile, throughput/capacity/SINR-related utility functions are always selected as the optimized objective functions . However, the energy efficiency (EE, or green communication) is another promising requirement especially when SeNB/MeNB is densely deployed to enhance the quality of user experience. As stated, most of previous works are focused on spectrum sharing and interference avoidance, and the EE aspect is largely ignored. Recently, heterogeneous networks, cognitive radios, and the smart grid are jointly studied to improve energy efficiency.

ENERGY MANAGEMENT TECHNIQUES

Necessity of Energy Management

Due to a full frequency reuse deployment, most of previous works focus on spectrum sharing and interference coordination/avoidance/mitigation to improve the spectral efficiency, but the energy efficiency (EE, or green communication) aspect is largely ignored. Actually, the EE is another promising requirement especially when small-cells are densely deployed to enhance the quality of user experience. In addition, future networks should be evolving towards to be environmentally friendly, and so the corresponding architecture design, resulting operation and implementation are envisioned to pursue minimal impacts on environment, whether from the energy consumption or from greenhouse gas emissions (Shakir, Qaraqe & Tabassum, et al., 2013). In fact, the concept of EE design/networking has widely spread during the past decades, recently gaining increasing popularity. The reasons why EE design/networking should be poured more attentions are summarized as follows from more extensive viewpoints of operators, networks and terminals.

The problems faced by wireless operators are the paradoxical trends between the more advanced quality of service (QoE) guarantees and the decreasing revenue earnings, which demonstrates a contradictory relationship between the operation/energy consumption expenditure and the monetary profit. Network system architectures, functional structures and wireless environments are getting more and more intelligent, dynamic and heterogeneous motivated by the diverse QoE requirements. Meanwhile, network scalability, robustness, flexibility and greenness are promisingly becoming the research focuses of wireless community. On the other hand, the terminals have capabilities of more intelligence and multi-homing with higher QoE requirements, which are largely determined by the promising cognitive radio and cooperative communication networking.

Therefore, no matter from the financial or the environmental considerations or better quality of user experience (QoE), reducing the amount of energy consumption has become an important way to increase the profits of both operators and users in mobile communications industry. In addition, in order not to repeat the same mistake of the one-sided pursuit of spectral efficiency, the next generation of communications should meanwhile care about the EE. Energy efficient design/networking means the monetary profit for the operators and much better QoE for prolonging the battery life of user terminals by deploying new network architectures with low signaling overhead.

Related Works

By now, we know that three investigated research points are most related to green communications and EE including Energy-Efficient Architectures, Energy-Efficient Resource Management and Energy-Efficiency Metric and Energy-Consumption Model. They are well investigated and summarized in several valuable surveys of (Feng, Jiang, Lim & Cimini, et al., 2012) for wireless networks, and (Hasan, Boostanimehr & Bhargava, 2011) for cellular networks. Towards 5G communication systems, we should discover the suitable energy-efficiency metrics and modelings, propose flexible EE optimization architectures and design efficient EE energy management schemes combining a multi-level considerations of Operators, Core networks, Radio access networks and Terminals (i.g., OCRT). To the knowledge of our best, there is no work well investigating these three EE-related issues in one unified optimization architecture.

To cope with EE resource managements, in (Xie, Yu, Ji & Li, 2012), the EE aspect of spectrum sharing and power allocation in heterogeneous cognitive radio networks with femtocells is investigated, where to fully exploit the cognitive capability, a wireless network architecture in which both the macrocell and the femtocell have the cognitive capability are considered. Meanwhile, cognitive radio resource managements (Saatsakis, Tsagkaris & Von-Hugo 2008; Gur & Alagoz, 2011) are fully employed to green wireless communications via cognitive dimension. In summary, heterogeneous networks evolve great challenges on the conventional network architecture, and dynamic topology, complex interference, rational strategic intelligent terminal, all of which call for more autonomous and cognitive resource management frameworks (Saatsakis, Tsagkaris & Von-Hugo, 2008; Gur & Alagoz, 2011). Also, cognition is considered to be one of the key features of the future networks, where cognitive femtocell (Elsawy, Hossain & Kim, 2013); Al-Rubaye, Al-Dulaimi & Cosmas, 2011), cognitive WiFi (Yang, Xu & Sheng, 2012) and cognitive LTE (Gharehshiran, Attar & Krishnamurthy, 2013) and others cognition-related applications (Wang, Ghosh & Challapali, 2011) are extensively introduced towards future wireless community.

Therefore, it is safe to conclude that cognitive-inspired distributed energy efficient decision-making for optimal radio resource usage and management have earned renewed interest, and can well enhance the energy efficient performance. On the other hand, conventionally, energy efficiency of wireless network has been extensively studied from various perspectives, such as decoding policy, dynamic planning, and network cooperation. Specially, network cooperation becomes an effective technique to improve the energy efficiency (Ismail & Zhuang, 2011; Niu, Zhou & Hua, et al., 2012); Bennis, Simsek & Czylwik, et al., 2013). An energy aware network planning scheme, which can guarantee both the coverage and traffic requirements, has been proposed to reduce the energy consumption with inter-cell coordination (Niu, Zhou & Hua, et al., 2012), by network collaboration (Ismail & Zhuang, 2011), through heterogeneous cooperation (Bennis, Simsek & Czylwik, et al., 2013), inter-network cooperation (Zou, Zhu & Zhang, 2013) or user cooperation (Nokleby& Aazhang, 2010). In heterogeneous networks, the smart multimode terminals can obtain the energy efficient gain by simultaneously combining transmissions over several multiple points by network cooperation.

Benefits of Cognitive Radio-Enabled Schemes in Future Heterogeneous Networks

By now, we can see that both cognition and cooperation techniques have been recognized as the most effective and efficient ways to meet the growing wireless network capacity and coverage demands, also they are well investigated to achieve the energy efficiency. Actually, heterogeneous networks provide more opportunities for exploring and exploiting cognition and cooperation to improve the spectral efficiency among multiple Nodes. To summarize typical characteristics of current network developments, we can see that ubiquitous networks are the ultimate goal, cognition is the inevitable means, and green communications are basic requirements of future wireless networks. In this chapter, we refer to such uniformly converged networks of above heterogeneous ubiquitous networks with cognitive radio capabilities and green as green composition networks, which is in line with the typical described scenarios of IEEE 1900.4. However, either cognitive radio potentiality or green requirements of resource management schemes are overlooked. Both cognitive radio and heterogeneous networks have been considered as promising techniques in wireless networks. However, most of previous works are focused on spectrum sharing and interference avoidance, and the energy efficiency aspect is largely ignored. However, the energy-aware design and how to save and harvest more energy should be paid enough attention. Specially, this situation will be challenged by the future Network and User Density, shown in Table 2

Cognitive radio-based radio resource management research based on the IEEE 1900.4 standard stoles the emerging spotlight of wireless community, which specifies a policy-based radio resource management framework in which the decision making process is distributed between network-terminal entities. Distributing radio resource management decision making in heterogeneous wireless networks can be delegated to mobiles by incorporating cognitive capabilities into mobile handsets, resulting in the reduction of signaling and processing burden. A novel cognitive radio resource management is proposed to improve the spectrum utilization efficiency in. The study of different radio resource management techniques to maintain either a load-or QoE-balanced system through dynamic load distribution across a

Table 2. Both network and user density challenge energy-aware design

Network Index	UMTS	LTE	WLAN
(Enhanced) Base Station	264 thousand	20 thousand ~200 thousand (2013)	382 thousand hotspots and 3.61 million APs~6 million (2015)
User	79 million(11% total use)		more than 14 million active users (standalone mode)

CWN is pivotal. On the other hand, the concept of energy-efficient networking has begun to spread in the past few years, gaining increasing popularity.

The problems faced by wireless operators are the paradoxical trends of the increasing data rate provisions and more advanced QoE guarantees, but, the decreasing earnings feed backed to it, which demonstrates a non-linear growth relationship between the operation expenditure and the monetary profit. Network system architectures, functional structures and environments motivated by the diverse needs of data rate transmission and QoE guarantees, are getting more complex, dynamic and heterogeneous. Meanwhile, network complexity, scalability, robustness, flexibility and greenness are promisingly becoming the research focuses of wireless community. The terminal equipments are with more intelligence, multi-homing and high-bandwidth rate transmission QoE and QoE requirements. All these call for more intelligent and flexible schemes, and we concentrate on the cognitive radio idea for the interference and energy management.

COGNITIVE INTERFERENCE MANAGEMENT AND ENERGY MANAGEMENT IN HETEROGENEOUS NETWORKS

Energy resource starvation and spectrum scarcity are newly encountered issues by wireless communities. Promisingly, we hold the view that cognitive radio technology can harvest energy/spectrum resources from current wireless network environments by the intelligent sensing and the advanced signal processing techniques. More importantly, cognitive radios provide more flexible and autonomous ways to manage these perceived resources. To achieve more energy management and better utilizing the management resource, in case of dynamic resource allocation, each cognitive radio should adapt its transmission parameters (e.g., power level, transmission rate) according to the varying spectrum/channel conditions

Since some cells such as picocells and femtocells will be user-deployed without operator supervision, their proper operation highly depends on their self-organizing features. The self-organizing capability of heterogeneous networks can be generally classified into three processes:

1. **Self-Configuration:** Where newly deployed cells are automatically configured by downloaded software before entering into the operational state.
2. **Self-Healing:** Where cells can automatically perform failure recovery or execute compensation mechanisms whenever failures occur.
3. **Self-Optimization:** Where cells constantly monitor the network status and optimize their settings to improve coverage and reduce interference.

The deployment of self-organizing heterogeneous networks is an intricate task due to the various type of coexisting cells and the increasing number of network parameters that need to be considered. The random, uneven and time-varying nature of user arrivals and their resulting traffic load also exacerbate the difficulties associated with deploying a completely self-organized heterogeneous network. Both the cognitive radios and self-organizing heterogeneous networks motivate the promising cognitive idea to save energy and motivate the interference.

Cognitive Energy Management

From an energy-saving perspective, we investigate the downlink power control issue of the two-tier heterogeneous networks using a cognitive radio train of thought in (Yang, Li, 2012). We consider the heterogeneous networks scenario of one macro-cell evolved-NodeB (eNB) and multiple femto-cell Home evolved NodeBs (HeNBs) cooperatively coexisting to provide better services.

Motivated by the promising framework of cognitive radio, a specific HeNB will allow macro-mobile station (macro-MS) who previously associated with eNB to access in for better signal-to-interference plus noise ratio (SINR) guarantee. This process is largely dependent on their specific locations and the significant interferences from the HeNBs around it. As a reward, the macro-MS pays a certain of revenue to HeNB as the incentive mechanism for this HeNB's downlink extra power consumption, which is manifested in the design of the price function. A newly-bulit pricing function is introduced to the SINR definition. Then, we select the SINR as the performance measure and formulate the power control of selected HeNBs as a multi-constrained optimization problem.

The proposed cognitive energy management algorithm is described as follows:

1. Each macro-MS determines the right associated node, for instance, the macro-MS is still associated to its original macrocell or turns to one specific HeNB for more SINR γ.
2. The HeNBs in the simulation scenario will be motivated to allow macro-MSs to access

in, which is characterized by pricing function c.
3. After the new association implementations of all macro-MSs, then both the eNB and the selected HeNB will adjust the transmission power during this round.

Note That: Here the referenced-x algorithm is the non-cognitive one, that is, we assume that the macro-MSs can't select the right node, but always associated to their original node.

During the simulation process, we always assume that the M macro-MSs can find the most suitable specific HeNB as the secondary service provider. Meanwhile, the available bandwidth for each macro-MS will not change. Here, both the HeNB and eNB will achieve the cognitive diversities of the macro-MSs, therefore, we respectively illustrate the "energy-per-bit" performance of the proposed-cognitive-HeNB and proposed-cognitive-eNB, which is shown in Figure 4.

Figure 4 depicts the energy efficiency measured by 'energy-per-bit' in the unit of j/b, which is with respect to the increasing number of macro-MSs. Here, we utilize the improved function of 'energy-per-bit' metric for HeNB and eNB, respectively shown as:

Figure 4. Energy efficiency measured by 'energy-per-bit'

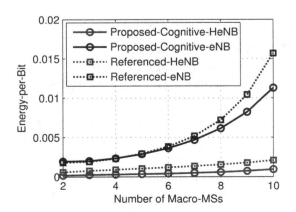

$$Energy\_per\_Bit\_HeNB = \frac{p^{\star}_{eNB} + \sum_{i=1}^{N} p^{\star}_i}{\sum_{m=1}^{M} C_m^{HeNB}},$$

$$Energy\_per\_Bit\_eNB = \frac{p^{\star}_{eNB} + \sum_{i=1}^{N} p^{\star}_i}{\sum_{m=1}^{M} C_m^{eNB}},$$

where $\sum_{m=1}^{M} C_m^{HeNB}$ and $\sum_{m=1}^{M} C_m^{eNB}$ are the total achievable rate when M macro-MSs are serviced by the HeNB and eNB, respectively. Moreover, $p^{\star}_{eNB} + \sum_{i=1}^{N} p^{\star}_i$ is the total power consumption, which represents the final optimal power selection of HeNBs and eNB using our 'Proposed-Cognitive-HeNB' and 'Proposed-Cognitive-eNB'.

Figure 5 illustrates the performance comparison of the 'energy-per-bit' between our 'Proposed-Cognitive-x' and 'Referenced-x'. On the Fig.\

Figure 5. Throughput comparison of the 'Proposed-Cognitive' algorithm with respect to the 'Referenced' one

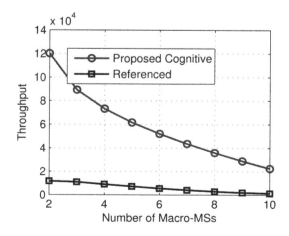

ref{Fig:figure1}, we know that the less 'energy per bit', the better energy efficiency performance. We can further conclude that: Both the 'Proposed-Cognitive-HeNB' and 'Referenced-HeNB' achieve much better energy efficiency with respect to 'Proposed-Cognitive-eNB' and 'Referenced-eNB', which means that M macro-MSs attain more energy performance improvement in HeNB than that in eNB. Both the 'Proposed-Cognitive-HeNB' and 'Proposed-Cognitive-eNB' achieve much better energy efficiency with respect to 'Referenced-HeNB' and 'Referenced-eNB', which shows that our 'Proposed-Cognitive-x' algorithms attain more energy performance improvement than that of 'Referenced-x'. Meanwhile, we can see that 'energy-per-bit' performance becomes less with the number of macro-MSs becomes increasingly larger. This is because that more macro-MSs will lead more interference power to the interference-limited system.

As above mentioned, more energy efficiency can be achieved using the 'Proposed-Cognitive' scheme with respect to the 'Referenced' one. From Figure 5, we conclude that we can achieve more throughput using the 'Proposed-Cognitive' scheme with respect to the 'Referenced' one. In addition, the achievable throughput becomes less with the increasing number of macro-MSs.

Cognitive Interference Shift (Capacity Offload)

We consider the heterogeneous network deployments where several femtocells are overlaid in a macrocell layout. Femtocells work in the hybrid access mode, which means that the macrocell user equipment (MUE) can access its adjacent femtocell for much higher SINR. For instance, in Figure 6 (A) the MUE is far away with its associated macrocell, meanwhile, this MUE is near to one specific femtocell. Therefore, the situation is the effectively received power from its macrocell is low, but the interference power from the femtocell is very high, which results a low SINR. However,

Figure 6. Cognitive interference shift

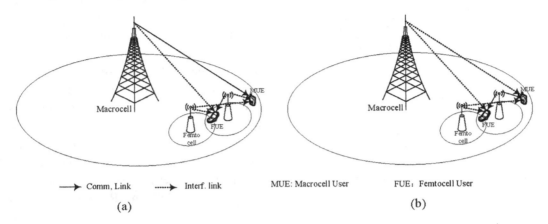

| → Comm, Link | ••••► Interf. link | MUE: Macrocell User | FUE: Femtocell User |

(a)   (b)

if the MUE can reassociate to the femtocell, then it will achieve an improved SINR, shown as Figure 6 (b). By now, several works have investigated the effectiveness and efficiency of the capacity offload of the femtocell, which can help to mitigate the interference.

Motivate by the cognitive radio idea in the downlink case of the two-tiered heterogeneous networks, here we evaluate the cognitive interference shift idea shown in Figure 6. Here, we assume that the users can perceive the interference context, and than the users will be transferred to its strongest interferer and the simulation parameters are given by Table 3.

Figure 7 shows SINR improvement of both FUE and MUE, respectively, before and after the cognitive interference shift. It can be clearly seen from the figure, the SINR is improved significantly after the interference shift. For the macrocell, MUEs can achieve the more average SINR, since the dynamic load transferring according to the perceived interference situations and multiple MUEs with the low SINR due to the serious interference from its nearest HeNB are transferred to the appropriately selected femtocell. For the FUEs, their average SINR improvement depends mainly on the interference compensation for the FUEs.

FUTURE RESEARCH DIRECTIONS

To summarize typical characteristics of future wirelss networks, we can see that ubiquitous/convergence are the ultimate goal, cognition/intelligence are the inevitable means, and green/energy-aware communications are basic requirements of future wireless networks. Energy resource starvation and spectrum scarcity are newly encountered issues by wireless communities. Promisingly, we hold the view that cognitive radio technology can harvest energy/spectrum resources from current wireless network environments by the intelligent sensing and the advanced signal processing techniques. In the future, first, we think the wide-bandwidth spectrum sensing and other network side information are important, which will provide the spectrum holes on the dimension of time, space or combination of them. These network information in the heterogeneous networks contain macrocell activity, channel gains, codebooks, and any message to mitigate interference and save energy. Here, we should emphasize the WiFi and TV spectrum utilization in the heterogeneous network scenario, which will be the practical dependent on the current popularity of the multimode, multi-frequency smart terminal and the awareness of the operator. Meanwhile, flexible and dynamic spectrum shifting will help

Table 3. System simulation parameters for down-link case

Simulation Parameter	Value
Deployment Scenario	10 HeNBs/sector
Number of UEs	60 UEs/sector
CF and Bandwidth	2GHz and 10MHz
Pathloss Models	$L = 127 + 30\log_{10} R$ $L = 128.1 + 37.6\log_{10} R$
Macro cell ISD	10s00m
Max Macro Tx Power	46dBm
Max Femto Tx Power	20dBm
Macro eNB Antenna Pattern Femto HeNB Antenna Pattern	Directional Antenna: three sectors Omni-directional antenna
Minimum Distance between HeNB and eNB	75m
Minimum Distance between UE and eNB	35m
Minimum Distance between UE and HeNB	3m
Minimum Distance among HeNBs	40m

to release the co-channel interference. In addition, we should provide the more cognitive and autonomous interference management scheme design for the extensive deployment of smallcells, which should care about both the spectral and the energy efficiency in one unified model to achieve the optimal tradeoff among them. Third, multiple intercell cooperation is another important method to mitigate the interference and save the energy.

CONCLUSION

This chapter will help to further understand the real meanings of the interference, meanwhile motivate more attentions of using these new sparking ideas for the current emerging interference management and energy management issues, for instance, cognitive radio and co-tier and cross-tier cooperation. In addition, the listed cognitive radio ideas for interference management and energy management will provide a good guidance in the future wireless community. Finally, our proposed algorithm can help to both mitigate interference and harvest energy in the two-tiered heterogeneous networks.

Figure 7. Efficiency of cognitive interference shift

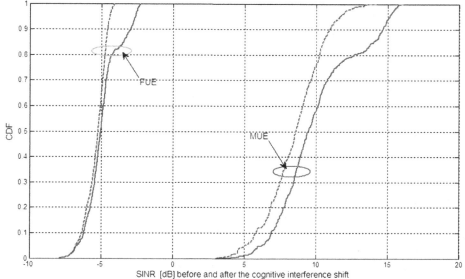

ACKNOWLEDGMENT

This work was supported in part by National Science Foundation of China under Grant 61201139, 61231008; by the Natural Science Basic Research Plan in Shaanxi Province of China under Grant no. 2012JQ8012; by the Fundamental Research Funds for the Central Universities K5051201033; by ISN02080001; by the 111 Project under Grant B08038; by the Program for Changjiang Scholars and Innovative Research Team in University, and by Shaanxi Province Science and Technology Research and Development Program (2011KJXX-40).

REFERENCES

R1-101369. (2010). *Considerations on interference coordination in heterogeneous networks.* 3GPP. Std.

R1-104661. (2010). *Comparison of time-domain eICIC solutions.* 3GPP. Std.

R1-104968. (2010). *Summary of the description of candidate eICIC solutions.* 3GPP. Std.

R4-110284. (2011). *Evaluations of RSRP/RSRQ measurement.* Austin, TX: 3GPP. Std.

Al-Rubaye, S., Al-Dulaimi, A., & Cosmas, J. (2011). Cognitive femtocell: Future wireless networks for indoor applications. *IEEE Veh. Technol. Mag.*, *6*(1), 44–51. doi:10.1109/MVT.2010.939902

Al-Zahrani, A. Y., & Yu, F. R. (2011). A game theory approach for inter-cell interference management in OFDM networks. [IEEE.]. *Proceedings of the IEEE, ICC*, 1–5.

Attar, A., Krishnamurthy, V., & Gharehshiran, O. N. (2011). Interference management using cognitive base-stations for UMTS LTE. *IEEE Communications Magazine*, *49*(8), 152–159. doi:10.1109/MCOM.2011.5978429

Bennis, M., Simsek, M., & Czylwik, A. et al. (2013). When cellular meets WiFi in wireless small cell networks. *IEEE Communications Magazine*, *51*(6), 35–41. doi:10.1109/MCOM.2013.6525594

Chandrasekhar, V., Andrews, J. G., & Muharemovic, T. et al. (2009). Power control in two-tier femtocell networks. *IEEE Transactions on Wireless Communications*, *8*(8), 4316–4328. doi:10.1109/TWC.2009.081386

Elsawy, H., Hossain, E., & Kim, D. (2013). Heterogeneous networks with cognitive smallcells: User offloading and distributed channel access techniques. *IEEE Communications Magazine*, *51*(6), 28–36. doi:10.1109/MCOM.2013.6525592

Feng, D.Q., Jiang, C.Z., Lim, G.B., Cimini, Jr., et al. (2012). A survey of energy-efficient wireless communications. *IEEE Communications Surveys and Tutorials.*

Fu, S., Wu, B., Ho, P., & Ling, X. (2012). Interference coordination in CoMP with transmission scheduling and game theoretical power reallocation. In *Proceedings of IEEE ICC 2012* (pp. 4212-4217). IEEE.

Gharehshiran, O. N., Attar, A., & Krishnamurthy, V. (2013). Collaborative sub-channel allocation in cognitive LTE femto-cells: A cooperative game-theoretic approach. *IEEE Transactions on Communications*, *61*(1), 325–334. doi:10.1109/TCOMM.2012.100312.110480

Gharehshiran, O. N., Attar, A., & Krishnamurthy, V. (2013). Collaborative sub-channel allocation in cognitive LTE femto-cells: A cooperative game-theoretic approach. *IEEE Transactions on Communications*, *61*(1), 325–334. doi:10.1109/TCOMM.2012.100312.110480

Ghosh, A., Mangalvedhe, N., & Ratasuk, R. et al. (2012). Heterogeneous cellular networks: From theory to practice. *IEEE Communications Magazine*, *50*(6), 54–64. doi:10.1109/MCOM.2012.6211486

Gur, G., & Alagoz, F. (2011). Green wireless communications via cognitive dimension: An overview. *IEEE Network*, *25*(2), 50–56. doi:10.1109/MNET.2011.5730528

Guruacharya, S., & Niyato, D., Dong In Kim, & Hossain, E. (2013). Hierarchical competition for downlink power allocation in OFDMA femtocell networks. *IEEE Transactions on Wireless Communications*, *12*(4), 1543–1553. doi:10.1109/TWC.2013.022213.120016

Hasan, Z., Boostanimehr, H., & Bhargava Vijay, K. (2011). Green cellular networks: A survey, some research issues and challenges. *IEEE Communications Surveys and Tutorials*, *13*(4), 524–540. doi:10.1109/SURV.2011.092311.00031

Ismail, M., & Zhuang, W. (2011). Network co-operation for energy saving in green radio communications. *IEEE Wireless Commun.*, *18*(5), 76–81. doi:10.1109/MWC.2011.6056695

Kang, X., Zhang, R., & Motani, M. (2012). Price-based resource allocation for spectrum-sharing femtocell networks: A Stackelberg game approach. *IEEE Journal on Selected Areas in Communications*, *30*(3), 538–549. doi:10.1109/JSAC.2012.120404

Li, X., Zhu, X., Wu, L., & Sandrasegaran, K. (2013). A distributed non-uniform pricing approach for power optimization in spectrum-sharing femtocell network. In *Proceedings of IEEE WCNC* (pp. 667-672). IEEE.

Li, Y., & Sousa, E. S. (2010). Cognitive interference management in 4G autonomous femtocells. [PIMRC.]. *Proceedings of PIMRC*, *2010*, 1567–1571.

Lopez-Perez, D., Guvenc, I., & Roche, G. (2011). Enhanced intercell interference coordination challenges in heterogeneous networks. *IEEE Wireless Comm.*, *18*(3), 22–30. doi:10.1109/MWC.2011.5876497

Niu, Z., Zhou, S., & Hua, Y. et al. (2012). Energy-aware network planning for wireless cellular system with inter-cell cooperation. *IEEE Transactions on Wireless Communications*, *11*(4), 1412–1423. doi:10.1109/TWC.2012.021412.110147

Nokleby, M., & Aazhang, B. (2010). User cooperation for energy-efficient cellular communications. In *Proceedings of ICC 2010*. ICC.

Rahman, M., & Yanikomeroglu, H. (2010). Enhancing cell-edge performance: A downlink dynamic interference avoidance scheme with inter-cell coordination. *IEEE Transactions on Wireless Communications*, *9*(4), 1414–1425. doi:10.1109/TWC.2010.04.090256

Rahman, M., & Yanikomeroglu, H. (2010). Interference alignment for cooperative femtocell networks-A game-theoretic approach. *IEEE Transactions on Wireless Communications*, *9*(4), 1414–1425. doi:10.1109/TWC.2010.04.090256

Saatsakis, A., Tsagkaris, K., & Von-Hugo, D. (2008). Cognitive radio resource management for improving the efficiency of LTE network segments in the wireless B3G world. In *Proceedings of 2008 IEEE Symposium on New Frontiers in Dynamic Spectrum Access Networks*. IEEE.

Shakir, M. Z., Qaraqe, K. A., & Tabassum, H. et al. (2013). Green heterogeneous small-cell networks: Towards reducing the CO_2 emissions of mobile communications industry using uplink power adaptation. *IEEE Communications Magazine*, *51*(6), 52–61. doi:10.1109/MCOM.2013.6525595

Supratim, D., Pantelis, M., Jerzy, M., & James, S.P. (2013). Algorithms for enhanced inter-cell interference coordination (eICIC) in LTE heterogeneous networks. *IEEE/ACM Trans. on Networking*.

Viering, I., Dottling, M., & Lobinger, A. (2011). On exploiting cognitive radio to mitigate interference in macro/femto heterogeneous networks. *IEEE Transactions on Wireless Communications*, *10*(8), 2196–2206.

Wang, J., Ghosh, M., & Challapali, K. (2011). Emerging cognitive radio applications: A survey. *IEEE Communications Magazine*, *49*(3), 74–81. doi:10.1109/MCOM.2011.5723803

Wang, W., Yu, G., & Huang, A. (2013). Cognitive radio enhanced interference coordination for femtocell networks. *IEEE Communications Magazine*, *51*(6), 37–43. doi:10.1109/MCOM.2013.6525593

Xiao, J., Hu, R. Q., Qian, Y., & Gong, L. (2013). Expanding LTE network spectrum with cognitive radios: From concept to implementation. *IEEE Wireless Communications*, *20*(2), 12–19. doi:10.1109/MWC.2013.6507389

Xie, R. C., Yu, F. R., Ji, H., & Li, Y. (2012). Energy-efficient resource allocation for heterogeneous cognitive radio networks with femtocells. *IEEE Transactions on Wireless Communications*, *11*(11), 3910–3920. doi:10.1109/TWC.2012.092112.111510

Yang, C., & Li, J. (2012). Green heterogeneous networks: A cognitive radio Idea. *IET Communications*, *6*(13), 1952–1959. doi:10.1049/iet-com.2011.0801

Yang, C., Xu, C., & Sheng, M. (2012). Cognitive wi-fi 2.0 networks: Future intelligent WLAN. *The Journal of Communication*, *33*(2), 71–80.

Yavuz, M., Meshkati, F., & Nanda, S. et al. (2009). Interference management and performance analysis of UMTS/HSPA+ femtocell. *IEEE Communications Magazine*, *47*(9), 102–109. doi:10.1109/MCOM.2009.5277462

Zou, Y., Zhu, J., & Zhang, R. (2013). Exploiting network cooperation in green wireless communication. *IEEE Transactions on Communications*, *61*(3), 999–1010. doi:10.1109/TCOMM.2013.011613.120358

KEY TERMS AND DEFINITIONS

Cognitive Radio: A radio can provide abundant new spectrum opportunities by exploiting underutilized or unutilized spectrum, temporarily and geographically.

Energy Management: Dynamic adjustment of energy to save energy according to the channel state information or the traffic situations.

Heterogeneous Network: Multiple types of smallcells including picocells, femtocells and RRH overlaid on the macrocell.

Interference Management: Any scheme to release, mitigate, use and control the interference, interference cancellation/mitigation/avoidance/alignment.

Long Term Evolution (LTE): Is a standard for wireless communication of high-speed data for mobile phones and data terminals. It is based on the GSM/EDGE andUMTS/HSPA network technologies, increasing the capacity and speed using a different radio interface together with core network improvements.

Power Control: Is the intelligent selection of transmit power in a communication system to achieve good performance within the system, which can improve the capacity of network and prolong the battery of mobile site.

Remote Radio Heads (RRHs): Have become one of the most important subsystems of today's new distributed base stations. The remote radio head contains the base station's RF circuitry plus analog-to-digital/digital-to-analog converters and up/down converters.

Resource Management: Is the efficient and effective deployment of a node's resources when they are needed.

Section 2
QoS Provisioning Solutions

Chapter 7
DASH:
A Solution for Improving Video Delivery Quality in Heterogeneous Network Environments

Lejla Rovcanin
Dublin City University, Ireland

Gabriel-Miro Muntean
Dublin City University, Ireland

ABSTRACT

Multimedia streaming has major commercial potential as the global community of online video viewers is expanding rapidly following the proliferation of low-cost multimedia-enabled mobile devices. These devices enable increasing amounts of video-based content to be acquired, stored, and distributed across existing best effort networks that also carry other traffic types. Although a number of protocols are used for video transfer, a significant portion of the Internet streaming media is currently delivered over Hypertext Transfer Protocol (HTTP). Network congestion is one of the most important issues that affects networking traffic in general and video content delivery. Among the various solutions proposed, adaptive delivery of content according to available network bandwidth was very successful. In this context, the most recent standardisation efforts have focused on the introduction of the Dynamic Adaptive Streaming over HTTP (DASH) (ISO, 2012) standard. DASH offers support for client-based bitrate video streaming adaptation, but as it does not introduce any particular adaptation mechanism, it relies on third party solutions to complement it. This chapter provides an overview of the DASH standard and presents a short survey of currently proposed mechanisms for video adaptation related to DASH. It also introduces the DASH-aware Performance-Oriented Adaptation Agent (dPOAA), which improves user Quality of Experience (QoE) levels by dynamically selecting best performing sources for the delivery of video content. dPOAA, in its functionality, considers the characteristics of the network links connecting clients with video providers. dPOAA can be utilised as a DASH player plugin or in conjunction with the DASH-based performance-oriented Adaptive Video Distribution solution (DAV) (Rovcanin & Muntean, 2013), which considers the local network characteristics, quantity of requested content available locally, and device and user profiles.

DOI: 10.4018/978-1-4666-5978-0.ch007

INTRODUCTION

Video delivery over the Internet is experiencing an outstanding growth. It is expected that the "video-on-demand traffic will nearly triple by 2017" (Cisco, 2013b, p. 2), while a sharp increase of up to 16-fold is predicted for mobile video between 2012 and 2017 (Cisco, 2013a). Among the many areas in which the online distribution of video content is expanding, education is one of the most important. Production of educational video content is becoming inexpensive and efficient (e.g. lecture podcasts, student generated videos, etc.) and it is easily made available online. Free educational video content is provided by many institutions, including Coursera (Coursera, n.d.) and edX (edX, n.d.). Increasing network connection support (e.g. wired and wireless connections such as WiFi as well as third and fourth Generation of mobile phone mobile communication technology standards - 3G/4G) together with processing power of mobile computing devices has led to their regular use for video retrieval and viewing. Decreasing costs of such devices has resulted in an explosion in the number of users and bandwidth demands. Such prolific use of portable devices is changing many aspects of today's life, including education, where millions of learners use diverse viewing devices to access and interact with online educational media content on a daily basis. This increase has added pressure on the network resources and solutions were needed to prevent negative effects of network congestion on user perceived quality or Quality of Experience (QoE) levels. Among the various solutions proposed, video delivery mechanisms which adapt the content to meet available network bandwidth, reduce loss and increase user QoE are very successful (Muntean & Murphy, 2002).

Dynamic Adaptive Streaming over HTTP (DASH) (Stockhammer, 2011; ISO, 2012) has been proposed to address problems with traditional approaches to streaming to a variety of Internet Protocol (IP) connected devices. DASH is a scalable client-based solution offering support for adaptive video streaming by enabling consecutive downloads of short video segments to match the viewer's current delivery conditions. It supports dynamic bitrate switching and live media services. This relatively new standard leverages existing HTTP-based multimedia content delivery infrastructure without the need for specialised media servers. Similar proprietary solutions such as Microsoft Silverlight Smooth Streaming (Zambelli, 2009), Apple HTTP Live Streaming (HLS) (Pantos, 2012) and Adobe Dynamic HTTP Streaming (HDS) ("Adobe HTTP Dynamic Streaming," n.d.) are widely used. However, DASH is a step towards standardised, cross-platform, efficient and cost-effective media streaming to a variety of IP enabled devices ranging from smartphones and tablets to PCs, TVs and set-top boxes.

In this chapter, we provide a short description of the DASH standard as it is considered the industry's most advanced standard for streaming multimedia content (Fisher, 2013). We also compare a number of current DASH-aware solutions in terms of the initial delivery delay control and throughput estimation. Furthermore, this chapter presents a DASH-based solution – DASH-aware Performance Oriented Adaptation Agent (dPOAA) and illustrates its benefits in an educational setting.

BACKGROUND

Currently Hypertext Transfer Protocol (HTTP) (Fielding et al, 1999) video streaming is a topic which attracts significant level of interest in the field of multimedia communications (Begen, Akgul, & Baugher, 2011). This complements the many existing solutions which were designed for video streaming over the Internet. Video streaming applications require real-time and steady throughput that is provided with efficient flow and rate control mechanisms. Real-time Transport Protocol (RTP) (Schulzrinne, Casner, Frederick, & Jacobson, 2003) is one such protocol and it is widely used over User Datagram Protocol (UDP). At the same time, protocols such as HTTP that were not designed with media streaming in mind, have begun to be employed for streaming due to their popularity, interoperability and availability. HTTP is a generic, stateless application-layer protocol that allows systems to be built independently of the data being transferred. Transmission Control Protocol (TCP) has been widely used in proprietary commercial video streaming systems for a decade and the majority of the adaptive multimedia streaming solutions deployed in practice are based on HTTP/TCP (Zambelli, 2009), which easily traverses firewalls and Network Address Translation (NAT) (Egevang & Francis, 1994) devices. This was a problem with the UDP-based video traffic and has severely affected the deployment of UDP-based solutions. Progressive download allows playing of incompletely downloaded videos using simple players or the fifth revision of HyperText Markup Language (HTML5) enabled browsers e.g. ("Progressive download," n.d.). Employing progressive download in general reduces the initial delay, however there is no mechanism for dynamic change of video quality if conditions on the client side change and therefore user QoE is often affected. Conversely, adaptive video streaming adjusts the video delivery to meet the delivery network constraints. The additive increase multiplicative decrease principle is employed in most solutions, drastically decreasing the delivery bitrate if loss is encountered indicating possible network congestion and conservatively increasing the bitrate when no loss is recorded. Various solutions address additional aspects such as energy-awareness, stream differentiation, different user interest in content, etc. (Muntean, Perry, & Murphy, 2005; Muntean, Ghinea, & Sheehan, 2008; Yuan, Venkataraman, & Muntean, 2010; Moldovan & Muntean, 2012). A nice overview of adaptive streaming approaches can be found in the work of Trestian (2012). End users are particularly sensitive to interruptions and frequent re-buffering (Tan, Gustafsson, & Heikkila, 2006) and their

expectations of the quality of the streamed video continue to grow, hence better approaches to video delivery are required, while retaining redeeming features of existing approaches.

Dynamic Adaptive Streaming over HTTP (DASH) (Stockhammer, 2011; ISO, 2012) was proposed by ISO/IEC Moving Picture Experts Group (MPEG) and the 3rd Generation Partnership Project (3GPP) to address the problems with interoperability and traditional approaches to Web streaming as well as to improve QoE levels. DASH is a standard for a client controlled media delivery model. Media content is typically stored on standard HTTP servers in multiple versions, further divided into segments of varying duration. The logic of a typical DASH-based adaptive system is located at the client side, which scales well. As a client/server paradigm, it leverages existing HTTP-based multimedia content delivery infrastructure, such as Web Servers, HTTP caches and Content Delivery Networks (CDN) without the need for specialised servers such as the Flash Media Server (or other competing products). DASH is HTTP/TCP based which eliminates firewall and NAT traversal issues. Unlike progressive download, DASH supports dynamic bitrate switching and live media services.

In a DASH context, Web servers host multiple presentations (versions/copies) of video content differing in temporal, spatial or fidelity quality (e.g. bit rate, resolution, colour depth, level of detail) ranging from lower quality renditions, up to very high quality. Each representation consists of segments (fragments, media chunks) of predefined duration, e.g. 10 seconds. DASH performs video streaming using consecutive downloads of these video segments. The process is controlled by the client, which requests content quality that matches initial conditions (available bandwidth, buffer size, remaining battery life) without the need for negotiation with the hosting server. After a segment is received, the client simply requests (via the HTTP GET method) the next segment of the quality that matches changes of the device state (e.g. buffer fill level, battery life, connection type), network traffic (e.g. drop/increase in estimated throughput) or user preferences (e.g. viewer profile, current task). A typical DASH system places decision-making at the client side and gives the client the control over the client-side queue fill level to avoid streaming buffer overflows. The client's insight into the system's performance yields the most informed adaptation decision on what to request from the server, which leads to higher QoE levels. While The DASH standard provides the means for client-driven maximization of QoE in this fragmented environment, by defining the content and structure of video description files used by DASH-enabled clients, it does not provide a specification for such a client (client-side behaviour is not defined). A comparison-based description of a number of DASH-based solutions is provided in this chapter.

Our solution is a DASH-based performance-oriented Adaptive Video Distribution Solution (DAV) (Rovcanin & Muntean, 2013) that enhances the performance of existing systems for personalised distribution of learning content. DAV considers both device and network characteristics and improves the content delivery process thereby increasing the video viewing experience. DAV involves two stages. First, it clusters local nodes based on user profile information provided by an associated personalised system. Second, it considers current network and local device characteristics, as well as data collected over time to select the most suitable (best performing) source for segment delivery. The source can either be one of the remote servers storing video segments belonging to the requested video stream or a DAV-enabled node within the local network that hosts required segments. This chapter introduces DASH-aware Performance Oriented Adaptation Agent (dPOAA) which rates servers based on their past performance. dPOAA could be utilised with DAV to provide remote server performance information to DAV Gateway.

MPEG DYNAMIC ADAPTIVE STREAMING OVER HTTP (DASH) STANDARD AND RELATED TOOLS

The standard defines the structure of Media Presentation description and the segment formats that typically contain efficiently coded media data and metadata in common media formats.

DASH Standard Outline

A *DASH Media Presentation* is a collection of encoded and deliverable versions of media content. Media content is composed of a single or multiple contiguous media content periods composed of one or multiple media content components (e.g. audio components in various languages and a video component). Each media content component (e.g. audio or video) may have several encoded versions (e.g. media streams with the properties of the encoding process such as sub-sampling, codec parameters, encoding bitrate, etc.).

The *Media Presentation Description (MPD* describes a DASH Media Presentation and reference media streams. It is an XML-formatted manifest file containing sufficient information for a client to request content from the server and support streaming services. MPD can contain various types of information including media-content description, accessibility features, required digital rights management (DRM), media-component locations on the network, uniform resource locator (URL), media characteristics such as video resolution and bitrates. The structure of an MPD file is illustrated in Figure 1, where the Media Presentation is a sequence of one or more Periods (temporal sections) containing one or more Adaptation Sets. Representations (content alternatives) are grouped into Adaptation Sets and consist of media segments of predefined duration (e.g. 6 seconds). At most one Representation within an Adaptation Set is selected to compose the delivered presentation. The client processes a video presentation on per

Figure 1. DASH MPD structure

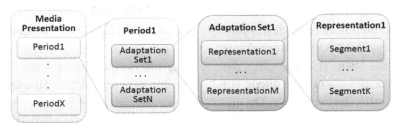

Period basis, first requesting metadata for a Period and consequently, requesting relevant segments within the Period. A consistent set of encoded versions of the Period media content is available (i.e. the set of available bitrates, languages, captions, subtitles etc.) and it does not change during a Period.

A segment is a fundamental element of the DASH standard. It is a unit of data associated with a HTTP URL and requested by DASH clients. Optionally, a segment can be associated with a byte range which may be requested individually. The DASH standard introduces four types of segments, namely *Media Segments* (contain and encapsulate media streams), *Intialization Segments* (any information necessary to enable the client to start decoding the payload), *Index Segments* (indexing information for the Media Segment) and *Bitstream Switching Segments* (essential data for seamless switching between Representations or for randomly accessing a Media Presentation).

A sample DASH system from (ISO, 2012) is illustrated in Figure 2. It indicates devices (green boxes) that either host or process the formats defined by DASH specification. In the considered deployment scenario, the DASH Client has access to an MPD file which provides sufficient information for a streaming service. The client requests segments from an HTTP server and performs demultiplexing, decoding and rendering of the included media streams.

The logical components of a conceptual DASH client model include the *DASH Access Engine* and the *Media Engine* as indicated in Figure 3. The DASH Access Engine first receives the MPD file, then constructs and issues requests and receives Segments (or parts of Segments). It processes the Segment Index (providing timing and stream access information) in order to access Segments by the use of HTTP (partial) GET requests. The output of the DASH Access Engine consists of media in an MPEG container format. The actual

Figure 2. Deployment architecture using DASH formats

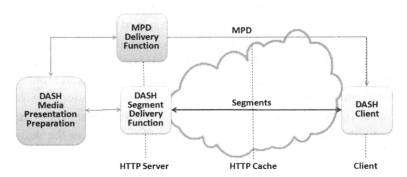

Figure 3. DASH client model

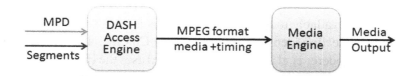

media playback is controlled by the Media Engine operating on the media streams contained in the Representations. Therefore, the Media Engine is not controlled by MPD and does not require any information from the MPD for successful decoding and presentation of the contained media streams. The Media Engine conceptually processes the Initialization Segment, which is media format specific. Initialization segment contains metadata describing the encoding of the media content, which initializes the engine, enabling it to start decoding the payload of any media stream within a Segment.

In DASH, the control of media delivery lies exclusively with the client, but the standard does not specify DASH client implementations, instead it provides an informative example of client behaviour, where clients:

1. Parse MPD to select a set of Adaptation Sets suitable for client delivery environment;
2. Select a Representation from each Adaptation Set;
3. Create a list of accessible Segments for each Representation;

4. Access the media content via requests for (entire or byte ranges of) Segments as given in the Segment list (step 3);
5. Buffer the requested media before starting the presentation;
6. Start rendering;
7. Continue the presentation with continuous requests for (parts of) Media Segments till the end of the viewed presentation.

The client may switch Representations when its environment changes (e.g. change of measured throughput) or when the MPD is updated (e.g. during live streaming). The switch to a different Representation takes place at a *Stream Access Point (SAP)*, where different Representations could be time-aligned to aid seamless switching. The switching points are announced in the MPD and/or the Segment Index. As time passes, the list of available Segments can be expanded for dynamic MPDs used in live streaming. Figure 4 illustrates DASH functionality assuming SAPs at the beginning of segments.

Figure 4. DASH functionality

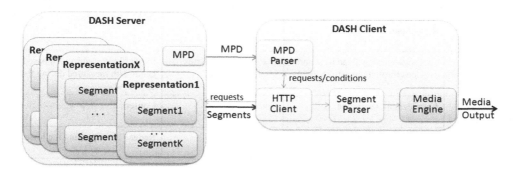

DASH Related Tools

There are a variety of freely available tools that are DASH-enabled, and this section identifies a number of them. D-DASH (Lederer et al., 2013) is an example of a distributed DASH Dataset suitable for CDN-based scientific evaluations. ITEC MPEG-DASH MPD validator ("ITEC MPEG-DASH MPD Validator," n.d.) is an online tool for testing MPD conformance to the DASH standard. GPAC MP4Box ("MP4Box | GPAC," n.d.) generates both segment files and corresponding MPDs. x264 (VideoLAN, n.d.) is a free software library and application for encoding video streams into the H.264/MPEG-4 AVC format. DASHEncoder (Lederer, Muller, & Timmerer, 2012) generates representations, segments, and MPD files according to the given configuration file or by command line parameters. It uses x264 for the video encoding and GPAC MP4Box for the multiplexing and the MPD generation to build a combined MPD file describing all representations.

There is a number of open-source clients which support playback based on the DASH standard. GPAC Osmo4 ("Osmo4 | GPAC," n.d.) is highly configurable multiplatform multimedia player which is integrated with the majority of Web browsers including Firefox, Opera and Internet Explorer. VLC Media player with DASH plugin (Muller & Timmerer, 2011) where VLC was extended with a DASH plugin (Firefox only) which

currently does not support all formats of MPDs. DASH-JS (Rainer, Lederer, Muller, & Timmerer, 2012) is a JavaScript based DASH library for Google Chrome. This integration of the DASH standard uses the HTML5 video element decoder unit and events dispatcher.

DASH-AWARE SOLUTIONS COMPARISON

This section provides a comparison of different DASH implementations in terms of bandwidth estimation as well as buffer level consideration and start-up delay constraints in the adaptation algorithms, as indicated in Table 1.

Bandwidth Estimation for HTTP Adaptive Streaming

HTTP adaptive streaming clients generally determine the quality of requested segments based on among other factors, their estimation of the current network connection bandwidth. They also consider the media buffer fill levels, and adjust the quality of the next requested segment to prevent buffer starvation and reduce interruptions for re-buffering.

A prototype of a DASH client proposed in (Miller et al., 2012) aims at properly estimating the dynamics of the available network throughput,

Table 1. Cross-comparison of proposed DASH adaptation algorithms

Solution	Bandwidth Estimation	Buffer Level	Start-Up Delay
(Miller, Quacchio, Gennari, & Wolisz, 2012)	Dynamics of the available network throughput	Considered	Reduce by requesting the lowest first
(Rainer et al., 2012)	Last segment download time and previous throughput estimation	Not considered in this implementation	Initial bitrate determined based on bandwidth measured during the MPD download
(C. Liu, Bouazizi, & Gabbouj, 2011)	Last segment fetch time	Considered	Conservative step-wise switch-up
(Thang, Ho, Kang, & Pham, 2012)	Past history and throughput variance used	Not considered	Reduce by requesting the lowest first

controlling the filling level of the client buffer, avoiding playback interruptions, maximizing the quality of the stream, avoiding unnecessary fluctuations in quality, while minimizing the initial delay. The adaptation algorithm uses information about the dynamics of the available throughput in the past and the buffer fill level to produce the quality level of the next segment and the minimum buffer level (in seconds of playback) at which the download of the next segment must start.

DASH-JS (Rainer et al., 2012) determines the throughput of next segment b_n based on the formula in Equation (2) where b_{n-1} is the throughput calculated for the previous segment, b_m denotes the actual measured throughput for the previous segment, and w_1 and w_2 are the weight factors for adjusting the influence of the recently measured segment throughput on the previous estimated throughput. As initialization value the bandwidth measured during the MPD download is used.

$$b_n = \frac{w_1 b_{n-1} + w_2 b_m}{w_1 + w_2} \quad (2)$$

A receiver-driven rate adaptation algorithm for adaptive HTTP streaming proposed in (C. Liu et al., 2011) detects bandwidth changes using a smoothed HTTP throughput measurement based on the segment fetch time (SFT). The smoothed HTTP throughput instead of the instantaneous TCP transmission rate is used to determine if the bitrate of the current media matches the end-to-end network bandwidth capacity. The proposed algorithm deploys a step-wise increase and aggressive decrease method to switch up/down between the different bitrates, without requiring transport layer information (e.g. round trip time (RTT), packet loss rates). The ratio of media segment duration (MSD) to segment fetch time (SFT) used to detect congestion and probe the spare network capacity as given in Equations (3).

$$\mu = \frac{MSD}{SFT}$$

$$(3)$$

$$\varepsilon = \max \left\{ \begin{array}{c} \dfrac{br_{i+1} - br_i}{br_i}, \\ \forall i = [0, 1, ..., N-1] \end{array} \right\}$$

Then the smoothed TCP throughput measurement can be estimated by multiplying with the media bitrate of the currently received segment. The switch to the next better quality level takes place if $\mu > 1+\varepsilon$ and the buffered media time is larger than the predefined minimum. Equations (3) define μ and ε, where br_i denotes the bitrate of quality i and N denotes the highest quality level. Switch to lower quality level takes place when $\mu < \gamma_d$ where γ_d is the switch down threshold related to the buffered media time and it is used to detect network congestion before the buffer drains.

The adaptation algorithm proposed in (Thang et al., 2012) calculates throughput based on Equations (4).

$$T_e(i) = \begin{cases} (1-\delta)T_e(i-2) + \delta T_s(i-1) \\ T_s(i-1) \end{cases}$$
$$i > 0$$
$$i = 1, 2$$

$$p = \frac{|T_s(i) - T_e(i)|}{T_e(i)}$$
$$\delta = \frac{1}{1 + e^{-k(p-P_0)}} \quad (4)$$

The estimated throughput is more sensitive to the last segment throughput for larger δs, whilst for smaller values the estimated throughput is smoothed (the value of δ is adaptively controlled). P is the normalized throughput deviation, indicating the significance of change in throughput. Larger changes in throughput, require quick reaction (δ close to 1). The values of k and P_0 (k = 21 and $P_0 = 0.2$) were determined based on the testbed observation and any change of segment throughput with p > 0.4 results in δ equal to 1, while changes with p < 0.1 result in $\delta < 0.1$.

Throughput smoothing by considering historic recordings is also used in (Gouache, Bichot, Bsila, & Howson, 2011) where the variance of throughput is used to compute a safety margin for estimated throughput in. However, it could be argued, that smoothing throughput delays the reaction of the client to significant drops in throughput, which in turn must be handled by having a large initial buffering and continuously checking whether the buffer level is lower than a safety threshold (Thang et al., 2012).

Start-Up Delay and Initial Buffering Considerations

The DASH standard (ISO, 2012) MPD element *@minBufferTime* attribute specifies a common duration used in the definition of the Representation data rate (e.g. minBufferTime="PT1.2S"). The client buffers media of for at least value of *@minBufferTime* attribute duration before starting the presentation. This attribute is linked with *@bandwidth* at Representation level. If the Representation is continuously delivered at *@bandwidth* bitrate, starting at any SAP, a client will have enough data for continuous playback providing playback begins after *@minBufferTime* * *@bandwidth* bits have been received (ISO, 2012).

Long start-up delay leads to a drop in user experience regardless of the received video quality (Alberi Morel, Kerboeuf, Sayadi, Leprovost, & Faucheux, 2010). The DASH standard considers start-up delays for video seek tasks and Initialization Segment. It suggests improving seek times with the use of partial HTTP GET to initially request the Segment Index from the beginning of the Media Segment. This Segment Index can be then used to map Segment timing to byte ranges of the

Segment. The standard then suggests continuous use of partial HTTP GET requests to access the relevant parts of the Media Segment which may reduce start-up delays and improve user experience (ISO, 2012). The Initialization Segment needs to be downloaded before any Media Segment can be processed, so keeping the Initialization Segment small may also reduce the start-up time significantly (ISO, 2012). A solution proposed in (Jarnikov & Ozcelebi, 2011) considered 15 s as the maximum start-up delay. The algorithm proposed in (Miller et al., 2012) aims at reducing the initial delay by requesting the lowest quality for the first segment downloaded. The fact that the quality of the first few seconds of the requested video will be of lowest quality is mitigated with an aggressive "fast start" phase where for each subsequent segment the next higher quality level bitrate was requested as long as the measured throughput is sufficiently higher that the requested bitrate and the buffer level monotonically increasing more aggressively when the buffer is fuller. While the initial delay was not explicitly discussed, the solution proposed in (Thang et al., 2012) assumes that the first segment is usually downloaded by simply requesting the lowest bitrate alternative.

Initial buffering is the minimum amount of pre-buffered media content (measured in seconds) that is required to start with video playback. Solution proposed in (Thang et al., 2012) uses initial buffering of two segment durations. A detailed analysis on the use of DASH for live service conducted in (Lohmar, Einarsson, Frojdh, Gabin, & Kampmann, 2011), recommends that the initial buffering should be about twice as long as the segment duration.

DASH-AWARE PERFORMANCE ORIENTED ADAPTATION AGENT

This section introduces a DASH-aware Performance Oriented Adaptation Agent (dPOAA).

This agent is inspired by the Performance Oriented Adaptation Agent (Rovcanin, Muntean, & Muntean, 2006, 2008), and aids intelligent selection of remote servers storing identical DASH content. dPOAA can be deployed at the campus gateway (Figure 5) to aid the server selection for the DASH-based performance-oriented Adaptive Video distribution solution (DAV) or at the user device, as a plugin for DASH players. dPOAA can be used to enhance the performance of Personalised Learning Systems (PLS) utilizing DASH video content.

Handling of multiple alternative base URLs is addressed in section 5.6.5. of the DASH standard (ISO, 2012). The standard supports the specification of an alternative base URLs through the BaseURL element at any level (i.e. MPD, Period, Adaptation Set or Representation level) of the MPD document. When alternative base URLs exist, identical Segments are available and accessible at multiple locations. The standard specifies that a DASH client may (a) use the first BaseURL element in the absence of other criteria, and (b) implement a suitable selection algorithm to determine URLs for segment requests (ISO, 2012). In line with the standard specification, we propose the use of dPOAA to compute server performance ratings which in turn can be used for selection of the best performing server where requested content is available from multiple servers.

DAV Outline

Communities of learners that have similar learning demands and watch the same educational video content while in close geographical proximity of a university campus, might introduce needless demands on the video hosting servers and the communication links between the hosting servers and the learner devices. In this setting, identical educational video content is requested and delivered multiple times to the clients within the local area network (LAN). Due to the nature of DASH client-based adaptation, any congestion at the host-player link will force the DASH player to request segments of lower quality in the attempt to avoid/reduce re-buffering interruptions. Consequently, a number of viewers will be subjected to low quality of video resulting in low levels of QoE. DAV enhances both user experience and the performance of existing PLSs by utilizing video segments available within the local network. DAV considers viewer preferences (i.e. learner profiles provided by the associated PLS), viewing device capabilities and utilizes content available locally, recruiting groups of active learners (watching the video within the campus) to share their partial copies of the video stream (i.e. video segments) with other students in the LAN. This solution requires no modification of the HTTP servers hosting video content and aids utilization of any

Figure 5. dPOAA deployed in conjunction with DAV

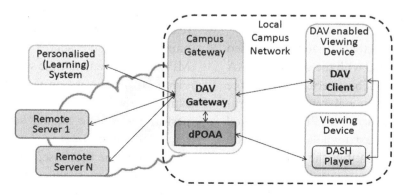

personalized distributed video delivery system. *DAV Gateway* (a DAV module) considers current network conditions and data collected over time to dynamically create a new MPD for the requested video based on the MPDs provided by the remote servers hosting the video. For each segment within a video, the *MPD Builder* (a component of DAV Gateway) selects a number of the best performing local hosts to add their URLs to the newly generated MPD file. When segments are unavailable locally the client reverts to the remote host. To build the new MPD constituents, DAV Builder selects video content from the hosts that are currently rated as the most efficient providers of the requested segments. *DAV Host Selector*, a component of DAV Gateway, uses a utility function to calculate local host rating, which is proportional to the freshness of the content stored at the host and limited by the number of simultaneous connections to the host.

When the requested video content resides on multiple remote servers, DAV Host Selector functionality can be extended with the rating generated by the *DAV Server Reputation Generator (SRG)*. SRG, as a component of DAV Gateway, generates remote server reputation based on historic performance information gathered over a number of recent sessions with the remote servers that store the requested video content. This reputation is then used to select the best performing remote server among the multiple video sources and to set its URL as the BaseURL at MPD level in the newly created MPD.

dPOAA Deployment

The performance a PLS that utilize DASH video content can be enhanced with the use of dPOAA for informed selection of best performing remote servers hosting the educational content. The learning content selection process in a PLS is triggered at every learner's request for learning content. At that time the PLS identifies the video content that best suits the learner. Once the video with matching learning objectives is identified, the PLS

builds a presentation suitable for the learner and learning context, and finally sends the presentation embedding the link to the relevant MPD file to the learner's device. Multiple server URLs are provided in the MPD file when the chosen video resides on multiple servers. When DAV is used, it intercepts messages to and from the PLS and uses the MPD file provided to build a new MPD. The new MPD is then sent to the learner's device. Once DASH player at the learner's device receives the MPD file, it parses it and requests relevant video segments from a server specified in the MPD.

When dPOAA is deployed in conjunction with DAV, it provides remote server performance information required by DAV SRG. In this case, dPOAA is installed on the campus gateway, as illustrated in Figure 5, and the server performance rating is inferred from historic network performance on the (remote server – campus gateway) link. In this deployment, the MPD that is received by the learner's device is modified by DAV Gateway, and it contains a single MPD BaseURL - the URL of the best performing host.

The proposed dPOAA solution could be easily applied as a plugin for DASH players to aid selection of the best performing server based on the historic information about segment downloads recorded at the client device. In this case, dPOAA is installed on the client device and it monitors links from the device to the remote servers, collects performance measurements and provides the performance information about each of the previously contacted servers storing the requested DASH content. In this setting, the original MPD reaches the learner's device, and it contains a number of remote server URLs (BaseURL at MPD level) when multiple servers are hosting the video. DASH player then uses server performance ratings provided by dPOAA to identify the best performing source among servers hosting the requested video.

While in the first case, dPOAA has access to more recent performance information, as DAV Gateway is aware of any node within the campus network currently downloading content from the remote servers, both deployments are expected to reduce both start-up delay and re-buffering.

dPOAA Architecture

The dPOAA enhances the remote host selection process by providing server performance ratings, so that the segments can be requested from the most efficient remote host. This in turn will result in smoother video playback and minimized start-up latency. The dPOAA depends on the information about network connection to remote hosts. Network parameter considered are the segment download time and the throughput as inferred from historic performance information gathered during the most recent sessions with the remote servers.

The block-level architecture dPOAA given in Figure 6, illustrates two dPOAA components, namely *dPOAA Performance Model* (dPOAA PM) and *dPOAA Performance Engine* (dPOAA PE).

dPOAA PM is the passive dPOAA component. It stores information used by the dPOAA algorithm. The dPOAA PM maintains a history log for each contacted hosting server. The log is a sliding-window structure that contains readings for the most recently requested segments from a given server. Each server is identified by its URL. The following readings are maintained for *X* last segments delivered by each server:

- *Throughput=8*Delivered / (DeliveryDuration*1024)* where:
  - ○ **Delivered:** The size of the segment delivered in KB.

- ○ **DeliveryDuration:** The difference between the end of delivery and request time in milliseconds.
  - ○ **Throughput:** Is calculated throughput of a link to the server, expressed in Mbps.
- **Round Trip Time (RTT):** The time that lapses from the segment request to the selected host until the client device receives first byte of the segment time in milliseconds.
- **Segment Duration:** The duration of the media contained in the requested segment when presented at normal speed expressed in milliseconds.

dPOAA PE is the active part of dPOAA. It calculates performance ratings for all remote servers hosting requested video on each learner request. The Server performance rating is based on the network condition, therefore dPOAA PE continuously needs fresh information on the state of the links to the server. The amount of additional traffic introduced with this process should be minimal as it may be resource consuming and wasteful in the ever changing Internet environment. The idea here is to collect as much information as possible without introducing extra traffic or deploying agents at the remote server side. Therefore POAA PE collects details for each segment requested from and delivered by a remote server, and stores this information to the server log. When deployed on the campus gateway, dPOAA collects performance information of (remote server – campus gateway) link for all requests from the local network, while when deployed as DASH player plugin, it collects

Figure 6. dPOAA block level architecture

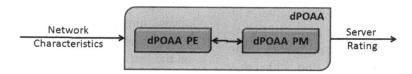

information of (remote server – viewing device) link for the requests from the local viewing device.

The hosting servers differ in their response time and availability (varying performance, load, etc.) as well as the quality of network connection in terms of throughput and delay. dPOAA generates the server rating - R_n, which is inferred from historic performance information including the throughput for the last downloaded segment from the server - Tp_{nL} and the average throughput over the X - 1 previous requests to the server - Tp_{nX}, to make the calculated rating less sensitive to short lived fluctuations in the server connection throughput. The weighted additive utility function is used to calculate R_n, as indicated in Equation (5).

$$R_n = (1 - w) \cdot Tp_{nX} + w \cdot Tp_{nL} \qquad (5)$$
$$0 < w < 1$$

Using previous throughput recordings to smooth the server throughput may result in slow reaction to drops in available bandwidth, which could result in re-buffering interruptions. The weight - w is dynamically computed using an exponential function and it depends on the severity of change in throughput. The value of w ranges from 0 to 1 and is particularly sensitive to larger drops in throughput when w is close to 1. Currently, a number of algorithms deploying the utility function in Equation (5) are being evaluated in a simulated setting. The evaluation results are available in (Rovcanin & Muntean, 2014).

dPOAA Benefits

Interactive video is an instructional technology with a long history in education. The amount and quality of free educational video content available online are growing rapidly. The increasing number of learners watching online videos together with their requirements (e.g. high data rate of the requested video content) introduces growing strain on the current Internet infrastructure, which may result in lower levels of Quality of Experience (QoE). A recent study (X. Liu et al., 2012) reports that 20% of user sessions suffer quality issues such as, more than 10% buffering time or more than 5 seconds start-up delay. At the same time, learners use a variety of viewing devices of differing capabilities, which can prolong start-up delays and introduce additional re-buffering pauses leading to even poorer levels of QoE. It could be argued that viewers who are interested in the content (e.g. when viewing a recommended video as part of graded homework) are more tolerant of longer start-up delays. Nevertheless, the tolerance drops after around 15 seconds (Dobrian et al., 2011). However, start-up delay that learners "experience while using an online instructional tool may have detrimental effects on performance and satisfaction" (Davis & Hantula, 2001, p. 250) and in general, it may reduce the likelihood of a viewer visiting the site again (Dobrian et al., 2011). In contrast, longer start-up delays typically result in fewer interruptions of playback for re-buffering at later stages. Online viewers are particularly sensitive to video playback interruptions (Tan et al., 2006) and small increases in the percentage of time spent in re-buffering negatively affects the video viewing time. For example, a 1% increase in the relative time spent in re-buffering (the total time of buffer starvation over the total length of video playback including pauses for re-buffering) can reduce viewing time for over 3 minutes for a 90 minute live event (Dobrian et al., 2011). Therefore, to increase viewing experience, dPOAA selects the best performing source of video content to minimise stops in playback while maintaining acceptable start-up delays, which is in line with evaluation criteria proposed (Dobrian et al., 2011; Miller et al., 2012).

Online video-based instruction is rapidly becoming an irreplaceable component of elearning and learning (e.g. university education) in general. The impact of the quality of viewing experience on the learning outcomes will be even more significant, as video viewing is becoming an integral part of the learning process. The proposed solution - dPOAA adjusts the learning content selection to network conditions in order to improve the overall viewing experience which in turn will positively affect the learning outcomes.

FUTURE RESEARCH DIRECTIONS

Utilization of smart phones for video viewing is becoming ubiquitous (e.g. Cisco (2013a) estimates that video traffic will account for more than two-thirds of global mobile data traffic by 2017). The idea behind DASH is to use available, inexpensive HTTP infrastructure to meet the current demands for streamed video. The HTTP servers can provide multiple versions of a video in terms quality (e.g. bitrate) ranging from lower quality renditions for 3G connections, up to high definition quality, thus meeting the requirements of heterogeneous viewing devices. This makes DASH a practical solution for addressing the surge in availability of free educational video content and inexpensive media-enabled mobile devices.

In this context, we propose the DASH-aware Performance Oriented Adaptation Agent (dPOAA) for DASH enabled Personalised Learning Systems to enhance remote host selection for DASH video delivery when content resides on multiple remote servers. Currently, dPOAA is being evaluated in a simulated setting. As future work, the authors are planning to conduct subjective evaluation tests that employ real video streaming traffic using a variety of different viewing devices.

CONCLUSION

The DASH standard is promising to end the need for the variety of vendor-specific video player solutions. The first section of this chapter provides an outline of this recent standard and identifies freely available DASH-based tools and players.

The standard proposes a client controlled adaptation in the face of changing network conditions but does not specify how it should be implemented. To respond to these changes, DASH player solutions must be able to estimate connection bandwidth, adjust initial buffering times and control buffer fill levels to provide good quality of playback. Therefore an overview of existing solutions is provided in the second section of this chapter.

The third section introduces the DASH-aware Performance Oriented Adaptation Agent (dPOAA) for DASH enabled Personalised Learning Systems where video content resides on multiple remote servers. In this case the relevant MPDs contain multiple server URLs and a DASH player can choose any of alternative URLs to request video content. While the standard allows specification of multiple URLs, it does not specify the selection algorithms. The video hosts differ in response time and availability as well as the quality of connection. dPOAA infers remote host performance based on historic performance information gathered over a number of recent sessions with the hosting servers. dPOAA can be deployed with the DASH-based performance-oriented Adaptive Video distribution solution (DAV) to provide remote server performance information. Alternatively, dPOAA can be used as a DASH player plugin to aid selection of the best performing server based on the historic information collected at the client device. In both cases, dPOAA deployment is expected to reduce both the start-up delay and re-buffering.

REFERENCES

Adobe HTTP Dynamic Streaming. (n.d.). *Using Adobe HTTP dynamic streaming*. Retrieved October 23, 2013, from http://help.adobe.com/en_US/HTTPStreaming/1.0/Using/index.html

Alberi Morel, M.-L., Kerboeuf, S., Sayadi, B., Leprovost, Y., & Faucheux, F. (2010). Performance evaluation of channel change for DVB-SH streaming services. In *Proceedings of IEEE International Conference on Communications (ICC)* (pp. 1–6). Cape Town, South Africa: IEEE.

Begen, A., Akgul, T., & Baugher, M. (2011). Watching video over the web: Part 2: Applications, standardization, and open issues. *IEEE Internet Computing, 15*(3), 59–63. doi:10.1109/MIC.2010.156

Cisco. (2013a, February 6). *Cisco visual networking index: Global mobile data traffic forecast update, 2012–2017.* Retrieved November 25, 2013, from http://www.cisco.com/en/US/solutions/ collateral/ns341/ns525/ns537/ns705/ns827/white_paper_c11-520862.html

Cisco. (2013b, May 29). *Cisco visual networking index: Forecast and methodology, 2012–2017.* Retrieved December 14, 2013, from http://www.cisco.com/c/en/us/solutions/collateral/service-provider/ip-ngn-ip-next-generation-network/white_paper_c11-481360.html

Coursera. (n.d.). *Coursera.* Retrieved October 13, 2013, from https://www.coursera.org/

Davis, E. S., & Hantula, D. A. (2001). The effects of download delay on performance and end-user satisfaction in an Internet tutorial. *Computers in Human Behavior, 17*(3), 249–268. doi:10.1016/S0747-5632(01)00007-3

Dobrian, F., Sekar, V., Awan, A., Stoica, I., Joseph, D., & Ganjam, A. … Zhang, H. (2011). Understanding the impact of video quality on user engagement. In *Proceedings of the ACM SIGCOMM 2011 Conference* (pp. 362–373). New York, NY: ACM. edX. (n.d.). *edX.* Retrieved October 13, 2013, from https://www.edx.org/

Egevang, K., & Francis, P. (1994). *RFC 1631: The IP network address translator (NAT).* Retrieved from http://www.hjp.at/doc/rfc/rfc1631.html

Fielding, R., Gettys, J., Mogul, J., Frystyk, H., Masinter, L., Leach, P., & Berners-Lee, T. (1999). *RFC 2616: Hypertext transfer protocol -- HTTP/1.1.* Retrieved from http://www.w3.org/Protocols/rfc2616/rfc2616.txt

Fisher, D. (2013). Harmonic powers virgin media's MPEG-DASH trial. *Harmonic Inc.* Retrieved October 10, 2013, from http://harmonicinc.com/news/harmonic-powers-virgin-media-s-mpeg-dash-trial

Gouache, S., Bichot, G., Bsila, A., & Howson, C. (2011). Distributed adaptive HTTP streaming. In *Proceedings of 2011 IEEE International Conference on Multimedia and Expo (ICME)* (pp. 1–6). Barcelona, Spain: IEEE.

ISO. (2012). *ISO/IEC 23009-1:2012 information technology -- Dynamic adaptive streaming over HTTP (DASH) -- Part 1: Media presentation description and segment formats.* Retrieved from http://www.iso.org/iso/catalogue_detail.htm?csnumber=57623

ITEC MPEG-DASH MPD Validator. (n.d.). Retrieved October 20, 2013, from http://www-itec.uni-klu.ac.at/dash/?page_id=605

Jarnikov, D., & Ozcelebi, T. (2011). Client intelligence for adaptive streaming solutions. *Signal Processing Image Communication, 26*(7), 378–389. doi:10.1016/j.image.2011.03.003

Lederer, S., Mueller, C., Timmerer, C., Concolato, C., Le Feuvre, J., & Fliegel, K. (2013). Distributed DASH dataset. In *Proceedings of the 4th ACM Conference on Multimedia Systems* (pp. 131–135). New York, NY: ACM.

Lederer, S., Muller, C., & Timmerer, C. (2012). Dynamic adaptive streaming over HTTP dataset. In *Proceedings of the 3rd ACM Conference on Multimedia Systems* (pp. 89–94). New York, NY: ACM.

Liu, C., Bouazizi, I., & Gabbouj, M. (2011). Rate adaptation for adaptive HTTP streaming. In *Proceedings of the Second Annual ACM Conference on Multimedia Systems* (pp. 169–174). New York, NY: ACM.

Liu, X., Dobrian, F., Milner, H., Jiang, J., Sekar, V., Stoica, I., & Zhang, H. (2012). A case for a coordinated internet video control plane. In *Proceedings of the ACM SIGCOMM 2012 Conference on Applications, Technologies, Architectures, and Protocols for Computer Communication* (pp. 359–370). New York, NY: ACM.

Lohmar, T., Einarsson, T., Frojdh, P., Gabin, F., & Kampmann, M. (2011). Dynamic adaptive HTTP streaming of live content. In *Proceedings of IEEE International Symposium on World of Wireless, Mobile and Multimedia Networks (WoWMoM)* (pp. 1–8). Lucca, Italy: IEEE.

MP4Box | GPAC. (n.d.). Retrieved October 18, 2013, from http://gpac.wp.mines-telecom.fr/mp4box/

Miller, K., Quacchio, E., Gennari, G., & Wolisz, A. (2012). Adaptation algorithm for adaptive streaming over HTTP. In *Proceedings of 19th International Packet Video Workshop (PV)* (pp. 173–178). Munich, Germany: Academic Press.

Moldovan, A., & Muntean, C. H. (2012). Subjective assessment of BitDetect - A mechanism for energy-aware multimedia content adaptation. *IEEE Transactions on Broadcasting, 58*(3), 480–492. doi:10.1109/TBC.2012.2191688

Muller, C., & Timmerer, C. (2011). A VLC media player plugin enabling dynamic adaptive streaming over HTTP. In *Proceedings of the 19th ACM International Conference on Multimedia* (pp. 723–726). New York, NY: ACM.

Muntean, G.-M., Ghinea, G., & Sheehan, T. N. (2008). Region of interest-based adaptive multimedia streaming scheme. *IEEE Transactions on Broadcasting, 54*(2), 296–303. doi:10.1109/TBC.2008.919012

Muntean, G.-M., & Murphy, L. (2002). Adaptive pre-recorded multimedia streaming. In *Proceedings of IEEE Global Telecommunications Conference (GLOBECOM)* (Vol. 2, pp. 1728–1732). Taipei, Taiwan: IEEE.

Muntean, G.-M., Perry, P., & Murphy, L. (2005). Objective and subjective evaluation of QOAS video streaming over broadband networks. *IEEE Transactions on Network and Service Management, 2*(1), 19–28. doi:10.1109/TNSM.2005.4798298

Osmo4 | GPAC. (n.d.). Retrieved October 20, 2013, from http://gpac.wp.mines-telecom.fr/player/

Pantos, R. (2012). *HTTP live streaming, IETF draft.* Retrieved November 11, 2013, from http://tools.ietf.org/html/draft-pantos-http-live-streaming-09

Progressive Download | Adobe Developer Connection. (n.d.). Retrieved October 23, 2013, from http://www.adobe.com/devnet/video/progressive.html

Rainer, B., Lederer, S., Muller, C., & Timmerer, C. (2012). A seamless web integration of adaptive HTTP streaming. In *Proceedings of the 20th European Signal Processing Conference (EUSIPCO)* (pp. 1519–1523). Bucharest, Romania: EUSIPCO.

Rovcanin, L., Muntean, C. H., & Muntean, G.-M. (2006). Performance enhancement for open corpus adaptive hypermedia systems. In V. P. Wade, H. Ashman, & B. Smyth (Eds.), *Adaptive hypermedia and adaptive web-based systems* (pp. 462–466). Berlin: Springer. doi:10.1007/11768012_70

Rovcanin, L., Muntean, C. H., & Muntean, G.-M. (2008). *Performance aware adaptation in open corpus e-learning systems.* Paper presented at the International Workshop on Technologies for Mobile and Wireless-Based Adaptive e-Learning Environments, Adaptive Hypermedia and Adaptive Web-Based Systems '08. Hanover, Germany.

Rovcanin, L., & Muntean, G.-M. (2013). A DASH-based performance-oriented adaptive video distribution solution. In *Proceedings of IEEE International Symposium on Broadband Multimedia Systems and Broadcasting.* London, UK: IEEE.

Rovcanin, L., & Muntean, G.-M. (2014). A DASH-aware performance oriented adaptation agent. In *Proceedings of IEEE International Symposium on Broadband Multimedia Systems and Broadcasting.* Beijing, China: IEEE.

Schulzrinne, H., Casner, S., Frederick, R., & Jacobson, V. (2003). RFC 3550: RTP: A transport protocol for real-time applications. *IETF.* Retrieved from https://tools.ietf.org/html/rfc3550

Stockhammer, T. (2011). Dynamic adaptive streaming over HTTP–Design principles and standards. In *Proceedings of the Second Annual ACM Conference on Multimedia Systems (MMSys11)* (pp. 133–144). New York, NY: ACM.

Tan, X., Gustafsson, J., & Heikkila, G. (2006). Perceived video streaming quality under initial buffering and rebuffering degradations. In *Proceedings of MESAQIN Measurement of Speech, Audio and Video Quality in Networks Conference.* Prague, Czech Republic: MESAQIN.

Thang, T. C., Ho, Q.-D., Kang, J. W., & Pham, A. T. (2012). Adaptive streaming of audiovisual content using MPEG DASH. *IEEE Transactions on Consumer Electronics, 58*(1), 78–85. doi:10.1109/TCE.2012.6170058

Trestian, R. (2012). *User-centric power-friendly quality-based network selection strategy for heterogeneous wireless environments.* (Doctoral dissertation). Dublin City University, Dublin, Ireland. Retrieved from http://doras.dcu.ie/16783/1/Ramona_Trestian_-_PhD_Thesis_Final.PDF

Video, L. A. N. (n.d.). *H.264/AVC encoder.* Retrieved October 17, 2013, from http://www.videolan.org/developers/x264.html

Yuan, Z., Venkataraman, H., & Muntean, G.-M. (2010). iPAS: An user perceived quality-based intelligent prioritized adaptive scheme for IPTV in wireless home networks. In *Proceedings of IEEE International Symposium on Broadband Multimedia Systems and Broadcasting.* Shanghai, China: IEEE.

Zambelli, A. (2009). IIS smooth streaming technical overview. *Microsoft Corporation.* Retrieved October 20, 2013, from http://www.microsoft.com/en-us/download/details.aspx?id=17678

KEY TERMS AND DEFINITIONS

DASH: Dynamic Adaptive Streaming over HTTP is a standard for a client controlled segmented media delivery where the most adequate segment version (quality) is requested to match user preferences, the viewing device capabilities and/or current connectivity characteristics.

DAV: DASH-based performance-oriented Adaptive Video distribution solution improves the quality of delivered video content by considering the local network, quantity of requested content available locally, and device and user profiles. It is deployed with personalised systems, such as a PLS.

dPOAA: DASH-aware Performance Oriented Adaptation Agent dynamically selects best performing sources for the video segment delivery by considering characteristics of the network links to the video sources. It can be used in conjunction with DAV or as DASH player plugin.

MPD: Media Presentation Description is a DASH manifest file containing sufficient information for a DASH client to request content from the server and support streaming services.

PLS: Personalised Learning Systems adjust their content and/or presentation to match learner's needs and characteristics.

POAA: Performance Oriented Adaptation Agent increases performance of Open Adaptive Educational Hypermedia Systems (OAEHS) which utilize remote learning content. POAA enhances content selection process in an OAEHS by considering network delivery conditions, so that the selected content can be smoothly delivered.

QoE: Quality of Experience refers to the viewer's experience - the degree of delight or annoyance with the delivered content, which enables more holistic understanding of the network quality.

Chapter 8

TraffCon:
An Innovative Vehicle Route Management Solution Based on IEEE 802.11p Sparse Roadside-Vehicle Networking

Kevin Collins
Dublin City University, Ireland

Gabriel-Miro Muntean
Dublin City University, Ireland

ABSTRACT

Traffic congestion is a major issue in the modern society, and unfortunately, it continues to worsen as the number of cars on the road grows behind the ability of existing road infrastructures to cope. Additionally, vehicle fuel consumption and gas emissions are increasing, and concentrated efforts to propose solutions to reduce these and consequently the pollution are needed. In this context, this chapter presents TraffCon, an innovative vehicle route management solution, which makes use of a novel best route selection algorithm for vehicular traffic routing and of vehicular wireless communications to reduce not only journey times but also fuel consumption and as a direct consequence vehicle gas emissions. The chapter shows how TraffCon can be supported by an IEEE 802.11p sparse roadside-vehicle network with very good results in comparison with classic approaches.

INTRODUCTION

Over the past number of years, employing vehicular communications to support intelligent traffic management services has garnered much attention in both industry and academia. A variety of communication technologies has been used including; optical (infrared) (Kwak and Lee, 2004), ultra-wideband (UWB) (Elbahhar, Rivenq, Heddebaut and Rouvaen, 2005),, Bluetooth (Sugiura and Dermawan, 2005), and cellular (Santa, Gómez-Skarmeta and Sánchez-Artigas, 2008). However it appears that IEEE 802.11 (Wi-Fi) based solutions are emerging as the most popular. This trend looks set to continue as the IEEE 802.11p (Jiang and Delgrossi, 2008), (Uzcátegui and Acosta-Marum, 2009) amendment to the standard is attracting increasing interest.

DOI: 10.4018/978-1-4666-5978-0.ch008

With the problem of a suitable communications technology for vehicular communications addressed, the next challenge is that of market introduction. A range of appealing applications are required to drive the uptake of vehicular communications and numerous solutions have already been proposed, with safety applications being the most prominent (Yang, Guo and Wu, 2009), (Zhang, Festag, Baldessari and Le, 2008), (Jiang, Chen and Delgrossi, 2008). Many safety applications rely on Inter-vehicle Communications (IVC) and the formation of Vehicle Ad-hoc Networks (VANET). Given the dearth of successfully deployed commercial examples of ad-hoc networks these types of application are unlikely to be viable in the early stages of vehicular communications. Also certain safety applications by their very nature require; very high up to 100% penetration rates of the technology e.g. co-operative collision avoidance (Taleb, Ooi and Hashimoto, 2008). The distribution method is also a problem with safety features being either fitted as standard or provided as optional extras in new cars, after-market introduction seems unlikely. This reduces the potential for them to be introduced quickly.

What is needed to drive the uptake of vehicular communications are other practical applications which benefit the user regardless of the number of other vehicles so equipped. The obvious platform for deployment is the widespread in-car satellite navigation system. This in-car technology can be provided as standard in new cars or added later with a portable solution. In Western Europe alone, approximately 14.4 million portable sat-nav systems were sold during 2007 and the number is expected to increase in the following years (Skog and Handel, 2009). There is already a trend toward allying this technology with wireless communications, many existing sat-nav units can receive live traffic data via FM traffic receivers or via connectivity provided by their mobile phone. However it is expected that most portable navigation devices will feature real-time two-way connectivity based on cellular or Wi-Fi technology.

For early adopters of Wi-Fi enabled sat-nav devices any enhanced functionality must be provided by roadside-vehicle communications (RVC). Assuming that a full infrastructure network is unavailable then the vehicle can be said to be travelling in a sparse infrastructure network. The connectivity availed by this network allows for the provision of new services as shown in Figure 1. Given the sat-nav platform it makes sense to offer location based services such as the traffic information services which have already proven popular.

This chapter presents TraffCon, an innovative vehicle route management solution (Collins and Muntean, 2008b) which makes use of the novel best route selection algorithm for vehicular traffic routing and of vehicular wireless communications to reduce not only journey times, but also fuel consumption and as a direct consequence, vehicle gas emissions. The best route selection algorithm is described and the provision of TraffCon as an enhanced traffic management service in the communications landscape outlined above is explored. Testing results shows how by employing TraffCon fuel consumption is greatly reduced in comparison with existing state-of-the-art solutions. The remainder of the chapter is structured as follows: in the next section Sparse Roadside-Vehicle Net-

Figure 1. Provision of in car services with a sparse infrastructure network

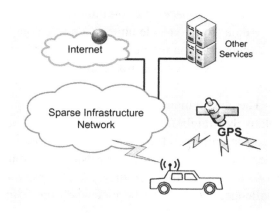

works are discussed in greater detail. The TraffCon system is introduced in a dedicated section and results from tests involving the proposed best route selection algorithm are presented in a section that follows immediately. The provision of traffic efficiency services in sparse roadside-vehicle networks and related test results are then presented. Related works are presented in a dedicated section just before the chapter finishes with conclusions and future work directions.

SPARSE ROADSIDE-VEHICLE NETWORKS

In the early stages of deployment of vehicular communications, services will be provided via roadside-vehicular communication. In the absence of full infrastructure this can be considered a sparse roadside-vehicle network. Vehicles communicate data with roadside infrastructure in order to provide services. These can be placed in two categories according to the communications involved:

- **Stand-Alone Services:** Communication occurs solely between the vehicle and a roadside unit which often serves a single purpose e.g. a petrol station or a speed limit sign advertising its existence.
- **Integrated Services:** The vehicle communicates with roadside units who share a common server via backhaul communications e.g. backhaul communications carry data from roadside units to a traffic control centre to enable the provision of traffic efficiency services across a city.

The deployment of stand-alone services is relatively straight forward as it only involves one roadside unit operating in isolation. To provide integrated services multiple roadside units must work together. However they are a variety of challenges which must be met when providing

integrated services over a sparse roadside-vehicle network. We will examine these in the next section.

Provision of Integrated Services

The integrated services which are likely to be provided to vehicles via vehicular communications are typically classified as follows (Kosch, Kulp, Bechler, Strassberger, Weyl, and Lasowski, 2009):

- Traffic safety (e.g. hazard warnings)
- Traffic efficiency (e.g. traffic updates)
- Value-added services (e.g., infotainment, business applications)

If these types of services are to be provided in this sparse roadside-vehicle communications environment they are number of issues which must be considered:

- **Connectivity:** In a sparse roadside-vehicle network vehicles are not always connected. Connectivity is provided intermittently at communication hotspots as seen in figure Figure 2.A. If providing a location based service for example the vehicle may not be connected at the location where information for a service is required. Therefore there are times when information must be gathered before it is needed.
- **Connection Time:** When a vehicle moves into range of a hotspot the connection window is often very short as its mobility can take it out of range quickly as shown in figure Figure 2.B. In order for services to function the necessary information must be exchanged in an efficient manner while connected. The problem can be addressed to some extent by infrastructure placement e.g. vehicles slow down and/or stop at intersections making them a good location for roadside units.

Figure 2. Connectivity, connection time and variant infrastructure density issues in a Manhattan grid

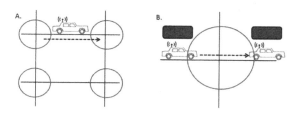
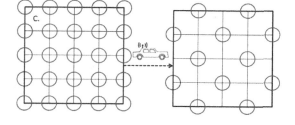

- **Variant Infrastructure Density:** The frequency with which a vehicle may encounter a roadside unit can vary widely depending on the infrastructure density in a given area. In figure Figure 2.C we see an example where a vehicle is moving from a region with a communications hotspot at every intersection to an area where hotspots are found at half the intersections. Variations in the density of roadside infrastructure affect the level of connectivity a vehicle receives which in turn effects the provision of services. Services should be capable of degrading and upgrading gracefully depending on the level of connectivity available.

These issues are dealbreakers for certain services e.g. a service such as video streaming which requires uninterrupted connectivity simply cannot be provided in a sparse roadside-vehicle network. Similarly co-operative collision avoidance and other safety applications which require vehicles in close proximity to be in constant radio contact cannot be provided in a sparse roadside-vehicle network. However a wide range of traffic safety, traffic efficiency and location based information services may still be provided in this chapter we focus on the provision of traffic efficiency services over sparse roadside to vehicle communications networks. We will first introduce and evaluate our own traffic efficiency solution entitled TraffCon. We will then show how this solution or others like it may be provide by a sparse roadside-vehicle network.

TRAFFCON SYSTEM

The TraffCon traffic management system presented in (Collins and Muntean, 2008b) has a client-server architecture. Vehicles act as client nodes and communicate with the server asynchronously in order to support two main functions: information gathering and traffic management as shown in figure Figure 3.

Information Gathering

With information gathering all nodes in the system collect useful temporal and spatially referenced traffic data e.g. speed, acceleration (i.e. Data Harvesting). This data is filtered, aggregated and refined to generate precise information regarding the state of the traffic network (i.e. Data Processing). This communication is not time critical as traffic information does not need to be up to the second. However, some threshold on the age of the information is required by the traffic management. In this phase inter-vehicle communication may be used to employ techniques such as data aggregation in order to reduce the load on the mesh network.

Traffic Management

In order to facilitate traffic management vehicles keep the server informed of their location and the server disseminates traffic instructions. The instructions are generated by a decision making process which uses the location information and the traffic network information provided by the

Figure 3. TraffCon system architecture

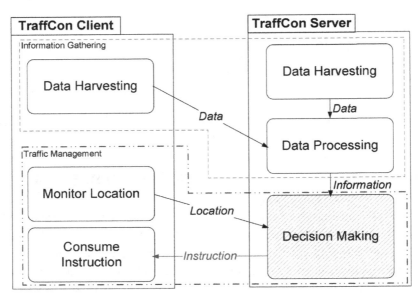

vehicular network. The decision making block is comprised of a number of algorithms which map to different traffic management services e.g. a best route selection algorithm manages route management. These communications are time sensitive as instructions will only be valid within a certain time frame. The best route selection which can be used to provide route management is described in the next section.

Best Route Selection Algorithm

The best route selection algorithm (summarised in Figure 4) is employed by TraffCon in its decision making process. A new decision making process starts when a vehicle begins a journey by sending its origin and desired destination to the server. The steps listed next are followed:

- Retrieve the k shortest routes from origin to destination. This is done by querying a cache of k-shortest paths using the origin and destination. It is possible to cache the paths as road layout changes infrequently relative to traffic conditions.

- A fitness function is evaluated for each route, resulting in an associated fitness score. This fitness function which considers overall road congestion, vehicle journey times and fuel consumption is presented in the next section.

- The best route is selected based on the fitness scores. The fitness function is the sum of weighted cost functions so the route with the lowest overall score is selected.

- The user is given an instruction on what to do at the next junction to follow the chosen route. After passing through a junction and onto a new road segment, the journey origin is updated to that position and the algorithm is repeated. In this way the route instructions remain valid even if the user does not obey all instructions, and the route may also be altered if changes in traffic conditions mean a better route now exists.

The cache of k shortest paths is created using the generalised Floyd Shortest-Path algorithm (Evans and Minieka, 1992). Constraint checking

Figure 4. One iteration of TraffCon's best route selection algorithm

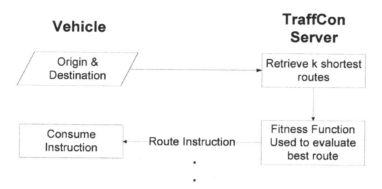

runs in parallel to ensure the *k* routes are valid i.e. no rules of the road are broken (e.g. going the wrong way down a one way street). The value of *k* is important as only that number of routes will be considered as possible solutions. The parameter was introduced to reduce the complexity of the solution space and speed up the solution finding process.

Other well known *k* shortest path algorithms exist including the double sweep algorithm and the generalised Dantzig algorithm (Evans and Minieka, 1992). However the double sweep algorithm is better suited to finding the k shortest paths between a specified vertex and all other vertices, while both Floyd and Dantzig algorithms are suited to finding the *k* shortest paths between every pair of vertices, as required. These two algorithms are of the same order of complexity so the choice for the Floyd algorithm does not influence system performance. The complexity of the proposed algorithm is discussed further in the next sub section.

One potential problem which can arise with the type of adaptation in the proposed algorithm is the "flash crowd " problem. The term arises from a 1971 novella called "Flash Crowd" by science fiction writer Larry Niven. In the story a teleportation booth that can transport one anywhere on Earth in milliseconds has been invented. One consequence not predicted by the builders of

the system was that with the near instantaneous reporting of newsworthy events, tens of thousands of people worldwide, including criminals, would flock to the scene of any interesting occurrence, to witness or exploit the event. This phenomenon termed a "flash crowd" results in widespread chaos. An equivalent behaviour can occur on the Web, when a Web site catches the attention of a large number of people, and gets an unexpected and overloading surge of traffic. The problem could occur with the best route selection algorithm if one section of road became popular because it was empty and vehicles gravitated towards it. This then frees up another section, making that section popular causing cars to gravitate back to that section. The result is an oscillating behaviour where cars are directed in circles not to their destination. To circumvent this problem a lag is introduced in the adaptation process. The vehicles route is not adapted from the next intersection but the succeeding intersection i.e. the second intersection in the list of those to be traversed according to the current chosen route.

Algorithm Complexity

In a network such as a wireless vehicular network where communication delays may be substantial it is important that delays introduced into any communication sequence by processing are kept to an absolute minimum. It was for this reason that the *k* parameter was introduced.

The generalised Floyd Shortest-Path algorithm is used to create the cache of paths offline, from the current roadmap. Constraint checking runs in parallel to ensure the *k* routes are valid i.e. no rules of the road are broken (e.g. going the wrong way down a one way street). The value of *k* is important as only that number of routes will be considered as possible solutions by the algorithm. If a permanent change is made to the road layout (e.g. new road constructed) then the cache of paths is regenerated using the new roadmap. Temporary changes in the road layout can be accounted for by associating special fitness scores to a road segment e.g. for a road closed due to roadworks the road segment can be assigned a fitness score of infinity so it is never selected.

In terms of computational complexity the algorithm is the simple operation of choosing the smallest number from a list of size *k* meaning a complexity of order $O(k)$. In practice *k* will be a small number i.e. approximately less than or equal to 20 so processing time will be negligible.

An obvious alternative to the proposed approach is to use a shortest path algorithm with the fitness scores as edge weights. However this results in a complexity of order $O(V^2)$ where *V* is the number of vertices in the road network. In a large-scale real-world road network, *V* is a very large number and consequently the proposed solution will be considerably more efficient.

Quantifying the Effect of Route on Fuel Consumption and Emissions

In this section an equation which quantifies the effect of route on fuel consumption and gas emissions is derived. It is used as part of the fitness function described in the next subsection.

Equation (1) can be used to estimate the value of the fuel consumed (ml), ΔF, during a time interval of duration Δt seconds (Akcilek and Besley, 2003).

$$\Delta F = \begin{bmatrix} \alpha + \beta_1 R_T v \\ + \left(\beta_2 M_v a^2 v / 1000 \right)_{a>0} \end{bmatrix} \Delta t \qquad (1)$$

where,

- R_T is the *total tractive force* (kN) required to drive the vehicle, which is the sum of the rolling resistance, air drag force, inertia force and grade force, and is given by equation (2)
- M_v is the *vehicle mass* (kg), including occupants and any other load,
- *v* is the *instantaneous speed* (m/s) = *v* (km/h) / 3.6,
- *a* is the *instantaneous acceleration rate* (m/s²), negative for deceleration,
- α is the *constant idle fuel rate* (mL/s), which applies during all modes of driving (as an estimate of fuel used to maintain engine operation),
- β_1 is the *efficiency parameter* which relates fuel consumed to the energy provided by the engine, i.e. \\ \indent \indent \indent fuel consumption per unit energy (mL/kJ), and
- β_2 is the *efficiency parameter* which relates fuel consumed during positive acceleration to the product of inertia energy and acceleration, i.e. fuel consumption per unit of energy-acceleration (ml/(kJ.m/s²))

$$\Delta R_t = \begin{bmatrix} b_1 + b_2 v^2 \\ + g \left(M_v a / 1000 \right) \left(G / 100 \right) \end{bmatrix} \qquad (2)$$

where,

- b_1 is the *tractive force* parameter for rolling resistance,
- b_2 is the *tractive force* parameter for aerodynamic resistance,
- *g* is *gravitational acceleration* (m/s²) and,

- *G* is the *road gradient* (percent).

Carbon Monoxide (CO), Hydrocarbons (HC) and Nitrogen Oxides (NO_x) emissions are calculated similarly. The differences are in terms of α = constant idle emissions rate (g/s), β_1 = efficiency parameter which relates pollutant emitted to the energy provided by the engine, i.e. emission per unit energy (g/kJ), and β_2 = efficiency parameter which relates pollutant emitted during positive acceleration to the product of inertia energy and acceleration, i.e. emission per unit of energy-acceleration ($ml/(kJ.m/s^2)$).

The values of Carbon Dioxide (CO_2) emission are estimated directly from fuel consumption as in equation (3):

$$\Delta F_{CO_2} = f_{CO_2} \Delta F \qquad (3)$$

where,

- ΔF is *fuel consumption* in ml and,
- f_{CO_2} is *the CO_2 rate* expressed in grams per millilitre of fuel (g/ml).

When comparing the fuel consumed or emissions produced by the same vehicle along a number of alternative routes M_v, α, β_1, β_2, b_1, b_2 and f_{CO_2} remain constant for all routes. Therefore, when evaluating the contribution of the route to fuel consumption typical values may be used for these constants. The typical values considered are those derived for light vehicles in Dia, Panwai, Boongrapue, Ton and Smith (2006) and are shown in Figure 5.

The following cost function Equation (4) is used to compare routes when evaluating routes in terms of fuel consumption and emissions. Given the case where the route is simply a link, the Fuel Consumption and Emissions Cost for a link *n* can be calculated as the summation of instantaneous fuel consumptions ΔF_j (computed as in Equation (1)) for all the time intervals along the given link from its origin O to destination D.

$$f_n = \sum\nolimits_{j=O}^{D} \Delta F_j \qquad (4)$$

This equation will be used as part of a larger function in the next section.

Fitness Function

The fitness function described in equation (5) is used to choose a vehicle route so that journey time, congestion and fuel consumption are minimised. Parameters for overall and individual benefits are used i.e. journey time and fuel consumption costs and used capacity cost, respectively.

The fitness function consists of weighted cost components including:

- **Journey Time Cost (T):** Encourages a routing solution with the minimum possible user journey time, e.g. a route which gives a journey time of 10 minutes would be chosen over a route which gives a journey time of 11 minutes.
- **Used Capacity Cost (C):** Encourages a less congested routed to be chosen, e.g. a route with 20\% of the road space occupied

Figure 5. Parameter values for the fuel cost equation

Parameter	M_v	α	β_1	β_2	b_1	b_2
Value	1400 kg	3.75 L/s	9x10e -4 L/J	3x10e -4 L/J	.233 N	7.9x10e -4 kg/m

by vehicles would be chosen over a route with 80\% occupancy.

- **Fuel Consumption and Emissions Cost (F):** Encourages a route which minimises fuel consumption and emissions to be taken, e.g. a route which results in 10 litres of fuel consumed would be chosen over one which requires 11 litres.

It may appear that the three metrics outlined are correlated and that time alone would suffice e.g. an increase in journey time would indicate an increase in used capacity or increased congestion and a shorter journey duration would mean reduced fuel consumption. However without considering capacity, congestion can only be identified when journey times rise which may be too late for many vehicles. By using the capacity component, congestion can be prevented without a rise in journey time. In the case of fuel consumption, the associated cost is indeed dependent on time, but also on velocity and acceleration characteristics. Take for example the stop, start driving behaviour prevalent in city driving, this is considerably more wasteful of fuel than driving at a constant speed. Consequently this component considers for example the effect of obstructions along the route which the time component alone cannot e.g. speed bumps, zebra crossings, etc.

Each of the components are weighted by w_i (see Equation (6)), to force the emphasis on a particular outcome. The more important a component is considered to be to the solution, the smaller the weighting factor associated with it, and therefore the stronger its contribution to the overall score R_{nv}.

$$R_{nv} = w_1 T_{nv} + w_2 C_{nv} + w_3 F_{nv} \qquad (5)$$

Given a certain vehicle v taking route n, the equation includes the following:

- **Journey Time Cost:** T_{nv}

- **Used Capacity Cost:** C_{nv}
- **Fuel Consumption and Emissions Cost:** F_{nv}
- **Weighting Factors:** w_i, which obey Equation (6).

$$\sum_{i=1}^{3} w_i = 1 \qquad (6)$$

It is possible to enhance this fitness function at a later date by considering additional parameters e.g. speed, emissions (i.e. CO_2, CO, HC, NO_x), operating cost etc.

Individual Cost Components

The information made available in the data gathering and processing stages of TraffCon is pulled as required by the fitness function to evaluate its constituent cost functions. Each cost function generates a cost score which is expressed as a percentage. These individual cost scores are calculated as follows.

Journey Time Cost

The journey time cost for a vehicle v taking route n is calculated as the summation of link times t from origin O to destination D along the given route over the maximum journey time from the K possible routes t_{maxv}, as described by Equation (7).

$$T_{nv} = \sum_{j=O}^{D} \frac{t_j}{t_{maxv}} \qquad (7)$$

This function encourages the fastest route (in temporal terms) to be selected.

Used Capacity Cost

The used capacity cost for a vehicle v taking route n is calculated as the average of the segment length l adjusted used capacities c of all the segments from origin O to destination D along the given route over the maximum average c_{maxv}. N is the number of segments along the route (see Equation (8)).

$$C_{nv} = \sum{}_{j=O}^{D} \left(\frac{c_j * l_j}{N} \right) / c_{maxv} \qquad (8)$$

This function encourages the least congested route to be selected.

Fuel Consumption and Emissions Cost

The Fuel Consumption and Emissions Cost for a vehicle v taking route n can be calculated as the summation of the individual link fuel consumption and emissions costs f Equation (4), for all the links along the given route from origin O to destination D over the maximum fuel consumption and emissions Cost from the K possible routes f_{maxv}, as shown in Equation (9).

$$T_{nv} = \sum{}_{j=O}^{D} \frac{f_j}{f_{maxv}} \qquad (9)$$

This function encourages the route which will result in the least amount of fuel being consumed and in the least amount of emissions being emitted, to be selected.

BEST ROUTE SELECTION: TESTING

In our previous papers (Collins & Muntean, 2008a) and (Collins & Muntean, 2008b) the effect of parameter k and adaptation/non-adaptation of the best route selection algorithm are studied. In this chapter we will examine the effect of varying the weights in the fitness function on the performance of the proposed route management solution. A weight selection will be suggested based on analysis of the results. In the above-mentioned papers, the TraffCon traffic management system

is shown to have a number of benefits including shorter journey times, improved fuel economy and a reduction in vehicle gas emissions. In this chapter we will examine in greater detail how these benefits are achieved and investigate whether the global improvements are achieved at expense of individual drivers.

Simulations are performed with the Scalable Wireless Ad-Hoc Network Simulator (SWANS) (Choffnes and Bustamante, 2005). This simulator supports realistic vehicular mobility modelling on real world roads. For testing two road networks are used: a sub network of the road network of Boston, MA, USA as highlighted in figure and of Chicago, IL, USA. Two distinct road networks were used to examine the impact of the road layout on performance; the Boston map has a non regular road network, whereas the Chicago map is a regular "Manhattan grid".

The analysis of results is divided into three investigations:

- Investigation into the effect of road layout on the algorithm performance.
- Investigation into the effectiveness of the fitness function's cost components.
- Investigation into how improvements are achieved.

Finally to complete the analysis the overall results are summarized.

Simulation-Based Testing

In order to evaluate proposed solution the following experiment was performed examining three different scenarios, which involved three competing approaches. In order to reduce the influence of noise in the results, the experiments were run three times using different seeds and the results were averaged. The experiment was performed twice: once using the Boston street map and a second time using the Chicago street map.

Case (1): Before each vehicle embarks on its journey it selects a shortest route using the A* shortest path algorithm (Goldberg and Ball, 2004). The vehicle does not deviate from this route. The shortest path algorithm factors in the speed limit and a turn penalty based on intersection type for each road segment.

Case (2): Each vehicle drives to its own destination according to the route management solution with dynamic adaptation during the journey. The *k* parameter was set to 15 and different values for the weights w_1, w_2 and w_3 are considered.

Case (3): Results for a hypothetical "ideal" solution are derived where suitable for a given parameter i.e. the solution is seen to perform well right up until the road network reaches vehicle saturation point (length of available road divided by average vehicle length).

A representative test set of 43 distinct weight settings was used and the complete set can be seen in Figure 6. The test set as shown in Figure 6 is divided into a number of subsets A through J. Set A examines what effect each of the three weights has in isolation, sets B through D have one weight

Figure 6. Set of weights examined during testing

SET A

w1	w2	w3
1	0	0
0	1	0
0	0	1

SET B

w1	w2	w3
.8	.2	0
.6	.4	0
.5	.5	0
.4	.6	0
.2	.8	0

SET C

w1	w2	w3
.8	0	.2
.6	0	.4
.5	0	.5
.4	0	.6
.2	0	.8

SET D

w1	w2	w3
0	.8	.2
0	.6	.4
0	.5	.5
0	.4	.6
0	.2	.8

SET E

w1	w2	w3
.8	.1	.1
.6	.2	.2
.4	.3	.3
.3	.3	.3
.2	.4	.4
0	.5	.5

SET F

w1	w2	w3
.1	.1	.8
.2	.2	.6
.3	.3	.4
.3	.3	.3
.4	.4	.2
.5	.5	0

SET G

w1	w2	w3
.1	.8	.1
.2	.6	.2
.3	.4	.3
.3	.3	.3
.4	.2	.4
.5	0	.5

SET H

w1	w2	w3
.7	.2	.1
.5	.3	.2
.7	.1	.2
.5	.2	.3

SET I

w1	w2	w3
.2	.1	.7
.3	.2	.5
.1	.2	.7
.2	.3	.5

SET J

w1	w2	w3
.2	.7	.1
.3	.5	.2
.1	.7	.2
.2	.5	.3

set to zero while the other two are varied, in sets E through G the weights are varied such that two of the weights remain equal and in sets H through J one weight is made dominant, while the relative strength of the other two is varied.

The simulation time was set at two hours. In each simulation, the number of vehicles on the road was varied and total completed journeys, and average, standard deviation in and best and worst individual speed and fuel economies were measured.

Total completed journeys is used to differentiate between traffic management solutions. The graph of completed journeys against number of vehicles should be similar to that of a Poisson distribution as seen in Figure 7. Three main phases should be evident in each solution as represented by the three sections marked on the graph in Figure 7. In section A of the graph there are not enough vehicles on the road for traffic congestion to be an issue and the number of completed journeys grows as the number of vehicles increases. In section B the graph flattens off around a peak value at this point the road network is at maximum utilisation. Finally in section C the road network becomes congested and the number of journeys completed decreases as the number of vehicles

increases. Eventually the saturation point of the road network with vehicles is reached and the graph tails off to zero. The better the solution is, the higher the peak of the wider the flat portion around it and the longer the tail.

In order to investigate how the performance improvements made by the TraffCon solution are achieved average, standard deviation in and best and worst individual speed and fuel economies are examined. The standard deviation and best and worst individual cases are used to explore whether global improvements are achieved at the expense of individual drivers. Solutions where global improvements are achieved but certain individuals are harshly punished would not be desirable.

Testing Results

Overview

The experiment described in the previous section produced a very large set of results for the 43 TraffCon solutions using distinct weight settings all of which could not possibly be displayed here. However a systematic process of elimination was used to isolate a smaller set of the best performing solutions. In this section we will first describe the

Figure 7. The poisson distribution type curve expected for completed journeys against number of vehicles

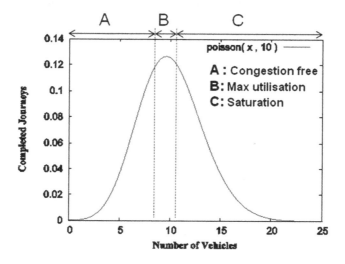

process of elimination and then analyse the set of best performing solutions.

The first measurement examined in other to reduce the solution set was the total number of journeys completed. On initial examination of the results for the Boston Map it was clear that the outliers were peaking around 12,000. The first step was to remove solutions below 75% of this observed upper bound i.e. those with a peak below 9,000. This removed the seven solutions in which the journey time cost was given a weight of zero. The next step was to remove all solutions which peaked below 12,000. After this 14 solutions remained and the 6 solutions with the highest peaks from that group are shown in Figure 8.

From first observations of the results for the Chicago Map it was clear that the outliers were peaking about 20,000 completed journeys. As for the Boston map the first step was to remove solutions below 75% of the observed upper limit i.e. those with a peak below 15,000. This removed the seven solutions in which the journey time cost was given a weight of zero. From this we can see that the worst performing solutions for both maps are the same i.e. those which do not consider journey time cost. The next step was to remove all solutions which peaked below 20,000. After this 15 solutions remained, the set of 14 solutions

remaining after this stage when examining the Boston map are a subset of the 15. From this we can see that the behaviour of the TraffCon solution is broadly similar irrespective of the road network i.e. whether the road network is irregular as in the Boston map or a "Manhattan grid" as found in the Chicago map. The 6 solutions with the highest peaks from the group of 15 are shown in figure 9.

For both maps as well as the top 6 solutions the solution with weights set to $w_1 = 1$, $w_2 = 0$ and $w_3 = 0$ i.e. the solution where only time is considered. This was done so that solutions which use all 3 parameters could be compared with a simpler approach where only time is considered.

Analysis of results is divided into three separate investigations and a summary of the overall results.

Investigation into the Effect of Road Layout on the Algorithm Performance

For both maps as shown in Figure 8 and Figure 9 the top two solutions are those with weights set to $w_1 = 0.7$, $w_2 = 0.2$, $w_3 = 0.1$ and $w_1 = 0.8$, $w_2 = 0.1$, $w_3 = 0.1$. This result further underlines that the behaviour of the best route selection algorithm is approximately the same irrespective of the road network i.e. whether the road

Figure 8. Completed journeys against number of vehicles for Boston map

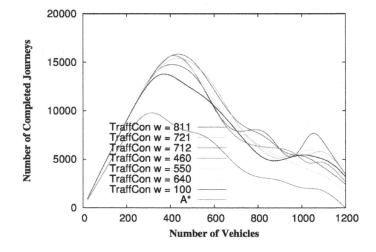

Figure 9. Completed journeys against number of vehicle

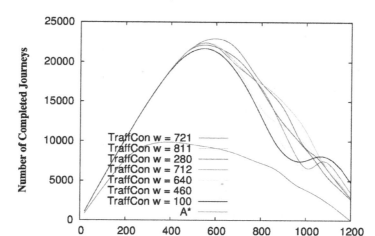

network is irregular as in the Boston map or a "Manhattan grid" as found in the Chicago map. As seen the experiments detailed in our previous papers (Collins and Muntean 2008a) and (Collins and Muntean, 2008b}, TraffCon solutions vastly improve on the A* shortest path solution. This can also be seen in Figures 8 and 9. For example in Figure 8 the shortest path solution peaks at 9615 completed journeys and the best TraffCon solution peaks at 16,152 an increase of 68%. In Figure 9, the shortest path solution peaks at 9950 completed journeys and the best TraffCon solution peaks at 22,310 an increase of 124%. It is clear from this result that the TraffCon solution achieves performance improvements whether the road network is irregular as in the Boston map or a "Manhattan grid" as found in the Chicago map.

Investigation into the Fitness Function's Cost Components Importance

The three cost components of the algorithms fitness function are Journey Time Cost, Used Capacity Cost and Fuel Consumption and Emissions Cost. The impact of the fitness function's cost components can be investigated using the

results from the previous section. The process of eliminating the more poorly performing solutions is described in a section. In this process the first solutions to be eliminated were those which did not consider time i.e. those in which $w_1 = 1$. This shows that journey time component plays a very important role in producing a good solution. In this section we will demonstrate that the other two cost components also play an important role.

The results for number of completed journey for Boston and Chicago street maps are shown in Figure 8 and Figure 9. They display the top 6 solutions from the set of 43 different weight settings examined in testing (outlined in Figure 6) as well as the solution with weights set to $w_1 = 1$, $w_2 = 0$ and $w_3 = 0$ i.e. the solution where only time is considered. This was done so that solutions which use all 3 weighted cost components can be compared with a simpler approach where only time is considered.

For both maps the top two solutions are shown to be those with weights set to $w_1 = 0.7$, $w_2 = 0.2$, $w_3 = 0.1$ and $w_1 = 0.8$, $w_2 = 0.1$, $w_3 = 0.1$. This result shows that best solutions consider Journey Time Cost, Used Capacity Cost and Fuel Consumption and Emissions Cost. If those two weight settings are averaged the best results are weighted at approximately 75%, 15% and 10% for Journey Time Cost, Used Capacity Cost and Fuel Consumption and Emissions Cost respectively.

To further under line how important the Used Capacity Cost and Fuel Consumption and Emissions Costs are to arriving at the best solution the results in Figure 9 can be examined more closely. The best performing solution in that graph has weights set to $w_1 = 0.7$, $w_2 = 0.2$ and $w_3 = 0.1$. In order to measure the statistical difference between that solution and a solution using weights set to $w_1 = 1$, $w_2 = 0$ and $w_3 = 0$ a t-test is used. The two solutions were compared in the region of the graph where the number of vehicles ranges from 500 to 1000. This is the congested region where the performance of the solutions is of most interest. The result of the t-test was as follows:

$$t = 4.038, \text{ given: } df = 25, \alpha = 0.001 \qquad (10)$$

Consequently it can be said with 99.9% certainty that there is a strong statistical difference in favour of the solution which has the weights set to $w_1 = 0.7$, $w_2 = 0.2$ and $w_3 = 0.1$. This proves beyond doubt that all three cost components play an important role in arriving at the best solution.

Investigation into How Improvements are Achieved

In order to investigate how the performance improvements made by the TraffCon solution are achieved; average, standard deviation in and best and worst individual speed and fuel economies are examined. The standard deviation and best and worst individual cases are used to explore whether global improvements are achieved at the expense of individual drivers. Solutions where global improvements are achieved but certain individuals are harshly punished would not be desirable. For the purposes of this investigation results obtained from the Chicago map will be used. The figures to be displayed were compiled in the same fashion as previously outlined for Figure 9. Any observa-

tions made here could similarly have been made using results from the Boston Map.

Figure 11 contains a graph of average speed against number of vehicles for the Chicago map. It was discerned in the previous section that the best performing solution for the Chicago Map was that with weights set to $w_1 = 0.7$, $w_2 = 0.2$ and $w_3 = 0.1$. It can be clearly seen in Figure 11 that this solution has highest results for average speed. It is clear that TraffCon solutions generate performance improvements by increasing the average speed of vehicles. The correlation between average speed and completed journeys is highlighted more clearly in Figure 10. In this diagram corresponding portion of the graphs between 500 and 1000 vehicles for Figures 9 and Figure 11 are expanded. The diagram illustrates the fact when a solution is seen to be the best in terms of completed journeys it also has the highest average speed. A similar trend can be seen if we look at results for average fuel economy as shown in Figure 12.

The average speed and fuel economy results can show how improvements are being achieved in an overall sense, but they do not indicate how individual vehicles are affected. To uncover the effect on individual drivers the following metrics will be examined standard deviation in and best and worst individual speed and fuel economies. Firstly looking at the best performing individual where speed and fuel economy are concerned as shown in Figure 13 and Figure 14. From these graphs it can be seen that when comparing TraffCon Solutions with the baseline A* shortest path solution that one of the contributing factors to the overall improvements is that there is an improvement in the best individual performances.

Next the worst individual performances are examined where speed and fuel economy are a concern, as shown in Figure 15 and Figure 16. From these graphs it can be seen that when comparing TraffCon Solutions with the baseline A* shortest path solution that one of the contributing factors

Figure 10. The correlation between average speed and completed journeys

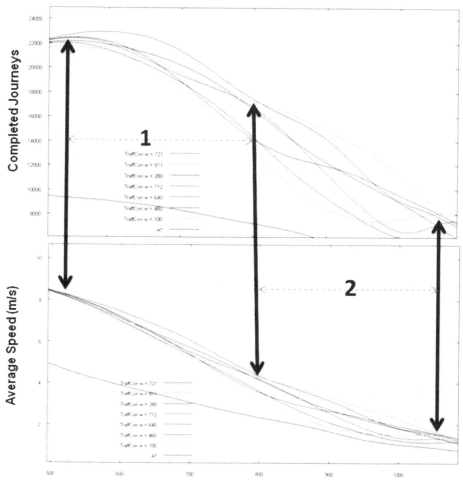

Number of Vehicles

to the overall improvements is that there is an improvement in the worst individual performances.

Finally the standard deviation in the results for speed and fuel economy is examined, as shown in Figure 17 and Figure 18. In the case of standard deviation in speed the deviation found in the TraffCon solution is lower than that of the baseline A* shortest path solution. This means that the speeds of individual vehicles vary less wildly in the TraffCon solutions. This along with the improvements in best and worst individual speeds for TraffCon would discount the possibility

of individual vehicles being excessively rewarded or punished by the TraffCon solution. It can be assumed rather that the global improvements in performance are achieved by improving the average speed of all vehicles.

For standard deviation in fuel economy as shown in Figure 18 the deviation found in the TraffCon solution is approximately equal to that of the baseline A* shortest path solution. This means that the fuel economy of individual vehicles do not vary anymore wildly in the TraffCon solutions. This along with the improvements in best and worst

Figure 11. Average speed against number of vehicles for Chicago map

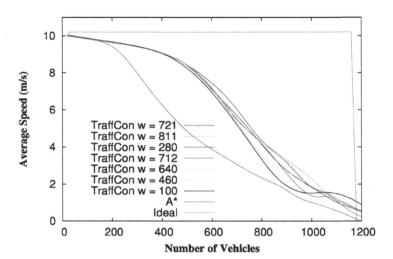

Figure 12. Average fuel economy against number of vehicles for Chicago map

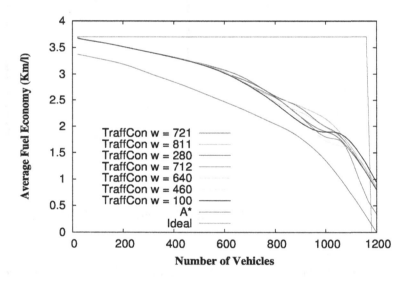

individual fuel economies for TraffCon would rule out the likelihood of extreme cases of punishment or reward of individual vehicles for the TraffCon solution. It can be assumed rather that the global improvements in performance are achieved by improving the fuel economy of all vehicles. In general it can be said that the global performance improvements achieved by the TraffCon solution do not come at the expense of individuals.

Summary of Results

In our previous papers (Collins and Muntean, 2008a) and (Collins and Muntean, 2008b) have demonstrated how the proposed solution reduces journey times, fuel consumption, fuel emissions and fuel costs. The solution brings improvements whether operated in a non-adaptive or adaptive fashion but solutions which use adaption perform

Figure 13. Best individual speed against number of vehicles for Chicago map

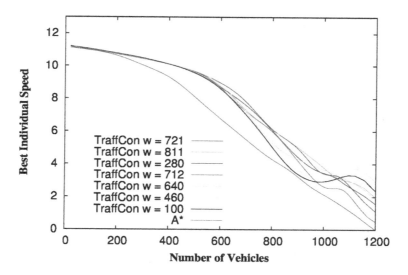

Figure 14. Best individual fuel economy vs number of vehicles for Chicago map

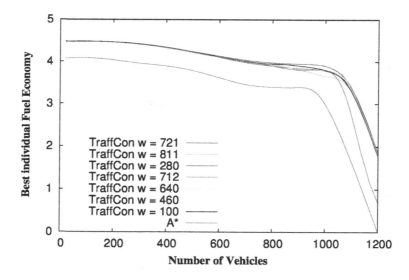

better. Performance of the algorithm increases as its k parameter increases but the majority of the increase occurs in the early increments as seen in a Pareto curve. Consequently in practice k may be set at a relatively low value approximately 20 to achieve good performance.

After performing analysis of results for the best route selection algorithm, this chapter demonstrates how the algorithm performs well irrespective of the road map used e.g. an irregular road network or a regular "Manhattan grid". All three cost components of the algorithms function contribute to finding the best solution. In practice for best performance the three cost components: Journey Time Cost, Used Capacity Cost and Fuel Consumption and Emissions Cost should

Figure 15. Worst individual speed against number of vehicles for Chicago map

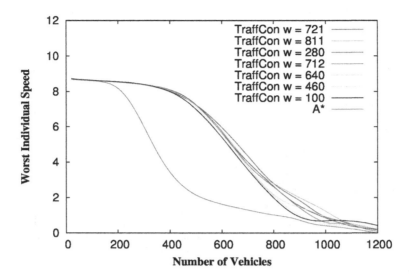

Figure 16. Worst individual fuel economy vs number of vehicles for Chicago map

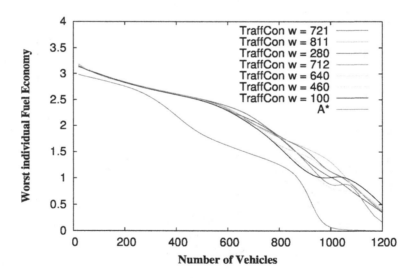

be assigned weight factors of 0.75, 0.15 and 0.1 respectively. Finally the global performance improvements achieved by the TraffCon solution do not come at the expense of individuals. This means that when using the TraffCon solution there is no concern that certain individuals will be harshly punished by the solution despite the overall improvement in performance.

Provision of Traffic Efficiency Services in Sparse Roadside-Vehicle Networks

Vehicles must be able to exchange a certain amount of data with roadside units in order to provide a given service in a sparse roadside-vehicle network setting. The required data exchange between ve-

Figure 17. Standard deviation in speed against number of vehicles for Chicago map

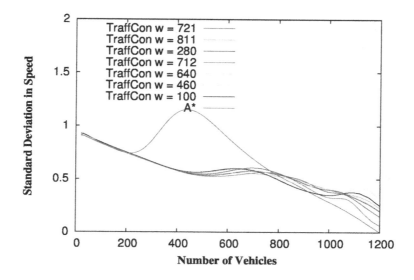

Figure 18. Standard deviation in fuel economy against number of vehicles for Chicago map

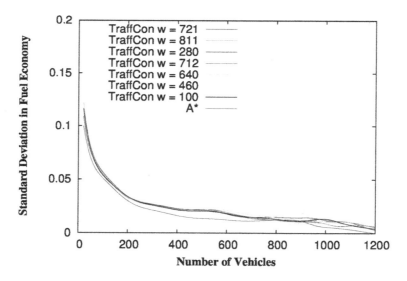

hicles and roadside infrastructure, to provide the route management service described and evaluated in this chapter is summarised in Figure 20. When a vehicle enters the range of a roadside unit it sends a service request. The information vehicles are asked to gather is piggybacked onto the request. In this case that consists of three parameters and the id for the road segment they describe. The data size is based on having a roadside unit at every intersection. It would increase if vehicles traversed more than one road segment between roadside units. The response from the roadside unit contains route information i.e. a list of the next 20 road segments the vehicle must take. This allows a typical navigation unit to display a look ahead of the route being taken. The data exchange algorithm required for this process is described in the next section.

Data Exchange Algorithm

The Data Exchange Algorithm (summarised in Figure 19) is employed by a location based service running in a sparse roadside-vehicle network. A new data exchange process is initiated when a vehicle begins a journey with a service requiring data exchange enabled. The steps listed next are as follows:

1. The vehicle continually checks if it is in range of a roadside unit.

If the vehicle is in range of a roadside unit it sends a service request to the roadside unit and sets a timer. If the timer expires before a response is received then another request is sent. The timer is set for certain duration according to Equation (11).

$$Time = \left[packet_{size} * Random\left(x,y\right)\right] / send\_rate \qquad (11)$$

where,

- *packet_size* is the size of the packet sent in mb

Figure 19. Data exchange algorithm

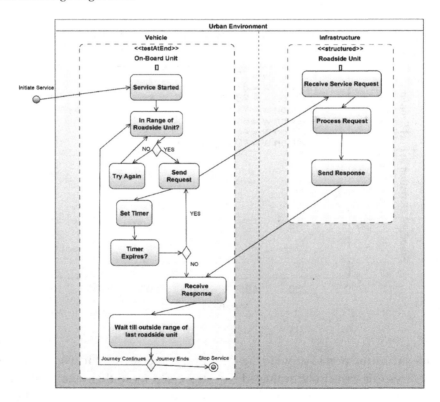

Figure 20. Summary of data exchange required for vehicle running route service

	Data Description	Data Size (bytes)	Payload Size (bytes)
Data Sent	Link ID & parameters	20	72
Data Received	Route i.e. list of 20 links	80	132

- $x > 1$, $y > x$ and *Random(x,y)* returns a random real number between x and y
- *send_rate* is the rate at which data is sent in mb/s

   3. If a response is received then the service has the necessary data required to update itself and no further requests are sent. The vehicle then waits till it has left the range of the roadside unit from which it received the request before beginning the process again.

   4. The algorithm stops when the journey is complete.

In the next section we will test the operation of this algorithm in an IEEE802.11p sparse roadside-vehicle network in order to demonstrate how traffic efficiency services may be provided using such an approach.

DATA EXCHANGE: TESTING

In this section we examine if sufficient amount of data can be exchanged between vehicles and a roadside unit in a sparse roadside-vehicle network in order to provide traffic efficiency services such as the TraffCon solution discussed earlier.

In order to evaluate the data exchange algorithm simulations were performed with Traffic and Network Simulation Environment (TraNS) (Piorkowski, Raya, Lugo, Papadimitratos, Grossglauser, and Hubaux, 2007), (Piorkowski, Raya, Lugo, Papadimitratos, Grossglauser, and Hubaux, 2008). TraNS uses the Simulation of Urban MObility (SUMO) traffic simulator to provide realistic modelling of vehicular mobility. The road network information can be taken from real world road map sources such as the US Census Bureau's TIGER/Line files: http://www.census.gov/geo/www/tiger/.

The NS-2 network simulator is used to provide simulation of wireless communications. Support for realistic IEEE 802.11p was possible using NS version 2.33 which has overhauled the modeling

and simulation of IEEE 802.11 for this purpose as outlined in (Chen, Schmidt-Eisenlohr, Jiang, Torrent-Moreno, Delgrossi and Hartenstein, 2007), (Chen, Jiang, Taliwal and Delgrossi, 2007). The test setup is described in the next section and results are discussed afterwards.

Simulation-Based Testing

To model a sparse roadside-vehicle communications network an infrastructure point is placed at a signalised intersection in the center of a sub-network of the road network of Chicago, as shown in Figure 21. Vehicles drive by the infrastructure point and exchange data according to the data exchange algorithm. Realistic vehicular traffic patterns are generated using TraNS. The access technology used is IEEE 802.11p. The NS-2 MAC and Phy settings used for IEEE 802.11p are shown below.

```
#IEEE 802.11p
#=====================================
Mac/802_11 set CWMin_                15
Mac/802_11 set CWMax_              1023
Mac/802_11 set SlotTime_      0.000009
Mac/802_11 set SIFS_          0.000016
Mac/802_11 set ShortRetryLimit_      7
Mac/802_11 set LongRetryLimit_       4
Mac/802_11 set PreambleLength_      60
Mac/802_11 set PLCPHeaderLength_    60
Mac/802_11 set PLCPDataRate_     6.0e6
Mac/802_11 set RTSThreshold_      2000
Mac/802_11 set basicRate_        6.0e6
Mac/802_11 set dataRate_         6.0e6

Mac/802_11Ext set CWMin_             15
Mac/802_11Ext set CWMax_           1023
Mac/802_11Ext set SlotTime_   0.000009
Mac/802_11Ext set SIFS_       0.000016
Mac/802_11Ext set ShortRetryLimit_   7
Mac/802_11Ext set LongRetryLimit_    4
Mac/802_11Ext set
  HeaderDuration_            0.000020
```

Figure 21. Sub network of Chicago road network visualised in SUMO with infrastrucure point indicated

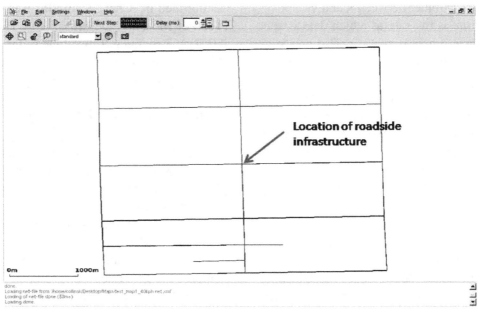

```
Mac/802_11Ext set                          Phy/WirelessPhyExt set
  SymbolDuration_           0.000004          CSThresh_              6.30957e-12
Mac/802_11Ext set                          Phy/WirelessPhyExt set Pt_       0.001
  BasicModulationScheme_           0       Phy/WirelessPhyExt set freq_    5.18e9
Mac/802_11Ext set use_802_11a_             Phy/WirelessPhyExt set
  flag_                         true          noise_floor_           2.51189e-13
Mac/802_11Ext set                          Phy/WirelessPhyExt set L_          1.0
  RTSThreshold_                 2000       Phy/WirelessPhyExt set
Mac/802_11Ext set MAC_DBG          0          PowerMonitorThresh_    2.10319e-12
                                           Phy/WirelessPhyExt set
Phy/WirelessPhy set                          HeaderDuration_           0.000020
  CSThresh_            6.30957e-12         Phy/WirelessPhyExt set
Phy/WirelessPhy set                          BasicModulationScheme_            0
  Pt_                          0.001       Phy/WirelessPhyExt set
Phy/WirelessPhy set                          PreambleCaptureSwitch_            1
  freq_                       5.18e9       Phy/WirelessPhyExt set
Phy/WirelessPhy set                          DataCaptureSwitch_                0
  L_                             1.0       Phy/WirelessPhyExt set
Phy/WirelessPhy set                          SINR_PreambleCapture_        2.5118
  RXThresh_                 3.652e-10      Phy/WirelessPhyExt set
Phy/WirelessPhy set bandwidth_    20e6       SINR_DataCapture_             100.0
Phy/WirelessPhy set CPThresh_     10.0
```

```
Phy/WirelessPhyExt settrace_dist_ 1e6
Phy/WirelessPhyExt set
  PHY_DBG_                          0
Phy/WirelessPhyExt set CPThresh_    0
Phy/WirelessPhyExt set RXThresh_    0
#====================================
```

Investigation into Amount of Data Which Can be Exchanged

In order to determine the limits of the algorithm, it was tested for the worst case scenario i.e. large numbers of cars present, all of which are trying to receive x amount of data from the roadside infrastructure. Three volumes of vehicular traffic are examined moderately heavy, heavy and very heavy traffic. For moderately heavy traffic vehicles are flown toward the intersection where the infrastructure point is located from all four adjoining roads at a rate of one every 8 seconds for 200 seconds. For heavy traffic the rate is one vehicle every 4 seconds and for very heavy traffic, the rate is set to one vehicle every 2.6667 seconds. In each case the simulation is allowed continue until all the traffic has passed through the intersection and is out of range of the infrastructure point. This results in 100 vehicles, 200 vehicles and 300 vehicles passing through the intersection in the moderately heavy, heavy and very heavy cases respectively.

For each of the three traffic patterns measurements are taken for three different cases:

Case (1): All vehicles try to receive 250kB of data from the roadside infrastructure.

Case (2): All vehicles try to receive 500kB of data from the roadside infrastructure.

Case (3): All vehicles try to receive 1000kB of data from the roadside infrastructure.

In each case the average data received and data received and lost is measured for each vehicle. In the simulations the infrastructure informs nearby vehicles of its presence with a beacon which is periodically broadcast. Vehicles respond to the beacon with a service request if they have not already received it. The infrastructure point then transmits data to the vehicle at a rate of 2MB. UDP is used at the transport layer and the access technology used is IEEE 802.11p.

Case (1) 250kB of Data Transmitted per Vehicle

In Figure 22 the average data received by each vehicle is shown for the case where vehicles are expected to receive 250kB of data. It can be seen that there is no data lost for the scenario with moderately heavy traffic as the average is 250kB. The average data received for the heavy traffic and very heavy traffic cases is 248.1kB and 249.2kB respectively. This means that the average amount of data received in those cases is 99.2% and 99.7% respectively.

It can be clearly seen where individual vehicles lost data, and how much data was lost in the heavy and very heavy traffic cases in Figure 24 and Figure 25

The percentage of vehicles which receive the full amount of data expected is shown in Figure 23. Again it is highlighted that 100\% of vehicles received the expected amount of data in the scenario with moderately heavy traffic. In the heavy and very heavy traffic cases 92.5% and 95% of vehicles respectively received the expected amount of data.

Case (2) 500kB of Data Transmitted per Vehicle

In Figure 26 the average data received by each vehicle is shown for the case where vehicles are expected to receive 500kB of data. The average data received for the moderately heavy traffic, heavy traffic and very heavy traffic cases is 497.53kB, 475kB and 488.2kB respectively. That

Figure 22. Average data received by each vehicle

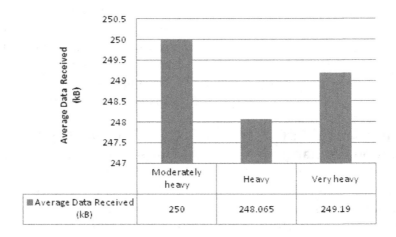

Figure 23. Percentage of vehicles which receive full amount of data

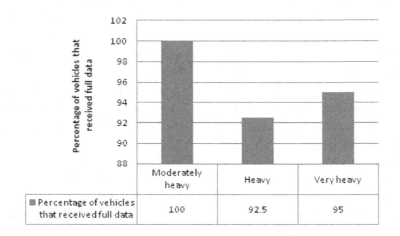

Figure 24. Data loss for each vehicle when traffic is heavy

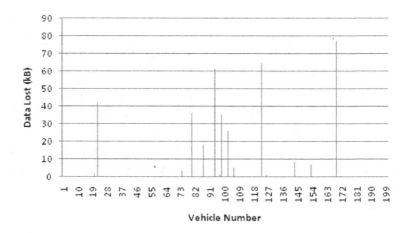

Figure 25. Data loss for each vehicle when traffic is very heavy

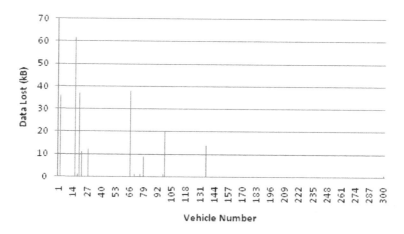

Figure 26. Average data received by each vehicle

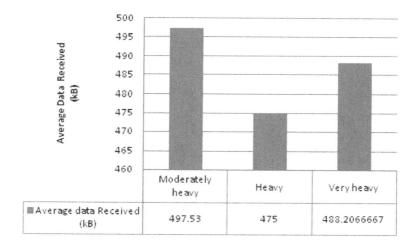

is 99.5%, 95% and 97.6% of the expected amount in each case.

Instances where individual vehicles lost data, and how much data was lost in the moderately heavy, heavy and very heavy traffic cases are shown in Figure 28, Figure 29 and Figure 30.

The percentage of vehicles which receive the full amount of data expected, when the expected amount is 500kB is shown in Figure 27. In the moderately heavy, heavy and very heavy traffic cases 91%, 70.5% and 79.3% of vehicles respectively received the expected amount of data.

Case (3) 1000kB of Data Transmitted per Vehicle

In Figure 31 the average data received by each vehicle is shown for the case where vehicles are expected to receive 1000kB of data. The average data received for the moderately heavy traffic, heavy traffic and very heavy traffic cases is 972.16kB, 799.12kB and 815.11kB respectively. That is 97.2%, 79.9% and 81.5% of the expected amount in each case.

Figure 27. Percentage of vehicles which receive full amount of data

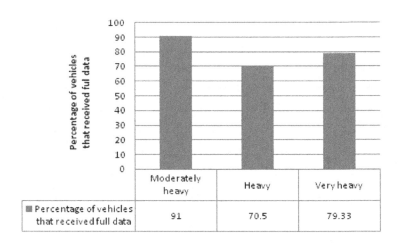

Figure 28. Data loss for each vehicle when traffic is moderately heavy

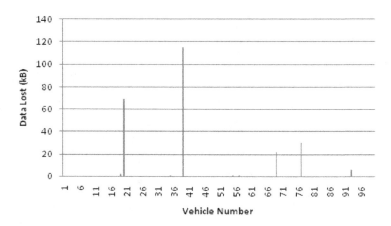

Figure 29. Data loss for each vehicle when traffic is heavy

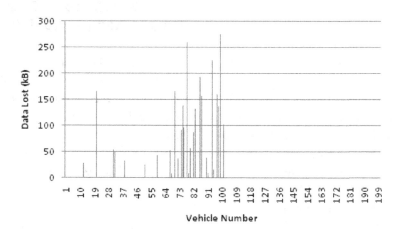

Figure 30. Data loss for each vehicle when traffic is very heavy

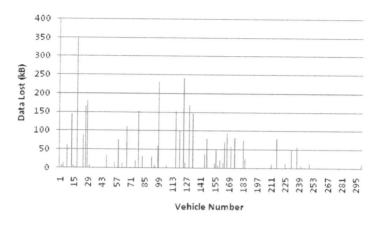

Figure 31. Average data received by each vehicle

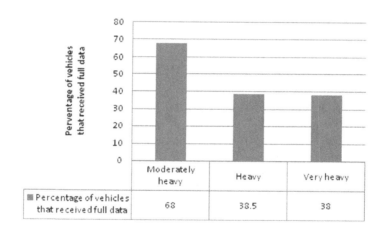

Instances where individual vehicles lost data, and how much data was lost in the moderately heavy, heavy and very heavy traffic cases are shown in Figure 33, Figure 34 and Figure 35.

The percentage of vehicles which receive the full amount of data expected, when the expected amount is 1000kB is shown in Figure 32. In the moderately heavy, heavy and very heavy traffic cases 68%, 38.5% and 38% of vehicles respectively received the expected amount of data.

Analysis of Results

In order to analyse the results of the investigation into the levels of data exchange being achieved by the data exchange algorithm the data requirements of the connected services being fed by it must be considered. The services being run can be categorised as traffic safety, traffic efficiency and value added services. The central system providing services will send data to services in that order of priority. In the worst case scenario outlined above i.e. large numbers of cars present, all of which are trying to receive x amount of data from the roadside infrastructure you would want traffic safety services to be supported, as many traffic efficiency services as possible and any data left over for value added services would be a bonus.

To give an indication of the levels of data required for traffic safety and traffic efficiency

Figure 32. Percentage of vehicles which receive full amount of data

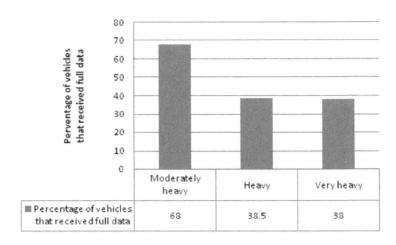

Figure 33. Data loss for each vehicle when traffic is moderately heavy

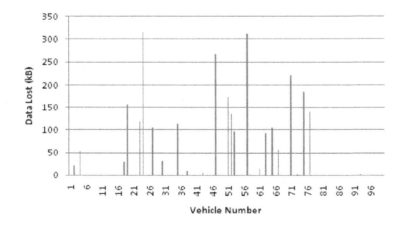

Figure 34. Data loss for each vehicle when traffic is heavy

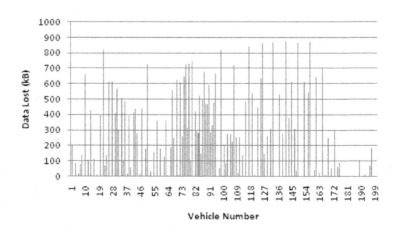

Figure 35. Data loss for each vehicle when traffic is very heavy

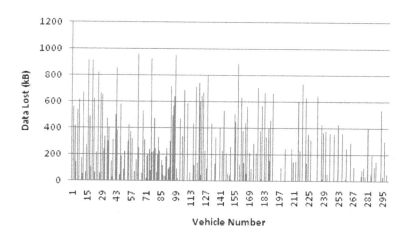

services lets take a route management service powered by the best route selection algorithm described earlier. Consider the service to be running on a sat-nav device in the vehicle. The required data exchange between vehicles and roadside infrastructure, to provide the service is summarised in Figure 20 and is of the order of tens of bytes. The levels of data involved are relatively small i.e. 20 bytes to be sent and 80 bytes to be received. From this example we can see that intelligent transport services have relatively low data requirements.

The results for case (1), where 250kB of data is transmitted to all vehicles, show that on average with moderately heavy traffic, heavy traffic and very heavy traffic; 100%, 99.2% and 99.7% of data is received respectively. In this instance a large number of intelligent transport services could be provided.

In cases (2) and (3) the amount of data transmitted to all vehicles is increased to 500kB and 1000kB. The amount of data getting through overall increases but lost data also goes up. This is where prioritisation becomes important because as long as the data being lost has the lowest priority essential services such as traffic safety and efficiency can be provided to vehicles and when the opportunity arises to receive more data value added services may also be supported.

To summarise even with worst case network scenario i.e. large numbers of cars present, all of which are trying to receive data from the roadside infrastructure, the data exchange algorithm can support a large number of intelligent transport type services. Consequently it can be said that Sparse Roadside-Vehicle Networks are capable of supporting intelligent transport type services.

Related Works

The IEEE 802.11p standard is attracting very much attention from the research community which mostly performs performance evaluation (Murray, Cojocari, and Fu, 2008), (Wang., Chao, Liu, He, Lin and Chou, 2008), (Wang, Ahmed, Krishnamachari and Psounis, 2008),. However work has already begun on enhancing the standard including this proposed MAC layer protocol for roadside-vehicle networks (Choi, Choi, Seok, Kwon, and Choi, 2007) and this rate adaptation based enhancement for the link layer (Shankar, Nadeem, Rosca, and Iftode, 2008).

The topic of roadside-vehicle communications is also an active research area, recent work includes; a highway lane reservation service (Iftode, Smaldone, Gerla, and Misener, 2008), a vehicle-to-roadside communication protocol for making secure payments (Isaac., Camara, Zeadally, and Marquez, 2008), and a roadside intelligent transport system data bus prototype (Cai and Lin, 2008).

Traffic efficiency services enabled by vehicular communications are also receiving significant attention from researchers. Recent work includes in the area includes; traffic light optimisation (Gradinescu, Gorgorin, Diaconescu, Cristea and Iftode, 2007), parking space management (Yan, Weigle, Olariu, 2009), dynamically varying speed limits Chuah, Du, Ghosal, Khorashadi, Liu, Smith and Zhang, 2008) and automated pothole detection (Eriksson, Girod, Hull, Newton, Madden, and Balakrishnan, 2008).

CONCLUSION AND FUTURE WORKS

This chapter describes the adaptive best route selection algorithm for use in the TraffCon traffic management system. Test results show that the algorithm gives shorter journey times, improves fuel economy and consequently lower harmful fuel emissions, while journey cost is also reduced in comparison with an existing scheme. In summary TraffCon's benefits are varied: social, economic and environmental i.e. shorter journey times, financial savings, potential increased productivity for commuters and professional drivers and a reduction in vehicle gas emissions.

In this chapter we have also shown how to fine tune the setting of the weights in the algorithm in order to achieve best performance. Having fine tuned the weight setting the algorithm will perform even better than previously demonstrated. It was demonstrated that the algorithm performs well irrespective of the road map used e.g. an irregular road network or a regular "Manhattan grid". Also it was shown that the global performance improvements achieved by the TraffCon solution do not come at the expense of individuals. This means that when using the TraffCon solution there is no concern that certain individuals will

be harshly punished by the solution despite the overall improvement in performance. Finally it was also demonstrated how such a route management service and many other intelligent transportation type services like it could comfortably be supported by an IEEE802.11p based sparse roadside-vehicle network.

Future works will include the development of other algorithms which can power other traffic management services for the Traffcon system. These algorithms would be designed to optimize the utilisation of existing road infrastructure and minimise time spent stuck in traffic and fuel consumed by moving vehicles like the best route selection algorithm. Example algorithms may include algorithms for vehicle lane management, vehicle speed management or many-on board prioritisation of vehicles.

ACKNOWLEDGMENT

The support of the Irish Research Council's Embark Initiative is gratefully acknowledged.

REFERENCES

Akcilek, R., & Besley, M. (2003). *Operating cost, fuel consumption and emission models in aaSIDRA and aaMotion*. Paper presented at the Conference of Australian Institutes of Transport Research. Adelaide, Australia

Cai, S. H., & Lin, Y. (2008). A roadside ITS data bus prototype for intelligent highways. *IEEE Transactions on Intelligent Transportation Systems*, 9(2), 344–348. doi:10.1109/TITS.2008.922873

Chen, Q., Jiang, D., Taliwal, V., & Delgrossi, L. (2007). IEEE 802.11 based vehicular communication simulation design for NS-2. In *Proceedings of ACM International Workshop on Vehicular Ad Hoc Networks* (VANET). New York, NY: ACM.

Chen, Q., Schmidt-Eisenlohr, F., Jiang, D., Torrent-Moreno, M., Delgrossi, L., & Hartenstein, H. (2007). Overhaul of IEEE 802.11 modeling and simulation in NS-2. In *Proceedings of ACM Symposium on Modeling, Analysis, and Simulation of Wireless and Mobile Systems* (MSWiM). New York, NY: ACM.

Choffnes, D. R., & Bustamante, F. E. (2005). *STRAW - An integrated mobility and traffic model for VANETs*. Paper presented at the International Command and Control Research and Technology Symposium. McLean, VA.

Choi, N., Choi, S., Seok, Y., Kwon, T., & Choi, Y. (2007). A solicitation-based IEEE 802.11p MAC protocol for roadside to vehicular networks. In *Proceedings of Mobile Networking for Vehicular Environments Conference*, (pp. 91–96). Anchorage, AK: Academic Press.

Chuah, C.-N., Du, H., Ghosal, D., Khorashadi, B., Liu, B., Smith, C., & Zhang, H. (2008). Distributed vehicular traffic control and safety applications with vgrid. In *Proceedings of IEEE Wireless Hive Networks Conference* (WHNC). IEEE.

Collins, K., & Muntean, G.-M. (2008a). Route based vehicular traffic management for wireless vehicular networks. In *Proceedings of IEEE Vehicular Technology Conference* (VTC Fall). Calgary, Canada: IEEE.

Collins, K., & Muntean, G.-M. (2008b). An adaptive vehicle route management solution enabled by wireless vehicular networks. In *Proceedings of IEEE Vehicular Technology Conference* (VTC-Fall). Calgary, Canada: IEEE.

Dia, H., Panwai, S., Boongrapue, N., Ton, T., & Smith, N. (2006). Comparative evaluation of powerbased environmental emissions models. In *Proceedings of IEEE Intelligent Transportation Systems Conference*, (ITSC '06), (pp. 1251–1256). IEEE.

Elbahhar, F., Rivenq, A., Heddebaut, M., & Rouvaen, J. M. (2005). Using UWB Gaussian pulses for inter-vehicle communications. *IEE Proceedings. Communications, 152*(2), 229–234. doi:10.1049/ip-com:20040572

Eriksson, J., Girod, L., Hull, B., Newton, R., Madden, S., & Balakrishnan, H. (2008). *The pothole patrol: Using a mobile sensor network for road surface monitoring*. Paper presented at the Annual International Conference on Mobile Systems, Applications and Services (MobiSys). Breckenridge, CO.

Evans, J., & Minieka, E. (1992). *Optimization algorithms for networks and graphs*. New York: Dekker.

Goldberg, A., & Ball, M. (2004). *Computing the shortest path: A* search meets graph theory* (Tech. Rep. MSR-TR-2004-24). Microsoft Research.

Gradinescu, V., Gorgorin, C., Diaconescu, R., Cristea, V., & Iftode, L. (2007). Adaptive traffic lights using car-to-car communication. In *Proceedings of IEEE Vehicular Technology Conference*. Dublin, Ireland: IEEE.

Iftode, L., Smaldone, S., Gerla, M., & Misener, J. (2008). Active highways (position paper). In *Proceedings of IEEE International Symposium on Personal, Indoor and Mobile Radio Communications* (PIMRC). IEEE.

Isaac, J. T., Camara, J. S., Zeadally, S., & Marquez, J. T. (2008). A secure vehicle-to-roadside communication payment protocol in vehicular ad-hoc networks. *Computer Communications, 31*(10), 2478–2484. doi:10.1016/j.comcom.2008.03.012

Jiang, D., Chen, Q., & Delgrossi, L. (2008). Optimal data rate selection for vehicle safety communications. In *Proceedings of ACM International Workshop on VehiculAr Inter-NETworking* (VANET). New York, NY: ACM.

Jiang, D., & Delgrossi, L. (2008). IEEE 802.11p: Towards an international standard for wireless access in vehicular environments. In *Proceedings of IEEE Vehicular Technology Conference* (VTC Spring 2008), (pp. 2036-2040). IEEE.

Kosch, T., Kulp, I., Bechler, M., Strassberger, M., Weyl, B., & Lasowski, R. (2009). Communication architecture for cooperative systems in Europe. *IEEE Communications Magazine, 47*(5), 116–125. doi:10.1109/MCOM.2009.4939287

Kwak, J. S., & Lee, J. H. (2004). Infrared transmission for inter-vehicle ranging and vehicle-to-roadside communication systems using spread-spectrum technique. *IEEE Transactions on Intelligent Transportation Systems, 5*(1), 12–19. doi:10.1109/TITS.2004.825082

Murray, T., Cojocari, M., & Fu, H. (2008). Measuring the performance of IEEE 802.11p using NS-2 simulator for vehicular networks. In *Proceedings of IEEE International Conference on Electro/Information Technology* (EIT), (pp. 498–503). IEEE.

Piorkowski, M., Raya, M., Lugo, A., Papadimitratos, P., Grossglauser, M., & Hubaux, J.-P. (2007). TraNS: Joint traffic and network simulator for VANETs. In *Proceedings of MobiCom*. Montreal, Canada: ACM.

Piorkowski, M., Raya, M., Lugo, A., Papadimitratos, P., Grossglauser, M., & Hubaux, J.-P. (2008). TraNS: Realistic joint traffic and network simulator for VANETs. *ACM SIGMOBILE Mobile Computing and Communications Review, 12*(1), 31–33. doi:10.1145/1374512.1374522

Santa, J., Gómez-Skarmeta, A. F., & Sánchez-Artigas, M. (2008). Architecture and evaluation of a unified V2V and V2I communication system based on cellular networks. *Computer Communications, 31*(12), 2850–2861. doi:10.1016/j.comcom.2007.12.008

Shankar, P., Nadeem, T., Rosca, J., & Iftode, L. (2008). Cars: Context-aware rate selection for vehicular networks. In *Proceedings of IEEE International Conference on Network Protocols* (ICNP), (pp. 1–12). IEEE.

Skog, I., & Handel, P. (2009). In-car positioning and navigation technologies—A survey. *IEEE Transactions on Intelligent Transportation Systems, 10*(1), 4–21. doi:10.1109/TITS.2008.2011712

Sugiura, A., & Dermawan, C. (2005). In traffic jam IVC-RVC system for ITS using bluetooth. *IEEE Transactions on Intelligent Transportation Systems, 6*(3), 302–313. doi:10.1109/TITS.2005.853704

Taleb, T., Ooi, K., & Hashimoto, K. (2008). An efficient collision avoidance strategy for ITS systems. In *Proceedings of IEEE Wireless Communications and Networking Conference* (WCNC), (pp. 2212-2217). IEEE.

Uzcátegui, R. A., & Acosta-Marum, G. (2009). WAVE: A tutorial. *IEEE Communications Magazine, 47*(5), 126–133. doi:10.1109/MCOM.2009.4939288

Wang, S.-Y., Chao, H.-L., Liu, K.-C., He, T.-W., Lin, C.-C., & Chou, C.-L. (2008). Evaluating and improving the TCP/UDP performances of IEEE 802.11(p)/1609 networks. In *Proceedings of IEEE Symposium on Computers and Communications* (ISCC). Marrakech, Morocco: IEEE.

Wang, Y., Ahmed, A., Krishnamachari, B., & Psounis, K. (2008). IEEE 802.11p performance evaluation and protocol enhancement. In *Proceedings of IEEE International Conference on Vehicular Electronics and Safety* (ICVES), (pp. 317–322). IEEE.

Yan, G., Weigle, M. C., & Olariu, S. (2009). A novel parking service using wireless networks. In *Proceedings of IEEE International Conference on Service Operations, Logistics and Informatics*. Chicago: IEEE.

Yang, L., Guo, J., & Wu, Y. (2009). Piggyback cooperative repetition for reliable broadcasting of safety messages in VANETs. In *Proceedings of IEEE Consumer Communications and Networking Conference* (CCNC). IEEE.

Zhang, W., Festag, A., Baldessari, R., & Le, L. (2008). Congestion control for safety messages in VANETs: Concepts and framework. In *Proceedings of International Conference on Telecommunications* (ITST), (pp. 199-203). ITST.

KEY TERMS AND DEFINITIONS

3G/4G: 3rd/4th Generation of mobile cellular communications.

RVC: Roadside-vehicle communications.

VANET: Vehicular ad-hoc networks.

WAVE: WIRELESS Access Vehicular Environment – V2X communications standardization.

WLAN: Wireless Local Area Network.

Chapter 9
Data Processing and Exchange Challenges in Video–Based Wireless Sensor Networks

Dan Pescaru
Politehnica University of Timisoara, Romania

Daniel-Ioan Curiac
Politehnica University of Timisoara, Romania

ABSTRACT

This chapter presents the main challenges in developing complex systems built around the core concept of Video-Based Wireless Sensor Networks. It summarizes some innovative solutions proposed in scientific literature on this field. Besides discussion on various issues related to such systems, the authors focus on two crucial aspects: video data processing and data exchange. A special attention is paid to localization algorithms in case of random deployment of nodes having no specific localization hardware installed. Solutions for data exchange are presented by highlighting the data compression and communication efficiency in terms of energy saving. In the end, some open research topics related with Video-Based Wireless Sensor Networks are identified and explained.

INTRODUCTION

Wireless Sensor Networks (WSNs) technology is nowadays widely used in various domains. It has applications in fields such as emergency rescue, environmental monitoring, military operations, at-home medical care or industrial systems. A wireless sensor network consists in a set of network nodes capable of sensing and wireless communication. It operates in the absence of a pre-deployed infrastructure and can work in hostile environments. Nodes are self-configurable, low power, low cost, and can be rapidly deployed in emergency situations. Their sensors interact with the physical environment by monitoring and measuring light, heat, position, movement, chemical presence, etc. The information from sensors is then delivered to the other nodes over the wireless

DOI: 10.4018/978-1-4666-5978-0.ch009

network. In many applications one more powerful node, known as central point (CP), gathers the information from sensor nodes, processes it, and interprets the results.

Special kinds of WSNs are represented by Video-based Wireless Sensor Networks (VWSNs), in which case large amounts of video data are sensed, processed in real-time and then transferred over the wireless networks (Sánchez, 2012). Among traditional applications, video monitoring for environment surveillance covers an area that focus attention nowadays due to more frequent threats posed by hurricanes, earthquakes or terrorist attacks.

One important problem in this context is related with data storage and exchange. Indeed, acquisition of a video sequence with reasonable frame rate implies significant amount of data that needs to be stored and transferred.

Handling video data usually required large storage buffers. These buffers help multi-frames video encoding/decoding process but also ensure temporary storage for multi-hop data transfer. Several hardware platforms where developed to provide large data buffers for such intensive data flows as eCAM (Chulsung, 2006), Cyclops (Mohammad, 2005) and RISE (Zeinalipour, 2005).

The wireless communication is characterized by noise, path loss, channel fading and interference. The result is a wireless channel having much lesser capacity than a wired one. Moreover, WSN multi-hop routing tends to generate more interference, delay, packet loss and higher number of errors during transmission. High packet loss rate on the path affects the bandwidth and delay values of transmission. Consequences depend on the application domain and on the kind of implemented system. All application has specific service requirements from the network usually expressed through a parameter named Quality of Service (QoS). Video surveillance using VWSNs in particular have a more constrained set of QoS requirements, aimed to sustain transmission of

high quality data at a high bit-rate. Many of them require strict end-to-end delay, bandwidth and jitter guarantees. These parameters are hard to be satisfied not only due to mentioned communication issues but also because video encoding/decoding algorithms that involve significant processing time.

The aim of the chapter is to debate various solutions for data processing and exchange in video-based wireless sensor networks and to point out some open issues in this field.

VIDEO-BASED WIRELESS SENSOR NETWORKS

Combining video surveillance with wireless sensor networks brings important advantages in many fields. Resulting video-based wireless sensor networks have a large applicability especially in surveillance of critical zones to detect suspect activities. Beside obvious military applications, a lot of systems were developed for surveillance in subway and train stations, airports, hospitals, parking zones, stores, and other public places (Fernandez, 2013). Along common intrusion detection tasks, these systems can be used also to identify persons, vehicles or other kind of targets.

Another class of applications was designed for environmental monitoring in the case of areas subject to earthquakes, flooding or other natural disasters (Dawood, 2013). Sensor nodes can be deployed in the risk area to collect images over a wide surface. A disaster headquarter will use the information to take the best management decisions to overcome the situation.

Despite the fact that object sensed by the camera can be at arbitrary locations, information quality strongly depends on camera's resolution, size of the object and distance between camera and object. Depending on particular application and on the size of the smallest interesting object, we can determine experimentally the medium distance D_q

which provide adequate quality. This distance is known as camera range or depth of view.

Data collection from video sensor assumes a target entering field of view (FoV) coverage area. Due FoV overlapping, multiple sensors could sense the same target simultaneously as depicted by Figure 1. Indeed, two camera sensors can collect visual data of the same object even if they are far from each other. Same time, a very close object may not be viewed by a particular visual sensor if it isn't inside its FoV. Generally, the collected information depends on the sensors orientation, resolution and depth of view but also on light or environment conditions (Costa, 2010).

Target discovery and tracking become more complex in case of mobile sensors or cameras with pan, tilt, and zooming facilities. In these scenarios, sensors movement or cameras' parameters variation allow dynamic adjustment of the FoV (Desai, 2009).

Figure 1. Collecting visual data in case of FoV overlapping

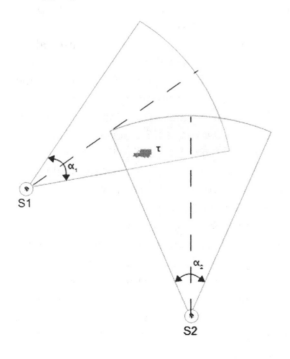

CHALLENGES AND SOLUTIONS IN VWSN VIDEO DATA PROCESSING

Issues Regarding Deployment, Coverage and Video Processing

Wireless sensor networks are generally composed of a large number of tiny sensors densely deployed over the area when the phenomenon of interest is happening. The deployment could be deterministic or random. In case of deterministic deployment, the process implies a prior prepared plan. This approach allows maximization of the covered area with the minimum number of sensors. Sometimes a number of redundant nodes are added for higher availability to ensure optimal performances. However, there are many real-life situations when deterministic deployment cannot be a solution. When we take into consideration a harsh or a hard-to-reach environment the random deployment might be the unique feasible solution.

In case of a random deployment the sensors will be scattered over a target area. Approaches varies from airdropping the sensors from a plain, launching them using a rocket or releasing them on the ocean. The chosen approach is strongly depending on the application monitoring requirements and the characteristics of the area under investigation. This may result in regions densely or sparsely covered by the sensor nodes. The solution is to increase the density of the deployment in regions of interest with higher relevance for the application to enhance the overall monitoring quality. Higher density ensures also a certain level of sensing redundancy. The redundancy is valuable for a WSN as it increases the precision of environment observations and network lifetime (Pescaru, 2008). Benefits of redundancy in coverage recovery are demonstrated in (Istin, 2011), where FoV recovery problem was debated in context of traffic surveillance applications. The problem of redundancy was deeply analyzed in (Curiac, 2009). In addition to obvious physical sensing redundancy, temporal sensing redundancy, temporal communication redundancy, and information redundancy adds high relevant data for deployment planning.

Obviously, not all visual sources have the same relevancy for a particular VWSN application. The significance of each of them is weighted with the importance of the target, the overlap with some regions of interest or with observation conditions. A well-defined concept of sensing relevance in video-based wireless sensor networks is proposed in (Costa, 2013). Five different groups of relevance related to the overall significance of the source nodes are identified as irrelevant, low relevance, medium relevance, high relevance and maximum relevance. Using this classification, redundant nodes are considered only if they fall in the same group of relevance.

The success of a VWSN application relies many times on area coverage. Although the problem of WSN coverage was intensively studied, in the case of a VWSN it becomes more difficult. Unlike omni-directional disc sensing model of general sensors, the sensing model for video cameras induces complex deployment-related situations.

Here the viewing direction of the sensor has significant impact on the quality of coverage over the target surface. Figure 2 demonstrates the large variation of coverage in two deployment scenarios that imply the same number of sensors.

After deployment, various classes of visual processing algorithms are required to fulfill the needs of VWSN applications. These include, but are not limited to:

- Image and video capturing and compression;
- Features extraction;
- Objects detection and tracking;
- Data aggregation, transfer and security;
- Distributed image processing.

Due to the limitation of communication bandwidth, it is not feasible to constantly stream video to a central server having high computation capabilities. On the other hand, many times it is unfeasible to move visual processing at the level of network nodes. Therefore, most solutions combine distributed processing, aggregation and central point processing to achieve desired result.

Figure 2. Area FoV coverage for two deployment scenarios involving four video sensors

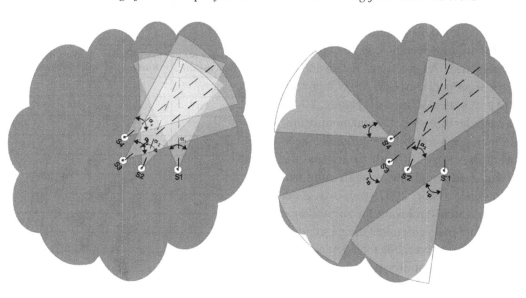

Proposed Solutions for Deployment, Coverage and Video Processing

Deployment and Coverage

Most of the VWSN applications are employed in surveillance tasks. The success of a surveillance operation relies not only on some sophisticated visual processing algorithms, but also it depends on good coverage of the investigated area. The problem of coverage has to be solved during the deployment/redeployment phases.

In the case of video-based wireless sensor networks, the deployment plan or the density variation has to take care of FoV coverage. For deterministic deployments, various algorithms for optimal camera placement (Oasis, 2010) have been proposed. In all of them, the goal is to find the minimal number of nodes that can view the larger or most interesting area of the monitored environment. This can be rather difficult in the case of a complex environment with significant number of visual obstacles. The work in (Adriaens, 2006) proposed a polynomial time algorithm to compute worst-case coverage, which is related with the maximal distance between the mobile target and the sensors. In case of random deployment, the optimal deployment density can be determined using various probabilistic approaches.

In general, deployment strategies are based on coverage estimation. Coverage can be expressed using various metrics. A Directional K-Coverage – *DKC* – metric is proposed in (Liu, 2008), adapting the concept previously defined in (Huang, 2003) in order to consider directional visual monitoring. *DKC* is defined as a probability guarantee, since 100% coverage is very difficult to achieve for randomly deployed visual sensors with a uniform density. Reference (Istin, 2007) proposes a set of metrics, particularly relevant for surveillance systems. The first metric denotes the percentage of covered surface relative to the total deployment surface – *CS/S*. Its computation is straightforward

and the conclusions drawn are useful for most applications. A refined variant of *CS/S* is the size of the Maximum Continuous Uncovered Surfaces over the monitored area – *MCUS*. It is especially important if we consider tracking applications. The aim is to reveal how much a target can move in the area without being noticed by the network. Several experiments demonstrate the saturation effect obtained for random deployments of VWSN with different number of nodes as presented in Table 1.

The deployment homogeneity could be analyzed using the total Number of Continuous Uncovered Surfaces – *NCUS*. To estimate the coverage closure, it is proposed a metric named Number of Crossing Paths – *NCP*. Here, a crossing path is considered a way between two borders of the guarded area uncovered by any sensor FoV. The *NCP* will count the number of different uncovered paths crossing the network. All paths, starting from the same uncovered surface and ending on other, have to be counted only once.

Table 1. The variation of Covered Surface and Maximum Continuous Uncovered Surface considering random deployments of wireless sensor networks with size variation between 0 and 10,000 nodes on a 1,000x1,000 m^2 monitored area

Network Size (# of nodes)	Covered Surface (%)	Maximum Continuous Uncovered Surface (%)
1,000	38.21	23.68
2,000	60.13	7.06
3,000	73.87	3.24
4,000	82.59	2.07
5,000	88.91	1.04
6,000	93.03	0.98
7,000	95.25	0.56
8,000	96.31	0.28
9,000	97.06	0.14
10,000	99.08	0.03

An analysis of the impact of coverage on surveillance quality after a random deployment over an area of interest is presented in (Pescaru, 2007). It is based on Relevant Camera Sensing Area – *RCSA* – parameter, which is defined as a sector resulting from the intersection of field o view and the monitored area. Based on that, the Network Relevant Sensing Area – *NRSA* – for whole video-sensor network is expressed as the union of all individual relevant cameras' sensing areas (1) as presented in Figure 3.

$$NRSA = \bigcup_{i=1}^{N} RCSA_i \qquad (1)$$

Using NRSA we can express an important deployment quality parameter calculated as the ratio between NRSA and network deployment area – *NDA*. We named it Deployment Coverage Quality – *DCQ*.

$$DCQ = \frac{NRSA}{NDA} \qquad (2)$$

The coverage can be used to switch off part of the redundant nodes. The lifetime of the sensor nodes is significantly longer in this case, as they do not have to operate the camera during idle time periods.

Localization

A wireless sensor network is often deployed in an ad-hoc manner in the absence of any knowledge on existing infrastructure or location characteristics. Moreover, redeployment of additional nodes could happen at any time when the upgrade of capabilities or replacements of malfunctioning nodes are necessary. Considering these situations, a central problem is the estimation of spatial-coordinates of the network nodes, known as topology extraction or localization. The solutions for this problem can

Figure 3. Network Relevant Sensing Area (NRSA)

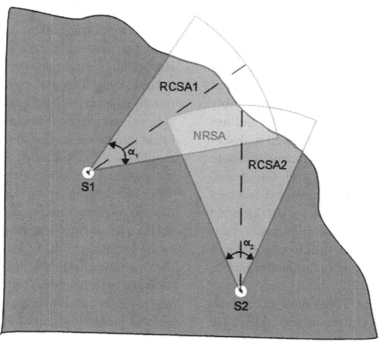

be classified into coarse-grained methods (Bulusu, 2000) based on proximity to a reference point, and fine-grained localization (Savvides, 2001) based on timing or signal strength.

Popular localization methods make use of Global Positioning System (GPS). Unfortunately, this solution can work only outdoors and the cost of GPS sensor is high. Therefore, it is not suitable for development of small cheap sensor nodes as desired for a massive deployment. Other coarse-grained solutions consider the network to be organized as a mixed hierarchy, built using both complex nodes and cheap low-level nodes. The complex high-level nodes are considered to know their location, by using GPS or other techniques. These nodes act as beacons and transmit their position periodically via the network. The low level nodes can run different localization proximity-based algorithms, including sophisticated iterative multi-lateration or multi-angulation (Langendoen, 2005).

Most of the fine-grained localization solutions are based on the timing of arrival or on the signal strength. Methods from the first category use the distance between the node and a reference point determined by measuring the communication signal arrival time (Meghani, 2012). The methods based on signal strength consider the signal attenuation proportional to the traveled distance and use this information to approximate the relative location (Elnahrawy, 2004). More elaborate methods rely on signal pattern matching techniques and use pre-scanned coverage area transmitted with signals. A central system assigns a unique signature for each square in the location grid. The system looks for a match between the signal received and those from the pre-constructed database and determines the correct location. A better solution uses measurements of the Doppler shifts of the transmitted signal and radio interferometric techniques (Kusy, 2007).

Reference (Pescaru, 2006) proposes a novel solution for node localization and video-filed overlap estimation. It starts from video images acquired from network sensors and computes the video fields' superposition. Data are gathered and processed on a central point, which extracts parameters for coordinates translation, rotation and scaling. Parameters are sent back to all nodes and used to calculate FoV overlaps between pairs of sensors. Processing consists on image registration algorithm applied on each pair of images, coming from individual sensors. Registration involves searching for corresponding elements between source and target images. In practice, correspondence is established based on features extracted from images or based on similarity between regions. As the region based registration is prone to errors generated by segmentation and cameras' color sensitivity, feature based registration is considered more reliable. As all registration algorithms are hard computational, a distributed solution based on node resources is not feasible.

The initial images have to represent the monitored area at a certain moment of time. Therefore a setup protocol was designed to ensure quasi-simultaneous data collecting. It retrieves images on an initialization phase and allows the central point to calculate all necessary transformation parameters between each pair of cameras.

The protocol was adapted from the one presented in (Cosma, 2006), which demonstrates good performance in case of large networks. It starts with a setup message broadcasted by the central point. This message embeds an empty routing table for paths information. Each node that receives the message should test if it is included or not into the message routing table. If not, it has to add itself to the routing table of the original message and broadcasts the modified message. After broadcasting, it starts a timer that manages the image capture and transmission. Each node acts as a router by propagating the server requests to the entire network. When a node receives for the first time a setup message it will forward this message to its neighbors. After that, an image is sent to the central point in an energy-efficient manner that preserves network integrity. To increase efficiency each node keeps routing information that will describe each of its neighbors by its current energy level and the hop-count until the sink. All received messages will update also the energy information of the sender into the receiver routing table. As long the next hop node energy is over 50% the only restriction considered in electing it is to have minimum hop count to the sink. When energy node is between 20%-50%, the node will be elected as next hop only if there are no other neighbors with equal hop-count and higher energy level. In case of multiple candidates the possible next hop is computed based on a LRU like algorithm. This strategy ensures an optimal balance for power consumption along the network during images collection process.

After gathering all the images from the network the central point starts to calculate geometric transform parameters between all pairs of matching images. This operation is based on image registration algorithms. The goal of image registration is to overlay two images of the same scene captured at different times, from different viewpoints and by different cameras. To accomplish this goal, a transformation has to be found so that several points in one image, called the reference image, can be mapped to corresponding points in a second one. In other words, registration geometrically aligns two images in an optimal manner. One of the first proposed registration methods was RANSAC (Fischler, 1981). It is based on a robust estimator. The main drawback of this solution is represented by the substantial computation time needed in most of the cases. Practical solutions do not consider all the available data if corresponding reduction of its precision is acceptable in the application context. Besides of that, due to the diversity of images to be registered and due to the various types of visual degradations encountered, it is practically impossible to design a universal method applicable to all situations. In addition to possible geometric deformations, radiometric deformations and noise have to be considered.

The registration method presented in reference (Pescaru, 2006) makes use of a mean shift algorithm for robust parameters estimation (Co-maniciu, 2002) to compute translation vector, rotation angle, and scaling factor. It relays on a semi-automated process to establish the set of corresponding features. Results are better than in case of using RANSAC, as this method considers all the available data samples. To deal with various errors that affect the algorithm in harsh situations, a post-processing phase could be applied.

The mean shift algorithm detects local maxima of a multivariate probability density. The computed parameters are selected from the values with the highest probability density in considered solution space. Estimation of the density vector δ starts from a sample of N k-dimensional data points χ_i, drawn from a distribution with multivariate probability density function $p(\delta)$

$$\hat{p}_B(\delta) = \frac{1}{N} \sum_{i=1}^{N} K_B(\delta - \chi_i), \qquad (3)$$

where K_B is the kernel function expressed by the equation

$$K_B(\delta) = |B|^{-1/2} K_B(B^{-1/2}\delta). \qquad (4)$$

The kernel function depends on the bandwidth matrix B, which is a symmetric positive $k \times k$ matrix. Frequently B has a diagonal form $diag[b_1^2, \ldots, b_d^2]$ or a proportional to the identity matrix $b^2 I$. Considering that, the profile of the radial symmetric kernel was defined as

$$K^R(\delta) = \xi K(\|\delta\|^2), \qquad (5)$$

where ξ represents a normalization constant, assumed strictly positive. A function $g(\delta) = -k'(\delta)$ could be now defined assuming existence of the derivate of the kernel profile for all $\delta \in [1, \infty)$, excepting a finite set of points. Considering this function, the mean shift algorithm is then used to find the location of the maxima of the estimated probability density function, which is closest with a starting location γ_i. The searching is conducted by iterating until reaching convergence the equation

$$\gamma_{j+1} = \frac{\sum_{i=1}^{n} \delta_i g\left(\left\|\frac{\gamma_j - \delta_i}{b}\right\|^2\right)}{\sum_{i=1}^{n} g\left(\left\|\frac{\gamma_j - \delta_i}{b}\right\|^2\right)}, \quad j = 1, 2, \ldots \quad (6)$$

for all $\{\gamma_j\}_{j=1,2,\ldots}$ representing the sequence of successive locations of the kernel G. In practice the convergence is very fast involving a very small number of iterations.

The registration model is based on a set of 2D transformations having the propriety of shape preserving mapping. The model is defined by Equation (7), which relates a pair of corresponding pixels (α, β) from two images.

$$\begin{bmatrix} \beta_x \\ \beta_y \end{bmatrix} =$$

$$\begin{bmatrix} \sigma & 1 \\ 1 & \sigma \end{bmatrix} \begin{bmatrix} \cos(\phi) & -\sin(\phi) \\ \sin(\phi) & \cos(\phi) \end{bmatrix} \begin{bmatrix} \alpha_x \\ \alpha_y \end{bmatrix} + \begin{bmatrix} \tau_x \\ \tau_y \end{bmatrix} \quad (7)$$

The σ, φ, τ_x and τ_y represents scaling, rotation and translation parameters. They can be unambiguously determined from the correspondence of two pairs of points. However, in real situations precision is affected by visual errors. A good solution exploits set of pairs of corresponding points for parameter estimation. As the angle between two line segments is not depending on translation or scaling, the rotation parameter φ can be estimated prior to translation or scaling parameters. Next, the scaling parameter can be computed prior to translation, based on the distances between known pairs of points. The last estimation concerns the translation vector, as it requires coordinates compensated accordingly to rotation and scaling parameters. Figure 4 presents an example of image registration on two sensor images in a typical outdoor environment.

The algorithm is affected by small errors due to noises and limited precision of point matching procedure. A fine-grade post-processing step could be used to reduce this error. In reference (Pescaru, 2006) the processing is based on chamfer matching (Borgefors, 1984). This technique relies on edges matching. The matching criterion is the correlation of a searched pattern with a distance map computed over a target image. It involves several steps. First, a distance transformation is computed and corresponding distance map is produced starting from the upper right corner of the second image. Then, a relevant pattern extracted from the first image is then moved over the relief

Figure 4. The results of registration process

defined by the distance map. Under the action of gravity, the pattern slides over the relief until it reaches the lowest possible altitude. If this altitude is close to zero, the result corresponds to an optimal matching pattern. The pattern is located where this correlation reaches an absolute minimum. Figure 5 depicts the result of post-processing in case of a complex view. Two sensors having different orientation have captured a pair images over the common area. To highlight the processing results, a pair of corresponding rectangular fragments from registered images was investigated. A Kenny edge detector (Kenny, 1986) was used to extract edges in considered fragments from original image coming from the first sensor and the image from the second sensor after registration process. Images from the figure present the binary difference between edges from the two fragments before, and after chamfer matching adjustment. It highlights minimization of non-aligned edges in case of post-processed image.

An improved version of discussed approach is presented in reference (Fuiorea, 2008). The aim was to replace user intervention in features selection through a full automatic procedure. The selection is based in this case on a Scale-Invariant Feature Transform – SIFT (Lowe, 1999). It is a computer vision algorithm designed to detect and describe local features in images. These local features are invariant to image scale and rotation. Detection is robust to changes in illumination,

noise, occlusion, and minor changes in view area. Extracted local features allow easy objects identification with high probability. Features extraction involves four steps. The first one is the scale-space extrema detection, followed by key-point localization, orientation assignment and computation of a local image descriptor. Key locations are defined as maxima and minima of the result of the difference of Gaussians function. They are applied in scale space over a series of resampled images. Scale-space extrema detection implies a convolution applied on the image using Gaussian filters at different scales. Then the difference of successive Gaussian-blurred images is computed. Key-points are generated as maxima/minima of the Difference of Gaussians (DoG) occurring at multiple scales.

$$DoG(x, y, \sigma) = L(x, y, k_i\sigma) - L(x, y, k_j\sigma) \tag{8}$$

The L represents the convolution of the original image I with a Gaussian blur G as presented in Equation (9).

$$L(x, y, k\sigma) = G(x, y, k\sigma) \cdot I(x, y) \tag{9}$$

Low contrast candidate and poorly localized points along an edge are discarded during key-point localization step. Orientation assignment

Figure 5. Differences between registered images before and after chamfer matching

step allows only dominant orientations to generate localized key-points. During this step gradient magnitude and direction are computed for every pixel in a neighboring region around the key-point that belongs to the Gaussian-blurred image *L*. These steps ensure invariance to image location, scale and rotation. The last step, which aims computation of local image descriptors, generates key-points that are highly distinctive and partially invariant to some other variations as illumination or 3D orientation. Following this procedure, SIFT descriptors robust to local affine distortion are obtained by considering pixels around a radius of the key location, blurring and resampling of local image orientation planes. This approach generates large numbers of features that densely cover the image over the full range of scales and locations.

After local feature extraction a robust estimation method could be used to give the best estimation of the geometrical transform parameters through features mapping between set of image pairs. The registration approach using automatic feature extraction proves strong benefit in terms of execution time, while losing in precision versus semi-automatic procedure is acceptable.

Data Processing

Data processing in VWSN represents an interdisciplinary field that combines networking, distributed and embedded computing and computer vision. Unlike wired camera networks, streaming video to a central server is not feasible due to limited bandwidth. Therefore, visual processing should be distributed between network nodes having very limited computing power and energy and the central point.

The problem implies high efficient solution at every level of VWSN. Regarding appropriate hardware, the main components include a powerful digital signal processor, a low power camera sensor and an efficient wireless module. A large variety of processors prove already enough capabilities

for such applications. As examples we can mention Cyclops, WiSN, WiCa, and Citric platforms.

Cyclops (Rahimi, 2005) was one of the first working solutions for VWSN applications. Cyclops consists of an Agilent Technology ADCM-1700 CMOS video sensor, an ATMEL ATmega128L micro-controller, a Xilinx XC2C256 CoolRunner complex programmable logic device, an external SRAM and a Flash memory. The platform was designed as an external attached sensor to a WSN mote such as one from the Mica family, and therefore it does not include a radio device. The video sensor is capable of 352×288 CIF resolution. The microcontroller operates at 7.37 MHz at 3.3V. The Xilinx XC2C256 device implements synchronization and memory control that is required for image capture. Cyclops technology was designed for minimal power consumption to enable large-scale deployment and extended lifetime. As a consequence, it has a strong limitation in processing capabilities and it was not designed for applications that require high-speed processing or high resolutions. However, it can be used for various applications that rely for example on detecting changes in size or shape of the objects.

The WiSN project (Downes, 2006) proposes flexible and expandable mote architecture for distributed image sensing and processing. The board is organized around an Atmel AT91SAM7S 32 bit processor, clocked at 48 MHz. It includes 64 MB of RAM and could operate two Agilent ADCM-1670 352×288 pixels at 15 fps sensor or up to four Agilent ADNS-3060 30×30 pixel image sensors at 100 fps. It has also a built-in IEEE 802.15.4 Chipcon CC2420 radio device. Target processing solutions includes the ability to learn from an environment and to control agents based on visual observations.

WiCa (Kleihorst, 2007) smart camera mote are based on a high performance single-instruction multiple-data processor. It contains a Xetal-II SIMD processor running at 84 MHz. The advantage of this solution is represented by the use of parallel processing to reduce the number of memory accesses, clock speed and instruction decoding. Despite the high computational capabilities, the power consumption is kept under 600 mW. The Xetal-II is coupled using a dual port RAM with a general purpose ATMEL8051 processor. The mote integrates one or two OM6802 camera sensors and a Texas Instruments CC2420 transceiver. Possible applications are Canny edge detection or real time gesture recognition.

The Citric platform (Chen, 2008) consists of an Intel XScale PXA270 processor running at up to 624 MHz clock speed, 32MB RAM, 32MB FLASH and an OmniVision OV9655 1.3 megapixel CMOS camera capable of SXGA 1280×1024 pixel resolution at 15 fps. The typical active power consumption of the camera is around 90mW at SXGA and the standby current is less than 20μA. The communication is ensured by a CC2420 radio component implementing IEEE 802.15.4 capable of 250 kbps transfers. This platform is powerful enough for medium intensive vision algorithms. It can ensure for image difference background subtraction and for bounding box computation a processing time per frame in the range of 0.2s – 0.4s at a resolution of 320×480.

CHALLENGES AND SOLUTIONS IN WSN MULTIMEDIA DATA EXCHANGE

Issues Regarding Data Exchange

Wireless Sensor Networks are used to sense the environment. Their applications require data to be collected in a central point in order to be processed and stored. Network nodes usually send these data when environment changes or when an event is detected. In case of VWSN systems, video frames captured by sensor camera represent the row data. A basic solution for data exchange implies in this case video streaming to the central point. However, real-time video streaming has stringent requirements for bandwidth, end-to-end delay and loss during transmission. These issues

are hard to be solved by nodes wireless communication modules. The wireless communication is characterized by high path loss, channel fading, interference, noise disturbances, and high error rate. In general, wireless channels have much lesser streaming capacity than wired channels. But for many monitoring applications, transient faults during transmissions can be tolerated. In addition, some error recovery mechanism could to be adopted to reduce the impact of packet losses, providing some level of reliability (Qaisar, 2009). In case of higher requirements, various solutions were proposed in form of data compression or flow congestion control mechanisms.

Recent versions of the VWSNs have the ability to perform local processing computations and data aggregation. The aim is to send only the relevant part of the sensed data to the central point. This represents a valuable improvement over their predecessors as it has been shown that the network nodes typically spend most of their energy in transmitting data. Therefore, in-node processing, compression and data aggregation often results in a reduction in the overall energy consumption.

Proposed Solutions for Data Exchange

The ability of a WSN to provide support for video streaming is restricted due to the hardware, communication capabilities, and power limitations of the sensor nodes. Relatively few applications have been proposed for multimedia streaming in such systems.

Data Streaming

Solutions in VWSN data streaming are limited due communication hardware restrictions. Early platforms as WeC, René and Dot2000 have very low 10kbps bandwidth. More recently platforms as Crossbow MICA and MICA2 rely on 38.4 kbps ChipCon1000 wireless module. Today, most WSN motes adopt the IEEE 802.15.4 communication standard (Bougard, 2005), and a transmission rate around 250kbps. To obtain it, Crossbow MicaZ, Tmote Sky and TelosB motes use ChipCon2420 module, while Arduino Mega-2560 and Waspmote adopt XBee-802.15.4. However, 250 kbps are not suitable to transmit high data rate media streams. A better solution is Bluetooth radio with maximum data rate of 3Mbps, used by Intel iMote1 with the drawbacks of quite limited size of the network. More advanced platforms, as Panoptes (Feng, 2005) or Intel Stargate1 (Nachman, 2005), use instead more capable 802.11 networking. Even so the main problem related to IEEE 802.11 devices is the high power-consumption that makes them suitable mainly for wireless local area computer network implementation.

Based on existing platforms one important direction of research in VWSN video streaming covers improvements of video transmission mechanisms. The reference (Maimour, 2009) addresses the problem of congestion control for information-intensive flows in surveillance WSN applications. They propose a multi-path routing solution and efficient congestion detection in case of packet losses due buffer overflow and the contention of radio channel. It relays on a mix of several mechanisms with the aim of ensuring a better handling of video flows. To solve congestions they develop several load repartition strategies on top of the multipart support. Using those strategies the video flow is split on multiple paths based on these strategies. This help in maintaining the transmission rate unchanged to ensure the effectiveness of the surveillance application. To evaluate performance they calculate a *fairness* metric defined as

$$\frac{\left(\sum_{i=1}^{N_s} r_i\right)^2}{N_s \sum_{i=1}^{N_s} r_i^2}, \tag{10}$$

where r_i represents the success rate achieved by the source i, and N_s is the total number of sources. The performance achieved in term of this metric for 250 nodes using an incremental approach to add new paths is around 80%. However, traffic distribution on multiple paths is not efficient in term of energy preservation.

The problem of loss recovery is treated in (Paek, 2007). They propose a Rate-Controlled Reliable Transport – RCRT protocol, which addresses emerging high-rate applications involving loss-intolerant multimedia data transfer. It uses end-to-end explicit loss recovery, but places all the congestion detection and rate adaptation functionality in the sinks. Sinks are able to achieve greater efficiency since they have a more comprehensive view of network behavior.

Other solutions use multiple paths for data transfer to alleviate the intensity of buffer usage at the intermediate sensor nodes and to reduce the required data rate on each wireless path. An example is COngestion Detection and Avoidance – CODA protocol described in (Wan, 2003). It allows a collection point to manage multiple sources associated with a single event in case of detecting network congestion. A drawback of the solution is the time delay in tacking action by the source.

Data Compression

One of the most commonly used communications standard for wireless sensor networks is the IEEE 802.15.4. Main advantages are low cost of equipments and power efficiency. This standard specifies a maximum data rate up to 250kB/s, which is relatively slow for video streaming. Hence, compression methods should be used to reduce the amount of data. They solve the problem of low data rate, but compression algorithms involved is high power demanding. Therefore the solution is most of the time comparable with the transmission cost of uncompressed image. Nevertheless some of them prove very reasonable power demands as for example JPEG compression using fixed-point discrete cosine.

A video clean sensor architecture based on IEEE 802.15.4 was proposed by (Shahidan, 2011). It consists in an Atmega644PV microcontroller unit operating at 3.3 V, an AT45DB321D data flash for data buffering, a C328-7640 VGA resolution camera module, and an XBee RF transceiver module for communication. Solution proves good performance in data compression and transfer for 640x480 video frames.

An alternative to classical video streaming is the image streams. In reference (Chiasserini, 2002) the solution is periodic transmission of compressed images. For efficiency they use JPEG with fixed-point discrete cosine transform for compression, in place of the commonly used floating-point transform. This approach provides good compression rates while computation complexity is not too high. The system runs on an Intel Strong-Arm 1110 platform at 59 MHz, the compression factor is around 8:1, and the maximum image transmission delay is 2s. However, the processed grayscale QCIF images are not suitable for complex applications.

Solution proposed in (Wu, 2004) adopts a multi-layer coding based on JPEG 2000 instead of JPEG change-difference coding. They use wavelet-based decomposition to create multiple bit-stream image encodings that are transmitted in small fragment bursts. The aim is to obtain an optimum balance between energy consumption for image coding and energy spent for wireless data transmission. Performance evaluation through simulations shows significant increasing of the system lifetime while satisfying application constraints related to image quality.

Routing Algorithms

Unlike routing in computers networks, in case of WSN several new issues have to be considered. The depletion of nodes battery power can result in broken links and affect the continuity of data transmission. Therefore, energy-aware routing is necessary to include policies for managing energy depletion. Low bandwidth, complex topology and harsh deployment environment should to be take into account by routing algorithms. Furthermore VWSN routing is expected to ensure also specific Quality of Service.

The reference (Wang, 2007) proposes an approach based on synchronized pipelined transmission for video data streaming. The route discovery process is based on a probabilistic method. The source node periodically sends out route probing packets. The probing packets are randomly relayed to a neighbor until they reach the central point. The subscriber node calculates the optimal path based on all received probing packets when a predefined timer expires. This algorithm is efficient if the source node is not significantly far from the central point. A certain level of energy conservation is achieved through reduction of packet retransmissions in the presence of node failures.

A location-based routing for video streaming is presented in (Cosma, 2006). The authors propose a topology extraction protocol using networks video cameras. There are two steps to accomplish the topology extraction. First the central point diffuse routing messages over the network and every node records routing information. After a path set-up phase, every node in the network captures an image using its video camera, and sends the image back to the central point. This node then performs image registration to extract the topology of the network. The authors further discuss possible optimizations for path routing and energy conservation. To accomplish that, every node maintains a record of their neighbors' energy level and hop count to the server. Any node with a relatively high energy (e.g. >20%) should be included in the candidate set for next hop selection during routing. The winner candidate will be the one with the smallest hop count.

The two-phase geographical greedy forwarding routing protocol (Shu et al. 2008) uses a greedy location-based scheme. In relays on a *step back and mark* process to explore possible paths to the sink. The aim is to find a route to the destination as if one exists. The method puts routing paths as close as possible to the centerline, and can cause very severe path coupling issues.

Other approaches are based on hierarchical schemes. Reference (Politis, 2008) describes a hierarchical solution for video data. The network architecture setup is derived from the architecture of Low-Energy Adaptive Clustering Hierarchy – LEACH – proposed by (Heinzelman, 2000). Instead of using a direct link between a cluster head and sink, cluster heads are permitted to establish links to each other. A video sensor node can select a number of available paths through other cluster heads in order to transmit its data. This improvement decreases the transmission power of a cluster head for shorter-range communication and saves energy.

Some interesting solutions are focused on energy saving. A possibility is to send data through the path of fewest hops and most longevity. This approach was proposed by (Li, 2007). The resulting global-energy-balancing routing – GEBR – scheme for real-time traffic is based on directed diffusion and balances node energy utilization to increase the network lifetime. The longevity of a path is measured with a metric called Minimum-Path-Energy, which express the minimum energy of all the nodes along a certain path. The path with fewer hops is considered to ensure the lowest data transmission delay.

CONCLUSION AND OPEN RESEARCH TOPICS

Advances in embedded systems, low power CMOS video sensors, and wireless communication have led to Video Wireless Sensor Networks. They add value to a large variety of application domains like civil or military surveillance, traffic management or environment monitoring. Challenges in designing VWSN applications are manly related with resource limitations. Video sensing is expensive in terms of energy consumption. In-node data processing as compression or feature extraction should be implemented on limited computational power and small memory buffers. Wireless data transmission over multiple hops is prone to errors and congestion, and overall distributed resource management is complex.

Among several solutions presented in this chapter we identify also some remaining open research issues concerned with various aspects of VWSN design and development.

As both video capturing and processing remains high power demanding, a main issue is related with node hardware design. A good perspective is offered here by development of specialized low power DSP chips or more complex controllers with vector processing capabilities.

More research should be done in embedded image and video processing to improve localization techniques, tracking and feature extraction. Good perspectives offer also 3D processing techniques and specialized stereovision devices.

Energy conservation is a critical design challenge for VWSN routing. An open issue here is how to ensure accurate network energy status measurement and to define accurate consumption models. Research should address improved protocols, distributed resource management and new low power/long range communication devices. High accurate simulation models and tools should be developed.

REFERENCES

Adriaens, J., Megerian, S., & Potkonjak, M. (2006). Optimal worst-case coverage of directional field-of-view sensor networks. In *Proceedings of IEEE Sensor, Mesh and Ad Hoc Communications and Networks* (pp. 336 – 345). Reston, VA: IEEE.

Borgefors, G. (1984). An improved version of the chamfer matching algorithm. In *Proceedings of the 7ᵗʰ International Conference on Pattern Recognition*. Montreal, Canada: Academic Press.

Bougard, B., Catthoor, F., Daly, D. C., Chandrakasan, A., & Dehaene, W. (2005). Energy efficiency of the IEEE 802.15.4 standard in dense wireless microsensor networks: Modeling and improvement perspectives. In Proceedings of Design, Automation and Test in Europe – DATE'05 (pp. 196-201). IEEE Computer Society.

Bulusu, N., Heidemann, J., & Estrin, D. (2000). GPS-less low cost outdoor localization for very small devices. *Proceedings of the IEEE Personal Communications, 7*(5), 28–34. doi:10.1109/98.878533

Canny, J. F. (1986). A computational approach to edge detection. *IEEE Transactions on Pattern Analysis and Machine Intelligence, 8*(6), 679–698. doi:10.1109/TPAMI.1986.4767851 PMID:21869365

Chen, P., Ahammad, P., Boyer, C., Huang, S., Lin, L., & Lobaton, E. … Sastry, S. (2008). Citric: A low-bandwidth wireless camera network platform. In *Proceedings of the Second ACM/IEEE International Conference on Distributed Smart Cameras ICDSC 2008*. Stanford, CA: ACM/IEEE.

Chiasserini, C., & Magli, E. (2002). Energy consumption and image quality in wireless video-surveillance networks. In *Proceedings of the 13th IEEE International Symposium on Personal, Indoor and Mobile Radio Communications – PIMRC'02* (pp. 2357–2361). IEEE.

Chiasserini, C. F., & Magli, E. (2002). Energy consumption and image quality in wireless video-surveillance networks. In *Proceedings of 13ᵗʰ IEEE International Symposium on Personal, Indoor and Mobile Radio Communications PIMRC'02* (pp. 2357–2361). IEEE Computer Society.

Comaniciu, D., & Meer, P. (2002). Mean shift: A robust approach toward feature space analysis. *IEEE Transactions on Pattern Analysis and Machine Intelligence, 24*(5), 603–619. doi:10.1109/34.1000236

Cosma, M., Pescaru, D., Ciubotaru, B., & Todinca, D. (2006). Routing and topology extraction protocol for a wireless sensor network using video information. In *Proceedings of the 3ʳᵈ Romanian-Hungarian Joint Symposium on Applied Computational Intelligence SACI'06*. Timisoara, Romania: SACI.

Costa, D., & Guedes, L. (2010). The coverage problem in video-based wireless sensor networks: A survey. *Sensors (Basel, Switzerland), 10*, 8215–8247. doi:10.3390/s100908215 PMID:22163651

Costa, D., & Guedes, L. (2013). Exploiting the sensing relevancies of source nodes for optimizations in visual sensor networks. *Multimedia Tools and Applications, 64*(3), 549–579. doi:10.1007/s11042-011-0961-4

Curiac, D., Volosencu, C., Pescaru, D., Jurca, L., & Doboli, A. (2009). View upon redundancy in wireless sensor networks. In *Proceedings of the 8ᵗʰ Wseas International Conference on Signal Processing, Robotics and Automation – ISPRA'09, Mathematics and Computers in Science and Engineering* (pp. 341-346). Cambridge, UK: ISPRA.

Dawood, M. S., Suganya, J., Devi, R. K., & Athisha, G. (2013). A review on wireless sensor network protocol for disaster management. *International Journal of Computer Applications Technology and Research, 2*(2), 141–146. doi:10.7753/IJCATR0202.1011

Desai, P., & Rattan, K. S. (2009). Indoor localization and surveillance using wireless sensor network and pan/tilt camera. In *Proceedings of the IEEE National Aerospace & Electronics Conference NAECON'09*. Fairborn, OH: IEEE.

Downes, I., Rad, L. B., & Aghajan, H. (2006). Development of a mote for wireless image sensor networks. In *Proceedings of COGnitive Systems with Interactive Sensors – COGIS'06*. Paris, France: COGIS.

Elnahrawy, E., Li, X., & Martin, R. P. (2004). The limits of localization using signal strength: A comparative study. In *Proceedings of the 1st IEEE International Conference on Sensor and Ad Hoc Communications and Networks SECON'04*. Santa Clara, CA: IEEE.

Feng, W. C., Kaiser, E., Feng, W. C., & Le Baillif, M. (2005). Panoptes: Scalable low-power video sensor networking technologies. *ACM Transactions on Multimedia Computing. Communications and Applications*, *1*(2), 151–167.

Fernandez, J., Calavia, L., Baladrón, C., Aguiar, J. M., Carro, B., & Sánchez-Esguevillas, A. et al. (2013). An intelligent surveillance platform for large metropolitan areas with dense sensor deployment. *Sensors (Basel, Switzerland)*, *13*(6), 7414–7442. doi:10.3390/s130607414 PMID:23748169

Fischler, M. A., & Bolles, R. C. (1981). Random sample consensus: A paradigm for model fitting with applications to image analysis and automated cartography. *Communication Magazine of the ACM*, *24*(6), 381–395. doi:10.1145/358669.358692

Fuiorea, D., Gui, V., Pescaru, D., Paraschiv, P., Istin, C., Curiac, D., & Volosencu, C. (2008). Sensor node localization using SIFT algorithm. In *Proceedings of the 9th International Conference on Automation and Information* (pp. 436-442). Bucharest, Romania: Academic Press.

Heinzelman, W., Chandrakasan, A., & Balakrishnan, H. (2000). Energy-efficient communication protocol for wireless microsensor networks. In *Proceedings of the 33rd Annual Hawaii International Conference on System Sciences*. IEEE.

Huang, C., & Tseng, Y. (2003). The coverage problem in a wireless sensor network. In *Proceedings of 2nd 909 ACM International Workshop on Wireless Sensor Networks and Applications* (pp. 115-121). San Diego, CA: ACM.

Istin, C., & Pescaru, D. (2007). Deployments metrics for video-based wireless sensor networks. *Transactions on Automatic Control and Computer Science*, *52*(66).

Istin, C., Pescaru, D., & Doboli, A. (2011). Stochastic model-based heuristics for fast field of view loss recovery in urban traffic management through networks of video cameras. *IEEE Transactions on Intelligent Traffic Systems*, *12*(3), 895–907. doi:10.1109/TITS.2011.2123095

Kleihorst, R., Abbo, A., Schueler, B., & Danilin, A. (2007). Camera mote with a high-performance parallel processor for real-time frame-based video processing. In *Proceedings of the IEEE Conference on Advanced Video and Signal Based Surveillance – AVSS'07* (pp. 69-74). IEEE.

Kusy, B., Ledeczi, A., & Koutsoukos, X. (2007). Tracking mobile nodes using RF doppler shifts. In *Proceedings of the 5th International Conference on Embedded Networked Sensor Systems SenSys'07*. Sydney, Australia: ACM Press.

Langendoen, K., & Reijers, N. (2005). Distributed localization algorithm. In *Embedded systems handbook*. Boca Raton, FL: CRC Press.

Li, P., Gu, Y., & Zhao, B. (2007). A global-energy-balancing real-time routing in wireless sensor networks. In *Proceedings of the 2nd IEEE Asia-Pacific Service Computing Conference* (pp. 89 - 93). Tsukuba, Japan: IEEE.

Liu, L., Ma, H., & Zhang, X. (2008). On directional k-coverage analysis of randomly deployed camera sensor networks. In *Proceedings of IEEE International Conference on Communications* (pp. 2707-2711). Beijing, China: IEEE.

Lowe, D. G. (1999). Object recognition from local scale-invariant features. In *Proceedings of the 7th IEEE International Conference on Computer Vision*, (Vol. 2, pp. 1150–1157). IEEE.

Maimour, M., Pham, C., & Hoang, D. (2009). A congestion control framework for handling video surveillance traffics on WSN. In *Proceedings of the 2009 International Conference on Computational Science and Engineering (CSE '09)*, (Vol. 2, pp. 943-948). Washington, DC: IEEE Computer Society.

Meghani, S. K., Asif, M., & Amir, S. (2012). Localization of WSN node based on time of arrival using ultra wide band spectrum. In *Proceedings of the 13th IEEE Annual Wireless and Microwave Technology Conference WAMICON'12*. IEEE.

Mohammad, R., Rick, B., Obimdinachi, I. I., Juan, C. G., Jay, W., Deborah, E., & Mani, S. (2005). Cyclops: In situ image sensing and interpretation in wireless sensor networks. In *Proceedings of the 3rd International Conference on Embedded Networked Sensor Systems SenSys '05* (pp. 192-204). ACM.

Nachman, L., Kling, R., Adler, R., Huang, J., & Hummel, V. (2005). The Intel® mote platform: A bluetooth-based sensor network for industrial monitoring. In *Proceedings of the 4th International Symposium on Information Processing in Sensor Networks – IPSN '05*. Piscataway, NJ: IEEE Press.

Osais, Y. E., St-Hilaire, M., & Fei, R. Y. (2010). Directional sensor placement with optimal sensing ranging, field of view and orientation. *Mobile Networks and Applications, 15*(2), 216–225. doi:10.1007/s11036-009-0179-0

Paek, J., & Govindan, R. (2007). RCRT: Rate-controlled reliable transport for wireless sensor networks. In *Proceedings of the 5th International Conference on Embedded Networked Sensor Systems – SenSys'07* (pp. 305-319). New York, NY: ACM.

Park, C., & Chou, P. H. (2006). eCAM: Ultra compact, high data-rate wireless sensor node with a miniature camera. In *Proceedings of the 4th International Conference on Embedded Networked Sensor Systems SenSys '06* (pp. 359-360). New York, NY: ACM.

Pescaru, D., Ciubotaru, B., Chiciudean, D., & Doboli, A. (2005). Experimenting motion detection algorithms for sensor network video surveillance applications. *Transactions on Automatic Control and Computer Science, 50*(64), 39–44.

Pescaru, D., Fuiorea, D., Gui, V., Toma, C., Muntean, G. M., & Doboli, A. (2006). Image-based node localization algorithm for wireless video sensor networks. In *Proceedings of the IT&T Conference*. Carlow, Ireland: Institute of Technology.

Pescaru, D., Gui, V., Toma, C., & Fuiorea, D. (2007). Analyses of post-deployment sensing coverage for video wireless sensor networks. In *Proceedings of the 6th International Conference RoEduNet-2007* (pp. 109-113). SITECH.

Pescaru, D., Istin, C., Curiac, D., & Doboli, A. (2008). Energy saving strategy for video-based sensor networks under field coverage preservation. In *Proceedings of the IEEE-TTTC International Conference on Automation, Quality and Testing, Robotics – AQTR'08* (pp. 289-294). IEEE.

Politis, I., Tsagkaropoulos, M., Dagiuklas, T., & Kotsopoulos, S. (2008). Power efficient video multipath transmission over wireless multimedia sensor networks. *Mobile Networks and Applications, 13*(3-4), 274–284.

Qaisar, S., & Radha, H. (2009). A reliability framework for visual sensor networks. In *Proceedings of Picture Coding Symposium*. Chicago: Academic Press.

Rahimi, M., Baer, R., Iroezi, O., Garcia, J., Warrior, J., Estrin, D., & Srivastava, M. (2005). Cyclops: In-situ image sensing and interpretation in wireless sensor networks. In *Proceedings of the 3rd International Conference on Embedded Networked Sensor Systems – SenSys'05* (pp. 192-204). New York, NY: ACM.

Sanchez, J., Benet, G., & Simó, J. E. (2012). Video sensor architecture for surveillance applications. *Sensors (Basel, Switzerland), 12*, 1509–1528. doi:10.3390/s120201509 PMID:22438723

Savvides, A., Han, C. C., & Srivastava, M. B. (2001). Dynamic fine-grained localization in ad-hoc networks of sensors. In *Proceedings of the 7th Annual International Conference on Mobile Computing and Networking (MobiCom'01),* (pp. 166-179). ACM Press.

Shahidan, A. A., Fisal, N., Fikri, A. H., Ismail Nor-Syahidatul, N., & Yunus, F. (2011). Image transfer in wireless sensor networks. In *Proceedings of the International Conference on Communication Engineering and Networks IPCSIT'2011,* (Vol. 19, pp. 158-165). Singapore: IACSIT Press.

Shu, L., Zhang, Y., Zhou, Z., Hauswirth, M., Yu, Z., & Hyns, G. (2008). Transmitting and gathering streaming data in wireless multimedia sensor networks within expected network lifetime. *Mobile Networks and Applications, 13*(3-4), 306–323.

Wan, C. Y., Eisenman, S. B., & Campbell, A. T. (2003). CODA: Congestion detection and avoidance in sensor networks. In *Proceedings of the ACM Conference on Embedded Networked Sensor Systems –SenSys.* Los Angeles, CA: ACM Press.

Wang, J., Masilela, M., & Liu, J. (2007). Supporting video data in wireless sensor networks. In *Proceedings of the 9th IEEE International Symposium on Multimedia* (pp. 310-317). Los Alamitos, CA: IEEE.

Wu, H., & Abouzeid, A. (2004). Energy efficient distributed JPEG 2000 image compression in multi-hop wireless networks. In *Proceedings of the 4th Workshop on Applications and Services in Wireless Networks – ASWN'04* (pp. 152–160). ASWN.

Zeinalipour, Y. D., Neema, S., Kalogeraki, V., Gunopulos, D., & Najjar, W. (2005). Data acquisition in sensor networks with large memories. In *Proceedings of the 21st International Conference on Data Engineering Workshops ICDEW '05.* IEEE Computer Society.

ADDITIONAL READING

Akyildiz, I. F., Melodia, T., & Chowdhury, K. R. (2007). A Survey on Wireless Multimedia Sensor Networks. [Elsevier USA.]. *Computer Networks, 51*(4), 921–960. doi:10.1016/j.comnet.2006.10.002

Horster, E., Lienhart, R., Kellermann, W., & Bouguet, J. Y. (2005). *Calibrating Visual Sensors and Actuators in Distributed Platforms. Computer Vision for Interactive and Intelligent Environment* (pp. 39–50). Lexington, Kentucky, USA: IEEE Computer Society. doi:10.1109/CVIIE.2005.2

Molina, J., Mora-Merchan, J., Barbancho, J., & Leon, C. (2010). Multimedia Data Processing and Delivery in Wireless Sensor Networks, Wireless Sensor Networks: Application - Centric Design, Yen Kheng Tan (Ed.), InTech.

Radke, R. (2010). A Survey of Distributed Computer Vision Algorithms. In H. Nakashima, H. Aghajan, & J. C. Augusto (Eds.), *Handbook of Ambient Intelligence and Smart Environments* (pp. 35–55). Springer, US. doi:10.1007/978-0-387-93808-0_2

Tarique, M., Tepe, K. E., Adibi, S., & Erfani, S. (2009). Survey of Multipath Routing Protocols for Mobile Ad-hoc Networks. *Journal of Network and Computer Applications*, *32*(6), 1125–1143. doi:10.1016/j.jnca.2009.07.002

Vieira, M. A. M., Coelho, C. N., Da Silva, D. C., & Da Mata, J. M. (2003). Survey on Wireless Sensor Network Devices. *In Proceedings of the IEEE Conference in Emerging Technologies and Factory Automation – ETFA '03*, vol.1 (pp. 537-544). IEEE.

KEY TERMS AND DEFINITIONS

CP: Central point, base station or sink is a special node of a WSN that have access to external energy source, and incorporates significant memory resources and processing power. Its role is to collect, process, and sometimes store data gathered from network sensors. It provides user interface to the WSN and/or transfers date to external systems and applications.

FoV: Field of View represents the entire angular expanse visible through a video camera objective at a given moment of time. The field of view is determined by the focal length of the lens and the size of the image sensor. Obstacles, illumination and weather conditions can affect it significantly.

GPS: Global Positioning System is a space-based satellite navigation system that provides location and time information. It can be used for WSN nodes localization under certain conditions.

Mote: A mote is a low power node in a wireless sensor network that is capable of reading sensory information, performing processing, and communicating with other nodes using wireless connection.

QoS: Quality of Service is a measure of overall performance of a network system. Quality of service is particularly important for the transport of traffic with special requirements as video streams in case of VWSNs.

VWSN: Video Wireless Sensor Networks is a WSN that incorporates video sensors and gather and transmit video information over wireless multi-hop connection.

WSN: Wireless Sensor Networks consists of distributed sensor nodes over a deployment area. The applications are related to monitoring physical events and conditions. They involve a large variety of sensors such as temperature, sound, pressure, light etc.

Chapter 10
Simulation of Competition in NGNs with a Game Theory Model

João Paulo Ribeiro Pereira
Polytechnic Institute of Bragança, Portugal

ABSTRACT

Like in a real competitive market situation, Next Generation Networks (NGN) competitors need to adapt their strategy to face/react the strategies from other players. To better understand the effects of interaction between different players, the authors build a Game Theory model in which the profit of each operator will be dependent not only on their actions but also on the actions of the other operators in the market. This chapter analyzes the impact of the price (retail and wholesale) variations on several output results: players' profit, consumer surplus, welfare, costs, and service adoption. The authors assume that two competing FTTH networks (incumbent operator and new entrant) are deployed in two different areas. They also propose in this chapter an adoption model use in a way that reflects the competition between players and that the variation of the services prices of one player has an influence on the market share of all players. Finally, the model uses the Nash equilibrium to find the best strategies.

INTRODUCTION

The rapid development of new-generation applications, such as high-definition television (HDTV), peer-to-peer (P2P) applications, video on demand, interactive games, e-learning, use of multiple personal computers (PCs) at home, and higher throughput requirements and communication demands make upgrading the access infrastructure a necessity. Ubiquitous broadband access requires a minimum bit rate that is sufficient to allow all citizens to benefit from these services.

The needs of telecommunication networks with higher capacity are becoming a reality all over the world. However, the limitation of local access networks is the major bottleneck to providing broadband access (OECD, 2008).

Service providers, network operators, and Internet access providers are faced with the challenge of providing higher capacity access to the end user and offering wider services (Kota, 2006). Consequently, new Internet infrastructure and technologies that are capable of providing high-speed and high-quality services are needed to ac-

DOI: 10.4018/978-1-4666-5978-0.ch010

commodate multimedia applications with diverse quality of service (QoS) requirements -Until a few years ago, Internet access for residential users was almost exclusively provided via public switched telephone networks (PSTN) over the twisted copper pair. The new quadruple play services (i.e., voice, video, data, and mobility), which require high-speed broadband access, created new challenges for the modern broadband wireless/wired access networks (J. P. Pereira & Ferreira, 2009). The new services led to both the development of several different last-mile solutions to make the access network capable of supporting the requirements and a stronger integration of optical and wireless access networks.

The broadband market is commonly subdivided into wholesale access (access provided to other operators, normally new entrants) and retail access (access provided to end users). The wholesale accesses are provided for fully unbundled lines, shared access, bitstream access, and resale. However, the availability of fixed wholesale access lines supplied by incumbent operators to new entrants is different between countries. As of January 2012, of DSL connections in Europe provided by new entrants, 63% (32% in 2007) were provided by local loop unbundling, 12.3% (17% in 2007) by shared access, 15.4% (38% in 2007) bitstream, and 8.1% (13% in 2007) were based on reseller products (J. P. R. Pereira, 2013b). The use of shared access, bitstream and resale decreased in recent years (however, full LLU increased).

Regulators must decide whether to promote competition on the basis of a single infrastructure with regulated access (service competition) or to encourage the build-up of competing, parallel infrastructures (infrastructure competition) (Höffler, 2007). Then, is important create the right incentive for operators to make an efficient build/buy choice and define the appropriate pricing principles. To obtain economic efficiency, a regulator should (Andersen.Management.International, 2004): (1) Encourage the use of existing infrastructure of the incumbent operator where

this is economically desirable, avoiding inefficient duplication of infrastructure costs by new entrants (incentive to buy); and (2) Encourage investment in new infrastructure where this is economically justified by (1) new entrants investing in competing infrastructure, and (2) the incumbent operator upgrading and expanding its networks (incentive to build).

To simulate competition we analyze the impact of retail and wholesale services price variations on NPV and operator's profit (payoffs). For that we propose one game to study the impact of retail price variation on NPV (wholesale prices are defined by regulator), and a second game to verify the impact of retail and wholesale price variations on players profit (different wholesale prices in each region). We adopt a scenario with two regions, two providers (players), two retail services, and one infrastructure layers (access to conduit and collocation facilities) – wholesale service. The two competing FTTH-PON networks (incumbent operator and new entrant) are deployed in both regions. We also propose an adoption model in a way that reflects the competition between players – The variation of the services prices of one player as an influence on the market share of all players.

MARKET CHALLENGES

Exist significant differences between the broadband access penetrations in OECD countries. The number of Internet users is still expanding rapidly, whereas the number of fixed broadband Internet users is increasing at an even greater rate. Since December 2004, broadband subscribers in the OECD have increased by 187%, reaching 221 million in June 2007 and 251 million in June 2008. Broadband is available to the majority of inhabitants, even within the largest OECD countries. A number of countries have reached 100% coverage with at least one wired broadband technology and up to 60% coverage with two (OECD, 2008). Wireless Internet connections at broadband speeds are also increasingly available. They are particularly important in underserved areas. These numbers clearly indicate the potential of broadband communications, not only for fixed, but also for mobile broadband services.

In fixed wireline accesses, DSL remains the dominant access technology preference in terms of number of connections. It has overtaken cable modems worldwide. DSL technology is available in 58% in OECD countries and 77.8% in the EU level compared to 29% (15.7% in the EU level) of lines consisting of cable modem technologies. Currently, only a minority of broadband connections are based on other technologies, such as fiber and wireless solutions. Table 1 illustrates the trends in fixed broadband access lines by technology in EU. As a result of DSL's technical limitations, several countries are considering the transition to very high-speed broadband. In the medium term, growing demand for multimedia content and the rise of simultaneous consumption in households appears to be an inescapable technological evolution. As FTTH appears to be the technology of choice, the challenge is bringing fiber as close as possible to the subscriber. Consistent with this major market, some players have already announced fiber deployments. For example, FTTx/Ethernet LAN has seen some growth in certain markets, such as Korea, Japan, Italy, and Sweden. The majority of active FTTH subscribers in Europe are currently concentrated in Sweden, Denmark, Norway, and The Netherlands. In other countries, such as Italy, France, Austria, and Germany, ambitious fiber deployment plans are being announced at the local level as well.

For fixed wireless accesses (FWA), wireless broadband is the "great equalizer" of broadband technologies. Further, it enables even those without technologies, such as twisted copper, coaxial cable, fiber, or satellite, to enter into competition for the broadband. Consequently, it expands the definition of who can be a carrier (Leary, 2004). In addition, new broadband wireless access (BWA) technologies, such as WiMAX and FLASH-OFDM, are next to be deployed. However, FWA penetration in Western Europe is increasing very slowly from 0.1% in 2002 till 0.6% in 2009 (Stordahl, 2010).

In mobile broadband penetration, Internet access via mobile phone or laptop computer connected to a 3G network (at broadband speeds) would theoretically have the potential to reach a much larger number of subscribers than wired broadband, even in the most advanced broadband countries (OECD, 2008). Across the OECD countries, an increasing number of subscribers are accessing the Internet with mobile broadband technologies. However, in contrast to 2G services, 3G growth has been stimulated by terminal manufacturers and application providers in the 3G market (OECD, 2009). The GPRS and EDGE offer limited capacity and are not classified as mobile broadband technologies. By other side, LTE technology is in an introduction phase. Hence statistics of the HSPA evolution so far reflects reasonable well the mobile broadband situation in Western Europe (Stordahl, 2010). Until the end of 2008 Austria has been in front. In 2009, Finland and Sweden are on the top followed by Portugal and Austria.

Table 1. Market share at EU level, 2006 - 2011 (as a % of total fixed broadband) (Source: EU)

Technology	Jan. 2006	Jul. 2006	Jan. 2007	Jul. 2007	Jan. 2008	Jul. 2008	Jan. 2009	Jul 2009	Jan 2010	Jul. 2010	Jan. 2011
DSL	80.9%	80.8%	80.8%	80.4%	80.3%	79.9%	79.5%	78.8%	78.7%	77.8%	77.2%
Cable	16.3%	16.0%	15.5%	15.5%	15.1%	15.2%	15.2%	15.3%	15.4%	15.8%	16.0%
Other (Fiber)	2.8%	3.2%	3.7%	4.1%	4.6%	4.9%	5.3%	5.9%	5.9%	6.4%	6.8%

Currently, service providers are determined to differentiate themselves from their competitors by searching for ways to brand and bundle new services, achieve operational cost reductions, and strategically position themselves in relation to their competition. Therefore, in order to maximize their revenues, network service providers must deliver NGN services to the market quickly while providing an excellent user experience. A new type of service is being incorporated into the traditional ones in the domains of voice, data, and video due to the capabilities offered by the new technologies and user demand in the information society (ITU-T, 2008).

The demand for broadband services has increased rapidly in the recent years. (Prasad & Velez, 2010) argues that the classification of broadband services and applications can be segmented into three main areas: Content providers (e.g., Video on demand, purchase/leasing of movies and music, online games, books, etc.); Information retrieval and storage (e.g., browsing, surfing, etc.); Peer to peer and person to person (video conference, exchange of personnel content, etc.). Based on the bandwidth requirements, downstream services can be divided into normal-speed services, including Web browsing, e-mail, and music downloads (up to approximately 3 to 5 Mbps), and high-speed services, including IPTV and video conferencing (over 10 Mbps) (Kirsch & Hirschhausen, 2008).

NEXT GENERATION NETWORKS (NGN)

In the traditional network architectures, different services (e.g., voice, data, and video) are integrated with the particular technology that transports and switches them (Sigurdsson, 2007). However, an NGN is a network in which all kinds of information is transported uniformly using packet-based transport and switching media. An NGN is a packet-based network that is able to provide telecommunication services, including data, voice, or video, using any physical network infrastructure, such as wireline (copper, coax, or fiber) or wireless facilities, to users and make use of multiple broadband transport technologies. Its service-related functions are independent of the underlying transport-related technologies (Gerami, 2010; Kirsch & Hirschhausen, 2008). Therefore, NGN refers to the networks using technologies (normally IP) that achieve convergence in order to carry voice, video, and data over the same infrastructure, rather than separate networks. It also has converged networks and services, with multiple networks with multiple services.

Besides the shift from circuit-switched to packet routed networking, the most important consequence of the migration to NGNs is the increasing modularity of the network and the separation and resulting independence of applications and services from the network through the introduction of an overarching middleware (ITU, 2006).

The term is usually used to describe the shift to higher network speeds using broadband, the migration from PSTN to an IP network, and a greater integration of services on a single network. NGN is expected to completely redesign the actual structure of communication systems and access to the Internet. The present structure of vertically independent but interconnected networks can be transformed into a horizontal structure of IP-based networks (see Figure 1). The convergence represents the shift from the refereed traditional vertical architecture (i.e., a situation in which different services were provided through separate networks, such as mobile, fixed, CATV, or IP, to a situation in which communication services will be accessed and used seamlessly across different networks and provided over multiple platforms in an interactive way.

However, convergence is taking place at different levels (Sarrocco & Ypsilanti, 2008), including the network, service, industry/market, legislative, institutional and regulatory, device, and converged

Figure 1. NGN structure

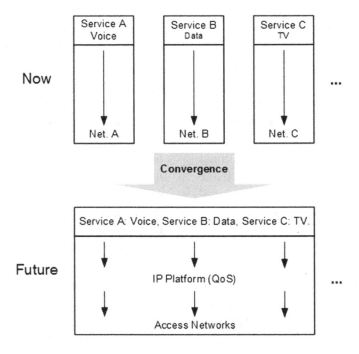

user experience levels. The different communication networks and services are now converging onto one network as a result of the digitalization of content, emergence of IP, and adoption of high-speed broadband. Traditional services, such as voice and video, are increasingly delivered over IP networks. Further, the development of new platforms is facilitating the provision of converged services. These converged services are appearing in markets as "triple" or "quadruple" play offers that provide data, television, fixed, and mobile voice services.

Together, next-generation core (NGC), next-generation access (NGA), and next-generation service platform (NGSP) create the IP NGN framework of the future. The core NGN is essentially the transport or backbone network. It uses digital technology to connect telephone calls and other network traffic more efficiently than traditional networks (Gerami, 2010). Access NGNs, also known as NGA networks or NGANs, involve an upgrade of the local loop to deliver broadband services, either through DSL and HCF technology or by deploying fiber into the loop for part. Building a core NGN does not directly influence these access technologies.

The global interest in NGNs has been driven by a confluence of technological and market factors like (Elixmann et al., 2007): (1) the migration of the network to IP; (2) the separation of the service from the network; (3) price reduction for computing and switching equipment; (4) general deployment and adoption of broadband Internet access; (5) technological improvements to enable higher speed and reliability (fiber deploys closer and closer to the consumer); and (6) convergence of fixed and mobile services. NGN also involves policy challenges for convergence and new networks. NGN network deployment requires significant investments. Therefore, policy strategies need to balance competition and investment.

Whether the population is primarily concentrated in villages or scattered areas affects the choice of technology with regard to both the access and the backhaul networks. The choice of technology with which to serve a particular customer or group of customers depends on a number of parameters. The key issue involves the aggregate bandwidth to be delivered to and from the customer site. If the network operator already possesses access infrastructure that enters the customer premises, it should provide services over existing infrastructure, if possible (France, Spirit, & Whitt, 1998).

NGNs provide to customer access to a large range of services, leading to the increase of the bandwidth demand - For example, if customers encounter their demand on a single network, a triple play product, the bandwidth demand for that network will increase. Moreover, the migration to NGN may require upgrades to the infrastructure to provide sufficient service quality (Kirsch & Hirschhausen, 2008). The entry of new competitors can be based on the resale of services from the incumbent, on building up their own infrastructures, on renting unbundled infrastructure from incumbents, or, on the combination of the above elements. The availability of these options to competitors and price definition are generally determined by regulatory policies. So, the introduction of NGNs by telecommunication network operators obligates the national regulators adapt their access regulation regimes to the new technological conditions. Regulation and/or promotion of competition by regulatory measures need to be analyzed and compared.

One of the main goals of regulated access is to prevent the incumbent from abusing a dominant market position (J. P. R. Pereira, 2013b). It is necessary to make sure that alternative operators can compete effectively. It is fundamental that incumbent operators give access to the civil works infrastructure, including its ducts, and to give wholesale broadband access (bitstream) to the local loop (be it based on copper, new fiber, etc.). However, at the same time, alternative operators should be able to compete on the basis of the wholesale broadband input while they progres-

sively roll out their own NGAN infrastructure. In some areas, especially with higher density, alternative operators have rolled out their own infrastructure and broadband competition has developed. This would result in more innovation and better prices to consumers (J. P. Pereira & Ferreira, 2011).

Many European incumbents and some alternative operators are starting to plan and in some cases deploy large-scale fiber investments, which has resulted in important changes for fixed-line markets (Amendola & Pupillo, 2007). The risk of alternative operators will take longer to deploy their own infrastructure and will give to incumbents the possibility to create new monopolies at the access level. The technologies used and the pace of development vary from country to country according to existing networks and local factors. Based on the different underlying cost conditions of entry and presence of alternative platforms, it may be more appropriate to geographically differentiate the access regulatory regime.

GAME THEORY

The main objective of a game-theory model is providing a mathematical description of a social situation in which two or more players interact, and every player can choose from different strategies. (J. P. Pereira & Ferreira, 2012; Yongkang, Xiuming, & Yong, 2005) define game theory as a collection of mathematical models formulated to study situations of conflict and cooperation, and concerned with finding the best actions for individual decision makers. (Machado & Tekinay, 2008) argue that game theory is a theory of decision making under conditions of uncertainty and interdependence. The players compete for some good or reward, and often in business cases, the customer will be the aim of the competition (J. P. R. Pereira, 2013a; Verbrugge, Casier, Ooteghem, & Lannoo, 2009).

The object of study in game theory is the game, where there are at least two players, and each player can choose amongst different actions (often referred to as strategies). The strategies chosen by each player determine the outcome of the game - the collection of numerical payoffs (one to each player). So, the game has three main key parts (Easley & Kleinberg, 2010): a) a set of participants; b) each player has a set of options for how to behave; we will refer to these as the player's possible strategies; and c) for each choice of strategies, each player receives a payoff that can depend on the strategies selected by everyone (in our model, the payoff to each player is the profit each provider gets).

After the calculation of the several payoffs, game theoretic concepts can be used for retrieving the most likely (set of) interactions between the players (Verbrugge et al., 2009). There are several different equilibrium-definitions of which probably the Nash equilibrium is the most commonly known - A broad class of games is characterized by the Nash equilibrium solution. In 1950, John Nash demonstrated that finite games always have a Nash equilibrium, also called a strategic equilibrium (Yongkang et al., 2005). A Nash equilibrium is a list of strategies, one for each player, which has the property that no player can unilaterally change his strategy and get a better payoff - each player's strategy is an optimal response to the other players' strategies. Even when there are no dominant strategies, it should be expected that players use strategies that are the best responses to each other. This is the central concept of noncooperative game theory and has been a focal point of analysis since then. For example, if player 1 chooses strategy S1 and player 2 chooses S2, the pair of strategies (S1 and S2) is a Nash equilibrium if S1 is the best response to S2, and S2 is the best response to S1. So, if the players choose strategies that are best responses to each other, then no player has an incentive to turn to an alternative strategy, and the system is in a kind of equilibrium, with no force pushing it toward a different outcome (Easley & Kleinberg, 2010).

One of the main goals of regulated access is to prevent the incumbent from abusing a dominant market position. It is necessary to make sure that alternative operators can compete effectively. It is fundamental that incumbent operators give access to the civil works infrastructure, including its ducts, and to give wholesale broadband access (bitstream) to the local loop (be it based on copper, new fiber, etc.). However, at the same time, alternative operators should be able to compete on the basis of the wholesale broadband input while they progressively roll out their own NGAN infrastructure. In some areas, especially with higher density, alternative operators have rolled out their own infrastructure and broadband competition has developed. This would result in more innovation and better prices to consumers (J. P. Pereira & Ferreira, 2011, 2012; J. P. R. Pereira, 2013a, 2013b)

Many European incumbents and some alternative operators are starting to plan and in some cases deploy large-scale fiber investments, which has resulted in important changes for European fixed-line markets. Many Europeans incumbents and some alternative operators are starting to plan and in some cases deploy large scale fiber investments, which results in important changes for European fixed line markets (Amendola & Pupillo, 2007). The risk of alternative operators will take longer to deploy their own infrastructure and will give to incumbents the possibility to create new monopolies at the access level. The technologies used and the pace of development vary from country to country according to existing networks and local factors. Based on the different underlying cost conditions of entry and presence of alternative platforms, it may be more appropriate to geographically differentiate the access regulatory regime.

MODEL OVERVIEW

This section focuses the development of a tool that simulates the impact of retail and wholesale price variation on provider's profit, welfare, consumer surplus, costs, market served, network size, etc.

The proposed model is divided into nine main parts (see Figure 2.): input parameters, retail prices modeling, wholesale prices modeling, total costs (build and lease infrastructures), revenues (retail and wholesale market), profit, consumer surplus, total welfare and Nash equilibrium analysis. Each of these parts are detailed described in the following sections.

In the proposed model, "Retail Prices" represents the set of retail prices charged by providers for each service to consumers in a given region/ area. We assume that retail providers cannot price

discriminate in the retail market. "Wholesale Prices" represents the prices that one provider charges to other provider to allow the later to use the infrastructure to reach consumers. We assume that wholesale price can be different in each area. Also, we assume that when a provider buys infrastructure access in the wholesale market, it cannot resell to another provider. The shared infrastructure consists of: conduit and collocation facilities; cable leasing (dark fiber requires active equipment to illuminate the fiber – for example repeaters); and bit stream.

For example, one or several wholesaler providers can sell Layer 0 access (conduit and collocation facilities) and/or Layer 1 access (cable leasing) or Layer 2 access (bitstream – network layer unbundling – UNE loop) only to retail providers and not directly to consumers. UNE loop is defined as the

Figure 2. Game-theoretic model structure

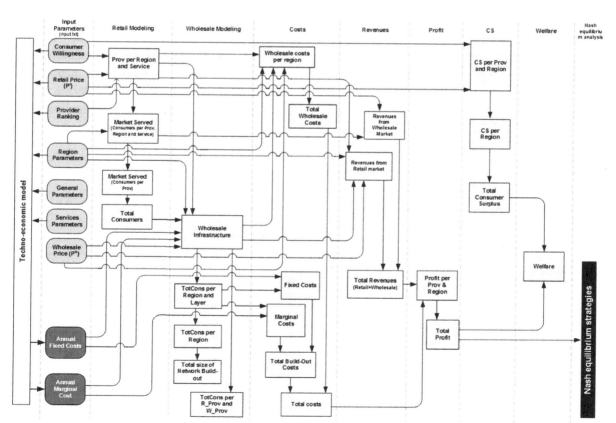

local loop network element that is a transmission facility between the central office and the point of demarcation at an end-user's premises.

The tool support scenarios with x providers (x>0), y regions (y>0), z services (z>0), and w infrastructure layers (see Table 2). For this study we propose a scenario with two regions, two providers, two services, and one infrastructure layers - Layer 0 access (conduit and collocation facilities) (see Figure 3.).

The scenario assumes that each provider has different wholesale prices in the two regions and the same retail price. Based on this scenario, is necessary identify the set of possible strategies, and for each strategy the tool calculates the results. To calculate the number of strategies required, we use the following formula:

$$TS = TVS^{\left(TProv*\left(TServ+\left(TReg*TLay\right)\right)\right)} \qquad (1)$$

Table 2. Wholesale layers

Wholesale Infrastructure	
0	Conduit
1	Cable
2	Bit-Stream (Conduit + Cable +Equipment)

where:

TS: Total strategies
TVS: Total values to simulate
TProv: Total providers
TServ: Total services
TReg: Total regions
TLay: Total layers

For the scenario presented above, and assuming that we want to simulate eight different prices (for retail and wholesale prices), we get 16.777.216 possible strategies or combinations (8 (2*(2+(2*1)))).

Some of the parameters to be defined include the number of competitors (both in the service market and access network provisioning), existent infrastructures, and the percentage shares of the competitors in these markets. The broadband access market is becoming increasingly more competitive, where time to market with new products and services is of vital importance. Operators and other market players need to frequently develop and refine new business models to remain competitive. For each market players (e.g., incumbents, competitors, or new entrants) we define the respectively market share. The proposed model is described more detailed in the next sections

Figure 3. Structure of the proposed scenario

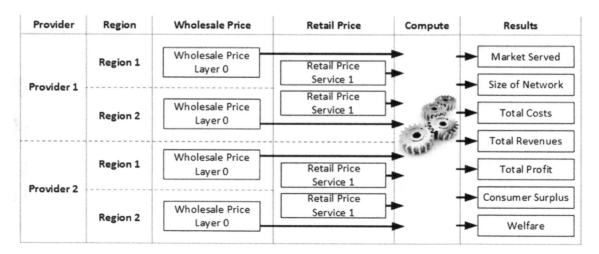

Input Parameter Assumptions

As we can see in Figure 2., our tool has several input parameters, computes several results and finds the strategies that are Nash equilibrium. The results are represented in tables and graphics. In this section, we describe the inputs: fixed and marginal costs and retail/wholesale variation values.

Fixed and Marginal Costs

In our model, we assume that providers incur in fixed costs to build network infrastructure to provide access to a region and in marginal costs to connect each consumer separately. The fixed and marginal costs are calculated in the techno-economic tool.

The fixed costs are detailed by provider, region and infrastructure layer. So, we assume that the fixed costs of each provider can be different in different regions - for example, if a provider has part of the infrastructure deployed in a region, and in the other is required all the infrastructure, the costs are different.

For marginal costs, we assume that each provider has different costs for deployment in each infrastructure layer. In each region, the marginal cost could be different for each provider depending of the total number of subscribers – scale economies. This means that the marginal cost can decrease when a specific provider buys higher quantities of equipment, cable, etc.

Pricing Strategy

Both suppliers and consumers aim at maximizing the benefit or surplus they receive (ITU-T, 2008). The suppliers aim at maximizing the profit, which is the difference between revenue and cost. The consumers aim at maximizing the consumer surplus, which is the difference between consumer value (also known as utility or maximum willingness to pay) and price. As discussed previously, some of the factors that are important in the de-

sign of pricing scheme include technology risks, availability of resources, competition, supplier and consumer behavior, price discrimination and regulation.

The definition of retail prices and trend was explained previously. For the game-theoretic tool, we need to define the variation in retail prices which we want to simulate. So, for each service, we define the price values we wish to simulate - the tool gives the possibility to simulate n values.

For wholesale prices, we define the variation in wholesale price layers that we want to simulate. Similarly, for retail price, for each layer we define the price values we wish to simulate—the tool gives the possibility to simulate n values. For infrastructure, the definition of which layer or combination of layers we would like to simulate is also required (Table 2). For example, if a provider wants to use (lease) the conduit from another provider, we choose option 0.

Simulation Model (Modeling Competition)

The simulation model can be sub-divided into seven main parts: retail and wholesale modeling, calculate total costs (build and lease infrastructure), calculate revenues (retail and wholesale market), calculate profit, calculate consumer surplus, and calculate welfare. The next sections describe all these parts.

Retail Modeling

In our model, we assume that consumers choose the service from the provider with the lowest price. However, consumers only buy a service if the price is less than their willingness to pay. This means that if there are two or more providers, consumers choose the service from the provider with the lowest price. Moreover, if several providers have the same price, we use the provider ranking. We also assume that consumers have a different willingness to pay for each service (e.g., voice, video and data).

First, the tool identify the retail provider for each service in the regions in study using information from providers, retail prices, consumer willingness to pay, and provider rank. Next, as we know which provider will provide each service, we can compute the total subscribers per region, service, and provider (market segment). The structure used is presented in Figure 4.

Wholesale Modeling

In wholesale modeling (Figure 5), we determine the infrastructure chosen by each provider to reach consumers. To model the wholesale market, we assume that if a provider does not have infrastructure, it uses the infrastructure (or part of the infrastructure, such as a conduit cable) of another provider if the price charged to access it is

lower than the cost to build an infrastructure. To achieve that goal, the algorithm uses information about wholesale prices, fixed costs, and marginal costs to identify the best solution (lease or build infrastructure) for each region and service. The algorithm also utilizes the information produced in retail modeling to determine which providers offer services to consumers in all the regions. The fixed and marginal costs are calculated in the techno-economic tool.

Calculate Total Costs (Build and Lease Infrastructures)

The calculation of the total costs incurred by each provider is divided in two main parts: wholesale costs and build-out costs (Figure 6). As sees in next figure, in order to compute the total wholesale costs, we use the wholesale infrastructure design computed previously and the wholesale

Figure 4. Retail market modeling

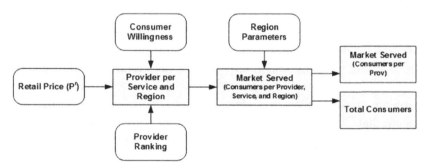

Figure 5. Wholesale market modeling

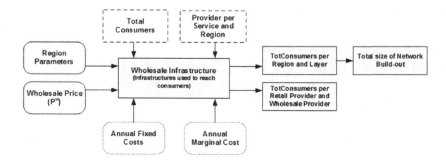

Figure 6. Total costs calculation

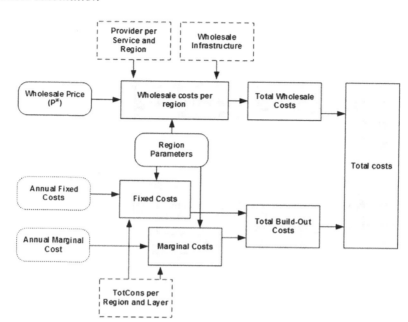

prices charged by the infrastructure owners (i.e., payments that a specific provider gives to the infrastructure owner to buy wholesale access in order to reach consumers). We assume that the network owner charges the same wholesale price to all providers.

To calculate the build-out costs, the algorithm uses the fixed and marginal costs parameters with region parameters to compute the total costs required to deploy an entire or part of an infrastructure. The total number of consumers per region and per provider is also used to add the effect of economies of scale. When a provider buys a large quantity of equipment, the probability of attaining better prices is higher.

Calculate Revenues (Retail and Wholesale Market)

To compute the total revenues per provider, we first calculate the revenues from the retail market. These are primarily based on the retail prices charged by providers and the total number of consumers

per provider and services computed in the retail modeling. Revenues from the retail market are equal to the product of the retail price of each service and the total customers of the service.

Next, we calculate the revenues from the wholesale market. The wholesale infrastructure provides information about the number of access leased. The revenues of a provider are the sum of all payments received from other providers that use its infrastructure to reach consumers. Finally, the total revenues of a given provider are the sum of the revenues from the retail and the wholesale market (Figure 7).

Calculate Profit, Consumer Surplus and Total Welfare

After computing the total costs and revenues in the previous algorithms, the formula we use to calculate total profit is the difference between total revenues and total profit (Figure 8). The total profit is also used in the identification of the Nash equilibrium strategies.

Figure 7. Revenues calculation

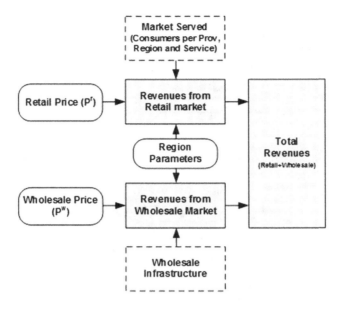

Figure 8. Profit calculation

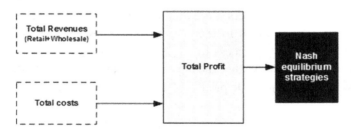

Consumer surplus (CS) is the difference between the total amount that consumers are willing and able to pay for each service and the total amount that they actually pay (i.e., the retail price) (Figure 9). So, the CS of a specific market is the sum of the individual consumer surpluses of all those customers in the market who actually

bought the service at the going retail price "Pr" (ACMA, 2009). To compute consumer surplus, we need information about consumer willingness to pay and retail prices for each service (Figure 9).

Total welfare is computed on base of the formula: welfare = consumer surplus + total profit. Like the previously calculations, the consumer

Figure 9. Consumer surplus calculation

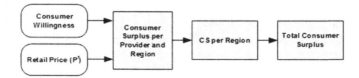

surplus and the profit are computed in the algorithms presented above. The block diagram is presented in Figure 10.

Analysis Model (Nash Equilibrium Analysis)

As discussed above, Nash equilibrium is a fundamental concept in the theory of games. It is also the most widely used method of predicting the outcome of a strategic interaction in the social sciences. A game consists of a set of players, a set of actions available to each player, and a payoff (in our model, profit) function for each player. A pure strategy Nash equilibrium is an action profile with the property that no single player can obtain a higher payoff by deviating unilaterally from this profile. Next, we explain the algorithm developed in our work for finding Nash equilibriums (i.e., finding each provider's best response to the other provider's strategy). Our algorithms support two or more players.

Consider a competitive situation with two players with a set of strategies available to the two players and the correspondent payoff (profit). The set of strategies for provider 1 are presented in column 1, and the strategies of provider 2 are listed in column 2 (see next figure). For example, when provider 1 uses strategy B and provider 2 uses strategy A, provider 1 has the profit of 6000 and provider B of 1000. The steps are:

Figure 10. Welfare calculation

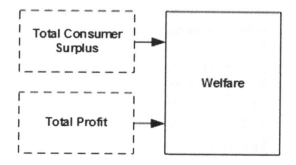

1. Select a specific provider and a specific strategy. For example, select strategy A for provider 1 (column 1). Next, find the provider2 best response (column 4) for strategy A from provider 1. This means that the best response for provider 2 to strategy A from provider 1 is 6000 (see Figure 11 – Step 1).
2. For provider 2, select strategy A (i.e., the same strategy selected in step 1) and find the provider 1 best response (column 3) for the strategy A from provider 2 (Figure 11 – Step 2).
3. Repeat steps 1 and 2 for strategy B.
4. When we finish, we will get the final table.

All of the lines with a circle in column 3 and 4 are a Nash equilibrium. That is, when both providers are playing their best response at the same time, that is a Nash equilibrium (provider 1 plays strategy B and provider 2 plays strategy B). Based on the algorithm described, our tool finds the strategies that are Nash equilibriums.

STRATEGIES AND MAIN ASSUMPTIONS

To analyze the impact of retail and wholesale services price variations, we propose two games (Figure 12.): (1) analysis the impact of retail price variation on NPV (wholesale prices are defined by regulator); and (2) analysis the impact of retail and wholesale price variations on profit, consumer surplus, welfare, and retail/wholesale market (different wholesale prices in each region). For the game-theoretic evaluation, the model calculates the NPV and operator's profit for both operators' pricing strategies. Operators' NPVs are used as payoffs for the players in the first and second game, and operators' profits for the third game.

From the several assumptions, we posit: (a) the price that players charge for their services (retail and wholesale) will be varied; (b) the retail price

Figure 11. Find Nash equilibrium

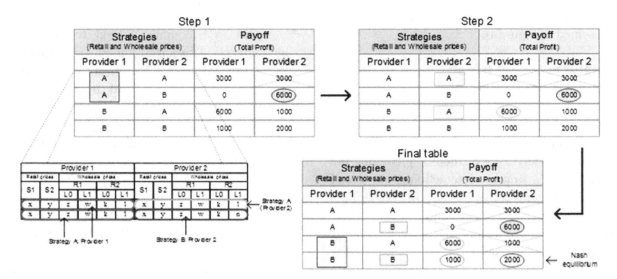

Figure 12. Games proposed

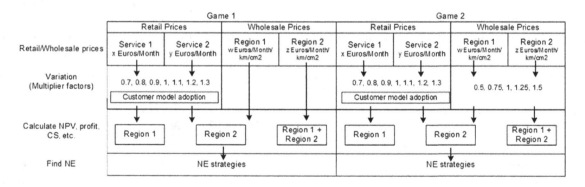

setting will influence the market share of both players (resulting in a higher or lower market share); and (c) consumers only buy a retail service if the price is less than their willingness to pay.

As stated above, we assume that when one player increases/decreases the retail price, the market share of all players will be affected. For example, if one player offers cheaper services, it will be able to capture a higher market share. If a price decreases to nearly zero, everyone will use the service, and the market share of this operator will be close to 100% (total market). On the other hand, if an operator charges a higher price for a service, no one will subscribe to the service from this player, and its market share will decrease to 0%.

The impact of changing prices in the market share (i.e., the estimate of the impact of the price on the service adoption) is modeled using the Boltzmann equation:

$$Y = \frac{V_i - V_f}{\left(1 + e^{(x - x0)/dx}\right)} + V_f \qquad (2)$$

in which the variables are defined as follows:

X_0: Is the mean base (or center)
dx: Is the width
V_i: Is the initial value of y
V_f: Is the final value of y

Figure 13 the s-curves of three functions. The slope (parameter b) of the market penetration should give an advantage or disadvantage to one of the players (Katsianis, Gyürke, Konkoly, Varoutas, & Sphicopoulos, 2007).

Main Assumptions

We assume that the willingness to pay for each retail service is different in both regions. In the urban area (region 1) the maximum amount subscribers would be willing to pay for service 1 is 26 euros and 65 euros for service 2. In the rural area we assume a willingness value of 22 euros for service 1 and 55 euros for service 2 (see Table 3).

For the wholesale infrastructure we assume a duct availability of player 1 100% in the urban area and 90% in the rural area. We also assume that operator 2 (new entrant) leases 100% of the ducts available in the urban area and 100% of the ducts available (operator 1 has only 90% and the remaining 10% are deployed by operator 2) in the rural area from operator 1 (incumbent operator). In the other hand, player 1 leases the 10% remain-

Table 3. Willingness assumptions

Parameters	Region 1 (Urban Area)		Region 2 (Rural Area)	
	Service 1	Service 2	Service 1	Service 2
Monthly Subscription Fee (Year1)	20€	50€	20€	50€
Willingness Value	26 €	65€	22€	55€
Willingness Multiplier	1.3	1.3	1.1	1.1

ing (in region 2) from operator 2. The wholesale prices assumptions are: 9.1€ (month / km / cm2) for urban area and 7.5€ (month / km / cm2) for the rural area. The wholesale infrastructure assumptions and described in Table 4.

The next sections present the three games results and analyses. In the first game, retail prices vary between tariff multiplier 0.7 and 1.3 (in increments of 0.1). For the second game, retail prices vary between 0.8 and 1.2, and wholesale prices between 0.5 and 1.5.

RESULTS

Based on the numerous input parameters described, our tool computes several results, including profit,

Figure 13. Models to estimate the impact of the price on the service adoption (a=0.4, b=3, dx=0.3)

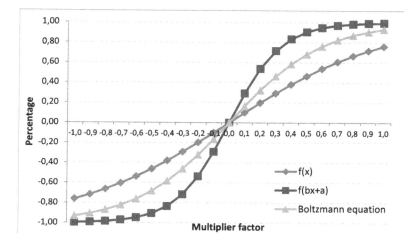

Table 4. Wholesale infrastructure assumptions

Parameters	Region 1 (Urban)		Region 2 (Rural)	
	Feeder Segment	Distribution Segment	Feeder Segment	Distribution Segment
Provider 1				
Duct Availability (# of ducts available for leasing)	100%	100%	90%	90%
Wholesale price charged to access owned ducts (€/Km)	€110	€110	€90	€90
Proportion of ducts leased	0%	0%	10%	10%
From operator	0	0	2	2
Proider 2				
Duct Availability (# of ducts available for leasing)	0%	0%	10%	10%
Wholesale price charged to access owned ducts (€/Km)	€110	€110	€90	€90
Proportion of ducts leased	75%	75%	100%	100%
From operator	1	1	1	1

consumer surplus, welfare, market served, network size, costs, and revenues, and finds the strategies that are Nash equilibriums. The results are saved in text files (see Figure 14.).

Figure 14 shows the structure of the results that correspond to a scenario of two providers, two retail services, two infrastructure layers, and two regions. Each line is a strategy. We consider a strategy to be a set of retail and wholesale prices. For each combination of prices, the tool calculates profit, CS, welfare, market served, network size, and total costs.

In addition to the results presented in the tables, the tool creates several types of graphs. For that, we incorporated a Gnuplot program in our C code. Gnuplot is a portable command-line-driven graphing utility for Linux, OS/2, MS Windows, OSX, VMS, and many other platforms. The source code is copyrighted but freely distributed.

Figure 14. Structure of the results produced (output from tool)

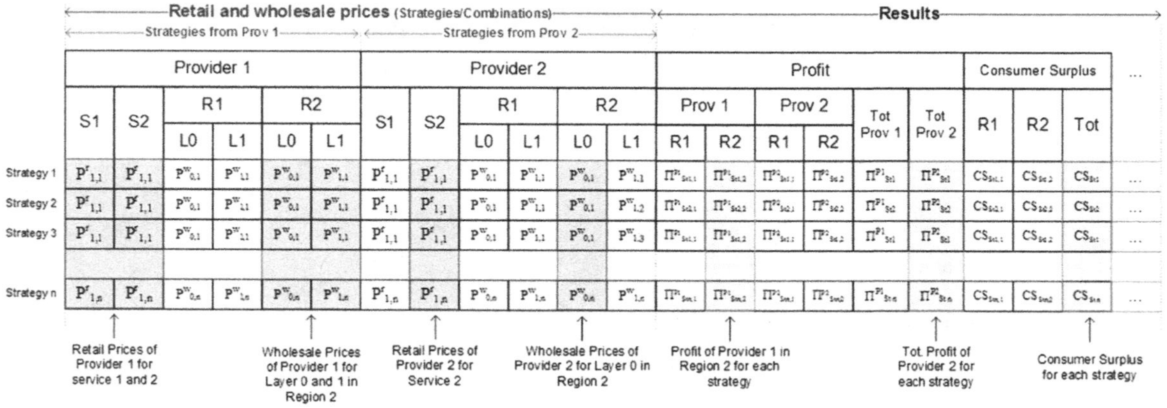

The graph shows the impact on profit of both providers and variation in wholesale and retail prices. This representation gives users a tool to gain a better perspective of the results.

Game 1: Impact of Retail Prices Variation on NPV

In this game we assume that wholesale prices are fixed and that operators choose retail prices to maximize their profit (see Figure 12). The impact of varying retail prices on market shares is estimated using the Boltzmann equation (described above). The main goal of this analysis is to determine the optimal retail price strategy for both players. The retail prices vary between −30% and 30%, with increasing steps of 10% (Table 5).

The combination of the two retail prices and seven multiplier factors leads to 49 possible strategies for each player (49x49 matrix) in each region (2,401 total strategies). Table 6 presents the structure of the combinations and calculated NPV.

The results (payoff matrix) of this game are presented in Table 7. for region 1 (urban area). Table 6. shows the sum of the payoffs of each player

in both regions. The following tables present the NPV for both players for each possible combination of strategies (one strategy for each player); Nash equilibrium strategies are also identified.

The first two rows represents the prices multiplier factor of player 2 (for services 1 and 2) and the first two columns show the variation (multiplier factors) of player 1. Each cell contains two values: The left value corresponds to the NPV of player 1, and the value on right side corresponds to the NPV of player 2. For example, the first value calculated (16,512,089 €) corresponds to the NPV of player 1 when the strategy of player 1 is to decrease the price of service 1 and service 2 by about 30% (multiplier factor 0.7), and the strategy of player 2 is also to decrease the price of service 1 and service 2 by about 30%.

We have analyzed the different strategies of the two players to find the game's Nash equilibria. (Our model includes a function for searching NE in the games). The NE strategies are formatted with a black background. From the analysis of these results, we find two NE strategies that are detailed in Table 8.

Table 5. Retail prices variation values

Tariff Multiplier Factor	0.7 (-30%)	0.8 (-20%)	0.9 (-10%)	1 (0%)	1.1 (10%)	1.2 (20%)	1.3 (30%)
Service 1 price	14	16	18	20	22	24	26
Serice 2 price	35	40	45	50	55	60	65

Table 6. Structure of combinations and results for game 1

Strategies	Player 1 Retail Price R1& R2		Player 2 Retail Price R1 &R 2		NPV					
					Player 1		Player 2		Total Player1	Total Player2
	S1	S2	S1	S2	R1	R2	R1	R2	R1+2	R1+R2
1	0.7	0.7	0.7	0.7	...	...	...	...	..	...
2	0.7	0.7	0.7	0.8	...	...	...	...	...	...
n	...	...	...	...	...	...	...	...	...	...

Table 7. Impact of retail prices variation (0.7 to 1.3) on NPV (€)—region 1 (urban area)

Price S1		0,70		...			...	1,30							
	Price S2	0,70		...	1,30		...	0,70		...	1,10		...	1,30	
0,70	0,7	16.512.089	-12.544.009		28.802.318	-24.111.799		18.536.768	-14.477.627		26.229.241	-19.253.255		30.826.996	-26.045.417
	0,8	15.251.728	-8.366.277		33.887.508	-24.111.799		17.276.406	-10.299.894		28.901.992	-16.816.923		35.912.186	-26.045.417
	0,9	13.130.606	-4.410.360		38.972.698	-24.111.799		15.155.285	-6.343.978		30.820.067	-13.978.016		40.997.376	-26.045.417
	1	10.487.574	-853.341		44.057.888	-24.111.799		12.512.253	-2.786.958		31.955.838	-10.820.742		46.082.566	-26.045.417
	1,1	7.648.610	2.199.270		49.143.078	-24.111.799		9.673.288	265.652		32.367.961	-7.486.434		51.167.756	-26.045.417
	1,2	-5.677.393	11.011.259		-5.564.353	-24.006.800		-3.652.715	9.077.642		-3.652.715	28.947.191		-3.539.674	-25.940.418
	1,3	-5.439.184	11.011.259		-5.326.143	-24.006.800		-3.414.505	9.077.642		-3.414.505	28.947.191		-3.301.465	-25.940.418
...	...														
0,90	0,7	15.905.526	-11.114.024		28.195.755	-22.681.814		20.201.491	-14.477.627		27.893.964	-19.253.255		32.491.720	-26.045.417
	0,8	14.645.164	-6.936.292		33.280.944	-22.681.814		18.941.129	-10.299.894		30.566.716	-16.816.923		37.576.910	-26.045.417
	0,9	12.524.043	-2.980.375		38.366.134	-22.681.814		16.820.008	-6.343.978		32.484.790	-13.978.016		42.662.100	-26.045.417
	1	**9.881.011**	**576.645**		43.451.324	-22.681.814		14.176.976	-2.786.958		33.620.561	-10.820.742		47.747.289	-26.045.417
	1,1	7.042.046	3.629.255		48.536.514	-22.681.814		11.338.012	265.652		34.032.684	-7.486.434		52.832.479	-26.045.417
	1,2	-6.283.956	12.441.245		-6.170.916	-22.576.815		-1.987.991	9.077.642		-1.987.991	28.947.191		-1.874.951	-25.940.418
	1,3	-6.045.747	12.441.245		-5.932.707	-22.576.815		-1.749.782	9.077.642		-1.749.782	28.947.191		-1.636.742	-25.940.418
...	...														
1,20	0,7	14.473.931	-9.509.528		26.764.160	-21.077.318		22.698.576	-14.477.627		30.391.049	-19.253.255		34.988.805	-26.045.417
	0,8	13.213.570	-5.331.796		31.849.350	-21.077.318		21.438.214	-10.299.894		33.063.801	-16.816.923		40.073.995	-26.045.417
	0,9	11.092.448	-1.375.879		36.934.540	-21.077.318		19.317.093	-6.343.978		34.981.875	-13.978.016		45.159.184	-26.045.417
	1	8.449.416	2.181.140		42.019.730	-21.077.318		16.674.061	-2.786.958		36.117.646	-10.820.742		50.244.374	-26.045.417
	1,1	5.610.452	5.233.751		47.104.920	-21.077.318		13.835.097	265.652		36.529.769	-7.486.434		55.329.564	-26.045.417
	1,2	-7.715.551	14.045.741		-7.602.510	-20.972.319		509.094	9.077.642		509.094	28.947.191		622.134	-25.940.418
	1,3	-7.477.342	14.045.741		-7.364.301	-20.972.319		**747.303**	9.077.642		**747.303**	**28.947.191**		860.343	-25.940.418
1,30	0,7	12.709.232	-8.402.733		24.999.461	-19.970.523		12.693.783	-14.481.984		20.386.256	-19.257.613		24.984.012	-26.049.774
	0,8	11.448.871	-4.225.001		30.084.651	-19.970.523		11.433.421	-10.304.252		23.059.008	-16.821.281		30.069.202	-26.049.774
	0,9	9.327.750	-269.084		35.169.841	-19.970.523		9.312.300	-6.348.335		24.977.082	-13.982.373		35.154.392	-26.049.774
	1	6.684.717	3.287.935		40.255.031	-19.970.523		6.669.268	-2.791.316		26.112.853	-10.825.099		40.239.582	-26.049.774
	1,1	3.845.753	6.340.546		45.340.221	-19.970.523		3.830.304	261.295		26.524.976	-7.490.792		45.324.771	-26.049.774
	1,2	-9.480.250	15.152.536		-9.367.209	-19.865.524		-9.495.699	9.073.285		-9.495.699	28.942.834		-9.480.250	-26.045.417
	1,3	-9.242.041	15.152.536		-9.129.000	-19.865.524		-9.257.490	9.073.285		-9.257.490	28.942.834		-9.242.041	-26.045.417

Row/column labels: Player 1 (Incumbent operator) strategies (left); Player 2 (New entrant) strategies (top).

Table 8. Pure NE strategies for region 1 (urban area)

Strategies	Player 1 (Incumbent Operator)		Player 2 (New Entrant)		NPV € Player 1	NPV € Player 2
	Retail Service 1	**Retail Service 2**	**Retail Service 1**	**Retail Service 2**		
1	0.9 (18€)	1 (50€)	0.7 (14€)	0.7 (35€)	9.881.001	576.645
2	1.2 (24€)	1.3 (65€)	1.3 (26€)	1.1 (55€)	747.303	28.947.191

Figure 15 shows the impact of service 2 price variation on the NPV of both operators (for the urban area).

In the previous tables and graphs we presented the results for region 1 and region 2 when isolated. However, operators are also interested in the results for both regions. So, Table 9 analyzes the sum of the payoffs of each player in both regions.

From these results presented in Table 9, we find three pure NE strategies (black cells) that are described in Table 10. The next table shows the three NE strategies that maximize the profit of both players. To maximize profit, in the first equilibrium strategy, operator 1 increases retail prices by 10%. Operator 2, in face of the imposed wholesale prices, decreases the price of service 1 and service 2 by 30% and 20%, respectively. A new entrant has to pay the wholesale to the incumbent, but if increase the retail prices their market share will decrease (see model above).

Figure 16 shows the impact of service 1 variation on NPV of both operators. We can verify that the variation of the retail price of service 1 does not have the same impact on NPV that it has on service 2.

From the analysis of Figure 17 we can conclude that the variation of retail prices of service 2 has a greater influence in the NPV than the variation of service 1 price. Service 2 price variation can drop the NPV of operator 1 to negative. On the other hand, operator 2 can turn the NPV positive when the tariff of service 2 increases.

Game 2: Impact of Retail and Wholesale Prices Variation on NPV

In this game we assume that wholesale prices are not pre-imposed and we investigate what is the reaction of operators when they can also choose

different wholesale prices in different regions (see Table 11). In game 2 we assume that has the same variation for both regions (see Figure 12). Retail prices vary between 0.8 (-20%) and 1.2 (20%) (in increments of 0.1). For wholesale price we assume a variation between 0.5 and 1.5 (in increments of 0.25).

In this context, the combination of the three prices and variation multipliers leads to 625(5^4) possible strategies for each player (625x625 matrix) in each region (390625 strategies in both regions).

As the matrix is to bigger, for this game we decide to present the NE strategies (players profit is used as payoff) and the graphs that show the impact of variation in the several results (presented in Table 12). The analysis of the results finds five

Figure 15. NPV variation: Provider 1 and 2/region 1/retail service 2

NPV - Region 1 / Retail Service 2

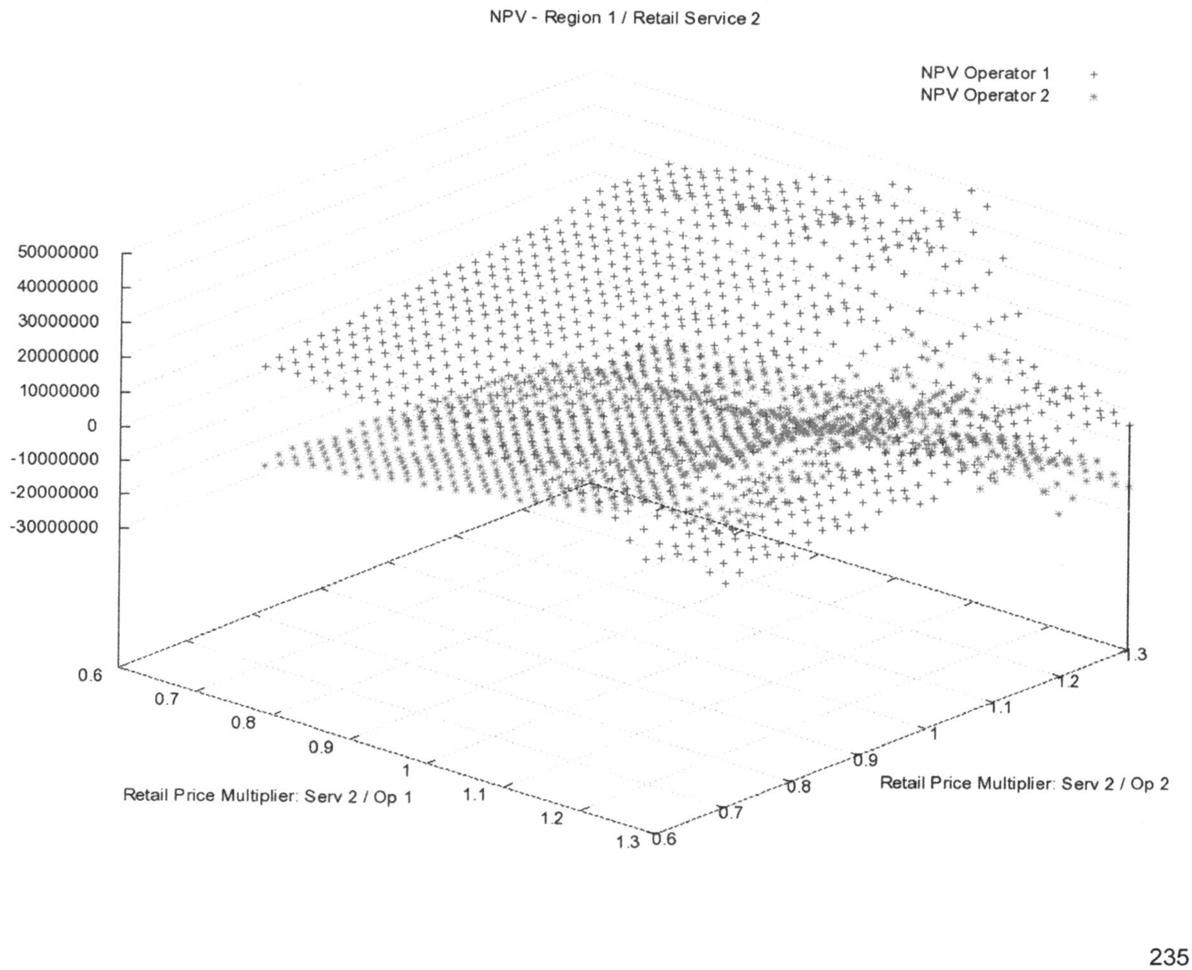

Table 9. Impact of retail prices variation (0.7 to 1.3) on NPV (€)—region 1 and 2

Price S1 (P1)	Price S2 (P1)	P2 S1=0,70 / S2=0,70		P2 S1=0,70 / S2=0,80		... / P2 S1=0,70 / S2=1,30		P2 S1=1,20 / S2=0,70		... / P2 S1=1,20 / S2=1,30		P2 S1=1,30 / S2=0,70		... / P2 S1=1,30 / S2=1,10	
0,70	0,7	15831024	-18582287	18183087	-19363781	28936533	-30770826	17496173	-19795217	30601681	-31983756	18113915	-20768607	26428738	-25938555
	0,8	14472132	-14083788	19556293	-16693988	34299456	-30618352	16137281	-15296719	35964604	-31831283	16755023	-16270109	29303695	-23304216
	0,9	12185918	-9824136	17582209	-11580297	39612688	-30427158	13851067	-11037066	41277837	-31640088	14468808	-12010456	31362952	-20234582
	1	9338223	-5994009	14713466	-6738115	44866176	-30195243	11003372	-7206939	46531325	-31408173	11621113	-8180329	32577289	-16820707
	1,1	6280874	-2707019	11341982	-2384199	50053039	-29925006	7946023	-3919949	51718187	-31137937	8563765	-4893339	33014991	-13215411
	1,2	-7258790	6298197	-6933535	11368737	-4619767	-29519466	-5593641	5085267	-2954619	-30732396	-4975899	4111877	-3280895	23715662
	1,3	-7216198	6452291	-6935595	11588571	-4402383	-29202072	-5551049	5239361	-2737234	-30415002	-4933308	4265971	-3375080	24186698
1,10	0,7	14054700	-15642494	16406763	-16423988	27160208	-27831033	19064485	-17729134	32169993	-29917673	21886956	-20768607	30201779	-25938555
	0,8	12695808	-11143995	17779969	-13754195	32523131	-27678559	17705593	-13230635	37532916	-29765199	20528064	-16270109	33076737	-23304216
	0,9	10409594	-6884343	15805885	-8640503	37836364	-27487364	15419379	-8970983	42846148	-29574004	18241850	-12010456	35135994	-20234582
	1	7561899	-3054215	12937141	-3798322	43089852	-27255449	12571684	-5140855	48099637	-29342089	15394155	-8180329	36350330	-16820707
	1,1	4504550	232775	**9565657**	**555595**	48276714	-26985213	9514335	-1853865	53286499	-29071853	12336806	-4893339	36788033	-13215411
	1,2	-9035114	9237991	-8709859	14308530	-6396091	-26579672	-4025329	7151351	-1386307	-28666312	-1202858	4111877	492146	23715662
	1,3	-8992522	9392085	-8711919	14528364	-6178707	-26262279	-3982737	7305445	-1168922	-28348918	-1160266	4265971	397962	24186698
1,20	0,7	13511514	-15140682	15863576	-15922176	26617022	-27329221	19138606	-17069339	32244114	-29257878	22830217	-20768607	31145040	-25938555
	0,8	12152622	-10642183	17236783	-13252383	31979945	-27176747	17779714	-12570840	37607037	-29105404	21471325	-16270109	34019997	-23304216
	0,9	9866407	-6382531	15262698	-8138692	37293177	-26985553	15493499	-8311188	42920269	-28914210	19185110	-12010456	36079254	-20234582
	1	7018712	-2552404	12393955	-3296511	42546666	-26753638	12645805	-4481060	48173758	-28682294	16337416	-8180329	37293591	-16820707
	1,1	3961364	734586	9022471	1057406	47733528	-26483401	9588456	-1194070	53360620	-28412058	13280067	-4893339	37731293	-13215411
	1,2	-9578300	9739802	-9253046	14810342	-6939278	-26077861	-3951208	7811146	-1312186	-28006517	-259597	4111877	**1435407**	**23715662**
	1,3	-9535709	9893896	-9255106	15030176	-6721894	-25760467	-3908617	7965240	-1094801	-27689124	-217006	4265971	1341222	24186698
1,30	0,7	11507889	-13885393	13859952	-14666887	24613397	-26073932	11507889	-9292724	24613397	-21481263	11492251	-20732168	19807074	-25902116
	0,8	10148997	-9386894	15233158	-11997094	29976320	-25921458	10148997	-4794225	29976320	-21328789	10133359	-16233669	22682032	-23267776
	0,9	7862782	-5127242	13259073	-6883402	35289552	-25730264	7862782	-534573	35289552	-21137595	7847145	-11974017	24741289	-20198142
	1	5015088	-1297114	10390330	-2041221	40543041	-25498349	**5015088**	**3295555**	40543041	-20905679	4999450	-8143889	25955625	-16784268
	1,1	1957739	1989876	7018846	2312695	45729903	-25228112	1957739	6582545	45729903	-20635443	1942101	-4856899	26393328	-13178971
	1,2	-11581925	10995092	-11256671	16065631	-8942903	-24822571	-11581925	15587761	-8942903	-20229902	-11597563	4148317	-9902559	23752102
	1,3	-11539334	11149186	-11258730	16285465	-8725518	-24505178	-11539334	15741855	-8725518	-19912509	-11554971	4302411	-9996743	24223138

Table 10. Pure NE strategies for both regions

Strategy	Player 1 (Incumbent Operator)		Player 2 (New Entrant)		NPV € Player 1	NPV € Player 2
	Retail Service 1	Retail Service 2	Retail Service 1	Retail Service 2		
1	1.1 (22€)	1.1 (55€)	0.7 (14€)	0.8 (40€)	9.565.657	555.595
2	1.2 (24€)	1.2 (60€)	1.3 (26€)	1.1 (55€)	1.435.407	23.715.662
3	1.3 (26€)	1 (50€)	1.2 (24€)	0.7 (35€)	5.015.088	3.295.555

NEs strategies. As player 2 do not operates in the wholesale market of region 1, the variation of this price is not significant.

We conclude that, in the business case defined, when operators can charge different retail and wholesale prices, they choose to increase wholesale prices. To maximize profits, operators increase wholesale prices and decrease retail prices. However, the increase in wholesale prices precludes entry of new operators into the market.

The main results of this game are summarized in the next figures. In the first two graphs we can see the impact of retail prices (top) and wholesale prices (bottom) on players profit. We can verify that both prices can turn profit positive/negative (Figure 18).

Consumer surplus decreases with the increase of prices (top graph). As also expected and modeled above the impact of retail prices variation has higher influence in the market share of competitors (see Figure 19).

CONCLUSION

Sensitivity analysis shows the impact that changes in a certain parameter will have on the model's outcome. As the interaction between all the players is important, we put the competition component in the business case. With game theory, we want to understand the effects of the interaction between the different players defined in our business case.

Figure 16. NPV variation: Operator 1 and 2/retail service 1

Total NPV (Euros) - Operator 1 (Region 1 and 2)

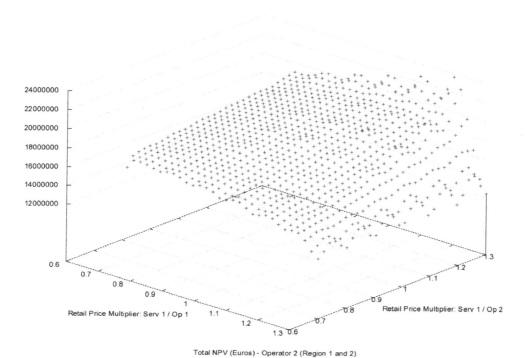

Total NPV (Euros) - Operator 2 (Region 1 and 2)

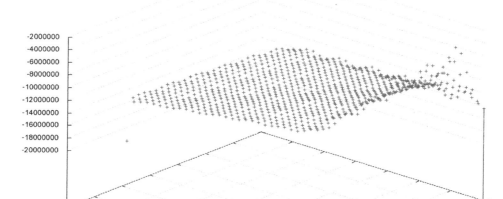

Figure 17. NPV variation: Operator1 and 2/retail service 2

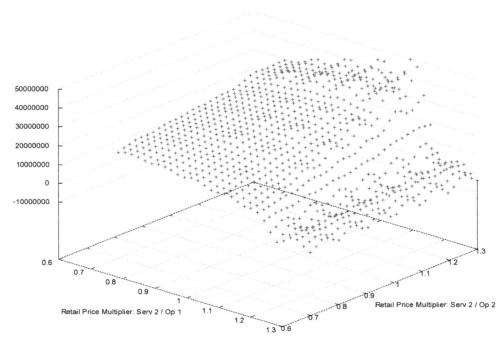

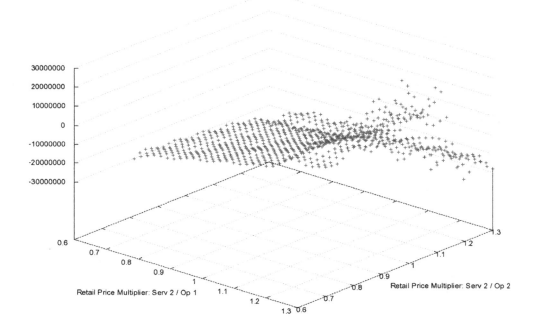

Table 11. Retail and wholesale prices variation values for game 2

Service	Tariff Multiplier Factor				
Retail Price	0.8	0.9	1	1.1	1.2
Wholesale Price	0.5	0.75	1	1.25	1.5

Table 12. Structure of combinations and results for game 2

Strategies	Player 1				Player 2				NPV						...
	Retail Price		Wholesale Price		Retail Price		Wholesale Price		Player 1		Player 2		Total Player1	Total Player2	Other Results: Profit, Consumer Surplus, Welfare, Retail & Wholesale Market, ...
	R1 & R2		R1	R2	R1 & R2		R1	R2					R1+R2	R1+R2	
	S1	S2	Duct Access		S1	S2	Duct Access		R1	R2	R1	R2			
1	0.8	0.8	0.8	0.8	0.8	0.8	0.8	0.8							
2	0.8	0.8	0.8	0.8	0.8	0.8	0.8	0.9							
n	...	...	...	...	...	...	...	...							

Table 13. Game 2 results - summary

R Price S1					Player 2 strategies												...
	R Price S2								0,80								...
		W Price R1								0,80							...
			W Price R2	0,50		0,75		0,50		1,00		1,25		1,50		0,50	...
		0,5	0,5	20981654	1704052	20954077	1728871	20926500	1753691	20898923	1778510	20871345	1803330	20981654	1704052
			0,75	21232678	1425137	21205100	1449956	21177523	1474776	21149946	1499595	21122369	1524415	21232678	1425137
			1	21483701	1146222	21456124	1171041	21428547	1195861	21400969	1220680	21373392	1245500	21483701	1146222
			1,25	21734724	867307	21707147	892127	21679570	916946	21651993	941766	21624416	966585	21734724	867307
			1,5	21985748	588392	21958171	613212	21930593	638031	21903016	662851	21875439	687670	21985748	588392
		0,75	0,5	21113446	1557616	21085869	1582436	21058292	1607255	21030715	1632075	21003137	1656894	21113446	1557616
			0,75	21364470	1278701	21336892	1303521	21309315	1328340	21281738	1353160	21254161	1377979	21364470	1278701
			1	21615493	999786	21587916	1024606	21560339	1049425	21532761	1074245	21505184	1099064	21615493	999786
			1,25	21866516	720872	21838939	745691	21811362	770511	21783785	795330	21756207	820150	21866516	720872
			1,5	22117540	441957	22089963	466776	22062385	491596	22034808	516415	22007231	541235	22117540	441957
		1	0,5	21245238	1411181	21217661	1436000	21190084	1460820	21162506	1485639	21134929	1510459	21245238	1411181
			0,75	21496261	1132266	21468684	1157085	21441107	1181905	21413530	1206724	21385953	1231544	21496261	1132266
0,8	0,8		1	21747285	853351	21719708	878171	21692130	902990	21664553	927809	21636976	952629	21747285	853351
			1,25	21998308	574436	21970731	599256	21943154	624075	21915577	648895	21887999	673714	21998308	574436
			1,5	22249332	295521	22221754	320341	22194177	345160	22166600	369980	22139023	394799	22249332	295521
		1,25	0,5	21377030	1264745	21349453	1289565	21321876	1314384	21294298	1339204	21266721	1364023	21377030	1264745
			0,75	21628053	985830	21600476	1010650	21572899	1035469	21545322	1060289	21517745	1085108	21628053	985830
			1	21879077	706916	21851500	731735	21823922	756555	21796345	781374	21768768	806194	21879077	706916
			1,25	22130100	428001	22102523	452820	22074946	477640	22047369	502459	22019791	527279	22130100	428001
			1,5	22381124	149086	22353546	173905	22325969	198725	22298392	223544	22270815	248364	22381124	149086
		1,5	0,5	21508822	1118310	21481245	1143129	21453668	1167949	21426090	1192768	21398513	1217588	21508822	1118310
			0,75	21759845	839395	21732268	864214	21704691	889034	21677114	913853	21649536	938673	21759845	839395
			1	22010869	560480	21983291	585300	21955714	610119	21928137	634939	21900560	659758	22010869	560480
			1,25	22261892	281565	22234315	306385	22206738	331204	22402607	101928	22151583	380843	22261892	281565
			1,5	22512915	2650	22485338	27470	22457761	52289	22430184	77109	22402607	101928	22512915	2650

In the proposed games, the profit (outcome) of each operator (player) will be dependent not only on their actions, but also on the actions of the other operators in the market.

The impact of the price (retail and wholesale) variations on several output results: players' profit, consumer surplus, welfare, costs, service adop-

tion, and so on. For that, two price-setting games are played. Players' profits and NPV are used as the payoff for the players in the games analyzed. The comparison of the two games above shows that when the regulator defines wholesale prices, operators increase retail prices to maximize profit. However, when wholesale prices are not regulated,

Table 14. Pure NE strategies in both regions (game 2)

Strategy	Player 1 (Incumbent Operator)				Player 2 (New Entrant)				NPV € Player 1	NPV € Player 2
	Retail		Wholesale		Retail		Wholesale			
	S1	S2	R1	R2	S1	S2	R1	R2		
1-4	0.8	0.8	1.5	1.25	0.8	0.8	0.50 0.75 1 1.25 1.5	1.25	22 402 606	101 928
5-9	0.8	0.9	1.25	1	0.8	0.8	0.50 0.75 1 1.25 1.5	1.25	19 543 660	6.198.799

Figure 18. Profit variation: Retail service 2 and wholesale service

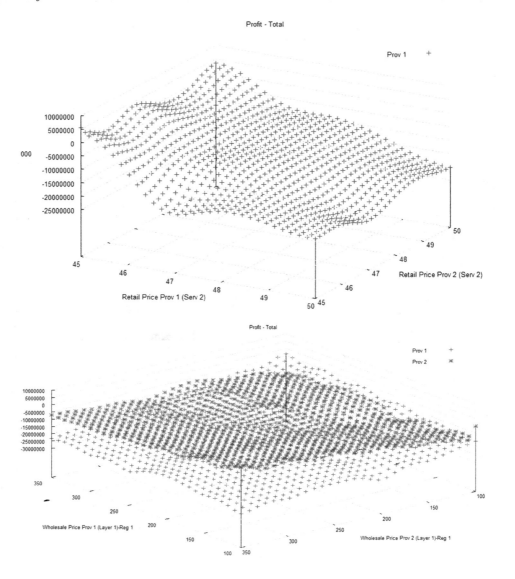

Figure 19. Consumer surplus retail market variation

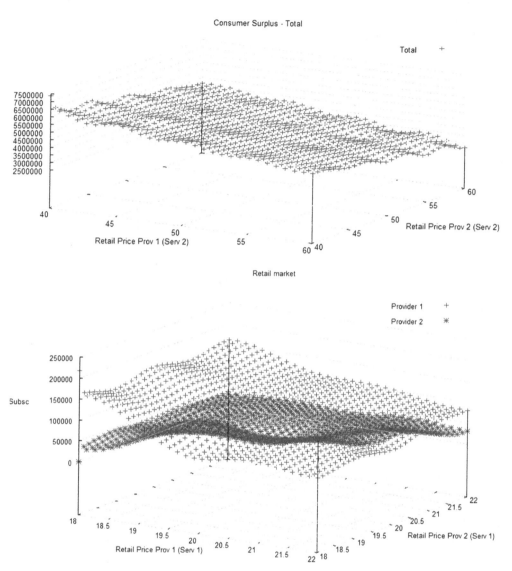

operators maximize profit by decreasing retail prices and increasing wholesale prices. However, without regulation, the higher wholesale prices will limit the entrance of new competitors.

The analysis of the two games show that the sharing of passive infrastructure (e.g., ducts, trenching, etc.) is a good option, particularly in the context of new building (in scenarios with developed access infrastructure). When an operator deploys an access network, the access to

existing civil engineering significantly reduces the investment.

It is fundamental that incumbent operators provide access to the civil works infrastructure, including its ducts, and give wholesale broadband access (bitstream) to the local loop, regardless of whether it is copper-based or fiber-based. However, at the same time, alternative operators should be able to compete on the basis of the wholesale broadband input while they progressively rollout their own NGA infrastructure. In some areas, especially those with higher density, alternative operators have introduced their own infrastructure. As a result, broadband competition has developed, which should result in more innovation and better prices for consumers. Regulators must guarantee to new entrant operators access to civil engineering; this will stimulate investment in new networks. The reduction of the barriers to new infrastructure investment by opening passive existing infrastructure would be key in the future. This study has shown that in rural areas, characterized by a small number of developed access infrastructure, the access to civil engineering does not make the scenario economically viable for the operator.

REFERENCES

ACMA. (2009). *Consumer benefits resulting from Australia's telecommunications sector.* Sydney, Australia: Australian Communications and Media Authority.

Amendola, G. B., & Pupillo, L. M. (2007). *The economics of next generation access networks and regulatory governance in Europe: One size does not fit all.* Paper presented at the 18th ITS Regional Conference. Istanbul, Turkey.

Andersen Management International. (2004). *Pricing shared access in Sweden.* Sweden: Post of Telestyrelsen.

Easley, D., & Kleinberg, J. (2010). *Networks, crowds, and markets: Reasoning about a highly connected world.* Cambridge, UK: Cambridge University Press. doi:10.1017/CBO9780511761942

Elixmann, D., Figueras, A. P., Hackbarth, K., Marcus, J. S., Nagy, P., Pápai, Z., & Scanlan, M. (2007). *The regulation of next generation networks (NGN)* (Final Report). Budapest.

France, P. W., Spirit, D. M., & Whitt, S. (1998). Developing the access network. *BT Technology Journal, 16*(4), 9–20.

Gerami, M. (2010). Evaluation of next generation networks. *International Journal on Computer Science and Engineering, 2*(2), 378–381.

Höffler, F. (2007). Cost and benefits from infrastructure competition: Estimating welfare effects from broadband access competition. *Telecommunications Policy, 31*(6-7), 401–418. doi:10.1016/j.telpol.2007.05.004

ITU. (2006). *Ruling the new and emerging markets in the telecommunication sector.* Paper presented at the ITU Workshop on What Rules for IP-Enabled NGNs? Geneva, Switzerland.

ITU-T. (2008). *Telecom network planning for evolving network architectures.* International Telecommunication Union.

Katsianis, D., Gyürke, A., Konkoly, R., Varoutas, D., & Sphicopoulos, T. (2007). A game theory modeling approach for 3G operators. *NETNOMICS: Economic Research and Electronic Networking, 8*(1), 71–90. doi:10.1007/s11066-008-9022-1

Kirsch, F., & Hirschhausen, C. V. (2008). *Regulation of next generation networks: Structural separation, access regulation, or no regulation at all?* Paper presented at the First International Conference on Infrastructure Systems and Services: Building Networks for a Brighter Future (INFRA). Rotterdam, The Netherland.

Kota, S. L. (2006). *Satellite multimedia networks and technical challenges.* Microwave Review.

Leary, P. (2004). *The wild world of wireless broadband and WiMAX.* Alvarion.

Machado, R., & Tekinay, S. (2008). A survey of game-theoretic approaches in wireless sensor networks. *Computer Networks, 52*(16), 3047–3061. doi:10.1016/j.gaceta.2008.07.003

OECD. (2008). *Broadband growth and policies in OECD countries*. OECD Publications.

OECD. (2009). *Mobile broadband: Pricing and services*. Organisation for Economic Cooperation and Development.

Pereira, J. P., & Ferreira, P. (2009). *Access networks for mobility: A techno-economic model for broadband access technologies*. Paper presented at the Testbeds and Research Infrastructures for the Development of Networks & Communities and Workshops. Washington, DC.

Pereira, J. P., & Ferreira, P. (2011). *Next generation access networks (NGANs) and the geographical segmentation of markets*. Paper presented at the Tenth International Conference on Networks (ICN 2011). St. Maarten, The Netherlands Antilles.

Pereira, J. P., & Ferreira, P. (2012). Game theoretic modeling of NGANs: Impact of retail and wholesale services price variation. *The Journal of Communication*. doi:10.4304/jcm.7.3.258-264

Pereira, J. P. R. (2013a). Effects of NGNs on market definition. In Á. Rocha, A. M. Correia, T. Wilson, & K. A. Stroetmann (Eds.), *Advances in information systems and technologies* (Vol. 206, pp. 939–949). Berlin: Springer. doi:10.1007/978-3-642-36981-0_88

Pereira, J. P. R. (2013b). Infrastructure vs. access competition in NGNs. In A. Selamat, N. Nguyen, & H. Haron (Eds.), *Intelligent information and database systems* (Vol. 7803, pp. 529–538). Berlin: Springer. doi:10.1007/978-3-642-36543-0_54

Prasad, R., & Velez, F. J. (2010). *WiMAX networks: Techno-economic vision and challenges*. New York: Springer. doi:10.1007/978-90-481-8752-2

Sarrocco, C., & Ypsilanti, D. (2008). *Convergence and next generation networks*. OECD.

Sigurdsson, H. M. (2007). *Techno-economics of residential broadband deployment*. (PhD Thesis). Technical University of Denmark - Center for Information and Communication Technologies. Retrieved from PhD_Thesis_Halldor_Sigurdsson.pdf

Stordahl, K. (2010). Market development up to 2015. *MARCH - Multilink architecture for multiplay services*.

Verbrugge, S., Casier, K., Ooteghem, J. V., & Lannoo, B. (2009). *White paper: Practical steps in techno-economic evaluation of network deployment planning*. Gent, Belgium: UGent/IBBT.

Yongkang, X., Xiuming, S., & Yong, R. (2005). Game theory models for IEEE 802.11 DCF in wireless ad hoc networks. *IEEE Communications Magazine, 43*(3), S22–S26. doi:10.1109/MCOM.2005.1404594

Chapter 11
Indoor Short Range Wireless Broadband Communications Based on Optical Fiber Distribution

Haymen Shams
University College London, UK

ABSTRACT

There is a continuous demand for increasing wireless access broadband services to the end users, especially with widespread high quality mobile devices. The Internet mobile applications and multimedia services are constantly hungry for broadband wireless bandwidth. In order to overcome this bandwidth limitation, a frequency band (57-64 GHz) has recently been assigned for short range indoor wireless broadband signals due to the large available bandwidth. However, the transmission at this band is limited to a few meters due to the high atmospheric absorption loss. Radio over Fiber (RoF) technology was considered an efficient solution to extend the distribution range and wireless capacity services. This chapter presents an introduction to RoF technology and its basic required optical components for indoor short range wireless millimeter waves (mm-waves). The limiting factors of RoF and its impairments are also described. Moreover, optical mm-wave generation solutions are explained and followed by the recent optical 60GHz activities and upcoming research areas such as THz and optical wireless.

INTRODUCTION

There is a global interest in wireless access broadband services based on optical fibers which provide a huge bandwidth needed for Internet users. Fiber to the home/premises (FTTH/FTTP) is also getting more and more attention to provide an ultimate solution for delivering different services to the customers' premises. A FTTH network constitutes a fiber-based network, connecting a large number of end user to a central point. In the future, the access bitrate requirements will soon expected to increase more than 10Gbps (IDate Consulting and Reserach, 2013).

Wireless broadband services for the last few meters have also attracted much interest from many academic researchers and many companies such as Panasonic, Samsung, LG, and Toshiba.

DOI: 10.4018/978-1-4666-5978-0.ch011

Services and multimedia applications such as Internet video, video communication, and video on demand are now available and need much greater bandwidth than that is offered today by available wireless channels. At the same time, new services such as high definition television (HDTV) and interactive video have been developed and are becoming commercially available in many countries ("WirelessHD Consortium," 2013). These applications and services drive the need for new wireless connections that can carry the increased bitrates inside homes, or buildings. According to Edholm's law, the wireless speed is being doubled for every 18 months over the last 25 years (Cherry, 2004). Therefore, in the next ten years, it is expected to reach to tens of Gbps. The use of 60 GHz radio techniques has become an enabler technology for many gigabit indoor applications that are constrained at lower frequency bands. These applications involve uncompressed Wireless HD streaming to wireless screens, wireless gigabit Ethernet that allows bidirectional Ethernet traffic and wireless docking stations that allow multiple peripherals to be connected without plugging and unplugging. A special frequency band in the 60 GHz has been globally allocated with 7 GHz of continuous spectrum for unlicensed use. The high path loss and the atmospheric absorption around 60 GHz make this band suitable for short range communication which mainly takes the form of the wireless local area network (WLAN), the wireless personal area network (WPAN), and the wireless body area network (WBAN). In addition, the short range coverage provides the cells with high security, anti-interference ability, and more densely packed communication links. The high available bandwidth and short range wireless signals enable broadband wireless access for in-building application such as HDTV and other multimedia services.

The combination of wireless and fiber optics was first introduced in the early 1980s for US military applications. This has been known as radio over fiber (RoF) technology and used also for RF distribution in cordless and mobile communication. The conventional way of RF signal distributions were transported via bulky copper cables and waveguides where all high frequency elements of a system have to be placed together to minimize the RF losses. The advantages of the low fiber losses, large bandwidth, and light weight features have enabled the optical fiber as an efficient transmission medium for transporting high frequency radio signals. Following this, many research centers and scientists across the world have developed new techniques to send wireless signals over fiber. RoF systems are now being used in many RF applications for transporting the radio signal from a central office (CO) to a remote antenna site such as cellular networks, indoor distributed antenna systems, and WLANs illustrated in Figure 1. The general RoF system is comprised of central location where the radio signal is generated and then distributed to a number of remote base stations using optical fibers in the building as shown in the Figure 1. Therefore, the most of the expensive and high frequency equipment have to be located at the central station where coding, modulation, multiplexing, and up-conversion are happening. Whereas, the remote antenna units (RAUs) should be simple, small in size, light and low cost (Jianjun et al., 2010).

Figure 1. Illustration diagram for fiber network distribution

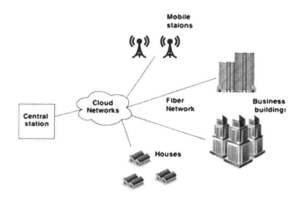

There has been a significant global research effort to design and implement RoF systems to distribute mm-wave with cost effective methods. This system can be easily integrated with the FTTH technology to provide wireless signal distribution in an indoor environment, and will match the requirements with the global plan towards enhanced wireless broadband delivery services.

This chapter presents an introduction to short range wireless communication over optical fiber networks. The chapter is divided into six sections. The first section represents the global interests for 60 GHz frequency bands and shows the assigned regulations from different countries for the unlicensed indoor use of the band. Section 2 discusses the methods for optical distribution of RF signal over fiber. Consequently, an overview of RoF technology and its basic components are represented in section 3. The conventional structure of a RoF system and its main optical components are described in details. Furthermore, the main limitation factors such as optical noise and nonlinear distortion that affect the performance of RoF systems are discussed in section 4. This has been shown as system impairments such as noise, distortion, and fiber dispersion degrade the signal-to-noise ratio and limit the system transmission lengths. Optical methods for mm-wave generation at 60 GHz using direct detection, and heterodyne detection are demonstrated at section 5 and then followed by the recent activities at

60 GHz for last three years. While section 6 is dedicated for the future direction for short range wireless communication and this introduce the research are more concerns for THz application, and optical wireless communication.

60 GHZ BAND FOR INDOOR WIRELESS COMMUNICATIONS

The large available bandwidth at the frequency band 60 GHz provides access to future wireless broadband services, and breaking the bandwidth limitation in the congestion lower microwave frequency band. Therefore, many regulation bodies have opened up the unlicensed frequency band around 60 GHz for broadband wireless services. Figure 2 shows the assigned 60 GHz for various regions around the world, and Table 1 shows the brief summary of the 60GHz regulations with the transmitted power and equivalent isotropic radiated power (EIRP). EIRP is defined as the amount of radiated power for a perfectly isotropic antenna needed to achieve the same measured value for an arbitrary antenna. Most of the countries have assigned the frequency band (57.0 - 64.0 GHz) for unlicensed utilization for indoor application with average transmitted power 10 dBm. For example, in USA/Canada, the 60 GHz band was regulated with 27 dBm for maximum transmitted power for 7 GHz emission bandwidth . While in South

Figure 2. 60 GHz frequency band regulations around the world

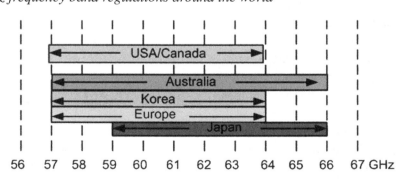

Table 1. The frequency band at 60GHz for different regulatory regions around the world

Region	Unlicensed Frequency Range (GHz)	Maximum Bandwidth	Transmitted Power	EIRP	Ref.
USA/Canada	57-64	7 GHz	27 dBm	40 dBm	(FCC, 2012); (M&Spec, 2010)
Europe	57-64	7 GHz	10 dBm	20 dBm	(ECC, 2012)
Germany	59-63	2 GHz	----	40 dBm	(BNetzA, 2008)
Japan	59- 66	2.5 GHz	10 dBm	58 dBm	(MPHPT, 2000)
Australia	57-66	9 GHz	10 dBm	43 dBm	(Media, 2011)
South Korea	57- 64	7 GHz	10 dBm	51.7 dBm	(KCC, 2006)

Korea, the same frequency band was allocated for unlicensed use with 10 dBm transmitted power (KCC, 2006). In March 2012, the Electronic Communication Committee (ECC) within the Commission for European Post and Telecommunications (CEPT) specified 7 GHz band for nonspecific short devices in Europe and 10 dBm maximum power without producing harmful interference to the fixed services (ECC, 2012). While, the radio regulations law in Japan allocated the frequency band 59.0-66 GHz for unlicensed use with transmission power 10 dBm and less than 2.5 GHz bandwidth (MPHPT, 2000). In Australia, only 3.5 GHz bandwidth (57- 66 GHz) was regulated with maximum transmitted power 10 dBm (Media, 2011). These assigned regulations pave the path for 60 GHz development and opened the interest to more research centers and industries.

RF DISTRIBUTION IN OPTICAL FIBER

Optical fibers are used to deliver high quality radio signals directly to a point of free space radiation (antenna site). The simplest system arrangement for radio signal transmission over fiber is shown in Figure 3. At the central office (CO), the light intensity of the laser diode is directly modulated with the wireless signal and then transmitted towards the photodiode through optical fiber links. The wavelength of the light can be either 1300 nm or 1550 nm for low transmission loss in silica fiber. In the downlink/uplink application, two optical fiber links can be used to provide full duplex transmission, or using the wavelength division multiplexing (WDM) technology for possible transmission in the two directions by using

Figure 3. Schematic diagram for basic radio signal distribution over fiber

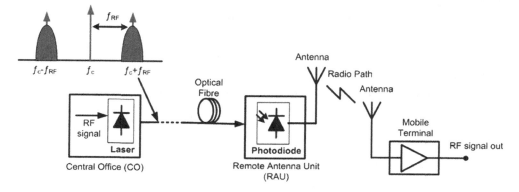

different wavelengths. The remote antenna unit (RAU) is a normal optical receiver that converts the optical signal back into electrical signal, where the RF power output is directly proportional to the square of the input optical power. Then, it radiates the electrical signal into free space via an antenna to the mobile terminal. This system is called intensity modulated-direct detection (IM-DD) which is widely used in cellular applications due to its simplicity and low cost. There are also other types of optical modulation by using an external modulator such as frequency or phase modulation which requires more complex system.

The RF wireless distribution can be classified into three possible transmission configurations based on RF frequency and the required applications (Lee, 2007; Lim et al., 2010). *RF-over-fiber*; where the radio signal is directly transmitted over the fiber link at the radio carrier transmission frequency without any need for frequency conversions at the base station. This is a simple configuration and easy to install, however it is limited with devices' bandwidth. The second scheme is *IF–over-fiber* where the wireless signals for downstream transmission can be distributed from the CO to the remote terminals at a lower intermediated frequency (IF) and then upconverted to RF at the RAU. This configuration uses lower speed opto-electronic devices and allows transmission over the multimode fiber (MMF) which is cheaper fiber link than single mode fiber (SMF) and widely used now in the infrastructure networks for many buildings. However, it requires a local oscillator (LO) and high speed electronic mixers at the RAUs which increase the complexity and cost at each remote terminal. *Baseband-over-fiber* is the third transport method. The laser light is modulated with baseband signal at the CO and then upconverted to RF at the RAU. This greatly reduces the limitations imposed by fiber chromatic dispersion and the need for high speed opto-electronic devices. In the other hand, the system complexity and cost increases due to the high LO frequency signal needed at the remote

terminals. For practical and cost effective system, it is necessary to keep most of the expensive and high frequency component at the central station. This brings all the system costs into the central station and allowing simple and compact size at the RAUs. In addition, it simplifies its installation, and easy maintenance.

ROF LINK COMPONENTS

The distribution of RF signal using fiber links shows numerous advantages of wireless signal distribution. Therefore, it is necessary to study the system components and parameters, and how these can affect the system performance. In this section, the basic principles and characteristics of the center station, RAU, and optical link are described in detail for the basic RoF system.

Central Office (CO)

In the CO, the laser diode is an essential element in fiber optic links since it generates the optical signal that carries the information. Normally, the laser wavelengths are placed at 1300 or 1550 nm, corresponding to the lowest known values of dispersion or attenuation, respectively. The RF microwave signal can be carried on the laser frequency (around 200 THz) and transported over the fiber links in several ways. The laser light is simply modulated either directly by injecting the electrical current into a semiconductor laser diode or externally using an external electro-optic modulator, as shown in Figure 4.

a. Direct Modulation Scheme

The direct modulation scheme as shown in Figure 4 (a) is achieved by applying the RF signal and DC bias together into the laser diode. The laser light output versus injection current (L-I) of a typical semiconductor laser is also shown in Figure 4(a). The biased laser diode at certain point over the

Figure 4. Optical transmitter using; (a) direct modulation, and (b) external modulation

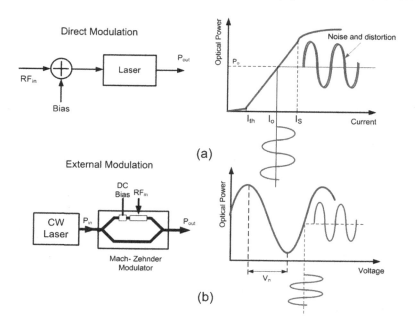

threshold value emits a constant output optical power P_o. If the RF signal is applied, the optical power is varied from bias point corresponds to the change of the applied RF signal. The optical output above the threshold increases linearly with the current until it reaches power saturation. This saturation is due to heating of the laser junction which results from internal losses or current leakage (Agrawal & Dutta, 1986). In the direct modulation scheme, the laser should be biased at a point in the linear region and driven with a limited RF power to avoid signal distortion and nonlinearity.

There are three types of semiconductor laser used in optical fiber communication; Fabry Perot (FP), distributed feedback laser diode (DFB-LD) and vertical cavity surface emitting laser (VCSEL). A FP-laser is a multimode semiconductor laser. It emits light in several longitudinal modes that only satisfy the condition of constructive interference of forward and backward travelling optical waves in the cavity. However, DFB-LD lases is a single longitudinal mode laser. The laser cavity has a periodic grating that provides optical feedback for the lasing wavelengths. This generates only a narrow band of wavelengths. In a typical DFB-laser, the modulation bandwidth is an important parameter in a RoF system where it sets the limit on the maximum RF frequency can be modulated in the laser carrier. A modulation bandwidth of 30 GHz was reported in multiple quantum well (MQW) laser at 1550 nm wavelength and 37 GHz for a distributed Bragg reflector (DBR) laser (Bach et al., 2003; Goutain et al., 1996). It has been shown that the modulation bandwidth enhanced for more than five times by using an injection locking technique. The improvement of the optical bandwidth can be obtained by injecting the semiconductor laser with another free running laser with a specific power and detuned frequency. An enhancement in modulation bandwidth using optical injection was recorded for DFB laser at 44 GHz, and VCSEL at 50 GHz (Chrostowski et al., 2005; Lau & Wu, 2006).

b. External Modulation Scheme

As mentioned before that the laser's light can also be modulated by using an external optical modulator. The externally modulated optical system has better advantages of increasing the limited modulation bandwidth of the laser, reducing the laser noise, and distortion in that occurs in the direct laser modulation (Stephens & Joseph, 1987). As a results many RoF system that have been proposed to use the external optical modulators.

There are two different principles of an external optical modulator used in optical fiber communication: *electro-optic* effect based on the changes of the refractive index, and *electro-absorption* effect based on the optical absorption under the influence of electric field. The electro-absorption materials are semiconductors that can be easily integrated with the continuous wave (CW) laser diode (Kingston, 1979). In electro-optic modulators, the Mach-Zehnder modulator (MZM) is the main widely used. It is made of an insulating material (lithium niobate (LiNbO3)) which has many advantages such as a refractive index that changes linearly with applied voltage, high electro-optic coefficient, and stability at normal electronic operating temperatures (Yu & Wu, 2002). This type of modulator can handle much higher optical powers (up to 400 mW) than electro-absorption modulators (limited to a few tens of milliwatts) (Williamson, Fellow, & Esman, 2008), and exhibits much higher extinction ratio (~25 dB) than EAMs (~10dB) but in general they also need higher drive voltages.

Figure 4 (b) shows the schematic diagram for employing a MZM and its transfer function. The input light is split into two paths in the upper and lower waveguide. The optical phase of the upper arm is changed by the applied voltage. Then, the two waveguides are recombined again in the output resulting into a constructive or destructive interference based on the relative phase shift of the light in the two arms. The output optical field (E_{out}) can be expressed as

$$
\begin{aligned}
E_{out}\left(t\right) \\
&= E_o cos\left[\frac{\varphi\left(V\left(t\right)\right)}{2}\right] cos\left(\omega_o t\right) \\
&= E_o cos\left[\frac{\pi}{2V_\pi}\left(V_{bias} + V_m cos\left(\omega_{RF} t\right)\right)\right] cos\left(\omega_o t\right)
\end{aligned}
\tag{1}
$$

where E_o and ω_0 denote the amplitude and angular frequency of the input optical carrier, respectively, and $\Phi(t)$ is the optical carrier phase change introduced by the applied $V(t)$ on one of the MZM arms. V_{bias} is the dc bias voltage, V_m and ω_{RF} are the amplitude and angular frequency of the electrical driving signal, respectively, and V_π is the half wave voltage (which means the necessary driving voltage for achieving a phase shift of π). This equation shows that the modulator has a sinusoidal transfer function as presented in Figure 4 (b). For a linear region operation, the modulator has to be biased at the quadrature (half power point) and the driven voltage should be less than V_π. The nonlinearity of the light output power, optical loss, and polarization sensitivity are the main disadvantages in this modulator. Moreover, this modulator cannot be integrated to the laser which increases the complexity and cost of the optical system (Kolner & Dolfi, 1987).

Remote Antenna Unit (RAU)

Remote antenna unit is simply an optical receiver that converts the received optical signal back into electrical form and radiates it via an antenna to the user's mobile terminal. The optical receiver is a photodetector connected to a transimpedance amplifier. The photodetector should have an enough large bandwidth that can handle the RF frequency used in the RoF system (Lee, 2007). There are two common types of photodiode used in the field of optical communications: the positive intrinsic negative (PIN) and avalanche photodiode (APD). PIN diode consists of three semiconductor layers p-type, intrinsic, and n-type layer. When the diode is reverse biased, it generates an electric current upon the incident light. The current generated is proportion to incident optical power. This is related to the diode responsivity and is normally around 0.5- 0.7 A/W. The generated current is very small in PIN diodes and therefore it is converted to voltage signal by using a transimpedance amplifier.

The avalanche photodiode (APD) improves greatly the receiver sensitivity by using impact ionization process. The device structure of an APD has more inserted layer p-type between i-layer and n+-layer. APD's diode is reversed biased at high electric field to produce an impact ionization process. This generates a secondary electron-hole pair and increases the diode responsivity over the PIN diode with several orders of magnitude. However, APD's bandwidth is limited due to the response time of the multiplication process. APD diode has higher noise and temperature gain dependent compared to the PIN diode. The bandwidth of APDs were normally limited to 5 -10 GHz. In optical fiber communications, APD diodes are generally used in long distance links for higher system sensitivity and for application with bandwidth less than 15GHz. However, PIN diodes are cost effective, less sensitive to temperature and require lower reverse bias voltage.

Transmission Media

The communication channel in most lightwave systems is the optical fiber which transports the optical signal from the transmitter to receiver. Therefore, it is important to consider the effect of the fiber during the propagation of the optical signal in RoF systems. Multimode and single mode fibers are common fiber types used in the field of optical communication. Optical fiber attenuation and dispersion are very important factors that degrade the system performance due to a reduction in signal to noise ratio (SNR) or result in an increase in the signal distortion.

Fiber attenuation is an important design issue in optical fiber systems and is relatively low, typically 0.5 dB/km or 0.2 dB/km for 1330 nm

and 1550 nm windows, respectively. This attenuation results decreasing the SNR at the optical receiver and limits the transmission distance of the fiber. The main source of the attenuation is due to the fiber impurities, and light scattering caused by the interactions between the photons and silica molecules, known as Rayleigh scattering (Agrawal, 2010). In some optical systems, optical amplifiers are used to increase the link length and provide distribution to a large number of users but this decreases the SNR due to the added amplifier's noise.

While fiber dispersion results in pulse broadening as the optical signal travels along the fiber causing intersymbol interference (ISI) between bits. There are three types of dispersion in the fiber. Intermodal dispersion results from the modes of a multimode fiber propagating with different velocities. This is also called modal dispersion and does not occur in the single mode fiber. While, material dispersion (chromatic dispersion) is refractive index dependent and varies with the light wavelength. Each wavelength travels with a different velocity and reaches to the receiver at different times. This dispersion occurs in all transmission systems since the light source and data signal has finite bandwidth. The third type of dispersion is a waveguide dispersion and it is very small and can be ignored compared to the other dispersions. It results from the waveguide characteristics such as fiber indices and the shape of the fiber core and cladding. The dispersion can be reduced to zero by adjusting the material and waveguide dispersion such as dispersion shifted fiber (DSF). Another way to decrease the effects of dispersion is to use a compensating fiber with a strong negative dispersion known as dispersion compensation fiber (DCF) (Keiser, 2000; Senior, 2009).

The effect of chromatic dispersion is more significant at higher modulation frequencies and severely limits the fiber transmission distance. In the conventional intensity modulated direct detection (IM-DD) RoF system, the information signal is generated on both sides of the optical carrier which is known as double sideband (DSB) modulation (Gliese, Norskov, & Nielsen, 1996). When the optical carrier and the two sidebands are transmitted over fiber, the chromatic dispersion causes a phase change for each sideband depending on the fiber length, modulation frequency, and chromatic dispersion parameter. This degrades the resulting RF power because the two RF signals by the two sidebands are generated out of phase at the receiver end. This can be fixed by using optical carrier suppression (OCS) or single side band (SSB) modulation as will be discussed later.

IMPAIRMENTS OF RADIO OVER FIBRE

All optical communication systems suffer from noise and distortions that limit system performance on the optical transmission link. Noise added to the optical signal produces bit errors at the decision gate in the receiver side, while distortion results in inter-symbol interference (ISI) due to the broadening of the optical pulses while propagating through the fiber which also increases the received bit errors. The system performance is determined by the measurement of the eyediagram and bit error rate (BER), usually plotted as a function of received optical power. Therefore, the determination of noise and distortion contribution is vital in digital and analogue optical communication systems and tends to limit the radio system distributions (Agrawal, 2010; Davies & Urey, 1992). In this section, it concerns about the main noise sources and the nonlinear distortions that affect RoF system.

Noise Sources in the RoF links

The sources of the noise in the RoF links are compromised of the laser's relative intensity noise (RIN), the laser's phase noise, amplified spontaneous emission (ASE) noise from optical amplifier, and receiver noise (Davies & Urey, 1992). In a semiconductor laser, the RIN is generated from laser intensity fluctuations even when the laser is biased at a constant current. These noise are translated into the received signal and degrade the signal quality. Another important phenomenon called mode partition noise (MPN) can also increase the effect of RIN. In practice, single mode semiconductor lasers oscillate by one or more side modes with the main longitudinal mode. The laser main and side modes fluctuates in their intensities. These mode fluctuations have no effect in the absence of fiber dispersion, as all modes are received at the same time on the photodiode. However, in the presence of the fiber transmission all modes do not arrive simultaneously at the receiver because they travel at slightly different speeds and cause an amplitude fluctuation of the signal at the decision circuit in the receiver. Therefore, MPN reduces the performance of an optical communication system and is related to the ratio of the main mode power to the power of the most dominant side modes. In practice, most commercial DFB semiconductor lasers are accompanied by one or more side bands that are suppressed by more than 30 dB (Agrawal, 2010).

During signal propagation over the fiber, the optical fiber channel does not contribute to noise generation in the optical signal but reduces the signal power through attenuation. However, optical amplifiers are used to increase the signal power but degrade the SNR value due to the generated ASE noise(Senior, 2009).

At the receiver end, the noise is composed of shot noise, photodiode dark current noise, and thermal noise from the RF amplifier. In most practical cases for low input power, the dominant noise source is the thermal noise which is due to random thermal motion of electrons and causes current fluctuations at the receiver output. This noise is decreased by increasing the optical power or using transimpedance amplifier at the front ends. However, if the incident power is large, the receiver performance is dominated by the shot noise where the electric current consists of a stream of electrons that are generated at random times (Palais, 2004). All these mentioned noise sources reduce the signal quality and limit the dynamic range of the RoF system.

Distortions in the RoF Systems

The distortions in optical communication systems are produced from the fiber dispersion and non-linearities in the laser. The effect of fiber dispersion as described previously severely limits the overall transmission distance and the maximum transmission rate (Davies & Urey, 1992). There are several methods in the literature showed how to compensate for fiber dispersion; pre-distortion, post-distortion, and during the fiber link (Agrawal, 2010). The nonlinearity in the transfer function of the laser or the external modulator is also a crucial parameter in the RoF systems. If we consider two input signals at frequencies f_1 and f_2 fed into the link. The nonlinearity in the systems generates spurious

output signals at the second and third harmonics of the input signals. The second harmonic signals located out of interested band, and can be easily filtered out for narrow band systems. While the third harmonics $2f_1 - f_2$ and $2f_2 - f_1$ known as the third order inter-modulation products (IM3) is important to be avoided (Williamson et al., 2008). These products are called spurious signals and fall in-band resulting in signal distortions. Figure 5 shows the relation between the input and output signal power. The fundamental signal varies linearly and the IM3 signal varies with the cube of the input power. The spur free dynamic range (SFDR) is defined as the range of the input signal power bounded by the intersection between the fundamental and IM3 with the noise floor. That means that the signal power should be higher than the noise floor and lower than the intersection point between the IM3 line and the noise floor. Dynamic range (DR) is an important parameter in wireless communication due to the wide range of the received power from MUs to the base station.

Figure 5. Output power versus input optical power for analogue optical links, illustrating spurious free dynamic range (SFDR)

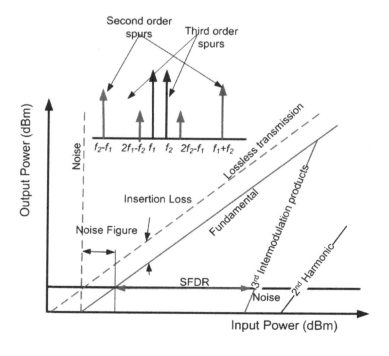

The received input RF power should not be more than 80 dB to the mobile terminals. However, this effect of DR can be neglected for in-building coverage systems where the cells are in range of pico and microcells. Many research techniques have been also proposed to combat these nonlinearities and increase the dynamic range in RoF links by using distortion cancellation methods (Hassin & Vahldieck, 1993; Roselli et al., 2003; Yaakob et al., 2006), or by reducing system's noise floor including the RIN, shot noise, and phase induced intensity noise (Esman & Williams, 1995; Mathai et al., 2001).

Nonlinearity in Fiber Links

Nonlinear effects in fiber are crucial factors on the multichannel performance for RoF systems. Fiber nonlinearities causes attenuation, distortion, and cross channel interference which result in restricted channel spacing, and limits maximum optical power on each channel. These nonlinearities are classified into stimulated Raman scattering, four wave mixing, and cross phase modulation (Agrawal, 2010; Wilson, etc., Darwazeh, & Ghassemlooy, 1995).

Stimulated Raman scattering is a non-linear effect where a small part of the incident light is scattered to a longer wavelength due to the interaction between the incident light and the fiber molecular. If there is any signal at this longer wavelength, then it will be amplified and cause crosstalk interference leading to degraded system performance. This Raman crosstalk occurs at a relatively high threshold incident power (about 500 mW near 1.55 μm) and can be avoided if the channel powers are made so small that Raman amplification is negligible over the fiber length.

Four wave mixing (FWM) is a major source of nonlinear interchannel crosstalk in multichannel systems and is caused by the nonlinear power dependence of the refractive index of the fiber. In the FWM process, new optical wavelengths are generated from the mixing of three wavelength signals propagating inside the fiber whenever the fiber dispersion is very small or close to zero. This impact of FWM can be reduced by decreasing the channel powers below 1 mW or using unequal channel spacing such that all the FWM-generated frequencies fall outside the signal spectra. The third nonlinear phenomenon is based on the intensity dependence of the refractive index and called the cross phase modulation (XPM). This causes channel phase fluctuation due to the power fluctuation on the other channels. It can be made very small or negligible if the channel power is reduced below 1 mW.

OPTICAL METHODS FOR GENERATING MILLIMETER WAVE SIGNALS

Electrical generation and distribution of high frequency signals at the mm-waves is still a challenge way in the contemporary electronic devices technology. This section presents the methods of generating mm-wave. This mm-wave can be obtained either by using intensity modulation and direct detection (IMDD) receivers, or remote heterodyning (RHD) receivers.

Intensity Modulation Direct Detection (IMDD) Receivers

The simplest and easiest way for optical mm-wave generation is to modulate the intensity of the laser output by either directly modulating the laser intensity or using an external modulator as shown in Figure 6. After transmission through the optical fiber, the mm-wave can be recovered by direct detection on a photodiode, amplified and transmitted by the antenna. However, even the simplest of this method, it suffered from the modulation bandwidth of the laser. Moreover, this method is also affected by the high laser noise due to intensity modulation, and the nonlinearity in the laser which leads to signal distortion. On

Figure 6. (a) Schematic diagram of optical mm-wave generation using direct and external modulation of the optical intensity, and (b) electrical power fading of the mm-wave signal due to fiber dispersion

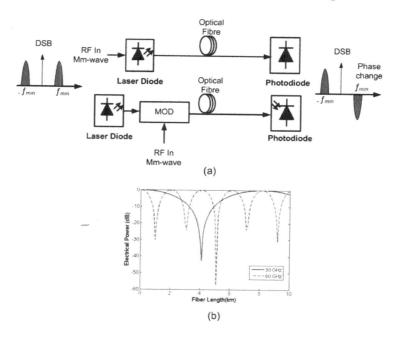

the other hand, external modulators suffer from limited bandwidth, high insertion loss and high driving voltages which in turn increase the cost and complexity of the system (Davies & Urey, 1992).

A further limitation of this method is the chromatic dispersion that reduces the transmission distance of the fiber. With this technique, the data signal is carried in sidebands on both sides of the optical carrier which is known as double side band (DSB) operation. Transmission of such a signal through a fiber will experience a phase shift between the two sidebands due to the chromatic dispersion effect as illustrated in Figure 6 (a). This can cause fading in the received power as a result of destructive interference as the two side bands add vectorially (Christina, Ka-Lun, Nirmalathas, Novak, & Waterhouse, 2008; Smith, Novak, & Ahmed, 1997). As shown in Figure 6 (b), the fiber dispersion results a periodic power fading of the recovered mm-wave with fiber transmission. This fiber effect extremely limits the transmission distance in optical DSB scheme. For a mm-wave

at 60 GHz transmitted on an optical carrier at a wavelength 1550 nm, and fiber dispersion 17 ps/nm.km, there is a significant decrease in the signal power at 1 km fiber transmission compared to the 30 GHz at 4 km. However, a single side band (SSB) modulation scheme can also reduce the power fading effect. This can be achieved by filtering one of the sidebands (Capmany et al., 2005), or using a dual drive intensity modulator (Smith et al., 1997). Nevertheless, this increases the complexity and cost of IMDD and has lower receiver sensitivity than DSB due to the large dc power component at the optical carrier (Ma et al., 2007; Schmuck, 1995; Zhao, Ibrahim, Gunning, & Ellis, 2011).

Remote Heterodyne Receivers

A mm-wave signal can also be generated optically by using a remote heterodyne receiver as illustrated in Figure 7 where two phases correlated optical carriers are generated at the center station with a

Figure 7. Optical remote heterodyne to generate microwave signal using two optical waves

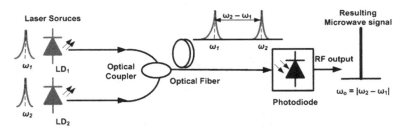

frequency offset equal to the desired frequency of the microwave or mm-wave signal, then they beat together at a high-speed photodetector.

If there is two optical fields from two independent lasers with angular frequencies ω_1 and ω_2, these can be written as follows (Gliese, Nielsen, Norskov, & Stubkjaer, 1998; Yao, Member, & Tutorial, 2009).

$$E_1 = E_{01} \cos\left(\omega_1 t + \varphi_1\right) \qquad (2)$$

$$E_2 = E_{02} \cos\left(\omega_2 t + \varphi_2\right) \qquad (3)$$

where E_{01}, E_{02} are the amplitude terms, and ϕ_1, ϕ_2 are the instantaneous phase terms of the two optical waves. When these fields are travelled through fiber and combined together at the photodetector with a limited bandwidth, a photocurrent that is generated at the output in the form of the fields square

$$
\begin{aligned}
I_{PD} &\alpha \left(E_1 + E_2\right)^2 \\
&= A \cos\left[\left(\omega_1 - \omega_2\right)t + \left(\varphi_1 - \varphi_2\right)\right] \\
&+ \; other\, terms
\end{aligned}
\qquad (4)
$$

where A is a constant which is determined by E_{01}, E_{02} and the responsivity of the photodetector. The first term is the only term of interest that shows that any frequency of the mm-wave can be generated by controlling the frequency difference between the two optical fields up to THz frequencies, limited

only by the bandwidth of the photodiode. The other terms are for higher frequency components, and can be neglected due to the limited bandwidth of the photodiode.

Using this technique can greatly reduce the bandwidth of the optical components required at the center station, and can also eliminate the power fading effect due to fiber transmission. However, the major problem in this technique is the phase noise in the generated mm-wave signal. If there are two optical carriers from two free running lasers they produce a mm-wave signal with high phase noise if they are not phase correlated. Therefore, it is necessary to either remove the actual laser signal phase noise or to correlate the phase noise of the two laser signals to generate a highly phase stable microwave or mm-wave signal. Several methods have been proposed to generate low phase noise microwave signals. The next subsections represent a number of common methods used in mm-wave generations and show recent reported examples. These mm-waves can be generated using multi-laser sources, external modulators, and optical comb generations.

Multi Laser Sources

The photonic generation of mm-waves can be obtained by using two optical carriers and can be classified into *optical injection locking* (OIL), *optical phase lock loop* (OPLL), *optical injection phase locking* (OIPL), and *integrated dual laser*. The OIL generates high quality microwave or mm-wave signal by injection locking of either two slave laser diodes (Goldberg, Taylor, Weller, & Bloom, 1983) or a multi-longitudinal mode slave laser (Goldberg, Yurek, Taylor, & Weller, 1985). In Figure 8 (a), the master laser is frequency modulated (FM) with an RF reference to generate optical sidebands spaced by the RF modulating frequency (f_m). The optical output of the master laser is injected into the two slave laser, and this is achieved by selecting the wavelengths of two slave lasers close to 2nd order sidebands as in Figure 8 (a) (Goldberg et al., 1983). This process produces two optical phase correlated carriers and would produce a low phase noise mm-wave signal determined by the reference RF source. A beat note at 35 GHz was generated by injection locking from a master laser modulated by an RF frequency of 5.846 GHz (Goldberg et al., 1985). However, this method needs a very precise temperature controller due to the small locking range (around few hundreds) for the slave lasers.

The OPLL works in the same manner as the electronic phase lock loop circuit. In Figure 8 (b), two free running optical waves spaced by the desired mm-wave frequency beat together at the photodiode and generate mm-wave signal at the output. The generated mm-wave is compared with an RF reference at the mixer and then filtered by low pass filter. The output voltage is then used to control the phase of the locked laser by changing the laser cavity length or the injection current. This method needs two narrow linewidth lasers, and a very short feedback loop. A microwave tuneable signal from 6- 34 GHz with a linewidth less than 1 MHz was obtained by using two Nd: YAG lasers (Williams, Goldberg, Esman, Dagenais, & Weller, 1989) and a package of OPLL system was produced with two semiconductor lasers capable of producing a microwave signal up to 14 GHz (Langley et al., 1999).

However, the OIPL is a combination of the OIL and OPLL as illustrated in Figure 8 (c). It produces a microwave signal with a lower phase

Figure 8. Schematic diagram of (a) OIL, (b) OPLL, and (c) OIPL

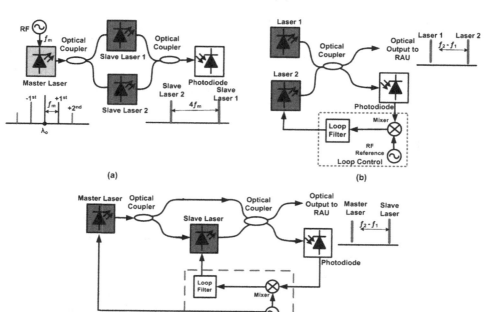

noise. The master laser is modulated with an RF signal to generate harmonic sidebands. One of the sidebands is then injected into the slave laser to phase locked it to the nth harmonic sideband of the master laser as in the OIL case. The generated microwave signal at the photodiode is phase locked as in the OPLL. This method does not require narrow linewidth lasers or narrow locking range compared to the other methods, however, it increases the complexity and the cost of the overall system (Walton, Bordonalli, & Seeds, 1998). The generation of a 36 GHz mm-wave was reported with a very narrow linewidth of a few kHz in (Johansson & Seeds, 2000) and a modulated 36 GHz mm-wave was also demonstrated with 140 Mbps data rate (Johansson & Seeds, 2001).

Another sophisticated approach is to use an integrated dual wavelength laser source where the optical modes are phase correlated because they are generated from the same laser cavity. At the output of the photodiode, the beat noise is cancelled. This method is a compact source for mm-wave generation. It does not need an optical injection or phase locking technique as in the other systems which greatly reduce the system cost and complexity. A 57 GHz mm-wave with a linewidth less than 10 Hz was reported using a dual multi-section semiconductor laser modulated with 6.3 GHz (Davies, Wake, & Lima, 1995; Wake, Lima, & Davies, 1995).

Microwave Generation using External Modulator

A high quality microwave signals can also be achieved by using the non-linearity of external modulators. Here the optical modulator is driven with an RF signal to produce sidebands spaced by same driving RF frequency and are phase correlated since they are generated from the same optical source. The use of external modulators has been widely used for generating frequency doubling and quadrupling of the RF sinusoidal drive signal. This can be achieved by controlling the bias of the Mach-Zehnder modulator (MZM). A frequency doubling is produced by biasing the MZM at the minimum transmission point to suppress the even order optical sidebands as illustrated in Figure 9 (a). This results two strong optical components centered at the optical carrier and separated by twice the RF drive frequency. At the photodetector, these components generate a frequency doubled of the RF driving signal with a linewidth dependent only on the driving signal purity. A quadrupled frequency signal can also be generated if the modulator is biased at the maximum transmission point of the transfer function to suppress the odd order optical sidebands shown in Figure 9 (b). The frequency doubler was first proposed by O'Reilly et al. in 1992 to generate a 36 GHz by driving the MZM modulator with an 18 GHz microwave signal (J. J. O'Reilly, Lane, Heidemann, & Hofstetter, 1992) and this was employed for video services by (J. O'Reilly & Lane, 1994). A frequency quadrupler was also achieved by applying 15 GHz to MZM for generating 60 GHz mm-wave (Lane & O'Reilly, 1994). However, to ensure a clean spectrum at the output of a photodetector, a Mach-Zehnder filter was used to select the two second order sidebands and suppress the unwanted optical spectral components. Another approach was used to generate a continuously tunable mm-wave signal based on external modulation using a MZM and a wavelength fixed optical filter which is used as a notch filter to remove the optical carrier as shown in Figure 9 (b) (Seregelyi, Paquet, & Belisle, 2005). In this approach, a 32-50 GHz mm-wave signal with low phase noise was generated when the electrical drive signal was tuned from 8-12.5 GHz. Both frequency doubling and quadrupling systems can produce a high quality mm-wave. However, these systems are based on biasing the MZM at the minimum or maximum transmission point to suppress the odd or even order optical sidebands, which would suffer from bias drifting, leading to poor system robustness. This can only be reduced by employing a complex bias control circuit.

Figure 9. Schematic diagram for generating a continuously tunable microwave signal based on external modulation and notch optical filter

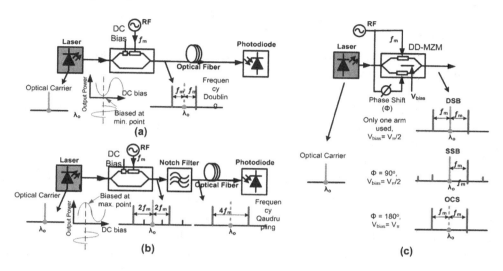

A dual drive MZM (DD-MZM) has also been used to generate mm-waves at the required RF frequency (Yi & Su, 2006). This modulator is comprised of two phase modulators in both arms and can be driven independently as shown in Figure 9 (c) (Cartledge, 1995; Seimetz, 2009). The output optical field (E_{out}) can be expressed as

$$E_{out}\left(t\right) = \frac{E_o}{2}\left(e^{j\varphi_1(t)} + e^{j\varphi_2(t)}\right) \qquad (5)$$

$$\varphi_1\left(V\left(t\right)\right) = \pi\,\frac{V_1\left(t\right)}{V_\pi}, \;\; \varphi_2\left(V\left(t\right)\right) = \pi\,\frac{V_2\left(t\right)}{V_\pi}$$

where $\varphi_1(t)$ and $\varphi_2(t)$ are the phase shift induced in both arms by the applied voltage. By controlling the bias voltage and the relative phase shift of the clocks between the two arms, this can produce an optical mm-wave with the DSB, SSB or OCS spectra. To generate DSB scheme, only one arm is driven by an RF clock and the dc bias voltage is at the quadrature point ($V_\pi/2$). While for SSB, the modulator is driven via the two arms by the two RF signals with equal amplitudes, biased

at ($V_\pi/2$) and 90° phase shift. The OCS spectral can be generated by dc biasing at V_π, and the two arm is driven with complementary phase (180°). As explained in the previous section, the DSB shows a periodic power fading in the signal power. However, the SSB and OCS optical mm-waves do not suffer from the fading effect but they only degraded by the time shift caused by different transmission velocities of the sidebands. The OCS optical mm-wave shows a superior performance to the optical SSB because it needs a lower frequency clock (Ma et al., 2007).

Optical Frequency Comb Generation (OFCG)

This method has gained much attention in the area of mm-wave generation as a low cost alternative to expensive broad bandwidth devices, flattened optical light tones, and easy to be tuned for the desired mm-wave frequency. The optical frequency comb means the generation of multiple optical tones equally spaced in frequency domain and phase correlated to each other. There are many techniques for generating optical comb have been reported in literature. This can be classified into multicarrier single optical source, two cascaded external modulators, and recirculating frequency shifting. Multicarrier single optical source such as mode locked laser (MLL), and gain switched laser (GSL) are based on generating very short periodic pulses in time domain and consequently equally spaced optical tones in the spectral domain. They are widely used sources for optical frequency comb generation, and have large number of optical applications such as clock extraction, optical time division multiplexing packet switching, and mm-wave signal generation. Gain switching method is realized in any laser diode structure that has no external cavity or sophisticated fabrication technologies. The gain switching method is simply achieved by biasing the laser diode below the threshold and driving it with an electrical comb generator or a large electrical sinusoidal signal at sub-gigahertz or gigahertz frequency as shown in Figure 10 (a). The idea of gain switching is to excite the first spike of relaxation oscillation by turning on the laser diode and terminate it before the onset of the second optical spike. When the

laser diode is biased below the threshold the photon density is negligible and the electron density is below the lasing threshold density. By applying a large sinusoidal signal, the carrier density increases above threshold until it reaches peak inversion density. At the same time, the photon density also increases slowly to such a level that stimulated emission begins to consume injected carriers significantly at the peak inversion point, and suppresses any further increase in carrier density. The laser produces a stream of optical pulses within picoseconds pulse widths with a repetition frequency of f_0, and the spectrum has a comb of multiple optical phase correlated tones equally spaced by driving frequency f_0. If two optical tones separated are filtered out, this generates a high stability mm-wave signal at the desired frequency when detected by using high speed photo-detector.

A passive MLL was used to generate 39.9 GHz tone in (van Dijk, Enard, Buet, Lelarge, & Duan, 2008) and 60 GHz in (Stöhr et al., 2010), and an active MLL is employed for generation

Figure 10. Schematic diagrams for (a) GSL mechanism, (b) two cascaded ex-modulators, and (c) recirculating frequency shifting

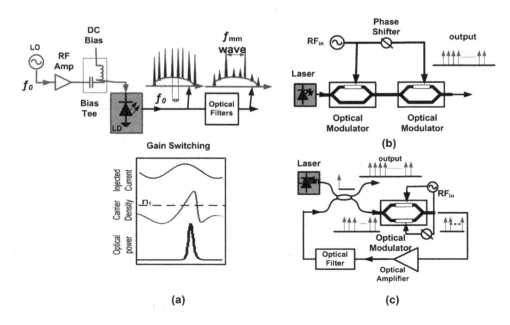

of 37.1GHz (Novak, Ahmed, Waterhouse, & Tucker, 1995). In RoF downlink transmission, the output of the MLL can be directly or externally modulated. Direct modulation of MLL has been used for generating 54.8 GHz with 3.03 Gbps by (Huchard et al., 2008; Khawaja & Cryan, 2010). However, a passive MLL externally modulated was demonstrated with 5 Gbps using EAM (Stöhr et al., 2010) and with a 3Gbps using MZM in (Ohno, Nakajima, Furuta, & Ito, 2005).

For GSL, The generation of 60 GHz by using gain switching technique was achieved at 3 Gbps OOK data and transmitted over 60 km fiber and 3 m free space. The direct modulation and external modulation was demonstrated, however the external modulation shows a superior performance in terms stability and less noise (H. Shams, Anandarajah, Perry, & Barry, 2010; Haymen Shams, Anandarajah, Perry, & Barry, 2010). Moreover, all optical up conversion to 60 GHz mm-wave was experimentally achieved by using an external injected gain switched laser with OOK at 2.5 Gbps (H. Shams, Perry, Anandarajah, & Barry, 2011; Haymen Shams, Perry, Anandarajah, & Barry, 2011). Another method for OFCG using two cascaded modulators shown in Figure 10(b). These cascaded optical modulators were also used to generate higher frequency microwave signal with a driving both with same sinusoidal signal. This approach can be performed by biasing the two MZMs at a combination of minimum and maximum transmission point or phase modulators (Dou, Zhang, & Yao, 2012; Zhang et al., 2013). Different methods have been proposed for this purpose to generate 60 GHz. A frequency sextuple optical mm-wave was demonstrated by using double cascaded MZM and 10 GHz driving RF signal for generating 60 GHz with 10 Gbps NRZ data (Chang, Ye, Gao, & Su, 2008). Recirculating frequency shifting technique is based on recirculating the output of the MZM as shown in Figure 10 (c). The loop consists of a laser, optical coupler, a double MZM, an optical amplifier, and optical filter. The optical signal is continuous injected in the loop and shifted by the applied RF signal. After many round trips the number of optical carriers is increased and limited by the filter bandwidth. The existence of the optical amplifier is to compensate the losses in the optical loop. A 100- and 300-GHz RoF and radio signal transmission for 10 Gbaud (20Gbps) QPSK using a coherent RoF technique was demonstrated by using an optical frequency shifter in an amplified optical loop set at a transmitter (Kanno et al., 2013), and 30Gbps QPSK was also achieved at 300 GHz by (Kanno et al., 2012).

RECENT ROF ACTIVITIES AT 60 GHZ FOR HIGHER BITRATES

The diversity of photonic generation methods for mm-wave shown in the previous section and advancing in opto-electronic devices inspired the researchers for the possibility of achieving higher bitrate transmission at 60 GHz using multilevel modulation formats. Figure 11 illustrates the recent activities for generating 60 GHz over the last 3 years. A 12.5 Gbps OOK at 60 GHz was realized using cascaded MZM for optical mm-wave generation and a coherent wireless receiver. Higher modulation format such as orthogonal frequency division multiplexing (OFDM) QPSK signal has been demonstrated by Huchard et.al for 3.03 Gbps at 60 GHz using direct modulation of mode locked Fabry Perot laser at 54.8 GHz pulses and transmitted it over 50 m fiber plus 5 m of air. In 2009, 27 Gbps photonic wireless 60 GHz 16-QAM OFDM was also achieved in the lab over 2.5 m using cascaded MZM. (A. Stohr, MWP 2009).

Optical generation for higher lever modulation formats such as quadrature amplitude modulation (QAM) and OFDM is now possible after the existence of the IQ modulator. IQ modulator consists of the dual arm MZMs with phase shift on one of the arm. It was used to achieve 28 Gbps 16QAM within 7 GHz and transmitted it over 100 km over SMF without dispersion compensation (LEOS

Figure 11. Recent activities at 60 GHz RoF

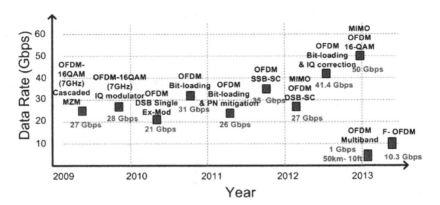

conference 2009). Ng'oma et al. experimental demonstrated 21 Gbps OFDM wireless signal using single drive MZM and optical frequency multiplication (A. Ng'oma OFC2010). Optical generation of high bitrates at 60 GHz was also realized over 30 Gbps within 7GHz bandwidth available based on OFDM.

There were also some works to compensate for the RoF impairments such as uneven frequency response was corrected by using bit loading (Levin- Campello) in OFDM modulation format and different data format (8, 16, 64 QAM) less than <5 km and wireless transmission over 3 m (A. Ng'oma et. al OFC 2011). A 26 Gbps OFDM signal wireless data after 100 km fiber transmission was also demonstrated by using PN mitigation and bit loading algorithm caused by walk off between optical carrier and optical OFDM signal (C.T. Lin, Optics express, 2011, and PTL, 2012). Single side band suppressed carrier modulation (SSB-SC) technique was used for 35 Gbps data rate with using matched filters and Hilbert transform (C.T. Lin, Tropical Meeting on Microwave photonics, 2011). The I/Q imbalance correction and bit loading algorithm were also used to increase the bitrate to 41.4 Gbps with 10 m wireless and compensate the degradation caused by frequency dependent amplitude and phase imbalance between in-phase and quadrature phase conversion (OFC 2012).

Multiple input multiple output OFDM (MIMO-OFDM), which deploys multiple antennas on both transmitter and the receiver, was proposed for 60 GHz RoF system to improve data rate (increase spectral efficiency) and the system reliability through spatial diversity. 2x2 MIMO OFDM employed with DSB-SC to produce 27Gbps, and 50 Gbps OFDM 16-QAM. (C.T. Lin, A. Ng'oma optics Express, 2012 and OFC 2012). Generation and transmission of multiband and multi-gigabit 60 GHz wireless over 50 km fiber and 10 ft wireless transmission was achieved at 1 Gbps at each band. (Optics Express 2013). Fast–OFDM, another multicarrier modulation format that can be achieved higher spectral efficiency compared to the conventional OFDM, has also been used for the first time at 60 GHz for 10.3 Gbps in RoF by (Haymen Shams & Zhao, 2013).

FUTURE RESEARCH DIRECTIONS

The emigration from lower frequency band to higher frequency has become necessary to increase the wireless speed due to the large available bandwidth. THz band has now shown an interest in academic and industry researches. It covers the range form 0.1-10 THz and can support wireless transmission for data rates above 10 Gbps (Kürner,

2012; Rouvalis, Renaud, Moodie, Robertson, & Seeds, 2010). However, the propagation loss is relatively high for the frequency range > 100 GHz compared to the microwave frequency bands due to the high absorption of H_2O and other atmospheric gas molecules. Three possible valleys in THz band can be acceptable to use for indoor wireless applications, where the attenuation is considered a minimum at these bands; W-band (75-100GHz), D-band (110-150 GHz), and G-band (220-270GHz). Wireless communication at THz system enables a wide variety of high speed promising applications and wireless extensions of broadband access fiber. THz pico-cells can be used as a part of the cellular network to provide high capacity in hot spots, and supplies high speed wireless links for kiosk application that requires fast content transfer of the kiosk server in shop or malls to mobile devices. In addition, the upcoming new generation of HDTV, known as Ultra HDTV (UHD-TV) needs 16 times higher resolution compared to the HDTV. However, THz frequency band is still largely unregulated. The interest group for THz (IGTHz) for IEEE 802.15 WPAN was initially established in 2008 to investigate the possibility of indoor/outdoor wireless communication at the THz range between 275-300 GHz (IEEE802.15, 2013).

The recent advanced in photonic techniques and opto-electronic devices enabled the possibility for photonic THz generation compared to the electronic devices in terms of their wide frequency bandwidth, tunability, and system performance and stability. In addition, the use of the optical links has great advantage for THz signal distribution with low losses. The generation of THz waves based on electronic devices is still considered a very challenge method at these high frequencies. The electronic generation of THz is obtained by using frequency multipliers that can provide milliwatts of THz power and several gigahertz bandwidths. However, most of the photonic methods are based on optical heterodyne receiver where two optical carriers spaced by the desired RF frequency beat together at the photodiode. There

are many papers in literature for THz waves on RoF systems. In 2003, an optical mm-wave generation at 120 GHz modulated with 3 Gbps was achieved by using MLLs or optical time division multiplexing (OTDM) pulses, while 10 Gbps was demonstrated over 2 km using incorporates both photonic and electronic technologies (Kosugi et al., 2003; Kukutsu et al., 2008). Moreover, wireless transmission of 8 Gbps OOK at 250 GHz carrier frequency over 0.5 m distance was demonstrated in (Song et al., 2009).

Advanced modulation formats have also applied to THz links in order to achieve higher spectral efficiency. Wireless transmission of optical generated 20 Gbps at 100 GHz was also proposed in (Kanno et al., 2011), and 16 Gbps QPSK at 100 GHz in wireless over fiber links using coherent detection in (Sambaraju et al., 2010). Even 100Gbps (25Gbaud QPSK) and 108 Gbps (12.5Gbaud 16QAM) hybrid fiber wireless transmission system at 100 GHz have also been demonstrated by using dual polarization division multiplexing and multiple-input multiple output wireless links (Li et al., 2012; Zibar et al., 2011). Moreover, an optical heterodyne IQ optical transmitter and IQ –MMIC at the receiver were used for 100 Gbps data transmission over 20 m at 237.5 GHz (Koenig et al., 2013).

Another interesting short range wireless broadband is an indoor optical wireless communication (OWC) that offers high unregulated spectrum in the infrared (IR) region (1550 nm wavelength). This technology is also becoming an attractive alternative medium to the RF channels, because of the ease implementation, no RF interference, and cheap optoelectronic devices. In addition, the privacy of the cells based network is preserved due to the incapability of the optical channel to pass through walls allowing the reuse of the same wavelength channels in different rooms of an office building. Furthermore, a wavelength division multiplexing (WDM) implemented on optical wireless system combines a number of independent data channels on a single optical beam thus providing a potential increase of bandwidth and data rates compared to that offered in RF channels. However, this system suffers from the high pass loss, dispersion, and receiver noise. In addition, there is also a limitation on average transmitted optical power due to the power consumption limits and the eye safety regulations. The laser light output is modulated and transmitted in a free space to the optical receiver. 10 Gbps data rate has been demonstrated in a simulated atmospheric environment, and using advanced modulation formats such as optical OFDM. Coherence detection and MIMO processing has been used to demonstrate a 100 Gbps per channel link. However, the IR free space communication suffers from transceiver misalignment, atmospheric turbulence, and humidity fluctuation. Moreover, the receiver sensitivity is lower compared to the THz receiver resulted for the ambient IR light noise, and the eye safety issue with IR wavelength set restriction in the IR transmitted power.

Both research areas in THz and IR free space communication are very attractive and show perspective solutions for future increase demand of the wireless broadband communications. However, there are still many challenges in both systems. These have to be resolved in order to obtain a complete reliable system for providing high speed wireless system.

CONCLUSION

This chapter presents a fiber based solution for indoor short range wireless mm-waves at 60 GHz. The wireless transmission at 60 GHz shows a huge interest due to the available bandwidth and capability for unlicensed use for high speed wireless applications. Regulation and characterization of 60 GHz has been shown for many organizations over the world. In order to extend this wireless signal and produce a low cost system, many photonics methods have been introduced to show the possibility to generate it. The introduction to RoF technology was demonstrated, in addition,

to its basic characterization and operation of the required optical components. The complexity and cost of the system were classified based on the transmitter configurations depending on the hardware components and cost. This shows that centralization of system complexity and simplification of RAUs can help to reduce installation and maintenance costs especially in large scale coverage areas (i.e. picocell networks) compared to the conventional distributed radio. System impairments such as noise, distortion, and fiber dispersion degrade the signal-to-noise ratio and limit the system transmission lengths. However, these impairments can be reduced with careful managing of the optical system. Overall, it can be seen that RoF systems have a very important role in radio signal distribution for cellular networks, and high speed applications in wireless personal networks. In the future trend, THz, and optical wireless systems (IR) are another short range wireless communication systems for providing a fast wireless speed for the future increase in the data loading applications.

REFERENCES

Agrawal, G. P. (2010). *Fiber-optic communication systems* (4th ed.). New York: John Wiley & Sons. doi:10.1002/9780470918524

Agrawal, G. P., & Dutta, N. K. (1986). *Long-wavelength semiconductor lasers*. Van Nostrand Reinhold. doi:10.1007/978-94-011-6994-3

Bach, L., Kaiser, W., Reithmaier, J. P., Forchel, A., Berg, T. W., & Tromborg, B. (2003). Enhanced direct-modulated bandwidth of 37 GHz by a multi-section laser with a coupled-cavity-injection-grating design. *Electronics Letters*, *39*(22), 1592. doi:10.1049/el:20031018

BNetzA. (2008). Allgemeinzuteilungen für punkt-zu-punkt rictfunk im frequenzbereich 217/2008, 59-64 GHz. *Bundesnetzagentur, Mitteilungenungen*.

Capmany, J., Ortega, B., Martinez, A., Pastor, D., Popov, M., & Fonjallaz, P. Y. (2005). Multiwavelength single sideband modulation for WDM radio-over-fiber systems using a fiber grating array tandem device. *IEEE Photonics Technology Letters*, *17*(2), 471–473. doi:10.1109/LPT.2004.840017

Cartledge, J. C. (1995). Performance of 10 Gb/s lightwave systems based on lithium niobate Mach-Zehnder modulators with asymmetric Y-branch waveguides. *IEEE Photonics Technology Letters*, *7*(9), 1090–1092. doi:10.1109/68.414712

Chang, Q., Ye, T., Gao, J., & Su, Y. (2008). *Generation of 60-GHz optical millimeter-wave and 20-GHz channel-spaced optical multicarrier using two cascaded 10-GHz modulators (pp. SaJ1)*. Optical Society of America. Retrieved from http://www.opticsinfobase.org/abstract.cfm?URI=AOE-2008-SaJ1

Christina, L., Ka-Lun, L., Nirmalathas, A., Novak, D., & Waterhouse, R. (2008). Impact of chromatic dispersion on 60 GHz radio-over-fiber transmission. In *Proceedings of IEEE Lasers and Electro-Optics Society*, (pp. 89–90). IEEE. doi:10.1109/leos.2008.4688502

Chrostowski, L., Zhao, X., Chang-Hasnain, C. J., Shau, R., Ortsiefer, M., & Amann, M. C. (2005). 50 GHz directly-modulated injection-locked 1.55 /spl mu/m VCSELs. In *Proceedings of OFC/NFOEC Technical Digest: Optical Fiber Communication Conference, 2005* (Vol. 4). IEEE. doi:10.1109/OFC.2005.192971

Davies, P. A., & Urey, Z. (1992). *Subcarrier multiplexing in optical communication networks*. Academic Press.

Davies, P. A., Wake, D., & Lima, C. R. (1995). Compact optical millimetre-wave source using a dual-mode semiconductor laser. *Electronics Letters*, *31*(5), 364–366. doi:10.1049/el:19950237

Dou, Y., Zhang, H., & Yao, M. (2012). Generation of flat optical-frequency comb using cascaded intensity and phase modulators. *IEEE Photonics Technology Letters*, *24*(9), 727–729. doi:10.1109/LPT.2012.2187330

ECC. (2012). *ECC report 176*. ECC.

Esman, R. D., & Williams, K. J. (1995). Wideband efficiency improvement of fiber optic systems by carrier subtraction. *IEEE Photonics Technology Letters*, *7*(2), 218–220. doi:10.1109/68.345928

Federal Communications Commissions. (2012). 15.255 operation within the: Vol. 57. *64 GHz* (pp. 851–853). Author.

Gliese, U., Nielsen, T. N., Norskov, S., & Stubkjaer, K. E. (1998). Multifunctional fiber-optic microwave links based on remote heterodyne detection. *IEEE Transactions on Microwave Theory and Techniques*, *46*(5), 458–468. doi:10.1109/22.668642

Gliese, U., Norskov, S., & Nielsen, T. N. (1996). Chromatic dispersion in fiber-optic microwave and millimeter-wave links. *IEEE Transactions on Microwave Theory and Techniques*, *44*(10), 1716–1724. doi:10.1109/22.538964

Goldberg, L., Taylor, H. F., Weller, J. F., & Bloom, D. M. (1983). Microwave signal generation with injection-locked laser diodes. *Electronics Letters*, *19*(13), 491. doi:10.1049/el:19830333

Goldberg, L., Yurek, A. M., Taylor, H. F., & Weller, J. F. (1985). 35 GHz microwave signal generation with an injection-locked laser diode. *Electronics Letters*, *21*(18), 814. doi:10.1049/el:19850574

Goutain, E., Renaud, J. C., Krakowski, M., Rondi, D., Blondeau, R., & Decoster, D. (1996). 30 GHz bandwidth, 1.55 micro sign]m MQW-DFB laser diode based on a new modulation scheme. *Electronics Letters*, *32*(10), 896. doi:10.1049/el:19960588

Hassin, D., & Vahldieck, R. (1993). Feedforward linearization of analog modulated laser diodes-theoretical analysis and experimental verification. *IEEE Transactions on Microwave Theory and Techniques*, *41*(12), 2376–2382. doi:10.1109/22.260731

Huchard, M., Chanclou, P., Charbonnier, B., van Dijk, F., Duan, G.-H., & Gonzalez, C. … Stohr, A. (2008). 60 GHz radio signal up-conversion and transport using a directly modulated mode-locked laser. In *Proceedings of 2008 International Topical Meeting on Microwave Photonics Jointly Held with the 2008 Asia-Pacific Microwave Photonics Conference* (pp. 333–335). IEEE. doi:10.1109/MWP.2008.4666705

IDate Consulting and Reserach. (2013). *Telecoms, internet, media*. Retrieved from http://www.idate.org/en/Research/FTTx-Watch-Service/World-FTTx-Markets_57_.html

IEEE802. 15. (2013). *THz interest group*. Retrieved from http://www.ieee802.org/15/pub/IGthz.html

Jianjun, Y., Gee-Kung, C., Zhensheng, J., Chowdhury, A., Ming-Fang, H., & Hung-Chang, C. et al. (2010). Cost-effective optical millimeter technologies and field demonstrations for very high throughput wireless-over-fiber access systems. *Journal of Lightwave Technology*, *28*(16), 2376–2397. doi:10.1109/JLT.2010.2041748

Johansson, L. A., & Seeds, A. J. (2000). Millimeter-wave modulated optical signal generation with high spectral purity and wide-locking bandwidth using a fiber-integrated optical injection phase-lock loop. *IEEE Photonics Technology Letters*, *12*(6), 690–692. doi:10.1109/68.849086

Johansson, L. A., & Seeds, A. J. (2001). 36-GHz 140-Mb/s radio-over-fiber transmission using an optical injection phase-lock loop source. *IEEE Photonics Technology Letters*, *13*(8), 893–895. doi:10.1109/68.935839

Kanno, A., Inagaki, K., Morohashi, I., Sakamoto, T., Kuri, T., & Hosako, I. et al. (2011). 20-Gb/s QPSK W-band (75-110GHz) wireless link in free space using radio-over-fiber technique. *IEICE Electronics Express*, *8*(8), 612–617. doi:10.1587/elex.8.612

Kanno, A., Kuri, T., Hosako, I., Kawanishi, T., Yasumura, Y., Yoshida, Y., & Kitayama, K. (2013). 100-GHz and 300-GHz coherent radio-over-fiber transmission using optical frequency comb source. In B. B. Dingel, R. Jain, & K. Tsukamoto (Eds.), *Broadband access communication technologies VII* (Vol. 8645, p. 864503–864503, 7). doi:10.1117/12.1000150

Kanno, A., Morohashi, I., Kuri, T., Hosako, I., Kawanishi, T., & Yasumura, Y. … Kitayama, K. (2012). 16-Gbaud QPSK radio transmission using optical frequency comb with recirculating frequency shifter for 300-GHz RoF signal. In *Proceedings of 2012 IEEE International Topical Meeting on Microwave Photonics* (pp. 298–301). IEEE. doi:10.1109/MWP.2012.6474117

KCC. (2006). *Frequency allocation comment on 60 GHz band*. Korea Communications Commission.

Keiser, G. (2000). *Optical fiber communications* (3rd ed.). New York: McGraw-Hill.

Khawaja, B. A., & Cryan, M. J. (2010). Wireless hybrid mode locked lasers for next generation radio-over-fiber systems. *Journal of Lightwave Technology*, *28*(16), 2268–2276. doi:10.1109/JLT.2010.2050461

Kingston, R. H. (1979). Electroabsorption in GaInAsP. *Applied Physics Letters*, *34*(11), 744. doi:10.1063/1.90657

Koenig, S., Boes, F., Antes, J., Henneberger, R., Schmogrow, R., Hillerkuss, D., & Palmer, R. (2013). 100 Gbit / s wireless link with mm-wave photonics, *1*(IL), 22–24.

Kolner, B. H., & Dolfi, D. W. (1987). Intermodulation distortion and compression in an integrated electrooptic modulator. *Applied Optics*, *26*(17), 3676–3680. doi:10.1364/AO.26.003676 PMID:20490122

Kosugi, T., Shibata, T., Enoki, T., Muraguchi, M., Hirata, A., Nagatsuma, T., & Kyuragi, H. (2003). *A 120GHz millimeter wave MMIC chipset for future broadband wireless access applications*. Academic Press.

Kukutsu, N., Hirata, A., Kosugi, T., Takahashi, H., Yamaguchi, R., Nagatsuma, T., & Kado, Y. (2008). 10-Gbit/s wireless link using 120-GHz-band MMIC technologies. In *Proceedings of 2008 33rd International Conference on Infrared, Millimeter and Terahertz Waves*. doi:10.1109/ICIMW.2008.4665692

Kürner, T. (2012). Towards future THz communications systems. *Terahertz Science and Technology*, *5*(1), 11–17.

Lane, P. M., & O'Reilly, J. J. (1994). Fibre-supported optical generation and delivery of 60 GHz signals. *Electronics Letters*, *30*(16), 1329–1330. doi:10.1049/el:19940850

Langley, L. N., Elkin, M. D., Edge, C., Wale, M. J., Gliese, U., Huang, X., & Seeds, A. J. (1999). Packaged semiconductor laser optical phase-locked loop (OPLL) for photonic generation, processing and transmission of microwave signals. *IEEE Transactions on Microwave Theory and Techniques*, *47*(7), 1257–1264. doi:10.1109/22.775465

Lau, E. K., & Wu, M. C. (2006). Ultra-high, 72 GHz resonance frequency and 44 GHz bandwidth of injection-locked 1.55-/spl mu/m DFB lasers. In *Proceedings of 2006 Optical Fiber Communication Conference and the National Fiber Optic Engineers Conference*. IEEE. doi:10.1109/OFC.2006.215716

Lee, C. H. (2007). *Microwave photonic*. Academic Press.

Li, X., Dong, Z., Yu, J., Chi, N., Shao, Y., & Chang, G. K. (2012). Fiber-wireless transmission system of 108 Gb / s data over 80 km fiber and 2 × 2 wireless links at 100 GHz W-band frequency. *Optics Letters*, *37*(24), 5106–5108. doi:10.1364/OL.37.005106 PMID:23258020

Lim, C., Nirmalathas, A., Bakaul, M., Gamage, P., Novak, D., & Waterhouse, R. (2010). Fiber-wireless networks and subsystem technologies. *Journal of Lightwave Technology*, *28*(4), 390–405. doi:10.1109/JLT.2009.2031423

Ma, J., Yu, J., Yu, C., Xin, X., Zeng, J., & Chen, L. (2007). Fiber dispersion influence on transmission of the optical millimeter-waves generated using LN-MZM intensity modulation. *Journal of Lightwave Technology*, *25*(11), 3244–3256. doi:10.1109/JLT.2007.907794

Management, S., & Specification, R. S. (2010). *Licence-exempt radio apparatus (all frequency bands)*. Category I Equipment.

Mathai, S., Cappelluti, F., Jung, T., Novak, D., Waterhouse, R. B., & Sivco, D. et al. (2001). Experimental demonstration of a balanced electroabsorption modulated microwave photonic link. *IEEE Transactions on Microwave Theory and Techniques*, *49*(10), 1956–1961. doi:10.1109/22.954814

Media, A. C. (2011). *Radiocommunications (low interference potential devices) class licence 2000* (Vol. 2011). Author.

MPHPT. (2000). *Specified low power radio station (12) 59-66 GHz band*. Regulation for the Enforcement of the Radio Law 6-4-2.

Novak, D., Ahmed, Z., Waterhouse, R. B., & Tucker, R. S. (1995). Signal generation using pulsed semiconductor lasers for application in millimeter-wave wireless links. *IEEE Transactions on Microwave Theory and Techniques*, *43*(9), 2257–2262. doi:10.1109/22.414573

O'Reilly, J., & Lane, P. (1994). Remote delivery of video services using mm-waves and optics. *Journal of Lightwave Technology, 12*(2), 369–375. doi:10.1109/50.350584

O'Reilly, J. J., Lane, P. M., Heidemann, R., & Hofstetter, R. (1992). *Optical generation of very narrow linewidth millimetre wave signals.* doi:10.1049/el:19921486

Ohno, T., Nakajima, F., Furuta, T., & Ito, H. (2005). A 240-GHz active mode-locked laser diode for ultra-broadband fiber-radio transmission systems. In *Proceedings of OFC/NFOEC Technical Digest: Optical Fiber Communication Conference,* (Vol. 6). IEEE. doi:10.1109/OFC.2005.193191

Palais, J. C. (2004). *Fiber optic communications* (5th ed.). Upper Saddle River, NJ: Prentice Hall.

Roselli, L., Borgioni, V., Zepparelli, F., Ambrosi, F., Comez, M., Faccin, P., & Casini, A. (2003). Analog laser predistortion for multiservice radio-over-fiber systems. *Journal of Lightwave Technology, 21*(5), 1211–1223. doi:10.1109/JLT.2003.810931

Rouvalis, E., Renaud, C. C., Moodie, D. G., Robertson, M. J., & Seeds, A. J. (2010). Traveling-wave uni-traveling carrier photodiodes for continuous wave THz generation. *Optics Express, 18*(11), 11105–11110. doi:10.1364/OE.18.011105 PMID:20588968

Sambaraju, R., Zibar, D., Caballero, A., Monroy, I. T., Alemany, R., & Herrera, J. (2010). 100-GHz wireless-over-fiber links with up to 16-Gb/s QPSK modulation using optical heterodyne generation and digital coherent detection. *Photonics Technology Letters, 22*(22), 1650–1652.

Schmuck, H. (1995). *Comparison of optical millimetre-wave system concepts with regard to chromatic dispersion.* Academic Press.

Seimetz, M. (2009). *High-order modulation for optical fiber transmission.* Berlin: Springer. doi:10.1007/978-3-540-93771-5

Senior, J. M. (2009). *Optical fiber communications.* Hoboken, NJ: Pearson Education.

Seregelyi, J., Paquet, S., & Belisle, C. (2005). Generation and distribution of a wide-band continuously tunable millimeter-wave signal with an optical external modulation technique. *IEEE Transactions on Microwave Theory and Techniques, 53*(10), 3090–3097. doi:10.1109/TMTT.2005.855123

Shams, H., Anandarajah, P. M., Perry, P., & Barry, L. (2010). Optical generation and wireless transmission of 60 GHz OOK signals using gain switched laser. In *Proceedings of Optical Fiber Communication Conference.* Washington, DC: OSA. doi:10.1364/OFC.2010.OThO7

Shams, H., Anandarajah, P. M., Perry, P., & Barry, L. P. (2010). Photonic generation and distribution of a modulated 60 GHz signal using a directly modulated gain switched laser. In *Proceedings of 21st Annual IEEE International Symposium on Personal, Indoor and Mobile Radio Communications* (pp. 1032–1037). IEEE. doi:10.1109/PIMRC.2010.5672089

Shams, H., Perry, P., Anandarajah, P. M., & Barry, L. (2011). Phase modulated optical millimeter wave generation based on externally injected gain switched laser. In *Proceedings of Optical Fiber Communication Conference/National Fiber Optic Engineers Conference 2011.* Washington, DC: OSA. doi:10.1364/OFC.2011.OWK7

Shams, H., Perry, P., Anandarajah, P. M., & Barry, L. P. (2011). Modulated millimeter-wave generation by external injection of a gain switched laser. *IEEE Photonics Technology Letters, 23*(7), 447–449. doi:10.1109/LPT.2011.2108277

Shams, H., & Zhao, J. (2013). First investigation of fast OFDM signals at 60GHz using direct laser modulation. In *Proceedings of CLEO/Europe-EQEC 2013*. Munich, Germany: CLEO.

Smith, G. H., Novak, D., & Ahmed, Z. (1997). Overcoming chromatic-dispersion effects in fiber-wireless systems incorporating external modulators. *IEEE Transactions on Microwave Theory and Techniques*, *45*(8), 1410–1415. doi:10.1109/22.618444

Song, H.-J., Ajito, K., Hirata, A., Wakatsuki, A., Furuta, T., Kukutsu, N., & Nagatsuma, T. (2009). Multi-gigabit wireless data transmission at over 200-GHz. In *Proceedings of 2009 34th International Conference on Infrared, Millimeter, and Terahertz Waves*. doi:10.1109/ICIMW.2009.5325768

Stephens, W., & Joseph, T. (1987). System characteristics of direct modulated and externally modulated RF fiber-optic links. *Journal of Lightwave Technology*, *5*(3), 380–387. doi:10.1109/JLT.1987.1075509

Stohr, A. (2010). Photonic millimeter-wave generation and its applications in high data rate wireless access. In Proceedings of Microwave Photonics (MWP), (pp. 7–10). IEEE. doi: doi:10.1109/mwp.2010.5664246

Stöhr, A., Member, S., Cannard, P., Charbonnier, B., van Dijk, F., & Fedderwitz, S. ... Weiß, M. (2010). Millimeter-wave photonic components for broadband wireless systems. Academic Press.

Van Dijk, F., Enard, A., Buet, X., Lelarge, F., & Duan, G.-H. (2008). Phase noise reduction of a quantum dash mode-locked laser in a millimeter-wave coupled opto-electronic oscillator. *Journal of Lightwave Technology*, *26*(15), 2789–2794. doi:10.1109/JLT.2008.927608

Wake, D., Lima, C. R., & Davies, P. A. (1995). Optical generation of millimeter-wave signals for fiber-radio systems using a dual-mode DFB semiconductor laser. *IEEE Transactions on Microwave Theory and Techniques*, *43*(9), 2270–2276. doi:10.1109/22.414575

Walton, C., Bordonalli, A. C., & Seeds, A. J. (1998). High-performance heterodyne optical injection phase-lock loop using wide linewidth semiconductor lasers. *IEEE Photonics Technology Letters*, *10*(3), 427–429. doi:10.1109/68.661432

Williams, K. J., Goldberg, L., Esman, R. D., Dagenais, M., & Weller, J. F. (1989). 6–34 GHz offset phase-locking of Nd:YAG 1319 nm nonplanar ring lasers. *Electronics Letters*, *25*(18), 1242. doi:10.1049/el:19890833

Williamson, R. C., Fellow, L., & Esman, R. D. (2008). Article. *RF Photonics*, *26*(9), 1145–1153.

Wilson, B., Darwazeh, I., & Ghassemlooy, F. (1995). *Analogue optical fibre communications*. Institution of Engineering and Technology. Retrieved from http://www.amazon.co.uk/Analogue-Optical-Fibre-Communications-Telecommunications/dp/0852968329

WirelessHD Consortium. (2013). Retrieved August 21, 2013, from http://www.wirelesshd.org/

Yaakob, S., Abdullah, W. R. W., Osman, M. N., Zamzuri, A. K., Mohamad, R., & Yahya, M. R. ... Rashid, H. A. A. (2006). Effect of laser bias current to the third order intermodulation in the radio over fibre system. In *Proceedings of 2006 International RF and Microwave Conference* (pp. 444–447). IEEE. doi:10.1109/RFM.2006.331123

Yao, J., Member, S., & Tutorial, I. (2009). Article. *Microwave Photonics*, *27*(3), 314–335.

Yi, L., & Su, Y. (2006). Optical millimeter-wave generation or up-conversion using external modulators. *IEEE Photonics Technology Letters, 18*(1), 265–267. doi:10.1109/LPT.2005.862006

Yu, P. K. L., & Wu, M. C. (2002). *RF photonic technology in optical fiber links* (W. S. C. Chang, Ed.). Cambridge, UK: Cambridge University Press.

Zhang, J., Yu, J., Chi, N., Dong, Z., Li, X., & Shao, Y. et al. (2013). Flattened comb generation using only phase modulators driven by fundamental frequency sinusoidal sources with small frequency offset. *Optics Letters, 38*(4), 552–554. doi:10.1364/OL.38.000552 PMID:23455133

Zhao, J., Ibrahim, S. K., Gunning, P., & Ellis, A. (2011). *Chromatic dispersion compensation using symmetric extension based guard interval in optical fast-OFDM*. Optical Society of America. doi:10.1364/ECOC.2011.We.8.A.3

Zibar, D., Caballero, A., Yu, X., Pang, X., Dogadaev, A. K., & Monroy, I. T. (2011). Hybrid optical fibre-wireless links at the 75–110 GHz band supporting 100 Gbps transmission capacities. In *Proceedings of 2011 International Topical Meeting on Microwave Photonics Jointly Held With the 2011 Asia-Pacific Microwave Photonics Conference*, (pp. 445–449). doi:10.1109/MWP.2011.6088767

ADDITIONAL READING

Agrawal, G. P. (2010). Fiber-Optic Communication Systems (4th Editio., p. 672). New York: John Wiley & Sons.

Agrawal, G. P., & Dutta, N. K. (1986). *Long-wavelength semiconductor lasers* (p. 473). Van Nostrand Reinhold. doi:10.1007/978-94-011-6994-3

Bach, L., Kaiser, W., Reithmaier, J. P., Forchel, A., Berg, T. W., & Tromborg, B. (2003). Enhanced direct-modulated bandwidth of 37 GHz by a multi-section laser with a coupled-cavity-injection-grating design. *Electronics Letters, 39*(22), 1592. doi:10.1049/el:20031018

BNetzA. (2008). [GHz. *Bundesnetzagentur, Mitteilungenungen.*]. *Allgemeinzuteilungen für Punkt-zu-Punkt Rictfunk im Frequenzbereich, 217/2008*, 59–64.

Capmany, J., Ortega, B., Martinez, A., Pastor, D., Popov, M., & Fonjallaz, P. Y. (2005). Multiwavelength single sideband modulation for WDM radio-over-fiber systems using a fiber grating array tandem device. *IEEE Photonics Technology Letters, 17*(2), 471–473. doi:10.1109/LPT.2004.840017

Cartledge, J. C. (1995). Performance of 10 Gb/s lightwave systems based on lithium niobate Mach-Zehnder modulators with asymmetric Y-branch waveguides. *IEEE Photonics Technology Letters, 7*(9), 1090–1092. doi:10.1109/68.414712

Chang, Q., Ye, T., Gao, J., & Su, Y. (2008). Generation of 60-GHz Optical Millimeter-Wave and 20-GHz Channel-Spaced Optical Multicarrier Using Two Cascaded 10-GHz Modulators (pp. SaJ1). Optical Society of America. Retrieved from http://www.opticsinfobase.org/abstract.cfm?URI=AOE-2008-SaJ1

Christina, L., Ka-Lun, L., Nirmalathas, A., Novak, D., & Waterhouse, R. (2008). Impact of chromatic dispersion on 60 GHz radio-over-fiber transmission. In *IEEE Lasers and Electro-Optics Society, 2008. LEOS 2008. 21st Annual Meeting of the* (pp. 89–90). doi:10.1109/leos.2008.4688502

Chrostowski, L., Zhao, X., Chang-Hasnain, C. J., Shau, R., Ortsiefer, M., & Amann, M. C. (2005). 50 GHz directly-modulated injection-locked 1.55 /spl mu/m VCSELs. In *OFC/NFOEC Technical Digest. Optical Fiber Communication Conference, 2005.* (Vol. 4, p. 3 pp. Vol. 4). IEEE. doi:10.1109/OFC.2005.192971

Davies, P. A., & Urey, Z. (1992). Subcarrier multiplexing in optical communication networks.

Davies, P. A., Wake, D., & Lima, C. R. (1995). Compact optical millimetre-wave source using a dual-mode semiconductor laser. *Electronics Letters*, *31*(5), 364–366. doi:10.1049/el:19950237

Dou, Y., Zhang, H., & Yao, M. (2012). Generation of Flat Optical-Frequency Comb Using Cascaded Intensity and Phase Modulators. *IEEE Photonics Technology Letters*, *24*(9), 727–729. doi:10.1109/LPT.2012.2187330

ECC. (2012). *ECC Report 176.*

Esman, R. D., & Williams, K. J. (1995). Wideband efficiency improvement of fiber optic systems by carrier subtraction. *IEEE Photonics Technology Letters*, *7*(2), 218–220. doi:10.1109/68.345928

Federal Communications Commissions. (2012). § 15.255 Operation within the band 57– 64 GHz (pp. 851–853).

Gliese, U., Nielsen, T. N., Norskov, S., & Stubkjaer, K. E. (1998). Multifunctional fiber-optic microwave links based on remote heterodyne detection. *IEEE Transactions on Microwave Theory and Techniques*, *46*(5), 458–468. doi:10.1109/22.668642

Gliese, U., Norskov, S., & Nielsen, T. N. (1996). Chromatic dispersion in fiber-optic microwave and millimeter-wave links. *IEEE Transactions on Microwave Theory and Techniques*, *44*(10), 1716–1724. doi:10.1109/22.538964

Goldberg, L., Taylor, H. F., Weller, J. F., & Bloom, D. M. (1983). Microwave signal generation with injection-locked laser diodes. *Electronics Letters*, *19*(13), 491. doi:10.1049/el:19830333

Goldberg, L., Yurek, A. M., Taylor, H. F., & Weller, J. F. (1985). 35 GHz microwave signal generation with an injection-locked laser diode. *Electronics Letters*, *21*(18), 814. doi:10.1049/el:19850574

Goutain, E., Renaud, J. C., Krakowski, M., Rondi, D., Blondeau, R., & Decoster, D. (1996). 30 GHz bandwidth, 1.55 [micro sign]m MQW-DFB laser diode based on a new modulation scheme. *Electronics Letters*, *32*(10), 896. doi:10.1049/el:19960588

Hassin, D., & Vahldieck, R. (1993). Feedforward linearization of analog modulated laser diodes-theoretical analysis and experimental verification. *IEEE Transactions on Microwave Theory and Techniques*, *41*(12), 2376–2382. doi:10.1109/22.260731

Huchard, M., Chanclou, P., Charbonnier, B., van Dijk, F., Duan, G.-H., & Gonzalez, C. … Stohr, A. (2008). 60 GHz radio signal up-conversion and transport using a directly modulated mode-locked laser. In *2008 International Topical Meeting on Microwave Photonics jointly held with the 2008 Asia-Pacific Microwave Photonics Conference* (pp. 333–335). IEEE. doi:10.1109/MWP.2008.4666705

IDate Consulting and Reserach. (2013). Telecoms, Internet, Media. Retrieved from http://www.idate.org/en/Research/FTTx-Watch-Service/World-FTTx-Markets_57_.html

IEEE802. 15. (2013). THz Interest Group. Retrieved from http://www.ieee802.org/15/pub/IGthz.html

Jianjun, Y., Gee-Kung, C., Zhensheng, J., Chowdhury, A., Ming-Fang, H., & Hung-Chang, C. et al. (2010). Cost-Effective Optical Millimeter Technologies and Field Demonstrations for Very High Throughput Wireless-Over-Fiber Access Systems. *Lightwave Technology. Journalism, 28*(16), 2376–2397. doi: doi:10.1109/jlt.2010.2041748

Johansson, L. A., & Seeds, A. J. (2000). Millimeter-wave modulated optical signal generation with high spectral purity and wide-locking bandwidth using a fiber-integrated optical injection phase-lock loop. *IEEE Photonics Technology Letters, 12*(6), 690–692. doi:10.1109/68.849086

Johansson, L. A., & Seeds, A. J. (2001). 36-GHz 140-Mb/s radio-over-fiber transmission using an optical injection phase-lock loop source. *IEEE Photonics Technology Letters, 13*(8), 893–895. doi:10.1109/68.935839

Kanno, A., Inagaki, K., Morohashi, I., Sakamoto, T., Kuri, T., & Hosako, I. et al. (2011). 20-Gb/s QPSK W-band (75-110GHz) wireless link in free space using radio-over-fiber technique. *IEICE Electronics Express, 8*(8), 612–617. doi:10.1587/elex.8.612

Kanno, A., Kuri, T., Hosako, I., Kawanishi, T., Yasumura, Y., Yoshida, Y., & Kitayama, K. (2013). 100-GHz and 300-GHz coherent radio-over-fiber transmission using optical frequency comb source. In B. B. Dingel, R. Jain, & K. Tsukamoto (Eds.), *Broadband Access Communication Technologies VII* (Vol. 8645, p. 864503–864503, 7). doi:10.1117/12.1000150

Kanno, A., Morohashi, I., Kuri, T., Hosako, I., Kawanishi, T., & Yasumura, Y. … Kitayama, K. (2012). 16-Gbaud QPSK radio transmission using optical frequency comb with recirculating frequency shifter for 300-GHz RoF signal. In *2012 IEEE International Topical Meeting on Microwave Photonics* (pp. 298–301). IEEE. doi:10.1109/MWP.2012.6474117

KCC. (2006). *Frequency Allocation Comment on 60 GHz band*. Korea Communications Commission.

Keiser, G. (2000). Optical fiber communications (3rd editio., p. 602). McGraw-Hill.

Khawaja, B. A., & Cryan, M. J. (2010). Wireless Hybrid Mode Locked Lasers for Next Generation Radio-Over-Fiber Systems. *Journal of Lightwave Technology, 28*(16), 2268–2276. doi:10.1109/JLT.2010.2050461

Kingston, R. H. (1979). Electroabsorption in GaInAsP. *Applied Physics Letters, 34*(11), 744. doi:10.1063/1.90657

Koenig, S., Boes, F., Antes, J., Henneberger, R., Schmogrow, R., Hillerkuss, D., & Palmer, R. (2013). 100 Gbit / s Wireless Link with mm-Wave Photonics, 1(IL), 22–24.

Kolner, B. H., & Dolfi, D. W. (1987). Intermodulation distortion and compression in an integrated electrooptic modulator. *Applied Optics, 26*(17), 3676–3680. doi:10.1364/AO.26.003676 PMID:20490122

Kosugi, T., Shibata, T., Enoki, T., Muraguchi, M., Hirata, A., Nagatsuma, T., & Kyuragi, H. (2003). A 120GHz Millimeter wave MMIC Chipset for Future Broadband Wireless Access Applications, 129–132.

Kukutsu, N., Hirata, A., Kosugi, T., Takahashi, H., Yamaguchi, R., Nagatsuma, T., & Kado, Y. (2008). 10-Gbit/s wireless link using 120-GHz-band MMIC technologies. *2008 33rd International Conference on Infrared, Millimeter and Terahertz Waves*, 1–2. doi:10.1109/ICIMW.2008.4665692

Kürner, T. (2012). Towards Future THz Communications Systems. *Terahertz Science and Technology, 5*(1), 11–17.

Lane, P. M., & O'Reilly, J. J. (1994). Fibre-supported optical generation and delivery of 60 GHz signals. *Electronics Letters*, *30*(16), 1329–1330. doi:10.1049/el:19940850

Langley, L. N., Elkin, M. D., Edge, C., Wale, M. J., Gliese, U., Huang, X., & Seeds, A. J. (1999). Packaged semiconductor laser optical phase-locked loop (OPLL) for photonic generation, processing and transmission of microwave signals. *IEEE Transactions on Microwave Theory and Techniques*, *47*(7), 1257–1264. doi:10.1109/22.775465

Lau, E. K., & Wu, M. C. (2006). Ultra-high, 72 GHz resonance frequency and 44 GHz bandwidth of injection-locked 1.55-/spl mu/m DFB lasers. In *2006 Optical Fiber Communication Conference and the National Fiber Optic Engineers Conference* (pp. 3 pp.). IEEE. doi:10.1109/OFC.2006.215716

Lee, C. H. (2007). *Microwave Photonic* (p. 440).

Li, X., Dong, Z., Yu, J., Chi, N., Shao, Y., & Chang, G. K. (2012). Fiber-wireless transmission system of 108 Gb / s data over 80 km fiber and 2 × 2 wireless links at 100 GHz W-band frequency. *Optics Letters*, *37*(24), 5106–5108. doi:10.1364/OL.37.005106 PMID:23258020

Lim, C., Nirmalathas, a., Bakaul, M., Gamage, P., Novak, D., & Waterhouse, R. (2010). Fiber-Wireless Networks and Subsystem Technologies. *Journal of Lightwave Technology*, *28*(4), 390–405. doi:10.1109/JLT.2009.2031423

Ma, J., Yu, J., Yu, C., Xin, X., Zeng, J., & Chen, L. (2007). Fiber Dispersion Influence on Transmission of the Optical Millimeter-Waves Generated Using LN-MZM Intensity Modulation. *Journal of Lightwave Technology*, *25*(11), 3244–3256. doi:10.1109/JLT.2007.907794

Management, S., & Specification, R. S. (2010). *Licence-exempt Radio Apparatus (All Frequency Bands)*. Category I Equipment.

Mathai, S., Cappelluti, F., Jung, T., Novak, D., Waterhouse, R. B., & Sivco, D. et al. (2001). Experimental demonstration of a balanced electroabsorption modulated microwave photonic link. *IEEE Transactions on Microwave Theory and Techniques*, *49*(10), 1956–1961. doi:10.1109/22.954814

Media, A. C. and. (2011). *Radiocommunications (Low Interference Potential Devices) Class Licence 2000* (Vol. 2011).

MPHPT. (2000). Specified Low Power Radio Station (12) 59-66 GHz band. *in Regulation for the Enforcement of the Radio Law 6-4-2*.

Novak, D., Ahmed, Z., Waterhouse, R. B., & Tucker, R. S. (1995). Signal generation using pulsed semiconductor lasers for application in millimeter-wave wireless links. *IEEE Transactions on Microwave Theory and Techniques*, *43*(9), 2257–2262. doi:10.1109/22.414573

O'Reilly, J., & Lane, P. (1994). Remote delivery of video services using mm-waves and optics. *Journal of Lightwave Technology*, *12*(2), 369–375. doi:10.1109/50.350584

O'Reilly, J. J., Lane, P. M., Heidemann, R., & Hofstetter, R. (1992). Optical generation of very narrow linewidth millimetre wave signals. doi:10.1049/el:19921486

Ohno, T., Nakajima, F., Furuta, T., & Ito, H. (2005). A 240-GHz active mode-locked laser diode for ultra-broadband fiber-radio transmission systems. In *OFC/NFOEC Technical Digest. Optical Fiber Communication Conference, 2005.* (Vol. 6, p. 3 pp. Vol. 5). IEEE. doi:10.1109/OFC.2005.193191

Palais, J. C. (2004). *Fiber Optic Communications* (5th ed., p. 456). Prentice Hall.

Roselli, L., Borgioni, V., Zepparelli, F., Ambrosi, F., Comez, M., Faccin, P., & Casini, A. (2003). Analog laser predistortion for multiservice radio-over-fiber systems. *Journal of Lightwave Technology*, *21*(5), 1211–1223. doi:10.1109/JLT.2003.810931

Rouvalis, E., Renaud, C. C., Moodie, D. G., Robertson, M. J., & Seeds, A. J. (2010). Traveling-wave Uni-Traveling Carrier Photodiodes for continuous wave THz generation. *Optics Express*, *18*(11), 11105–11110. Retrieved from http://www.opticsexpress.org/abstract.cfm?URI=oe-18-11-11105 doi:10.1364/OE.18.011105 PMID:20588968

Sambaraju, R., Zibar, D., Caballero, A., Monroy, I. T., Alemany, R., & Herrera, J. (2010). 100-GHz Wireless-Over-Fiber Links With Up to 16-Gb/s QPSK Modulation Using Optical Heterodyne Generation and Digital Coherent Detection, *22*(22), 1650–1652.

Schmuck, H. (1995). Comparison of optical millimetre-wave system concepts with regard to chromatic dispersion.

Seimetz, M. (2009). *High-Order Modulation for Optical Fiber Transmission* (p. 251). Springer. doi:10.1007/978-3-540-93771-5

Senior, J. M. (2009). Optical Fiber Communications, 3/E (pp. 1128). Jersy: Pearson Education.

Seregelyi, J., Paquet, S., & Belisle, C. (2005). Generation and distribution of a wide-band continuously tunable millimeter-wave signal with an optical external modulation technique. *IEEE Transactions on Microwave Theory and Techniques*, *53*(10), 3090–3097. doi:10.1109/TMTT.2005.855123

Shams, H. Anandarajah, P. M., Perry, P., & Barry, L. (2010). Optical Generation and Wireless Transmission of 60 GHz OOK Signals Using Gain Switched Laser. In *Optical Fiber Communication Conference* (pp. OThO7). Washington, D.C.: OSA. doi:10.1364/OFC.2010.OThO7

Shams, H. Perry, P., Anandarajah, P. M., & Barry, L. (2011). Phase Modulated Optical Millimeter Wave Generation Based on Externally Injected Gain Switched Laser. In *Optical Fiber Communication Conference/National Fiber Optic Engineers Conference 2011* (pp. OWK7). Washington, D.C.: OSA. doi:10.1364/OFC.2011.OWK7

Shams, Haymen, & Zhao, J. (2013). First Investigation of Fast OFDM Signals at 60GHz using Direct Laser Modulation. In *CLEO/Europe-EQEC 2013*. Munich.

Shams, H., Anandarajah, P. M., Perry, P., & Barry, L. P. (2010). Photonic generation and distribution of a modulated 60 GHz signal using a directly modulated gain switched laser. In *21st Annual IEEE International Symposium on Personal, Indoor and Mobile Radio Communications* (pp. 1032–1037). IEEE. doi:10.1109/PIMRC.2010.5672089

Shams, H., Perry, P., Anandarajah, P. M., & Barry, L. P. (2011). Modulated Millimeter-Wave Generation by External Injection of a Gain Switched Laser. *IEEE Photonics Technology Letters*, *23*(7), 447–449. doi:10.1109/LPT.2011.2108277

Smith, G. H., Novak, D., & Ahmed, Z. (1997). Overcoming chromatic-dispersion effects in fiber-wireless systems incorporating external modulators. *IEEE Transactions on Microwave Theory and Techniques*, *45*(8), 1410–1415. doi:10.1109/22.618444

Song, H.-J., & Ajito, K. Hirata, a., Wakatsuki, a., Furuta, T., Kukutsu, N., & Nagatsuma, T. (2009). Multi-gigabit wireless data transmission at over 200-GHz. *2009 34th International Conference on Infrared, Millimeter, and Terahertz Waves*, 1–2. doi:10.1109/ICIMW.2009.5325768

Stephens, W., & Joseph, T. (1987). System characteristics of direct modulated and externally modulated RF fiber-optic links. *Journal of Lightwave Technology*, *5*(3), 380–387. doi:10.1109/JLT.1987.1075509

Stohr, A. (2010). Photonic millimeter-wave generation and its applications in high data rate wireless access. In *Microwave Photonics (MWP), 2010 IEEE Topical Meeting on* (pp. 7–10). doi:10.1109/mwp.2010.5664246

Stöhr, A., Member, S., Cannard, P., Charbonnier, B., Van Dijk, F., & Fedderwitz, S. (2010). *Weiß, M.* Millimeter-Wave Photonic Components for Broadband Wireless Systems.

Van Dijk, F., Enard, A., Buet, X., Lelarge, F., & Duan, G.-H. (2008). Phase Noise Reduction of a Quantum Dash Mode-Locked Laser in a Millimeter-Wave Coupled Opto-Electronic Oscillator. *Journal of Lightwave Technology*, *26*(15), 2789–2794. Retrieved from http://jlt.osa.org/abstract.cfm?URI=jlt-26-15-2789 doi:10.1109/JLT.2008.927608

Wake, D., Lima, C. R., & Davies, P. A. (1995). Optical generation of millimeter-wave signals for fiber-radio systems using a dual-mode DFB semiconductor laser. *IEEE Transactions on Microwave Theory and Techniques*, *43*(9), 2270–2276. doi:10.1109/22.414575

Walton, C., Bordonalli, A. C., & Seeds, A. J. (1998). High-performance heterodyne optical injection phase-lock loop using wide linewidth semiconductor lasers. *IEEE Photonics Technology Letters*, *10*(3), 427–429. doi:10.1109/68.661432

Williams, K. J., Goldberg, L., Esman, R. D., Dagenais, M., & Weller, J. F. (1989). 6–34 GHz offset phase-locking of Nd:YAG 1319 nm nonplanar ring lasers. *Electronics Letters*, *25*(18), 1242. doi:10.1049/el:19890833

Williamson, R. C., Fellow, L., & Esman, R. D. (2008).. *RF Photonics*, *26*(9), 1145–1153.

Wilson, B. etc., Darwazeh, I., & Ghassemlooy, F. (1995). *Analogue Optical Fibre Communications* (pp. 338). Institution of Engineering and Technology. Retrieved from http://www.amazon.co.uk/Analogue-Optical-Fibre-Communications-Telecommunications/dp/0852968329

Wireless, H. D. Consortium. (2013). Retrieved August 21, 2013, from http://www.wirelesshd.org/

Yaakob, S., Abdullah, W. R. W., Osman, M. N., Zamzuri, A. K., Mohamad, R., & Yahya, M. R. … Rashid, H. A. A. (2006). Effect of Laser Bias Current to the Third Order Intermodulation in the Radio over Fibre System. In 2006 International RF and Microwave Conference (pp. 444–447). IEEE. doi: doi:10.1109/RFM.2006.331123

Yao, J., Member, S., & Tutorial, I. (2009).. *Microwave Photonics*, *27*(3), 314–335.

Yi, L., & Su, Y. (2006). Optical millimeter-wave generation or up-conversion using external modulators. *IEEE Photonics Technology Letters*, *18*(1), 265–267. doi:10.1109/LPT.2005.862006

Yu, P. K. L., & Wu, M. C. (2002). *RF Photonic Technology in Optical Fiber Links* (W. S. C. Chang, Ed.). Cambridge: Cambridge University Press.

Zhang, J., Yu, J., Chi, N., Dong, Z., Li, X., & Shao, Y. … Tao, L. (2013). Flattened comb generation using only phase modulators driven by fundamental frequency sinusoidal sources with small frequency offset. *Optics letters*, *38*(4), 552–4. Retrieved from http://www.ncbi.nlm.nih.gov/pubmed/23455133

Zhao, J., Ibrahim, S. K., Gunning, P., & Ellis, A. (2011). *Chromatic Dispersion Compensation Using Symmetric Extension based Guard Interval in Optical Fast-OFDM (pp. We.8.A.3).* Optical Society of America.

Zibar, D., Caballero, A., Yu, X., Pang, X., Dogadaev, A. K., & Monroy, I. T. (2011). Hybrid optical fibre-wireless links at the 75–110 GHz band supporting 100 Gbps transmission capacities. *2011 International Topical Meeting on Microwave Photonics jointly held with the 2011 Asia-Pacific Microwave Photonics Conference*, 445–449. doi:10.1109/MWP.2011.6088767

KEY TERMS AND DEFINITIONS

Fiber to the Home: This term used for broadband network connection to the home using optical fiber cables.

Microwave Photonics: A term refers to the combination between the radiofrequency and optoelectronics.

Optical Fiber Communication: A method of communication for transmitting information from one place to another by using light.

Optical Millimeter Waves: This refers to the method of optical generation and distribution of millimeter waves.

Optical Up Conversion: refers to the optical up conversion for the baseband and IF signal using optical methods.

Optical Wireless Communication: A method of communication using an optical fiber and free space air for optical signal transmission.

Radio Frequency Photonics: This is the same term used to describe microwave photonics; however, this includes any radio frequency processed by photonic methods.

Radio Over Fiber: A term for a technology uses the light source to transmit radio signals over an optical fiber.

RF Photonics: A term used to refer for RF and optoelectronic technologies.

THz Communication Systems: A future wireless channel that can provide high speed communication.

Chapter 12
Broadband NG-PON Networks and Their Designing Using the HPON Network Configurator

Rastislav Róka
FEI STU Bratislava, Slovakia

ABSTRACT

With the emerging applications and needs of ever increasing bandwidth, it is anticipated that the Next-Generation Passive Optical Network (NG-PON) with much higher bandwidth is a natural path forward to satisfy these demands and for network operators to develop valuable access networks. NG-PON systems present optical access infrastructures to support various applications of many service providers. Therefore, some general requirements for NG-PON networks are characterized and specified. Hybrid Passive Optical Networks (HPON) present a necessary phase of the future transition between PON classes with TDM or WDM multiplexing techniques utilized on the optical transmission medium – the optical fiber. Therefore, some specific requirements for HPON networks are characterized and presented. For developing hybrid passive optical networks, there exist various architectures and directions. They are also specified with emphasis on their basic characteristics and distinctions. Finally, the HPON network configurator as the interactive software tool is introduced in this chapter. Its main aim is helping users, professional workers, network operators and system analysts to design, configure, analyze, and compare various variations of possible hybrid passive optical networks. Some of the executed analysis is presented in detail.

INTRODUCTION

Demands for modernizing advanced applications and new multimedia broadband Internet services to both residential and business customers imply that the broadband access network will be faced with the challenge of transmitting an increasing volume of dynamic data-centric traffic with higher bit rates (up to a few Gbit/s). Although a huge capital cost were invested in creating of metallic (homogeneous lines or coaxial cables) or wireless infrastructures together with signal transmitting technologies, market demands for very broadband transmission paths are still expanding. At the

DOI: 10.4018/978-1-4666-5978-0.ch012

same time, wireless communication networks represent a rapidly growing market whereby new standards enable higher capacity, reliability and a larger number of supported users. Metallic access solutions (Digital Subscriber Lines, Power Line Communications or Hybrid Fiber-Coax) as well as emerging Worldwide Interoperability for Microwave Access and Long Term Evolution wireless technologies are realizable with severe limitations in both network reach and offered bandwidth per user. Such constraints can be indisputably solved by the necessity of Fiber-To-The-x architectures.

Common key advantages of FTTx architectures are a reliable and safety transmission medium (the optical fiber), a reachability of remote communities compared with other access technologies, a flexibility of signal transmission rates up to Gbit/s directly to particular residences, a scalability of system components, a utilization of passive optical components only, a local power supply and a low energy consumption, a possibility for implementations of various WDM technologies (Čuchran & Róka, 2006). As can be seen, a broad mix of services for full-filling of customer requirements is provided by diverse topologies and infrastructures in the access network. However, there exist three extensive problems – a low throughput, a service variety and a traffic irregularity. Therefore, current solutions do not seem to adequately address the stringent requirements identified regarding next generation passive optical access networks. Thus,

the convergence of optical, metallic and wireless networks (Figure 1) is also a crucial requirement which will enable boosting network penetration and correspondingly justify operational expenditures and capital expenditures for the broadband access network.

One of the prominent technologies for offering the FTTH architecture is the passive optical network (PON). Architectures of optical access networks must be simple – from a viewpoint of service provisioning for subscribers. It means that passive architectures with no switching and control elements in the optical distribution network (ODN) are preferable against active ones. Moreover, optical network terminals (ONT) on the subscriber side must be simple, cheap and high reliable. These conditions separate out utilization of sophisticated optical lasers and other complex optical components in common ONT equipment. Optical ONT components must be also able working in the environment without any temperature control. The optical line terminal (OLT) on the central office side can be more sophisticated because it is located in the temperature controlled environment and costs are amortized between several connected end subscribers.

Emerging applications of advanced end users can be associated with increasing bandwidth demands. Except technological improvements of mobile broadband and broadcast technologies, it is avoidable to consider a reliable support in access

Figure 1. Connectivity options for the next generation passive optical access network architecture

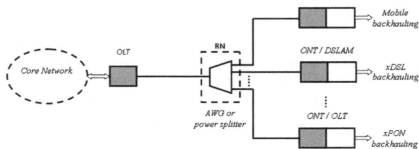

networks by appropriate modern and advanced technologies utilizing the fixed transmission medium, above all optical fibers. Optical access networks designed for those applications are called passive optical networks (PON) because only passive optical power splitters are located in the remote node (RN). Their main advantages are high reliability, simple maintenance and no need of external power supplies. Moreover, present optical infrastructure is transparent to bit rates and modulation formats of optical information signals. Complete passive optical access networks can be upgraded without substantial changes of its fundamental infrastructure. Also, the WDM technology with separated wavelengths assigned to particular subscribers can be implemented into passive optical networks and, by this way, various specific broadband and multimedia services can be provisioned to each end subscriber (Čuchran & Róka, 2006).

The PON network is in its substance a bi-directional point-to-multipoint system that contains passive (optical fibers, passive optical splitters, couplers, connectors) optical elements in a distribution part of the access network and active (the OLT terminal, multiple ONT terminals) optical elements placed in end terminating points of the access network. The downstream data signal is created by the optical OLT transmitter in the central office. Passive optical couplers located between end terminating points distribute this optical signal from one input to various output optical fibers that deliver the same optical data signal to all end subscribers. The optical ONT receiver on the subscriber side selects from received optical signals just data routed to the appropriate ONT terminal and ignores data addressed to other subscribers. The upstream traffic is transmitted by the same optical fiber as the downstream traffic. Because all optical signals are directed back to the one optical OLT receiver in the central office, stand-alone different timeslots are adequate allocated using the TDMA protocol (or DBA algorithms) for each subscriber terminal, so these upstream optical signals from different ONT terminal don't interfere mutually in the common optical fiber. The key advantage of this PON approach is locating only passive optical components in the optical distribution network. Optical transmitters and receivers are located inside buildings; other active optical components are not utilized in the outside plant. By this way, total network costs for installing, operating and maintenance of optical network equipment are markedly decreased.

Current standardized PON networks based on the Time-Division Multiple Access (TDMA) have evolved as an access solution to provide simplicity and low operational cost. The most effective utilization of the optical transmission medium can be attained using more wavelengths per one fiber by means of WDM technologies. Moreover, scaling up TDMA-PON networks to several tens of gigabits per second of the aggregate capacity is extremely challenging due to the complexity of optical components and burst mode receivers at such high data rates. Therefore, WDM-PON networks are increasingly considered to deliver ultra-high-speed services by enabling service providers to offer a dedicated wavelength straight to a home or business with limitations in terms of scalability and bandwidth granularity.

From a viewpoint of the architecture, we can classify passive optical networks into following classes with basic characteristics (Ramaswami & Sivarajan, 2001):

- **All-Fiber Passive Optical Network (AFPON):** The simplest PON architecture utilizes a standalone optical fiber from a central office to each subscriber. From a viewpoint of the logical topology, a standalone optical fiber is used for connecting each ONU terminal. From a viewpoint of the physical topology, all optical fibers can be located in the ring configuration. Total network costs for its building and creating present a main problem of this approach.

- **Time Division Multiplexing-Passive Optical Network (TDM-PON):** In this simple and wide-spread PON architecture (Figure 2), the downstream traffic is transmitting from the optical OLT transmitter to all optical ONT receivers through a passive optical power splitter. This architecture is broadcasting; however, switching services can be also supported by allocating specific time slots to individual ONT terminals based on their requests for transmission bandwidths. At the upstream traffic, subscriber terminals share a common transmission channel created by using a passive coupler. For this aim, a fixed time-division multiple access protocol or appropriate dynamic bandwidth algorithms must be utilized. This architecture allows sharing of CO equipment by all end subscribers and utilizing cheap optical components. A number of supported ONT terminals is limited above all by splitting losses in the passive optical power splitter.
- **Wavelength Division Multiplexing-Passive Optical Network (WDM-PON):** In this advanced PON architecture, a simple optical OLT transmitter is replaced by a field of WDM transmitters or by one tunable laser source. This approach allows utilizing subscriber terminals working on specified wavelengths with corresponding electronic equipment on specified receiving rates, not on maximum transmission rates of the passive optical network. However, a limitation given by splitting losses in the passive optical power splitter is still present.
- **Wavelength Routing-Passive Optical Network (WR-PON):** This superior PON architecture introduces a wavelength routing that solves splitting losses problem and simultaneously supports other WDM-PON advantages. In the remote node, passive splitters are replaced by AWG elements. Moreover, this approach allows provisioning point-to-point services to ONT subscriber ONT terminals.

The next-generation PON (NG-PON) with much higher bandwidth is a natural path forward to satisfy demands of ever increasing bandwidth. Many network operators are motivated to further develop a valuable optical access network and to leverage such NG-PON systems as a common access infrastructure to support broader market segments.

The NG-PON technology must be able to protect the investment of legacy passive optical networks. There are several migration scenarios to meet disparate service provider`s needs. Two of

Figure 2. The general PON network architecture

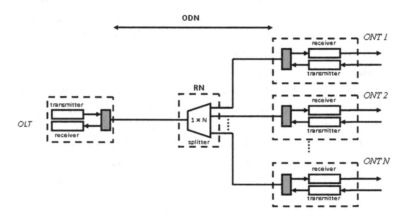

them – service-oriented and service-independent scenarios – reflect recognition that differing service introduction strategies might affect requirements for the NG-PON specifications.

NG-PON technologies can be divided into two categories. The NG-PON1 presents an evolutionary growth with supporting the coexistence with the GPON on the same ODN. The coexistence feature enables seamless upgrade of individual customers on active optical fibers without disrupting services of other customers. The NG-PON2 presents a revolutionary change with no requirement in terms of coexistence with the GPON on the same ODN (Kani et al., 2009; Effenberger et. al., 2009). From another view, there are several possible architectures that could meet the NG-PON requirements. The 10GPON system is referred to as the XG-PON, where the Roman numeral X signifies 10 Gbit/s transmission speed, and we can expect its various versions – the XG-PON1, the XG-PON2, the extended reach and wavelength controlled XG-PON, the hybrid DWDM/XG-PON (Effenberger et. al., 2009; Tanaka, 2010).

At present days, two basic development trends of WDM systems are boosted. The first approach is the dense wavelength division multiplexing (DWDM) that can have conventional spectral spacing of 25 GHz, 50 GHz or 100 GHz (corresponding to 0,2 nm, 0,4 nm or 0,8 nm at wavelengths around the 1,5 µm). The second approach is the coarse wavelength division multiplexing (CWDM) that promises all the key characteristics of network architectures (transparency, scalability and low cost), especially for building metro/access networks (Róka, 2003). The metro/access network does not require the same bandwidth and distance requirements as the long-haul network. The challenge for metro/access networks is in distributing the capacity delivered by the long-haul network core and in aggregating from the network edge back to the long-haul core. Multiple topologies have been proposed to provide solutions to this challenge (Róka & Khan, 2011; Róka, 2012).

Now, we can shortly present basic steps of a consistent transition from the existing TDM-PON network to the WDM-PON network:

- In the first step, a change of the central office equipment is executed. Specifically, a coupler is adding to combine the original OLT TDM-PON system equipment and the new OLT WDM-PON system equipment into the one-fiber transmission.
- In the second step, appropriate changes in ONU equipment are executed, specifically with adding new ONT WDM-PON equipment assigned to specific wavelengths for ONU transceivers. These new ONT WDM-PON terminal can be connected only to the new AWG element, not to a common power splitter. Also, a coupler must be added into the remote node to combine the original 1:N power splitter and the new AWG element with 32 specific wavelength outputs into the one-fiber transmission.
- In the final status, only new WDM-PON system with appropriate OLT and ONT equipment and the AWG element is working. All old TDM-PON system parts in the outside plan are removed, including old OLT TDM-PON equipment, power splitters and old ONT TDM-PON equipment.

For a reason of comparison, we can present basic steps of a consistent transition from the existing TDM-PON network to the hybrid passive optical network:

- In the first step, a coupler is adding to combine the original OLT TDM-PON system and the new OLT TDM/WDM-PON system into the one-fiber transmission. The OLT TDM/WDM-PON equipment is connected to the coupler through dedicated outputs of the common power splitter.

- In the second step, new ONT TDM/WDM-PON equipment is adding and connected to outputs of the original 1:N power splitter.
- In the final status, new hybrid TDM/WDM-PON system with appropriate OLT and ONT equipment and the OLT power splitter is working. Only the old OLT TDM-PON equipment is exchanged, power splitters in the outside plan and old ONT TDM-PON can be re-used without changes.

In this chapter, we focus on a design of a transition stage between TDM-PON and WDM-PON networks. A main reason for this motivation is that at first a number of operating TDM-PON networks is even now high and still rising and at second a utilization of installed optical infrastructures is maximized for transmission capacity's increasing. On the other side, a creating the hybrid HPON network can be used as the upgrade of old networks in many cases with a utilization of relevant parts of the original infrastructure with minimum financial costs. It's a question whether only a consistent transition from the TDM-PON to the HPON network is requested or further to the full-value WDM-PON network is suitable. Therefore, it is important to identify a right time for creating and building of the full-value WDM-PON network. For this purpose, the HPON network configurator as an interactive software tool can be used.

REQUIREMENTS FOR NG-PON NETWORKS

The largest requirement for NG-PON networks is its coexistence with the operational GPON on the same ODN infrastructure. This presents a challenge due to multiplexing new systems with old ones. For this purpose, we can use both WDM and/or TDM techniques. Each of these methods will have different requirements for the wavelength plan (Effenberger et. al., 2009):

- **The WDM in both Directions:** The simplest scheme is created by using wavelengths to separate NG-PON1 signals from GPON signals. This system requires GPON ONU terminals to be equipped with a wavelength blocking filter, so that additional NG-PON1 wavelengths are ignored. If the existing OLT equipment is expected for a smooth migration, the wavelength branching filter must be placed between the ODN and the existing GPON OLT.
- **The WDM Downstream, The TDMA Upstream:** The upstream channel spectrum of the NG-PON1 may need to be shared with the previous PON system using the TDMA channel sharing. In this scheme, the existing GPON OLT would be replaced with the OLT that supports both the GPON and NG-PON1 systems. The NG-PON1 OLT would be installed between the ODN and the existing GPON OLT and would perform two additional functions – amplifying the upstream signal and mimicking GPON ONU terminals connected to the GPON OLT and thereby requesting and obtaining upstream timeslots to allocate NG-PON1 ONU terminals connected to it.
- **The TDM Downstream, The TDMA Upstream:** It is possible to construct different information signals that are sufficiently orthogonal, where same wavelengths can be used to transmit both signals. In this approach, the bit-stacked signal is generated by two differential optical sources at the OLT. The relative optical modulation depth of signals is adjusted in the ratio of about 30%. This offers very simple upgrade opportunities for legacy GPONs by simply adding a second optical source. This upgrade can be accomplished by either replacing the GPON OLT by a new hybrid GPON/NG-PON OLT or by combining optical data streams by employing an additional separate combiner box.

In present days, PON networks with the TDM multiplexing technique are creating in many countries, including also Slovakia (Róka, 2008). In the near future, we can expect NG-PON technologies with different motivations for developing of HPON networks:

1. Creating the new PON network overcoming TDM-PON network possibilities with minimum financial costs. In this case, various optical resources are utilized, but it isn't the full-value WDM-PON network, and the TDM approach is still utilized from various reasons. This HPON network is not very expensive created (in a comparison with the WDM-PON network) and provides a sufficient transmission capacity for customer needs in a long-time horizon.

This variation can be included in the NG-PON1 category, where the WDM filter is installed to combine and separate G-PON and XG-PON1 signals into and out of the common ODN infrastructure. The ODN, i.e. optical fibers and the remote node, is not replaced or changed during the migration to the NG-PON1 network (Kani et. al., 2009).

2. Preparing the transition from the TDM-PON to the WDM-PON network with minimum costs for rebuilding of the existing TDM-PON infrastructure. Such HPON network should satisfy following features:
   a. A backward compatibility with the original TDM-PON architecture and a coexistence of TDM and WDM approaches,
   b. A maximum exploitation of the existing optical infrastructure, optical fibers and optical equipment,
   c. New bonus functions for the network protection and fast traffic restoration in a case of failures.

This variation can be included in the NG-PON2 category, where separate optical fibers and power splitters may be used. Also, a different device replacing the simple power splitter may be used (Kani et. al., 2009). In a case of the extended reach and wavelength controlled NG-PON version, the basic feature is a more controlled ONU wavelength. If we use a wavelength-controlled ONU, then the bandwidth of optical amplifiers can be reduced to about 0,5 nm and this reduction allows a sensitivity to be improved by many dB. By this way, a wavelength-controlled ONU also opens possibility for WDM-based multiplexing upgrades in a future. In a case of the hybrid DWDM/XG-PON network, multiple NG-PON are combined with using a DWDM MUX/DEMUX and a colorless technology for the ONU equipment. Key components for the new system are colorless transmitters (the seed light injected reflective semiconductor optical amplifiers and tunable laser diodes) and WDM filters (Effenberger et. al., 2009).

REQUIREMENTS FOR THE HPON NETWORK

Features of the HPON Network

The passive optical network HPON is a hybrid in a way that utilizes both TDM and WDM multiplexing principles together on a physical layer. The HPON network utilizes similar or soft revised topologies as TDM-PON architectures. For downstream and upstream transmissions, TDM and WDM approaches are properly combined, i.e. it is possible to utilize the time-division or wavelength-division multiplexing of transmission channels in the common passive optical architecture.

The first HPON network design is based on principles of the evolutionary architecture from the TDM-PON network utilizing few WDM components (Figure 3). A basic architecture of the optical distribution network that distributes

Figure 3. The general WDM/TDM-PON network architecture

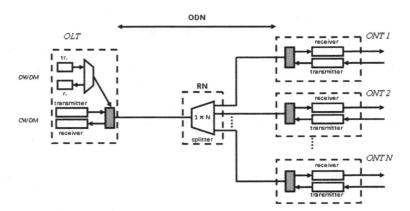

signals to users consists of the one-fiber topology and several topological links connected to the optical network terminals through the remote node. Logically, a connection of the point-to-point type is created between the optical line terminal and the remote node. The remote node consists of either a passive optical power splitter (TDM-PON) or an arrayed waveguide grating (WDM-PON). As resources of optical radiations, two different types of tunable lasers based on dense or coarse wavelength multiplexing for various wavelength areas can be utilized in order to decrease a number of necessary optical sources. A number of OLT tunable lasers is smaller than a number of transmission channels utilized in a network; therefore various subscribers can dynamically share tunable lasers. Of course, there are other possible HPON architectures that can be also included in the HPON network simulator.

Except the original WDM/TDM-PON network, we can propose other variations of hybrid passive optical networks. In the second design, besides utilizing few WDM components in the original TDM PON infrastructure, changes of the network topology can be considered with modifications of WDM techniques' utilizing in both transmission directions (SUCCESS). In this case, there exists a backward compatibility with previous TDM PON networks, however, an exchange of TDM ONU equipment is necessary. In the third design, an integration of metropolitan and access networks is included into utilizing WDM technologies (SARDANA). In this case, a combination of the WDM distribution network ring with add/drop nodes and TDM access subnetwork trees seems to be very profitable for the implementation.

Hybrid Networks for a Smooth Transition

Hybrid networks for a smooth transition from TDM-PON to WDM-PON networks allow a possibility for simultaneous provisioning of both TDM and WDM services. However, new WDM subscribers can be added by exchanging TDM ONU equipment. Configuration changes are controlled from the OLT and no other interventions are necessary on the original TDM subscribers' side. There can be considered three various architectures:

- The self-renewable HPON with a tree topology (Ahsan et. al., 2009),
- The HPON with a video overlay (Lee et. al., 2009),
- The SUCCESS HPON (An et. al., 2005).

Comparison of WDM/TDM-PON and SUCCESS HPON Networks

The WDM/TDM-PON network represents a hybrid network based on the combined WDM/TDM approach (Banerjee et. al., 2005; Kazovsky et. al., 2007; Lee et. al., 2010). The SUCCESS HPON network introduces a sequential transition to the pure WDM PON network in a compliance with the TDM and WDM technology coexistence (An et. al., 2005; Banerjee et. al., 2005; Kazovsky et. al., 2007). A number of WDM subscribers in the SUCCESS HPON is limited by a number of available wavelengths (max. 150 without TDM nodes). This number can be increased by wavelengths and the AWG port sharing as in a case of the WDM/TDM-PON network up to quadruple at the maintenance of acceptable attenuation values.

In Table 1, output values from the HPON simulation model for few selected configurations are presented. As we can see, until the 1:8 splitting ratio, the total attenuation in the WDM/TDM-PON is lower or equal to the original TDM-PON. In addition, a number of subscribers is much higher. In the SUCCESS HPON, the attenuation for TDM nodes is higher at 4 network nodes. For a comparable number of subscribers, the attenuation in the SUCCESS HPON is around 10 dB above the value in the WDM/TDM-PON. In the first place, it is due to utilizing of CWDM wavelength with higher attenuation values.

Due to a summary of simulation results and hybrid network comparison (Róka, 2010; Róka, 2011), we can see that both HPON network designs overcome actual TDM-PON network possibilities. Because the SUCCESS HPON has a high attenuation of TDM nodes, it is not possible to realize this network without modifications. For improvement of power relationships, it is necessary to utilize fewer nodes with CWDM wavelengths in the lower attenuation band, ADM multiplexors with the lower attenuation, the lower splitting ratio in TDM nodes. Another possibility is an exploitation of optical amplifiers, however, with increasing of noise levels and other nonlinear effects. By contrast, the WDM/TDM-PON is balanced and utilizes a more easily concept that is identical in the entire network. Average capacities per subscribers can be very high (in the order of Gbit/s). From a total standpoint, the WDM/TDM-PON is

Table 1. The WDM/TDM-PON and SUCCESS HPON comparison

The TDM-PON with the 1:32 Splitting Ratio/ Subscribers	The WDM/TDM-PON (AWG Ports/ Splitting Ratio/subsCribers)	The TDM Node Attenuation [dB]
2 / 64	32 / 1:4 / 128	19.5
4 / 128	32 / 1:8 / 256	23.0
6 / 192	48 / 1:8 / 384	23.0
8 / 256	32 / 1:16 / 512	26.1
10 / 320	48 / 1:16 / 768	26.1
The TDM-PON with the 1:32 Splitting Ratio/ Subscribers	The SUCCESS HPON (TDM Nodes/ WDM Nodes/Subscribers)	The TDM/WDM Node Attenuation [dB]
2 / 64	3 / 1 / 128	30.4 / 15.3
4 / 128	6 / 2 / 256	33.0 / 18.0
6 / 192	9 / 3 / 384	35.7 / 20.7
8 / 256	11 / 4 / 480	37.6 / 22.6
10 / 320	12 / 4 / 511	38.3 / 23.3

preferable to the SUCCESS HPON for utilization in access networks. Even though financial costs of these network components are above actual TDM-PON components, costs per subscriber's capacity in the HPON are much below the TDM-PON.

Hybrid Networks with an Integration

Hybrid networks with an integration of the WDM technology with present TDM networks bring an increasing the number of subscribers, transmission rates and network reaches. By this way, a network design can concatenate and combine functionalities of metropolitan and access networks. This integration utilizes the common central office equipment and combines WDM distribution networks with a bidirectional ring topology and OADM nodes that are connecting to TDM access subnetworks. As an example, the SARDANA HPON can be presented (Lee et. al., 2010).

The SARDANA network architecture is created by a two-fiber ring with connected remote nodes that insure a bidirectional signal amplifying and dropping, respectively adding DWDM wavelengths for particular TDM trees (Prat et. al., 2009). By using EDFA amplifiers, a transmission band is limited to the C-band. At HPON network constellation, selected values for parameters of TDM network are preferred and 1G (EPON), 2,5G (GPON) and 10G (10G-EPON, XG-PON) transmission rates are considered. Also, various splitting ratios of optical power splitters in the TDM network can be selected.

Comparison of SUCCESS and SARDANA HPON Networks

The SUCCESS HPON network allows the WDM and TDM coexistence within one access networks and introduces a sequential transition of TDM subscribers to the pure WDM PON network (An et. al., 2005; Banerjee et. al., 2005). A number of WDM subscribers is limited by a number of available wavelengths (max. 150 at the 0,8 nm channel spacing). A total number of DWDM carriers is reduced by a number of connected TDM nodes. A maximum of joinable subscribers is possible to achieve in a case of the full DWDM band availability. At more than 11 TDM nodes networked by the ITU-T G.652D optical fiber, the CWDM band is overlapping with the DWDM band and therefore a number of joinable WDM subscribers is starting to decrease. The availability of DWDM and CWDM wavelengths can be graphically presented.

At this architecture, a number of subscribers is limited by high attenuation values of TDM nodes. A problem of the ring topology is a high attenuation caused by a utilization of longer optical fibers and by higher inserted losses of particular nodes. A solution can be found in positioning of optical amplifiers in remote nodes. However, an effective spectral band is then reduced and a number of joinable TDM nodes is decreased.

At the configuration, it is possible to set network parameters manually or by using default preferences described in Table 2. They represent model scenarios of the network employment –

Table 2. Parameters of SARDANA HPON configuration preferences

Scenario	L_k [km]	L_s [km]	N	K
Urban 1	17	3	16	1:64
Urban 2	10	10	16	1:32
Metro	50	10	8	1:32
Rural	80	20	8	1:16

from small-scale and populous areas (Urban) to large-scale and sparsely populated (Rural) areas (Lee et. al., 2009).

At the SUCCESS network, it is necessary to take into account a smaller number of TDM nodes due to their higher attenuation values. At the TDM transmission, the CWDM multiplexing is utilizing. Therefore, it is possible to utilize with high constraints all transmission bands supported by selected optical fibers. However, an adding of optical amplifiers into TDM nodes brings a restriction of band utilizations.

At the SARDANA network, this bandwidth restriction presents no problem because the applied DWDM multiplexing technique provides a sufficient number of transmission channels in the one band. In the C-band, only 1 TDM node could be connected with the EDFA amplifier. By using of AWG elements, WDM nodes can be considered with lower attenuation values. In both network architectures, a ring topology allows a selection of transmission directions in dependence on network power relationships and insures a traffic protection in a case of fiber failures. Transmission rates for TDM subscribers are equal in both networks. Transmission rate for WDM subscribers can achieve values up to a few Gbit/s.

For comparison of both hybrid networks, basic characteristics of SUCCESS and SARDANA HPON network configurations can be presented (Figure 4). In this case, following parameters were selected: the ITU-T G.652D optical fiber, the 0,2 nm DWDM channel spacing, the ring length 15 km, the access fiber length 2 km, the 1:32 splitting ratio in TDM nodes. A number of remote nodes equals to 17 as a maximum joinable quantity in the SUCCESS network. As we can see, a number of SUCCESS subscribers is the highest for 11 TDM nodes, however, with their attenuation values approaching to 40dB. On the other side, a number of SARDANA subscribers is continuously increasing with comparable attenuation values not exceeded of 25 dB.

THE HPON NETWORK CONFIGURATOR

The HPON network configurator allows comparing possibilities of various passive optical access networks. Our HPON network simulator (Róka, 2010) represents real possibilities for a consistent transition from the TDM-PON to the HPON based on various specific parameters – a network

Figure 4. Characteristics of the SUCCESS and SARDANA HPON networks

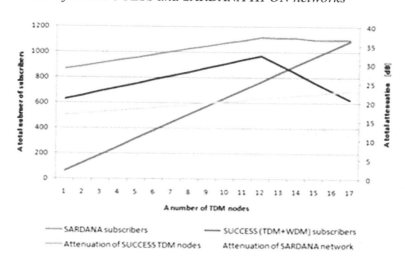

capacity from a viewpoint of the physical layer, a number of TDM and WDM network subscribers, a number of exploited wavelength types, a growth of the channel capacity by connecting of new subscribers and other feasibilities. This HPON network simulator has main dialogue window for designing a transition from TDM-PON to HPON networks. Additional dialogue windows with basic network schemes and short interactive descriptions serve for the specific HPON configuration setup.

At the creating of simulated HPON configurations, it is necessary to deal with these problems:

- A total network capacity.
- An availability of wavelengths.
- Power relationships (a transmitting power of light sources, a sensitivity of receivers, an attenuation of the transmission path and optical components.

Based on primary input values of the deployed TDM-PON network (a number of TDM nodes, a capacity of the node, a number of subscribers per node), a total capacity of the deployed network and an average capacity per one subscriber are calculated (only for the downstream direction) and possible network extensions with adding WDM nodes are also displayed. Thereafter, changes of the topology and a subsequent transition to the HPON network are presented to the user. By this way, a user can take a decision to regulate or to exchange primary input values for adapting to demands of the HPON network.

Then, a number of new DWDM subscribers and a required capacity per one subscriber are inserted. Based on given values, a total capacity of the hybrid network (only for the downstream direction), a growth of the capacity due to connecting of new subscribers, a number of necessary DWDM transmitters and receivers, a number of utilized CWDM and DWDM wavelengths are evaluated. Thereafter, further possible network extensions are displayed. By this way, a user can take a decision to regulate or to exchange

primary input values for adapting to demands of the HPON network.

A Configuration of the HPON Environment, its Capabilities and Parameters

Our simulation model for comparing possibilities of various passive optical access networks is created by using the Microsoft Visual Studio 2008 software in the IDE development environment (Róka, 2010; Róka & Khan, 2011; Róka, 2011; Róka, 2012). There exist possibilities for the graphical interface created by using the MFC (Microsoft Foundation Class) library for the C++ programming language. The simulation model has one main interactive dialogue window (Figure 5) for inserting and presenting parameters of transitions from TDM-PON to HPON networks. It allows comparing and analyzing three principal approaches for designing and configuring of hybrid passive optical networks. Therefore, additional dialogue windows with basic network infrastructures and relations can be used for the specific HPON configuration setup. For WDM/TDM-PON and SUCCESS HPON networks, transitions from the original TDM-PON architecture are expressed by GIF animations. For their presentation, a free available CPictureEx class is used.

Our simulation model is working in several steps:

1. **Setting Parameters of the Optical Fiber:** A type of the optical fiber (according to the ITU-T), the DWDM multiplexing density.
2. **Evaluating Optical Fibers:** Standard or inserted specific attenuation values in dB/km, a calculation of numbers of CWDM and DWDM carrier.
3. **Inserting Input Parameters of the TDM-PON Network:** A number of TDM networks, a type of the network, a number of subscribers per one network, a distance between the ONT and the OLT.

Figure 5. The main window of the HPON network configurator

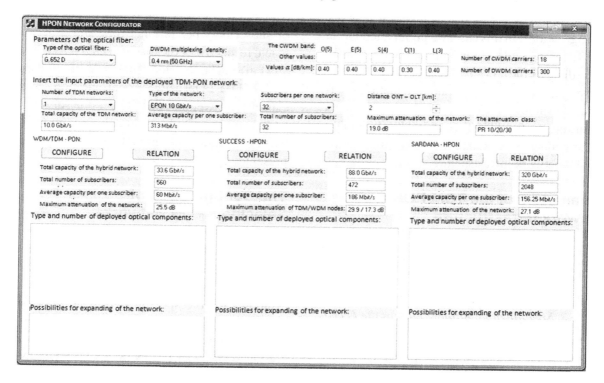

4. **Evaluating Input Parameters:** A calculation of the total transmission capacity of the TDM network together with the average capacity per one subscriber, the total number of subscribers and the maximum attenuation of the TDM network; also, the attenuation class is presented. This step is terminating with the selection of detailed hybrid PON configuration design.

5. **Setting Input Parameters for the Hybrid PON Configuration:** Based on the stored TDM-PON network data and selecting one from HPON types.

6. **Application Input Parameters and Specific Parameters of the HPON Network Configuration:** (The total capacity of the hybrid network, the total number of subscribers, the average capacity per one subscriber, the maximum attenuation of the hybrid network between the OLT and the ONT, a number and type of used active and passive components) with summing up a type and number of deployed optical components and presenting possibilities for future expanding of hybrid HPON network types.

Parameters of the Optical Fiber

In the first step, a selection of the optical fiber's type and the DWDM multiplexing density can be executed. A selected type of the optical fiber is presented by the specific attenuation values and by a number of transmission bands. For specifications, various ITU-T recommendations – ITU-T G.652A, G.652B, G.652C, G.652D, G.656, G.657 – together with the "Other values" option can be inserted. Then, specific attenuation coefficients are concretely displayed. Also, a total number of CWDM and DWDM carrier wavelengths for particular bands are presented.

Also, an attenuation of optical fibers for available wavelengths is calculated in specific network configurations. In this case, we prefer attenuation coefficients (Table 3) for common optical fibers according to the ITU-T G.652 (ITU-T, 2009a). However, we can incorporate attenuation coefficients (Table 4) for new types of optical fibers according to the ITU-T G.657 (ITU-T, 2009b) and, by this way, evaluate their utilization in the HPON network infrastructure.

Parameters of the TDM PON Network Infrastructure

In the second step, a selection and a listing of parameters for the deployed TDM-PON network

Table 3. Specific attenuation values of the ITU-T G.652 optical fibers

Class	Wavelength	Specific Attenuation
A	maximum at 1310 nm	0.5 dB/km
	maximum at 1550 nm	0.4 dB/km
B	maximum at 1310 nm	0.4 dB/km
	maximum at 1550 nm	0.35 dB/km
	maximum at 1625 nm	0.4 dB/km
C	maximum from 1310 nm to 1625 nm	0.4 dB/km
	maximum at 1550 nm	0.3 dB/km
D	maximum from 1310 nm to 1625 nm	0.4 dB/km
	maximum at 1550 nm	0.3 dB/km

Table 4. Specific attenuation values of the ITU-T G.657 optical fibers

Class	Wavelength	Specific Attenuation
A	maximum from 1310 nm to 1625 nm	0,4 dB/km
	maximum at 1383 nm ± 3 nm	0,4 dB/km
	maximum at 1550 nm	0,3 dB/km
B	maximum at 1310 nm	0,5 dB/km
	maximum at 1550 nm	0,3 dB/km
	maximum at 1625 nm	0,4 dB/km

can be executed. A number and type of networks (EPON, GPON, 10G-EPON, XG-PON), a number of subscribers per one network and a network reach, respectively the distance OLT-ONT (max. 999 km) can be selected. Then, features of the selected TDM-PON network configuration – a total capacity, an average capacity per one subscriber, a total number of subscribers, the maximum network attenuation and the attenuation class - are presented.

The Configuration of Selected HPON Networks

In the third step, three hybrid networks are reserved. By using CONFIGURE push buttons in the main dialogue window, autonomous dialogue windows for the specific hybrid network configuration are opened. Then, a configuration of specific network parameters can be proceeding for the WDM/TDM-PON, SUCCESS HPON or SARDANA HPON option. Finally, a short list of basic characteristics – a total capacity of the hybrid network, a total number of subscribers, an average capacity per one subscriber, the maximum network attenuation – calculated for each option are displayed.

Applications of the HPON Selection

Finally, a selection of one from three various hybrid passive optical network approaches. In the first case, the WDM/TDM-PON configuration window (Figure 6) is opened. After inserting requested parameters of the hybrid WDM/TDM-PON network and also a number of TDM subnetworks, the Apply button can be pushed. Then, a complete set introducing type and number of optical components is introduced together with their basic characteristics.

In the second case, the SUCCESS HPON configuration window (Figure 7) is opened. After inserting requested input parameters for TDM nodes and WDM nodes, the Configure button can be pushed. Then, a complete set introducing type

Figure 6. The window of the WDM/TDM-PON configuration

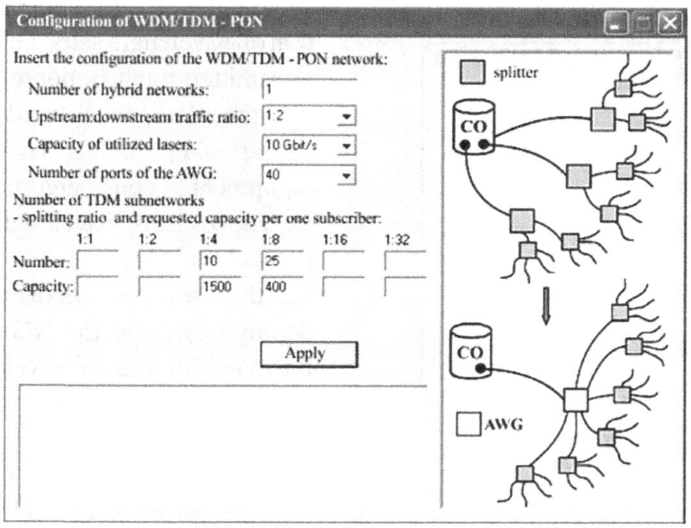

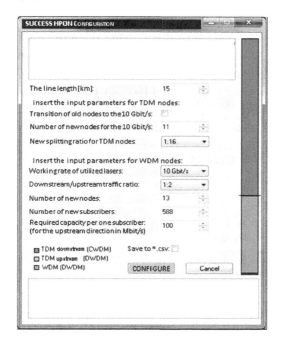

Figure 7. The window of the SUCCESS HPON configuration

and number of optical components is introduced together with their basic characteristics. Moreover, a graphical presentation of the bandwidth allocation between TDM downstream, TDM upstream and WDM wavelengths is presented.

In the third case, the SARDANA HPON configuration window (Figure 8) is opened. After inserting requested input parameters for remote nodes, TDM trees and the WDM ring length, the Configure button can be pushed. Then, a complete set introducing type and number of optical components is introduced together with their basic characteristics.

Other Considered Parameters

A Total Network Capacity

In the TDM network, a capacity is based on selected architectures and on the OLT transmitter capacity. In the WDM network, a capacity is depending on the transmitter capacity, because each subscriber has a dedicated own wavelength. Therefore, the total WDM capacity is a number of subscribers (or wavelengths) multiplied by the transmission capacity of transmitters. In the HPON network, TDM parts are unchanged and WDM tunable lasers can be shared by several subscribers, then a total network capacity is depending also on a number of utilized tunable lasers.

Figure 8. The window of the SARDANA HPON configuration

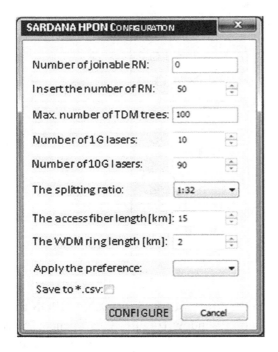

An Availability of Wavelengths

One of the issues with any DWDM scheme is provisioning of available wavelengths. For the OLT side, there is no issue with equipment – a new OLT interface supporting all the channels in

a single module. However, each ONU terminal should support only a single wavelength and an option of wavelength selectable sources for upstream transmitters might be possible. Alternatively, ONU interfaces may be colored and this may present operational problems. Therefore, colorless ONU equipment is considered in some architecture.

The overall wavelength plan for NG-PON networks is shown in Figure 9. This plan pulls together the diverse set of requirements from PON deployments and the NG-PON system concept into a minimal set of wavelength assignment (Effenberger et. al., 2009):

1. **The XG-PON1:** The downstream wavelength band of 1575 – 1580 nm is used since it is the only wavelength band that is left in the system with the video overlay. For the upstream, 5 channel assignments can be discussed – within the L-band (channel A), the C-band (channel B), the video-compatible C-band (channel C), the O-plus band (channel D) and the O-minus band (channel E). According to the ITU-T G.987 series (ITU-T, 2010), parameters for the upstream wavelength allocation are determined to 1260 – 1280 nm.

Figure 9. The NG-PON wavelength spectrum plan

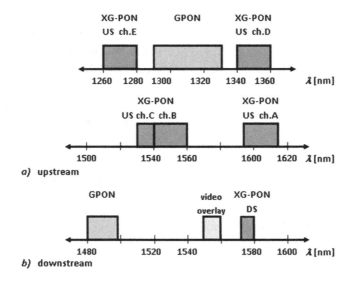

2. **The ER+WC XG-PON1:** The 0,5 nm wide wavelength windows (the 200 GHz channel spacing) are specified.

3. **The XG-PON2:** The downstream band is the same as for the XG-PON1. The upstream band spans 1260–1280 nm that corresponds to the O-band placement and permits using of directly modulated lasers without excessive dispersion penalties and also using of uncooled lasers.

4. **The Hybrid DWDM/XG-PON:** The channel spacing can be selected at either 100 GHz or 50 GHz. It requires the C-band upstream allocation (channel B) because it is sensitive to fiber losses, but this is in conflict with the video overlay. The downstream wavelengths are located from 1575 to 1582 nm.

Now, it is appropriate to clarify a relationship between a number of available CWDM and DWDM wavelengths in the network. The less CWDM wavelengths are used, the more DWDM wavelengths can be utilized in a relevant spectrum. Simulation calculations are based on a following relationship (1):

$$\lambda_D = \frac{20 \cdot (18 - \lambda_C) \cdot 125}{\Delta\lambda} - \lambda_C \qquad (1)$$

where λ_C assigns a number of used TDM nodes, respectively CWDM wavelengths, λ_D is a maximum number of available DWDM wavelengths for WDM subscribers, $\Delta\lambda$ is the interval between DWDM channels (25, 50 or 100 GHz). This relationship describes a maximum possible number of available DWDM wavelengths that can be utilized by WDM subscribers in a dependency on a number of utilized CWDM wavelengths.

The allocation of CWDM and DWDM carriers in particular transmission bands is presented in Table 5. By reducing of DWDM channel spacing, negative influences of nonlinear effects (e.g. FWM) can be increased in the real optical transmission media.

In the WDM/TDM-PON network, 2 sets of wavelengths can be utilized - for CWDM and for DWDM systems. Because these bands are overlapped, a number of available wavelengths is depending on utilized bandwidths and on a density of the wavelength allocation (100 GHz, 50 GHz or 25 GHz channel spacing). In the simulation program, a dependency between wavelengths is exactly scheduled (Róka, 2010; Róka, 2011).

In the SUCCESS HPON network, a situation is different. In the first step of a transition to the HPON, a network topology is changing from various point-to-multipoint infrastructures to the one ring by means of the one optical fiber. There-

Table 5. A number of DWDM and CWDM wavelengths for particular transmission bands

Bands	O 1260-1360 nm	E 1360-1460 nm	S 1460-1530 nm	C 1530-1565 nm	L 1565-1625 nm	Total Number of Possible Wavelengths
DWDM (0.8 nm, 100 GHz)	-	-	50	25	75	150
DWDM (0.4 nm, 50 GHz)	-	-	100	50	150	300
DWDM (0.2 nm, 25 GHz)	-	-	200	100	300	600
CWDM (20 nm)	5	5	4	1	3	18

fore, DWDM wavelengths (one wavelength per one TDM node) are utilizing in the downstream direction. In the upstream direction, each TDM node utilizes a different wavelength from the CWDM grid.

In the SARDANA HPON network, transmissions in both directions are limited by using of wavelengths in the C-band due to the EDFA operational range. So, the utilization of DWDM systems can be varied with different densities of the DWDM channel spacing.

Power Relationships

In the HPON network, power relationships are depending on specific network characteristics and applied optical component parameters. We prefer real values of optical components utilized in passive optical networks (Table 6).

Also, total power relationships for specific network configurations are calculated in the HPON network configurator. For the XG-PON, there will be two loss budgets denoted Normal and Extended. The Normal loss budget is defined with a Class B+ loss budget plus an insertion loss from a WDM1 filter. The link loss will be approximately 28,5 dB to 31 dB at BER = 10^{-12}. The Extended loss budget is defined with a Class C+ loss budget plus an insertion loss from a WDM1 filter (Effenberger et al., 2009).

FUTURE RESEARCH DIRECTIONS

NG-PON systems present optical access infrastructures to support various applications of many service providers. Technological improvements of mobile broadband and broadcast technologies will require a reliable support in access networks. Therefore, appropriate advanced technologies utilizing the fixed transmission medium can be expected in a near future and more reasons begin effect on utilization and implementation of the WDM multiplexing technique in passive optical networks.

Table 6. Attenuation specifications of HPON optical components

Symbol	Description	Value
α_{FIBER}	the maximum fiber attenuation in wavelength bands	ITU-T standards
α_{DWDM}	the maximum fiber attenuation in the DWDM wavelength bands	0.25 dB/km
L_{ACCESS}	the access fiber length	optional
L_{RING}	the ring length	optional
a_{FILTER}	the attenuation of the WDM filter	0.4 dB
a_{AWG}	the AWG attenuation	5 dB
$a_{50:50}$	the 50:50 power splitter attenuation	4.4 dB
$a_{90:10}$	the 90:10 power splitter attenuation	0.8:12 dB
	the 1:4 splitter attenuation	7.5 dB
	the 1:8 splitter attenuation	11 dB
	the 1:16 splitter attenuation	14.1 dB
$a_{SPLIT1:N}$	the 1:32 splitter attenuation	17.4 dB
	the 1:64 splitter attenuation	21.0 dB
	the 1:128 splitter attenuation	22.5 dB
	the 1:256 splitter attenuation	26.4 dB
a_{TDM-RN}	the TDM node attenuation (including connectors)	1.5 dB
a_{WDM-RN}	the WDM node attenuation (including connectors)	1 dB
$a_{ADD/DROP}$	the attenuation of added/dropped wavelengths	1.2 dB
$a_{ISOLATOR}$	the attenuation of the isolator	0.3 dB
a_{CON}	the connector attenuation	0.2 dB
	loss of a splice	0.15 dB
	loss of the fiber span	0.25 dB/km

On the other hand, the NG-PON technology must be able to protect the investment of legacy passive optical networks. Therefore, a strong interest for utilization of old TDM equipment in passive optical networks is present. Naturally, an expansion of hybrid passive optical networks seems to be a practical solution. However, an area of research directions in HPON networks is very wide and can include e.g. a mutual convergence of functionalities between metropolitan and access networks, an enlarging of network reaches by using of optical amplification, etc.

CHALLENGES AND OPEN ISSUES

In the near future, a convergence of optical, metallic and wireless technologies will be continued. Mobile base stations can be backhauled through the normal passive optical network and they can be thought of as normal PON ONU elements. Between the central office and the remote base station will be introduced another intermediate node responsible for generation and transmission of control data streams over shorter fiber distances. Broadband NG-PON networks can be deployed by three main scenarios to address different cases with diverse degrees of consolidation – the urban, the passive extended reach and the active extended reach. With these, also various HPON deployments could be included into possible future extensions. Moreover, a variety of users - residential, corporate/business and telco – must be considered. And, therefore, more flexible HPON architectures should be considered.

For practical implementation, there are some open issues. A high importance is dedicated to the energy saving in long-reach broadband access networks and the energy efficient efforts on both OLT and ONU sides and in converged broadband wireless-optical access networks. From this viewpoint, the HPON possibilities can also play an important role. For enhancing broadband NG-PON networks, DSP-based approaches can be utilized for flexible per-wavelength rate upgrades and for extending reach of optical access systems. Together with the virtualization of access networks with reconfigurable OLT/ONU elements, the HPON network configurator must be ready also for these future deployments. Moreover, a virtualization of heterogeneous wireless-optical network and IT infrastructures can be mentioned for support of wireless and metallic access and backhauling solutions and for cloud and mobile cloud service.

Therefore, possible HPON deployments must be ready for these prospective variations of future broadband NG-PON networks.

CONCLUSION

With the emerging applications and needs of ever increasing bandwidth, it is anticipated that the next-generation passive optical network with much higher bandwidth is a natural path forward to satisfy these demands and for network operators to develop valuable access networks. NG-PON systems present optical access infrastructures to support various applications of many service providers, thus also for emerging applications of advanced mobile broadband and broadcast technologies associated with increasing bandwidth demands.

Hybrid passive optical networks present a necessary phase of the future transition between PON classes with TDM or WDM multiplexing techniques utilized on the optical transmission medium – the optical fiber. For developing hybrid passive optical networks, there exist various architectures and directions. We focused on a design of a transition stage between TDM-PON and WDM-PON networks. A main reason for this motivation is that at first a number of operating TDM-PON networks is even now high and still rising and at second a utilization of installed optical infrastructures is maximized for transmission capacity's increasing. On the other side, a creating the hybrid HPON network can be used as the upgrade of old networks in many cases with a utilization of relevant parts of the original infrastructure with minimum financial costs. It's a question whether only a consistent transition from the TDM-PON to the HPON network is requested or further to the full-value WDM-PON network is suitable.

The HPON network configurator as an interactive software tool can be used for identifying a right time for creating and building of the full-value WDM-PON network. Its main aim is helping users, professional workers, network operators and system analysts to design, configure, analyze and compare various possible hybrid passive optical networks. This software program can be simply, fast and effectively upgraded for further variations of future broadband NG-PON networks.

ACKNOWLEDGMENT

This work is a part of research activities conducted at Slovak University of Technology Bratislava, Faculty of Electrical Engineering and Information Technology, Institute of Telecommunications, within the scope of the project VEGA No. 1/0106/11 "Analysis and proposal for advanced optical access networks in the NGN converged infrastructure utilizing fixed transmission media for supporting multimedia services".

REFERENCES

Ahsan, M. S., et al. (2009). Migration to the next generation passive optical network. In *Proceedings of International Conference on Computers and Information Technology* (vol. 12, pp. 79-84). Dhaka, India: Academic Press.

An, F. T. et al. (2005). Success HPON: A next-generation optical access architecture for smooth migration from TDM-PON to WDM-PON. *IEEE Communications Magazine*, *43*(11), S40–S47. doi:10.1109/MCOM.2005.1541698

Banerjee, A. et al. (2005). WDM-PON technologies for broadband access – A review. *Journal of Optical Networking*, *4*(11), 737–758. doi:10.1364/JON.4.000737

Čuchran, J., & Róka, R. (2006). *Optocommunication systems and networks*. Bratislava, Slovakia: Slovak University of Technology Publishing House.

Effenberger, F. et al. (2009a). Next-generation PON – Part II: Candidate systems for next-generation PON. *IEEE Communications Magazine*, *47*(11), 50–57. doi:10.1109/MCOM.2009.5307466

Effenberger, F. et al. (2009b). Next-generation PON – Part III: System specification for XG-PON. *IEEE Communications Magazine*, *47*(11), 58–64. doi:10.1109/MCOM.2009.5307467

Kani, J. et al. (2009). Next-generation PON – Part I: Technology roadmap and general requirements. *IEEE Communications Magazine*, *47*(11), 43–49. doi:10.1109/MCOM.2009.5307465

Kazovsky, L. G. et al. (2007). Next-generation optical access networks. *Journal of Lightwave Technology*, *25*(11), 3428–3442. doi:10.1109/JLT.2007.907748

Lee, J. H. et al. (2009). Seamless upgrades from a TDM-PON with a video overlay to a WDM-PON. *Journal of Lightwave Technology*, *27*(15), 3116–3123. doi:10.1109/JLT.2008.2006861

Lee, J. H. et al. (2010). First commercial deployment of a colorless gigabit WDM/TDM hybrid PON system using remote protocol terminator. *Journal of Lightwave Technology*, *28*(4), 344–351. doi:10.1109/JLT.2009.2037979

Prat, J., et al. (2009). Passive optical network for long-reach scalable and resilient access. In *Proceedings of International Conference on Telecommunications* (vol. 10, pp. 271-275). Zagreb, Croatia: Academic Press.

Ramaswami, R., & Sivarajan, K. N. (2001). *Optical networks – A practical perspective*. San Francisco, CA: Morgan Kaufmann Publishers.

Róka, R. (2003). The utilization of the DWDM/CWDM combination in the metro/access networks. In *Proceedings of Joint 1st Workshop on Mobile Future & Symposium on Trends in Communications* (vol. 10, pp. 160-162). Bratislava, Slovakia: Academic Press.

Róka, R. (2008). The evolution of optical access networks for the provisioning of multimedia services in the NGN converged networks. In *Design of forms in the marketing communication for support of implementation in new multimedia products in the praxis* (pp. 138–143). Žilina, Slovakia: Žilina University Publishing House.

Róka, R. (2010). The designing of passive optical networks using the HPON network configurator. *International Journal of Research and Reviews in Computer Science, 1*(3).

Róka, R. (2010). The utilization of the HPON network configurator at designing of passive optical networks. In *Proceedings of International Conference on Telecommunication and Signal Processing* (vol. 33, pp. 444-448). Baden near Vienna, Austria: Academic Press.

Róka, R. (2011). The extension of the HPON network configurator at designing of NG-PON networks. In *Proceedings of International Conference on Telecommunication and Signal Processing* (vol. 34, pp. 79-84). Budapest, Hungary: Academic Press.

Róka, R. (2012). The designing of NG-PON networks using the HPON network configurator. *Journal of Communication and Computer, 9*(6), 669–678.

Róka, R., & Khan, S. (2011). The modeling of hybrid passive optical networks using the network configurator. *International Journal of Research and Reviews in Computer Science, 2*, 48–54.

Tanaka, K. et al. (2010). IEEE 802.3av 10G-EPON standardization and its research and development status. *Journal of Lightwave Technology, 28*(4), 651–661. doi:10.1109/JLT.2009.2038722

ITU-T Telecommunication Standardization Sector. (2009a). *Characteristics of a single-mode optical fiber and cable*. Recommendation G.652.

ITU-T Telecommunication Standardization Sector. (2009b). *Characteristics of a bending-loss insensitive single-mode optical fiber and cable for the access network*. Recommendation G.657.

ITU-T Telecommunication Standardization Sector. (2010). *10-gigabit-capable passive optical network systems: Definitions, abbreviations, and acronyms*. Recommendation G.987.

KEY TERMS AND DEFINITIONS

HPON Network Configurator: The interactive software tool for designing, configuring, analyzing and comparing various possible hybrid passive optical networks.

HPON: The hybrid passive optical network with utilization of both TDM and WDM multiplexing principles together on a physical layer.

NG-PON: The next-generation PON as a natural path forward to satisfy demands of ever increasing bandwidth and to protect the investment of legacy passive optical networks.

PON: The access network based on the optical transmission medium with only passive optical components locating in the outside environment.

TDM Multiplexing: Sharing a common optical path by various transmission channels in the upstream direction assigning different time slots for particular subscriber terminals.

WDM Multiplexing: Sharing a common optical path by various transmission channels in downstream or upstream directions assigning different wavelengths for particular subnetworks or subscriber terminals.

Compilation of References

Aberer, K., & Despotovic, Z. (2004). *On reputation in game theory application on online settings* (Working Paper). Unpublished.

ACMA. (2009). *Consumer benefits resulting from Australia's telecommunications sector.* Sydney, Australia: Australian Communications and Media Authority.

Adobe HTTP Dynamic Streaming. (n.d.). *Using Adobe HTTP dynamic streaming.* Retrieved October 23, 2013, from http://help.adobe.com/en_US/HTTPStreaming/1.0/Using/index.html

Adriaens, J., Megerian, S., & Potkonjak, M. (2006). Optimal worst-case coverage of directional field-of view sensor networks. In *Proceedings of IEEE Sensor, Mesh and Ad Hoc Communications and Networks* (pp. 336 – 345). Reston, VA: IEEE.

Agrawal, G. P. (2010). *Fiber-optic communication systems* (4th ed.). New York: John Wiley & Sons. doi:10.1002/9780470918524

Agrawal, G. P., & Dutta, N. K. (1986). *Long-wavelength semiconductor lasers.* Van Nostrand Reinhold. doi:10.1007/978-94-011-6994-3

Ahlgren, B., Dannewitz, C., Imbrenda, C., Kutscher, D., & Ohlman, B. (2012). A survey of information-centric networking. *IEEE Communications Magazine, 50*(7), 26–36. doi:10.1109/MCOM.2012.6231276

Ahn, J. W., Brusilovsky, P., Grady, J., He, D., & Syn, S. Y. (2007). Open user profiles for adaptive news systems: Help or harm? In *Proceedings of ACM International Conference on World Wide Web.* Alberta, Canada: ACM.

Ahsan, M. S., et al. (2009). Migration to the next generation passive optical network. In *Proceedings of International Conference on Computers and Information Technology* (vol. 12, pp. 79-84). Dhaka, India: Academic Press.

Akcilek, R., & Besley, M. (2003). *Operating cost, fuel consumption and emission models in aaSIDRA and aaMotion.* Paper presented at the Conference of Australian Institutes of Transport Research. Adelaide, Australia

Akkarajitsakul, K., Hossain, E., Niyato, D., & Dong, I. K. (2011). Game theoretic approaches for multiple access in wireless networks: A survey. *IEEE Communications Surveys & Tutorials, 13*(3), 372–395. doi:10.1109/SURV.2011.122310.000119

Alberi Morel, M.-L., Kerboeuf, S., Sayadi, B., Leprovost, Y., & Faucheux, F. (2010). Performance evaluation of channel change for DVB-SH streaming services. In *Proceedings of IEEE International Conference on Communications (ICC)* (pp. 1–6). Cape Town, South Africa: IEEE.

Alexious, A., Bouras, C., Kokkinos, V., & Tsichritzis, G. (2010). *Communication cost analysis of MBSFN in LTE.* Paper presented at the Institute of Electrical and Electronics Engineers 21st International Symposium on Personal Indoor and Mobile Radio Communications. Istanbul, Turkey.

Alkhawlani, M., & Ayesh, A. (2008). Access network selection based on fuzzy logic and genetic algorithm. *Advances in Artificial Intelligence,* (1): 1–12. doi:10.1155/2008/793058

Almalag, M. S., & Weigle, M. C. (2010). Using traffic flow for cluster formation in vehicular ad-hoc networks. In Proceedings of Local Computer Networks (LCN), (pp. 631-636). IEEE.

Alpcan, T., Basar, T., Srikant, R., & Altman, E. (2002). CDMA uplink power control as a noncooperative game. *Wireless Networks*, *8*(6), 659–670. doi:10.1023/A:1020375225649

Al-Rubaye, S., Al-Dulaimi, A., & Cosmas, J. (2011). Cognitive femtocell: Future wireless networks for indoor applications. *IEEE Veh. Technol. Mag.*, *6*(1), 44–51. doi:10.1109/MVT.2010.939902

Altman, E., Boulogne, T., El-Azouzi, R., Jimenez, T., & Wynter, L. (2006). A survey on networking games in telecommunications. *Computers & Operations Research*, *33*(2), 286–311. doi:10.1016/j.cor.2004.06.005

Altman, E., El-Azouzi, R., Hayel, Y., & Tembine, H. (2009). The evolution of transport protocols: An evolutionary game perspective. *Computer Networks*, *53*(10), 1751–1759. doi:10.1016/j.comnet.2008.12.023

Al-Zahrani, A. Y., & Yu, F. R. (2011). A game theory approach for inter-cell interference management in OFDM networks.[IEEE.]. *Proceedings of the IEEE, ICC*, 1–5.

Amendola, G. B., & Pupillo, L. M. (2007). *The economics of next generation access networks and regulatory governance in Europe: One size does not fit all.* Paper presented at the 18th ITS Regional Conference. Istanbul, Turkey.

Anastasopoulos, M. P., Arapoglou, P. D., Kannan, R., & Cottis, P. G. (2008). Adaptive routing strategies in IEEE 802.16 multi-hop wireless backhaul networks based on evolutionary game theory. *IEEE Journal on Selected Areas in Communications*, *26*(7), 1218–1225. doi:10.1109/JSAC.2008.080918

Anderegg, L., & Eidenbenz, S. (2003). Ad hoc-VCG: A truthful and cost-efficient routing protocol for mobile ad hoc networks with selfish agents. In *Proceedings of the ACM International Conference on Mobile Computing and Networking*, (pp. 245-259). ACM.

Andersen Management International. (2004). *Pricing shared access in Sweden.* Sweden: Post of Telestyrelsen.

An, F. T. et al. (2005). Success HPON: A next-generation optical access architecture for smooth migration from TDM-PON to WDM-PON. *IEEE Communications Magazine*, *43*(11), S40–S47. doi:10.1109/MCOM.2005.1541698

Araniti, G., Scordamaglia, V., Condoluci, M., Molinaro, A., & Iera, A. (2012). *Efficient frequency domain packet scheduler for point-to-multipoint transmissions in LTE networks.* Paper presented at the IEEE International Conference on Communications. Ottawa, Canada.

Araniti, G., Campolo, C., Condoluci, M., Iera, A., & Molinaro, A. (2013). LTE for vehicular networking: A survey. *IEEE Communications Magazine*, *51*(5), 148–157. doi:10.1109/MCOM.2013.6515060

Attar, A., Krishnamurthy, V., & Gharehshiran, O. N. (2011). Interference management using cognitive base-stations for UMTS LTE. *IEEE Communications Magazine*, *49*(8), 152–159. doi:10.1109/MCOM.2011.5978429

Awada, A., Wegmann, B., Viering, I., & Klein, A. (2013). A SON-based algorithm for the optimization of inter-RAT handover parameters. *IEEE Transactions on Vehicular Technology*, *62*(5), 1906–1923. doi:10.1109/TVT.2013.2251923

Axelrod, R. (1981). The emergence of cooperation among egoists. *The American Political Science Review*, *75*(2), 306–318. doi:10.2307/1961366

Bach, L., Kaiser, W., Reithmaier, J. P., Forchel, A., Berg, T. W., & Tromborg, B. (2003). Enhanced direct-modulated bandwidth of 37 GHz by a multi-section laser with a coupled-cavity-injection-grating design. *Electronics Letters*, *39*(22), 1592. doi:10.1049/el:20031018

Bakmaz, B. M. (2013). Network selection equilibrium in heterogeneous wireless environment. *Electronics and Electrical Engineering*, *19*(4), 91–96. doi:10.5755/j01.eee.19.4.4058

Banerjee, A. et al. (2005). WDM-PON technologies for broadband access – A review. *Journal of Optical Networking*, *4*(11), 737–758. doi:10.1364/JON.4.000737

Bansal, S., & Baker, M. (2003). *Observation-based cooperation enforcement in ad hoc networks (Stanford Technical Report).* Palo Alto, CA: Stanford University.

Barth, M., Mandava, S., Boriboonsomsin, K., & Xia, H. (2011). Dynamic ECO-driving for arterial corridors. In Proceedings of Integrated and Sustainable Transportation System (FISTS), (pp. 182-188). IEEE.

Basagni, S. (1999). Distributed clustering for ad hoc networks. In Proceedings of Parallel Architectures, Algorithms, and Networks, (pp. 310-315). IEEE.

Begen, A., Akgul, T., & Baugher, M. (2011). Watching video over the web: Part 2: Applications, standardization, and open issues. *IEEE Internet Computing, 15*(3), 59–63. doi:10.1109/MIC.2010.156

Bell, L., & Bull, G. (2010). Digital video and teaching. *Contemporary Issues in Technology & Teacher Education, 10*(1), 1–6.

Bennis, M., Guruacharya, S., & Niyato, D. (2011). Distributed learning strategies for interference mitigation in femtocell networks. In *Proceedings of IEEE Global Telecommunications Conference* (GLOBECOM). IEEE.

Bennis, M., Simsek, M., & Czylwik, A. et al. (2013). When cellular meets WiFi in wireless small cell networks. *IEEE Communications Magazine, 51*(6), 35–41. doi:10.1109/MCOM.2013.6525594

Benslimane, A., Taleb, T., & Sivaraj, R. (2011). Dynamic clustering-based adaptive mobile gateway management in integrated VANET—3G heterogeneous wireless networks. *IEEE Journal on Selected Areas in Communications, 29*(3), 559–570. doi:10.1109/JSAC.2011.110306

Blum, J., Eskandarian, A., & Hoffman, L. (2003). Mobility management in IVC networks. In *Proceedings of Intelligent Vehicles Symposium,* (pp. 150-155). IEEE.

BNetzA. (2008). Allgemeinzuteilungen für punkt-zu-punkt rictfunk im frequenzbereich 217/2008, 59-64 GHz. *Bundesnetzagentur, Mitteilungenungen.*

Borgefors, G. (1984). An improved version of the chamfer matching algorithm. In *Proceedings of the 7th International Conference on Pattern Recognition*. Montreal, Canada: Academic Press.

Bougard, B., Catthoor, F., Daly, D. C., Chandrakasan, A., & Dehaene, W. (2005). Energy efficiency of the IEEE 802.15.4 standard in dense wireless microsensor networks: Modeling and improvement perspectives. In Proceedings of Design, Automation and Test in Europe – DATE'05 (pp. 196-201). IEEE Computer Society.

Bucciol, A., & Zarri, L. (2013). *Financial risk aversion and personal life history.* Retrieved September 16, 2013, from http://leonardo3.dse.univr.it/home/workingpapers/risk_events_BZ.pdf

Buchegger, S., & Boudec, J.-Y. L. (2002). Performance analysis of the CONFIDANT protocol. In *Proceedings of the 3rd ACM International Symposium on Mobile Ad Hoc Networking & Computing* (MobiHoc '02), (pp. 226-236). ACM.

Bulusu, N., Heidemann, J., & Estrin, D. (2000). GPS-less low cost outdoor localization for very small devices. *Proceedings of the IEEE Personal Communications, 7*(5), 28–34. doi:10.1109/98.878533

Buttyán, L., & Hubaux, J.-P. (2000). Enforcing service availability in mobile ad-hoc WANs. In *Proceedings of the 1st ACM International Symposium on Mobile Ad Hoc Networking & Computing* (MobiHoc '00), (pp. 87-96). ACM.

Buttyán, L., & Hubaux, J.-P. (2001). *Nuglets: A virtual currency to stimulate cooperation in self organized ad hoc networks* (Technical Report DSC/2001/001). Lausanne, Switzerland: Swiss Federal Institute of Technology.

Buttyán, L., & Hubaux, J.-P. (2003). Stimulating cooperation in self-organizing mobile ad hoc networks. *Mobile Networks and Applications, 8*(5), 579–592. doi:10.1023/A:1025146013151

Cai, S. H., & Lin, Y. (2008). A roadside ITS data bus prototype for intelligent highways. *IEEE Transactions on Intelligent Transportation Systems, 9*(2), 344–348. doi:10.1109/TITS.2008.922873

Canny, J. F. (1986). A computational approach to edge detection. *IEEE Transactions on Pattern Analysis and Machine Intelligence, 8*(6), 679–698. doi:10.1109/TPAMI.1986.4767851 PMID:21869365

Capmany, J., Ortega, B., Martinez, A., Pastor, D., Popov, M., & Fonjallaz, P. Y. (2005). Multiwavelength single sideband modulation for WDM radio-over-fiber systems using a fiber grating array tandem device. *IEEE Photonics Technology Letters*, *17*(2), 471–473. doi:10.1109/LPT.2004.840017

Cartledge, J. C. (1995). Performance of 10 Gb/s lightwave systems based on lithium niobate Mach-Zehnder modulators with asymmetric Y-branch waveguides. *IEEE Photonics Technology Letters*, *7*(9), 1090–1092. doi:10.1109/68.414712

Chan, V., Chapin, J., Elson, P., Fisher, D., Frost, V., Jones, K., & Miller, G. (2011). *Workshop on future heterogeneous networks*. Mountain View.

Chandrasekhar, V., Andrews, J. G., & Muharemovic, T. et al. (2009). Power control in two-tier femtocell networks. *IEEE Transactions on Wireless Communications*, *8*(8), 4316–4328. doi:10.1109/TWC.2009.081386

Chang, J., Li, Y., Feng, S., Wang, H., Sun, C., & Zhang, P. (2009). A fractional soft handover scheme for 3GPP LTE-advanced system. In *Proceedings of IEEE International Conference on Communications Workshops* (pp. 1-5). IEEE.

Chang, Q., Ye, T., Gao, J., & Su, Y. (2008). *Generation of 60-GHz optical millimeter-wave and 20-GHz channel-spaced optical multicarrier using two cascaded 10-GHz modulators (pp. SaJ1)*. Optical Society of America. Retrieved from http://www.opticsinfobase.org/abstract.cfm?URI=AOE-2008-SaJ1

Charilas, D. E., Panagopoulos, A. D., Vlacheas, P., Markaki, O. I., & Constantinou, P. (2009). *Mobile lightweight wireless systems congestion avoidance control through non-cooperative games between customers and service providers*. Berlin: Springer.

Charilas, D., Athanasios, E., & Panagopoulos, D. (2010). A survey on game theory applications in wireless networks. *Computer Networks*, *54*(18), 3421–3430. doi:10.1016/j.comnet.2010.06.020

Charilas, D., & Panagopoulous, A. (2010). Multiaccess radio network enviroments. *IEEE Vehicular Technology Magazine*, *5*(4), 40–49. doi:10.1109/MVT.2010.939107

Charilas, D., Vassaki, S., Panagopoulos, A., & Constantinou, P. (2011). Cooperation incentives in 4G networks. In *Game theory for wireless communications and networking*. Boca Raton, FL: CRC Press. doi:10.1201/b10975-17

Chen, K., & Nahrstedt, K. (2004). iPass: An incentive compatible auction scheme to enable packet forwarding service in MANET. In *Proceedings of the 24th International Conference on Distributed Computing Systems*, (pp. 534-542). Academic Press.

Chen, K., Yang, Z., Wagener, C., & Nahrstedt, K. (2005). Market models and pricing mechanisms in a multihop wireless hotspot network. In *Proceedings of the Second Annual International Conference on Mobile and Ubiquitous Systems: Networking and Services* (MOBIQUITOUS '05), (pp. 73-84). Academic Press.

Chen, P., Ahammad, P., Boyer, C., Huang, S., Lin, L., & Lobaton, E. … Sastry, S. (2008). Citric: A low-bandwidth wireless camera network platform. In *Proceedings of the Second ACM/IEEE International Conference on Distributed Smart Cameras ICDSC 2008*. Stanford, CA: ACM/IEEE.

Chen, Q., Jiang, D., Taliwal, V., & Delgrossi, L. (2007). IEEE 802.11 based vehicular communication simulation design for NS-2. In *Proceedings of ACM International Workshop on Vehicular Ad Hoc Networks* (VANET). New York, NY: ACM.

Chen, Q., Schmidt-Eisenlohr, F., Jiang, D., Torrent-Moreno, M., Delgrossi, L., & Hartenstein, H. (2007). Overhaul of IEEE 802.11 modeling and simulation in NS-2. In *Proceedings of ACM Symposium on Modeling, Analysis, and Simulation of Wireless and Mobile Systems* (MSWiM). New York, NY: ACM.

Cherif, M. O., Senouci, S. M., & Ducourthial, B. (2009). A new framework of self-organization of vehicular networks. In *Proceedings of Information Infrastructure Symposium*, (pp. 1-6). IEEE.

Chiasserini, C. F., & Magli, E. (2002). Energy consumption and image quality in wireless video-surveillance networks. In *Proceedings of 13ᵗʰ IEEE International Symposium on Personal, Indoor and Mobile Radio Communications PIMRC'02* (pp. 2357–2361). IEEE Computer Society.

Choffnes, D. R., & Bustamante, F. E. (2005). *STRAW - An integrated mobility and traffic model for VANETs*. Paper presented at the International Command and Control Research and Technology Symposium. McLean, VA.

Choi, N., Choi, S., Seok, Y., Kwon, T., & Choi, Y. (2007). A solicitation-based IEEE 802.11p MAC protocol for roadside to vehicular networks. In *Proceedings of Mobile Networking for Vehicular Environments Conference*, (pp. 91–96). Anchorage, AK: Academic Press.

Christina, L., Ka-Lun, L., Nirmalathas, A., Novak, D., & Waterhouse, R. (2008). Impact of chromatic dispersion on 60 GHz radio-over-fiber transmission. In *Proceedings of IEEE Lasers and Electro-Optics Society*, (pp. 89–90). IEEE. doi:10.1109/leos.2008.4688502

Chrostowski, L., Zhao, X., Chang-Hasnain, C. J., Shau, R., Ortsiefer, M., & Amann, M. C. (2005). 50 GHz directly-modulated injection-locked 1.55 /spl mu/m VCSELs. In *Proceedings of OFC/NFOEC Technical Digest: Optical Fiber Communication Conference, 2005* (Vol. 4). IEEE. doi:10.1109/OFC.2005.192971

Chuah, C.-N., Du, H., Ghosal, D., Khorashadi, B., Liu, B., Smith, C., & Zhang, H. (2008). Distributed vehicular traffic control and safety applications with vgrid. In *Proceedings of IEEE Wireless Hive Networks Conference* (WHNC). IEEE.

Cisco Data Traffic Forecast Update, 2012–2017. (n.d.). Retrieved from http://www.cisco.com/en/US/solutions/collateral/ns341/ns525/ns537/ns705/ns827/white_paper_c11-520862.pdf

Cisco. (2012). *Architecture for mobile data offload over wi-fi access networks* (Cisco White Paper). Cisco.

Cisco. (2012). *Cisco visual networking index, 2012-2017*. Cisco.

Cisco. (2013a, February 6). *Cisco visual networking index: Global mobile data traffic forecast update, 2012–2017*. Retrieved November 25, 2013, from http://www.cisco.com/en/US/solutions/ collateral/ns341/ns525/ns537/ns705/ns827/white_paper_c11-520862.html

Cisco. (2013b, May 29). *Cisco visual networking index: Forecast and methodology, 2012–2017*. Retrieved December 14, 2013, from http://www.cisco.com/c/en/us/solutions/collateral/service-provider/ip-ngn-ip-next-generation-network/white_paper_c11-481360.html

Ciubotaru, B., Muntean, G. M., & Ghinea, G. (2009). Objective assessment of region of interest-aware adaptive multimedia streaming quality. *IEEE Transactions on Broadcasting*, *55*(2), 202–212. doi:10.1109/TBC.2009.2020448

Collins, K., & Muntean, G.-M. (2008). Route based vehicular traffic management for wireless vehicular networks. In *Proceedings of IEEE Vehicular Technology Conference* (VTC Fall). Calgary, Canada: IEEE.

Collins, K., & Muntean, G.-M. (2008). An adaptive vehicle route management solution enabled by wireless vehicular networks. In *Proceedings of IEEE Vehicular Technology Conference* (VTC-Fall). Calgary, Canada: IEEE.

Comaniciu, D., & Meer, P. (2002). Mean shift: A robust approach toward feature space analysis. *IEEE Transactions on Pattern Analysis and Machine Intelligence*, *24*(5), 603–619. doi:10.1109/34.1000236

Condoluci, M., Militano, L., Araniti, G., Molinaro, A., & Iera, A. (2013). *Multicasting in LTE-A networks enhanced by device-to-device communications*. Paper presented at the IEEE Global Telecommunications Conference. Atlanta, GA.

Cosma, M., Pescaru, D., Ciubotaru, B., & Todinca, D. (2006). Routing and topology extraction protocol for a wireless sensor network using video information. In *Proceedings of the 3rd Romanian-Hungarian Joint Symposium on Applied Computational Intelligence SACI'06*. Timisoara, Romania: SACI.

Costa, D., & Guedes, L. (2010). The coverage problem in video-based wireless sensor networks: A survey. *Sensors (Basel, Switzerland)*, *10*, 8215–8247. doi:10.3390/s100908215 PMID:22163651

Costa, D., & Guedes, L. (2013). Exploiting the sensing relevancies of source nodes for optimizations in visual sensor networks. *Multimedia Tools and Applications*, *64*(3), 549–579. doi:10.1007/s11042-011-0961-4

Coursera. (n.d.). *Coursera*. Retrieved October 13, 2013, from https://www.coursera.org/

Čuchran, J., & Róka, R. (2006). *Optocommunication systems and networks*. Bratislava, Slovakia: Slovak University of Technology Publishing House.

Curiac, D., Volosencu, C., Pescaru, D., Jurca, L., & Doboli, A. (2009). View upon redundancy in wireless sensor networks. In *Proceedings of the 8th Wseas International Conference on Signal Processing, Robotics and Automation – ISPRA'09, Mathematics and Computers in Science and Engineering* (pp. 341-346). Cambridge, UK: ISPRA.

Dahlman, E., Parkvall, S., & Skold, J. (2008). *3G evolution: HSPA and LTE for mobile broadband*. Burlington, MA: Academic Press.

Davies, P. A., & Urey, Z. (1992). *Subcarrier multiplexing in optical communication networks*. Academic Press.

Davies, P. A., Wake, D., & Lima, C. R. (1995). Compact optical millimetre-wave source using a dual-mode semiconductor laser. *Electronics Letters, 31*(5), 364–366. doi:10.1049/el:19950237

Davis, E. S., & Hantula, D. A. (2001). The effects of download delay on performance and end-user satisfaction in an Internet tutorial. *Computers in Human Behavior, 17*(3), 249–268. doi:10.1016/S0747-5632(01)00007-3

Dawood, M. S., Suganya, J., Devi, R. K., & Athisha, G. (2013). A review on wireless sensor network protocol for disaster management. *International Journal of Computer Applications Technology and Research, 2*(2), 141–146. doi:10.7753/IJCATR0202.1011

Demir, C., & Comaniciu, C. (2007). An auction based AODV protocol for mobile ad hoc networks with selfish nodes. In *Proceedings of IEEE International Conference on Communications* (ICC '07), (pp. 3351-3356). IEEE.

Desai, P., & Rattan, K. S. (2009). Indoor localization and surveillance using wireless sensor network and pan/tilt camera. In *Proceedings of the IEEE National Aerospace & Electronics Conference NAECON'09*. Fairborn, OH: IEEE.

Dia, H., Panwai, S., Boongrapue, N., Ton, T., & Smith, N. (2006). Comparative evaluation of powerbased environmental emissions models. In *Proceedings of IEEE Intelligent Transportation Systems Conference*, (ITSC '06), (pp. 1251–1256). IEEE.

Ding, R., & Muntean, G. M. (2013). Device characteristics-based differentiated energy-efficient adaptive solution for video delivery over heterogeneous wireless networks. In *Proceedings of IEEE Wireless Communications and Networking Conference*. Shanghai, China: IEEE.

Ding, X., Hartog, J., & Sun, Y. (2010). *Can we measure individual risk attitudes in a survey?* (IZA Discussion Paper No 4807). Retrieved August 22, 2011, from http://ftp.iza.org/dp4807.pdf

Djahel, S., Salehie, M., Tal, I., & Jamshidi, P. (2013). Adaptive traffic management for secure and efficient emergency services in smart cities. In *Pervasive computing and communications* (pp. 340–343). Academic Press. doi:10.1109/PerComW.2013.6529511

Dobrian, F., Sekar, V., Awan, A., Stoica, I., Joseph, D., & Ganjam, A. ... Zhang, H. (2011). Understanding the impact of video quality on user engagement. In *Proceedings of the ACM SIGCOMM 2011 Conference* (pp. 362–373). New York, NY: ACM. edX. (n.d.). *edX*. Retrieved October 13, 2013, from https://www.edx.org/

Dohmen, T., Falk, A., David, H., & Sunde, U. (2008). *The intergenerational transmission of risk and trust attitudes* (IZA Discussion Paper No 2380). Retrieved August 22, 2011, from http://www.swarthmore.edu/Documents/academics/economics/huffman/Intergenerational_ReStud_revision2_v6.pdf

Dohmen, T., & Falk, A. (2011). Performance pay and multidimensional sorting - Productivity, preferences and gender. *The American Economic Review, 101*(2), 556–590. doi:10.1257/aer.101.2.556

Dohmen, T., Falk, A., Huffman, D., Sunde, U., Schupp, J., & Wagner, G. (2011). Individual risk attitudes: Measurement, determinants and behavioural consequences. *Journal of the European Economic Association, 9*(3), 522–550. doi:10.1111/j.1542-4774.2011.01015.x

Doolan, R., & Muntean, G. M. (2013). VANET-enabled eco-friendly road characteristics-aware routing for vehicular traffic. In *Proceedings of IEEE Vehicular Technology Conference* (pp. 1-5). IEEE.

Dou, Y., Zhang, H., & Yao, M. (2012). Generation of flat optical-frequency comb using cascaded intensity and phase modulators. *IEEE Photonics Technology Letters, 24*(9), 727–729. doi:10.1109/LPT.2012.2187330

Downes, I., Rad, L. B., & Aghajan, H. (2006). Development of a mote for wireless image sensor networks. In *Proceedings of COGnitive Systems with Interactive Sensors – COGIS'06*. Paris, France: COGIS.

Dror, E., Avin, C., & Lotker, Z. (2011). Fast randomized algorithm for hierarchical clustering in vehicular ad-hoc networks. In *Proceedings of Ad Hoc Networking Workshop (Med-Hoc-Net),* (pp. 1-8). IEEE.

Dror, E., Avin, C., & Lotker, Z. (2013). Fast randomized algorithm for 2-hops clustering in vehicular ad-hoc networks. *Ad Hoc Networks, 11*(7), 2002–2015. doi:10.1016/j.adhoc.2012.02.006

Dutta, P. (1999). *Strategies and games, theory and practice.* Cambridge, MA: MIT Press.

Easley, D., & Kleinberg, J. (2010). *Networks, crowds, and markets: Reasoning about a highly connected world.* Cambridge, UK: Cambridge University Press. doi:10.1017/CBO9780511761942

ECC. (2012). *ECC report 176.* ECC.

Effenberger, F. et al. (2009). Next-generation PON – Part II: Candidate systems for next-generation PON. *IEEE Communications Magazine, 47*(11), 50–57. doi:10.1109/MCOM.2009.5307466

Effenberger, F. et al. (2009). Next-generation PON – Part III: System specification for XG-PON. *IEEE Communications Magazine, 47*(11), 58–64. doi:10.1109/MCOM.2009.5307467

Egevang, K., & Francis, P. (1994). *RFC 1631: The IP network address translator (NAT).* Retrieved from http://www.hjp.at/doc/rfc/rfc1631.html

Eidenbenz, S., Resta, G., & Santi, P. (2008). The commit protocol for truthful and cost-efficient routing in ad hoc networks with selfish nodes. *IEEE Transactions on Mobile Computing, 7*(1), 19–33. doi:10.1109/TMC.2007.1069

Elbahhar, F., Rivenq, A., Heddebaut, M., & Rouvaen, J. M. (2005). Using UWB Gaussian pulses for inter-vehicle communications. *IEE Proceedings. Communications, 152*(2), 229–234. doi:10.1049/ip-com:20040572

Elixmann, D., Figueras, A. P., Hackbarth, K., Marcus, J. S., Nagy, P., Pápai, Z., & Scanlan, M. (2007). *The regulation of next generation networks (NGN)* (Final Report). Budapest.

Elnahrawy, E., Li, X., & Martin, R. P. (2004). The limits of localization using signal strength: A comparative study. In *Proceedings of the 1st IEEE International Conference on Sensor and Ad Hoc Communications and Networks SECON'04.* Santa Clara, CA: IEEE.

Elsawy, H., Hossain, E., & Kim, D. (2013). Heterogeneous networks with cognitive smallcells: User offloading and distributed channel access techniques. *IEEE Communications Magazine, 51*(6), 28–36. doi:10.1109/MCOM.2013.6525592

Ericson. (2012). *Traffic and market report.* Ericson.

Eriksson, J., Girod, L., Hull, B., Newton, R., Madden, S., & Balakrishnan, H. (2008). *The pothole patrol: Using a mobile sensor network for road surface monitoring.* Paper presented at the Annual International Conference on Mobile Systems, Applications and Services (MobiSys). Breckenridge, CO.

Esman, R. D., & Williams, K. J. (1995). Wideband efficiency improvement of fiber optic systems by carrier subtraction. *IEEE Photonics Technology Letters, 7*(2), 218–220. doi:10.1109/68.345928

Evans, J., & Minieka, E. (1992). *Optimization algorithms for networks and graphs.* New York: Dekker.

Fadlullah, Z. M., Nozaki, Y., Takeuchi, A., & Kato, N. (2011). A survey of game theoretic approaches in smart grid. In *Proceedings of International Conference on Wireless Communications and Signal Processing* (WCSP), (pp. 1-4). WCSP.

Fan, P., Haran, J. G., Dillenburg, J., & Nelson, P. C. (2005). Cluster-based framework in vehicular ad-hoc networks. In *Proceedings of Ad-Hoc, Mobile, and Wireless Networks* (pp. 32–42). Berlin: Springer. doi:10.1007/11561354_5

Federal Communications Commissions. (2012). 15.255 operation within the: Vol. 57. *64 GHz* (pp. 851–853). Author.

Felegyhazi, M., & Hubaux, J. (2006). *Game theory in wireless networks: A tutorial (EPFL Technical Report, 2006-002).* EPFL.

Feng, D.Q., Jiang, C.Z., Lim, G.B., Cimini, Jr., et al. (2012). A survey of energy-efficient wireless communications. *IEEE Communications Surveys and Tutorials.*

Feng, W. C., Kaiser, E., Feng, W. C., & Le Baillif, M. (2005). Panoptes: Scalable low-power video sensor networking technologies. *ACM Transactions on Multimedia Computing. Communications and Applications, 1*(2), 151–167.

Fernandes, S., & Karmouch, A. (2012). Vertical mobility management architectures in wireless networks: A comprehensive survey and future directions. *IEEE Communications Surveys & Tutorials, 14*(1), 45–63. doi:10.1109/SURV.2011.082010.00099

Fernandez, J., Calavia, L., Baladrón, C., Aguiar, J. M., Carro, B., & Sánchez-Esguevillas, A. et al. (2013). An intelligent surveillance platform for large metropolitan areas with dense sensor deployment. *Sensors (Basel, Switzerland), 13*(6), 7414–7442. doi:10.3390/s130607414 PMID:23748169

Fielding, R., Gettys, J., Mogul, J., Frystyk, H., Masinter, L., Leach, P., & Berners-Lee, T. (1999). *RFC 2616: Hypertext transfer protocol -- HTTP/1.1*. Retrieved from http://www.w3.org/Protocols/rfc2616/rfc2616.txt

Fischler, M. A., & Bolles, R. C. (1981). Random sample consensus: A paradigm for model fitting with applications to image analysis and automated cartography. *Communication Magazine of the ACM, 24*(6), 381–395. doi:10.1145/358669.358692

Fisher, D. (2013). Harmonic powers virgin media's MPEG-DASH trial. *Harmonic Inc.* Retrieved October 10, 2013, from http://harmonicinc.com/news/harmonic-powers-virgin-media-s-mpeg-dash-trial

France, P. W., Spirit, D. M., & Whitt, S. (1998). Developing the access network. *BT Technology Journal, 16*(4), 9–20.

Frey, B. J., & Dueck, D. (2007). Clustering by passing messages between data points. *Science, 315*(5814), 972–976. doi:10.1126/science.1136800 PMID:17218491

Fu, S., Wu, B., Ho, P., & Ling, X. (2012). Interference coordination in CoMP with transmission scheduling and game theoretical power reallocation. In *Proceedings of IEEE ICC 2012* (pp. 4212-4217). IEEE.

Fuiorea, D., Gui, V., Pescaru, D., Paraschiv, P., Istin, C., Curiac, D., & Volosencu, C. (2008). Sensor node localization using SIFT algorithm. In *Proceedings of the 9th International Conference on Automation and Information* (pp. 436-442). Bucharest, Romania: Academic Press.

Gazdar, T., Belghith, A., & Benslimane, A. (2010). A cluster based secure architecture for vehicular ad hoc networks. In Proceedings of Computer Systems and Applications (AICCSA), (pp. 1-8). IEEE.

Gazdar, T., Benslimane, A., & Belghith, A. (2011). Secure clustering scheme based keys management in VANETs. In *Proceedings of Vehicular Technology Conference (VTC Spring)*, (pp. 1-5). IEEE.

Gerami, M. (2010). Evaluation of next generation networks. *International Journal on Computer Science and Engineering, 2*(2), 378–381.

Gharehshiran, O. N., Attar, A., & Krishnamurthy, V. (2013). Collaborative sub-channel allocation in cognitive LTE femto-cells: A cooperative game-theoretic approach. *IEEE Transactions on Communications, 61*(1), 325–334. doi:10.1109/TCOMM.2012.100312.110480

Ghazvini, M., Movahedinia, N., Jamshidi, K., & Moghim, N. (2013). Game theory applications in CSMA methods. *IEEE Communications Surveys & Tutorials, 15*(3), 1062–1087. doi:10.1109/SURV.2012.111412.00167

Ghosh, A., Mangalvedhe, N., & Ratasuk, R. et al. (2012). Heterogeneous cellular networks: From theory to practice. *IEEE Communications Magazine, 50*(6), 54–64. doi:10.1109/MCOM.2012.6211486

Gibbons, R. (1992). *A primer in game theory*. Upper Saddle River, NJ: Pearson Education Limited.

Girinath, D. R., & Selvan, S. (2010). A novel cluster based routing algorithm for hybrid mobility model in VANET. *International Journal of Computers and Applications, 1*(15), 35–42. doi:10.5120/326-495

Gliese, U., Nielsen, T. N., Norskov, S., & Stubkjaer, K. E. (1998). Multifunctional fiber-optic microwave links based on remote heterodyne detection. *IEEE Transactions on Microwave Theory and Techniques, 46*(5), 458–468. doi:10.1109/22.668642

Gliese, U., Norskov, S., & Nielsen, T. N. (1996). Chromatic dispersion in fiber-optic microwave and millimeter-wave links. *IEEE Transactions on Microwave Theory and Techniques, 44*(10), 1716–1724. doi:10.1109/22.538964

Goldberg, A., & Ball, M. (2004). *Computing the shortest path: A* search meets graph theory* (Tech. Rep. MSR-TR-2004-24). Microsoft Research.

Goldberg, L., Taylor, H. F., Weller, J. F., & Bloom, D. M. (1983). Microwave signal generation with injection-locked laser diodes. *Electronics Letters*, *19*(13), 491. doi:10.1049/el:19830333

Goldberg, L., Yurek, A. M., Taylor, H. F., & Weller, J. F. (1985). 35 GHz microwave signal generation with an injection-locked laser diode. *Electronics Letters*, *21*(18), 814. doi:10.1049/el:19850574

Goldsmith, A. (2012). Beyond 4G: What lies ahead for cellular system design. In *Proceedings of Wireless Communications and Networking Conference* (WCNC). IEEE.

Gomes, P., Vieira, F., & Ferreira, M. (2013). Sustainable highways with shadow tolls based on VANET advertising. In *Proceeding of the Tenth ACM International Workshop on Vehicular Inter-Networking, Systems, and Applications* (pp. 71-76). ACM.

Goonewardene, R. T., Ali, F. H., & Stipidis, E. L. I. A. S. (2009). Robust mobility adaptive clustering scheme with support for geographic routing for vehicular ad hoc networks. *Intelligent Transport Systems*, *3*(2), 148–158. doi:10.1049/iet-its:20070052

Gouache, S., Bichot, G., Bsila, A., & Howson, C. (2011). Distributed adaptive HTTP streaming. In *Proceedings of 2011 IEEE International Conference on Multimedia and Expo (ICME)* (pp. 1–6). Barcelona, Spain: IEEE.

Goutain, E., Renaud, J. C., Krakowski, M., Rondi, D., Blondeau, R., & Decoster, D. (1996). 30 GHz bandwidth, 1.55 micro sign]m MQW-DFB laser diode based on a new modulation scheme. *Electronics Letters*, *32*(10), 896. doi:10.1049/el:19960588

Gradinescu, V., Gorgorin, C., Diaconescu, R., Cristea, V., & Iftode, L. (2007). Adaptive traffic lights using car-to-car communication. In *Proceedings of IEEE Vehicular Technology Conference*. Dublin, Ireland: IEEE.

Gritter, M., & Cheriton, D. R. (2000). *TRIAD: A new next-generation internet architecture*. Retrieved from http://www-dsg.stanford.edu/triad/

Grossman, P. J. (2013). Holding fast: The persistence and dominance of gender stereotypes. *Economic Inquiry*, *51*(1), 747–763. doi:10.1111/j.1465-7295.2012.00479.x

Guiso, L., Sapienza, P., & Zingales, L. (2013). *Time varying risk aversion*. The National Bureau of Economic Research. Retrieved September 16, 2013, from http://www.econ.yale.edu/~shiller/behfin/2013_04/Guiso_Sapienza_Zingales.pdf

Gunter, Y., Wiegel, B., & Großmann, H. P. (2007). Medium access concept for VANETs based on clustering. In *Proceedings of Vehicular Technology Conference,* (pp. 2189-2193). IEEE.

Guo, C., Guo, Z., Zhang, Q., & Wenwu, Z. (2004). A seamless and proactive end-to-end mobility solution for roaming across heterogeneous wireless networks. *IEEE Journal on Selected Areas in Communications*, *22*(5), 834–848. doi:10.1109/JSAC.2004.826921

Gur, G., & Alagoz, F. (2011). Green wireless communications via cognitive dimension: An overview. *IEEE Network*, *25*(2), 50–56. doi:10.1109/MNET.2011.5730528

Guruacharya, S., Niyato, D., Hossain, E., & Kim, D. I. (2010). Hierarchical competition in femtocell-based cellular networks. In *Proceedings of IEEE Global Telecommunications Conference* (GLOBECOM), (pp. 1-5). IEEE.

Guruacharya, S., & Niyato, D., Dong In Kim, & Hossain, E. (2013). Hierarchical competition for downlink power allocation in OFDMA femtocell networks. *IEEE Transactions on Wireless Communications*, *12*(4), 1543–1553. doi:10.1109/TWC.2013.022213.120016

Guruprasad, K. R. (2011). Generalized Vornoi partition: A new tool for optimal placement of base stations. In *Proceedings of IEEE International Conference on Advanced Networks and Telecommunication Systems* (pp. 1-3). IEEE.

Hafeez, K. A., Zhao, L., Liao, Z., & Ma, B. N. W. (2011). Clustering and OFDMA-based MAC protocol (COMAC) for vehicular ad hoc networks. *EURASIP Journal on Wireless Communications and Networking*, (1): 1–16.

Hammitt, J., & Haninger, K. (2010). Valuing fatal risks to children and adults: Effects of disease, latency, and risk aversion. *Journal of Risk and Uncertainty*, *40*(1), 57–83. doi:10.1007/s11166-009-9086-9

Han, Z., Niyato, D., Saad, W., Basar, T., & Hjorungnes, A. (Eds.). (2012). *Game theory in wireless communications and networks: Theory, models, and applications*. Cambridge, UK: Cambridge University Press.

Harikrishnan, Y., & He, J. (2013). Clustering algorithm based on minimal path loss ratio for vehicular communication. In Proceedings of Computing, Networking and Communications (ICNC), (pp. 745-749). IEEE.

Harsanyi, J. (1967). Games with incomplete information played by Bayesian players, part I, the basic model. *Management Science, 14*(3), 159–182. doi:10.1287/mnsc.14.3.159

Hartenstein, H., Bochow, B., Ebner, A., Lott, M., Radimirsch, M., & Vollmer, D. (2001). Position-aware ad hoc wireless networks for inter-vehicle communications: The Fleetnet project. In *Proceedings of the 2nd ACM International Symposium on Mobile Ad Hoc Networking & Computing* (pp. 259-262). ACM.

Hasan, Z., Boostanimehr, H., & Bhargava Vijay, K. (2011). Green cellular networks: A survey, some research issues and challenges. *IEEE Communications Surveys and Tutorials, 13*(4), 524–540. doi:10.1109/SURV.2011.092311.00031

Hassin, D., & Vahldieck, R. (1993). Feedforward linearization of analog modulated laser diodes-theoretical analysis and experimental verification. *IEEE Transactions on Microwave Theory and Techniques, 41*(12), 2376–2382. doi:10.1109/22.260731

He, Q., Wu, D., & Pradeep, K. (2004). SORI: A secure and objective reputation-based incentive scheme for ad-hoc networks. In *Proceedings of IEEE Wireless Communications and Networking Conference* (WCNC'04), (vol. 2, pp. 825-830). IEEE.

Heinzelman, W., Chandrakasan, A., & Balakrishnan, H. (2000). Energy-efficient communication protocol for wireless microsensor networks. In *Proceedings of the 33rd Annual Hawaii International Conference on System Sciences*. IEEE.

Höffler, F. (2007). Cost and benefits from infrastructure competition: Estimating welfare effects from broadband access competition. *Telecommunications Policy, 31*(6-7), 401–418. doi:10.1016/j.telpol.2007.05.004

Huang, C., & Tseng, Y. (2003). The coverage problem in a wireless sensor network. In *Proceedings of 2nd 909 ACM International Workshop on Wireless Sensor Networks and Applications* (pp. 115-121). San Diego, CA: ACM.

Huang, C. J., Lin, C. F., Li, C. Y., Lee, C. Y., Chen, H. M., Shen, H. Y., & Chen, I. F. (2011). Service-oriented routing and clustering strategies for vehicle infotainment dissemination. *International Journal of Innovative Computing, Information, & Control, 7*(3), 1467–1480.

Huang, H. C., Wang, T. Y., & Hsieh, F. M. (2012). Constructing an adaptive mobile learning system for the support of personalized learning and device adaptation. *Procedia-Social and Behavioral Sciences, 64*, 332–341. doi:10.1016/j.sbspro.2012.11.040

Huang, J. (in press). Economic viability of dynamic spectrum management. In *Mechanisms and games for dynamic spectrum allocation*. Cambridge, UK: Cambridge University Press. doi:10.1017/CBO9781139524421.018

Huang, J. H., & Han, Z. (2010). Game theory for spectrum sharing. In *Cognitive radio networks: Architectures, protocols, and standards*. Auerbach Publications, CRC Press. doi:10.1201/EBK1420077759-c10

Huchard, M., Chanclou, P., Charbonnier, B., van Dijk, F., Duan, G.-H., & Gonzalez, C. ... Stohr, A. (2008). 60 GHz radio signal up-conversion and transport using a directly modulated mode-locked laser. In *Proceedings of 2008 International Topical Meeting on Microwave Photonics Jointly Held with the 2008 Asia-Pacific Microwave Photonics Conference* (pp. 333–335). IEEE. doi:10.1109/MWP.2008.4666705

Hügelschäfer, S., & Achtziger, A. (2013). On confident men and rational women: It's all on your mind (set). *Journal of Economic Psychology*. ISSN 0167-4870

Hwang, J., Shin, A., & Yoon, H. (2008). Dynamic reputation-based incentive mechanism considering heterogeneous networks. In *Proceedings of the 3rd ACM Workshop on Performance Monitoring and Measurement of Heterogeneous Wireless and Wired Networks* (PM2HW2N '08), (pp. 137-144). ACM.

IDate Consulting and Reserach. (2013). *Telecoms, internet, media*. Retrieved from http://www.idate.org/en/Research/FTTx-Watch-Service/World-FTTx-Markets_57_.html

IEEE Standard for Local and Metropolitan Area Networks-Part 16. (2005) Air interface for fixed broadband wireless access systems (Incorporated into IEEE Standard 802.16e-2005 and IEEE Standard 802.16-2004/Cor 1-2005 E). *IEEE Standard P802.16/Cor1/D5*. IEEE.

IEEE802. 15. (2013). *THz interest group.* Retrieved from http://www.ieee802.org/15/pub/IGthz.html

Iftode, L., Smaldone, S., Gerla, M., & Misener, J. (2008). Active highways (position paper). In *Proceedings of IEEE International Symposium on Personal, Indoor and Mobile Radio Communications* (PIMRC). IEEE.

Ileri, O., Siun-Chuon, M., & Mandayam, N. B. (2005). Pricing for enabling forwarding in self-configuring ad hoc networks. *IEEE Journal on Selected Areas in Communications, 23*(1), 151–162. doi:10.1109/JSAC.2004.837356

Isaac, J. T., Camara, J. S., Zeadally, S., & Marquez, J. T. (2008). A secure vehicle-to-roadside communication payment protocol in vehicular ad-hoc networks. *Computer Communications, 31*(10), 2478–2484. doi:10.1016/j.comcom.2008.03.012

Islam, M. H., Dziong, Z., Sohraby, K., Daneshmand, M. F., & Jana, R. (2012). Capacity-optimal relay and base station placement in wireless networks. In *Proceedings of International Conference on Information Networking* (pp. 358-363). Academic Press.

Ismail, M., & Zhuang, W. (2011). Network cooperation for energy saving in green radio communications. *IEEE Wireless Commun., 18*(5), 76–81. doi:10.1109/MWC.2011.6056695

ISO. (2012). *ISO/IEC 23009-1:2012 information technology -- Dynamic adaptive streaming over HTTP (DASH) -- Part 1: Media presentation description and segment formats.* Retrieved from http://www.iso.org/iso/catalogue_detail.htm?csnumber=57623

Istin, C., & Pescaru, D. (2007). Deployments metrics for video-based wireless sensor networks. *Transactions on Automatic Control and Computer Science, 52*(66).

Istin, C., Pescaru, D., & Doboli, A. (2011). Stochastic model-based heuristics for fast field of view loss recovery in urban traffic management through networks of video cameras. *IEEE Transactions on Intelligent Traffic Systems, 12*(3), 895–907. doi:10.1109/TITS.2011.2123095

ITEC MPEG-DASH MPD Validator. (n.d.). Retrieved October 20, 2013, from http://www-itec.uni-klu.ac.at/dash/?page_id=605

ITU. (2006). *Ruling the new and emerging markets in the telecommunication sector.* Paper presented at the ITU Workshop on What Rules for IP-Enabled NGNs? Geneva, Switzerland.

ITU-T Telecommunication Standardization Sector. (2009). *Characteristics of a single-mode optical fiber and cable.* Recommendation G.652.

ITU-T Telecommunication Standardization Sector. (2009). *Characteristics of a bending-loss insensitive single-mode optical fiber and cable for the access network.* Recommendation G.657.

ITU-T Telecommunication Standardization Sector. (2010). *10-gigabit-capable passive optical network systems: Definitions, abbreviations, and acronyms.* Recommendation G.987.

ITU-T. (2008). *Telecom network planning for evolving network architectures.* International Telecommunication Union.

Jang, J.-S. R. (2002). ANFIS: Adaptive-network-based fuzzy inference system. *IEEE Transactions on Systems, Man, and Cybernetics, 23*(3), 665–685. doi:10.1109/21.256541

Jaramillo, J. J., & Srikant, R. (2007). Darwin: Distributed and adaptive reputation mechanism for wireless ad-hoc networks. In *Proceedings of the 13th Annual ACM International Conference on Mobile Computing and Networking* (MobiCom '07), (pp. 87-98). ACM.

Jarnikov, D., & Ozcelebi, T. (2011). Client intelligence for adaptive streaming solutions. *Signal Processing Image Communication, 26*(7), 378–389. doi:10.1016/j.image.2011.03.003

Jiang, D., & Delgrossi, L. (2008). IEEE 802.11p: Towards an international standard for wireless access in vehicular environments. In *Proceedings of IEEE Vehicular Technology Conference* (VTC Spring 2008), (pp. 2036-2040). IEEE.

Jiang, D., Chen, Q., & Delgrossi, L. (2008). Optimal data rate selection for vehicle safety communications. In *Proceedings of ACM International Workshop on Vehicular Inter-NETworking* (VANET). New York, NY: ACM.

Jianjun, Y., Gee-Kung, C., Zhensheng, J., Chowdhury, A., Ming-Fang, H., & Hung-Chang, C. et al. (2010). Cost-effective optical millimeter technologies and field demonstrations for very high throughput wireless-over-fiber access systems. *Journal of Lightwave Technology*, *28*(16), 2376–2397. doi:10.1109/JLT.2010.2041748

Johansson, L. A., & Seeds, A. J. (2000). Millimeter-wave modulated optical signal generation with high spectral purity and wide-locking bandwidth using a fiber-integrated optical injection phase-lock loop. *IEEE Photonics Technology Letters*, *12*(6), 690–692. doi:10.1109/68.849086

Johansson, L. A., & Seeds, A. J. (2001). 36-GHz 140-Mb/s radio-over-fiber transmission using an optical injection phase-lock loop source. *IEEE Photonics Technology Letters*, *13*(8), 893–895. doi:10.1109/68.935839

Kang, X., Zhang, R., & Motani, M. (2012). Price-based resource allocation for spectrum-sharing femtocell networks: A Stackelberg game approach. *IEEE Journal on Selected Areas in Communications*, *30*(3), 538–549. doi:10.1109/JSAC.2012.120404

Kani, J. et al. (2009). Next-generation PON – Part I: Technology roadmap and general requirements. *IEEE Communications Magazine*, *47*(11), 43–49. doi:10.1109/MCOM.2009.5307465

Kanno, A., Morohashi, I., Kuri, T., Hosako, I., Kawanishi, T., & Yasumura, Y. … Kitayama, K. (2012). 16-Gbaud QPSK radio transmission using optical frequency comb with recirculating frequency shifter for 300-GHz RoF signal. In *Proceedings of 2012 IEEE International Topical Meeting on Microwave Photonics* (pp. 298–301). IEEE. doi:10.1109/MWP.2012.6474117

Kanno, A., Inagaki, K., Morohashi, I., Sakamoto, T., Kuri, T., & Hosako, I. et al. (2011). 20-Gb/s QPSK W-band (75-110GHz) wireless link in free space using radio-over-fiber technique. *IEICE Electronics Express*, *8*(8), 612–617. doi:10.1587/elex.8.612

Kanno, A., Kuri, T., Hosako, I., Kawanishi, T., Yasumura, Y., Yoshida, Y., & Kitayama, K. (2013). 100-GHz and 300-GHz coherent radio-over-fiber transmission using optical frequency comb source. In B. B. Dingel, R. Jain, & K. Tsukamoto (Eds.), *Broadband access communication technologies VII* (Vol. 8645, p. 864503–864503, 7). doi:10.1117/12.1000150

Karadeniz, S. (2011). Effects of gender and test anxiety on student achievement in mobile based assessment. *Procedia Social and Behavioral Sciences*, *15*, 3173–3178. doi:10.1016/j.sbspro.2011.04.267

Karagiannis, G., Altintas, O., Ekici, E., Heijenk, G., Jarupan, B., Lin, K., & Weil, T. (2011). Vehicular networking: A survey and tutorial on requirements, architectures, challenges, standards and solutions. *IEEE Communications Surveys & Tutorials*, *13*(4), 584–616. doi:10.1109/SURV.2011.061411.00019

Karhunen, P., & Ledyaeva, S. (2010). Determinants of entrepreneurial interest and risk tolerance among Russian university students: Empirical study. *Journal of Enterprising Culture*, *18*(3), 229–263. doi:10.1142/S0218495810000574

Katsianis, D., Gyürke, A., Konkoly, R., Varoutas, D., & Sphicopoulos, T. (2007). A game theory modeling approach for 3G operators. *NETNOMICS: Economic Research and Electronic Networking*, *8*(1), 71–90. doi:10.1007/s11066-008-9022-1

Kayis, O., & Acarman, T. (2007). Clustering formation for inter-vehicle communication. In *Proceedings of Intelligent Transportation Systems Conference*, (pp. 636-641). IEEE.

Kazovsky, L. G. et al. (2007). Next-generation optical access networks. *Journal of Lightwave Technology*, *25*(11), 3428–3442. doi:10.1109/JLT.2007.907748

KCC. (2006). *Frequency allocation comment on 60 GHz band*. Korea Communications Commission.

Keiser, G. (2000). *Optical fiber communications* (3rd ed.). New York: McGraw-Hill.

Khan, M. A., Sivrikaya, F., Albayrak, S., & Mengaly, K. Q. (2009). Auction based interface selection in heterogeneous wireless networks. In *Proceedings of Second IFIP Wireless Days* (pp. 1-6). IFIP.

Khan, M. A., Toseef, U., Marx, S., & Goerg, C. (2010). Auction based interface selection with media independent handover services and flow management. In *Proceedings of European Wireless Conference* (pp. 429-436). Academic Press.

Khan, M. A., Toseef, U., Marx, S., & Goerg, C. (2010). Game-theory based user centric network selection with media independent handover services and flow management. In *Proceedings of Eighth Annual Communication Networks and Services Research Conference* (pp. 248-255). Academic Press.

Khan, M., Tembine, H., & Vasilakos, A. (2012). Evolutionary coalitional games: design and challenges in wireless networks. *IEEE Wireless Communications*, *19*(2), 50–56. doi:10.1109/MWC.2012.6189413

Khan, M., Tembine, H., & Vasilakos, A. (2012). Game dynamics and cost of learning in heterogeneous 4G networks. *IEEE Journal on Selected Areas in Communications*, *30*(1), 198–213. doi:10.1109/JSAC.2012.120118

Khawaja, B. A., & Cryan, M. J. (2010). Wireless hybrid mode locked lasers for next generation radio-over-fiber systems. *Journal of Lightwave Technology*, *28*(16), 2268–2276. doi:10.1109/JLT.2010.2050461

Kingston, R. H. (1979). Electroabsorption in GaInAsP. *Applied Physics Letters*, *34*(11), 744. doi:10.1063/1.90657

Kirsch, F., & Hirschhausen, C. V. (2008). *Regulation of next generation networks: Structural separation, access regulation, or no regulation at all?* Paper presented at the First International Conference on Infrastructure Systems and Services: Building Networks for a Brighter Future (INFRA). Rotterdam, The Netherland.

Kleihorst, R., Abbo, A., Schueler, B., & Danilin, A. (2007). Camera mote with a high-performance parallel processor for real-time frame-based video processing. In *Proceedings of the IEEE Conference on Advanced Video and Signal Based Surveillance – AVSS'07* (pp. 69-74). IEEE.

Koenig, S., Boes, F., Antes, J., Henneberger, R., Schmogrow, R., Hillerkuss, D., & Palmer, R. (2013). 100 Gbit / s wireless link with mm-wave photonics, 1(IL), 22–24.

Kolner, B. H., & Dolfi, D. W. (1987). Intermodulation distortion and compression in an integrated electro-optic modulator. *Applied Optics*, *26*(17), 3676–3680. doi:10.1364/AO.26.003676 PMID:20490122

Kosch, T., Kulp, I., Bechler, M., Strassberger, M., Weyl, B., & Lasowski, R. (2009). Communication architecture for cooperative systems in Europe. *IEEE Communications Magazine*, *47*(5), 116–125. doi:10.1109/MCOM.2009.4939287

Kosugi, T., Shibata, T., Enoki, T., Muraguchi, M., Hirata, A., Nagatsuma, T., & Kyuragi, H. (2003). *A 120GHz millimeter wave MMIC chipset for future broadband wireless access applications*. Academic Press.

Kota, S. L. (2006). *Satellite multimedia networks and technical challenges*. Microwave Review.

Kuklinski, S., & Wolny, G. (2009). Density based clustering algorithm for VANETs. In Proceedings of Testbeds and Research Infrastructures for the Development of Networks & Communities and Workshops, (pp. 1-6). IEEE.

Kukutsu, N., Hirata, A., Kosugi, T., Takahashi, H., Yamaguchi, R., Nagatsuma, T., & Kado, Y. (2008). 10-Gbit/s wireless link using 120-GHz-band MMIC technologies. In *Proceedings of 2008 33rd International Conference on Infrared, Millimeter and Terahertz Waves*. doi:10.1109/ICIMW.2008.4665692

Kuo, Y., Wu, E., & Chen, G. (2004). Non-cooperative admission control for differentiated services in IEEE 802.11 WLANs. In *Proceedings of the IEEE Global Telecommunications Conference* (GLOBECOM 2004), (vol. 5, pp. 2981-2986). IEEE.

Kürner, T. (2012). Towards future THz communications systems. *Terahertz Science and Technology*, *5*(1), 11–17.

Kusy, B., Ledeczi, A., & Koutsoukos, X. (2007). Tracking mobile nodes using RF doppler shifts. In *Proceedings of the 5th International Conference on Embedded Networked Sensor Systems SenSys'07*. Sydney, Australia: ACM Press.

Kwak, J. S., & Lee, J. H. (2004). Infrared transmission for inter-vehicle ranging and vehicle-to-roadside communication systems using spread-spectrum technique. *IEEE Transactions on Intelligent Transportation Systems*, *5*(1), 12–19. doi:10.1109/TITS.2004.825082

Lai, L., & el Gamal, H. (2008). The water-filling game in fading multiple-access channels. *IEEE Transactions on Information Theory*, *54*(5), 2110–2122. doi:10.1109/TIT.2008.920340

Lane, P. M., & O'Reilly, J. J. (1994). Fibre-supported optical generation and delivery of 60 GHz signals. *Electronics Letters*, *30*(16), 1329–1330. doi:10.1049/el:19940850

Langendoen, K., & Reijers, N. (2005). Distributed localization algorithm. In *Embedded systems handbook*. Boca Raton, FL: CRC Press.

Langley, L. N., Elkin, M. D., Edge, C., Wale, M. J., Gliese, U., Huang, X., & Seeds, A. J. (1999). Packaged semiconductor laser optical phase-locked loop (OPLL) for photonic generation, processing and transmission of microwave signals. *IEEE Transactions on Microwave Theory and Techniques, 47*(7), 1257–1264. doi:10.1109/22.775465

Larsson, E. G., Jorswieck, E. A., Lindblom, J., & Mochaourab, R. (2009). Game theory and the flat-fading Gaussian interference channel: Analyzing resource conflicts in wireless networks. *IEEE Signal Processing Magazine, 26*(5), 18–27. doi:10.1109/MSP.2009.933370

Latouche, M., Rauschen, C., Oszabó, O., Creusat, J.-B., & Belmans, W. (2013). *Mobile data explosion how mobile service providers can monetize the growth in mobile data through value-added services* (Cisco White Paper). Cisco Internet Business Solutions Group (IBSG).

Lau, E. K., & Wu, M. C. (2006). Ultra-high, 72 GHz resonance frequency and 44 GHz bandwidth of injection-locked 1.55-/spl mu/m DFB lasers. In *Proceedings of 2006 Optical Fiber Communication Conference and the National Fiber Optic Engineers Conference*. IEEE. doi:10.1109/OFC.2006.215716

Lauriola, M., Panno, A., Levin, I. P., & Lejuez, C. W. (2013). Individual differences in risky decision making: A meta-analysis of sensation seeking and impulsivity with the balloon analogue risk task. *Journal of Behavioral Decision Making*. doi: doi:10.1002/bdm.1784

Leary, P. (2004). *The wild world of wireless broadband and WiMAX*. Alvarion.

Lecompte, D., & Gabin, F. (2012). Evolved multimedia broadcast/multicast service (eMBMS) in LTE-advanced: Overview and Rel-11 enhancements. *IEEE Communications Magazine, 50*(11), 68–74. doi:10.1109/MCOM.2012.6353684

Lederer, S., Mueller, C., Timmerer, C., Concolato, C., Le Feuvre, J., & Fliegel, K. (2013). Distributed DASH dataset. In *Proceedings of the 4th ACM Conference on Multimedia Systems* (pp. 131–135). New York, NY: ACM.

Lederer, S., Muller, C., & Timmerer, C. (2012). Dynamic adaptive streaming over HTTP dataset. In *Proceedings of the 3rd ACM Conference on Multimedia Systems* (pp. 89–94). New York, NY: ACM.

Lee, C. C., & Steele, R. (1998). Effect of soft and softer handoffs on CDMA system capacity. *IEEE Transactions on Vehicular Technology, 47*(3), 830–841. doi:10.1109/25.704838

Lee, C. H. (2007). *Microwave photonic*. Academic Press.

Lee, H., Son, H., & Lee, S. (2009). Semisoft handover gain analysis over OFDM-based broadband systems. *IEEE Transactions on Vehicular Technology, 58*(3), 1443–1453. doi:10.1109/TVT.2008.927041

Lee, J. H. et al. (2009). Seamless upgrades from a TDM-PON with a video overlay to a WDM-PON. *Journal of Lightwave Technology, 27*(15), 3116–3123. doi:10.1109/JLT.2008.2006861

Lee, J. H. et al. (2010). First commercial deployment of a colorless gigabit WDM/TDM hybrid PON system using remote protocol terminator. *Journal of Lightwave Technology, 28*(4), 344–351. doi:10.1109/JLT.2009.2037979

Lee, K. C., Lee, U., & Gerla, M. (2009). Survey of routing protocols in vehicular ad hoc networks. In *Advances in vehicular ad-hoc networks: Developments and challenges*. Hershey, PA: IGI Global.

Li, P., Gu, Y., & Zhao, B. (2007). A global-energy-balancing real-time routing in wireless sensor networks. In *Proceedings of the 2nd IEEE Asia-Pacific Service Computing Conference* (pp. 89 - 93). Tsukuba, Japan: IEEE.

Li, X., Zhu, X., Wu, L., & Sandrasegaran, K. (2013). A distributed non-uniform pricing approach for power optimization in spectrum-sharing femtocell network. In *Proceedings of IEEE WCNC* (pp. 667-672). IEEE.

Lim, C., Nirmalathas, A., Bakaul, M., Gamage, P., Novak, D., & Waterhouse, R. (2010). Fiber-wireless networks and subsystem technologies. *Journal of Lightwave Technology, 28*(4), 390–405. doi:10.1109/JLT.2009.2031423

Liu, C., Bouazizi, I., & Gabbouj, M. (2011). Rate adaptation for adaptive HTTP streaming. In *Proceedings of the Second Annual ACM Conference on Multimedia Systems* (pp. 169–174). New York, NY: ACM.

Liu, H., & Krishnamachari, B. (2006). A price-based reliable routing game in wireless networks. In *Proceedings of the ACM Workshop on Game Theory for Communications and Networks* (GameNets '06). ACM.

Liu, L., Ma, H., & Zhang, X. (2008). On directional k-coverage analysis of randomly deployed camera sensor networks. In *Proceedings of IEEE International Conference on Communications* (pp. 2707-2711). Beijing, China: IEEE.

Liu, X., Dobrian, F., Milner, H., Jiang, J., Sekar, V., Stoica, I., & Zhang, H. (2012). A case for a coordinated internet video control plane. In *Proceedings of the ACM SIGCOMM 2012 Conference on Applications, Technologies, Architectures, and Protocols for Computer Communication* (pp. 359–370). New York, NY: ACM.

Li, X., Dong, Z., Yu, J., Chi, N., Shao, Y., & Chang, G. K. (2012). Fiber-wireless transmission system of 108 Gb / s data over 80 km fiber and 2 × 2 wireless links at 100 GHz W-band frequency. *Optics Letters*, 37(24), 5106–5108. doi:10.1364/OL.37.005106 PMID:23258020

Li, Y., & Sousa, E. S. (2010). Cognitive interference management in 4G autonomous femtocells.[PIMRC.]. *Proceedings of PIMRC, 2010*, 1567–1571.

Lohmar, T., Einarsson, T., Frojdh, P., Gabin, F., & Kampmann, M. (2011). Dynamic adaptive HTTP streaming of live content. In *Proceedings of IEEE International Symposium on World of Wireless, Mobile and Multimedia Networks (WoWMoM)* (pp. 1–8). Lucca, Italy: IEEE.

Lopez-Perez, D., Guvenc, I., & Roche, G. (2011). Enhanced intercell interference coordination challenges in heterogeneous networks. *IEEE Wireless Comm.*, 18(3), 22–30. doi:10.1109/MWC.2011.5876497

Louta, M., Zournatzis, P., Kraounakis, S., Sarigiannidis, P., & Demetropoulos, I. (2011). Towards realization of the ABC vision: A comparative survey of access network selection. In *Proceedings of IEEE Symposium on Computers and Communications* (ISCC), (pp. 472-477). IEEE.

Lowe, D. G. (1999). Object recognition from local scale-invariant features. In *Proceedings of the 7th IEEE International Conference on Computer Vision*, (Vol. 2, pp. 1150–1157). IEEE.

Low, T. P., Pun, M. O., Hong, Y. W. P., & Kuo, C. C. J. (2009). Optimized opportunistic multicast scheduling (OMS) over wireless cellular networks. *IEEE Transactions on Wireless Communications*, 9(2), 791–801. doi:10.1109/TWC.2010.02.090387

Luo, Y., Zhang, W., & Hu, Y. (2010). A new cluster based routing protocol for VANET.[NSWCTC]. *Proceedings of Networks Security Wireless Communications and Trusted Computing, 1*, 176–180.

Lu, R., Lin, X., Zhu, H., & Shen, X. (2009). SPARK: A new VANET-based smart parking scheme for large parking lots.[IEEE.]. *Proceedings of INFOCOM, 2009*, 1413–1421.

Machado, R., & Tekinay, S. (2008). A survey of game-theoretic approaches in wireless sensor networks. *Computer Networks*, 52, 3047–3061. doi:10.1016/j.gaceta.2008.07.003

Mackenzie, A., & DaSilva, L. (2006). *Game theory for wireless engineers*. Morgan & Claypool Publishers.

Maimour, M., Pham, C., & Hoang, D. (2009). A congestion control framework for handling video surveillance traffics on WSN. In *Proceedings of the 2009 International Conference on Computational Science and Engineering (CSE '09)*, (Vol. 2, pp. 943-948). Washington, DC: IEEE Computer Society.

Ma, J., Yu, J., Yu, C., Xin, X., Zeng, J., & Chen, L. (2007). Fiber dispersion influence on transmission of the optical millimeter-waves generated using LN-MZM intensity modulation. *Journal of Lightwave Technology*, 25(11), 3244–3256. doi:10.1109/JLT.2007.907794

Management, S., & Specification, R. S. (2010). *Licence-exempt radio apparatus (all frequency bands)*. Category I Equipment.

Marina, N., Saad, W., Han, Z., & Hjorungnes, A. (2011). Modeling malicious behavior in cooperative cellular wireless networks. In *Cooperative cellular wireless networks*. Cambridge, UK: Cambridge University Press. doi:10.1017/CBO9780511667008.015

Martinez, F. J., Toh, C. K., Cano, J. C., Calafate, C. T., & Manzoni, P. (2010). Emergency services in future intelligent transportation systems based on vehicular communication networks. *IEEE Intelligent Transportation Systems Magazine*, 2(2), 6–20. doi:10.1109/MITS.2010.938166

Maslekar, N., Boussedjra, M., Mouzna, J., & Houda, L. (2009). Direction based clustering algorithm for data dissemination in vehicular networks. In *Proceedings of Vehicular Networking Conference (VNC)*, (pp. 1-6). IEEE.

Maslekar, N., Boussedjra, M., Mouzna, J., & Labiod, H. (2011). A stable clustering algorithm for efficiency applications in VANETs. In *Proceedings of Wireless Communications and Mobile Computing Conference (IWCMC)*, (pp. 1188-1193). IEEE.

Maslekar, N., Mouzna, J., Labiod, H., Devisetty, M., & Pai, M. (2011). Modified C-DRIVE: Clustering based on direction in vehicular environment. In *Proceedings of Intelligent Vehicles Symposium (IV)*, (pp. 845-850). IEEE.

Mateus, A., & Marinheiro, R. N. (2010). A media independent information service integration architecture for media independent handover. In *Proceedings of Ninth International Conference on Networks* (ICN), (pp. 173-178). ICN.

Mathai, S., Cappelluti, F., Jung, T., Novak, D., Waterhouse, R. B., & Sivco, D. et al. (2001). Experimental demonstration of a balanced electroabsorption modulated microwave photonic link. *IEEE Transactions on Microwave Theory and Techniques, 49*(10), 1956–1961. doi:10.1109/22.954814

Media, A. C. (2011). *Radiocommunications (low interference potential devices) class licence 2000* (Vol. 2011). Author.

Meghani, S. K., Asif, M., & Amir, S. (2012). Localization of WSN node based on time of arrival using ultra wide band spectrum. In *Proceedings of the 13th IEEE Annual Wireless and Microwave Technology Conference WAMICON'12*. IEEE.

Milan, F., Jaramillo, J. J., & Srikant, R. (2006). Achieving cooperation in multihop wireless networks of selfish nodes. In *Proceedings from the 2006 ACM Workshop on Game Theory for Communications and Networks* (GameNets '06). ACM.

Miller, K., Quacchio, E., Gennari, G., & Wolisz, A. (2012). Adaptation algorithm for adaptive streaming over HTTP. In *Proceedings of 19th International Packet Video Workshop (PV)* (pp. 173–178). Munich, Germany: Academic Press.

Mohammad, R., Rick, B., Obimdinachi, I. I., Juan, C. G., Jay, W., Deborah, E., & Mani, S. (2005). Cyclops: In situ image sensing and interpretation in wireless sensor networks. In *Proceedings of the 3rd International Conference on Embedded Networked Sensor Systems SenSys '05* (pp. 192-204). ACM.

Mohammed, A., Kamal, H., & AbdelWahab, S. (2007). 2G/3G inter-RAT handover performance analysis. In *Proceedings of the Second European Conference on Antennas and Propagation* (pp. 1-8). Academic Press.

Moldovan, A. N., & Muntean, C. H. (2011). Towards personalized and adaptive multimedia in m-learning systems. In *Proceedings of 16th AACE World Conference on E-Learning in Corporate, Government, Healthcare, and Higher Education* (E-Learn). AACE.

Moldovan, A.-N. & Muntean, C. H. (2012). Subjective assessment of BitDetect – A mechanism for energy-aware adaptive multimedia. *IEEE Transactions on Broadcasting Journal, 58*(3), 480-492.

Moldovan, A. N., Molnar, A., & Muntean, C. H. (2011). EcoLearn: Battery power friendly e-learning environment for mobile device users. In *Learning-oriented technologies, devices and networks-Innovative case studies*. Saarbrücken, Germany: LAP LAMBERT Academic Publishing.

Moldovan, A., & Muntean, C. H. (2012). Subjective assessment of BitDetect - A mechanism for energy-aware multimedia content adaptation. *IEEE Transactions on Broadcasting, 58*(3), 480–492. doi:10.1109/TBC.2012.2191688

Molnar, A. (2011). *Cost efficient educational multimedia delivery*. (Doctoral thesis). National College of Ireland, Dublin, Ireland. Retrieved August 26, 2013, from http://trap.ncirl.ie/762/

Molnar, A., & Frias-Martinez, V. (2011). EducaMovil: Mobile educational games made easy. In *Proceedings of AACE EDMEDIA 2011 World Conference on Educational Multimedia, Hypermedia & Telecommunications*. Lisbon, Portugal: AACE.

Molnar, A., & Muntean, C. H. (2009). Performance aware and cost oriented adaptive e-learning framework. In *Proceedings of IADIS International Conference e-Learning*. Algarve, Portugal: IADIS.

Molnar, A., & Muntean, C. H. (2010). *Educational content delivery: An experimental study assessing student preference for multimedia content when monetary cost is involved*. Paper presented at the 10th International Conference on Intelligent Systems Design and Applications. Cairo, Egypt.

Molnar, A., & Muntean, C. H. (2012). Consumer' risk attitude based personalisation for content delivery. In *Proceedings of Consumer Communications and Networking Conference*. Las Vegas, NV: Academic Press.

Molnar, A., & Muntean, C. H. (2013). Comedy: Viewer trade-off between multimedia quality and monetary benefits. In *Proceedings of IEEE International Symposium on Broadband Multimedia Systems and Broadcasting*. London, UK: IEEE.

Molnar, A., & Weerakkody, V. (2013). Defining key performance indicators for evaluating the use of high definition video-to-video services in eHealth. In *Proceedings of Artificial Intelligence Applications and Innovations, 2nd Workshop on Intelligent Video-to-Video Communications in Modern Smart Cities*. Paphos, Cyprus: Academic Press.

Molnar, A., & Muntean, C. H. (2011). Mobile learning: An economic approach. In *Intelligent and adaptive learning systems: Technology enhanced support for learners and teachers*. Hershey, PA: IGI Global. doi:10.4018/978-1-60960-842-2.ch020

Molnar, A., & Muntean, C. H. (2013). Cost oriented adaptive multimedia delivery. *IEEE Transactions on Broadcasting, 59*(3), 484–499. doi:10.1109/TBC.2013.2244786

Mondal, A., Trestian, I., Qin, Z., & Kuzmanovic, A. (2012). P2P as a CDN: A new service model for file sharing. *Computer Networks, 56*(14), 3233–3246. doi:10.1016/j.comnet.2012.06.010

Moura, J., Silva, J., & Marinheiro, R. N. (2012). A brokerage system for enhancing wireless access. In *Proceedings of International Conference on Communications and Signal Processing* (MIC-CSP), (vol. 1, pp. 45-50). Academic Press.

Moustafa, H., Senouci, S. M., & Jerbi, M. (2009). Introduction to vehicular networks. In H. Moustafa, & Y. Zhang (Eds.), *Vehicular networks: Techniques, standards and applications*. Boca Raton, FL: CRC Press. doi:10.1201/9781420085723

MP4Box | GPAC. (n.d.). Retrieved October 18, 2013, from http://gpac.wp.mines-telecom.fr/mp4box/

MPHPT. (2000). *Specified low power radio station (12) 59-66 GHz band*. Regulation for the Enforcement of the Radio Law 6-4-2.

Muller, C., & Timmerer, C. (2011). A VLC media player plugin enabling dynamic adaptive streaming over HTTP. In *Proceedings of the 19th ACM International Conference on Multimedia* (pp. 723–726). New York, NY: ACM.

Mundinger, J., & Boudec, J.-Y. L. (2005). Analysis of a robust reputation system for self-organized networks. *European Transactions on Communications, 16*(5), 375–384.

Muntean, C. H., McManis, J., & Murphy, J. (2002). The influence of web page images on the performance of the web servers. In *Proceedings of Int. Conference of Networking (ICN 2001)* (LNCS), (vol. 2093, pp. 821–828). Berlin: Springer.

Muntean, G.-M., & Murphy, L. (2002). Adaptive pre-recorded multimedia streaming. In *Proceedings of IEEE Global Telecommunications Conference (GLOBECOM)* (Vol. 2, pp. 1728–1732). Taipei, Taiwan: IEEE.

Muntean, C. H., & Muntean, G. M. (2009). Open corpus architecture for personalized ubiquitous e-learning. *Personal and Ubiquitous Computing, 13*(3), 197–205. doi:10.1007/s00779-007-0189-5

Muntean, G. M., Ghinea, G., & Sheehan, T. N. (2008). Region of interest-based adaptive multimedia streaming scheme. *IEEE Transactions on Broadcasting, 54*(2), 296–303. doi:10.1109/TBC.2008.919012

Muntean, G.-M., Perry, P., & Murphy, L. (2005). Objective and subjective evaluation of QOAS video streaming over broadband networks. *IEEE Transactions on Network and Service Management, 2*(1), 19–28. doi:10.1109/TNSM.2005.4798298

Murray, T., Cojocari, M., & Fu, H. (2008). Measuring the performance of IEEE 802.11p using NS-2 simulator for vehicular networks. In *Proceedings of IEEE International Conference on Electro/Information Technology* (EIT), (pp. 498–503). IEEE.

Nachman, L., Kling, R., Adler, R., Huang, J., & Hummel, V. (2005). The Intel® mote platform: A bluetooth-based sensor network for industrial monitoring. In *Proceedings of the 4th International Symposium on Information Processing in Sensor Networks – IPSN '05*. Piscataway, NJ: IEEE Press.

Nasser, N., Hasswa, A., & Hassanein, H. (2006). Hand-offs in fourth generation heterogeneous networks. *IEEE Communications Magazine*, 96–103. doi:10.1109/MCOM.2006.1710420

Nazir, M., Bennis, M., Ghaboosi, K., MacKenzie, A. B., & Latva-Aho, M. (2010). Learning based mechanisms for interference mitigation in self-organized femtocell networks. In *Proceedings of Conference Record of the Forty Fourth Asilomar Conference on Signals, Systems and Computers*, (pp. 1886-1890). Academic Press.

Nemoianu, I. D., & Pesquet-Popescu, B. (2013). Network coding for multimedia communications. In *Intelligent multimedia technologies for networking applications: Techniques and tools*. Academic Press.

Niu, Z., Zhou, S., & Hua, Y. et al. (2012). Energy-aware network planning for wireless cellular system with inter-cell cooperation. *IEEE Transactions on Wireless Communications*, 11(4), 1412–1423. doi:10.1109/TWC.2012.021412.110147

Niyato, D., & Hossain, E. (2007). Radio resource management games in wireless networks: An approach to bandwidth allocation and admission control for polling service in IEEE 802.16 (Radio Resource Management and Protocol Engineering for IEEE 802.16). *IEEE Wireless Communications*, 14(1), 27–35. doi:10.1109/MWC.2007.314548

Niyato, D., & Hossain, E. (2008). A noncooperative game-theoretic framework for radio resource management in 4G heterogeneous wireless access networks. *IEEE Transactions on Mobile Computing*, 7(3), 332–345. doi:10.1109/TMC.2007.70727

Nokleby, M., & Aazhang, B. (2010). User cooperation for energy-efficient cellular communications. In *Proceedings of ICC 2010*. ICC.

Novak, D., Ahmed, Z., Waterhouse, R. B., & Tucker, R. S. (1995). Signal generation using pulsed semiconductor lasers for application in millimeter-wave wireless links. *IEEE Transactions on Microwave Theory and Techniques*, 43(9), 2257–2262. doi:10.1109/22.414573

Nurmi, P. (2006). *Bayesian game theory in practice: A framework for online reputation systems* (Technical Report C-2005-10). Academic Press.

O'Reilly, J. J., Lane, P. M., Heidemann, R., & Hofstetter, R. (1992). *Optical generation of very narrow linewidth millimetre wave signals*. doi:10.1049/el:19921486

O'Reilly, J., & Lane, P. (1994). Remote delivery of video services using mm-waves and optics. *Journal of Lightwave Technology*, 12(2), 369–375. doi:10.1109/50.350584

OECD. (2008). *Broadband growth and policies in OECD countries*. OECD Publications.

OECD. (2009). *Mobile broadband: Pricing and services*. Organisation for Economic Cooperation and Development.

Oeldorf-Hirsch, A., Donner, J., & Cutrell, E. (2012). How bad is good enough? Exploring mobile video quality trade-offs for bandwidth-constrained consumers. In *Proceedings of ACM 7th Nordic Conference on Human-Computer Interaction: Making Sense through Design*. Copenhagen, Denmark: ACM.

Ohno, T., Nakajima, F., Furuta, T., & Ito, H. (2005). A 240-GHz active mode-locked laser diode for ultra-broadband fiber-radio transmission systems. In *Proceedings of OFC/NFOEC Technical Digest: Optical Fiber Communication Conference*, (Vol. 6). IEEE. doi:10.1109/OFC.2005.193191

Ong, E. H., & Khan, J. (2008). Dynamic access network selection with QoS parameters estimation: A step closer to ABC. In *Proceedings of IEEE Vehicular Technology Conference* (pp. 2671-2676). IEEE.

Ormond, O., Murphy, J., & Muntean, G. M. (2006). Utility-based intelligent network selection in beyond 3G systems. In *Proceedings of IEEE International Conference on Communications* (pp. 1831-1836). IEEE.

Osais, Y. E., St-Hilaire, M., & Fei, R. Y. (2010). Directional sensor placement with optimal sensing ranging, field of view and orientation. *Mobile Networks and Applications*, 15(2), 216–225. doi:10.1007/s11036-009-0179-0

Osmo4 | GPAC. (n.d.). Retrieved October 20, 2013, from http://gpac.wp.mines-telecom.fr/player/

Paek, J., & Govindan, R. (2007). RCRT: Rate-controlled reliable transport for wireless sensor networks. In *Proceedings of the 5th International Conference on Embedded Networked Sensor Systems – SenSys'07* (pp. 305-319). New York, NY: ACM.

Page, M., Molina, M., & Jones, G. (2013). The mobile economy. *GSMA*. Retrieved November 1, 2013, from http://www.atkearney.com/documents/10192/760890/The_Mobile_Economy_2013.pdf/

Palais, J. C. (2004). *Fiber optic communications* (5th ed.). Upper Saddle River, NJ: Prentice Hall.

Pantos, R. (2012). *HTTP live streaming, IETF draft.* Retrieved November 11, 2013, from http://tools.ietf.org/html/draft-pantos-http-live-streaming-09

Park, C., & Chou, P. H. (2006). eCAM: Ultra compact, high data-rate wireless sensor node with a miniature camera. In *Proceedings of the 4th International Conference on Embedded Networked Sensor Systems SenSys '06* (pp. 359-360). New York, NY: ACM.

Peng, M., Liu, Y., Wei, D., Wang, W., & Chen, H.-H. (2011). Hierarchical cooperative relay based heterogeneous networks. *IEEE Wireless Communications Magazine, 18*(3), 48–56. doi:10.1109/MWC.2011.5876500

Pereira, J. P., & Ferreira, P. (2009). *Access networks for mobility: A techno-economic model for broadband access technologies.* Paper presented at the Testbeds and Research Infrastructures for the Development of Networks & Communities and Workshops. Washington, DC.

Pereira, J. P., & Ferreira, P. (2011). *Next generation access networks (NGANs) and the geographical segmentation of markets.* Paper presented at the Tenth International Conference on Networks (ICN 2011). St. Maarten, The Netherlands Antilles.

Pereira, J. P. R. (2013). Effects of NGNs on market definition. In Á. Rocha, A. M. Correia, T. Wilson, & K. A. Stroetmann (Eds.), *Advances in information systems and technologies* (Vol. 206, pp. 939–949). Berlin: Springer. doi:10.1007/978-3-642-36981-0_88

Pereira, J. P. R. (2013). Infrastructure vs. access competition in NGNs. In A. Selamat, N. Nguyen, & H. Haron (Eds.), *Intelligent information and database systems* (Vol. 7803, pp. 529–538). Berlin: Springer. doi:10.1007/978-3-642-36543-0_54

Pereira, J. P., & Ferreira, P. (2012). Game theoretic modeling of NGANs: Impact of retail and wholesale services price variation. *The Journal of Communication.* doi:10.4304/jcm.7.3.258-264

Pervaiz, H., & Bigham, J. (2009). Game theoretical formulation of network selection in competing wireless networks: An analytic hierarchy process model. In *Proceedings of Third International Conference on Next Generation Mobile Applications, Services and Technologies* (pp. 292–297). Academic Press.

Pescaru, D., Fuiorea, D., Gui, V., Toma, C., Muntean, G. M., & Doboli, A. (2006). Image-based node localization algorithm for wireless video sensor networks. In *Proceedings of the IT&T Conference.* Carlow, Ireland: Institute of Technology.

Pescaru, D., Gui, V., Toma, C., & Fuiorea, D. (2007). Analyses of post-deployment sensing coverage for video wireless sensor networks. In *Proceedings of the 6th International Conference RoEduNet-2007* (pp. 109-113). SITECH.

Pescaru, D., Istin, C., Curiac, D., & Doboli, A. (2008). Energy saving strategy for video-based sensor networks under field coverage preservation. In *Proceedings of the IEEE-TTTC International Conference on Automation, Quality and Testing, Robotics – AQTR'08* (pp. 289-294). IEEE.

Pescaru, D., Ciubotaru, B., Chiciudean, D., & Doboli, A. (2005). Experimenting motion detection algorithms for sensor network video surveillance applications. *Transactions on Automatic Control and Computer Science, 50*(64), 39–44.

Piorkowski, M., Raya, M., Lugo, A., Papadimitratos, P., Grossglauser, M., & Hubaux, J.-P. (2007). TraNS: Joint traffic and network simulator for VANETs. In *Proceedings of MobiCom.* Montreal, Canada: ACM.

Piorkowski, M., Raya, M., Lugo, A., Papadimitratos, P., Grossglauser, M., & Hubaux, J.-P. (2008). TraNS: Realistic joint traffic and network simulator for VANETs. *ACM SIGMOBILE Mobile Computing and Communications Review, 12*(1), 31–33. doi:10.1145/1374512.1374522

Ploeg, J., Serrarens, A. F., & Heijenk, G. J. (2011). Connect & drive: Design and evaluation of cooperative adaptive cruise control for congestion reduction. *Journal of Modern Transportation, 19*(3), 207–213. doi:10.1007/BF03325760

Politis, I., Tsagkaropoulos, M., Dagiuklas, T., & Kotsopoulos, S. (2008). Power efficient video multipath transmission over wireless multimedia sensor networks. *Mobile Networks and Applications, 13*(3-4), 274–284.

Prasad, R., & Velez, F. J. (2010). *WiMAX networks: Techno-economic vision and challenges.* New York: Springer. doi:10.1007/978-90-481-8752-2

Prat, J., et al. (2009). Passive optical network for long-reach scalable and resilient access. In *Proceedings of International Conference on Telecommunications* (vol. 10, pp. 271-275). Zagreb, Croatia: Academic Press.

Progressive Download | Adobe Developer Connection. (n.d.). Retrieved October 23, 2013, from http://www.adobe.com/devnet/video/progressive.html

Qaisar, S., & Radha, H. (2009). A reliability framework for visual sensor networks. In *Proceedings of Picture Coding Symposium.* Chicago: Academic Press.

R1-101369. (2010). *Considerations on interference coordination in heterogeneous networks.* 3GPP. Std.

R1-104661. (2010). *Comparison of time-domain eICIC solutions.* 3GPP. Std.

R1-104968. (2010). *Summary of the description of candidate eICIC solutions.* 3GPP. Std.

R4-110284. (2011). *Evaluations of RSRP/RSRQ measurement.* Austin, TX: 3GPP. Std.

Rahimi, M., Baer, R., Iroezi, O., Garcia, J., Warrior, J., Estrin, D., & Srivastava, M. (2005). Cyclops: In-situ image sensing and interpretation in wireless sensor networks. In *Proceedings of the 3rd International Conference on Embedded Networked Sensor Systems – SenSys'05* (pp. 192-204). New York, NY: ACM.

Rahman, M., & Yanikomeroglu, H. (2010). Enhancing cell-edge performance: A downlink dynamic interference avoidance scheme with inter-cell coordination. *IEEE Transactions on Wireless Communications, 9*(4), 1414–1425. doi:10.1109/TWC.2010.04.090256

Rainer, B., Lederer, S., Muller, C., & Timmerer, C. (2012). A seamless web integration of adaptive HTTP streaming. In *Proceedings of the 20th European Signal Processing Conference (EUSIPCO)* (pp. 1519 –1523). Bucharest, Romania: EUSIPCO.

Raj, H., Saroiu, S., Wolman, A., & Padhye, J. (2013). Splitting the bill for mobile data with SIMlets. In *Proceedings of ACM Workshop on Mobile Computing Systems and Applications.* Santa Barbara, CA: ACM.

Rakha, H., & Kamalanathsharma, R. K. (2011). Eco-driving at signalized intersections using V2I communication. In Proceedings of Intelligent Transportation Systems (ITSC), (pp. 341-346). IEEE.

Ramakrishnan, B., Rajesh, R. S., & Shaji, R. S. (2011). CBVANET: A cluster based vehicular adhoc network model for simple highway communication. *J. Advanced Networking and Applications, 2*(4), 755–761.

Ramaswami, R., & Sivarajan, K. N. (2001). *Optical networks – A practical perspective.* San Francisco, CA: Morgan Kaufmann Publishers.

Razzaq, A., & Mehaoua, A. (2010). Video transport over VANETs: Multi-stream coding with multi-path and network coding. In Proceedings of Local Computer Networks (LCN), (pp. 32-39). IEEE.

Razzaque, M. A., Dobson, S., & Nixon, P. (2010). *Enhancement of self-organisation in wireless networking through a cross-layer approach.* Berlin: Springer. doi:10.1007/978-3-642-11723-7_10

Reumerman, H. J., Roggero, M., & Ruffini, M. (2005). The application-based clustering concept and requirements for intervehicle networks. *IEEE Communications Magazine, 43*(4), 108–113. doi:10.1109/MCOM.2005.1421913

RFC 793. (1981). *Transmission control protocol.* Retrieved August 26, 2013, from http://www.ietf.org/rfc/rfc793.txt

Richard, A., Dadlani, A., & Kim, A. (2013). Multicast scheduling and resource allocation algorithms for OFDMA-based systems: A survey. *IEEE Communications Surveys and Tutorials, 15*(1), 240–254. doi:10.1109/SURV.2012.013012.00074

Rich, E. (1979). User modelling via stereotypes. *Cognitive Science, 3*(4), 329–354. doi:10.1207/s15516709cog0304_3

Róka, R. (2003). The utilization of the DWDM/CWDM combination in the metro/access networks. In *Proceedings of Joint 1st Workshop on Mobile Future & Symposium on Trends in Communications* (vol. 10, pp. 160-162). Bratislava, Slovakia: Academic Press.

Róka, R. (2010). The utilization of the HPON network configurator at designing of passive optical networks. In *Proceedings of International Conference on Telecommunication and Signal Processing* (vol. 33, pp. 444-448). Baden near Vienna, Austria: Academic Press.

Róka, R. (2011). The extension of the HPON network configurator at designing of NG-PON networks. In *Proceedings of International Conference on Telecommunication and Signal Processing* (vol. 34, pp. 79-84). Budapest, Hungary: Academic Press.

Róka, R. (2008). The evolution of optical access networks for the provisioning of multimedia services in the NGN converged networks. In *Design of forms in the marketing communication for support of implementation in new multimedia products in the praxis* (pp. 138–143). Žilina, Slovakia: Žilina University Publishing House.

Róka, R. (2010). The designing of passive optical networks using the HPON network configurator. *International Journal of Research and Reviews in Computer Science*, *1*(3).

Róka, R. (2012). The designing of NG-PON networks using the HPON network configurator. *Journal of Communication and Computer*, *9*(6), 669–678.

Róka, R., & Khan, S. (2011). The modeling of hybrid passive optical networks using the network configurator. *International Journal of Research and Reviews in Computer Science*, *2*, 48–54.

Roselli, L., Borgioni, V., Zepparelli, F., Ambrosi, F., Comez, M., Faccin, P., & Casini, A. (2003). Analog laser predistortion for multiservice radio-over-fiber systems. *Journal of Lightwave Technology*, *21*(5), 1211–1223. doi:10.1109/JLT.2003.810931

Rouvalis, E., Renaud, C. C., Moodie, D. G., Robertson, M. J., & Seeds, A. J. (2010). Traveling-wave uni-traveling carrier photodiodes for continuous wave THz generation. *Optics Express*, *18*(11), 11105–11110. doi:10.1364/OE.18.011105 PMID:20588968

Rovcanin, L., & Muntean, G.-M. (2013). A DASH-based performance-oriented adaptive video distribution solution. In *Proceedings of IEEE International Symposium on Broadband Multimedia Systems and Broadcasting*. London, UK: IEEE.

Rovcanin, L., & Muntean, G.-M. (2014). A DASH-aware performance oriented adaptation agent. In *Proceedings of IEEE International Symposium on Broadband Multimedia Systems and Broadcasting*. Beijing, China: IEEE.

Rovcanin, L., Muntean, C. H., & Muntean, G.-M. (2008). *Performance aware adaptation in open corpus e-learning systems*. Paper presented at the International Workshop on Technologies for Mobile and Wireless-Based Adaptive e-Learning Environments, Adaptive Hypermedia and Adaptive Web-Based Systems '08. Hanover, Germany.

Rovcanin, L., Muntean, C. H., & Muntean, G.-M. (2006). Performance enhancement for open corpus adaptive hypermedia systems. In V. P. Wade, H. Ashman, & B. Smyth (Eds.), *Adaptive hypermedia and adaptive web-based systems* (pp. 462–466). Berlin: Springer. doi:10.1007/11768012_70

Saad, W., Han, Z., Poor, H. V., & Başar, T. (2012). *Game theoretic methods for the smart grid*. Eprint arXiv:1202.0452.

Saad, W., Han, Z., & Hjorungnes, A. (2011). Coalitional games for cooperative wireless cellular networks. In *Cooperative cellular wireless networks*. Cambridge, UK: Cambridge University Press. doi:10.1017/CBO9780511667008.014

Saatsakis, A., Tsagkaris, K., & Von-Hugo, D. (2008). Cognitive radio resource management for improving the efficiency of LTE network segments in the wireless B3G world. In *Proceedings of 2008 IEEE Symposium on New Frontiers in Dynamic Spectrum Access Networks*. IEEE.

Sambaraju, R., Zibar, D., Caballero, A., Monroy, I. T., Alemany, R., & Herrera, J. (2010). 100-GHz wireless-over-fiber links with up to 16-Gb / s QPSK modulation using optical heterodyne generation and digital coherent detection. *Photonics Technology Letters*, *22*(22), 1650–1652.

Sanchez, J., Benet, G., & Simó, J. E. (2012). Video sensor architecture for surveillance applications. *Sensors (Basel, Switzerland)*, *12*, 1509–1528. doi:10.3390/s120201509 PMID:22438723

Santa, J., Gómez-Skarmeta, A. F., & Sánchez-Artigas, M. (2008). Architecture and evaluation of a unified V2V and V2I communication system based on cellular networks. *Computer Communications*, *31*(12), 2850–2861. doi:10.1016/j.comcom.2007.12.008

Santi, P. (2012). *Mobility models for next generation wireless networks*. Sussex, UK: Wiley. doi:10.1002/9781118344774

Saraydar, C. U., Mandayam, N. B., & Goodman, D. (2002). Efficient power control via pricing in wireless data networks. *IEEE Transactions on Communications*, 50(2), 291–303. doi:10.1109/26.983324

Sarrocco, C., & Ypsilanti, D. (2008). *Convergence and next generation networks*. OECD.

Savvides, A., Han, C. C., & Srivastava, M. B. (2001). Dynamic fine-grained localization in ad-hoc networks of sensors. In *Proceedings of the 7th Annual International Conference on Mobile Computing and Networking (MobiCom'01)*, (pp. 166-179). ACM Press.

Schmuck, H. (1995). *Comparison of optical millimetre-wave system concepts with regard to chromatic dispersion*. Academic Press.

Schulzrinne, H., Casner, S., Frederick, R., & Jacobson, V. (2003). RFC 3550: RTP: A transport protocol for real-time applications. *IETF*. Retrieved from https://tools.ietf.org/html/rfc3550

Scutari, G., Palomar, D., & Barbarossa, S. (2008). Competitive design of multiuser MIMO systems based on game theory: A unified view. *IEEE Journal on Selected Areas in Communications*, 26(7), 1089–1103. doi:10.1109/JSAC.2008.080907

Seimetz, M. (2009). *High-order modulation for optical fiber transmission*. Berlin: Springer. doi:10.1007/978-3-540-93771-5

Sen, S., Joe-Wong, C., Ha, S., Bawa, J., & Chiang, M. (2013). When the price is right: Enabling time-dependent pricing of broadband data. In *Proceedings of SIGCHI Conference on Human Factors in Computing Systems*. Paris, France: ACM.

Seregelyi, J., Paquet, S., & Belisle, C. (2005). Generation and distribution of a wide-band continuously tunable millimeter-wave signal with an optical external modulation technique. *IEEE Transactions on Microwave Theory and Techniques*, 53(10), 3090–3097. doi:10.1109/TMTT.2005.855123

Sgora, A., Chatzimisios, P., & Vergados, D. D. (2010). *Mobile lightweight wireless systems: Access network selection in a heterogeneous environment using the AHP and fuzzy TOPSIS methods*. Berlin: Springer.

Shahidan, A. A., Fisal, N., Fikri, A. H., Ismail Nor-Syahidatul, N., & Yunus, F. (2011). Image transfer in wireless sensor networks. In *Proceedings of the International Conference on Communication Engineering and Networks IPCSIT'2011*, (Vol. 19, pp. 158-165). Singapore: IACSIT Press.

Shakir, M. Z., Qaraqe, K. A., & Tabassum, H. et al. (2013). Green heterogeneous small-cell networks: Towards reducing the CO_2 emissions of mobile communications industry using uplink power adaptation. *IEEE Communications Magazine*, 51(6), 52–61. doi:10.1109/MCOM.2013.6525595

Shams, H., & Zhao, J. (2013). First investigation of fast OFDM signals at 60GHz using direct laser modulation. In *Proceedings of CLEO/Europe-EQEC 2013*. Munich, Germany: CLEO.

Shams, H., Anandarajah, P. M., Perry, P., & Barry, L. (2010). Optical generation and wireless transmission of 60 GHz OOK signals using gain switched laser. In *Proceedings of Optical Fiber Communication Conference*. Washington, DC: OSA. doi:10.1364/OFC.2010.OThO7

Shams, H., Anandarajah, P. M., Perry, P., & Barry, L. P. (2010). Photonic generation and distribution of a modulated 60 GHz signal using a directly modulated gain switched laser. In *Proceedings of 21st Annual IEEE International Symposium on Personal, Indoor and Mobile Radio Communications* (pp. 1032–1037). IEEE. doi:10.1109/PIMRC.2010.5672089

Shams, H., Perry, P., Anandarajah, P. M., & Barry, L. (2011). Phase modulated optical millimeter wave generation based on externally injected gain switched laser. In *Proceedings of Optical Fiber Communication Conference/National Fiber Optic Engineers Conference 2011*. Washington, DC: OSA. doi:10.1364/OFC.2011.OWK7

Shams, H., Perry, P., Anandarajah, P. M., & Barry, L. P. (2011). Modulated millimeter-wave generation by external injection of a gain switched laser. *IEEE Photonics Technology Letters*, 23(7), 447–449. doi:10.1109/LPT.2011.2108277

Shankar, P., Nadeem, T., Rosca, J., & Iftode, L. (2008). Cars: Context-aware rate selection for vehicular networks. In *Proceedings of IEEE International Conference on Network Protocols* (ICNP), (pp. 1–12). IEEE.

Shastry, N., & Adve, R. S. (2006). Stimulating cooperative diversity in wireless ad hoc networks through pricing. In *Proceedings of IEEE International Conference on Communications* (ICC '06.), (vol. 8, pp. 3747-3752). IEEE.

Shea, C., Hassanabadi, B., & Valaee, S. (2009). Mobility-based clustering in VANETs using affinity propagation. In *Proceedings of Global Telecommunications Conference*, (pp. 1-6). IEEE.

Shen, D. M. (2010) The QoE-oriented heterogeneous network selection based on fuzzy AHP methodology. In *Proceedings of the Fourth International Conference on Mobile Ubiquitous Computing, Systems, Services and Technologies* (pp. 275-280). Academic Press.

Shen, W., & Zeng, Q.-A. (2007). Cost-function-based network selection strategy in integrated wireless and mobile networks. In *Proceedings of 21st International Conference on Advanced Information Networking and Applications Workshops* (vol. 2, pp. 314-319). Academic Press.

Shen, S., Yue, G., & Cao, Q. (2011). A survey of game theory in wireless sensor networks security. *Journal Networks, 6*(3), 521–532. doi:10.4304/jnw.6.3.521-532

Shi, H.-Y., Wang, W.-L., Kwok, N.-M., & Chen, S.-Y. (2012). Game theory for wireless sensor networks: A survey. *Sensors (Basel, Switzerland), 12*, 9055–9097. doi:10.3390/s120709055 PMID:23012533

Shoaib, M., Song, W. C., & Kim, K. H. (2012). Cluster based data aggregation in vehicular adhoc network. In *Proceedings of Communication Technologies for Vehicles* (pp. 91–102). Berlin: Springer. doi:10.1007/978-3-642-29667-3_8

Shu, L., Zhang, Y., Zhou, Z., Hauswirth, M., Yu, Z., & Hyns, G. (2008). Transmitting and gathering streaming data in wireless multimedia sensor networks within expected network lifetime. *Mobile Networks and Applications, 13*(3-4), 306–323.

Sigurdsson, H. M. (2007). *Techno-economics of residential broadband deployment*. (PhD Thesis). Technical University of Denmark - Center for Information and Communication Technologies. Retrieved from PhD_Thesis_Halldor_Sigurdsson.pdf

Silva, J. C., Moura, J. A., Marinheiro, R. N., & Almeida, J. (2013). Optimizing 4G networks with flow management using an hybrid broker. In *Proceedings of International Conference on Advances in Information Technology and Mobile Communication* (AIM). Academic Press.

Silva, J., Marinheiro, R., Moura, J., & Almeida, J. (2013). Differentiated classes of service and flow management using an hybrid broker. *ACEEE International Journal on Communication, 4*(2), 13–22.

Singhal, C., Kumar, S., De, S., Panwar, N., Tonde, R., & De, P. (2012). Class-based shared resource allocation for cell-edge users in OFDMA networks. *IEEE Transactions on Mobile Computing, 99*(PrePrints), 1.

Sivaraj, R., Gopalakrishna, A. K., Chandra, M. G., & Balamuralidhar, P. (2011). QoS-enabled group communication in integrated VANET-LTE heterogeneous wireless networks. In Proceedings of Wireless and Mobile Computing, Networking and Communications (WiMob), (pp. 17-24). IEEE.

Skog, I., & Handel, P. (2009). In-car positioning and navigation technologies—A survey. *IEEE Transactions on Intelligent Transportation Systems, 10*(1), 4–21. doi:10.1109/TITS.2008.2011712

Skraparlis, D., Sakarellos, V. K., Panagopoulos, A. D., & Kanellopoulos, J. D. (2009). *Outage performance analysis of cooperative diversity with MRC and SC in correlated lognormal channels* (p. 707839). Article, ID: EURASIP Journal on Wireless Communications and Networking.

Smith, G. H., Novak, D., & Ahmed, Z. (1997). Overcoming chromatic-dispersion effects in fiber-wireless systems incorporating external modulators. *IEEE Transactions on Microwave Theory and Techniques, 45*(8), 1410–1415. doi:10.1109/22.618444

Solomon, M. R., Bamossy, G., Askegaard, S., & Hogg, M. K. (2010). *Consumer behaviour: A European perspective*. New York: Prentice Hall.

Song, H.-J., Ajito, K., Hirata, A., Wakatsuki, A., Furuta, T., Kukutsu, N., & Nagatsuma, T. (2009). Multigigabit wireless data transmission at over 200-GHz. In *Proceedings of 2009 34th International Conference on Infrared, Millimeter, and Terahertz Waves*. doi:10.1109/ICIMW.2009.5325768

Srivastava, V., Neel, J., MacKenzie, A. B., Menon, R., Dasilva, L. A., & Hicks, J. E. et al. (2005). Using game theory to analyze wireless ad hoc networks. *IEEE Communications Surveys & Tutorials*, 7(4), 46–56. doi:10.1109/COMST.2005.1593279

Stephens, W., & Joseph, T. (1987). System characteristics of direct modulated and externally modulated RF fiber-optic links. *Journal of Lightwave Technology*, 5(3), 380–387. doi:10.1109/JLT.1987.1075509

Stockhammer, T. (2011). Dynamic adaptive streaming over HTTP–Design principles and standards. In *Proceedings of the Second Annual ACM Conference on Multimedia Systems (MMSys11)* (pp. 133–144). New York, NY: ACM.

Stohr, A. (2010). Photonic millimeter-wave generation and its applications in high data rate wireless access. In Proceedings of Microwave Photonics (MWP), (pp. 7–10). IEEE. doi: doi:10.1109/mwp.2010.5664246

Stöhr, A., Member, S., Cannard, P., Charbonnier, B., van Dijk, F., & Fedderwitz, S. … Weiß, M. (2010). Millimeter-wave photonic components for broadband wireless systems. Academic Press.

Stordahl, K. (2010). Market development up to 2015. *MARCH - Multilink architecture for multiplay services.*

Sugiura, A., & Dermawan, C. (2005). In traffic jam IVC-RVC system for ITS using bluetooth. *IEEE Transactions on Intelligent Transportation Systems*, 6(3), 302–313. doi:10.1109/TITS.2005.853704

Su, H., & Zhang, X. (2007). Clustering-based multichannel MAC protocols for QoS provisionings over vehicular. *IEEE Transactions on Vehicular Technology*, 56(6), 3309–3323. doi:10.1109/TVT.2007.907233

Supratim, D., Pantelis, M., Jerzy, M., & James, S.P. (2013). Algorithms for enhanced inter-cell interference coordination (eICIC) in LTE heterogeneous networks. *IEEE/ACM Trans. on Networking.*

Tal, I., & Muntean, G. M. (2012). User-oriented cluster-based solution for multimedia content delivery over VANETs. In Proceedings of Broadband Multimedia Systems and Broadcasting (BMSB), (pp. 1-5). IEEE.

Tal, I., & Muntean, G. M. (2013). User-oriented fuzzy logic-based clustering scheme for vehicular ad-hoc networks. In *Proceedings of Vehicular Technology Conference* (pp. 1-5). IEEE.

Tal, I., & Muntean, G.-M. (2013). V2X communication-based power saving strategy for electric bicycles. In *Proceedings of Global Telecommunications Conference Workshops,* (pp. 1-6). Academic Press.

Tal, I., Tianhua, Z., & Muntean, G.-M. (2013). On the potential of V2X communications in helping electric bicycles save energy. In *Proceedings of Vehicular Networking Conference,* (pp. 1-4). Academic Press.

Taleb, T., & Benslimane, A. (2010). Design guidelines for a network architecture integrating VANET with 3G & beyond networks. In *Proceedings of Global Telecommunications Conference (GLOBECOM 2010),* (pp. 1-5). IEEE.

Taleb, T., Ooi, K., & Hashimoto, K. (2008). An efficient collision avoidance strategy for ITS systems. In *Proceedings of IEEE Wireless Communications and Networking Conference* (WCNC), (pp. 2212-2217). IEEE.

Tan, X., Gustafsson, J., & Heikkila, G. (2006). Perceived video streaming quality under initial buffering and re-buffering degradations. In *Proceedings of MESAQIN Measurement of Speech, Audio and Video Quality in Networks Conference*. Prague, Czech Republic: MESAQIN.

Tanaka, K. et al. (2010). IEEE 802.3av 10G-EPON standardization and its research and development status. *Journal of Lightwave Technology*, 28(4), 651–661. doi:10.1109/JLT.2009.2038722

Taylor, J. W. (1974). The role of risk in consumer behaviour. *Journal of Marketing*, 38, 54–60. doi:10.2307/1250198

Taylor, P., & Jonker, L. (1978). Evolutionary stable strategies and game dynamics. *Mathematical Biosciences*, 40, 145–156. doi:10.1016/0025-5564(78)90077-9

Teshima, S., Ohta, T., Kohno, E., & Kakuda, Y. (2011). A data transfer scheme using autonomous clustering in VANETs environment. In Proceedings of Autonomous Decentralized Systems (ISADS), (pp. 477-482). IEEE.

Thang, T. C., Ho, Q.-D., Kang, J. W., & Pham, A. T. (2012). Adaptive streaming of audiovisual content using MPEG DASH. *IEEE Transactions on Consumer Electronics*, *58*(1), 78–85. doi:10.1109/TCE.2012.6170058

Third Generation Partnership Project. (2012). *TS 36.300, evolved universal terrestrial radio access (E-UTRA) and evolved universal terrestrial radio access network (E-UTRAN) (Release 11)*. Academic Press.

Tian, D., Wang, Y., Lu, G., & Yu, G. (2010). A VANETs routing algorithm based on Euclidean distance clustering. [ICFCC]. *Proceedings of Future Computer and Communication*, *1*, V1–V183.

Tielert, T., Rieger, D., Hartenstein, H., Luz, R., & Hausberger, S. (2012). Can V2X communication help electric vehicles save energy? In *Proceedings of ITS Telecommunications (ITST)*, (pp. 232-237). IEEE.

Tonguz, O. K., & Boban, M. (2010). Multiplayer games over vehicular ad hoc networks: A new application. *Ad Hoc Networks*, *8*(5), 531–543. doi:10.1016/j.adhoc.2009.12.009

Toulminet, G., Boussuge, J., & Laurgeau, C. (2008). Comparative synthesis of the 3 main European projects dealing with Cooperative Systems (CVIS, SAFESPOT and COOPERS) and description of COOPERS demonstration site 4. In Proceedings of Intelligent Transportation Systems, (pp. 809-814). IEEE.

Traverso, S., Huguenin, K., Trestian, I., Erramilli, V., Laoutaris, N., & Papagiannaki, K. (2012). Tailgate: Handling long-tail content with a little help from friends. In *Proceedings of ACM International Conference on World Wide Web*. Lyon, France: ACM.

Trestian, R. (2012). *User-centric power-friendly quality-based network selection strategy for heterogeneous wireless environments*. (Doctoral dissertation). Dublin City University, Dublin, Ireland. Retrieved from http://doras.dcu.ie/16783/1/Ramona_Trestian_-_PhD_Thesis_Final.PDF

Trestian, R., Moldovan, A. N., Muntean, C. H., Ormond, O., & Muntean, G. M. (2012). Quality utility modelling for multimedia applications for android mobile devices. In *Proceedings of IEEE International Symposium on Broadband Multimedia Systems and Broadcasting*. Seoul, Republic of Korea: IEEE.

Trestian, I., Ranjan, S., Kuzmanovic, A., & Nucci, A. (2012). Taming the mobile data deluge with drop zones. *IEEE/ACM Transactions on Networking*, *20*(4), 1010–1023. doi:10.1109/TNET.2011.2172952

Trestian, R., Ormond, O., & Muntean, G.-M. (2011). Reputation-based network selection mechanism using game theory. *Physical Communication*, *4*(3), 156–171. doi:10.1016/j.phycom.2011.06.004

Trestian, R., Ormond, O., & Muntean, G.-M. (2012). Game theory-based network selection: Solutions and challenges. *IEEE Communications Surveys & Tutorials*, *14*(4), 1212–1231. doi:10.1109/SURV.2012.010912.00081

Trivedi, H., Veeraraghavan, P., Loke, S., Desai, A., & Singh, J. (2011). SmartVANET: The case for a cross-layer vehicular network architecture. In Proceedings of Advanced Information Networking and Applications (WAINA), (pp. 362-368). IEEE.

Tung, L.-C., Mena, J., Gerla, M., & Sommer, C. (2013). A cluster based architecture for intersection collision avoidance using heterogeneous networks. In *Proceedings of Annual Mediterranean Ad Hoc Networking Workshop* (Med-Hoc-Net 2013). IFIP/IEEE.

Ucar, S., Ergen, S. C., & Ozkasap, O. (2013). VMaSC: Vehicular multi-hop algorithm for stable clustering in vehicular ad hoc networks. In *Proceedings of Wireless Communications and Networking Conference* (WCNC), (pp. 2381-2386). IEEE.

Uzcategui, R. A., & Acosta-Marum, G. (2009). Wave: A tutorial. *IEEE Communications Magazine*, *47*(5), 126–133. doi:10.1109/MCOM.2009.4939288

Van Dijk, F., Enard, A., Buet, X., Lelarge, F., & Duan, G.-H. (2008). Phase noise reduction of a quantum dash mode-locked laser in a millimeter-wave coupled optoelectronic oscillator. *Journal of Lightwave Technology*, *26*(15), 2789–2794. doi:10.1109/JLT.2008.927608

Varela, G. (2013). Autonomous adaptation of user interfaces to support mobility in ambient intelligence systems. In *Proceedings of ACM SIGCHI Symposium on Engineering Interactive Computing Systems* (pp. 179-182). ACM.

Vassaki, S., Panagopulos, A., & Constantinou, P. (2009). *A game-theoretic approach of power control schemes in DVB-RCS networks*. Paper presented at the 15ᵗʰ Ka and Broadband Communications, Navigation and Earth Observation Conference. Cagliari, Italy.

Verbrugge, S., Casier, K., Ooteghem, J. V., & Lannoo, B. (2009). *White paper: Practical steps in techno-economic evaluation of network deployment planning*. Gent, Belgium: UGent/IBBT.

Video, L. A. N. (n.d.). *H.264/AVC encoder*. Retrieved October 17, 2013, from http://www.videolan.org/developers/x264.html

Viering, I., Dottling, M., & Lobinger, A. (2011). On exploiting cognitive radio to mitigate interference in macro/femto heterogeneous networks. *IEEE Transactions on Wireless Communications, 10*(8), 2196–2206.

Vodopivec, S., Bester, J., & Kos, A. (2012). A survey on clustering algorithms for vehicular ad-hoc networks. In Proceedings of Telecommunications and Signal Processing (TSP), (pp. 52-56). IEEE.

Wahab, O. A., Otrok, H., & Mourad, A. (2013). VANET QoS-OLSR: QoS-based clustering protocol for vehicular ad hoc networks. *Computer Communications.* doi:10.1016/j.comcom.2013.07.003 PMID:23805013

Wake, D., Lima, C. R., & Davies, P. A. (1995). Optical generation of millimeter-wave signals for fiber-radio systems using a dual-mode DFB semiconductor laser. *IEEE Transactions on Microwave Theory and Techniques, 43*(9), 2270–2276. doi:10.1109/22.414575

Walton, C., Bordonalli, A. C., & Seeds, A. J. (1998). High-performance heterodyne optical injection phase-lock loop using wide linewidth semiconductor lasers. *IEEE Photonics Technology Letters, 10*(3), 427–429. doi:10.1109/68.661432

Wan, C. Y., Eisenman, S. B., & Campbell, A. T. (2003). CODA: Congestion detection and avoidance in sensor networks. In *Proceedings of the ACM Conference on Embedded Networked Sensor Systems –SenSys*. Los Angeles, CA: ACM Press.

Wang, J., Masilela, M., & Liu, J. (2007). Supporting video data in wireless sensor networks. In *Proceedings of the 9ᵗʰ IEEE International Symposium on Multimedia* (pp. 310-317). Los Alamitos, CA: IEEE.

Wang, S.-Y., Chao, H.-L., Liu, K.-C., He, T.-W., Lin, C.-C., & Chou, C.-L. (2008). Evaluating and improving the TCP/UDP performances of IEEE 802.11(p)/1609 networks. In *Proceedings of IEEE Symposium on Computers and Communications* (ISCC). Marrakech, Morocco: IEEE.

Wang, Y., Ahmed, A., Krishnamachari, B., & Psounis, K. (2008). IEEE 802.11p performance evaluation and protocol enhancement. In *Proceedings of IEEE International Conference on Vehicular Electronics and Safety* (ICVES), (pp. 317–322). IEEE.

Wang, B., Wu, Y., & Liu, K. (2010). Game theory for cognitive radio networks: An overview. *Computer Networks, 54*(14), 2537–2561. doi:10.1016/j.comnet.2010.04.004

Wang, B., Wu, Y., Liu, K. J. R., & Clancy, T. C. (2011). An anti-jamming stochastic game for cognitive radio networks. *IEEE Journal on Selected Areas in Communications, 29*(4), 877–889. doi:10.1109/JSAC.2011.110418

Wang, J., Ghosh, M., & Challapali, K. (2011). Emerging cognitive radio applications: A survey. *IEEE Communications Magazine, 49*(3), 74–81. doi:10.1109/MCOM.2011.5723803

Wang, W., Yu, G., & Huang, A. (2013). Cognitive radio enhanced interference coordination for femtocell networks. *IEEE Communications Magazine, 51*(6), 37–43. doi:10.1109/MCOM.2013.6525593

Wang, Z., Liu, L., Zhou, M., & Ansari, N. (2008). A position-based clustering technique for ad hoc intervehicle communication. *IEEE Transactions on Systems, Man and Cybernetics. Part C, Applications and Reviews, 38*(2), 201–208. doi:10.1109/TSMCC.2007.913917

Wanner, L. (2004). *Introduction to clustering techniques*. International Union of Local Authorities.

Watanabe, E. H., & Menasché, D. S. de Souza e Silva, E., & Leao, R. M. M. (2008). Modeling resource sharing dynamics of VoIP users over a WLAN using a game-theoretic approach. In *Proceedings of IEEE Conference on Computer Communications* (INFOCOM 2008), (pp. 915-923). IEEE.

Weerakkody, V., Molnar, A., Irani, Z., & El-Haddadeh, R. (2013). A research proposition for using high definition video in emergency medical services. *Health Policy and Technology*, 2(3), 131–138. doi:10.1016/j.hlpt.2013.04.001

Wen, Y. F. (2009). Heterogeneous base station placement for wireless networks. In *Proceedings of IEEE Mobile WiMAX Symposium* (pp. 87-92). IEEE.

Williams, K. J., Goldberg, L., Esman, R. D., Dagenais, M., & Weller, J. F. (1989). 6–34 GHz offset phase-locking of Nd:YAG 1319 nm nonplanar ring lasers. *Electronics Letters*, 25(18), 1242. doi:10.1049/el:19890833

Williamson, R. C., Fellow, L., & Esman, R. D. (2008). Article. *RF Photonics*, 26(9), 1145–1153.

Wilson, B., Darwazeh, I., & Ghassemlooy, F. (1995). *Analogue optical fibre communications*. Institution of Engineering and Technology. Retrieved from http://www.amazon.co.uk/Analogue-Optical-Fibre-Communications-Telecommunications/dp/0852968329

WirelessHD Consortium. (2013). Retrieved August 21, 2013, from http://www.wirelesshd.org/

Wolny, G. (2008). Modified DMAC clustering algorithm for VANETS. In *Proceedings of Systems and Networks Communications* (pp. 268–273). IEEE.

Wu, H., & Abouzeid, A. (2004). Energy efficient distributed JPEG 2000 image compression in multi-hop wireless networks. In *Proceedings of the 4th Workshop on Applications and Services in Wireless Networks – ASWN'04* (pp. 152–160). ASWN.

Xiao, J., Hu, R. Q., Qian, Y., & Gong, L. (2013). Expanding LTE network spectrum with cognitive radios: From concept to implementation. *IEEE Wireless Communications*, 20(2), 12–19. doi:10.1109/MWC.2013.6507389

Xie, R. C., Yu, F. R., Ji, H., & Li, Y. (2012). Energy-efficient resource allocation for heterogeneous cognitive radio networks with femtocells. *IEEE Transactions on Wireless Communications*, 11(11), 3910–3920. doi:10.1109/TWC.2012.092112.111510

Xu, J., & Bull, S. (2010). Encouraging advanced second language speakers to recognise their language difficulties: A personalised computer-based approach. *Computer Assisted Language Learning*, 23(2), 111–127. doi:10.1080/09588221003666206

Yaakob, S., Abdullah, W. R. W., Osman, M. N., Zamzuri, A. K., Mohamad, R., & Yahya, M. R. … Rashid, H. A. A. (2006). Effect of laser bias current to the third order intermodulation in the radio over fibre system. In *Proceedings of 2006 International RF and Microwave Conference* (pp. 444–447). IEEE. doi:10.1109/RFM.2006.331123

Yan, G., Weigle, M. C., & Olariu, S. (2009). A novel parking service using wireless networks. In *Proceedings of IEEE International Conference on Service Operations, Logistics and Informatics*. Chicago: IEEE.

Yang, L., Guo, J., & Wu, Y. (2009). Piggyback cooperative repetition for reliable broadcasting of safety messages in VANETs. In *Proceedings of IEEE Consumer Communications and Networking Conference* (CCNC). IEEE.

Yang, Q., Lim, A., & Agrawal, P. (2008). Connectivity aware routing in vehicular networks. In *Proceedings of Wireless Communications and Networking Conference*, (pp. 2218-2223). IEEE.

Yang, Z., Li, M., & Lou, W. (2010). Codeplay: Live multimedia streaming in VANETS using symbol-level network coding. In Proceedings of Network Protocols (ICNP), (pp. 223-232). IEEE.

Yang, C., & Li, J. (2012). Green heterogeneous networks: A cognitive radio Idea. *IET Communications*, 6(13), 1952–1959. doi:10.1049/iet-com.2011.0801

Yang, C., Xu, C., & Sheng, M. (2012). Cognitive wi-fi 2.0 networks: Future intelligent WLAN. *The Journal of Communication*, 33(2), 71–80.

Yao, J., Member, S., & Tutorial, I. (2009). Article. *Microwave Photonics*, *27*(3), 314–335.

Yap, K.-K. (2013). *Using all networks around us*. (PhD Thesis). Stanford University, Palo Alto, CA.

Yavuz, M., Meshkati, F., & Nanda, S. et al. (2009). Interference management and performance analysis of UMTS/HSPA+ femtocell. *IEEE Communications Magazine*, *47*(9), 102–109. doi:10.1109/MCOM.2009.5277462

Yeh, S., Talwar, S., Wu, G., Himayat, N., & Johnsson, K. (2011). Capacity and coverage enhancement in heterogeneous networks. *IEEE Wireless Communications*, *18*(3), 32–38. doi:10.1109/MWC.2011.5876498

Yi, L., & Su, Y. (2006). Optical millimeter-wave generation or up-conversion using external modulators. *IEEE Photonics Technology Letters*, *18*(1), 265–267. doi:10.1109/LPT.2005.862006

Yin, C., Ogata, H., Tabata, Y., & Yano, Y. (2010). JAPELAS2: Japanese polite expressions learning assisting system in ubiquitous environments. *International Journal of Mobile Learning and Organisation*, *4*(2), 214–234. doi:10.1504/IJMLO.2010.032637

Yongkang, X., Xiuming, S., & Yong, R. (2005). Game theory models for IEEE 802.11 DCF in wireless ad hoc networks. *IEEE Communications Magazine*, *43*(3), S22–S26. doi:10.1109/MCOM.2005.1404594

Yuan, Z., Venkataraman, H., & Muntean, G.-M. (2010). iPAS: An user perceived quality-based intelligent prioritized adaptive scheme for IPTV in wireless home networks. In *Proceedings of IEEE International Symposium on Broadband Multimedia Systems and Broadcasting*. Shanghai, China: IEEE.

Yu, J. Y., & Chong, P. H. J. (2005). A survey of clustering schemes for mobile ad hoc networks. *IEEE Communications Surveys and Tutorials*, *7*(1-4), 32–48. doi:10.1109/COMST.2005.1423333

Yu, P. K. L., & Wu, M. C. (2002). *RF photonic technology in optical fiber links* (W. S. C. Chang, Ed.). Cambridge, UK: Cambridge University Press.

Zambelli, A. (2009). IIS smooth streaming technical overview. *Microsoft Corporation*. Retrieved October 20, 2013, from http://www.microsoft.com/en-us/download/details.aspx?id=17678

Zaydoun, Z. Y., & Mahmud, S. M. (2009). Toward strongly connected clustering structure in vehicular ad hoc networks. In *Proceedings of Conference on Vehicular Technology*, (pp. 1-5). IEEE.

Zeinalipour, Y. D., Neema, S., Kalogeraki, V., Gunopulos, D., & Najjar, W. (2005). Data acquisition in sensor networks with large memories. In *Proceedings of the 21st International Conference on Data Engineering Workshops ICDEW '05*. IEEE Computer Society.

Zhang, D., Ileri, O., & Mandayam, N. (2008). Bandwidth exchange as an incentive for relaying. In *Proceedings of 42nd Annual Conference on Information Sciences and Systems*, (pp. 749-754). Academic Press.

Zhang, W. (2004). Handover decision using fuzzy MADM in heterogeneous networks. In *Proceedings of IEEE Wireless Communications and Networking Conference* (vol. 2, pp. 653-658). IEEE.

Zhang, W., Festag, A., Baldessari, R., & Le, L. (2008). Congestion control for safety messages in VANETs: Concepts and framework. In *Proceedings of International Conference on Telecommunications* (ITST), (pp. 199-203). ITST.

Zhang, Y., Lou, W., & Fang, Y. (2004). SIP: A secure incentive protocol against selfishness in mobile ad hoc networks. In *Proceedings of IEEE Conference Wireless Communications and Networking* (WCNC), (vol. 3, pp. 1679-1684). IEEE.

Zhang, J., Yu, J., Chi, N., Dong, Z., Li, X., & Shao, Y. et al. (2013). Flattened comb generation using only phase modulators driven by fundamental frequency sinusoidal sources with small frequency offset. *Optics Letters*, *38*(4), 552–554. doi:10.1364/OL.38.000552 PMID:23455133

Zhang, Y., & Guizani, M. (Eds.). (2011). *Game theory for wireless communications and networking*. Boca Raton, FL: CRC Press.

Zhao, J., Ibrahim, S. K., Gunning, P., & Ellis, A. (2011). *Chromatic dispersion compensation using symmetric extension based guard interval in optical fast-OFDM*. Optical Society of America. doi:10.1364/ECOC.2011.We.8.A.3

Zhong, S., Chen, J., & Yang, Y. R. (2003). Sprite: A simple, cheat-proof, credit-based system for mobile ad hoc networks.[]. INFOCOM.]. *Proceedings of INFOCOM*, *3*, 1987–1997.

Zhu, K., Niyato, D., & Wang, P. (2010). Network selection in heterogeneous wireless networks: Evolution with incomplete information. In *Proceedings of IEEE Wireless Communications and Networking Conference* (pp. 1-6). IEEE.

Zibar, D., Caballero, A., Yu, X., Pang, X., Dogadaev, A. K., & Monroy, I. T. (2011). Hybrid optical fibre-wireless links at the 75–110 GHz band supporting 100 Gbps transmission capacities. In *Proceedings of 2011 International Topical Meeting on Microwave Photonics Jointly Held With the 2011 Asia-Pacific Microwave Photonics Conference*, (pp. 445–449). doi:10.1109/MWP.2011.6088767

Zoubir, A., & Boashash, B. (1998). The bootstrap and its application in signal processing. *IEEE Signal Processing Magazine*, *15*(1), 56–76. doi:10.1109/79.647043

Zou, Y., Zhu, J., & Zhang, R. (2013). Exploiting network cooperation in green wireless communication. *IEEE Transactions on Communications*, *61*(3), 999–1010. doi:10.1109/TCOMM.2013.011613.120358

About the Contributors

Ramona Trestian is a Lecturer with the Computer and Communications Engineering Department, School of Science and Technology, Middlesex University, London, UK. She was previously an IBM-IRCSET Exascale Postdoctoral Researcher with the Performance Engineering Laboratory (PEL) at Dublin City University (DCU), Ireland since December 2011. She was awarded the PhD from Dublin City University in March 2012 and the B.Eng. degree in Telecommunications from the Electronics, Telecommunications, and the Technology of Information Department, Technical University of Cluj-Napoca, Romania in 2007. She has published in prestigious international conferences and journals and has two edited books. She is a reviewer for international journals and conferences and an IEEE member. Her research interests include mobile and wireless communications, multimedia streaming, handover and network selection strategies, and software-defined networks.

Gabriel-Miro Muntean received his Ph.D. degree from Dublin City University (DCU), Ireland for research in the area of quality-oriented adaptive multimedia streaming in 2003. He is a Senior Lecturer with the School of Electronic Engineering at DCU, Ireland, co-Director of the DCU Performance Engineering Laboratory, Director of the Network Innovations Centre, Rince Institute, Ireland, and Consultant Professor with Beijing University of Posts and Telecommunications (BUPT), China. His research interests include quality-oriented and performance-related issues of adaptive multimedia delivery, performance of wired and wireless communications, energy-aware networking, and personalised e-learning. Dr. Muntean has published over 170 papers in prestigious international journals and conferences, has authored 3 books and 12 book chapters and has edited 4 other books. Dr. Muntean is Associate Editor for the *IEEE Transactions on Broadcasting* and *IEEE Communications Surveys and Tutorials* and reviewer for other important international journals, conferences, and funding agencies. He is a member of ACM, IEEE, and IEEE Broadcast Technology Society.

* * *

Giuseppe Araniti is an Assistant Professor of Telecommunications at the University Mediterranea of Reggio Calabria, Italy. From the same University he received the Laurea (2000) and the Ph.D. Degree (2004) in Electronic Engineering. His major area of research includes Personal Communications Systems, Enhanced Wireless and Satellite Systems, Traffic and Radio Resource Management in 4G Mobile Radio Systems, Multicast and Broadcast Services, and Digital Video Broadcasting-Handheld. He is a Member of IEEE.

Massimo Condoluci received the B.S. (July 2008) and the M.S. (July 2011) Degrees in Telecommunications Engineering from the University Mediterranea of Reggio Calabria, Italy. Currently, he is a Ph.D. student in Telecommunications Engineering at the same University. His main research activities focus on Radio Resource Management (RRM) over Long Term Evolution (LTE) and LTE-Advanced (LTE-A) radio mobile systems, with particular attention to the management of multicast transmissions and their coexistence with unicast services and to the resource allocation for Device-to-Device communications over LTE-A. He is a Student Member of IEEE.

Kevin Collins is a postdoctoral researcher with Insight Research Centre, School of Electronic Engineering, Dublin City University, Ireland. He was awarded PhD and B.Eng. degrees from the same university in 2011 and 2008, respectively. His research interests focus on mobile and wireless systems and in particular on vehicular ad-hoc networks.

Daniel-Ioan Curiac received the M.S. degree in automation and computer engineering in 1990 and the Ph.D. degree in control system engineering in 1996, from the Politehnica University of Timisoara, Romania. Since 1990, he has been with the Automation and Applied Informatics Department at Politehnica University of Timisoara, where he is currently a professor and a doctoral supervisor in computer engineering. His scientific researches, evidenced by numerous journal and conference publications, cover a wide variety of scientific domains including intelligent control systems, applied artificial intelligence, chaotic systems and their applications to autonomous robots path planning, and unconventional methods for data security.

Swades De received his PhD in Electrical Eng. from the State Univ. of New York at Buffalo in 2004. He is currently an associate professor of Electrical Eng. at IIT Delhi. His research interests include performance study, resource efficiency in wireless networks, broadband wireless access, and communication and systems issues in optical networks. Dr. De currently serves as an associate editor of *IEEE Communications Letters* and *Springer Photonic Network Communications* journal. He is a member of IEEE, IEEE Communications and Computer Societies, and IEICE.

Jiandong Li was graduated from Xidian University with Bachelor Degree, Master Degree, and Ph. D in Communications and Electronic System, respectively, in 1982, 1985, and 1991. He is with Xidian University from 1985, an associate professor from 1990 to 1994, professor from 1994, Ph.D student supervisor from 1995, and Dean of School of Telecommunication Engineering, Xidian University from 1997, respectively. Now, he also serves as Executive Vice Dean Graduate School, Xidian University. Dr. Li is a senior member of IEEE and China Institute of Electronics (CIE) and the fellow of China Institute of Communication (CIC). He was the member of PCN specialist group for China 863 Communication high technology program between Jan. 1993 and Oct. 1994 and from 1999 to 2000. He is also the member of Communication specialist group for The Ministry of Information Industry. His current research interest and projects are funded by the 863 High Tech Project, NSFC, National Science Fund for Distinguished Young Scholars, TRAPOYT, MOE, and MOI.

Rui M. Neto Marinheiro is an Assistant Professor, with a tenured position, at ISCTE – Lisbon University Institute, Portugal. In 1995, he obtained a Licenciatura degree in Electrical and Computer Science Engineering with a specialization in Telecommunications from the Faculty of Engineering of the University of Porto, Portugal. He graduated with the highest-grade average of his class. In 2001, he defended his PhD dissertation titled "Using Context to Integrate Hypermedia with Information Retrieval Systems" at the University of Southampton, United Kingdom, under the supervision of Professor Dame Wendy Wall. He was awarded a FCT – PRAXIS XXI grant for his PhD studies. Dr. Marinheiro has an extensive teaching experience and researched in many R&D institutions in field of Telecommunications, Wireless Communications, Computer Networks and Hypermedia. Dr. Marinheiro has coordinated and participated in many national and international research projects and he has also authored and co-authored numerous scientific works.

Antonella Molinaro is an Associate Professor of Telecommunications at University Mediterranea of Reggio Calabria, Italy. She was with the University of Messina (1998-2001) and the University of Calabria (2001-04) as an Assistant Professor, and with the Polytechnic of Milano (1997-98) with a research contract. She worked at Telesoft, Rome (1992-93), and at Siemens, Munich (DE) (1994-95) with an European fellowship contract. Her current research interests focus on vehicular networking and future Internet architectures. She is a Member of IEEE.

Andreea Molnar is a Postdoctoral Research Associate in the College of Technology and Innovation, Department of Engineering at Arizona State University, USA. She has her PhD from National College of Ireland and BSc and MSc from Babes-Bolyai University, Romania. Her research interests include cost effective multimedia delivery, mobile learning, serious games, innovation impact, public e-services adoption, and diffusion. She has been involved in several projects, including the NSF-funded project Deep Insights Anytime, Anywhere, and FP7 European project Live Video-to-Video supporting Interactive City Infrastructure (LiveCity). One of the projects she was involved in, EducaMovil, is the recipient of the "We Help With You" award given for outstanding projects in ICTs for Development.

José André R. S. Moura received the B.S. degree for Electronics and Telecommunications from the Universidade de Aveiro (UA) – Aveiro University, in 1989. From 1989 to 2000, he worked as a project manager for assembling and testing Supervisory Control and Data Acquisition (SCADA) systems on EFACEC Sistemas Electrónica, SA. From 2000 to 2002, he worked as a researcher in the VESPER project developing the Virtual Home Environment (VHE) paradigm on INESC-Porto. Since 2001, he has been working on computer networks in ISCTE-IUL. He finished his PhD thesis at Lancaster University in 2011, focusing on managing the mobile access in heterogeneous wireless networks. Since 2011, he is an assistant professor on ISCTE-IUL. He is currently a researcher with IT-IUL, Lisbon, Portugal. His research interests include Wireless Networks, Game Theory, Virtualization, Cloud Computing, and Big Data.

Cristina Hava Muntean is a Lecturer with the School of Computing, National College of Ireland. She received the B.Eng. degree from the Computer Science Department, Politehnica University of Timisoara, Timisoara, Romania, in 2000, and the Ph.D. degree from Dublin City University, Dublin, Ireland, in 2005, for research on end user quality of experience-aware adaptive hypermedia systems.

Currently, she coordinates the NCI Research Laboratory and supervises M.Sc. and Ph.D. students. She is actively involved in research in the areas of technology enhanced personalised m/e-learning, gaming-based e-learning, adaptive multimedia delivery over wireless networks, and energy saving solutions. She has published 1 book, 6 book chapters, and over 50 peer-reviewed journal and conference papers and she was awarded four best paper awards. Dr. Muntean is also a reviewer for important international journals and conferences.

João Paulo Ribeiro Pereira earned his Ph.D. in Engineering and Management from Technical University of Lisbon. He is professor in the School of Technology and Management, Polytechnic Institute of Bragança (IPB) since 1999. During his time at the IPB, he held a number of positions. He has published numerous articles and book chapters.

Dan Pescaru was born in Timisoara, Romania. He received the M.S. in computer science from the Politehnica University of Timisoara in 1995 and the Ph.D. degree in computer science from the Politehnica University of Timisoara in 2004. He is currently an Associate Professor with the Department of Computers, Faculty of Automation and Computers, Politehnica University of Timisoara. He has been involved in various projects related with wireless communication, sensor networks, and cyber physical systems. He has authored or coauthored more than 60 journal and conference papers. His research interests include wireless sensors networks, cyber-physical systems, artificial intelligence, and image processing.

Rastislav Róka (Assoc. Prof.) was born in Šaľa, Slovakia on January 27, 1972. He received his MSc. and PhD. degrees in Telecommunications from the Slovak University of Technology, Bratislava, in 1995 and 2002. Since 1997, he has been working as a senior lecturer at the Institute of Telecommunications, FEI STU, Bratislava. Since 2009, he is working as an associated professor at this institute. At present, his research activity is focused on the signal transmission through optical transport and access networks by means of new WDM and TDM technologies using advanced optical signal processing included various modulation and coding techniques and through metallic access networks by means of xDSL and PLC technologies. His main effort is dedicated to effective utilization of the optical fiber's transmission capacity of the broadband passive optical networks by means of DBA and DWA algorithms.

Lejla Rovcanin received the M.Sc degree from Dublin City University (DCU), Ireland in 1999. She is a PhD Student in the Performance Engineering Laboratory, Network Innovations Centre, Rince Institute in the School of Electronic Engineering, DCU. Her research interests include the application of technology for learning as well as quality-oriented and performance-related issues of adaptive multimedia delivery. She is a student member of IEEE.

Haymen Shams received his PhD degree in electrical engineering from Dublin City University (DCU), Ireland in 2011, and his M.Sc degree in electronic and electrical department from Alexandria University, Egypt in 2006. His PhD dissertation addressed the optical technologies for generation and distribution of millimetre waves and ultra-wideband RF signals in Radio over Fiber (RoF) systems. His current research interests are on RF-over-fiber for wireless communication including ultra wideband and millimetre wave signals, different optical modulation level formats (such as DQPSK, DDQPSK, and CO-OFDM), digital coherent receivers, digital signal processing, and optical coherent THz. He is currently a research associate in photonic groups, department of electrical and electronic engineering, University College London (UCL). Dr. Shams is a member of Institute of Electronic and Electrical Engineering (IEEE), and European Physical Society (EPS).

João Carlos M. Silva received the B.S. degree for Aerospace Engineering from the Instituto Superior Técnico (IST) – Lisbon Technical University, in 2000. From 2000-2002 he worked as a business consultant on McKinsey & Company. He finished his PhD thesis at IST in 2006, focusing on spread spectrum techniques, Multi-User Detection schemes and MIMO systems. Since 2006, he has been working on computer networks, as an assistant professor in Instituto Superior das Ciências do Trabalho e da Empresa (ISCTE). Recently, he started to undertake an MBA in 2013, at ISEG (Instituto Superior de Economia e Gestão).

Chetna Singhal received her B.Eng. in Electronics and Telecommunications from Univ. of Pune in 2008 and M.Tech. in Computer Technology from Electrical Eng. Dept., IIT Delhi in 2010. She worked in IBM Software Lab, New Delhi, as a Software Engineer, from June 2010 to July 2011. She is currently pursuing Ph.D. from Bharti School of Telecommunications, IIT Delhi, since July 2011. Her research interests include handoff schemes and cross-layer optimization in wireless networks, adaptive multimedia multicast and broadcast schemes and technologies. She is a student member of ACM, IEEE, and IEEE Computer and Communications Societies.

Irina Tal is a Ph.D. researcher with the Performance Engineering Laboratory, School of Electronic Engineering, Dublin City University, Ireland. She was awarded the M.Eng. degree (2011) in Software Engineering and B.Eng. degree (2009) in Computer Science from the Computers Department, "Politehnica" University of Timisoara, Romania. Her research interests include vehicular ad-hoc networks, clustering algorithms, Fuzzy Logic and software solutions for a sustainable transport. She is a student member of IEEE, VTS and The Research Institute for Networks and Communications Engineering Institute (The Rince Institute) Ireland.

Chungang Yang received the Bachelor and Doctoral Degree in the Department of Electrical and Information Engineering, Xidian University, Xi'an, China in 2006 and 2011, respectively. Between Sep. 2010 and March 2011, he held the visiting scholar position in the department of electrical and computer engineering at Michigan Technological University. From July 2011, he has been with Xidian University as an assistant professor and was promoted to associated professor in July 2013. Dr. Yang is a member of IEEE. His research interests include cognitive radio networks, heterogeneous networks, resource and interference management and network optimization, cognitive media access protocol and algorithm design, and game theory for wireless networks.

Index